Through the Back Door

STUDIES IN CONTEMPORARY HISTORY
Edited by Dariusz Stola / Machteld Venken

VOLUME 5

PETER LANG
EDITION

Jerzy Kochanowski

Through the Back Door

The Black Market in Poland 1944-1989

Translated by Anda MacBride and Anna Wróbel

PETER LANG
EDITION

Bibliographic Information published by the Deutsche Nationalbibliothek
The Deutsche Nationalbibliothek lists this publication in the Deutsche Nationalbibliografie; detailed bibliographic data is available in the internet at http://dnb.d-nb.de.

Library of Congress Cataloging-in-Publication Data
Names: Kochanowski, Jerzy, author.
Title: Through the back door : the black market in Poland, 1944-1989 / Jerzy Kochanowski.
Other titles: Tylnymi drzwiami. English
Description: Frankfurt am Main ; New York : Peter Lang Edition, 2017. | Series: Studies in contemporary history, ISSN 2364-2874 ; vol. 5 | Translation of: Tylnymi drzwiami : "czarny rynek" w Polsce, 1944-1989; Warszawa : Wydawnictwo "Neriton", 2010. | Includes bibliographical references.
Identifiers: LCCN 2016051003| ISBN 9783631655856 (print) | ISBN 9783653048018 (PDF) | ISBN 9783631704363 (ePub) | ISBN 9783631704370 (MOBI)
Subjects: LCSH: Black market–Poland–History–20th century. | Scarcity–Poland–History–20th century. | Poland–Economic conditions–1945-1981. | Poland–Economic conditions–1981-1990. | Poland–Social conditions–1945-
Classification: LCC HF5482.65.P7 K6313 2017 | DDC 381–dc23 LC record available at https://lccn.loc.gov/2016051003

Cover illustration: A vendor, Warsaw, 1970s
Photograph by Jacek Sielski, FORUM Polish Photography Agency

Copy edited by Anda MacBride and Seamus MacBride

NATIONAL PROGRAMME
FOR THE DEVELOPMENT OF HUMANITIES

The publication has been founded by Ministry of Science and Higher Education of the Republic of Poland as part of the National Programme for the Development of Humanities. This publication reflects the views only of the authors, and the Ministry cannot be held responsible for any use which may be made of the information contained therein.

This publication has also been financially supported by the University of Warsaw.

ISSN 2364-2874
ISBN 978-3-631-65585-6 (Print)
E-ISBN 978-3-653-04801-8 (E-PDF)
E-ISBN 978-3-631-70436-3 (EPUB)
E-ISBN 978-3-631-70437-0 (MOBI)
DOI 10.3726/b10771

Peter Lang Edition is an Imprint of Peter Lang GmbH.

Peter Lang – Frankfurt am Main · Bern · Bruxelles · New York · Oxford · Warszawa · Wien

This publication has been peer reviewed.

www.peterlang.com

Table of Contents

Foreword

Małgorzata Mazurek, Columbia University

The pursuit of profit, accompanied by acquisitiveness and avarice, has never been the exclusive domain of capitalism, as Max Weber pointed out almost a century ago, arguing that it could be found throughout the world in any epoch, whether among Chinese officials or Roman aristocrats, pirates or modern peasants. Jerzy Kochanowski tells the story of the pursuit of profit under state socialism, something that many would see as a contradiction in terms. And yet – argues the author – organized, profit-oriented black markets were an organic part of the communist era.

In the course of World War One, and later during World War Two, much of what had previously been considered the legitimate pursuit of profit became classified in Poland as *spekulacja*, or profiteering: a morally condemned, politically risky and illegal mode of enrichment at the cost of others. In many post-1918 European democracies, the specters of profiteering and hyperinflation loomed as large as those of radical right- and left-wing ideologies. Taking this lesson into account, during, and most of all, after the second world war, many European nation states introduced food rationing and price controls which, they hoped, would protect the consumer purchasing power of their citizens. In the occupied territories of East Central Europe, however, where the predatory extraction of human and material resources and the violence of war had led to mass starvation on a much greater scale than in the West, the black market offered salvation from the occupier's state intervention.

In the Warsaw of 1945, as in many European cities of the time, the female street vendor symbolized the rebirth of life amidst the ruins and rubble, where the "wind carried russet dust from the ruins onto bread, sausages and fruit, and made street vendors wipe the foodstuff with an alarmingly dirty rag." One should not forget that the postwar reconstruction went hand in hand with ethnic cleansing and anti-Semitism, historical themes which Jerzy Kochanowski explores elsewhere. In 1949, Załma Gerber, a butcher sentenced to a fine of 500 000 zloty – or a two-year work camp imprisonment – for overcharging, wrote in his appeal to the state Special Commission for Combating Fraud and Corruption: "I find it unjustifiable that I have been sentenced on the basis of an accusation by a single client. After all, everyone knows that Jewish shops are not welcome in local society. [...] What makes the severity of the penalty so unfair is the fact that

I have already lost my life's work because of the war and the time I had spent in concentration camps."

In Poland and other East Central European states, consumer self-welfare and the black market undermined the communist welfare state project well beyond the period of postwar reconstruction. As the food shortages dragged on, despite the repeated attempts of government to buy social peace through pro-consumer policies, profit-oriented activities continued to be part of daily experience. This was due not only to flaws in the planned economy, but also because, striving to hold onto their power, communist officials continually restrained and criminalized market mechanisms related to supply and demand as illegal profiteering. Thus, state socialism fought "speculation" as much as it reproduced it.

Jerzy Kochanowski portrays these profit-oriented, illegal self-welfare activities in defiance of state-imposed social welfare as a game. These shenanigans, he argues, lasted half a century, resulting in a pro- and anti-profiteering "sinusoid" that eventually peaked in 1989, when profit-making was confirmed not only as a social, but also political norm. The author of *Through the Back Door: The Black Market in Poland 1944–1989* makes it clear that the institutions designed to deal with black markets were in fact helpless. They did not determine reality; they merely reacted to it. Yet in no way was this game a matter of resistance by a heroic society to a villainous one-party state. Rather, the black market was the result of a complex interplay, in which the boundaries between the public and the private, the state and the individual, the legal and the criminal, were often blurred. As Paulina Bren and Mary Neuburger have noted, elsewhere in socialist Eastern Europe, developments in the sphere of consumption proved that the "confounding binaries of 'official' and 'unofficial' were in many respects far more complex than under capitalism, and certainly more overtly political."

Today's historiography on state socialism still carries imprints of the Cold War mindset. Many normative assumptions, idealizations and negative stereotypes of communism or the free market remain unarticulated or taken for granted. History, especially in today's East Central Europe, has been a hotbed of political claim-making. Historical narratives are created with the aim of establishing yet another edifice of the one-and-only truth, a new gateway to a righteous past. In this world of political passions, stories of everyday life that shed light on mundane details in specific contexts and which show a concern for historical precision are much needed. Jerzy Kochanowski's is a book that delivers just such a complex and ethnographic representation of the ordinary. Its great virtue is its perspective: through the eponymous "backdoor", we zoom in on the countless individuals who participated in everyday profiteering, smuggling, and barter. Rather than pinpointing the essence of the black market – a futile undertaking if we accept the idea of history as changing reality – *Through the Back Door* describes the myriad ways in which the profit-oriented informal economy shaped the lives of ordinary people.

Indeed, the historical geography of profiteering in communist Poland is as complex as it is fascinating. While much has been said about the social inequalities created by the state socialist economy and its shadowy underbelly, the black market, we learn here a great deal about the regional diversity of postwar Polish society and its economy. Kochanowski's spatial history of communist Poland leads us to that affluent mountain resort, Zakopane, where a dollar-based private tourist sector successfully challenged, if not supplanted, the official one. We visit port cities, those traditional hives of illegal money and commodity exchange. We also become acquainted with provincial socialist-era "speakeasies," where illegal alcohol was produced and sold on a mass scale. Finally, we get a tour across East Central Europe, following cross-border trade routes including the "cosmetics-cum-clothing" pathway to Romania, the "crystal glass and hard currency" channel between Poland and Yugoslavia, and the "linen trail" to Hungary. In the 1970s and 1980s, these established routes flourished and were further extended. Towards the end of communism, cross-border trafficking, often one way to cover the cost of summer vacation, became a truly global affair with its own complex know-how and logistics, based on shared knowledge, which was passed on by word of mouth. *Through the Back Door* we uncover this fascinating, arcane world, gripped as if following a detective yarn. The transnational centers of tourist trading – the *Polenmarkt* on the Mexicoplatz in Vienna or Romanian beaches – turned into commodity exchanges for socialist goods reveal the true scale and wealth of the Soviet Bloc's black markets.

It is always tricky to attempt a single-cause explanation of why communism fell, or why it lasted as long as it did. Jerzy Kochanowski chooses not to venture into these muddy waters, but he does leave us some clues. If we were to picture the East Central European counterpart of the Western "entrepreneur" (in the parlance of the 1980s neoliberals) – an individual both resourceful and creative, perhaps what would appear before our eyes might well turn out to be a woman laden with bags and swathed in a peasant shawl: the ubiquitous "*baba* with veal," the villager that sold meat to urbanites. Although this familiar figure disappeared with the fall of communism, she remained an icon of popular and shrewd profit-making. This book gives the *baba* more than just an engaging contextualization – it gives her a face and a history, as well as affording the reader an informed and sympathetic view.

1. Terms and Methods

"During the war one could get anything at all", reminisced the Polish painter Franciszek Starowieyski, "but once the socialist shambles began its reign, even trivial things became unavailable. Very quickly people realized that socialism was a force of "desertification." "What will happen in the Sahara once the socialists arrive? They will run out of sand," ran a popular joke that did the rounds in 1945, when it became clear how quickly everything was disappearing and falling apart, once socialism took hold."[1] This book is dedicated to all the efforts undertaken by post-war Polish society to irrigate the "socialist desert" and squeeze from it as much as possible. Bearing in mind that most of the oases and water reserves and oases had been nationalized; Poles were obliged to engage in a complicated, and usually illegal, game playing with the state. This went on for almost half a century.

1.1 What Color was the Black Market?

This book does not aspire to be an economic, sociological or anthropological analysis. It aims at an interdisciplinary (albeit history-focused) reconstruction of various behaviors, mechanisms, phenomena, practices, processes and strategies united under the shared umbrella of the term "black market". These mechanisms and strategies were unusually multilayered; they varied in time and geography. They reacted instantly to external and internal circumstances. Black market players spoke their own language and had a distinct set of values. They were involved in the black market sometimes purposefully and exclusively for profit, and sometimes under duress and against their will.[2] As with any other mass phenomenon, with this one also there are controversial and debatable issues, starting with the terminology and the methodology; these require some clarification.

No state can completely control its citizens and their economic life. No society consists solely of those who put the common good above the individual one. The economy of a state often brings to mind a river that at times dips under the surface, its flow becoming subterranean. Its depth, the strength of the current, the type of river bed, fauna and flora of the underground flows (to stay with the fluvial terminology) depend on many factors and look different in every

1 *Franciszka Starowieyskiego opowieść o końcu świata czyli reforma rolna*, written down by K. Uniechowska, Warszawa 1994, p. 132.

2 See: M. Kosewski, *Ludzie w sytuacjach pokusy i upokorzenia*, Warszawa 1985, pp. 12–73.

country; this does not make it any easier for researchers. This much is clear both from the variety of terms used to describe it (Poland's black market economy has been variously referred to as the "gray sphere", or shadow, black, second, parallel, hidden, informal, unofficial, secret, unobservable, unregistered, or unquantifiable economy), and also from the absence of a universally satisfying definition. While trying to create one, some reach for moral yardsticks and others for legal, institutional, statistical (especially if they are able to register the black market activities) or, as a last resort, ideological criteria. Regardless of the perspective adopted, the term "black market" is used to refer to the production and exchange of goods or services conducted for profit (whether monetary or not) outside of formal institutions (also implying that it remains outside of legally binding regulations) and unaccounted for in the gross national product.[3]

Everywhere in the world the gray sphere faithfully accompanies the official economy. It always has its own, often endemic, characteristics dependent on the economic and social structure, tradition, and legal system. However, one can assume that in countries where the free market system is established and developed, the gray sphere is mostly about avoiding taxes and taking advantage of illegal labor. Criminal activities, such as selling drug and weapons, the trade in fissile material, and human trafficking are a different matter. These tend to hog the headlines and bring enormous profits but at the same time they barely influence the everyday life of an average Frenchman, German or Finn.

The average citizen of any "people's democracy", whether a Pole, a Russian or a Romanian, did not care much about the black market in tanks or uranium, but wanted to know how and where they could get shoes, gas, furniture, and pots (and what to put in the latter), since the supply of even the most ordinary goods could never be taken for granted. To have money in one's purse or wallet was

---

3 *The Second Economy in Marxists States*, ed. M. Łoś, Houndmills–London 1990, pp. 2–4; E. Klinkmüller, G. Leptin, *Terminologische Anmerkungen zum Begriff der Schattenwirtschaft*, in: *Beiträge zum Problem der Schattenwirtschaft*, ed. G. Hedtkamp, Berlin 1983, pp. 11–13; *Gospodarka nieformalna. Uwarunkowania lokalne i systemowe*, ed. K.Z. Sowa, Rzeszów 1990; M. Bednarski, *Drugi obieg gospodarczy. Przesłanki, mechanizmy i skutki w Polsce lat osiemdziesiątych*, Warszawa 1992, pp. 15, 34; F. Schneider, D.H. Enste, *The Shadow Economy: An International Survey*, Cambridge 2002, pp. 6–9. See also: *The Unofficial Economy: Consequences and Perspectives in Different Economic Systems*, ed. S. Alessandrini, B. Dallago, Aldershot 1987 (especially articles: E. Feige, *The Anatomy of the Underground Economy* and P. Wiles: *The Second Economy: Its Definitional Problems*; M. Göke, K.-H. Hartwig, *Schwarzmärkte*, in: *Ökonomische Theorie der Rationierung*, ed. M. Tietzel, München 1998, pp. 106–137.

not enough to succeed in making a successful purchase; it was a common experience to stand in line in front of a store with no guarantee that the item of one dreams, or indeed anything else at all, would be there when one finally arrived at the front of the line hours later. Chronic shortages in the socialist economies are a well-known fact and much has been written about them. János Kornai's work on this topic has become a classic (which, incidentally, does not mean that his conclusions are immune to debate).[4] What matters more for our purposes is, rather than showing how the shortages came about, looking at how they were alleviated. There were two possible approaches: either the state rationed the goods and services, or society took over the (re)distribution. From the point of view of the totalitarian/authoritarian state, such an alternative was unacceptable and the liberal slogan "What is not forbidden is allowed" was generally substituted with the clear guideline: "What is not explicitly allowed is forbidden".[5]

Citizens were disinclined to conform to the dictatorial economy and, especially where the shortages were particularly painful, they constantly perfected adjustment strategies. Through the "back door", they would drain the state sector and develop social networks based on mutual but not exactly gratuitous help in acquiring goods and services that were absent from the market. Poles jokingly defined the worst possible punishment as "sentenced to two years with no cronies". Similar sentiments had their equivalents in almost all socialist countries; in the Soviet Union they used to say "*Blat* is stronger than Stalin"; the Polish "cronies" and Soviet "blat" both meaning "good ol' boy networks". The whirlpool of the second economy sucked out the supplies from the first one thus creating shortages, which increased various informal economic activities.[6] In the socialist countries this vicious circle not only produced the second economy, but also the

4 J. Kornai, *Economics of Shortage*, Amsterdam–New York 1980; J. Kornai, *The Socialist System: The Political Economy of Communism*, Princeton 1992; *Models of Disequilibrium and Shortage in Centrally Planned Economies*, ed. Ch. Davis, W. Charemza, London 1989. See: K. Nowakowski, *Niedobory w gospodarce a społeczeństwo i jednostka*, Katowice 1993; M. Jastrząb, *Puste półki. Problem zaopatrywania ludności w artykuły powszechnego użytku w Polsce w latach 1949–1956*, Warszawa 2004, p. 130.
2004; M. Mazurek, *Społeczeństwo kolejki. O doświadczeniach niedoboru 1945* J. Kornai, *The Socialist System: The Political Economy of Communism 1989*, Warszawa 2010; M. Mazurek, *Antropologia niedoboru w NRD i PRL 1971–1989*, Wrocław 2010.

5 *The Second Economy in Marxists States...*, p. 4; A.V. Ledeneva, *Russia's economy of favours: Blat, Networking and Informal Exchange*, Cambridge–New York 1998, p. 87.

6 A.V. Ledeneva, *Russia's Economy of Favours...*, p. 87.

"second society"[7] guided by its own ethical rules, goals, models, and mentality. Its existence was probably most in evidence when viewing society from the economic angle.

When the entire economy not only depends on the state but also belongs to it, it is hard to call the "underground" economy a parallel one. Parallel equals independent, and independence was certainly not a characteristic of the socialist *second economy*. In the Soviet Bloc countries, the connections between the two economies were very tight and usually of a parasitic kind. The official economy provided money, natural resources and products for private (legal and illegal) artisans and merchants or smugglers. Private houses were built with state-owned bricks and cement; cars ran on state-owned gas.[8] But there was also a certain symbiosis. The state enterprises could not operate, nor meet their production goals, without using the strategies of the grey sphere both in dealings with the state and private co-operants. The managers of state enterprises often knowingly flouted the law, because they knew that without the proverbial "nuts and bolts" supplied by canny artisans the factory would have not been able to function. Not too many questions were asked, such as enquiring too closely into the source of steel used for the production of parts. In this context, the shades used to define the informal economic arrangements of the time – ranging as they do from gray to black – are clearly insufficient. No wonder that researchers into the socialist second economy were obliged to broaden the palette considerably.

Although the model described below was evolved to apply to the Soviet Union, it nevertheless applies to a great degree also to other states of the eastern bloc (and not just in Europe).[9]

---

7 E. Hankiss, *The "Second Society": Is There an Alternative Social Model Emerging in Contemporary Hungary?*, in: "Social Research" p. 55, 1988/1–2 & 13–42. See: M. Marody, *Od społeczeństwa drugiego obiegu do społeczeństwa obywatelskiego*, in: "Studia Socjologiczne" 1999, p. 4 (155)/35–51. See: J.R. Wedel, *The Private Poland: An* Anthropologist's Look at Everyday Life, New York 1986; *Herrschaft und Eigen-Sinn in der Diktatur. Studien zur Gesellschaftsgeschichte der DDR*, ed. T. Lindenberger, Köln–Weimar–Wien 1999; U. Brunnbauer, *"Die sozialistische Lebensweise". Ideologie, Gesellschaft, Familie und Politik in Bulgarien (1944–1989)*, Köln–Weimar–Wien 2007.

8 J. Brodacz, *Mali ludzie – wielkie interesy. Afera skórzana w Radomiu*, "Polityka", 45/Nov 5 1960; Central Archives of Modern Records in Warsaw (Archiwum Akt Nowych – AAN), The Office of the Council of Ministers (Urząd Rady Ministrów – URM), 32/115, fol. 38.

9 Based on: A. Katsenelinboigen, *Coloured Markets in the Soviet Union*, in: "Soviet Studies" 29/1977/1, pp. 62–85; F. Haffner, *Ist die Schattenwirtschaft ein Reformansatz? Das Verhältnis der Wirtschaftsreformen in Osteuropa zur Schattenwirtschaft*, "Vierteljahreshefte

1.1.1 Legal Markets

The market called, for more than one reason, **red** was in fact the inefficient and inflexible system of state distribution. It was aided by the **pink market,** in which privately, legally owned goods changed hands. The state created a network of *komis* (second-hand) stores (*skupochnyie* in Russian) where one could sell clothes, books, furniture and so on, for prices no higher than in regular stores. *Komis* stores were one of the few places where traces of market behavior occurred – for example, the price was negotiable, and the un-cleared stock was put on sale. However, there were not many *skupocznyie* and so their influence on the market was negligible.

The **white markets** were of greater importance. They included the town marketplaces where one could sell used goods (*barakholki* were often closed down due to their taking liberties with the interpretation of the term "second-hand items"), and also the *kolkhoz* markets which sold food. The prices in both markets were not regulated by the state (apart from times of exceptional shortage, when maximum prices were introduced but rarely respected).

1.1.2 Semi-legal Markets

The gray market included apartment and holiday cottage (*dacha*) rental services (and also house renovation, car repair, tailoring and shoe services) carried out after – or sometimes during – working hours by *shabashnikovs*. Income acquired from tutoring or medical advice was also included in that group. The illegal but commonly accepted barter between enterprises (without which production goals were often impossible to meet) was part of the grey market. The authorities usually turned a blind eye to the grey market, especially in the areas where the supply of goods and services was insufficient.

1.1.3 Illegal Markets

The brown market dealt with goods theoretically available on the red market but in reality subject to chronic shortages. In the case of meat, dairy products, clothes, refrigerators, cars, mechanised equipment, and building materials, the demand was vastly greater than the supply. As a result, numerous means of back

zur Wirtschaftsforschung" 1985, pp. 177–187; L.I. Shelley, *The Second Economy in the Soviet Union*, in: *The Second Economy in Marxist states…*, pp. 11–26; G. Grossman, *The Second Economy of the USSR*, in: *The Underground Economy in the United States and Abroad*, ed. V. Tanzi, Lexington–Massachusetts–Toronto 1982.

door distribution became available. Producers, employees of trade headquarters and warehouses, transport drivers and salesmen, all took part in these dealings. People engaged in such actions in order to create social capital, hoping for a reciprocated "service" in other shortage areas. A separate segment of the brown market dealt with coveted imported items, considered as luxuries in the Soviet Union – mostly clothes, and in the 1980s, also video cassettes or cars, vast numbers of which were brought into the country, often legally, by sailors, athletes, and artists. Theoretically, these were to be distributed by the small network of *komis* stores but since the vendors did not want to leave a paper trail (their IDs had to be shown and their details recorded during each transaction), more discreet and less formal channels of distribution were soon created.

Factories and enterprises also took advantage of the brown market. For example, the management of the *kolkhozes*, the collective farms, were constantly obliged to grapple with lack of parts and being in possession of illegally acquired cash (*lewa kasa*) obtained the needed items through informal channels by buying items that had been stolen or produced as side jobs.

Although the participants in the *brown market* were tolerated, both the state and a large part of society viewed those engaged in the black market as criminals. Draining the red market for profit (via shoplifting, theft from warehouses and factories or from transport and generating a fake surplus, usually by lowering the quality of the product) was also considered a black market activity. Alcohol played an extremely important role on the black market. Its retail distribution was under special state control, which on the one hand led to a growth in the production of moonshine, and on the other to the private distribution of state alcohol, of course at higher prices.

Soviet luxury items (jeans, wigs, etc.) legally imported and distributed on the *brown market* were but a drop in the ocean of need. It is hard to estimate how many were smuggled into the Soviet Union and how many were purchased from tourists (this was the domain of *fartsovshchiks*, who also sold tourists local souvenirs or hard-to-get-items such as caviar). The higher caste of the black marketers, *valutchiks* (from Russian *valuta* – currency), monopolized the illegal trade in hard currency and gold, which, along with precious stones, were used as a store of value and were thus the main items subject to hoarding. This kind of illegal trading carried the most severe punishment, including the death penalty.

1.2 The Black Market in Communist Poland: Problems with Definition

We can assume that, following World War II, and in particular in the late 1940s and early 1950s after the communist regime had established itself, the structure of the internal market in Poland was not very different from that outlined above. At the same time, thanks to a singular coincidence of historical, political, economic, and social factors, the Polish second economy had its own characteristics and indeed endemic traits, compared to other Soviet bloc countries.[10]

Among the historical factors, a significant role was played by the instrumental and pragmatic attitude that a large part of society had toward the state and its institutions, which they perceived as something external and unconnected to them, an attitude that was a legacy of the Second World War and, earlier, of the partitions of Poland. This was particularly prevalent in the part of Poland formerly under Russian occupation. The average Polish citizen identified first of all with his family and his close-knit social network, for example in a work place or a neighborhood, next – with the nation (in its 19th century sense), and finally – with the state. "This ambivalent attitude," wrote the Polish historian Andrzej Friszke, "with its strong undertow of rebelliousness and contrariness weakened the executive abilities of the totalitarian state".[11] As a result, compared with other countries in the bloc, institutional control was much weaker both in the sphere of national symbolism and the economy.

On the other hand, already during the interwar period, the state had exerted a firm grip on the economy, which caused a sizeable part of the population to consider it a force capable of solving economic problems; the perceived degree of its ability to do that colored society's evaluation of the government and its legitimacy. After the war, this point of view was reinforced, especially in the context of fervent egalitarian propaganda, which inflated the aspirations and expectations of society in regards to consumption. However, when the economy, underachieving on all possible fronts, especially since the 1970s, became increasingly less and less capable of solving the economic problems, with increasing pain for

10 See: A. Korbonski, *"The Second Economy" in Poland*, in: "Journal of International Affairs" 35/1981/1, pp. 1–13; M. Łoś, *The Dynamics of the Second Economy in Poland*, in: *The Second Economy in Marxists States…*, pp. 27–49; S. Tellenbach, *The Logic of Development in Socialist Poland*, "Social Forces" 57/1978/2 (special), pp. 436–456.

11 A. Friszke, *Kultura polityczna w PRL 1948–1989*, in: A. Friszke, *Przystosowanie i opór. Studia z dziejów PRL*, Warszawa 2007, p. 398.

the population, citizens changed their attitude to the state and its institutions by taking the initiative to battle on their own against the shortages.[12]

Polish society was already well prepared to undertake independent, if unofficial, economic activities. It was the crisis of the 1930s that had inspired the multitude deprived of jobs and the means of survival to engage in trade. "Higher categories of workers (lower rank state officials, railroad workers, employees of local government and social services) are being absorbed on a massive scale into the ranks of the petty bourgeoisie," wrote Stanisław Rychliński, "which does not directly 'enhance' the cultural and social position of the middle class [...]. The petty bourgeoisie has lost its static character of a middle stratum, separating the upper echelons of society from the underprivileged. It has become a makeshift bridge with a dynamic undercurrent."[13] During the German occupation, the range of acceptable social behavior became stretched. The ability to adjust to a new situation and to survive became more important than social status. Trade, smuggling, and cottage industry made survival possible both for those from the social margins and the intelligentsia.[14] The ghettoization of the Jews, followed by their annihilation, created a blank space on the economic map, which quickly filled with Poles. "New kinds of enterprises emerged," wrote Jan Szczepański, "run by people without professional qualifications, from different social classes. It was a particular kind of small manufacturing functioning usually in breach of the then current law, all kinds of 'shady businesses' that disregarded the official regulations, bribed the German authorities and focused on quick profit. At that time, new models of operating a business appeared, and remained after the war."[15] After returning from England, the lawyer and economist Stanisław M. Korowicz noted the poignant joke circulating in the late 1940s which encapsulated the new reality with the comment that in post-war Poland "a large number of Catholics are doing business and a large number of Jews wear army uniforms. It's a crazy world!"[16] We cannot overestimate the influence of private property in agriculture (from 1956),

---

12 Ibid., 399. See: W. Narojek, *Socjalistyczne "welfare state". Studium z psychologii społecznej Polski Ludowej*, Warszawa 1991. The shortages in Poland were worse than those in the GDR, Czechoslovakia or Hungary, and occasionally than those in the Soviet Union, Romania and Bulgaria.

13 *Drobnomieszczaństwo w strukturze i świadomości społecznej*, ed. Z. Zagórski, Wrocław 1988 (Acta Universitatis Wratislaviensis. Prace Filozoficzne. Socjologia 2), p. 3.

14 See: M. Walczak, *Walka ekonomiczna narodu polskiego* 1939–1945 Warszawa 1983, pp. 63–99; K. Wyka, *Gospodarka wyłączona* in *Życie na niby*, Kraków 2010, pp. 274–311.

15 *Drobnomieszczaństwo...*, p. 5.

16 S.M. Korowicz, *W Polsce pod sowieckim jarzmem*, London 1955, p. 31.

private trade, artisanry and services on the shape and size of communist Poland's second economy. In 1979, the private economy (including agriculture) employed 23.9% of the labor force. Polish peasants, who already during the German occupation had proved that they were capable of adapting to difficult circumstances, adapted to the new reality and actively participated in all kinds of economic activities, usually at the shadier end of the market. On the one hand, they skillfully and creatively took advantage of food shortages, particularly of meat, in the cities. On the other, as representatives of the private – that is, the disadvantaged sector, they were constantly struggling with shortages in the means of production, often acquiring them in an unofficial way. Private trade and artisanry were strongly tied up with the state in a parasitic/symbiotic way. At the same time, small-time entrepreneurs were some of the most important clients of the gold and hard currency black market.

As an aside, the Polish hard currency black market was sustained and stimulated (an unprecedented situation in the Soviet Bloc) by the state currency policies, for instance on foreign currency bank accounts and internal export. Thus, a dual currency system effectively existed in Poland in the last several years before the fall of communism. Also, beginning with the late 1950s, Polish authorities presented an attitude that differed from that of the authorities of other countries of the Bloc towards emigration, with the exception of political emigration of course. The extent of permitted contacts was relatively wide, which meant a greater flow of hard currency, goods, and technology as well as a wider penetration of models of consumption. Beginning in the 1970s, Polish regulations regarding travel outside the Iron Curtain countries were much more liberal than those in the rest of the Soviet Bloc (except Yugoslavia, with its special status). All this had various consequences: from smuggling and the tourist trade to copycat activities emulated by those who keenly watched the goings-on. This mattered – since as in all poor countries, the ability to access goods and services offered in developed western countries was a synonym for wealth.[17] The long-term isolation of the Soviet Bloc states produced in its citizens the so-called "fire-victim syndrome", of those who had "lost their belongings in a fire and who were now trying to rebuild their life in the mode of developed societies with mass consumption.

17 R.L. Chugh, J.S. Uppal, *Black Economy in India*, New Dehli 1986, p, 14 See: K. Karcz, *Efekt naśladowania zewnętrznych wzorców konsumpcji jako czynnik utrudniający sterowanie spożyciem indywidualnym*, in: *Narzędzia polityki gospodarczej i społecznej w procesie kształtowania konsumpcji*. All-Poland academic and didactic conference of Faculties of Trade in Goods and Services of higher economic schools, September 1987, vol. 1, Katowice 1987, pp. 201–205.

Those patterns reach us through films, TV, newspapers and magazines, tourism, family visits, etc."[18] The difference between the reality of the Soviet Bloc and the western ideal could to a large extent (or sometimes only) be eliminated using black market strategies.

It is not easy to paint a picture of the black market in communist Poland. Certainly, this could not be the work of a realist painter but rather a pointillist, with overlapping colors, and the full image only to be appreciated from a distance. Neither do traditional definitions have a perfect fit here. It makes sense to go along with Jerzy Tomaszewski, an acclaimed historian and economist, who describes the black market as a "casual term for illegal or clandestine trade taking place within controlled trade in goods [...]; it emerges when the supply of particular items, despite being strictly regulated (official prices, provision cards, trade monopoly etc.) does not meet the demand."[19]

Subsequent chapters will show, however, that the black market in communist Poland did not coincide with this definition. For example, the rationing of consumer goods was only periodically in effect in Poland (from 1944 until 1953, and from 1976 until 1989), and then only in respect of selected items, whereas the black market existed during the entire post-war period.[20] However, during the forty-five post-war years, the regulations were enforced in big enterprises, which had to follow the rules of distribution in respect of energy, cement, machinery, and money. But even the large factories had to take on board black market strategies when selling such strictly regulated goods as meat, sugar, and alcohol to their employees or when exchanging goods with other producers. These practices were endemic in the 1980s. It's important to stress that without this inter-factory barter, factories would often not have been able to operate at all.[21] In particular, the monographic chapters that follow (dealing for instance with meat, alcohol or gas) will provide numerous examples of such practices.

Can we include phenomena not connected with shortages and rationing under the black market umbrella? The unofficial gas trade functioned in Poland,

---

18 J. Szczepański, *Zagadnienia konstruowania i realizacji modelu i wzorów konsumpcji socjalistycznej*, in: *Badania nad wzorami konsumpcji*, ed. J. Szczepański, Wrocław–Warszawa–Kraków 1977, p. 33.

19 J. Tomaszewski, *Czarny rynek*, in: *Encyklopedia historii gospodarczej Polski do 1945 roku*, ed. A. Mączak, vol. 1, Warszawa 1981, p. 114.

20 During the post-war period there existed various quasi-regulatory measures such as coupons, branch allowances, special stores, sailors' or miners' ration books, etc. See: *Ökonomische Theorie der Rationierung...*

21 AAN, URM, 32/119, fol. 67.

and also in the USSR, Romania and other countries, regardless of temporary shortages and regulations; during such periods, it increased and specialized. Similarly, illicit alcohol distilling existed also in times when alcohol stores were well supplied. It is worth mentioning that until the crisis of the 1980s, the black market prices of moonshine and gas coming from state resources were lower than those of the official market. Should the proverbial *baba* – the peasant woman selling meat, which she brought from the countryside directly to private apartments in Warsaw or Krakow when meat was not being rationed – be treated as a black market phenomenon, or rather as a form of a traditional local distribution system? How should we view the informal taking over of the function of inefficient stores in order to shift even goods not subject to market restrictions? For example, in 1984 two resourceful men got in on the act of the not-very-dynamic, state-owned Fish Market. They bought two tons of herring for 50zl a kilo in the port of Świnoujście and sold it for a much higher price in the city of Zielona Góra, some 300 km away.[22] Later the same year, the agent of a store on the Baltic coast, who had "first sunk one million zloty of his own renovating the space and had then later tried in vain to stock it with goods bought on the local market, in the end bought them in Silesia, added his costs to the price and found himself in prison accused of speculation."[23] A year later, newspapers covered the story of a saddler from Przemyśl, who supplied bread at a small surcharge to nearby Stubno, where there was no bakery, and as a result was hit with a fine and suspended sentence."[24] The concept of a "market" implies trading, albeit not necessarily money-based.[25] This allows us to no longer consider such phenomena as tax evasion, embezzlement, or corruption, leaving us at the same time with a question: where is the boundary between the black market (or indeed a market of any other hue) and economic crime? How to classify for example the "meat affair" in Warsaw, when a surplus of meat intentionally produced in state enterprises was distributed in official stores at official prices in the early 1960s? How can we classify artisans who produced goods using materials often illegally obtained from state-owned sources but who distributed their product through legal store networks? Such activities – although not part of the black market per se – yielded large, often untaxed or unreported profits, later converted into

22 AAN, URM, 32/121, fol. 83.

23 S. Podemski, *Niech nie lecą wióry*, Polityka 18/1984.

24 *Szczęście w nieszczęściu*, Polityka 48/1985, Szlachetny spekulant, Polityka 8/1986.

25 D. O'Hearn, *The Consumer Second Economy: Size and Effects*, Soviet Studies 32/1980/2, p. 219.

black-market hard currency and gold. They also encouraged the development of smuggling techniques, which brought in luxury and hoarding articles unavailable on the official market.

In addition, the Polish authorities had problems with an accurate definition of black market phenomena. They struggled with a lack of precise legal language and at times, obliged to do so by the circumstances, allowed the accused the benefit of the doubt. More than that! In the 1980s, when the illegal trade encompassed practically all goods, not infrequently the sentences that the communist authorities meted out in cases involving the black market were strikingly lenient, often in direct contrast to the expectations of the public opinion that had demanded an intervention. When in 1984, a war veteran asked the authorities to curtail the speculation of goods, such as appliances and clothes, bought in official stores, an apparatchik from the Council of Ministers' Committee for Obeying the Law, Public Order and Social Discipline ruled that the law had not been broken. One was allowed to resell a product at a higher price if one had bought it earlier solely for private use. Only deliberate re-sale, planned in advance – and this was hard to prove – would be prosecuted. State lawyers agreed that tightening the law would do little to improve the situation.[26] From September 1981, anti-speculation law (see chapter 3) dealt only with "products in daily use". A telling exchange of letters between the District Office of Interior Affairs in Kalisz and the General Prosecutor's Office took place in 1985. "Kalisz," wrote the deputy chief of the Kalisz police, "is the location of a well-known manufacturer of pianos; the famous Calisia is located here. When the pianos are delivered to the local music store, the line in front of it is just as long as the one waiting for citrus fruit in front of the deli next door. It means that people are eager to buy pianos. Police investigated the purchase of pianos outside the state-regulated system. It turned out that on January 17 [1985], the District Prosecutor's Office in Kalisz took the position, expressed in writing, that a piano meets higher-level needs and, as such, is not a product of everyday use." When the prosecution dismissed the charges against the potential black marketeer, the Kalisz police, afraid that this could make case law ("Tomorrow, we may no longer be able to say that a fur coat is not an article of everyday use...!") asked Warsaw for an opinion. Ultimately, the General Prosecutor upheld the decision of the Kalisz lawyers.[27] The terminology used in post-war Poland did not help. Officially, the term "black market" did not exist. Initially, in the less formal official language the traditional term "profiteering"

26 AAN, URM, 32/184, fol. 59–62.
27 AAN, URM, 32/116, K 73, p. 166.

(*paskarstwo*) was used; in the more formal language – wartime, or goods, usury (*lichwa wojenna* or *lichwa towarowa*) was quickly substituted by the key term "speculation" (*spekulacja*),[28] which defined only a part of the phenomenon we are talking about: "an economic crime, which consists of a person, who was not authorized to do so, buying goods in order to re-sell them at a profit " or "a crime, which involves an illegal middleman in the process of distributing goods in order to gain profit." In post-war Poland, the term "black market" denoted rather the trade in hard currency and gold (the term "black-market exchange rate" was used also in the official correspondence). In the late 1950s and the early 1960s, the phrase "black market" appears more often both in the press and in the less official pronouncements of the authorities. The term is not clearly defined and generally depicts the activities of those black marketeers trading in various articles – from hard currency and gold, meat and alcohol to cars and construction materials. Only after 1980, when the illegal trade became a significant problem, was the term "black market" – often in quotation marks, often preceded by the adjectives food, gas, currency etc. – widely employed by journalists and MPs. The official term "speculation" was also used. It seems therefore that the approach of the Indian economists may be more useful in defining the black market in communist Poland. Already at the beginning of the 1980s they had concluded that "in recent decades the black market has become a way of life [for the Indian people]."[29] No wonder their definition is much broader than the ones accepted in the West and fits the Eastern European realities much better: "When by (artificial) manipulation of the economic forces of demand and supply, of both currency and produce (or either), trade or industry (or both) create an artificial situation of scarcity or glut, and in the process amass huge returns on their investments [...], we have a black market situation."[30]

---

28 "Goods usury" usually occurring under disrupted economic conditions (war or natural disaster) meant that the manufacturer or the merchant obtained extraordinary and unsubstantiated economic profits. "Speculation" implied that, additionally, a profit-taking middleman was involved. M. Bednarski, *Drugi obieg gospodarczy...*, p. 152.

29 S.K. Ray, *Economics of the Black Market*, Boulder 1981, p. 1. In the 1980s the size of the second economy, mostly consisting of black market practices such as gold smuggling, was estimated at over 50 per cent of the GNP. A. Kumar, *The Black Economy in India*, New Delhi 202, p. 55.

30 S.K. Ray, *Economics...*, p. 4.

1.3 Literature, Sources, Method

Polish literature on the subject has not been very helpful in helping one get a grip on the topic of the Polish black market (or sorting out the definitions). It is economists and lawyers – and not historians or anthropologists – that have long dominated this area of research. In 1957, on the wave of political changes triggered by the momentous events of October 1956, the newly established, as part of the Council of Ministers, Economic Council, led by the Polish economist Oskar Lange (who later lived in the USA and became a professor at the University of Chicago), attempted to evaluate the illegal income of Poles.[31] Research on economic crimes continued in the following years within the Supreme Audit Office (Najwyższa Izba Kontroli, NIK) and the Committee for Research on Social Issues of the Polish People's Republic (Komitet Badań nad Zagadnieniami Społecznymi Polski Ludowej), chaired by the distinguished economist Michał Kalecki (who was later to serve as the deputy director of the United Nations Economic Department). At the beginning of the 1960s, the research was cancelled by Władysław Gomułka's government in an attempt to avoid the scientific confirmation and popularization of a well-known fact – that the involvement of Polish society in illegal transactions had reached a mass scale. It was more convenient to focus on individual economic scandals. As a result, bookstores and the libraries tended to offer only legal expertise (written by Tadeusz Cyprian, Stanisław Galarski, Oktawia Górniok, Bronisław Koch, and others). In 1974 the Institute for Criminal Problems (Instytut Problematyki Przestępczości) was established at the Prosecutor General's Office.[32] It also dealt with economic crimes, but only a very small group of people had access to the often fascinating conclusions of its research. The uniformed services such as the Central Customs Office (Główny Urząd Ceł, GUC), the police (Milicja Obywatelska, MO; nota bene, in spite of the name "militia", these were not community vigilantes but a fully professional force), and the Security Service (Służba Bezpieczeństwa, SB) also prepared evaluations but only for internal distribution.

At the turn of the 1970s and the 1980s, a Warsaw sociologist complained: "in Poland [black market] issues are not researched systematically, and then only by the media, where they are treated as marginal or pathological phenomena

31 See: *Szara strefa Października. "Notatka" o nielegalnych dochodach w Polsce 1956–1957*, ed. J. Kochanowski, Przegląd Historyczny (PH), 95 2004/1, pp. 77–96.

32 Monitor Polski 1974/9/68.

(economic crime, speculation)."[33] Scientific dissertations written at that time by sociologists or economists who departed from the "pathological" perspective were unlikely to see the light of day in print.[34] Outside of Poland very little was written about the Polish second economy, especially in comparison with the USSR, which was the center of attention. This changed in the 1980s, when the second economy became a subject that slowly began to find its way into Poland. In 1984, the first article by Marek Bednarski,[35] a pioneer of black market research, and a brochure by Rudolf Jaworek became available.[36] By the end of the year, the weekly *Polityka* had published a series of articles about the parallel economy.[37] In the following years the black market became the subject of both presentations at scholarly conferences[38] and of books with limited distribution.[39]

In spite of it being the year in which Poland's transition from People's Republic to democracy began, 1989 was by no means a watershed year in research on communist Poland's second economy. The times of transformation brought other current topics to cover. In the early 1990s the only relevant book to be published was that of Marek Bednarski, a summary of his earlier work.[40] That monograph with its focus on the 1980s remains to this day the most exhaustive picture of the economy of that period. In the middle of the 1990s, as the archives continued to open their doors to scholars and research on the institutions of the communist state moved ahead, the second economy caught the attention of Polish historians. One pioneer was Grzegorz Sołtysiak, who in 1991 published several sources on

33 P. Gliński, *Ekonomiczne uwarunkowania stylu życia. Rodziny miejskie w Polsce w latach siedemdziesiątych*, 1983, PhD dissertation, IFIS PAN, p. 112.

34 The above-mentioned PhD dissertation by P. Gliński and Paweł Wyczański's PhD dissertation, the Dept. of Finance and Statistics at the SGiPS (now called the SGH) 1987, *Czarny rynek walutowy w Polsce 1970–1984.*

35 M. Bednarski, *Drugi obieg*, Życie Gospodarcze 1984/35 See also *Gospodarka "drugiego obiegu" a kryzys lat osiemdziesiątych in: Rzeczywistość polska i sposoby radzenia sobie z nią*, ed. M. Marody, A. Sułek, Warszawa 1987.

36 R. Jaworek *Gospodarka nieformalna-czwarty sektor gospodarczy*, Warszawa 1984.

37 J. Kleer, *W cieniu*, L.Będkowski, *Jak sąsiad z sąsiadem*, K. Krubski, *Góra lodowa*, M. Przybylik, *Słonina i schab spod serca*, W. Markiewicz, *Poemat pedagogiczny*, J. Baczyński, *Policzyć sztuki, godziny i do kasy,* Polityka 1984/49.

38 J. Rogoziński, *Kryzys jako weryfikator w sferze rynku i konsumpcji*, in: *Narzędzia polityki gospodarczej i społecznej…*, vol. 1, pp. 151–161.

39 J. Misala, *Nieoficjalna wymiana handlowa obywateli polskich z zagranicą*, Warszawa 1989; P. Wyczański, *Dwuwalutowość w gospodarce polskiej oraz metody i możliwości jej ograniczenia*, Warszawa 1989.

40 M. Bednarski, *Drugi obieg gospodarczy…*

the activities of the Special Commission for Combating Fraud and Corruption (Komisja Specjalna do Walki z Nadużyciami i Szkodnictwem Gospodarczym) in the period 1945–1954.[41] Another was Marcin Kula, a professor at the University of Warsaw and co-founder of the school of the researchers of People's Poland, who encouraged his students to use the Special Commission's materials while researching social history;[42] other pioneers were Dariusz Jarosz and Tadeusz Wolsza, who in 1995 published, in book format, a selection of documents about the Special Commission. It is undoubtedly the best researched institution of those dealing with the illegal economic activity of Polish society (among the researchers were Piotr Fiedorczyk, Roman P. Smolorz, Bogdan Sekściński, Ludwik S. Szuba, Ryszard Tomkiewicz, and Waldemar Tomczyk). In the late 1990s, information about the Polish black market began to appear in publications on a wider spectrum of problems – Dariusz Jarosz and Maria Pasztor wrote about the context of the "meat affair", Paweł Sowiński about tourism and recreation, Dariusz Stola – about migration, Małgorzata Mazurek and Mariusz Jastrząb – about shortages, Krzysztof Kosiński – about alcoholism, Krzysztof Madej – about the policies of Gomułka's regime with regard to criminal economic activities.[43]

The primary sources also posed significant problems for researching the Polish second economy. The black market is an illegal, informal sphere of social behavior, existing as it does at the margin of the law or in conflict with it. Not surprisingly, black market players are never eager to document their activities. It was the institutions that controlled, investigated and punished those activities that produced the majority of sources. Such materials were mainly generated by the Polish Workers' Party and the Polish United Workers' Party, popularly, although incorrectly, referred to in the West as the "Communist Party" (Polska Partia Robotnicza / Polska Zjednoczona Partia Robotnicza, PPR/PZPR), the Ministry of Public Security / the Ministry of Internal Affairs (Ministerstwo Bezpieczeństwa Publicznego/Ministerstwo Spraw Wewnętrznych , MBP/MSW), the SB and MO, NIK, the General Prosecutor Office, the Ministry of Justice, the GUC and the civic institutions engaged in the fight against speculation, such as, between 1945 and 1954, the Special Commission or, between 1981 and 1987, the Central Commission for Combating Speculation (Centralna Komisja do Walki ze Spekulacją).

41 *Komisja do walki,* ed. G. Sołtysiak, Karta 1991/1, pp. 81–97.

42 T. Grosse, J. Grużewski, M. Kozak, M. Kula, M. Meller, K. Piasecki, P. Piskorski, P. Salak, M. Woźniak, P. Zalewski, *Szarzy ludzie zaplątani w codzienności komunizmu*, PH 1993/3, pp. 335–350.

43 See the bibliography.

Other sources included materials from central and local state archives,[44] which at first glance had nothing to do with the black market – such as the Ministry of Foreign Affairs, (Ministerstwo Spraw Zagranicznych, MSZ) or the Central Committee of Physical Culture and Tourism (Główny Komitet Kultury Fizycznej i Turystyki, GKKFiT) or the Central Committee of Tourism (Główny Komitet Turystyki, GKT) but which were ultimately a repository of valuable information. Much information on the behavior of the authorities can be retrieved from official reports but these are always written from the perspective of those authorities. In the absence of any sociological research into the black market[45] and the understandable reluctance of the black market protagonists to document their activities, the grass-roots perspective is painfully absent. This gap is only to a certain degree filled by letters and complaints received by the authorities, by the institutions, and newspaper editors (stored in the archives of the Polish United Workers' Party or Polish Television [TVP] archives) or reports gathered by the employees of Radio Free Europe from visitors out of Poland. The credibility of those sources is, however, questionable. The newspapers and magazines were no more credible, despite the fact that the topic of black market pathology was one always in demand in communist Poland. And yet, it was only the press (and then only for an astute reader) that constituted an invaluable source of grass-roots information.

During the almost decade-long process of researching and writing this book, I talked with close to a hundred people about the black market in communist Poland. I have never met anyone who lived in Poland during that time who had not experienced the black market phenomenon in one way or another (provided they were reasonably observant). There are twenty odd million similar potential witnesses. The sheer numbers make it difficult to use oral history testimonies in a representative way (not to mention other logistical challenges that this method would entail). Theoretically, I could have interviewed a random cross-section of people. The scale of such research would have exceeded, however, the resources of an individual scholar. I used the interview technique cautiously and only after exhausting other sources. The weekly *Polityka* and the daily *Gazeta Wyborcza* ran, on several occasions, competitions on black market memoirs; they proved to be useful and interesting for this author.

---

44 See the bibliography – list of archives.

45 With the exception of J. Węgleński, for the research on tourist commerce from the beginning of 1960s, see: chapter 9.

The type of primary sources, the great time span, and the sheer diversity of black market phenomena forced the author to limit radically the range of problems and focus on the most representative ones. It is important to stress that strict differentiation between economic crimes and black market activities turned out to be impossible. Often common sense and intuition remained the only valid criteria and then, just in case, the label "black market" was put in quotation marks.[46] In defining any market (including the black market), the main criterion is the existence of an act of trading in order to gain a profit. We are also looking for elements of organized action, deliberateness and specialization suggesting some kind of professionalism. A black market strategy should include visible stages of planning, execution, and evaluation of profitability. Black market activities also involve the presence of deliberate bending or breaking of the existing law. The product traded on the black market has to be subject to specific restrictions, such as monopoly, rationing, or a ban on distribution) on the manufacturer and distributor, imposed in this case by the communist state in Poland, which leaves no doubt with regard to its legal status. In order to be successful, economic activity requires favorable conditions and sufficient time to develop and perfect appropriate techniques and strategies. It is best to investigate the black market mechanisms that take place over a great duration with attention to possible changes and mutations. The interest of the authorities in a particular sector of an illegal trade is also one of the determining factors. A further important criterion is the mass scale of the phenomenon. It was certainly not possible to live during the times of "real socialism" without being involved in some way in black market transactions. It is important to pinpoint which sector of economy was most likely to engage in black market trading for the greatest time, preferably between 1944 and 1989. Often it is not easy to pigeon-hole some of the phenomena that at first sight seem quintessentially black market in character. For example, the illegal tobacco trade, which infringed one of the main monopolies of the state, disappeared at the turn of the 1940s and the 1950s. Tobacco trading returned to the black market in the early 1980s but only briefly and accompanied by practically all other goods. Nor do black market sales of books fit in here since they took place mostly in the 1980s and were limited to the narrow circles of book aficionados. The same can be said of the so-called *koniki*, the touts selling tickets for movies and sports events. Although they survived throughout the entire duration of the

46 in 1987, K. Rogoziński had proposed putting the word "black" in "black market" in quotation marks; K. Rogoziński, *Kryzys jako weryfikator...*, p. 161.

Polish People's Republic and continued throughout its collapse, their operations were confined to the big cities. For the same reasons I eliminate from my spectrum pornography and drugs.[47] Geography seems to be one of the most crucial criteria. The phenomena that existed continuously, reached a mass scale and were ubiquitous in most of Poland (with allowances for regional differences) would be the best to observe and study. The complexity of the subject determined the division of the chapters into two types: general and monographic. The first general chapter provides a short survey of the world history of the black market until the 1940s. It is followed by a chapter, which presents the development of the black market phenomenon in post-WWII Poland, with emphasis on the three institutions established specifically in order to combat speculation in the country. This chapter also presents the broad political, social and economic context of the Polish black market. The last chapter in this cluster offers an analysis and the correlations of the black market and its historical and geographical determinants. After considering the criteria of trade, profit, specialization, mass scale, continuity and geography on the battlefield that was the black market, there were only three armies left: those that traded in meat, those that traded in alcohol, and those that traded in both hard currency and gold. Of course the graph of the fluctuations of their black market trading was never linear. It looked more like a very irregular wave. We can definitely say though that in post-war Poland unofficial trade in those articles was an important element of the game playing between society and the authorities. It thus made sense to dedicate a separate, monographic chapter to each of the above specialized branches of the black market. The inclusion of the automobile sector of illegal trading (including cars, gas and spare parts) posed more questions. On the one hand, the black market in automobiles came into play at the beginning of motorization at the turn of the 1950s and the 1960s and reached a mass scale in the 1980s. On the other, most of the transactions, especially those involving gas, were one-sided. The state was the sole distributor of gas, which could not be produced independently (unlike meat and alcohol) or brought from abroad (unlike currency, gold or even cars). The only way of introducing gas to the black market was to "repossess" it in various ways

47 Drugs appear to be a separate issue. While other sectors of the black market enjoyed a certain level of social acceptance, this was not the case with drugs. Drug dealing was widely perceived in the rightly so, as a criminal activity. Pornography was also viewed negatively but not overly rigidly, although it is difficult to define it precisely and impossible to determine the scale of the phenomenon.

from the state. I therefore came to the conclusion that the illegal distribution of gas merited a chapter of its own.[48]

Black market phenomena were, to some extent, homogenous: despite changing economic, political, and social circumstances, certain specific goods continued to change hands illegally. More difficult to tackle is the topic of smuggling, which constituted a discrete and singular black market category. On the one hand, smuggling broke the state monopoly in international trading,[49] as well as tax and currency laws; on the other – it involved a very wide range of goods. Hard currency and gold always stayed on the smugglers' list; other wares came and went depending on the economic situation, the consumption aspirations of society, the type of shortages etc. Despite those complexities, smuggling meets our criteria: it was significant throughout the post-war era, highly profitable, and specialized. If earlier on, smuggling was regional, took place mostly in areas close to the Polish borders and involved the lower classes, in communist Poland it became a countrywide phenomenon. With the appearance of mass tourism in the late 1950s, millions of Poles began to participate in this activity. The part of the book dedicated to "currency values" presents highly specialized gold and currency smugglers. A separate monograph chapter is focused on "tourist commerce" commonly practiced within the Soviet Bloc countries. The above classification is proposed in the full knowledge that maintaining clear boundaries between each sector of the black market is extremely difficult. As always, what is not clearly defined and of an informal nature is usually full of empty spaces, margins and overlaps. As a result, some repetitions were unavoidable. It was also not possible to avoid highlighting some themes at the cost of others. The over-representation of Warsaw, evident in the book, does not mean that the role of the provinces is intentionally diminished, or that it was simply the Warsaw perspective that was the easiest to research. This approach certainly does not reflect any bias on the part of the author. There is no doubt that Warsaw remained over the years the black

48 I did not include, however, the unofficial trade in construction materials despite the fact it was a widespread, long-term practice prevalent throughout Poland. To analyze the problem would not have contributed many new details to flesh out the picture of the black market but it would have required a separate set of research methods and tools. The unofficial methods of acquiring apartments were a separate phenomenon that operated outside of the black market spectrum. See: D. Jarosz, *Peerelowskie lamenty mieszkaniowe,* in: *Od Piłsudskiego do Wałęsy. Studia z dziejów Polski XX wieku*, ed K. Persak, Warszawa 2008, 307–320, D. Jarosz, *Mieszkanie się należy… Studium z peerelowskich praktyk społecznych*, Warszawa 2010.

49 M. Bednarski, *Drugi obieg gospodarczy…*, p. 40.

market capital of the country. All the source limitations forced the author to look at the topic through the eyes of a state official or a policeman rather than those of an illegal money changer (*cinkciarz*) or the "baba" selling veal. Thus themes presenting the strategies undertaken by the black market insiders, their motivations, opinions, ethical considerations, and rituals are certainly debatable and do not exhaust the topic. The same can be said about relations between the black market and the official economy or about estimating the real profit from unofficial operations. Here, a more general question arises: how should we define black market "profit"? I am fully aware that this book can do no more than open the door; behind it there lie paths that can take us in many very different directions.

This book is the result of research financed by the Ministry of Science and Higher Education, Grant No 1 H01G074 29.

I would not have been able to write this book without help from countless friends, colleagues, acquaintances and strangers, who supported my project by bringing to my attention the existence and location of the materials, by sharing their knowledge, often very particular and unsurpassed, or by facilitating the logistic of the research. I am most grateful to Włodzimierz Borodziej, Błażej Brzostek, Katarzyna Chimiak, Katarzyna Czajka, Andrzej Garlicki, Tomasz Gleb, Grażyna Godziejewska, Bogdan Górski, Heidi Hein-Kirchner, Maria Hrnova, Iwona Jakimowicz-Ostrowska, Dariusz Jarosz, Włodzimierz Kalicki, Mariusz Kardas, Ondrej Klipa, Jacek Kochanowicz, Maria Koczerska, Jeff Kopstein, Krzysztof Kosiński, Éva Kovács, Andrzej Krajewski, Marcin Kula, Jan Kusber, Andreas Lawaty, Włodzimierz Lengauer, Tomasz Markiewicz, Ewa and Przemysław Matusik, Małgorzata Mazurek, Maria and Mikołaj Morzycki-Markowski, Jana Oldfield, Krzysztof Persak, Błażej Popławski, Joachim von Puttkamer, Jolanta Rudzińska, Maika Sach, Bożena Skarżyńska, Emilia Słomanowska-Kamińska, Grzegorz Sołtysiak, Anna and Jacek Soszyński, Paweł Sowiński, Andrzej Stach, Dariusz Stola, Grażyna Szelągowska, Philip Ther, Janina Tomala-Steinhauer, Romuald Turkowski, Maciej Wojtyński, Marcin Woźniczko, Andrzej Wroński, Anna and Piotr Wróbel, Marcin Zaremba, Jonathan Zatlin and Klaus Ziemer. The present edition is the fruit of the collaboration between Anna Wróbel and Anda and Seamus MacBride. To all others whom my less-than-perfect memory has caused me to omit I sincerely apologize.

Finally, my special thanks to my wife Iwona, who has always listened patiently to my reports on black market discoveries and was my first critical reader. Also thanks to my children Róża and Antek, for whom the shortages of the, for them pre-historic, Polish People's Republic turned into a very noticeable shortage of a father.

2. Shortage, Greed, Protest: A Short Course in the History of the Black Market in the First Half of the 20th Century

2.1 The Beginnings

As soon as man began to engage in the exchange of goods with the participation of money, attempts appeared to limit, ration, and control the process. These could be triggered by anything: a war, a natural disaster, an empty treasury, or the fear of rioting. The Code of Hammurabi introduced control over prices and earnings. In the 11th century BC, Chinese clerks supervised the harvest and set the acceptable range of prices. Seven hundred years later, the Athenians were setting maximum prices for grain. Emperor Diocletian went much further in 301 CE by setting the maximum price for 900 products and a maximum wage for 160 types of work. Both merchants and artisans tried to by-pass the constraints, whereas state officials tried to find and punish the offenders.[50] Interference in markets took place also in the Middle Ages; for instance, in 13th century England, the size of a loaf of bread was standardized and its price was set according to the price of grain. It was also in England, in 1351, that wage regulation was first introduced.[51] Attempts were made to restrict trade, for example by licensing the markets, or by applying the *jus stapulae*, the obligation on travelling salesmen passing by to offer their goods for sale for a period, which offered a privileged position to local merchants (triggering protests from others who tried to by-pass the restrictions). The restrictions imposed by the guilds were expected not only to impede access to professions but also to maintain adequate quality and price. Those contemptuously called "bunglers" (*partacze*) manufactured outside of the guild system products that were usually just as good and certainly cheaper and were, in effect, dabbling in the black market.

In the modern era, along with the establishment of centralized, bureaucratized states, which divided up the world into spheres of influence, market regulations began to take on a new, global shape. Colonial empires – Portugal, Spain, France or England – aimed at increasing the profits by introducing monopolies in trade with overseas territories. Pirates were black market buccaneers, undermining the

50 R. Sèdillot, *Histoire des marchés noirs*, Paris 1985, pp. 13–28; J. Butterworth, *The theory of price control and black markets*, Hong Kong–Singapore–Sydney 1994, pp. 3–4.

51 J. Butterworth, *The theory...*, pp. 6–7.

monopoly of the (foreign) state. In fact, it was not only foreign but also internal trade that was subject to monopoly. It included luxury items, grain, salt, tobacco, or much later, matches. Breaking the state monopoly by smuggling or producing wares illegally was a dangerous undertaking, but at the same time highly profitable, as were most other black market activities. The smugglers, who either transported goods on their own backs or reached English or French shores in their boats, were the most long-standing professional players in the black market.[52]

The French Revolution – with its continuous critical failures of supply, exorbitant prices, and anti-speculation laws can be seen as the beginning of the "modern" black market. These phenomena affected all social groups, even the most privileged, without exception. You could buy grain, sugar (especially after France had lost San Domingo), soap, and candles only by infringing the centrally imposed laws. The fast-growing inflation enhanced by the compulsory use of paper money put pressure on consumer durables and luxury items. Gold was also sought after, since its trade was controlled by the state. All these goods found themselves on the black market. The introduction of the Continental Blockade caused smuggling to flourish; as a result, new trade routes were developed via the ports of Portugal and Spain and Turkey as well as those on the Baltic.[53] The American Civil War, dominated by a black market, was a true dress rehearsal for the arrival of the 20th century. The front line stretched almost across the entire continent, some 3.5 million Americans put on military uniforms and 620 thousand lost their lives (more than American losses in two World Wars and the Korean War put together). For the first time, the railroads, the telegraph, armored ships and even a submarine were used on a large scale. This was the first total war in history that engaged the whole of society, as well as pauperizing it, and mobilized all resources, which then had to be rigidly controlled, including the rationing of oil.

2.2 The First World War and the Interwar Period

What the Americans had experienced in the 1860s was just a taste of European reality half a century later. When dispatching his troops in 1914, Kaiser Wilhelm promised that they would be back home "before the leaves fall from the trees". Those that survived returned to their families after the leaves had fallen for the fifth time. The winning side had not only had the strongest army but also the greatest material resources. The army's needs were a priority so they devoured

52 R. Sédillot, *Histoire…*, pp. 38–52.

53 R. Sédillot, op. cit. pp. 57–79, p. 87; J. Debû-Bridel, *Histoire du marché noir* (1939–1947), Paris 1947, pp. 18–23.

the majority of industrial and agricultural output. Civilians came second and received articles of lesser quality. Britain was the only country not to introduce rationing during WWI, considering it a violation of economic freedom. Trading, however, was controlled by the state, which supervised about 85% of consumption. But even in Britain, as in the rest of Europe, shortages, food lines, inflation, and high prices were common, everyday occurrences.

Despite all that, the situation was not tragic – that is not until 1916. It was only the abysmal harvest of that year in Europe, Canada and the USA as well as the painfully felt shortage of labor in agriculture and industry that brought about the collapse in supplies. In 1917, in Britain women spent so much time standing in food lines that husbands had to take time off work from their factory jobs and children miss school to take their place. There was no coal. Trucks transporting potatoes to towns were stopped and plundered. The authorities introduced maximum prices but were not able to guarantee the supply – as a result, food drifted on to the black market. Introducing fines for black marketeers made little difference; during the War no more than 290 people were fined in excess of £50, of whom only three had been involved in large scale black market trading. In the final year of the war, thirteen people were sent to prison and seven sentenced to pay high fines (in excess of £500).[54]

France introduced food rationing in March 1917, asking its citizens to change their eating habits and substitute potatoes for white bread. In Germany, the War Food Office (*Kriegsernährungsamt*) set up in May 1916 did nothing to alleviate the provision crisis. Not for nothing was the winter of 1916/1917 called the "turnip winter" – there was almost nothing else to eat.[55] Food and industrial goods were available virtually only on the black market. In April 1918, the Reichstag declared it the "only effective way of distributing food".[56] To a large extent, the shortages contributed to the radicalization of society and accounted for the support for the revolution in 1918. In Russia, the February Revolution was triggered by women rebelling at standing in lines for the bakeries.[57]

The First World War was the black market lab where strategies were initiated and later developed not only during times of conflict. Getting round food rationing by making a trip directly to the countryside became common

54 E. Smithies, *The Black Economy in England since 1914*, Dublin 1984, 19–21, pp. 28–30.

55 M. Wildt, *Der Traum vom Sattwerden. Hunger und Protest, Schwartzmarkt und Selbsthilfe in Hamburg 1945–1948*, Hamburg 1986, p. 12.

56 E. D. Kohler, *Inflation and Black Marketeering in the Rhenish Agricultural Economy 1919–1922, "German Studies Review"* no. 8, 1985/1, p. 48.

57 See: A. Û. Davydov, *Mešočniki i diktatura v Rossii: 1917–1921*, St. Petersburg 2007.

throughout Europe. In Poland (or at least in the Polish Kingdom), the terms "smuggling" (*szmugiel*) and "smuggler" (*szmugler*) in reference to someone who brought butter, meat, or potatoes to the city (often using sophisticated methods) were already in use in 1916 and 1917. Ration stamp fraud and gold and currency speculation became a common practice, gold-backed currency having disappeared as soon as the war broke out). The corruption allowed supplies to reach the military and from there food, textiles, forage, and fuel were siphoned off to the civilian market.

The First World War black market (*paskarstwo*) quietly percolated into peacetime, without changing its scale or range of products. The destroyed and pauperized Europe was unable to supply its people with enough jobs or desired products. Under the circumstances, the practice of ramping-up prices or breaking rationing (which continued in most European countries) did not disappear; on the contrary – the turnover of the black market increased. For example, in the spring of 1919 an estimated one third of food products in Germany were sold through black market channels.[58] Inflation, and indeed hyperinflation), which affected some European countries, did not help to calm the mood. In Britain, the Ministry of Supply continued to exist until 1921 and price controls and rationing of some articles carried on until 1922.[59] At that time strict market regulation ceased in other countries.

During the First World War there were attempts to limit the availability of alcohol and to introduce prohibition. Similar attempts undertaken in Russia in 1914 were completely unsuccessful. A ban on alcohol sales, officially in force in Russia until 1925, was from the outset widely ignored, which helped to encourage unofficial production and distribution. "Officially, alcohol vending is prohibited in Moscow," a Polish officer serving in the Russian army remembered at the turn of 1916/1917, "but, as Russians say, 'the law is like the shaft of a cart, it points the way you turn it', so in Russia, in every decent restaurant they'll serve in a teapot enough alcohol for anyone to have their fill."[60]

The Russian lesson had not been learnt in the USA, where prohibition was introduced in 1919. This led to the development of a huge, criminalized black market in alcohol, which embraced illegal production, smuggling and retailing. Drinking alcohol became de rigueur, partly as a protest against the state's efforts to limit personal freedom. For the first time ever, the black market began to

---

58 *Ibid.*

59 J. Butterworth, *The Theory…*, 10; E. Smithies, *The Black Economy…*, pp. 38–40.

60 I.B. Ataman (J. Pietrucin-Pietruszewski), *W wichrze rewolucji*, ed. J. Kochanowski, Karta 1991/1, p. 4.

threaten state structures, leading to the development of organized crime, which penetrated the legal sphere and successfully corrupted the justice system, local government, the police, and the customs service. The last of these was particularly significant, since smuggling became one of the chief sources of alcohol. For example, residents of St. Pierre and Miquelon, islands located close to US shores, although formally part of France (France and Canada did not recognize American prohibition law), abandoned fishing and instead used their boats for smuggling – a much more profitable pursuit. On St. Pierre, a crate of whisky went for $12 but could be sold for as much as $96 in New York City! No wonder that only in the first year of prohibition alone, the islanders shifted over 10 million (old!) dollars' worth of liquor to the USA. For owners of speedboats in the Bahamas, Cuba and Mexico, this was also a time of prosperity.[61]

Prohibition also proved how dangerous state manipulation of the market and human needs and habits could be, and how utterly futile the efforts of the state against resistance by large sections of society. All that the expansion of the apparatus of repression seems to achieve is an increase of evermore specialized and effective techniques for evading restrictions.

In independent Poland, the first decree on protection of the consumer and the market was issued as early as December 5, 1918. Based on the act of January 11, 1919, the Office for Combating Usury and Speculation (Urząd do Walki z Lichwą i Spekulacją) was created in the Ministry of Supply. It was authorized to punish "acts of usury and all kinds of illegal trade in essential articles" with penalties of up to three months jail and fines of up to 50 thousand marks.[62] Soon, the dire economic situation, made even worse by the war effort, forced the authorities to implement comprehensive measures. A bill on "combating war usury" was passed on July 2, 1920.[63] The Office for Combating Usury and Speculation had wide powers, including the ability to issue warrants for searching apartments. Departments of State were empowered to conduct investigations and, on their own authority, punish minor offenders, with fines and detention of six months. For particularly severe crimes, the death penalty was not out of the question. The Office operated until the summer of 1922; subsequently, its powers were transferred to the voivodships. In the years that followed (1923–1924), with the currency stabilized, supply improved, and rationing ended – the black market faded away. Particular branches of it such as smuggling or distilling moonshine

61 J. Paxton, J. Wroughton, *Smuggling*, Basingstoke–London, 1971, pp. 39–41.

62 Journal of Laws, Dziennik Ustaw, Dz. U. 7/109, Jan 18, 1919; A. Mogilnicki, *Lichwa*, in: Z. Cybichowski, *Encyklopedia podręczna prawa publicznego,* vol 1, Warszawa, 373.

63 Dz. U. 67/449, August 4, 1920.

would reappear as a result of the Great Depression (between 1931 and 1936, each year the authorities uncovered a few thousand illegal distilleries).[64] The terms "smuggler" and "speculator" returned to the pages of Polish newspapers in the last weeks of peace in 1939, when fear of war caused a panic that resulted in runs on shops. This in turn was used by store-owners as a pretext to raise prices. The authorities tried to put the fear of God into ruthless traders; posters proclaimed that 'speculators' would be carted off to the Bereza Kartuska prison camp.

2.3 Second World War

Runs on stores demonstrated that society had not forgotten the dramatic shortages of the First World War (and its aftermath). The authorities were well aware of the problem, especially those in countries that conducted aggressive, conflict-oriented policies, reliant on food imports. Both Japan and Germany were in that group; the latter, despite its attempts at self-sufficiency, had to import half of its meat, fats, and dairy requirements. Both countries froze wages and prices. Just before the war, most foodstuffs and industrial goods were rigidly controlled and rationed. The authorities asked citizens to cut back and use ersatz products. "Luxury is your enemy!" ran a propaganda campaign slogan. Regulatory bodies were established.

In Japan, as early as July 1939 a special economic police force was set up. During the first 15 months of its operation, it arrested more than two million people – 3.5% of all citizens. In spite of that, the Japanese market systematically weakened and the real cost of goods exceeded the prices set by the authorities to such an extent that trading became simply not worthwhile. This forced both vendors and buyers to work towards a strategy that would preserve the appearance of legality and give the authorities a pretext to turn a blind eye to their activities. The traditional Japanese custom of bestowing gifts was revived; any discrepancy between the official and the market price was adjusted soon after the transaction had taken place, and accounted for as its "gift" value. "The wartime strategies formed the basis for the post-war period, when an estimated 17 000 local black markets were identified. They were the basis for the development of yakuza.[65]

In Germany, the National Socialists prepared for war not only the military but also the supply chain. Shortly before Germany attacked Poland, State Boards (*Reichsstellen*) were set up; these were responsible for different sectors of the food market such as grain, fat, and meat. At all administrative levels, Food Offices

64 J. Łukasiewicz, *Gorzelnictwo*, in: *Encyklopedia historii gospodarczej Polski do 1945 roku*, ed. A. Mączak, vol. 1, Warszawa 1981, p. 205.

65 O. Griffith, *Need, Greed and Protest…*, pp. 828–830, pp. 834–835.

(*Ernährungsämter*) were established – as a matter of fact this system survived the fall of the Third Reich.[66] The German authorities were well aware of how people behaved in times of crisis. That is why as early as July 1939, they banned the hoarding of goods, and continued to expand the rationing and trade controls. As long as supplies were sufficient and ration stamps covered the main needs, unofficial trade was limited to barter and side trade (*Tauschhandel, Schleichhandel*), mainly among friends. However, when in 1941 and 1942 it became increasingly difficult to buy the radically diminished rations, unofficial trade showed all characteristics of a black market (*Schwarzmarkt*). Thanks to Germany's brutal exploitation of the occupied countries, its rationing system functioned much more effectively than those of other countries.

Until the end of the Second World War, a significant number of Nazi policy-makers believed that by tightening the restrictive measures they would be able to harness the illegal transactions. In January 1942, Goebbels started a propaganda campaign directed against the illegal trade.

Two months later, only trading exclusively between consumers (households) was permitted; trading between manufacturers and consumers was prohibited. Despite the fact that death sentences for black market crimes continued to be carried out as late as April 1945, it was hard to expect that millions of people would accept cold and hunger without any protest. Nothing could stop the Germans from travelling to the countryside looking for food (*Hamsterfahrten*) or prevent the clandestine slaughter of animals and selling of the meat, or the distribution of forged ration stamps.[67] Black market activities were endemic: peasants, industrialists, the SS-men guarding concentration camps (where a separate black market existed), and soldiers (who had looted goods or bought them illegally in the occupied territories – a major source of contraband) all played their part in black market transactions on a big scale. Small fry of the black market felt exonerated when looking at Party elites who, even as they urged "extreme saving measures", were themselves involved in consumer scandals. At the turn of 1942 and 1943, the German public learned of an affair involving August Nöthling, the owner of a Berlin delicatessen who had supplied products unavailable to most Germans to many prominent figures (including Richard Darré, the Third Reich's Minister of Food and Agriculture. The scandal was, at Hitler's personal wish, quickly hushed up (Nöthling committed suicide, probably "assisted" by the SS).[68]

---

66 M. Wildt, *Der Traum…*, pp. 14–15.

67 W.A. Boelcke, *Der Schwarz-Markt 1945–1948. Vom Überleben nach dem Kriege*, Braunschweig 1986, pp. 11–13.

68 *Ibid.*, pp. 2021, pp. 26–28.

On the other side of the front line, the black market was a common phenomenon connected with never-ending problems with provisions. In 1939 Britain instituted a system of rationing. It was fully implemented by 1942. The British system was clear, egalitarian, and easy to use and control. Some products, for example cigarettes or hard liquor, were not rationed but heavily taxed and supplied in small amounts (alcohol was mostly reserved for export). Those products immediately became black market items (they were stolen, smuggled, or manufactured). It was the same story with textiles, soap, cosmetics, and razors. Due to war priorities, there was a ban on production of toys, jewelry, glass, and leather goods. Naturally, they also appeared on the black market.[69]

The black market and trade restrictions took a somewhat different form overseas. In particular, Canada, a member of the British Commonwealth, adopted restrictive measures at the very beginning of the war. The Wartime Prices and Trade Board (WPTB), which controlled prices, production and allocation was established[70] as early as September 3, 1939. Both in Canada and the USA, the war was a time of prosperity, economic growth, and pay increases. Between 1939 and 1942 wages in Canada increased by 100%. The problem was that there was nothing to buy. Canada, as did Europe, radically limited production for civilian consumers. For example between 1940 and 1943, the production of furniture fell by half, refrigerators from 53 161 to 358, and washing machines – from 117 512 to 13 200 units. The WPTB had to introduce special price lists for used articles. They were usually ignored and the difference was paid "under the table". This practice applied especially to automobiles. The production of cars for the civilian market fell from 102 664 in 1940 to 11 966 in 1943 (and half of these were reserved for physicians, policemen and firemen). Theoretically, car depreciation was expected to be 25% in the first year and 10% in subsequent years. In reality – as happened in the 1980s in Poland – used cars were sold for twice the official price. Similar practices applied to spare parts and gas (often sold by soldiers), textiles, and coal.

The list of rationed food products also gradually lengthened: in 1942 it included coffee, tea, sugar, and alcohol, in 1943 – also beef and canned food (the rations were often three times as high as in Britain). In Canada, black market means of acquiring meat from farms, warehouses, and factories spread with lightning

69 E. Smithies, *The Black Economy…*, pp. 64–67, E. Smithies, *Crime in Wartime: A Social History of Crime in World War II*, London 1982, I. Zweiniger-Bargiełowska, *Austerity in Britain: Rationing, Controls, and Consumption, 1939–1955*, Oxford-New York 2000, pp. 151–202, M. Roodhouse, *Black Market Britain: 1939–1945*, Oxford 2013.

70 See: J. Keshen, *One for All or All for One: Government Controls, Black Marketing and the Limits of Patriotism, 1939–1947*, Journal of Canadian Studies 29, 1994/4, pp. 111–143.

speed. The alcohol shortage affected moonshine production and smuggling from the USA (cigarettes were also "imported" from there). In 1944 the restrictions were eased, in 1946 – most of them were abolished altogether.

Rationing (and the black market) was similar in the USA. Already by1942, sales of tires were subject to rationing, as the supply of natural rubber had been cut off; next came gas rationing (beginning in May 1942 in the eastern states only; which were supplied mostly by sea by oil tankers; and from December, throughout the whole country). From November 1943, the rationing included almost all products that were crucial for the war effort or that were using resources needed for the war effort, such as cars, sugar, bicycles, shoes, coffee, cheese, butter, meat, canned food, dried fruit, coal etc. Gas, meat, and sugar became the main items sold on the back market.[71]

Characteristically, even in Britain, where the supply problems were much more severe than overseas, there was not a single case of the black market monopolizing or in any way controlling a section of the market. Organized crime did not develop. On the one hand, Britain was cut off from its neighbors and smuggling on a large scale was out of the question. On the other – most British, American, and Canadian citizens supported the actions of their authorities. This strong social control was based more on a sense of community and responsibility than on fear. "Supply" propaganda played on patriotism and was more effective in the Allied states than in Germany, Japan or Italy. The British or Americans could easily notice all the tangible effects of restrictive measures. The common-sense approach of the British and American authorities, which treated illegal trade as a necessary safety valve to regulate the market, cannot be underestimated. Convictions in connection with black market activities were few; the majority involved inflating the prices of goods or breaking the rationing rules.[72]

Europe at war constituted a tightly woven system which included the neutral states. Almost all countries introduced rationing, which quickly generated black market phenomena. This was most noticeable in Sweden, where a large proportion of food products had to be imported. There, food rationing started on March 27, 1940, just before Germany's attack on Denmark and Norway. Until the end of 1941, the rationing system in Sweden encompassed most basic products. The black market, at first insignificant, began to grow in 1943, and by the end of the war its turnover encompassed between 20 and 30% of all trade. Transactions

71 World War II Rationing, www.u-s-history.com/pages/h1674.html (accessed: March 5, 2014).

72 E. Smithies, *The Black Economy…*, pp. 68–69, J. Butterworth, *The Theory…*, p. 16.

took place mostly in official stores, which commonly broke the rationing rules (of the 1 300 surveyed stores, 65% sold meat outside the ration coupons system). Between 1940 and 1952, Swedish courts sentenced 67 thousand people for taking part in unofficial transactions.[73]

In Britain, the USA, Canada, Sweden, Germany, Japan or Italy participation in the black market had been prompted by need and greed; it was not an activity that functioned as a form of social protest. It was different in occupied countries; participation in black market activities was on the one hand often the only way of surviving on a daily basis and, on the other, a form of resistance. Kazimierz Wyka wrote: "In the winter of 1939/40, the population of the General Government faced a clear dilemma: accept the size of rations and starve to death, or – somehow or other manage. Naturally, the first alternative was never considered seriously; the important thing was: how to survive without accepting the restrictions?"[74]

This was the dilemma that faced citizens of all the occupied countries. However, in each country a different percentage of the population asked themselves such questions. On the one hand, permanent features of the occupation landscape were shortages, unemployment, low wages, food lines, rationing, hunger, and as their consequence a black market. On the other, the occupation systems differed significantly from one another.[75] There were different ideologies but also different practices. While in the economically developed Western countries the occupiers tried to take advantage rationally of opportunities and resources using the existing administrative and economic system, in the backward East and South they effectively adopted colonial experience, subjected the conquered lands to ruthless exploitation and viewed them as a source of food, cheap labor and resources.

While in the west negotiations, often successful, were arranged between the invaders and representatives of the occupied population, in the east and south, coercive measures and terror were the tools of communication. The peoples of Denmark, Holland, and Czechoslovakia were allowed by the occupiers to

73 J. Wijk, *Svarta börsen-samhällslojalitet i kris. Livsmedelsransoneringarna och den illegalahandeln i Sverige 1940–1949*, Stockholm 1992.

74 K. Wyka, *Życie na niby*, Kraków 2010, p. 276.

75 See P. Voglis, *Surviving Hunger: Life in the Cities and Countryside during the Occupation*, in: *Surviving Hitler and Mussolini: Daily Life in Occupied Europe*, ed. R. Gildea, O. Wieviorka, A. Warring, Oxford–New York 2006, pp. 16–41. In Polish historiography: C. Madajczyk, *Faszyzm i okupacje 1938–1945*, vol 2: *Mechanizmy realizowania okupacji*, Poznań 1984.

consume a much greater part of their industrial and agricultural output than the citizens of conquered Poland, Greece, Serbia or the Soviet Union. This affected directly the size of the ration and in consequence turned permanent shortages into chronic hunger. It is not surprising that in the east and south, the motivation to create new strategies for survival and the drive to abandon old habits was the strongest. Earlier black market experiences also played their part, such as those of Poland during World War I, as did the lower level of acceptance of authority compared to Western Europe. Ignoring bans and restrictions imposed by the occupier became a patriotic duty. Legal sanctions, including the death penalty, were unable to put a stop to this state of affairs.

Even though in different occupied countries the black market came in different shapes and hues;[76] it usually consisted of corresponding sectors and used similar

---

76 In German-occupied Poland, the black market was most developed in the territory of the General Government, where (especially in Warsaw) it became a specialized field practiced officially and professionally. See: W. Jastrzębowski, *Gospodarka niemiecka w Polsce 1939–1944, Warszawa 1946, M. Walczak, Walka ekonomiczna narodu polskiego 1939–1945,* Warszawa 1983, T. Szarota, *Okupowanej Warszawy dzień powszedni. Studium historyczne*, Warszawa 1988. In the territories incorporated in the Reich, where the center-liberal measures were much stricter and rations larger, the illegal trade was smaller in scope and limited to groups of trusted participants. See: T. Janicki, *Czarny rynek w Poznaniu podczas II Wojny Światowej, Kronika Miasta Poznania,* 2009–3, pp. 94–116. The black market in the Russian occupation zone was limited due to similar reasons. See: G. Hryciuk, *Polacy we Lwowie 1939–1944. Życie codzienne*, Warszawa 2000, S. Lewandowska, *Życie codzienne Wilna w latach II wojny światowej*, Warszawa 1997. In **France,** by the end of the German occupation 10–30 per cent of all transactions were occurring on the black market. In 1942–43 in Vichy France, it is estimated that 92 billion francs' worth of basic food products were sold on the black market. At that time, the budget of the French state was 135 billion. See: R. Sédillot, *Histoire*, p. 143, L. Taylor, *The Black Market in Occupied Northern France, 1940–44*, Contemporary European History, 1997/6, pp. 158–167, P. Sanders, *Histoire du marché noir 1940–46*, Paris, 2001, D. Veillon, *Vivre et survive en France 1939–1947*, Paris 1995, F. Grenard, *La France du marché noir 1940–49*, Paris 2008, Y. Lecouturier, *Le marché noir en Normandie 1939–1945*, Rennes 2010. On **Greece,** see: V. Hionidou, *Black market, Hyperinflation and Hunger: Greece 1941–44*, Food & Foodways, 2004/12, 81–106, M. Mazower, *Inside Hitler's Greece: The Experience of Occupation 1941–44*, New Haven–London 1993, S. Thomadakis, *Black Market, Inflation and Force in the Economy of Occupied Greece*, in: *Greece in the 1940s. A Nation of Crisis*, ed. J.O. Iatrides, Hanover (USA), London 1981. On **Holland** see: H.A. van der Zee, *The Hunger Winter: Occupied Holland 1944–5,* London 1982. On **Belgium** see: R. Miry, *Zwarte Handel in levensmiddelen*, Brussels 1946, P. Struye, G. Jacquelyns, *La Belgique sous l'occupation allemande 1940–44*, Brussels 1950. On **Denmark** see: C. Bundgård Christensen, *Den sorte børs. Fra besættelsen til*

strategies. The inhabitants of big cities, subject to the greatest pauperization, were always among the losers. They were the most affected by frozen wages, unemployment and poverty-level food rations, which covered only a small portion of the human calorie requirement (no more than one third of it in the General Government!). They were forced to rely on the black market, where prices tended to be many times higher than the official ones.[77] The effects of the high prices were often dismal: in Athens and Piraeus, some 40 thousand people died of malnutrition between the fall of 1941 and late 1942! For city dwellers, to participate in the black market, whether as customers, vendors or middlemen was a necessity, a basic condition of survival. The rural population, especially from areas close to the city, benefited from this situation. For example, small towns located in the vicinity of Warsaw specialized in selling different black market products: Karczew supplied meat (not for nothing was it called "Prosiaków", "prosię" meaning "a piglet" in Polish), Jabłonna and Legionowo – moonshine, Rembertów – tobacco, Piaseczno, Góra Kalwaria and Grójec – flour.[78]

The countryside, increasingly exploited under strict control since 1942, was nevertheless still able to produce a surplus destined for the cities. Villagers in eastern and southern Europe were managing much better than French, Dutch or Danish modern farmers. Thanks to traditional methods of running farms, the peasants of eastern and central European were better at creating defense mechanisms.[79] They were better both at avoiding the distribution networks of rationed goods and at deliberately frustrating any surveillance. Often, thanks to corruption, they were able more easily to reach mutually advantageous compromises with lower level occupation authorities. In Europe, a grand redistribution of wealth was taking place: money, gold, hard currency, jewelry, furniture, carpets, clothing, anything and everything. All migrated from the cities to the countryside.

---

efterkrigstid, Copenhagen 2010. On **Italy** see: R. Mariano, *Borsari neri in Roma citta aperta,* Rome 1989. On **Soviet Union** see: V.S. Puzškarēv, *"Cernyj" rynek w SSSR v gody velikoj otecestvennoj wojny i ego vlijanie na sostajanie vnutrennego rynka strany*, Ekonomiceskij Žurnal, 2006/12, pp. 212–225.

77 P. Voglis, *Surviving Hunger*…, 2, M. Walczak, Walka ekonomiczna…, 28–29. In General Government, food staples prices rose on the free market 10 times for bread, p. 120 times for pork fat, while wages were mostly frozen at pre-war levels. M. Walczak, Walka ekonomiczna…, pp. 23–27.

78 M. Walczak, Walka ekonomiczna…, pp. 67–8, see also T. Szarota, Okupowanej Warszawy…, pp. 220–39.

79 A. Jezierski, C. Leszczyńska, *Historia gospodarcza Polski*, Warszawa 1999, pp. 354–5, P. Voglis, *Surviving Hunger*…, p. 17.

Trips to the countryside to get food became a commonplace occurrence. City inhabitants, both workers and the intelligentsia, laden with suitcases and bundles, were an everyday sight in Paris, Athens, Amsterdam and Warsaw. Out-of-town trips could supply the family and provide a bit of an income, which allowed the black market sharks to make enormous profits. Sometimes these were full-blown illegal enterprises, with their own supply and distribution networks, and their own transportation, as well as a good relationship with the occupation authorities.

Most of the food smuggled in from the countryside was sold in the cities in official stores or restaurants, where the owners regularly violated the rationing regulations. Let us note that ration stamp trading was an important part of black market activity in Europe. The stamps were stolen from the occupation authorities, forged, and used multiple times. The emergence in Paris or Warsaw of illicit restaurants that served luxury dishes and drinks was a brand-new phenomenon.[80] The fact that you could get Russian caviar in Paris restaurants and smoked salmon and French cognac in those in Warsaw was made possible by the widespread participation in the black market of soldiers and occupation officials, who were often the conduits for contraband between the far-flung regions of occupied Europe.

Indeed, participation in the black market by the occupiers was much wider and multi-layered, even in the General Government where the chasm dividing the occupiers and the occupied was at its deepest. In all the occupied countries the attitude of the invaders to the black market was, on the one hand suffused with ideology, on the other, with pragmatism. Usually, the latter prevailed. Everywhere, illicit trade was fought either through dogged persistence or sporadic large-scale anti-black-market operations (usually followed by price hikes). These "repression spectaculars" were mostly for show, a cover for turning a blind eye to black market transactions, which to a certain extent solved local supply problems and constituted a source of additional and often sold by soldiers), textiles, and coal.

The sometimes considerable profit, both for the gendarme happy to accept a bribe from a street vendor and for the high official dealing in often vast quantities of goods – since the spiriting of goods out of military warehouses or transport was carried out not only by stealing but also by corrupting representatives of the occupying authorities. Food, fuel and textiles often entered the black market in this manner. There were sometimes surprises; for example, in May 1943 Warsaw

80 J. Debû-Bridel, Histoire…, pp. 124–131, A. Strzeżek, *Od konsumpcji do konspiracji czyli warszawskie lokale gastronomiczne 1939–1944*, Warszawa 2012.

was "inundated" with live turtles, several train cars of which had been bought from German convoys.[81]

The General Government and especially Warsaw, situated as it was on the communication highway between occupied western Europe and the eastern front, became a destination for selling luxury items brought from France. Likewise, it was only thanks to the black market that German soldiers and officials could buy and send to their families products unavailable at home such as fats or alcohol. Factory owners and managers often distributed their products through black market channels, outside of the rationing system and for a much higher price. And it was also on the black market that they had to buy food and industrial articles that they passed on to their workers as a form of payment in kind; this "oiled the wheels", helping to keep productivity at a relatively high level. The occupation authorities were aware of this practice and in 1943 estimated that the black market covered between 30 and 50% of all demand.[82]

There is no in-depth comparative analysis of the black markets in different European countries.[83] The existing research mainly concentrates on legal trade and overshadows the illicit production. The territory of the General Government seemed to have been in the lead not only in the highly-developed clandestine food industry, which encompassed moonshine distilleries, mills, bakeries, meat and oil processing plants, but also in illegal plants manufacturing cosmetics, shoes, clothes and other everyday items.[84] Smuggling food to the Jewish ghettos especially the Warsaw ghetto, was a regional specialty of the General Government black market.[85]

The vast majority of the goods smuggled into the Warsaw ghetto were paid for with hard currency (gold, jewelry, cash) or with objects of item The art trade constituted a very significant part of the black market in all the occupied countries.

---

81 T. Szarota, *Okupowanej Warszawy…*, pp. 230–1.

82 AAN, Government Delegation for Poland, (AAN, DRnK), 202/IV-1, fol. 82, S. Schwaneberg, The economic policy of the German occupation authorities in the General Government 1939–1945, manuscript shared by the author.

83 See: T. Szarota, *Życie codzienne w stolicach okupowanej Europy. Szkice historyczne, kronika wydarzeń*, Warszawa 1995.

84 M. Walczak, *Walka ekonomiczna…*, pp. 73–4.

85 M. Passenstein, *Szmugiel w getcie warszawskim*, Biuletyn Żydowskiego Instytutu Historycznego 1958/26, C. Battrick, Smuggling as a Form of Resistance in the Warsaw Ghetto, "Journal of Holocaust Education" 4, 1995/2, pp. 199–224, B. Engelking, J. Leociak, *Getto warszawskie. Przewodnik po nieistniejącym mieście*, 2013, pp. 481–496, H. Grynberg, J. Kostański, *Szmuglerzy*, Warszawa 2001.

There was also strong demand for stores of value such as hard currency and gold coins, which was fueled by inflation and massive profits made both by the occupation apparatus and the local population, including the black market racketeers. Another factor in seeking a tangible form of investment was the considerable likelihood of suddenly losing one's entire worldly possessions. Each of the occupied countries had their favorites. While in Poland, gold dollars and roubles were the main objects of hoarding (see chapter 8), in France it was gold twenty-franc coins.[86] Everybody, however – including the Germans and the Italians – placed great trust in the American "greenback".

It is impossible to assess the black market during the Second World War and under German occupation unequivocally. Undoubtedly, the second economy was for many a means of survival, keeping the wolf from the door. After the war, it became a significant element of memory politics, construed into the most common form of political resistance. This was most apparent in those countries where armed resistance was not significant but collaboration with the occupiers was common. In France, for example, as soon as the war ended, research focused on the symbolic and heroic aspects of the black market.[87] *The Black Market in Paris*, a French film released in 1956 had a similar message.

There was, however, a flipside. The black market was far from being a charitable activity. It punished the poor but rewarded the brave, the dynamic and the ruthless. Some it made rich, others it pauperized. It was kind to those who had no qualms in taking advantage of the situation or who chose to collaborate with the occupier. Prevailing public opinion on the black market was ambivalent; for example the Polish underground press was full of warnings about profiteering storeowners and their exorbitant prices. Even in France, where the black market eventually came to be glorified as a form of wartime resistance against the occupier, after the liberation the courts were still convicting people for involvement in illegal trade during the occupation.[88]

2.4 After the War

The courts had, however, a much greater problem with post-war participants in the black market. The end of the war did not halt black market operations, which continued in peace time without a hitch. The circumstances were already favorable. On the one hand, people were fed up with restrictions and did not perceive

86 R. Sédillot, *Histoire…*, pp. 134–135.
87 M. David, *Le marché noir*, Paris 1945, J. Debû-Bridel, Histoire…
88 L. Taylor, *The Black Market*, p. 174.

them as reasonable once the war was over. Sacrifices for the sake of "our boys on the front line" were no longer necessary and did not prevent anyone from participating in illegal transactions. The survivors were eager to make up the wartime losses. What they now wanted was to get a life in more sense than one. That is why for example the black market in Britain concentrated on luxury items (usually smuggled) such as the coveted nylon stockings or watches, as well as American cigarettes and gas, which was in such short supply that a monthly allowance would barely suffice for a trip from London to Brighton.[89] A vast part of Europe was in ruins and an even larger part was impoverished. Even such a powerful state such as Britain was on the brink of bankruptcy. Keeping consumption at a low level while focusing on exports could help pay off the debts. Other countries, including Poland, were in a similar situation.

There were many other factors that fueled the black market mechanisms. The war had broken down social barriers, shaken moral standards and spread pathological behavior of which the illicit trade was one of the mildest. Poverty has always been one of the most important engines of the black market. Alcohol and cigarettes were considered remedies for stress and gold and hard currencies – insurance against hardship. The displaced masses that spread out over the European continent were a natural reservoir of potential black market participants. Millions of people were traversing the globe, whether voluntarily or forced to do so by circumstances and they were widening the channels of illegal trade by canny arbitrage, facilitating the flow of goods between areas of abundance and those of shortages. The victorious troops, the US army with the greatest resources at its disposal, joined in the mass transfer of goods. The long, cold and snowy winter of 1946/47 and a catastrophic draught in the summer of 1947 posed an additional challenge. All European countries, from Spain to the Soviet Union, had to deal with supply shortages worse than those of the war; this continued to stimulate new black market strategies.

In post-war Britain and France, the black market complemented the official distribution channels. In Italy and especially in Germany, just as it had been in occupied Poland and Greece, making use of the black market was a prerequisite for survival. "If you wanted to eat, you had to trade," a Romanian DP reminisced.[90] The black market had not only a practical but also a psychological impact. In a country that had been destroyed, occupied and divided, and was grappling with

---

89 E. Smithies, *The Black Economy*, p. 91, p. 110, p. 130. Roodhouse *ibid*. Gas rationing ended in May 1950.

90 J. Sandulescu, *Hunger's Rogues: On the Black Market in Europe 1948*, New York–London 1974, p. 18.

enormous economic and demographic problems (with millions of displaced people and refugees) while coming to terms with the bitterness of defeat, the black market played a therapeutic role. The popular German saying "God helps those who help themselves"[91] took on a slightly different meaning. Participation in the black market attested to one's creativity and self-reliance. If in France it was a mythologized form of resistance, in Germany it was one of the founding myths of the new state. Germany was the only country where the immediate post-war years were commonly called, as indeed they still are now, the "Schwarzmarktzeit", the time of the black market. There, the black market became a vital component of the collective memory, often portrayed in literature and films and the subject of academic research.[92]

It is worth dwelling on the German black market since it demonstrates persuasively the universal pervasiveness of black market strategies, regardless of place and time. If a large number of Germans, both civilians and soldiers, were involved in the black market transactions during the war; as soon as the war ended – they all were. During the so called "no man's time" when the old wages were not paid anymore and the new ones had not yet started to be paid, when the old food stamps had expired and the new ones were not yet available, with cash reserves gone and banks still closed, pantries and store shelves emptied – the black market was all that stood between the people and certain perdition.[93]

The situation was not desperate as long as the reserves remained. Soon they too were gone, and at the beginning of 1946, the Combined Food Board in Washington

---

91 M. Wildt, *Der Traum…*, p. 103.

92 See: M. Wildt, *Der Traum…*, W.A. Boelcke, *Der Schwarz-Markt…*, J. Lenzner, *Brennende Kehle. Schwarzer Markt 1945–1948 oder: Der authentische Bericht eines Kenners der dunkelsten Schattenwirtschaft zwischen Stunde Null und Währungsreform von ihm selbst aufgezeichnet*, Bremen 1988; P. Erker, *Ernährungskrise und Nachkriegsgesellschaft. Bauern und Arbeiterschaft in Bayern 1943–1953*, Stuttgart 1990; R. Gries, *Die Rationengesellschaft. Versorgungskampf und Vergleichsmentalität. Leipzig, München und Köln nach dem Kriege*, Münster 1991; J. Roesler, *The Black Market in Post-war Berlin and the Method Used to Counteract It*; "German History: The Journal of the German History Society" 7, 1989/1, pp. 92–107; M. Zierenberg, *Stadt der Schieber. Der Berliner–Schwarzmarkt 1939–1950*, Göttingen 2008; F. Grube, G. Richter, *Die Schwarzmarktzeit. Deutschland zwischen 1945 und 1948*, Hamburg 1979; P. Steege, *Black Market, Cold War. Everyday Life in Berlin, 1946–1949*, New York 2007; S. Mörchen, *Schwarzer Markt: Kriminalität, Ordnung und Moral in Bremen 1939–1949*, Frankfurt/Main 2011. About Austria: E. Holzer, *Schleichhändler vor Gericht. Der Schwarzmarkt in der Steiermark nach dem 2. Weltkrieg*, Graz 2007.

93 W.A. Boelcke, *Der Schwarz-Markt…*, p. 76.

drastically limited allocations for the western occupation zones, which instantly cut food rations down to a quarter of their previous level. In 1946 the situation became critical in many places. For example between April and July of 1946, 160 out of the 700 hundred patients at the psychiatric clinic in Grafenberg near Düsseldorf died, and the rest were on their last legs. By June, fresh meat had disappeared from the market (only cans were issued).[94] The situation was not much better in the Russian zone. When it seemed that life could not get any worse, the severe winter of 1946/7 arrived (which triggered a transport collapse; securing coal deliveries became the primary task of the police), followed by the summer drought. As a result, the food supply diminished further, and at the turn of 1947/48 fats became unavailable. All that the promise of currency reform, with its implicit devaluation, at first achieved was to invigorate the black market. Peasants were reluctant to get rid of their products, preferring to wait for the new, "good" money. When, finally, it did arrive in the western occupation zones, it created the basis for the free market. As a mass phenomenon, the black market had to leave the stage.

The German post-war black market consisted in fact of many different phenomena – from the self-organised *Hamsterfahrten*, foraging expeditions to the countryside, to large-scale trade operations (often run by crime groups), theft, and supply ration scams. Germans had to develop the same strategies as the Poles, Greeks or French had earlier done. The difference was that they no longer faced the threat of being sent to a concentration camp if they were caught. In Germany and in the German speaking territories, members of all social classes, from peasants to the aristocracy, were to be found using the black market.[95] Because there was a shortage of adult men, young people and women made up the greater part of the black-market traders; another group consisted of Displaced Persons, the so-called DPs. After the war, the DPs, who lived on United Nations Relief and Rehabilitation Administration (UNRRA) supplies, had time and opportunity on their hands as well as little to lose, and much to gain. Both those who were planning to return to their homeland and those who wanted to emigrate tried to gather as many resources as possible to make the beginning of a new life easier in due course. The black market offered a perfect opportunity.[96] Trading between the city and the countryside constituted the foundation of the black market. Interestingly,

94 M. Wildt, *Der Traum…*, p. 37, p. 43, p. 45.

95 In 1946 the *Schwarzmarktring* was uncovered. Agathe Prinzessin von Preußen, Elisabeth Prinzessin von Preußen and Luise Henriette Schmalz nee Prinzessin von Preußen were part of it; J. Lenzner, *Brennende Kehle…*, p. 13.

96 *Ibid*. 34–35; W.A. Boelcke, *Der Schwarz-Markt…*, p. 82. See: J. Sandulescu, *Hunger's rogues…*

peasants who to a large extent had carried on with survival strategies well-rehearsed during the First World War did not consider their black market activities as law-breaking but rather a way of combating their own poverty. Not without reason – from mid-1945 to mid-1948, peasants had no way of laying their hands legally on more than between one and two percent of the indispensable means of production. Out of necessity, they turned to the black market.[97] They made no pretense of it being a charitable activity. In time, they became quite savvy in the realm of alternative business. As a rule, they refused to accept currency that was depreciating at the speed of light, but instead demanded payment from their trading partners in the cities in the form of clothing, bedding, carpets, jewelry and clocks.[98] The longer the provisions crisis lasted, the more specialized became the actions of the peasants who waited for seasonal dips in supply and then sold food at a higher price. In spite of frequent controls and restrictions they always found a way to produce a surplus or to explain the sudden disappearance of products meant for central distribution. It is possible that as much as half of all production was distributed through unofficial channels. For example in the Russian occupation zone at the turn of 1947 and 1948, some 57% of the livestock was found to have 'disappeared'.[99] As a result, peasants (for example, in Bavaria)[100] were the only group that could afford to make investments.

In the cities, the black market, or rather the black markets were unofficially institutionalized, usually in streets and squares not far from the railroad stations. The greatest centers of unofficial trading were in Berlin (Alexanderplatz, the Tiergarten, the ruins of the Reichstag, and in the vicinity of the Potsdamer Bahnhof) and also in Hamburg, Munich, Hanover, Düsseldorf, and Frankfurt-am-Main.[101]

Everything could be, and was, sold on the black market; however, some articles played a particularly important role. These were coffee, sugar, alcohol, and above all cigarettes. Beginning in 1943/44 when the anti-inflation measures failed and the German mark was depreciating rapidly, cigarettes emerged as the main substitute for money, a "measure of all things" (Erich Kästner noted in his diary in February 1945 that cigarettes should be counted not in numbers but in copies).[102] Cigarettes had some characteristics of good money, since they were countable and convenient to handle, but they were certainly not sustainable legal tender. After

---

97 P. Erker, *Ernährungskrise…*, p. 75.

98 R. Gries, *Die Rationengesellschaft…*, p. 107, p. 109.

99 W.A. Boelcke, *Der Schwarz-Markt…*, p. 141.

100 P. Erker, *Ernährungskrise…*, p. 177.

101 W.A. Boelcke, *Der Schwarz-Markt…*, pp. 84–88.

102 P. Erker, *Ernährungskrise…*, p. 28.

the war they not only maintained but also strengthened their position as a "money substitute". Since 60% of all adult Germans (and an unknown percentage of youngsters) smoked, they were all potential clients of the black market. The most valuable were American cigarettes, a "gold standard", which – measured in items, packages, and cartons – formed the baseline for other black market prices.[103]

While in the spring of 1945 the price of tobacco products was a hundred times higher than before the war, the price of coffee and alcohol skyrocketed three hundredfold.[104] It was still possible to produce alcohol at home. Moonshine distilling caught on like wildfire. Bootleg liquor was produced in the city and in the countryside, in basements, kitchens, and scientific labs (including those of the university in Greifswald).[105] It was more difficult to acquire (whether by buying or stealing) coffee from the occupiers than to distil spirits at home. As for coffee, it was only available as contraband. Coffee was usually smuggled in, together with hard currency, gold or industrial products from France, Belgium and Holland – countries that had colonies, and thus coffee. "People transported all kinds of things," Tomasz Domaniewski noted in Antwerp in the spring of 1946, "but mostly cars, which they filled with parts, machinery, chemicals and other items which in Germany they had paid a pittance for but which in Belgium or France could be sold for a lot of money. On the way back they brought mostly coffee, the basic currency of the time without which Germans could not survive and of which they never had enough.[106] The porous border was quickly sealed, which forced smugglers to devise sophisticated or ruthless new methods of operation.[107]

Dealing on the black market was a crime and thus subject to prosecution. Demands to curtail it came from the occupation authorities, the unions, and political parties (on the left, especially from the KPD, the Communist Party of Germany which called for the setting-up of labor camps for those involved in illegal trading[108]). And there were indeed genuine attempts to combat the underground trade. Special police units were created, in Munich already in 1945. In Hamburg,

---

103 J. Sandulescu, *Hunger's Rouges...*, p. 19, G. Schmölders, *Die Zigarettenwährung, in: Sozial-ökonomische Verhaltenforschung. Ausgewählte Aufsätze von Günter Schmölders*, ed. G. Brinkmann, B. Strümpel, H. Zimmermann, Berlin 1973, pp. 166–71.

104 W.A. Boelcke, *Der Schwarz-Markt...*, p. 109.

105 *Ibid.*, pp. 172–173.

106 T. Domaniewski, *Błogosławieni ubodzy duchem, in: Uśmiech z dalekich dróg. Opowiadania*, Warszawa 1973, p. 9.

107 *Ibid.* ; J. Sandulescu, *Hunger's Rogues...*, W. Trees, Schmuggler, *Zöllner und die Kaffeepanzer. Die wilden Nachkriegsjahren an der deutschen Westgrenze*, Aachen 2002.

108 M. Wildt, *Der Traum...*, p. 39.

in March 1946 alone, more than 1400 checks and 150 round-ups were carried out. However, the best that could be done was to limit the black market and remove it from sight. The dealers moved the larger transactions to private apartments or restaurants, and carried with them nothing more than "samples". Official countermeasures could certainly diminish the scale of the illegal activities but could not get eradicate their political, economic, and social roots.[109] The illegal markets, in a topographical sense, revived immediately after any attempt to eliminate them. The authorities tried instead to fight "organized crime" groups, which often resembled smoothly-run businesses with access to the occupation authorities and German police. In 1946, US Military Police liquidated such a headquarters located in a bakery in Frankfurt-am-Main. It turned out that the bakery's phone number had been the most frequently dialed long distance telephone number in all Germany.[110]

War on the black market was doomed to failure; for one thing, the phenomenon was too widespread and, for another, illicit transactions enjoyed public support, since they delivered products unavailable on the legal market and also generated profits. People were forced to lead a double life, just as had been the case in the occupied countries during the war. The historian Kazimierz Wyka, who wrote about everyday life in occupied Poland, called it "pretend life". The majority of citizens had problems telling apart things that were accepted and permitted from those that were prohibited, since these were all thoroughly mixed-up in the context of both ethics and the law. It was often a schizophrenic situation: a prosecutor would write down the charges against a black market dealer on a piece of paper bought on the black market while drinking black market coffee served by his wife who was wearing a dress acquired on the black market. It is not surprising that a poll conducted by students from Freiburg im Breisgau at the end of 1947 showed that the majority (76%) of respondents were convinced participants in the black market should be protected and only 6% believed they should be persecuted.[111]

---

109 R. Gries, *Die Rationengesellschaft…*, 220; M. Wildt, *Der Traum…*, p. 110.

110 W.A.Boelcke, *Der Schwarz-Markt…*, p. 198.

111 *Ibid.*, 123–125. In 1947 a book was published as part of the series "Law for Everyone" (Recht für jeden) written by a well-known lawyer Karl Kromer; *Schwarzmarkt, Lausch- und Schleichhandel. In Frage und Antwort mit 500 praktischen Beispielen* (Schloss Bleckende an der Elbe 1947). It was written not only for lawyers but mostly for black market dealers to let them know what was allowed and how they could defend themselves if caught.

The fight against the black market was even more difficult due to the widespread involvement of representatives of the occupation authorities, both uniformed and civilian, who effectively protected their German trading partners. Whereas, during the war, Germans had enjoyed a business bonanza in Warsaw, Amsterdam or Paris, after the war ended the Americans, the Russians and the British coined it hand over fist in Frankfurt-am-Main, Berlin and Hamburg. In July 1945, the United States authorities in Berlin paid their soldiers one million dollars in wages. The soldiers in turn sent back home goods worth three million dollars, having deftly turned a handsome profit through black market operations.[112] For a carton of cigarettes, Americans paid a dollar; they could sell it for a thousand marks. With such a staggeringly advantageous conversion rate, cameras, antiques, jewelry, gold watches, and diamonds came almost free. No wonder that the US Mail delivered to West Berlin and the American occupation zone three thousand cartons of cigarettes a day. Likewise, food, alcohol, nylons, and gas kept flooding the market. A sergeant in Frankfurt-am-Main specialized in bringing dentures from the USA and selling them to local dentists. The American authorities estimated that their soldiers were able to transfer goods worth $500 million in this way. What was the value of the items that went back home? That was impossible to determine since all the estimates were unreliable.[113] No one has ever attempted to assess the scale of transactions carried out by Soviet soldiers who participated in the black market just as eagerly, selling their own supplies and items confiscated in Germany, including cars. Russian strategies were somewhat different – the buyers were not so much interested in antiques or jewelry as in items in demand in the Soviet Union such as watches or sewing machines.

And there was another difference. If, after the monetary reform, the black market had lost its significance in the western occupation zones, in the East it was only just entering a new phase. It would last for the next forty years.

---

112 K.C. Ruffner, *The Black Market in Post-war Berlin: Colonel Miller and an Army Scandal*, "Prologue Quarterly of the National Archives and Records Administration" 34, 2002/3, pp. 170–183.

113 W.A. Boelcke, *Der Schwarz-Markt...*, 127, pp. 131–132.

3. The Polish (anti) Speculation Curve: 1944–1989

Even though the shortages in post-war Poland were not always acute, there never existed a balanced market, crucial for the elimination of the black market. These shortages were curve-shaped – rising briefly in times of prosperity, then quickly falling again, when store shelves emptied and the lines got longer. The Polish authorities and the Polish people faced the necessity of having to invent increasingly sophisticated strategies. The critical turning point came when the authorities decided it was time for an unorthodox approach, reaching new highs in repression. In post-war Poland there had always existed professional, both uniformed and civilian, institutions for dealing with economic crime. They could be effective but at the same time even under an authoritarian regime they had limitations imposed by rules. The status attached to an institution of the state was a stigma and they could not count on social acceptance. Additional institutions were therefore set up, neutrally called "commissions" or "teams" in order to create the illusion that the state was loosening its grip. These commissions combined the structures of the state, labor unions, and social organizations and gave an impression of mass social participation or popular support for their activities. Until 1980, the authorities had a monopoly on information and propaganda, so they found it easy to manipulate public opinion, characterizing certain groups as a threat and enemy of the state and fanning citizens' wrath against them. This was not hard – since the more difficult everyday living conditions, the easier it was to drum up support, especially from low income citizens, to attack scapegoats.

There were three occasions in post-war Poland on which special institutions in charge of "extraordinary measures" for controlling and regulating the market were appointed: in 1945, 1957, and 1981. On each occasion they had different names and the political, social, and economic context was different. What they had in common was their target: "speculation" – this referred to any sector of the black market – and a shared ideological foundation. With their fighting slogans lifted as if straight from wartime reports, and an almost fanatical conviction of their own efficacy and righteousness, they were populist and egalitarian. At the same time, the commissions were helpless in the face of a reality that they could not fully control and to which they could only react. As a result, the commissions became an arena for a game of two players – the state and the people. The former had more pawns and set the rules, which they changed at will as they went along.

But the latter were quicker, more creative and quick to adjust. In the game of The State versus The People, it was The People that ultimately won.

3.1 Commission I: 1945–1950/54

The Special Commission for Combating Fraud and Economic Corruption, which was active between 1945 and 1954, did not progress in a linear manner. The first year and a half could be called a trial period and it involved looking for a formula, researching the possibilities, and acting on intuition. The unleashing in 1947 of the "battle for trade" marked the beginning of the Commission's golden era. It lasted until 1950, when the Commission was deprived of most of its powers and left only with decision-making functions. We will focus therefore mainly on the first five years of its operations.

3.1.1 Trial Period: 1944–1947

Once the euphoria of liberation had passed, Poles found themselves once again obliged to try and answer the ubiquitous question: "How can one make a living?" Trading offered the simplest solution, so it is not surprising that the occupation-era black market instantly adjusted to the new, post-war circumstances. The pauperized intelligentsia and famished workers were pushed into the black market by post-war circumstances. Stanisław M. Korowicz wrote, "Even the sporadic black-market trading proved much more advantageous financially than the wages of either blue, or white-collar workers."[114]

The very same situation could be observed in all the war-scarred European countries. And everywhere, Poland included, in the muddy post-war waters there swam not just minnows but also sharks. The period of chaos, political destabilization, and mass internal and external migrations created opportunities for big-time, profitable business operations. The Second World War shattered many social, moral, and ethical barriers. New ways of behaving, unacceptable and

114 S.M. Korowicz, *W Polsce pod sowieckim jarzmem*, London 1955, p. 31. There was much truth in a joke that did the rounds in post-war Krakow: "Two men are chatting. 'What do you do for a living?' 'Well, I work at the post office, my wife's a teacher, one daughter works for the county council, the other is a clerk at the tobacco factory, and my son is unemployed. But we all live quite well.' Appalled, the first man exclaims: 'How come your son has no job? How can you let him remain unemployed?' The father replies: 'My friend, but he cannot *afford* to work – *someone* has to make the money to keep us all, or we'd all soon kick the bucket on those four miserly paychecks!" *Ibid*.

indeed unimaginable before 1939, became commonplace. "Everywhere", an inspector wrote in 1945, "in trade, industry and state or local government offices, fraud goes on, for the sake of making a personal profit."[115]

The legal aspect of the economy also posed problems. Small-scale manufacturing and commerce were rapidly coming back to life and geared up for maximum profit in the shortest possible time. In a country destroyed by the war and suffering from acute shortages, where those who had jobs earned hunger wages and many others such as orphans, widows, the elderly and the disabled required aid from the state, this caused conflicts and tension. Introducing full rationing was logistically impossible – it would have required the involvement of a huge apparatus, expropriating all production surpluses from the peasants, which would have resulted only in expanding the black market. In the end, a half-way system was introduced, with the assumption that food rationing would do no more than complement the free market. This partial rationing was expected to protect the weakest and also the "most important" citizens from the state's point of view – big-city inhabitants, miners, and railroad workers.[116] The latter two groups received allocations of basic food articles, enabling bare survival at low, fixed prices, which were expected to keep in check the number of those using the black market.[117]

The reality, as always, departed from the theory. Merchants looking for profit tried to avoid the regulated prices by selling (legally or not) most of their wares at commercial prices. They were not controlled; this led to absurd situations where food prices in agricultural areas (in which inspections were infrequent) were 50–100% higher than in big cities.[118] In large agglomerations such as Łódź, the price differential between different districts reached 100%. In the first half of 1945, rationed bread cost 0.75–1.50 zl, whereas commercial (free-market) bread between 45 and 50 zl; similarly, pork fat respectively 2.75 – 10 zl compared to 350 – 500 zl, meat 2.25 – 4.50 zl against 70–180 zl, and wheat flour 1.10 – 1.15 zl in shops and between 57.50 zl and 95.60 zl on the black market.[119] As a result, there was not much to be bought in shops, due to the fact that the official, low prices were hardly an incentive to suppliers. Just as it had under the German occupation, this

115 AAN, URM, 5/31, fol. 15. See: M. Zaremba, *Wielka trwoga. Polska 1945–1947. Ludowa reakcja na kryzys*, Kraków 2012.

116 Z. Grodek, *Zaopatrzenie kartkowe w okresie Rządu Tymczasowego (31 December 1944 – June 1945)*, PH, 60, 1969/4, p. 691.

117 L. Beskid, *Ekonomiczne uwarunkowania rozwoju konsumpcji*, in: *Badania nad wzorami konsumpcji*, ed. J. Szczepański, Wrocław–Kraków 1977, p. 100.

118 AAN, URM, 5/31, fol. 3.

119 Z. Grodek, *Zaopatrzenie...*, p. 697.

encouraged black market strategies and unsurprisingly, enhanced the yearning for "order"[120] – since in the summer of 1945, the average wage covered no more than 38% of the cost of living. Against the backdrop of starving workers and intelligentsia, those who enjoyed conspicuous consumption – thanks to hard currency and goods brokerage (*maklerstwo towarowe i dewizowe*) or wholesale looting (*szaber hurtowy*) – stuck out like a sore thumb[121] and attracted public wrath.

An unbalanced market at all times encourages an egalitarian mood. This was especially the case in post-war Poland, where social equality was the chief premise of the socialist system, with official propaganda based on the slogan that the socialist state would provide for "each according to his need", and emphasis on the equality of all citizens in terms of their biological, material, and cultural needs.[122] Beside loudly expressed discontent, there were frequent grass-roots demands for the implementation of "the appropriate provision of necessary articles for all working people in the spirit of democratic equality, or [for] raising wages to the minimum subsistence level."[123] Citizens expected the state to act decisively and use whatever methods were necessary.[124] The authorities were themselves well aware that half-measures would no longer suffice, particularly as they had already proved ineffective.

---

120 See: M. Zaremba, *Trzej jeźdźcy: strach przed głodem, drożyzną, chorobami zakaźnymi w Polsce 1944–1947*, in: *Gospodarka i społeczeństwo w czasach PRL-u (1944–1989)*, ed. E. Kościk, T. Głowiński, Wrocław 2007, pp. 182–206; M. Zaremba, *Wielka trwoga…*, pp. 509–552.

121 "We don't have it as good as we should," a woman living in Przedecz near Włocławek wrote on June 6 1945. "We do have a church, two priests, beautiful services and sermons but we don't enjoy it because of the very high prices. We have one store here, the co-op. Everything is expensive there, there is one butcher but there is no meat for us there, they have sausage [*kiełbasa*], leberka [*Leberwurst*] but they don't sell it to food-stamp holders. Well, they did, two or three times, because they sell everything under the table and it's very expensive and not everybody can afford it. Those who have a lot of money and smuggle can pig out and booze but those who don't have money for all that, have to look at it through the crack in the door, they can only complain and say it was better when the Germans were here because they gave equal rations to all and we could get everything…" AAN, Biuro Kontroli przy Prezydium KRN, 225, fol. 2.

122 J. Szczepański, *Zagadnienia konstruowania i realizacji modelu i wzorów konsumpcji socjalistycznej*, in: *Badania nad wzorami konsumpcji…*, p. 33; L. Beskid, *Przemiany spożycia w gospodarstwach domowych w Polsce w latach siedemdziesiątych*, in: *Diagnozy społeczne w okresie narastającego kryzysu. Ekspertyzy Instytutu Podstawowych Problemów Marksizmu-Leninizmu*, ed. Z. Sufin, 1981, p. 40.

123 AAN, URM, 5/640, k. 148–149.

124 AAN, URM, 5/252, k. 24.

The period directly after the war was a golden age not only for the small fry but also for black market sharks: So, the Director has lost 60 bales of cotton, the President has lost 15 wagons of coal, I have only lost two cars and Dr Szaberski won them all… *[a pun based on 'Szaber' – in Polish, looting]. Karol Baraniecki,* Clients of the Special Commission, *"Szpilki", no. 9, 26 February 1946.*

Klienci Komisji Specjalnej

rys. Karol Baraniecki

– A więc pan dyrektor przegrał 60 bel bawełny, pan prezes 15 wagonów węgla, ja przegrałem tylko 2 samochody, a wszystko wygrał szanowny doktór Szaberski…

The first decree on combating wartime usury and speculation was issued on October 25, 1944. In early 1945, the Central Office for Combating Wartime Usury and Speculation (Główny Urząd do Walki z Lichwą i Spekulacją Wojenną, GUWLS or GU) was established in the Office of the Council of Ministers. It dealt mostly with illegal trade, speculation, and the illicit production of alcohol.[125] The institution had only a few dozen employees – not many, considering its wide-ranging objectives. By August 1, 1945 it had been possible to establish regional departments solely in the "old Poland", that is within its pre-1939 borders – in the Warsaw, Lublin, Łódź, Krakow, and Katowice voivodships; the "recovered",

125 AAN, URM, 5/31, fol. 3.

post-German territories were still terra incognita. There were problems with the city of Białystok where it proved impossible to recruit locally, which prompted the idea of sending in sporadic inspection brigades a month at a time.[126] Nor was it smooth sailing in other cities. The setting up of an anti-usury and speculation department in Łódź, in June 1945 caused such a stir amongst local merchants and black marketeers that they threatened to create a separate Department for the city of Łódź, staffed by their own "ol' boy networks".[127] The results of the GU-WLS's activities were modest. In July 1945, in Warsaw the Office confiscated a mere 20 kg of tobacco, 1330 headache medications, 3.25 kg saccharine, 20 liters of moonshine, and in Lublin 17.5 liters of moonshine, 3.7 kg counterfeit yeast and 3.6 kg of tobacco.[128]

The first institutions set up to fight speculation functioned like those depicted in Jerzy Zaruba's cartoon The Office for Fighting Speculation, *"Szpilki", no. 9, 1 May 1945.*

126 AAN, URM, 5/252, fol. 21.
127 AAN, URM, 5/31, fol. 15.
128 *Ibid.*, fol. 21–22.

Prime Minister Edward Osóbka-Morawski's hopes that the GUWLS would replicate the Soviet *cherezvychaika* office, which controlled all walks of life where official routes were being by-passed, no matter what position the fraudsters held, did not materialize.[129] The GU was a weak and bureaucratized structure dependent on the coalition government (from the end of June 1945), not revolutionary enough and much too politicized. For conservative bureaucrats, the GU became a fifth wheel and on August 18, 1945 the decision was reached to incorporate the GU in the Ministry of Treasury. However, neither the conservatives nor the supporters of the GU's independence applauded that decision.[130] The latter worried that the GU would now be censored and supervised by the Central Inspectorate of Treasury Protection (Główny Inspektorat Ochrony Skarbowej, GIOS). They postulated the "establishment of an Office or Inspectorate for Combating Wartime Usury and Speculation, parallel to the Central Inspectorate of Treasury Protection (at the Treasury), which would be able to introduce initiatives, and with the existing duplication with other Offices, would bring about reciprocal control, desirable in our opinion."[131] Ultimately, the Office would be included in the GIOS as a subordinate unit, but "with the existing powers".[132] This did not end the problems and it turned out that the Treasury Protection team would not be able to tackle usury and speculation, since it lacked the necessary legal authority. According to the Finance Minister, there were plans to amend the decree from August 25, 1944.[133] There was no need to do this. The Politburo of the Central Committee of the Polish Workers' Party (KC PPR), the real center of decision-making, was not interested in bringing to life another bureaucratic institution, which was difficult to control, to boot. So the Politburo took the initiative, while trying to keep up appearances. It is hard to believe that the appeal directed to the government by the Central Commission of the Labor Unions (Komisja Centralna Związków Zawodowych) on August 31, 1945 urging it to create a "special commission to fight corruption, bribery, speculation, and banditry" had not been inspired by the Party. Especially since ideology began clearly to dominate the economy: "through their propaganda and support for thievery, bribery and speculation as well as acts of industrial sabotage and disorganization of the state apparatus, reactionary groups in Poland […] want to exacerbate our difficulties and keep our cities starving in order to spread discontent amongst the working masses so that on the wave of that discontent they, the

129 AAN, URM, 5/252, fol. 1.
130 *Ibid.*
131 *Ibid.*, fol. 5.
132 *Ibid.*
133 AAN, URM, 5/253, fol. 2.

reactionaries, may again reach out for power and drive the working masses into enslavement by the capitalist and the landowner."[134] It did not take long for the Party authorities to react. By September 2, 1945, the Politburo of the Central Committee of the Communist Party established a Special Commission for Combating Fraud (Specjalna Komisja do Walki z Nadużyciami). Administered personally by Władysław Gomułka, the Commission was set up at the State National Council, (Krajowa Rada Narodowa, KRN), headed by Bolesław Bierut, which served at that time as a kind of super-government.[135] The Commission faced an enormous task and was also granted enormous powers. It was expected to combat the theft of state property, corruption and fraud in the "state, local government, and economic apparatus", and it could avail itself of all other state structures.[136] Unlike the professional institutions, the Special Commission was to rely on the "participation of the social entities, and especially on supervision by municipal councils, on social invigilation by the labor unions, and on the activities of complaints offices established for the purpose."[137]

Bolesław Bierut and Jakub Berman were in charge of developing the appropriate decrees. After more than two months of deliberations, on November 16, 1945 the package of decrees was accepted together with the establishment of the Special Commission for Combating Fraud and Corruption. Published side by side (sections 300–302) in the Journal of Laws, Issue 53, they were an important step on the path to stabilizing not so much the economy but rather the power of the new regime.

Since there is an ample body of literature[138] on the historic and legal aspects of the Special Commission (even though there is less coverage of its sociological

134 *Komisja Specjalna do Walki z Nadużyciami i Szkodnictwem Gospodarczym 1945–1954*, selection of documents, introduction and ed. D. Jarosz, T. Wolsza, 1995 (later: Jarosz, Wolsza, *Komisja*), p. 15.

135 About Prezydium see: *Protokoły posiedzeń Prezydium Krajowej Rady Narodowej 1944–1947*, selection, introduction and ed. J. Kochanowski, Warszawa 1995.

136 P. Fiedorczyk, *Komisja…*, p. 36; *Protokoły Posiedzeń Biura Politycznego KC PPR 1944–1945*, ed. A. Kochański, Warszawa 1992, pp. 100–101.

137 A. Kochański, *Polska 1944–1991. Informator historyczny*, vol 1: *Podział administracyjny, ważniejsze akty prawne, decyzje i enuncjacje państwowe (1944–1956)*, Warszawa 1996, p. 100.

138 Books on the topic: Jarosz, Wolsza, *Komisja*; R. Tomkiewicz, *Olsztyńska Delegatura Komisji Specjalnej do Walki z Nadużyciami i Szkodnictwem Gospodarczym 1945–1954*, Olsztyn 1995; *Działalność Delegatury Komisji Specjalnej do Walki z Nadużyciami i Szkodnictwem Gospodarczym w Szczecinie w latach 1945–1954. Materials from the Scientific Conference March 20 1998*, ed. Z. Chmielewski, Szczecin 1998;

or cultural contexts), we need only focus here on the most important issues. During the nine years of existence of the Commission, its chairman was Roman Zambrowski. It seems, however, that Bolesław Bierut and members of the Special Commission Bureau had more sway (among others Kazimierz Jasiński – the director of the Executive Office, Jan Grubecki, Leon Chajn, Eugeniusz Gajewski, Mieczysław Mietkowski, Marek Porowski and Konrad Świetlicki). The institution that they were put in charge of had been equipped with executive means that were at odds with the rule of law. It had the powers to charge, prosecute, and pass and carry out sentences, sending convicts to labor camps that were also run by the same authority. The Commission's officials – paid better than in other state agencies and allowed to carry weapons – were meant to be the new and trusted personnel of the justice system.[139]

The Commission's executive authority and simultaneously its core – the Warsaw-based Executive Office – took care of the more serious cases. In 1945/46, there were many multi-million zloty cases, in which the perpetrators were high-ranking state officials.[140] The Commission was also involved with prominent cases such as the illegal trade in pharmaceuticals or thefts of UNRRA gifts, however small-scale. These mattered all the more in view of the fact that the Commission's success rate in the provinces had not been that impressive.[141] One does have to acknowledge, however, that those in power were realists, fully aware that on the one

---

P. Fiedorczyk, *Komisja…*; R. P. Smolorz, *Verwaltung mit Rechtsbefugnissen im stalinistischen Polen. Die Spezialkommission zur Bekämpfung von Wirtschaftsschädigung und Wirtschaftsmissbrauch,* Regensburg 2004; L.S. Szuba, *Komisja Specjalna do Walki z Nadużyciami i Szkodnictwem Gospodarczym i jej delegatura bydgoska (1945–1954)*, Toruń 2009; B. Sekściński, *Ogniwo terroru. Delegatura Komisji do Walki z Naudużyciami i Szkodnictwem Gospodarczym w Lublinie,* Warszawa 2012; W. Tomczyk, *Delegatura Komisji Specjalnej do Walki z Nadużyciami i Szkodnictwem Gospodarczym w Rzeszowie 1946–1954*, Rzeszów 2007, PhD dissertation written under the supervision of Prof. W. Bonusiak. http://www.pbc.rzeszow.pl/dlibra/docmetadata?id=959&from=publication (access: March 7 2014). In the above publications – detailed bibliography (especially: W. Tomczyk, *Delegatura…*, pp. 3–4; L.S. Szuba, *Komisja…*, pp. 334–344.

139 P. Fiedorczyk, *Komisja…*, p. 27, p. 42, 83, p. 97.

140 AAN, Krajowa Rada Narodowa (KRN), 214, fol. 180–181.

141 The work on establishing delegations ended in February, (Poznań, Szczecin, Wrocław). The Executive Office acted as the Warsaw delegation (*delegatura warszawska*). In 1947, there were 294, and in 1949 – 420 county inspectorates; P. Fiedorczyk, *Komisja…*, p. 72, p. 73, p. 77.

hand the illegal market posed a threat but on the other did rescue people in need. Alceo Valcini, an Italian diplomat who arrived in Warsaw in late 1945 and stayed for a year, was astounded to find how well supplied Warsaw was in comparison with starving Rome. "This abundance," he recalled, "was eloquent testimony to the reign of chaos and lack of discipline that prevailed in Poland, and especially in Warsaw, immediately after the war. It tempted the authorities to implement drastic solutions, a temptation to which they did not succumb because these would have been resented by a part of the population, and would have had undesirable political effects in view of the unstable political situation."[142]

The Commission's first year and a half of activity was based more on pragmatism than ideology, all the more so as the cases brought before the Commission covered thirty different kinds of crimes – from hard currency and gold trading, speculation, and smuggling to sabotage, corruption and fraud – which turned out to be too much even for such a specialized and well-trained and equipped institution. The Commission's focus turned then to easier cases such as illegal alcohol production, slaughter and tanning, and hard currency trading, which were more burdensome for both the state treasury and the average citizen. The particular characteristics of the periphery where the boundaries between the authorities and the society are always less clear (see chapter 4) and difficulties in assembling appropriate personnel made any more sophisticated activity difficult. Six months after the Commission had been established, reports from Poznań stated, "practically no member of the delegation has at their disposal even the most rudimentary information necessary to maintain adequately such an important institution as the Special Commission. They are individuals with no conception of law and order."[143] As a consequence, instead of combating fraud, the Commission often preserved the existing "ol' boy networks", thus guaranteeing their stability.

At the same time, it was not unusual for the Commission to engage in excessive repression or for its employees to settle private scores. Walenty Preiss, the chairman of the Szczecin delegation, who had earlier worked in the prison system, treated the Commission like a form of the Bolshevik *cherezvychaika*: "During an interrogation he makes the accused stand at attention a few meters away, does not allow the smallest movement; there is a handgun on his desk with the safety catch off. The interrogation usually lasts several hours (up to five) and the alternating interrogators ask the accused the very same question a hundred times even when the accused has pleaded guilty [...]. At a particular

142 A. Valcini, *Bal w hotelu "Polonia"*, transl. A. Dutka, Warszawa 1983, p. 56.
143 Jarosz, Wolsza, *Komisja*, p. 69.

moment, Preiss approaches the accused from behind and acts as if he is about to shoot him. Preiss uses the same methods even when dealing with witnesses and outsiders [...]. Preiss's excessive temperament has found its release in fighting smugglers. He has been in charge of field operations, often risking his own life. Blowing-off steam at the railroad station where the chairman of the delegation was personally catching women with small-time loot did nothing to lend dignity to the Commission's image."[144]

In the Łódź voivodship there was a shortage of employees authorised to conduct investigations and independently prepare the minutes.[145] The Voivodship Office of Public Security (Wojewódzki Urząd Bezpieczeństwa Publicznego, WUBP) in Olsztyn tried to use the local Special Commission's delegation for its own political ends.[146] The delegation in Rzeszów was unable to cope with the smugglers.[147] In the Warsaw voivodship, no-one took seriously the meat-free and cake-free (sic) days introduced by the authorities (and theoretically supervised by the Special Commission).[148] In mid-May 1946, Wilhelm Garncarczyk the voivod of Warsaw complained that the war on illicit alcohol production had "so far really been a fiction. The bylaws are strict and they should be observed. The Special Commissions must join the war against moonshine and keep track of the police (Milicja Obywatelska, MO) to ensure that they do not take bribes."[149] Such actions were doomed to failure, due as much to the low level of ethics as to the low wages of the officials. For example in May 1946, a policeman from Warsaw could not present himself for duty because he had no shoes.[150] Functionaries were therefore more likely to take bribes and engage in their own dealings than prosecute the black marketeers. In June 1947, the civil authorities of the Polish capital urged policemen who owned vending kiosks to "stop selling vodka and abide by the law because they are demoralizing the neighboring kiosk owners."[151] Soon enough there was no one left to be demoralized.

---

144 *Ibid.*, p. 73. See: *Komisja do Walki*, ed. G. Sołtysiak, Karta 1991/1, pp. 81–97.

145 AAN, URM, 5/754, fol. 26.

146 *Ibid.*

147 *Ibid.*, fol. 32.

148 AAN, KRN, 487, fol. 34.

149 AAN, KRN, 508, fol. 5.

150 State Archive of the City of Warsaw (Archiwum Państwowe m. st. Warszawy, APW), Starostwo Grodzkie Śródmiejsko-Warszawskie, 14, fol. 36.

151 *Ibid.*, fol. 65.

3.1.2 "We Have Won the Trade War": 1947–1950

On July 1, 1946 the peasants were released from the compulsory submission of food provisions (*świadczenia rzeczowe*). It was a canny move from the propaganda point of view, but less so as far as food supplies were concerned. Now it became more difficult to induce peasants to deliver food to collection stations, especially since the cities had nothing attractive to offer – except for a modest and not very appealing choice of industrial articles; former German supplies were exhausted and UNRRA rations limited.[152] To make things worse, extreme weather hit most of Europe hard in 1946 and 1947 – first came a severe winter, followed by spring flooding and summer drought. This had serious long-term consequences and led to increased tension in international relations.[153] But even before nature struck, the food supply in Poland had worsened. Peasants were now consuming more, thus selling less; especially since their profit margins were improving. Free market prices, and inflation, began to grow while purchasing power was sliding; all this made the already long-suffering wage earners even worse off. The state-imposed prices ceased to have any foundation in reality, since they were set much below the cost of production, and merchants tried all they could to avoid accepting them on a scale not seen before.[154] The official market was in disarray, due to profiteering that fed on ever more acute shortages, and periodical panics brought on by rumors about price hikes, a looming currency replacement, or the possibility of a new war.

These circumstances allowed the authorities, which had just "won" the parliamentary election and eliminated the legal opposition, to start dealing with the small private sector, as a pretext evoking the "righteous wrath of society". In April 1947, during a session of the Polish Workers' Party Central Committee (KC PPR), the blame for the market situation was put down to the excessive purchasing power of the cities, unwarranted enrichment of the peasants but mostly the "mess, disorganization, anarchy, barbarity and demoralization" of commerce.[155]

---

152 J. Kaliński, *Wpływ sytuacji rynkowej na warunki bytowe ludności. Lipiec 1946 – grudzień 1948 r.*, Kwartalnik Historyczny 76, 1969/2, pp. 319–320.

153 See: R.G. Kaiser, *Cold Winter, Cold War*, New York 1974; A.J. Robertson, *The Bleak Midwinter: Britain and the Fuel Crisis 1947*, Manchester 1987; A. Häusser, G. Maugg, *Hungerwinter. Deutschlands humanitäre Katastrophe 1946/47*, Berlin 2009.

154 J. Kaliński, *Bitwa o handel 1947–1948*, 1970, pp. 61–69; C. Bobrowski, *Wspomnienia ze stulecia*, Lublin 1985, p. 183.

155 Quote from: J. Kaliński, *Wpływ sytuacji...*, p. 326; AAN, The Ministry of Recovered Territories (Ministerstwo Ziem Odzyskanych, MZO), 340, circular 34, 10 May 1947, fol. 1.

Unsurprisingly, it was traders who were first in the line of fire; they were often meted out the highest penalty available in the Special Commission's repertoire – two years labor camp. At its session on May 6, 1947 the Commission announced that it would embark on a "path of strict coercion in order to deter speculators". The Special Commission sought permission to impose huge fines (up to five million zloty) and to close down the black marketeers' stores.[156] The Special Commission received all those powers (and more[157]), based on the Act of June 2, 1947 on Combating High Prices and Excessive Profits in Trade. Together with other Acts passed on that day,[158] it became a foundation of the "battle for trade".

Warsaw, 1 May 1947, propaganda banner of the Special Commission for Combating Economic Fraud and Corruption on the route of the parade; photo from the archives of the Polish Press Agency (PAP).

The Special Commission played a major role in this battle. The administrative authorities, which until then had been able to mete out legal penalties, were now expected to do no more than "cooperate in unveiling crimes liable to prosecution

156 AAN, KS, 8, fol. 34.

157 Jarosz, Wolsza, *Komisja*, pp. 5–6.

158 The Act on Combating High Prices was published in the Journal of Laws/43/218. No. 219: Act on Citizens Tax Commissions and Public Inspectors; No. 220: Act on Permits for Operating Trade Enterprises and Trading in a Professional Capacity.

by the special commissions."[159] During the Fourth Convention of the Special Commission that took place on June 16, 1947 it became clear that "combating speculation is now the most important economic issue in the country. Following the war, speculation has become a mass phenomenon in Poland and it threatens the economic balance of the State".[160] All the members of the Commission (925 in 1947 and 1 300 by 1949) were suddenly removed from their on-going tasks and without any special preparation sent out to inspect the mostly private stores, which at that time constituted 90% of all stores.[161] By the end of the year, more than 70 thousand public controllers[162] had inspected 213 353 retail sales premises and prepared 45 thousand penalty reports. The outcome was that almost 22 thousand people received fines totaling more than 531 million zloty. 1 850 people were sent to labor camps (where the conditions were made drastically harsher).[163] The fast pace continued in the following year when 153 thousand people participated in more than 23 700 control actions. They inspected 455 400 stores (some repeatedly) and wrote 77 744 criminal reports.[164]

The Commission was becoming an increasingly convenient and specialized tool, used to suit the government's immediate needs. It was involved in all new areas of the battle – against wholesale and retail trade, against the agricultural products (mostly meat) trade, against the skilled trades, against private commerce (or what was left of it) and artisans, who at this point operated illegally. The sheer numbers of those sent to labor camps clearly showed the trend. When the Commission's focus shifted to small trade, the number of people sent to the camps for black marketing rose from 518 in 1947 to 1 072 in 1949. First in the line of fire was the illegal trade in industrial articles. By the end of 1948, in a propaganda effort intended to demonstrate a semblance of normalization, the Commission proudly announced that "only a very limited range" of industrial articles was now subject to speculation."[165] It was also for this reason that rationing was abolished with effect from January 1, 1949, as was the circular of December

159 AAN, MZO, 340, no. 51, fol. 11.

160 AAN, KS, 10, fol. 92.

161 AAN, KS, 8, fol. 59.

162 The introduction of "people's" control was a new phenomenon. According to the Act of June 2, 1947 public commissions for price control, citizens' tax commissions, and public inspectors in treasury offices were to be created immediately; AAN, 190, fol. 28.

163 Jarosz, Wolsza, *Komisja*, p. 81.

164 *Ibid.*, p. 104.

165 AAN, KS, 8, k. 103.

29, 1948, which recommended the use of fines and advised mass arrests only in the "most glaring cases".[166]

At the turn of 1948 and 1949, this provision applied mainly to meat supply. When the worst meat crisis since the war came in September 1948, the authorities began to tackle the meat trade, which remained mostly in private hands. In the fall, they unleashed a press campaign, accompanied by stringent control of butcher stores. The government had been clandestinely working on its "H" (husbandry) legislation, which it launched on January 28, 1949. Again, the Commission rose to the challenge: whilst in 1947 no-one was sent to the camp for illegal slaughter, in 1948 there were already 314 arrests and in 1949 – the number soared to 2 119.[167]

As long as the targets of the Commission were the black market tycoons, it had reasonable support from the public. As soon, however, as it started to poke around in the pots and pockets (and lives) of ordinary people, who were simply trying to survive, it came to be seen as a typical state institution, an object of hate. The labor camps, supposedly intended to put away and re-educate the "enemies of the people" – black marketeers, now started to fill with ordinary folk. "In the camp [Mielęcin]," stated an anonymous letter sent to the Ministry of Justice in December 1947, "80 to 90% [of the prisoners] belong to the proletariat and land up in the camp because of the difficult economic situation."[168] If the number of anonymous letters is a measure of social trust and faith in the effectiveness of the state, the flurry of denunciations diminished in step with the change of operational mode implemented by the Special Commission: in 1946 – private letters constituted 28.3% of all reports, in 1947 – 8.8%, in 1948 – 6.5%, and in 1949 – only 2.3%.[169]

The revolution devours its own children. Nor was the Special Commission spared. It had been effective at the time that the communists seizing power but, once the state's structures had become entrenched, it began to interfere more than help. A state, and especially a totalitarian state, cannot have two prosecuting institutions simultaneously (in this case, the Special Commission and the State Prosecutor's Office). These two Polish institutions in were in direct competition with each other. This led to the paradoxical situation that other organizations were free to pick which of the two institutions it wanted to deal with crimes committed within their own structures. The Commission was generally the preferred

---

166 Jarosz, Wolsza, *Komisja*, p. 85.

167 Ibid, p. 105.

168 *Ibid.*, p. 159.

169 *Ibid.*, 98; P. Fiedorczyk, *Komisja…*, pp. 178–179.

option for a good reason: the sentences that it passed were lighter than those that would be delivered by the courts.[170] The Act of July 20, 1950 redefined the powers of the Polish Republic's Prosecutor's Office, stripping the Special Commission of its investigative and prosecution functions as well as of the right to accept reports of crimes directly from citizens. The Commission was left with dealing with cases that had already gone through the prosecutor's office and with meting out the sentences, be they a fine, confiscation of assets, or a labor camp sentence. All these options were made use of, especially since – beside sentences for dealing on the black market, illegal slaughter and tanning, taking benefits in kind or clandestine distilling – the Commission also passed judgment in political cases. Whereas between 1945 and 1950, the Commission sent to the camps some 25 thousand people, between 1951 and 1954, the number more than doubled to 59.5 thousand.[171]

As late as June 1954, the General Prosecutor approvingly described the Commission as a "sharp instrument of the class struggle created to implement harsh and quick penal repression";[172] as such, it had made a lasting impact in the delivery of the coercive state. Once the state became less repressive, however, the Commission had to go. The decree disbanding the Special Commission was issued on December 23, 1954. What was left was the personnel (indeed, many Special Commission functionaries embarked on successful careers also after 1956), the memory (both collective and institutional) and a lesson to learn that an institution like that is useful as long as it does not go "over the top": it is fine to combine invigilation and prosecution in one body but sentencing should be left to others.[173]

3.2 Intermedium I: 1950–1956

Both the curtailing of the Commission's powers in 1950 and the disbanding of it in 1954 were explained on the grounds of the supposedly stabilizing economic situation and diminishing number of prosecutions. This was no more than wishful thinking. The black market is like a flu virus: under favorable conditions, it rapidly develops new mutations, resistant to the most sophisticated vaccines. Even the hard currency and gold trade, heavily persecuted and drastically

170 P. Fiedorczyk, *Komisja...*, p. 50.

171 Jarosz, Wolsza, *Komisja*, 8. See: A. Zaćmiński, *Przestępstwa polityczne w orzecznictwie Komisji Specjalnej do Walki z Nadużyciami i Szkodnictwem Gospodarczym 1950–1954*, "Pamięć i Sprawiedliwość" 2008/1, pp. 321–343.

172 A. Kochański, *Polska 1944–1991. Informator...*, vol. 1, p. 533.

173 P. Fiedorczyk, *Komisja...*, pp. 325–326.

penalized, did not disappear but rather went deeper underground, giving rise to new, fancier, and authority-resistant strategies. Smuggling, illegal slaughter and alcohol production followed suit.[174]

Just as had happened under the German occupation, the oppressiveness of the state and systemic shortages precipitated the emergence of a black market-based society, in which the creation of social capital and multi-branched networks of dependency were geared mostly towards the acquisition of goods unavailable on the market. Again, the market supply worsened to the point that in the middle of 1951, food stamps for basic articles were re-introduced (and remained until the beginning of 1953).[175] Industrial goods, coal, and construction materials were unofficially rationed during that time, using special coupons and allocations. The rapacious redenomination of the currency in October 1950, which in one fell swoop wiped out two thirds of Poles' savings, completely destroyed their trust in the national currency and inspired spending rather than saving.[176] And the constant fear of a new war, prevalent in the early 1950s, coupled with periodic runs on shops, encouraged stockpiling.

On the one hand, all these goings-on intensified the war on profiteering, on the other – they fostered the development of illegal commerce. At the same time, the Polish black market diversified. On the one side there were the experienced and highly specialized, wily operators, who had often undergone their baptism of fire during wartime; they kept a low profile and were cautiously adjusting themselves to the new circumstances, with networks of intermediaries at their disposal often outside of Poland, for example in Berlin or in port cities such as Szczecin or Gdynia. On the other side were the non-professionals; they only made occasional sallies into the black market and treated illicit trade as an additional source of income to eke out the hunger-level state wages.[177] The nationalized industries created a new re-distribution channel, readily available to a multitude of participants – from those employed in wholesale to transport and retail store workers. As a result, everyone who got a chance to do so was dealing on the black market, regardless of their position or income. At the beginning of 1950, there were three phenomena involved in the "chain trade": buying goods at state-owned stores, then re-selling them on the free market or to the private

174 See the monographic chapters.

175 M. Jastrząb, *Puste półki. Problem zaopatrywania ludności w artykuły powszechnego użytku w Polsce w latach 1949–1956*, 2004, pp. 43–87.

176 J. Kochanowski, *Dziesięć dni, które wstrząsnęły portfelem, Polityka,* 30 Oct 2010.

177 Herder-Institut Marburg (HIM), Pressearchiv, P 6221, Item 3608/1954, The Black Market in Poland.

retail stores, and re-customizing or repackaging goods for retail trade.[178] The risk taken was cost-effective, considering that at the beginning of the 1950s there was a fourfold differential in price between retail stores and local marketplaces. Exchanging goods for food products in rural areas and distributing them in the cities was also highly advantageous.[179]

Taking the wind out of the black marketeers' sails was one of the pretexts for the drastic price hike implemented on January 3, 1953, which almost equalized the retail and black market prices. The price increase, aimed at emptying citizens' pockets instead of reforming the market, changed little. A mere two months later, the decree on the protection of the interests of buyers enhanced the impact of the resolutions of the Act of June 2, 1947 that had combated high prices by introducing more severe sanctions with obligatory prison sentences, which could not be substituted by a fine. "All acts that interfere with the trade in goods with the motive of profiteering" were subject to prosecution and punishment.[180]

The decree was tailored to purge small-time retailers. Meanwhile, talented entrepreneurs soon realized that the centralized and nationalized economy was a true Eldorado and a potential source of enormous profits. If one knew where to invest and was also familiar with the law and skilled in filling the pockets of corrupt functionaries, one could operate successfully and safely for a long time. Between 1954 and 1957, a Warsaw resident, one Stefania Husiatyńska, together with eleven partners in crime, successfully managed to run a foreign trade enterprise in Warsaw. They "received nylons from the USA and England, which they exchanged for cash and then gave the money to families in Poland indicated by their bosses in the USA".[181] The group's turnover was estimated at 36.5 million zloty, the profit – at 14 million zloty.[182] This story was not an exception.

Husiatyńska (and those who ran similar operations) avoided as a rule any contacts with official structures, with the exception of the postal and custom services. The Stalinist state allowed its citizens quite a large margin of (economic)

178 "Konfekcjonowanie" meant improving state-manufactured goods. For example, scarves and shawls were made (illegally) from linen bought in Białystok or Olsztyn and sold at no less than a 100% markup. AAN, KS, 10, k. 103.

179 AAN, KS, 11, fol. 265.

180 Dz.U. no. 16, item 64, Dekret o ochronie interesów nabywców w obrocie handlowym, 4 March 1953; M. Madej, *O ukrywaniu i gromadzeniu towarów jako formie spekulacji*, "Prawo", 1953/11, pp. 19–23.

181 APW, Warsaw Committee of the Polish United Workers' Party (Komitet Warszawski PZPR, KWar. PZPR), 30/XVIII-7, vol. 1, fol. 39.

182 Trybuna Ludu, TL, no. 297 from October 27, 1957.

latitude, whether due to omission, neglect, corruption and inability to control everything or deliberately as a result of its dependency on the economic activity of the public players. A case of a certain Mr. Kowarski is a good example here. Mr. Kowarski, who had acquired some capital by trading hard currency in 1953, "organized near Warsaw an illegal production of fruit juices necessary to manufacture wine. The business was set up as a regular enterprise. Kowarski kept accounts and paid his workers and clerks modest wages. However, the business was not registered and did not pay tax.[183] Kowarski's business thrived to such an extent that he was soon able to buy a farm, then add or rent orchards, developing his own production, which practically monopolized the supply. By 1956 he had sold to the state products worth approximately 50 million zloty.[184]

Often, this "inter-sector cooperation", which was allowed by the law, would turn into more or less hidden privatization of the state. Managers soon noticed that by using the existing legislation, which afforded considerable flexibility to all kinds of cooperatives (permitting for example purchases outside of the state channels), one could scoop up nice profits as a middleman. It is hardly surprising that such cooperatives "became hotbeds of a variety of private profiteers, in the process losing the character of nationalized enterprises."[185] This was skillful brokerage, and effectively drained the state's less-than-bottomless coffers. It is worth providing a detailed illustration of how the mechanism of a typical, large-scale speculation from the first half of the 1950s functioned, even if this necessitates quoting at length:

The profiteers, (from all over Poland, and especially from Łódź, the northern region of Kurpie, the mountainous southern region of Podhale, and the southern counties of the Lublin district) bought, on a mass scale, cottage industry products such as homespun cloth, wadding, and others. The basic material for the production of homespun cloth was wool that came from the farms of individual peasants or else had been stolen from state textile plants. The profiteers delivered the textiles, wadding and other materials to tailors working from home who made coats and other ready-to-wear clothing. The profiteers also bought from the state-owned retail stores haberdashery and various household items, to which they "added value" with the help of their cottage industry workers and then (often without bothering to "add" any value at all) sold for wholesale prices to the state-owned stores or coop stores at a huge profit.

183 J. Wołowski, *Wina i kara*, "Nowe Drogi" 1957/7, p. 53.

184 *Ibid.*

185 AAN, URM, 9/261, fol. 11.

A certain hierarchy was born within this procedure – from small, local black marketeers who hoarded or purchased supply straight from the cottagers to the profiteers acquiring large amount of goods [...]. The latter put them on the market and were paid in cash.

Disregarding the bans and limitations, the profiteers usually disposed of the goods through the stores of the Consumers' Cooperative (Powszechna Spółdzielnia Spożywców, PSS), and other multi-branch coops, and also to a smaller degree in the Community Cooperative (GS) stores. They could take advantage of the regulations, which between 1953 and 1955 allowed PSS outlets to buy goods from private individuals in certain circumstances (such as shortages in the state-owned wholesalers or in coops). The rules of the workers' cooperatives (auxiliary, handicapped and others) permitted the buying of resources and "other products" necessary for their own production from decentralized sources.

Since the cooperatives had limited opportunities for using the purchased products or resources in production, and had difficulties disposing of them in their retail stores (in the case of the GS and the PSS), they embarked on re-selling them to other trade enterprises. The profiteers delivered the goods – and paid the bribes – directly to these enterprises (usually the MHD, the CPLiA, the Centrogal, and similar chains), received the receipts and accepted new orders for the board of the cooperative designated by the profiteer. After recording in the books the fictitious purchase and re-sale transaction, the management of the coop made payments to the profiteer in cash either via their own cashier or via the National Bank of Poland (NBP). Subsequently, the payment due was levied from the state trade enterprise by a bank transfer. Beside the state trade enterprises, the Polish State Railroad (PKP), coal mines, construction material suppliers, mills and meat processing plants were among the recipients of goods sold via the profiteers' re-invoicing."[186]

In a similar way, hundreds of tons of cement, steel products, and means of transportation were turned over. The profits from such operations, after deducting the costs (which included huge bribes), were estimated at millions of zlotys.

As ever, the only cases that we are aware of are those exposed by prosecutions. Between the second half of 1954 and February 1956, six hundred people were under investigation (no doubt, the tip of the iceberg – it is quite impossible to assess the size of the entire iceberg); half of them were arrested – and 40% were members of the Communist Party. At the beginning of 1956, Polish trade was corrupted to such a degree that "one could only buy the more attractive products from black marketeers or acquaintances that worked in state trade or by paying a

186 *Ibid.*, fol. 3–7.

bribe, typically 10% of the price of the product."[187] No exception was Toruń, where in 1956 there was allegedly "not a single trade or service enterprise, where the management had not been arrested or prosecuted for profiteering."[188] According to cautious estimates (excluding smuggling, illegal tanning, slaughter, distilling etc.), in 1956, the illegal income of Poles constituted more than 8% of the national income (21.4 billion out of 256.7 billion zloty).[189] This was only a prelude to the next year's events.

3.3 Team I (and II): 1957 (and Later)

The political, economic and social problems, which crawled out of the Polish Pandora's box in 1956, gave sleepless nights to those in power, especially in the first months of 1957. The brutally suppressed Poznań riots of June 1956 were what prised open this particular Pandora's box. The weakened authorities tried to stifle the subsequent conflagration. They did it against the urgent pressure of unfolding events; their method of choice was to throw money at the emerging problems, which was disastrous for the unstable economy and the leaky market. In 1956, the purchasing power of wages began to climb (for the next such boom, Poles would have to wait until 1971, when it went on until 1975). In 1956 alone, the payroll budget rose by as much as 17.7% and peasants' income by 20.4%.[190] And that without including illicit earnings!

Increased cash flow stimulated market demand but despite the government flooding the official market with goods before they were informally rationed, such as radio sets, motorcycles and citrus fruit, Polish wallets continued to bulge with an excess of "hot" money.[191] The reason was that consumers had become choosier; they were unwilling to buy the usual shoddy goods that had littered the stores for weeks. By 1956, it had been noted that the needs of the Polish customer had gotten more sophisticated, both in respect of food products and material goods. In mid-1956 it was noted that the "consumer now demands prettier, more aesthetically appealing products of higher quality, as well as modern and fashionable, which industry does not deliver in satisfying quantities either because of technical difficulties or due

187 AAN, URM, 22/210, fol. 1–16; *Szara strefa Października. "Notatka" o nielegalnych dochodach w Polsce 1956–1957*, ed. J. Kochanowski, PH, 95, 2004/1, pp. 77–96, p. 90.
188 AAN, URM, 9/261, fol. 10.
189 *Szara strefa Października...*; *Rocznik statystyczny 1958*, Warszawa 1958, p. 57.
190 M. Jastrząb, *Puste półki...*,117–118; C. Bobrowski, *Wspomnienia...*, pp. 254–255.
191 A. Jezierski, C. Leszczyńska, *Historia gospodarcza Polski*, Warszawa 1999, p. 538.

to its total disregard of customer demand."[192] Not much changed in 1957; consumers continued to buy some products only "out of necessity or because they could not afford anything better."[193] Not only were the goods available in nationalized stores usually shoddily made but they were also very expensive. Anyone fashion-conscious and anyone who gave a fig about quality and design went shopping in the incredibly popular "ciuchy" flea-market, or visited the network of "komis" sale-or-return stores (which were rapidly expanding, especially since March 1957 when the anonymous purchasing of supplies was introduced), turning to the state distributors only as a last resort.[194]

The unfulfilled demand was only one of the factors that drove the rapid growth of the black market in 1956 and 1957. The decriminalization of the operations of private craftsmen and private trade had many different consequences. Private entrepreneurs needed resources, goods, semi-finished products, machinery, and tools. They found it difficult to acquire them legally so would turn to a gamut of illicit solutions.[195] Sometimes the method of choice was simply theft from the state sector. At other times entrepreneurs had to run complex trade operations requiring much capital, including hard currency, and excellent knowledge of the market, including the non-Polish market. For foreign products they paid with foreign currency, most often acquired on the black market. Selling the manufactured product was not much easier. Usually the best solution was to find a state or coop trading partner. It often required corrupting a state official or store manager.

Those on both sides of the transaction rarely showed any moral qualms. No reader can doubt that by now that the authorities had no such considerations; as for the entrepreneurs, who could now operate legally, they had not rid themselves of the underhand ways and clandestine habits practiced in the recent past. In mid-1957, even the conservative Krakovians bemoaned the absence in the reviving private sector of honest businesses based on pre-war tradition and complained about the "post-war, newcomer speculators, determined to siphon off a significant part of the national income."[196] The press wrote: "many people

192 AAN, URM, 27/2, fol. 8.

193 W. Szymańska, *Za ile warto siedzieć*, *Prawo i Życie*, *PiŻ*, 1957/11. See: *Ekonomiści warszawscy o spekulacji*, *Życie Gospodarcze* 1957/21.

194 HIM, Pressearchiv, P 6221, Item 5276/57, Free Market and Black Market in Warsaw, 1957.

195 Z. Broncel, *Październik i dolary*, "Kultura" 1957/116, 39–40; AAN, KC PZPR, 237/XXXII–28, fol. 4.

196 State Archive in Krakow, Archiwum Państwowe w Krakowie (APKr), Komitet Wojewódzki PZPR (KW PZPR), p. 229, k. 174; AAN, Ministerstwo Sprawiedliwości (MS), 558, fol. 186.

without any serious capital, experience, or qualifications have rushed into commerce. They evaluated the economic situation as uncertain, new economic policy as short-term and counted on quick profits, not planning any long-term operations. In their favor was legislation passed by the Ministry of Interior Trade on the re-instatement of travelling salesmen. Such are the people who constitute the core of the profiteers: discharged administration personnel and former door-to-door salesmen. They deal in goods purchased from nationalized stores or in foreign goods, the easiest to come by."[197]

The private, mostly illegal, foreign trade erupted and spread like wildfire. Whereas previously it had been next to impossible to travel beyond the borders of Poland, now the gates to freedom opened a little wider and relaxed passport regulations encouraged Poles to travel in their masses. Emigration, mostly of Jews and Germans, increased as did the repatriation of Poles from the countries to the east of Poland; contacts with the Polish diaspora abroad (the "Polonia") intensified – this all added to the cross-border traffic. In 1957, as many as 59 thousand people travelled to the West as tourists, compared with only 14 thousand a year earlier! Trips to the capitalist and Soviet Bloc countries were "tourist" only in name – usually they were connected with trade activities (see chapter 9).[198] Professional smugglers now also had better "work opportunities" and could operate on a truly large scale. Hard currency, Polish currency, silver and objects of art were leaving Poland; the imports were gold coins, watches, nylons, and clothing. Just a single speculator, one Mieczysław Dudek, between October 1956 and March 1957 sent to Vienna 40 thousand dollars, 400 kg of silver, and 2 400 000 zloty, receiving in return 11 thousand Swiss watches.[199]

It was not difficult to sell even luxury goods smuggled into Poland. The demand was enormous. The small but fast growing fortunes of the black marketeers had to be invested quickly – the memory of the savage currency redenomination

197 E. Kaczmarczyk, *Handel prywatny a zjawisko spekulacji*, "Tygodnik Demokratyczny" 1957/22.

198 P. Sowiński, *Wakacje w Polsce Ludowej. Polityka władz i ruch turystyczny (1945–1989)*, 2005; P. Sowiński, *Merchand adventures komunizmu. Handlowe podróże Polaków na Zachód w latach 1956–1970*, in: *Od Piłsudskiego do Wałęsy. Studia z dziejów Polski w XX wieku*, ed. K. Persak et al, Warszawa 2008, pp. 291–306; D. Stola, *Kraj bez wyjścia? Migracje z Polski 1949–1989*, Warszawa 2010; J. Kochanowski, "*Jesteśmy za biedni, aby urlop spędzać w kraju". Masowa turystyka i nielegalny handel w latach sześćdziesiątych XX w. Perspektywa polska*, "Roczniki Dziejów Społecznych i Gospodarczych, 2008/68, pp. 125–150.

199 APW, KWar. PZPR, 30/XVIII-7, vol. 1, 1958, fol. 36–37.

in 1950 was still fresh. There was high demand for objects that were stores of value, such as jewelry, watches, and gold coins (which from 1956 could once again be owned legally). Construction of single-family homes was on the rise, fueling demand for construction materials. The sales of automobiles increased and were quickly followed by the illegal sale of gas (the appearance of speculation in cars was noted in 1957).

At first, the black market operations were relatively safe and, to a large extent, helped by society's open-minded attitude. "People are used to the black market and it doesn't bother them in everyday life, even if some complain," a diarist noted in 1957. "We are used to backstreet shopping. People have also got used to the fact that those with modest earnings lead luxurious life styles, buy cars or even build villas. The atmosphere of tolerance is accompanied by a sense of impunity. The profiteers […] feel quite safe among us. Snitching happens rarely".[200] Even when it did, especially after October 1956, there was a good chance that the authorities would ignore incriminating information. The police, earlier accused of brutality or lawlessness, played it safe by restraining their more radical actions, often to the point of idleness. "The incorrect approach to tackling [the abuses of] the previous period," the Warsaw District Committee of the Polish United Workers' Party complained in 1957, "and the relatively great influx of cases in relation to the number of employees […] further formalized the prosecution proceedings."[201] The police were accused of trying not to "harm" the suspect, of being skeptical about the evidence and often uncritical towards the suspect and their defense.[202] Ultimately, the "condemnation of severe sentences issued in the past had led in some cases to much too lenient punishments"[203] and until the second half of 1957 "many actions considered criminal before were no longer prosecuted, such as […] obligatory deliveries, general profiteering, etc."[204] The courts and the prosecutor's office trod lightly. Reality made it clear that the existing legislation was unable to categorize some of the black market activities as criminal; as a result, prosecutions were often dropped.[205]

Neither did the regulatory institutions have much sway. The National Trade Inspectorate (Państwowa Inspekcja Handlowa PIH) had no powers to inspect

200 W. Szymańska, *Za ile warto siedzieć*, PiŻ, 1957/ 11.
201 APW, Warszawski Komitet Wojewódzki PZPR, 60/X–6, vol. 1, fol. 14.
202 *Ibid.*, fol. 15.
203 *Ibid.*
204 *Ibid.*, fol. 1.
205 AAN, MS, 558, fol. 65–73; M. Regent, *Z zagadnień spekulacji (Uwagi na tle orzecznictwa sądów okręgu kieleckiego)*, "Nowe Prawo" 1956/10, p. 118.

production, especially that of the cooperatives and crafts. Often, it was the hostility of people openly siding with the profiteers that was more of a problem for the Inspectorate's employees than the actual fraud. The Commissions for Combating Corruption and Fraud in Trade (Komisje do Walki ze Spekulacją i Nadużyciami w Handlu KWS) operating at the National Councils based their operations on the activists and, in the revolutionized atmosphere of late 1956 and early 1957 stood practically no chance of functioning effectively. Paradoxical as it may seem, the National Trade Inspectorate (PIH) itself contributed to the demise of the said Commissions, even though it was its official brief to direct them. The professional inspectors would no longer hide their negative attitude toward their "amateur" colleagues whom they considered a hindrance rather than a help.[206]

It is not surprising that the black market, built up for many years, now rapidly provided a foundation for a solid structure. In 1957, the number of economic crimes detected in Warsaw rose by 26% in comparison with the previous year. There were numerous cases involving large amounts of capital and profit. For the authorities, the black market operations had both economic, especially with regard to the "distribution of the national product",[207] and political repercussions. They shook the foundations of the system and brought about an economic diversification of society. Krzysztof Madej noted that, in its own way, the Gomułka government had tried to acknowledge the rule of law.[208]

By early 1957, the new administration had entrenched itself sufficiently to begin to quench the hopes awakened during the thaw and trim the existing margins of freedom. What it needed, however, was a proxy enemy that could distract society. The "kulaks and reactionaries" were now bogeymen of the past but the profiteers fit perfectly the role of Public Enemy No. 1, particularly since cases of conspicuous wealth stuck out like a sore thumb against the widespread poverty and grayness. In the spring of 1957, the anti-black market rhetoric in the press and elsewhere began to resemble the "battle for trade" campaign of the past. JacekWołowski wrote in *Nowe Drogi*: "The battle against fraud, bribery and profiteering is the battle that the government and society need to fight. Appropriate decrees are necessary. Public opinion demands fair sentences but we also need a wide and active social inspection (national councils, workers councils, and the unions)."[209] Debates on the topic swamped the media. Some called for restraint

206 AAN, MS, 558, fol. 37.

207 C. Bobrowski, *Wspomnienia...*, p. 255.

208 K. Madej, *Bezradność lub represja: władze wobec przestępczości gospodarczej w PRL (1956–1970)*, Warszawa 2010.

209 J. Wołowski, *Wina i kara*, "Nowe Drogi" 1957/7, p. 57.

and argued that, with the improving economy and supply, the black market would disappear – but they were outnumbered by those who were in favor of the traditional approaches such as control, prosecution and severe punishment. More importantly, the authorities themselves also had faith in the saving grace of institutionalized repression.

In mid-March 1957, the press reported that the government was working on establishing a team at the Prime Minister's office to co-ordinate a wide front (of professional and social institutions) for the war on the black market.[210] One can assume that the debate conducted on May 3, 1957 by Warsaw economic activists was representative of the whole country. The consensus of the meeting was to maintain private trade (although not necessarily in city centers) but was adamantly against "all attempts by speculators to conduct black market operations under the label of crafts (*rzemiosło*), and against the diversion of goods produced in state or coop factories in order to line the profiteers' pockets, thereby depriving the state of part of the national income."[211] Some speakers opted for bringing back the public "commissions for combating corruption and fraud in trade", which were still active in some areas, albeit on their last legs, and spoke in favor of energizing the labor unions but most of all for obligatory participation in the battle by Party members, for whom fighting the profiteers should be an "important part of the class struggle on the economic front".[212] The pragmatists were less than impressed; they reckoned that the public activists might be able to encourage housewives to get involved in inspecting markets and stores, but would be helpless when faced with seasoned profiteers. "Comrade Directors," they argued, "keep sending out as inspectors not the best but the worst employees. Often, instead of carrying out the inspection, they go somewhere else. They quickly jot down some negative conclusions, take a stroll around the city, then come back, and return their report convinced that they have fulfilled their party duty."[213] The participants agreed that the most important issue was not ineffective inspection but the lack of updated legislation, which would serve both as a deterrent and a tool facilitating the punishment of "economic criminals".[214]

This two-pronged approach was indeed implemented. In May 1957, the Politburo established regional commissions to combat profiteering. On May 23, 1957, the Council of Ministers issued a decree to set them up in a traditional manner,

210 *Walka ze spekulacją na warsztacie Rządu*, Trybuna Ludu (TL), 133, March 16, 1957.
211 APW, KWar. PZPR, 30/VII–3, vol. 8, fol. 13.
212 *Ibid.*, fol. 15. See: APKr, KW PZPR, 229, fol. 179.
213 APW, KWar. PZPR, 30/VII–3, t. 8, fol. 72–73.
214 *Ibid.*, fol. 71.

attached to the county, municipal, and city district presidiums.[215] Simultaneously, the Polish parliament (Sejm) was working on an anti-profiteering decree and passed it on July 13.[216] Taking advantage of the relative freedom of speech still existed, the debate on the decree spread outside the corridors of parliament, government and Party offices. Not all newspapers were prepared to echo the positive tone of the Party newspapers *Trybuna Ludu* and *Nowe Drogi*. Some did not hide their skepticism. They criticized the decree for its lack of consistency,[217] and pointed out the senselessness of fighting the black market with punishments and court sentences rather than aiming for economic normality.[218] The journalist Józef Kuśmierek went even farther by pointing out the absurdity of the "battle with the black market", which "slowly saturates our whole political life and which has already become a new political theory, an almost conservative dogma."[219]

There was no unanimity on whose job it should be to combat economic crime. Some, analyzing the events of the previous year, doubted if the police and the Prosecutor's Office would be able to rise to the challenges of "organized crime", against which, wrote Władysław Kopaliński, "one should act in an organized way. There should be an institution, which would systematically combine experience and facts [...]. I don't have in mind, however, those extraordinary or special commissions but a permanent institution, whose job it would be to supply the investigative authorities with indispensable information about the object of the crime."[220] There were others who were, though, of the opinion that the state already had at its disposal sufficient apparatus to deal with the profiteers. "I would like to point out quietly," wrote Jerzy Milewski in *Kierunki*, "that there already exists in Poland an institution with a Latin-sounding name, charged with

215 *Ochotnicze komitety do walki ze spekulacją. Inicjatywa z krakowskiego*, TL/224/Aug 15, 1957.

216 Act of 13 July 1957 on combating speculation and protection of the interests of buyers and agricultural producers in trading, Dz.U. 1957, no 39, item 171. The most severe penalties (up to ten years of imprisonment and a hefty fine) were reserved for those employed in nationalized outlets that sold to "unauthorized persons, for commercial purposes, goods not designated for direct sale". "Unauthorized buyers and those who distributed goods bought at the stores risked up to five years of prison. Speculation in goods "purchased with foreign currency paid locally and abroad" was now criminally liable. There was no mention of special institutions designated to supervise the execution of the law.

217 *Dar jasnowidzenia*, PiŻ, 1957/11.

218 G. Pisarski, *Nie tylko tędy droga*, "Życie Gospodarcze" 1957/19.

219 J. Kuśmierek, *Czego się obawiam?*, "Polityka"/24 /7 August 13, 1957.

220 W. Kopaliński, *Z siatką na wieloryby*, ŻW, 1957/160.

prosecuting crime. It is the Prosecutor's Office of the Polish People's Republic. Auxiliary organs such as the National Trade Inspectorate and [...] the Citizens' Police [the state police] cooperate with the Prosecutor's Office."[221]

A large section of society took with a large pinch of salt yet another 'anti-fraud commission' set up in 1957. In the cartoon by Zbigniew Ziomecki, The Economic Underground, *an apparatchik from such a commission asks the workers, "If you happen upon any trace of the economic underground, do please let us know." "Szpilki", nos. 51–52 of 22–29 December 1957 (courtesy of the author)*

221 J. Milewski, *Jeszcze jeden urząd?*, "Kierunki" 1957/30.

The pragmatic approach and common sense pointed to the latter solution. This required time, however, and the authorities were after a quick and spectacular success. On August 39, 1957, by an edict of Prime Minister Józef Cyrankiewicz, the Teams for Combating Corruption and Economic Fraud (Zespoły do Spraw Zwalczania Spekulacji i Nadużyć Gospodarczych) were created. The Central Team was at the Prime Minister office; the chairmen of the Voivodship National Councils (WRN) nominally governed the regional sections. The main goal of the headquarters was to co-ordinate the methods and direction of the ministries and institutions "established to prosecute profiteering and fraud" (since October 3, 1957, this had included all economic crimes). The headquarters mapped out the projects and drafted the motions requiring government decisions, and supervised the regional teams. Konstanty Dąbrowski, the Minister of State Inspection (Ministerstwo Kontroli Państwowej) and, following its dismantling, the president of the Supreme Audit Office NIK, became the chairman of the Prime Minister's team. Its members were the deputy minister of interior trade, the Chief of the Police (Komendant Główny MO), representatives of the Ministry of Justice and Finance, the Supreme Court, the Prosecutor General, the Central Committee of the PUWP/PZRP, the Main Council of the Trade Unions (CRZZ), Społem, Farmers Self-Help, Samopomoc Chłopska, the youth organizations, and the Women's League.[222] The structure of the regional teams reflected that of the Central Team: it was headed by the WRN chairman, with the president of the District Court, the prosecutor, the chairman of the NIK delegation and the Voivodship Chief of Police as team members.

The structure of the teams was expected to facilitate the execution of the basic tasks of the teams: the intensification of legal penalties, the strengthening of the enforcement apparatus (including the re-animated Commissions for Combating Corruption), and in the most newsworthy cases the expediting of court decisions. The teams focused on the most visible and easiest to prove crimes – "goods profiteering". Naturally, this focus resulted in increased scrutiny of private enterprise. However, the teams needed "big operations", which would demonstrate the effectiveness both of the new decree and the newly established teams. On September 26, 1957, some 700 policemen and employees of the regulation enforcement bodies participated in the roundup at the Bazar Różyckiego marketplace in Warsaw. On September 29 and 30, the "largest-scale enforcement operation since its inception" was conducted in the CDT Main Department Store in Warsaw. The sting revealed major "speculation leaks", especially in the high-end fur

222 AAN, MS, 558, fol. 197–198.

department, whose target clientele were certainly not ordinary people. Despite press articles hailing the confiscation of hundreds of sacks of illegal goods at marketplaces, actual results on the ground were much more modest. And no amount of obfuscation could hide the fact that the first anniversary of October 56 followed a year that had been less than successful both economically and politically (bearing in mind the riots that had followed the shutting-down of *Po Prostu* magazine).[223]

In second-hand goods street markets, people tussled excitedly over coveted Western fashion items and any clothes that looked markedly "foreign" – which was the highest accolade for a piece of clothing, and was in fact a euphemism for "Western". The inspectors' own "clothes battles" usually ended in Pyrrhic victories, the illegal trade resuming the moment the inspectors left. Moreover, the dealers could easily reach a mutually beneficial consensus with the inspectors. "The war on profiteering and the profiteering live side happily by side", wrote Józef Kuśmierek. "One can buy anything and everything on the black market, for almost none of the attractive goods is available legally. As for the profiteering-enforcement squads, they will buy lemons for their rickety children in plain sight and legally on the illegal market as soon as they have finished their public inspection round."[224] Whilst voivodship-level achievements were easier to demonstrate – for instance, the questioning of light sentences passed by the county courts, checking the licenses of private stores and restaurants and imposing on them the appropriate taxes (in Warszawa, Szczecin, Wrocław, Kielce), or combating the "marketplace black market",[225] attempts to activate the teams at county level were not successful. County teams were usually left to their own devices; not only were their employees poorly paid but at all times subject to local scrutiny, which at times resulted in physical assaults on the inspectors. And without any means of transport at their disposal, unsurprisingly, they "did not develop effective methods".[226]

More and more frequently it had to be admitted that the battles coordinated by the teams were a fiction. Only small fry were arrested, whereas "most of the black marketeers keep selling meat on the side, deal in goods purchased at nationalized stores, and sell clothes door-to-door".[227] The workplaces – under a formal obligation to delegate public inspectors – as a rule sent out their

223 HIM, Pressearchiv, P 6221, Item 5729/57, "Speculation" scare is smokescreen for drive against private enterprise.

224 J. Kuśmierek, *Czego się obawiam?*

225 AAN, MS, 558, fol. 226–227.

226 "Kurier Polski", 10, January 13, 1958.

227 *Ibid.*,

"unsophisticated, lowest-qualified employees, just so that the onerous formalities and 'feudal' duties were fulfilled."[228] People were reluctant to join the commission, since it required time-consuming post-enforcement procedures involving the prosecution, court, testimonies, etc. – all the more so if the case was found to have merit. And, after all, refusal to participate did not entail any serious consequences.[229] In 1959 in Praga Północ, a large, and not very safe, district of Warsaw, from 31 plants only 148 public inspectors volunteered, despite interventions by Party organizations.[230] Unsurprisingly, many of the cases uncovered and documented by the inspectors were not followed up "due to irregularities in the filing of charges, securing of evidence and other infringements".[231] When the head of the team took his tasks seriously (as was the case in Wrocław), those interested in maintaining the status quo tried to get rid of him by accusing him of corruption.[232] Even after his acquittal, an air of ambiguity remained, effectively pre-empting any future anti-black market initiatives on his part.

In mid-1959, exactly two years after the start of the anti-black market offensive, it became clear that economic crime activities were not showing any downward trend. Crimes were being committed "within groups with a mutual understanding involving people who should have been keeping an eye on each other."[233] Faced with robust local social networks, both the anti-profiteering Act of July 1957 and the actions of various commissions and teams proved ineffectual; in fact, it was the police (MO) and the apparatus of state control that detected the majority of offences.[234] The era of professionalism had arrived. The police and the Trade Inspectorate (the latter often rejected any attempts to be part of the public control teams) as well as the highest offices of the government understood this very well. The resolution of the Third Congress of the Polish United Workers' Party in March 1959 declared that the "protection of public property requires the implementation of harsher measures" and that, for the Party, a "constant battle

228 M. Chrzanowski, *Komisje do walki ze spekulacją są potrzebne*, "Rada Narodowa" 1958/42.

229 D. Pick, *Fenomen "prywaciarza" w PRL. Warszawa w latach 1956–1970*, Warszawa 2003, M.A. Thesis under the supervision of prof. W. Borodziej, Historical Institute, University of Warsaw (copy in the author's possession).

230 A. Bondarewski, *KWS – magiczne literki*, PiŻ, 1960/11.

231 AAN, MS, 558, fol. 218–220.

232 J. Krak, A. Mag, *Nie strzelać! Rezerwat*, PiŻ, 1959/6.

233 AAN, MS, 5489, fol. 67. In 1957 police revealed 7384 cases of economic crimes, in 1958–8780, in 1959 – 9287, in 1960 – 10 372; AAN, PZPR, 237/XIV–246, fol. 66.

234 AAN, MS, 5489, fol. 67.

against the plague of fraud is of utmost importance as is instilling in the public a sense of the indefatigable hammering of corruption and thievery."[235] What the resolution did not mention, however, was that this goal should be achieved by using "social" tools, that is – community input. Even the former apologists of the anti-black market legislation from 1957, two years later were much more restrained in their pronouncements and pointed to legal infringements, incompatibilities with the criminal code, ambiguities and doubts.[236] They stressed that the cutting edge of a decree forged in haste "is quickly blunted".[237] Nevertheless, the legislation remained in use until a new criminal code was introduced in 1969 (the decree was repealed in 1972).[238] The teams and commissions were finally disbanded by the end of the 1950s.

3.3.1 Excursus: Team II

As pointed out earlier, in the investigations of economic crime conducted from mid-1954 until February 1956, members of the PUWP made up some 40% of all those arrested. These were not some rank-and-file activists from the local, regional committees but usually leading Party apparatchiks, who held "positions of power"[239] – managers, directors, and chairmen. Whether in the metropolises or small, provincial towns, a Party membership card was a ticket to a higher position and provided a greater scope of action for the holder, while also providing him with a protective umbrella. While an average black marketeer was a small-time trader, party members were typically involved in large-scale theft, corruption, and embezzlement,[240] activities that fall outside of the proposed field of research of the present work. Nevertheless, we ought to refer briefly to the discrete team set up between 1957 and 1958 to combat crime among Party members. It is difficult to make a firm distinction between the different types of profiteering, especially since it often involved both the public and the private sector. It was, however, unique in the history of communist Poland that a formal body was set up to deal exclusively with the wrong-doings of Party members.

---

235 "Nowe Drogi" 1959/ 4, p. 656.

236 K. Buchała, *Ustawa o zwalczaniu spekulacji – a inne normy karne*, "Palestra" 1959/5, pp. 39–51.

237 T. Cyprian, *Spekulacja*, "Palestra, 1960/ 4, pp. 13–24.

238 AAN, Institute of Crime Problems, Instytut Problematyki Przestępczości IPP, p. 107, Adam Krukowski, *Przestępczość gospodarcza w polskim prawie karnym*, fol. 86.

239 AAN, MS, 5489, fol. 67.

240 AAN, KC PZPR, 237/XXXII–28, fol. 3.

Until at least the 1960s, black-marketeers were depicted as a cross between hoodlum and petit-bourgeois, with workers shown fighting them. Jan Sochacki, Speculator, *1959. Photo: Warsaw Museum of Caricature, sign. 4302.*

On October 31, 1957 the Central Committee of the PUWP appointed the Team for Combating Fraud and Corruption, (Zespół do Walki z Nadużyciami i Korupcją), with Jerzy Albrecht at the helm; the team had voivodship, municipal, county, and city district branches. Its goal was to "cleanse sections of state and economy administration of corrupted and criminal elements."[241] With no sources available on the actual process, we can only speculate about how the teams were set up. The economic context was bound to have played a part, since we know how much the

241 AAN, KC PZPR, 237/XXXII-1, fol. 1.

economy and what he considered its pathologies mattered to Gomułka. All the more so, since the numbers of corruption cases, inflicting tangible, and increasing, losses on the state sector systematically increased. Only radical action could put an end to the growing anarchy in the ranks of the PUWP, tighten discipline and abate the mood of "liberalism and helplessness in the executive bodies set up to prosecute economic crimes."[242] Their aim was two-pronged: to calm the mood of the lower echelons of the Party – which, emboldened by the events of October 56 – had ever since, more and more openly, criticized the abuses and irregularities. But it was also important to prove, especially now that the end of the "thaw" was in sight, how uncompromising the leading ideology of the state was capable of being, also towards its own members. Far be it from me to indulge in a conspiracy version of history but one cannot exclude the possibility that the spur to action came from the Party's desire to get rid of its negative image by washing its own dirty linen, or at least selecting the items for the laundry, away from public scrutiny.

The teams consisted of members of various rungs of the Party administration, in particular, those employed in the Prosecutor's Office, the judiciary system, state security services, the Police, the Trade Inspectorate and Treasury security as well as Party activists from major factories, Party members within the Union of Socialist Youth (ZMS), the Union of Rural Youth (ZMW), and the trade unions. The teams were to focus on "Party organizations active in trade, restaurants and catering establishments, in construction, on State Agricultural Farms (PGR), and in institutions and enterprises in close contact with 'private initiative'"[243] – as all private enterprise was referred to. It was not an easy task. Even when the Party auditors tried to carry out their duties thoroughly, they usually hit a brick wall built by the local cliques. Insiders were fully aware that only through solidarity would they be able to wait out the actions of the Party's *cherezvychaika*. For example, members of the "economic activist group" in City Meat Trade (Miejski Handel Mięsem) in Chorzów "organized a clandestine meeting [...] and swore an oath that in case of an investigation, [they would] not wreck the situation [...] and all put up their hands to swear they would not snitch on one another."[244] The teams at the regional committees were so passive that by mid-1958, the Secretariat of the Central Committee remarked on it in a special circular.[245] This is not to

242 AAN, KC PZPR, 237/XXXII-2, fol. 1.

243 *Ibid.*

244 AAN, KC PZPR, 237/XXXII-7, fol. 141.

245 K. Madej, *Siermiężna i dolarowa – korupcja w PRL w latach 1956–1980*, in: *PRL – trwanie i zmiana*, ed. D. Stola, M. Zaremba, Warszawa 2003, p. 252.

say that there was no resistance in the big cities. For example in Warsaw, where "absolutely no one is in charge of the fraud-fighting team", by the end of 1957 only eight cases out of a hundred had been investigated. In the Old Town district of Warsaw and in the city center not a single case had been pursued; the situation was similar in Łódź.[246]

In spite of the lack of prosecution, by April 15, 1 958 charges had been laid against approximately 14 thousand party members. Of those, 9 112 were sentenced, 5 809 excluded from the party and 3 280 – reprimanded. In 3 255 cases, there was an attempt to remove the targeted members from their position (it is unknown how many were indeed removed); 4 020 cases ended up at the Prosecutor's Office.[247] Some were of the opinion that the teams had uncovered too much, while others thought it was not enough. What is certain, however, is that the fraud-fighting teams became dangerous – a double-edged weapon. With effect from the spring of 1958, the representatives of prosecuting bodies (the police, the Prosecutor's Office) could no longer be part of the teams (and let us not forget that it was the police who uncovered and reported most of the cases).[248] By mid-1958, the teams had been transformed into advisory bodies operating within the voivodship and regional Party committees, and from that moment on did not have any real impact.

While much has been written on the anti-profiteering commissions from the 1945–1954 and 1981–1987, very scant source material remains concerning the post-October 1956 commissions. This was not so much due to the efforts of overactive archivists to remove the relevant files but rather the absence of documentation reflected the lack of any real significance of the teams and commissions operating after 1957. There were several reasons. The modus operandi used during the times of chaos and brutal compulsory nationalization of the economy, which accompanied the formation of the totalitarian structures of the state, did not work in times heralded as a return to the rule of law. The fact that the 'rule of law' was no longer an empty phrase had given society a real chance to defend itself.

A certain reversal of roles had taken place. After 1956, Polish society found itself on the revolutionary, and the authorities on the "reactionary" side of the barricade. As a result, the authorities could no longer use methods from the revolutionary repertory without appearing anachronistic. Such methods were

246 AAN, KC PZPR, 237/XXXII–7, fol. 121, 123, 126.

247 AAN, KC PZPR, 237/XXXII–8, fol. 209–210. Social makeup of those prosecuted was more important: there were 1 756 workers, 825 peasants, 6 385 white collar/intelligentsia (of which 4.5 thousand held positions); *ibid.*

248 AAN, KC PZPR, 237/XXXII–28, fol. 2.

tolerated when store shelves were empty and people desperate. The shortages of the late 1950s were limited to more attractive articles, which were at the time considered luxury items. The average citizen was now more likely to be improving his strategies for laying his hands on desirable goods rather than engaging in anti-profiteering activities. The prevailing perception was that, since the state was unable to minimize the shortages, the least it should do was to exhibit benevolent neutrality.

The acclaimed poet Tadeusz Różewicz called the 1960s the times of "minor stabilization" but it seemed that it was Marcin Zaremba who had got it right when he called them the era of "minor de-stabilization".[249] There were crises, tensions, and conflicts, at times solved with radical methods (such as the death penalty in the notorious "meat affair"). Resisting temptation, the central authorities did not utilize the social mood to recreate anti-profiteering institutions. The idea, however, had not been forgotten. If need be, it was the trade unions that were given the task of implementation, then held responsible for the results. More than two decades were to pass before the authorities would again be involved in anti-black market operations.

3.4 Intermedium II: The 1960s and 1970s

This chapter does not aspire to present the economic history of the period or to analyze the steps taken by the authorities on the road to combating economic crime. The latter was researched thoroughly (especially in regards to the crucial period of the 1960s) by Krzysztof Madej, Maria Pasztor, and Dariusz Jarosz.[250] Instead, I would like to focus on the factors that supported and strengthened the black market in Poland. Some had been inherited from the earlier period and adapted themselves gradually to the new era. The changing political, social, and economic circumstances encouraged not only the assimilation of the old strategies but also the creation of new ones such as the tourist trade, which became an element of everyday life and paved the way for the black market boom of the 1980s.

---

249 M. Zaremba, *Społeczeństwo polskie lat sześćdziesiątych – między "małą stabilizacją" a "małą destabilizacją"*, in: *Oblicza marca 1968*, ed. K. Rokicki, S. Stępień, Warszawa 2004, pp. 24–51.

250 K. Madej, *Siermiężna i dolarowa…*; K. Madej, *Bezradność lub represja..*; K. Madej, *Milicja Obywatelska wobec przestępczości gospodarczej (1956–1970). Ewolucja struktur i jej uwarunkowania*, PH, 98, 2007/1, pp. 49–70; D. Jarosz, M. Pasztor, *Afera mięsna: fakty i konteksty*, Toruń 2004.

The title of this chapter emphasizes the division into two different eras, with not only different first secretaries of the PUWP but also distinct economic, social, and black market landscapes. Each period had its own turning point when the growing economic crisis decreased the supply of goods, leading to a deterioration of the general mood; on both occasions, this resulted in citizens engaging more vigorously in unofficial trade strategies, and the authorities responding with increased vigor with counter strategies.

3.4.1 The 1960s

The Teams for Combating Corruption and Economic Fraud were officially disbanded in 1961, but had already disappeared from the headlines and official communiqués a year earlier. Just as had been the case with the Special Commission, the change was accompanied neither by economic stabilization nor by a slowdown in unofficial trading. On the contrary, the numbers of "speculation cases" prosecuted rose, especially in the meat industry. Problems with a strategic product such as meat, smuggling and trading of hard currency and gold quickly became the main characteristic of the decade.

The Polish black market was fueled both by shortages – of meat and luxury items – and panic breaking-out periodically on the market. The panics were triggered by internal tensions or by a growing fear of war during international crises, such as the building of the Berlin Wall in 1961,[251] the Cuban crisis in 1962, the Middle East war in 1967, the Soviet intervention in Czechoslovakia in August 1968 and skirmishes at the Soviet-Chinese border. While in the 1950s people had focused on buying large amounts of "crisis" goods (pasta, kasha, salt, canned food, candles, and soap), in the 1960s the waves of war panic increased the demand for store-of-value articles, that is to say gold coins and bars, and hard currency. Although trade in those was still prohibited, ownership was not a crime. Recurring rumors of an impending currency revaluation (in September 1961, September and October 1963, January 1968, October and November 1969) served their purpose – not only did Poles deposit their savings in bank accounts but they were also buying gold and dollars hand over fist, which caused their price to rise rapidly, and they were storming luxury item stores, buying jewelry,

251 In this case, the list of concerns was longer: "The buying panic is triggered by rumors about: war, lack of food supply in warehouses, price hikes of essentials, looming currency reform, the introduction of food coupons (which allegedly had already been introduced in Czechoslovakia)"; APW, KWar. PZPR, 30/VII–43, vol. 20, fol. 183.

furs, furniture and technical and mechanical appliances.[252] In accordance with the laws of supply and demand, a large volume of such articles entered illegal circulation. The waves of market panic accompanied by continuous shortages boosted and fanned further the speculation fever and brought about a phenomenon that could be called "(anti)-speculation allergy".

In the 1960s there were many additional factors that unexpectedly stimulated the black market. For example, advantage was taken of the rights of those returning from abroad, in the 1960s – mostly from the West, to import personal effects without paying any customs duty. Often, literally tons of pepper, polyethylene, imitation leather, cosmetics, and fake furs were brought into the country under such a guise. Once in Poland, the goods were distributed on the black market and sold to state warehouses.[253]

The millennial festivities in 1966 were a headache for the Polish authorities, and not just because of their religious and political implications. The numerous celebrations boosted the illegal production and distribution of devotional articles, toys, and probably alcohol.[254] Their production often relied on resources, which had been earlier smuggled into Poland. Private craftsmen would not have been able to continue their production without zippers and haberdashery brought illegally from Czechoslovakia.[255] Every time goods were confiscated at the border, prices in the Nowy Targ and Zakopane markets went up.[256] In the 1960s, tourism became a mass pursuit and was unapologetically used as a means of cross-border trade (more in chapter 9).

---

252 AAN, KC PZPR, XI/775, fol. 25–26.

253 Archive of the Institute of National Remembrance in Warsaw (Archiwum Instytutu Pamięci Narodowej w Warszawie-AIPN), Ministry of Internal Affairs II (Ministerstwo Spraw Wewnętrznych II-MSW II), 4369, Circular of the Investigations Office of the Ministry of Interior, no. 123/64, November 2, 1964, fol. 214–215. In 1963, on behalf of a returnee from Canada, some Polish "entrepreneurs" brought to Poland almost four thousand sheets of artificial foam (from West Germany) and 14 tons of plastics (from England); *ibid.*, fol. 21–22; AIPN, MSW II, 4368 Circular of the Investigations Office of the Ministry of Interior, 1964, fol. 92.

254 AIPN, Police Headquarters (MO-KG MO), 35/3178, 1–2, 29–30.

255 HIM, Pressearchiv, P 6221, RFE-Research, Item No 2823, 3 IX 1961, "Gorale" (the highlanders) – the privileged class in Poland; *Przemytnicy w potrzasku*, TL/249 from September 10, 1961; J. Kochanowski, *Naczynia połączone, czyli polsko-czechosłowackie Schleichwege 1945–1989*, in: *Amicus Poloniae. Teksty ofiarowane Profesorowi Heinrichowi Kunstmannowi w osiemdziesiątą piątą rocznicę urodzin*, ed. K. Ruchniewicz, M. Zybura, Wrocław 2009, pp. 205–207.

256 M. Różycki, *Prawo pogranicza*, ŻW/307–309, December 24–26, 1959.

In 1957, the private sector in Poland consisted of almost 190 thousand enterprises.[257] With such solid foundation, it could effectively defend itself from the recurrent government tightening of the screw (in 1957 for the first time and then in 1961-1965 and 1969-1971). The registered decrease in the numbers of private enterprises did not reflect reality. Some artisans or merchants turned to the grey zone, which was probably as wide-spread as the legal one.[258] Or they would accept a job in the state sector during economic declines only to return to their illicit business when the economic environment again turned more permissive. The number of private operators grew significantly in the 1960s with the appearance of franchising (*ajencja*). The authorities were more likely to accept stores, restaurants, and service businesses run as franchises than as strictly private businesses.

A large group (over a thousand in 1966) of private manufacturers took advantage of the export opportunities, which emerged in 1957. What was much more common, however, since more profitable and demanding less effort, was cooperation with the state sector, which had at its disposal unlimited resources. Despite the periodic hounding of private entrepreneurs, who were allegedly "draining" state resources, factories and offices could no longer operate without them. Not without significance was the fact that such cooperation was financially beneficial to state officials. The inflated budgets or dubious origin of resources and machineries were regarded leniently. "No-one officially knows and no-one wants to know what the source of craftsmen's supply is," wrote in *Życie Gospodarcze*, in 1968, Jerzy Urban – who in the 1950s and 1960s was a journalist so unpopular with the government that he was eventually banned from any journalistic activity, yet in the 1980s was to become a government spokesman, wildly detested by society – "because in the current atmosphere of spontaneity finding this out would mean closing down private artisan industry."[259] In the late 1960s the trend reversed – in 1965 the non-agricultural private sector employed around 350 thousand but in 1969 the number rose to 512 thousand. That translated into 43% growth in comparison to the 11% increase in the nationalized economy.[260]

---

257 134 000 craft businesses, 25–27 000 sales outlets (not counting marketplaces!), some 3 000 larger manufacturing plants, some 18 000 transportation companies, some 4.5 thousand service outlets; D. Pick, *Fenomen "prywaciarza" w PRL…*, p. 30.

258 *Ibid.*, p. 36.

259 Ibid., p. 94.

260 AAN, KC PZPR, XII/1795, report on social and economic problems on the Gdańsk coast, 1971, fol. 45–46. Only in 1967 r. the number of those employed in craft business rose 8.2%; AAN, KC PZPR, XI/773, fol. 13, 15, 44.

Being a private operator (or employed by one) was probably more demanding but also more profitable. Even if the stories about the fantastically wealthy private artisans or merchants were not always true, their average income allowed them a relatively high standard of living, enabling them also to put some money in such stores of value as hard currency and gold, and they were also the most important clients of the hard currency and gold black markets. "We have just seized from 'private initiative'," reported the chief of the Warsaw Police Antoni Fryden, "62 kg of gold intended for the market and $30 000, to the total value of over 20 million zloty."[261] In 1970, the police (MO) seized 36.5 kg in gold bars, seven thousand 10-rouble gold coins, and 3.5 kg gold jewelry. They were sold "mostly to the owners of private artisan shops, usually for hard currency."[262] The private entrepreneurs had competition from sailors, athletes, scientists and state officials, that is, groups with high if not always declared or legally obtained income, who invested their profits from dubious sources, embezzlement or other fraudulent operations in a similar way.

With the hoarding of gold and hard currency, the internal black market thrived; contraband operations became more efficient and professionalized. Since the early 1960s, the numbers of "hard currency smuggling crimes" had steadily risen. For example in 1963, a 47% increase was reported in comparison to the previous year.[263] In 1962, ten big "affairs" (including three cases involving hard currency) were investigated, with convictions in some of the cases; a year later there were already 18 prosecutions (with four involving hard currency). The authorities attributed the growth to increased criminal activity and an "improved detection rate".[264]

1964 was a watershed year. The "meat affair" made the authorities more vigilant, which resulted in an avalanche of fraud exposure, greater and lesser. Small-time black market dealers were again targeted en masse by the authorities, along with black market sharks; this was due both to the worsening provisions and Gomułka's regime trying to hide the fact that it was tightening the screws. Diverting attention on to the traditional populist enemy – the swindler and the profiteer – seemed to do the trick, especially since parts of society were openly demanding harsher penalties for economic crimes. "There is public demand", the Warsaw Committee of the PUWP reported in July 1964, "for bringing in social inspectors, overcoming the existing chaos, and changing the methods of fighting

261 APW, KWar. PZPR, 30/XVIII-7, vol. 1, fol. 171.
262 APW, KWar. PZPR, 30/VII-43, vol. 49, fol. 68–69.
263 APW, KWar. PZPR, 30/XVIII-7, vol. 1, fol. 169.
264 *Ibid.*, fol. 169–170. See: K. Madej, *Bezradność lub represja.*

criminals. Many point to the effectiveness of the system used in Bulgaria. A relatively large number of people note that despite the fact that the swindlers are being locked up, there has been no improvement in the meat supply."[265]

The idea of public anti-speculation commissions was being revisited, now, however, introduced by and accountable only to the trade unions. Warsaw, commonly perceived as the seedbed of the black market evil, was also at the forefront of anti-speculation activity. In January and February 1965, more than 600 activists participated in inspections of stores and marketplaces. By mid-March, workplaces volunteered 1 200 "public", that is community, inspectors.[266] They were apparently not very competent, since the following year not only was it recommended that the "number of activists delegated for public controls" be increased but also that there be "careful selection"; nevertheless, the drive was towards a simplification of recruitment in order to achieve a "mass character of public inspection."[267] Periodically, for instance before holidays, mass-scale inspections were to be conducted. These operations were to be decentralized with the help of special city district teams. There was a call to set up community courts at the manager's offices of state plants to deal with petty crime, hitherto dealt with by police courts (*kolegia*).[268] Varsovians were urged to lend a hand in the enhancement of community invigilation by snitching on any known culprits.[269]

If one did no more than glance at the statistics published in official reports, the overall impression was of a spectacular success – while in 1965 in Warsaw, only 220 inspections took place, by November 30,1966 the number had risen to 8 829, and for 1967, a staggering 20 thousand were planned! Among the participants were the members of the unions, police functionaries, employees of the PIH and the Prosecutor's Office, and Socialist Youth Organization (ZMS) activists. However, on closer scrutiny of the comments that accompanied the figures, a less ideal picture emerged: attendance at the inspection raids was extremely low and the public courts, which had been launched with such aplomb, barely functioned.[270] All this was mostly just a lot of hot air: at the turn of 1966 and 1967 in Warsaw,

265 APW, KWar. PZPR, 30/VII–43, vol. 24, fol. 269.

266 *Ibid.*, vol. 26, fol. 180, 182.

267 *Ibid.*, vol. 28, fol. 113.

268 The public courts law came into force on July 7, 1965 (Dz.U. no. 13, item 92). With amendments it was in place until 1990. A. Kochański, *Polska 1944–1991. Informator historyczny*, vol. 2: *Ważniejsze akty prawne, decyzje i enuncjacje państwowe (1957–1970)*, Warszawa 2000, p. 422.

269 APW, KWar. PZPR, 30/VII–43, vol. 28, fol. 113.

270 *Ibid.*, vol. 30, IS 3/I/1121, fol. 19–21.

the estimated number of all kinds of speculation cases was 1 500 annually.[271] This was not an impressive number, considering that in 1966 and 1967 Poles had more and more "hot" money burning their pockets, and store shelves were emptying at a dramatic rate.[272] The international situation (including the war in the Middle East) had also had an impact on internal Polish politics and had further complicated the situation. In early 1968, the black market exchange rate with the US dollar reached its highest level since 1957. The fear of war and the anxiety around the possibility of a currency reform not only pushed people (especially those who were about to emigrate) toward exchanging zloty into dollars but also brought about increasing bank account deposits (in April 1968, these increased by 23% compared with a year earlier). Stores were brimming with customers searching high and low for "consumer durables with investment potential such as refrigerators, vacuum cleaners, TV sets, furs, jewelry etc."[273]

It is difficult to state unequivocally whether this was the reason for the unprecedented emphasis on speculation in the new criminal code implemented in 1969. Distinctions were made between crimes linked to the nationalized and non-nationalized sectors and those related to manufacturing and retail trade. Harsher penalties were meted out to perpetrators who turned an illegal trade into a regular source of income. Black market operations connected with internal export were dealt with separately. The legislation retained quaint wartime wording, referring to penalties for "unauthorized persons" who stockpiled goods in "incommensurable quantities".[274] It seemed that the anti-speculation articles in the criminal code would be implemented swiftly. Meanwhile, throughout 1970, the Ministry of Internal Trade was flooded with complaints about shortages of: butter, margarine, cottage cheese, milk (condensed and powdered), coffee, chocolate, chocolate sweets, cocoa, citrus fruits, pork, cured meats, lard, pork fat, fish, some types of bread, and, among industrial products, textile articles, underwear, wool, cotton, clothing, paper and paper products, lavatory paper, crystal, ceramics, household glass items, coal, coke, construction materials, shoes, furniture, collapsible bikes, silver-plated cutlery, some cosmetics, and spare parts."[275] Salvation for the market was sought in a price hike. We all know how that plan worked out: bringing a bloody end to the decade – and to the Gomułka regime.

---

271 APW, KWar. PZPR, 30/VII–43, vol. 30, fol. 24.

272 AAN, KC PZPR, XI/773, fol. 13, 15, 44.

273 APW, KWar. PZPR, 30/VII–43, vol. 33, fol. 118–119.

274 *Mała encyklopedia prawa*, Warszawa 1980, pp. 693–694.

275 AAN, Ministry of Internal Trade and Services (Ministerstwo Handlu Wewnętrznego i Usług, MHWiU), 15/1, report on complaints and suggestions, 1970.

3.4.2 The 1970s

At the beginning of the Gierek decade it looked like small-scale, traditional 'speculation' was about to vanish from the everyday vocabulary. Even though the number of detected "speculation crimes" did not decrease,[276] they disappeared from the front-page headlines. The prosecuting bodies were focusing rather on the rapidly growing problem of hard currency contraband, a more spectacular pursuit than chasing petty black traders. The battle against hard currency offences waned with the arrival of an unofficial dual currency system. In 1974 the government launched the chain of Pewex stores, which soon drew Poles like a magnet with an assortment of goods that were irresistible, whether because they were foreign and thus much coveted, such as electronics, Levi's jeans or Western brand name spirits, or because they were simply indispensable – humble toilet paper, for one – and not available elsewhere much of the time. The name "Pewex" was short for "Przedsiębiorstwo Eksportu Wewnętrznego" – "Internal Export Company", a contradiction in terms. This was, however, a euphemism: in fact, what it meant was that the stores only accepted payment in hard currencies – not something that most citizens, with obvious exceptions such as seafarers, had readily available. To shop in Pewex they were obliged to buy German marks or most often US dollars on the black market, which came conveniently courtesy of the illegal currency dealer (*cinkciarz*), loitering conspicuously near the entrance. The government turned a blind eye to this ubiquitous illegal currency dealing, since the chain had been introduced to ease the country's foreign currency deficit and the authorities were only too happy to harvest the dollars and other currency circulating in society, however they might have been come by. This meant that the illegal street money dealers, the chief source of hard currency for an average Pole, were now – paradoxically – involved in a pro-state activity. The illegal foreign trade practiced by the Poles now focused on obtaining hard currency. Its scope widened due to the rapidly growing number of participants, now in the millions, as well as the fact that it spanned a widening geographical area. Besides the hard-currency stores, another policy designed to drain the private hard currency supply was the significant relaxation of the rules governing hard currency bank accounts (1976).

Opening Poland to the world was one of the modernizing goals of the new government's policies. In the early 1970s, the growth rates of real wages and

276 In 1970, there were 2 921 "speculation crimes" uncovered, and 1 644 sentences passed, of these – 13.5% were a jail term. In 1973, there were 3 009 such crimes, with 2 161 (13.2%) convictions; AAN, URM, 32/2, fol. 13.

personal income household expenditure were among the highest in the world, and the highest among the Soviet Bloc countries (51.5% in 1971–1975).[277] Between 1971 and 1975, the average wage in the nationalized economy grew 7.3% annually, compared to only 1.8% in the decade 1961–1970. Wages were spent mainly on consumption: industrial articles, services (including tourism), and food, including higher quality products. While between 1970 and 1975 the consumption of grains decreased by 13 kg and potatoes by 20 kg per capita, the consumption of butter rose by over one kilogram, sugar – more than four,and milk and milk products by nine liters, reflecting an improved standard of living for the average Pole, measured by the size of the archetypal national dish on his plate: the pork chop. Between 1960 and 1970, the consumption of meat per person grew in Poland by 10.5 kg but in the first part of 1970 alone, it soared by 17.5 kg. "Such an acceleration of the growth rate of meat consumption had never before been recorded in Poland or probably in any other country."[278] Had it occurred to Gierek, he could have truthfully told Poles, in the words that Harold Macmillan had addressed to the British in 1957, that they "have never had it so good".

By 1971, there were fewer complaints about inadequate supplies, in particular of cars.[279] People expressed cautious optimism when luxury articles such as TV (including color) sets, radios, and domestic appliances became commonplace in Polish apartments, which were now bigger and of a higher standard than the cramped cubicles of the Gomułka era. In 1975, Poles purchased one million TV sets – almost twice as many as in 1970; sales of refrigerators also doubled. The number of washing machines sold rose by 50%. There was great progress in the automobile sector. In 1970, Poles owned some 453 400 cars; this grew to 1 041 600 by 1975, and to 2 069 4 000 by 1979. The cars were relatively cheaper now. In 1971, one had to spend 70 monthly paychecks in order to buy a Fiat 125p; by 1974 this had gone down to "only" 55 – still an alarming ratio by Western standards.[280]

Polish society was becoming accustomed to growing and more sophisticated consumption and to constant prices, which to a large extend ceased to mark the

277 L. Beskid, *Ewolucja konsumpcji w latach siedemdziesiątych w Polsce*, in: *Systemy wartości*, p. 346. See: M. Zaremba, *"Bigosowy socjalizm". Dekada Gierka*, in: *Polacy wobec PRL. Strategie przystosowawcze*, ed. G. Miernik, Kielce 2003, pp. 183–200.

278 *Polityka i organizacja żywienia ludności*, ed. W. Kamiński, Warszawa 1980, p. 46.

279 AAN, MHWiU, 15/1, fol. 95–97.

280 Z. Krasiński, H. Mruk, P. Rzepczyński, *Handel i usługi na tle rozwoju motoryzacji indywidualnej*, Warszawa 1977, p.11; *Rynek motoryzacyjny*, ed. Z. Krasiński, Warszawa 1980, pp. 44–45.

limits of demand.[281] The good times were all too brief. The more the appetite for consumption grew, the more painful every successive market wobble became. By 1974, the writing was on the wall. The growth of individual income recorded in September exceeded earlier projections, a stark harbinger of growing inflation. Store deliveries could not keep pace with the thicker and thicker wads of cash bulging in people's wallets.[282] In 1974, at the turn of August and September, even in usually well-stocked Warsaw there were shortages of quality cuts of meat, washing machines, refrigerators, furniture, radio and TV equipment. To be eligible to buy a sought-after consumer industrial article, you now had to put your name on a pre-registration list, and well in advance.[283] The statistics still looked encouraging, especially in the five-year range. However, an average consumer does not think in terms of macro-economics but rather in the context of his kitchen table, refrigerator or garage. "The political team treated the period of 1971–1975 as a whole," wrote Piotr Bożyk, Edward Gierek's economic advisor between 1971 and 1975, "taking the total numbers of goods delivered to the market as a whole, and dividing them per year and per capita. The consumer was not interested in such an approach. When he had the money in his wallet, he looked to buy a specific item – when this was not available, his disillusionment with politics grew. The buyers who came between 1974 and 1975 were not the same people who had been the lucky ones buying goods between 1971 and 1973. Thus the new buyers were not interested in the government's argument that, taking the 5-year period as a whole, things were just fine: since the first three years had been very good, and the last two not so good, on average, the five-year period was not too bad."[284]

The situation was, however, getting worse. An expert's report (written in the early 1980s) on the economy of the years 1974–1977 pointed out that the "growing difficulties in purchasing goods and services, the diminishing variety and quality of supply, the rapidly growing prices, the rising black-market dollar exchange rate, the widening of the range of goods only available to those holding hard currency, the limiting of the availability of goods through the introduction of coupon and allocation schemes, and the pessimistic view of the future caused by the overall worsening market and general social and economic situation prompted increased spending of current earned income on 'jam today' (the general perception

281 L. Beskid, *Ekonomiczne…*, pp.168–169.

282 AAN, KC PZPR, XIA/465, fol. 1–2.

283 APW, KWar. PZPR, 30/VII–43, vol. 55, fol. 61–63.

284 P. Bożyk, *Marzenia i rzeczywistość czyli Anatomia polskiego kryzysu*, Warszawa 1983, p. 89.

was that 'tomorrow it's all bound to be more expensive and there will be less of everything'). This whittled away savings, put aside with the goal of buying a specific product, directing instead life savings accumulated to safeguard the future towards investing in goods, hard currency, luxury items, and gold."[285]

In 1974, the rising cost of living drove many people, especially those for whom the raison d'être had become "to have" rather than merely "to be", to develop various sophisticated extramural income generating operations among which black market strategies played an increasingly important role.[286] Between 1975 and 1980, employment in the more lucrative private sector (excluding agriculture) grew significantly. Between 1970 and 1975, the number of private operators rose from 442 300 to 469 200 and in 1980 the official number was 602 000 (the greatest growth was recorded among enterprise owners and co-owners). During the 1970s, the previously negative collective image of the private entrepreneur, derogatively referred to as a "prywaciarz", changed noticeably: the "cult of successful business, energy, initiative was coming to the fore. The entrepreneurial spirit, the ability to get things done, involvement in "business" were valued by families. Children were raised with those values in mind and their parents contrasted them with the apathy and passivity in workplaces throughout the nationalized sector."[287] These different perceptions were, however, accompanied by a slackening of moral norms and increasing condoning of actions incompatible with the letter of the law.[288]

In the mid-1970s, terms such as the "black market" and "speculation" gradually made a reappearance; first, in Party or police confidential reports, then – in the press. They were in continual use from the summer of 1976 onwards when due to the quickly called off price hike, panic on the market, and the introduction of sugar rationing, unofficial distribution channels immediately sprang into life (based on illicit "leaking" of goods from the nationalized trade system, illegal produce trading etc.). The authorities reacted swiftly, setting up teams authorized to combat illegal food trading (mostly of meat) and to inspect trade and transportation.[289] The teams were to be created at all levels, from the municipality to voivodship, and include representatives of the PIH, financial offices, and the labor unions. In June 1977, the Politburo of the Polish United Workers' Party adopted a resolution to continue actions to protect "public order and social

---

285 AAN, Instytut Rynku Wewnętrznego i Usług, p. 317, fol. 42–43.

286 See: P. Gliński, *Ekonomiczne uwarunkowania…*, op. cit.

287 *Ibid.*, p.163.

288 See: *Prywaciarze 1945–89*, ed. A. Knyt, A. Wancerz-Gluza, Warszawa 2001; the author's correspondence with R. Grzelak, September–November 2002.

289 AAN, KC PZPR, WO, 1075, unpag.

discipline in the country."[290] That they did so is hardly surprising – in 1977, the crime rate rose by 6% with economic crime up by 8%. The food sector, trade, construction, transportation (the huge amount of 3.6 billion zloty worth of gas had been stolen!) were considered the most threatened branches of the economy.[291]

In the early 1977, sociologists from Poznań researched the extent of the shortages and found that they had been experienced by 83% of households. In the cities around 85% of households had searched unsuccessfully for a product, 41% had been looking for three products (71% and 33% respectively in rural areas).[292] In the third quarter of 1977, there were shortages of 130 products to a total value of 15.6 billion zloty, which was one third more than the "highest shortages recorded during the most difficult periods for the markets."[293] In the following quarter, the shortages rose to some 25 billion zloty! Not only were there shortages of meat but also of textiles, clothing, shoes, household appliances, TV and radio equipment, cars, furniture, coal, and even soap and toothpaste.[294]

In a poll conducted in 1975, five thousand people were asked to identify negative phenomena in Poland. Fifty nine percent of the respondents named alcoholism, 51% arrogance and rudeness of bureaucrats, 48% mismanagement and wastefulness, 47% hooliganism, 38% nepotism and 31% bribery. At that time, no-one mentioned speculation.[295] Two years later, alcoholism had become even more prominent (62.7%) but in second place came "selling under the counter" – as many as 59.1% of the respondents had encountered the practice very often or often (16.1% had encountered it rarely, 17% – never).[296] As was to be expected, there were calls for increased vigilance. Almost 40% of respondents stressed the importance of public supervision. "There is a need for frequent and unexpected inspections, especially in stores and local community offices. People should get used to having their every step watched and know that they cannot get away with

290 *Ibid.*, 3210, unpag.

291 J. Maziarski, *Przestępczość gospodarcza*, "Polityka"/43, Oct 28, 1978. The report of July 1977 *Social and economic policies after Fifth Session of CC of the PUWP* stated blatantly that "the black market and speculation keep growing"; *Raporty dla Edwarda Gierka*, Warszawa 1988, p. 65.

292 W. Krasucka, *Spekulacja (wybrane zagadnienia)*, "Studia Kryminologiczne, Kryminalistyczne i Penitencjarne" 10/1979, pp. 152–153.

293 AAN, KC PZPR, XI/790, fol. 23.

294 *Ibid.*, fol. 68–73.

295 Z. Sufin, *Tendencje w opiniach i postawach społeczeństwa polskiego w latach 1975–1976*, in: *Diagnozy społeczne w okresie narastającego kryzysu…*, p. 10.

296 AAN, KC PZPR, XIA/396, fol. 87; *Społeczeństwo polskie w drugiej połowie lat siedemdziesiątych. Raporty z badań*, ed. Z. Sufin, Warszawa 1981, p. 191.

anything." There were also voices that "trade inspections will not help much if they are not accompanied by additional supplies of goods."[297]

The increased trade supervision executed by professional institutions such as the state Police (MO), the National Trade Inspectorate (PIH), the National Price Commission (PKC) and the public commissions still affiliated with the Main Council of Labor Unions (CRZZ) was clearly noticeable (with 182 762 inspections in 1976 and 228 637 in 1977).[298] The press also took up more frequently the issue of public involvement in inspections. "Informal, public supervision", wrote Jacek Maziarski in the *Polityka* weekly, "has a good chance of becoming the best tool for combating fraud."[299] Only under certain conditions, however: "In order to arouse public opinion the enclaves of ambiguity need to be consistently reduced. Where the public interest is at stake, we must ensure decisively that there is no question of holy cows, taboos or shameful dissembling."[300] The journalist got to the root of the problem here – faced with the critical market situation, Poles were getting used to unorthodox methods of finding ways round problems. For the hundreds of thousands inspections and countrywide actions, hailed as a huge success (for example the operation Rynek, conducted in December 1979 by the police, the PIH and public inspectors[301]), brought meagre results, disproportionate to the effort. While in 1975, 3 140 cases of speculation had been prosecuted in Poland and 2 805 people had been sentenced (of which 11.2% had been sent to jail), in 1977 there were 4351 cases (3 090 sentences including 18.6% of unsuspended prison sentences). In 1979, 4 727 speculation cases had been reported, in 1980 – 5 229; respectively 4 102 and 4 700 people had been put before a judge. A smaller percentage ended in prison (7.5% in 1979 and 5.6% in 1989).[302] Was this a sign of the weakness of the authorities – or the power of society? The summer of 1980 brought answers to this question.

297 *Społeczeństwo polskie w drugiej połowie lat siedemdziesiątych…*, pp. 193–194.

298 W. Krasucka, *Spekulacja…*, p. 161. See: AAN, KC PZPR, XI/790, Note on the functioning of retail trade in Warsaw, October 11, 1977, fol. 96.

299 J. Maziarski, *Przestępczość gospodarcza*, "Polityka", 43, October 28, 1978.

300 *Ibid.*

301 *Milicyjna akcja "Rynek"*, ŻW, no. 302 /December 24–26, 1979.

302 AAN, URM, 32/2, fol. 13.

3.5 Commission II: 1981–1987

3.5.1 The Road to "Speculation Hell"

Following the fiasco of the so-called price reform of June 1976, the authorities tried to fight the growing crisis by limiting (not very successfully) wage increases and by raising prices, often by introducing "commercial prices", as they were known. Both the shortages and the methods of dealing with them aggravated the public mood. "There is a negative perception of commercial stores and the Pewex chain", the Ministry of Internal Affairs (MSW) noted in the early August of 1978, which "gives rise to a well-founded suspicion that society has been divided into 'sectors' or 'castes' of 'haves' and 'have-nots', and that the stores service private entrepreneurs, thieves, and black marketeers. This situation is perceived as a contradiction of socialist principles…"[303] It is not surprising that the poor were the first to rebel. The decision of the Government Price Commission (PKC) on June 24, 1980 to raise the prices of meat products with effect from July 1 was the last straw. Poles could have probably got over "commercializing", that is to say raising, the prices of the already expensive, and thus out of reach, meat cuts such as beef tenderloin, goose, and duck. But the sudden increases in price of run-of-the-mill basic subsistence foods in workplace cafeterias were a different story altogether. The price hike was introduced in the same arrogant way as the previous one: abruptly, without consultation, often without informing the workplace management or the local Party cells. For example in Wrocław, the "Party secretaries were generally shocked by the new prices they saw in the cafeterias and buffets. In most places, the managers only learnt about the new prices from their cafeteria workers."[304] Strikes erupted at several factories, the largest – in Lublin, in mid-July.[305] The authorities assumed that the strikes could be extinguished with money. It turned out, however, that this method was only tinkering with the flames. The real blaze exploded on the Baltic coast on August 14, 1980.

The lists of demands put forward in August 1980 included economic items (often prioritized before political): wage increases, full market provision, and doing away with the [high] "commercial" prices, internal export, and meat

303 AAN, KC PZPR, XIA/815, fol. 11.

304 AAN, KC PZPR, WO, 3337, fol. 8.

305 See: *Zapowiedź sierpniowego przełomu. Meldunki MSW o sytuacji w kraju w okresie 1 lipca – 16 sierpnia 1980,* ed. K. Dubiński, "Zeszyty Historyczne" (Paris) 2000, no. 133, pp. 69–164.

rationing.[306] The historic *21 Demands* that the Strike Committee presented to the government delegation at the Gdańsk Shipyard on August 17, 1980 were no exception. The easiest for the authorities to accept were the wage demands; as far as the demands concerning provisions were concerned (no. 10, no. 11, and no. 13), all they could do was show good will and make promises. Little could the strikers and the authorities know that the then-existing level of market supplies, perceived as critically inadequate at the time, would soon – with hindsight – be remembered fondly.

The rationing, already promised in the August agreements, was a lesser evil and had been accepted by most of the population.[307] After long and stormy consultations, on April 1, 1981 the authorities introduced meat ration stamps, and in the following months also ration stamps for grain, rice, fats, soap, washing detergent, chocolate, alcohol, and cigarettes. These ration stamps are not to be confused with the federal aid system that has functioned in the USA as a form of food-purchasing assistance for no-income and low-income people, where a stamp entitles the bearer to swap it for food without payment. The Polish ration stamps were no free-meal ticket. All that the Polish food stamps and other stamps in Poland entitled the bearer to – and that only after having spent many hours in the interminably long lines that came to be synonymous with the era – was being eligible to *buy* the item for which the stamp had been issued. Without a ration stamp, no purchase was possible at all. Moreover, the allocations of food and daily utility items were far from quantities that we now think adequate for average needs and the allocation was based on the government's assessment of an individual's needs. For example, an office worker was entitled to buy 2.5 kg of meat a month, a manual worker – 4.5 kg whereas a miner – a more acceptable eight kg.

Food ration stamps further upset the market and created an even bigger mess. Paradoxically, what the rationing, which applied to half of the total value of food sales (more, if one includes alcohol) did was to limit radically buying opportunities. Poles had money (the August wage increases had provided them with additional cash) and they were anxious to spend it on any kind of durable. In mid-1981, the stampede for industrial products began – they immediately disappeared from the market. In 1979, market shortages amounted to 22 billion zloty; in 1980 they reached 81 billion zloty. In 1981, they were estimated at 278

306 *Postulaty 1970–71 i 1980. Materiały źródłowe do dziejów wystąpień pracowniczych w latach 1970–1971 i 1980 (Gdańsk i Szczecin)*, ed. B. Chmiel, E. Kaczyńska, Warszawa 1998.

307 See articles in: *Umowa o kartki*, ed. J. Kurczewski, Warszawa 2004; K. Cegieła, *Kartki na szczęście. Reglamentacja dóbr w Polsce Ludowej*, "Mówią Wieki" 2002/4, pp. 23–29.

billion zloty, while the disposable financial resources at the time were estimated (including pre-payments etc.) at 496 billion (129 billion zloty in 1979 and 173 billion zloty in 1980).[308]

The huge, unquenchable demand for food, alcohol, cigarettes and industrial articles triggered new, unofficial ways of accessing goods and improved the existing methods. This had also happened during provision crises in the past but this time the huge scale of the phenomenon was in a league of its own. "Every shortage of output," an official report noted in August 1981, "is immediately taken advantage of by speculators, [...] who intercept the goods in question and put them on the market using channels that enable them, whether semi-legally or entirely illegally, to gain high profits at the expense of consumers. As a result, the black marketeers hold the whole of society in a dictatorial economic grip."[309] The economic exchange between cities and rural areas became, to a large degree, privatized (see chapter 5). Barter exchange developed between retail stores and factories. Goods travelled between producers and wholesale or retail (they were stolen or re-distributed through other channels at higher prices, while all that the retail stores received was the payment due at the official prices, and invoices). Barter also took place between individuals. For example, even tee-totalers made sure that they had bought their allocation of vodka in the knowledge that it would be useful to swap for some other item in short supply. Some goods delivered to the stores stayed at the back of the store and were distributed through the back door, in more senses than one. From there they often ended up in street booths or marketplaces. The leaky rationing system created numerous opportunities – the coupons could be altogether ignored by the store personnel, or illegally obtained, which allowed those who knew the store personnel, to shop at state prices. Indeed, "contacts" in shops was the byword of the era. This led to new modes of social behavior. The shop assistant in the local butcher's, baker's or grocer's was a person to cultivate and shower with small gifts, if one wanted to ensure that the family was not to run short of food.

The strategies described above developed both on a large scale resulting in effective black market enterprises as well as on an individual scale, helping the most underprivileged groups such as pensioners, and people with disabilities to survive on day-to-day basis. A "professional" black marketeer complained to a reporter: "Thousands of riffraff are hanging around, thousands of rookies who

---

308 AAN, Instytut Rynku Wewnętrznego i Usług (IRWiU), 317, Warszawa, fol. 47–48, 52–54.

309 AAN, URM, 32/112, fol. 3.

are trying to work an angle; grandmas, pensioners, salesgirls, drivers, assorted petty floaters and bunglers, they have all made a mess of a decent business."[310]

From the end of 1980, the terms "speculation" and "black market" (especially in relation to food) permanently entered both the media and colloquial Polish. The police (MO), and the operations of the PIH and those undertaken by the Teams for Market Control (Zespoły ds Kontroli Rynku) set up in September 1980 were not very effective. A journalist commented that "fighting speculation is reminiscent of fighting the proverbial dragon: when you cut off the head, another one immediately grows in its place."[311]

Let's not forget that it was the higher, "commercial" prices – set a year earlier and only on a small part of goods, at that, and which were far from stable – that had triggered the public protests. Now, even though the prices asked, and obtained, on the black market were much higher, it became an important and sometimes only way of filling the gaps in supply. However, only groups in economically and politically privileged positions could satisfy their needs by taking advantage of the black market. The weak and the poor were left behind. The social stratification was becoming increasingly delineated by the individual's ability to access goods. As had happened the year before, by mid-1981, the threat of social revolt became real. Only, this time, the protesters enjoyed the support of the 10-million strong Independent Self-governing Trade Union Solidarity. The authorities were forced into taking a stand.

3.5.2 Provisorium: The Extraordinary Commission: August 10 – October 12, 1981

The government's reaction was surprisingly slow in coming, considering that already by February 1981, Wojciech Jaruzelski had described the combating of speculation as "one of the main tasks for the state and economic administration apparatus",[312] when presenting a program for economic and social stabilization before the Sejm. In Częstochowa, an anti-speculation commission was set up in February 1981, and by mid-March – in Gdańsk. In early June, the District Coordination Team for Combating Fraud (Wojewódzki Zespół Koordynacyjny ds Zwalczania Spekulacji) was established in Łódź. It included a "rapid response

310 S. Drozdowski, *Tajne kanały czarnego rynku*, "Słowo Powszechne" September 8, 1981.

311 A. Kołodziejski, *Cielęcina... za dolary. Czy nie można opanować czarnego rynku żywnościowego?*, TL/ 298, December 15, 1980.

312 AAN, URM, 32/2, fol. 4.

team to deal with all irregularities in trade".[313] The authorities had considered an anti-speculation law already in April when they introduced the rationing, however, the Rubicon was not yet being crossed. We can only assume that although the authorities hoped that the existing institutions and legislation[314] would prove effective, they were also aware that society's willingness to accept radical steps would increase in proportion to the length of the lines in front of the almost empty stores. If so, they were right. In spring 1981, a significant media campaign started – and not necessarily instigated by the authorities –urging them to undertake an anti-speculation drive. "The newspapers," Anna Matałowska wrote in *Polityka*, "following in the footsteps of the government, are pushing for an onslaught against speculation. The factory workers and other state employees are echoing the demands, putting the policy forward as the number one priority for trade in the near future."[315] At the same time, there was no shortage of others, who pointed out the senselessness and futility of the institutionalization of anti-speculation activities.[316] In front of the TV cameras on August 3 1981, Deputy Prime Minister Mieczysław Rakowski did not hide his concern. He pointed out the lessons of Poland under the Nazi occupation: even the prospect of death or the concentration camp had not held back the illegal trade.

In the spring and summer of 1981, very few heeded such voices. Radical and decisive actions were gaining popular support.[317] In June 1981, the market collapsed. Even those who had until recently praised the introduction of rationing because it put had ham back on their tables, now started complaining. The rationing spread to include more and more products. People waited in long lines even to buy bread. It was not unusual to see on the shelves of a general grocery store nothing but an artful stretch of bottles of vinegar – the store manager making a vain attempt to detract from the absence of any other products in stock. But finally, sometimes even the vinegar vanished from the shelves. "Generally speaking, the market has collapsed," noted Mieczysław Rakowski on July 27, 1981. "There are nightmarish lines, people buying out anything that shows up. Workers

313 AAN, URM, 32/9, k. 27–28; *Ibid.*, 21/113, fol. 57, 64–65. About Łódź, see: W. Pawłowski, *Współczesne Janosiki*, "Polityka", no. 35, August 29, 1981. Such a commission appeared in the Warsaw voivodship only at the turn of July and August 1981: ŻW, no. 182, August 7, 1981.

314 *Projekt ustawy o zwalczaniu spekulacji przekazany do Sejmu. Wypowiedź profesora Zygmunta Rybickiego dla PAP*, ŻW, no. 188, August 14, 1981.

315 A. Matałowska, *Bazar pod obstrzałem*, "Polityka", no. 19, May 9, 1981.

316 S. Podemski, *Spekulacja i prawo*, "Polityka", no. 33, August 15, 1981.

317 See: ŻW, July 30, and August 5, 1981.

from big plants are protesting against the lower rations. The government is being accused of deliberately starving the nation, of its biological annihilation and similar nonsense."[318]

Indeed, already in June 1981, the Independent Trade Union Solidarity began to blame the authorities for their helplessness in the face of the crisis and repeatedly organized protests against insufficient supplies.[319] A serious conflict erupted when on July 23, the government announced it would simultaneously decrease meat rations and raise prices. In its meeting the following day, Solidarity's National Cooordinating Commission (Krajowa Komisja Porozumiewawcza) hammered the economic policy of the government. "The daily life of Polish families," the Commission communiqué read, "is a torment." The union's main goal was to guarantee "basic living conditions for the nation". This time, Solidarity did more than merely call on the authorities to carry out reforms – it promised to take the initiative into its own hands. A call went out to local government and Solidarity branches to organize effective distribution of goods. There was a plan to organize commissions throughout all the regions "to control the continuing production, supply, and distribution of food and day-to-day industrial articles."[320] On July 30, "hunger marches" filled the streets of Łódź and other Polish cities. At the talks between the government and the Solidarity on August 3 and 6, with food supplies prominent on the agenda, both sides entrenched their positions further.

The authorities had no intention of allowing Solidarity to take the initiative. During the parliamentary session on July 30 and 31, due to a reshuffle of the government, General Jaruzelski's confidant Czesław Kiszczak became Minister of Interior Affairs. From August 3 onward, 1 700 policemen were directed daily to fight speculation. They were reinforced by soldiers, professional inspectors, and community, or the so-called "public" inspectors.[321] On August 10, 1981, the Council of Ministers passed resolution No. 156, which created, at central, voivodship, and local levels, the Extraordinary Commissions for Combating Fraud (Nadzwyczajne Komisje do Walki ze Spekulacją). Simultaneously a legislative draft was submitted to parliament, proposing to "provide increased consumer protection within commercial activities concerning articles of daily necessity and

318 M.F. Rakowski, *Dzienniki polityczne 1981–1983*, Warszawa 2004, p. 9.

319 See:W. Kuczyński, *U progu wytrzymałości*, "Tygodnik Solidarność", no. 17, July 24, 1981.

320 "Tygodnik Solidarność", no. 18, July 31, 1981.

321 AAN, KC PZPR, Administration Department (Wydział Administracyjny, WA), LI/116, fol 64.

the introduction of more effective means of combating the speculation."[322] Both decisions were justified on the grounds that lower-income citizens had been cut off "from basic goods outside the rationing system", whereas "all kinds of crooks and embezzlers" continued to make huge profits. It was pointed out that both phenomena "offended the public sense of justice".[323] It is not surprising that a large part of the Second Session of the Party's Central Committee (KC PZPR) on August 11 was dedicated to discussing ways of combating the speculation.

The authorities had to show determination. Immediately they began to build the structures of the Extraordinary Commission (Nadzwyczajna Komisja): the headquarters (Krajowa NK with Deputy Prime Minister Stanisław Mach at the helm) and the voivodship commissions with Deputy Voivods at the top. The commissions tried to give the impression of creating a wide "anti-speculation front" by involving both the institutions specifically designated to deal with the black market and public organizations. From the very beginning the new construct took on a quasi-military shape and employed, in the headquarters and voivodship sections, fifty four carefully selected retired police officers. The Commissions' reports were to land directly on General Jaruzelski's desk.[324]

Undoubtedly, many of the decision makers, including the Prime Minister, believed in the effectiveness and the validity of such undertakings. PR considerations (as we would put it today) also played a role. Actions aimed at sustaining so-called social justice could boost confidence in the government, its popularity massively undermined in favor of Solidarity, which also proclaimed concern about the standard of living. "Public support and acceptance for anti-speculation undertakings is noticeable [...]" wrote *Trybuna Ludu*, "People clearly demand that the war on speculation must be won."[325] For the large groups marginalized by the Solidarity revolution such as members of the old unions, youth activists, members of ORMO (the Police Volunteer Reserve), veterans, military, police retirees, and so on, the Commission provided an opportunity to return to public

322 AAN, URM, 32/119, fol. 1.

323 AAN, URM, 32/112, fol. 3.

324 He continued to receive them until the end of commission's existence and it seems he read them carefully. On the margin of the report from July 1982, which covered mostly the topic of wastefulness, he wrote: "This is very interesting material. Due to its explosive character, it should be added to propaganda materials as soon as August". A special note was addressed to the government spokesman, Jerzy Urban: "For proper use"; AAN, URM, 1.4 /21, fol. 80.

325 *Nie ustają działania kontrolne i represyjne. Mniej spekulantów na bazarach*, TL, no. 187, August 12, 1981.

life. During the first all-Poland conference of the representatives of voivodship and local commissions on September 15, 1981, the delegates demanded not only more repressions against the black marketeers but also an immediate expansion of the public inspectorate participation. "They fondly remember," wrote Teresa Kuczyńska ironically, "the era of CRZZ when we had 60 000 public inspectors. We need, as they put it, a whole army of people if we want to see any effects of the battle against speculation. It is not enough to hound the black marketeers in the marketplaces. There must also be more invigilation in the factories where the scarce goods are produced. Since all goods are today in very short supply, this means invigilation of all factories."[326]

The delegates were in a triumphalist mood, no doubt boosted by the vigorous efforts of the Extraordinary Commission which, only a few weeks into its existence, even before its structures had settled down, took ostentatious action – supervised personally by General Stanislaw Zaczkowski, the Chief of Police. Between August 10 and 23, almost 24 000 policemen, over 6 000 soldiers (including some from the Internal Military Security!), nearly 5 000 professional inspectors, and 7 500 "public" activists conducted inspections of warehouses, stores, marketplaces, transportation, and purchasing stations (*punkty skupu*).[327] The courts were told to increase sentences and submit transcripts to headquarters. The Commission planned a session – to be attended by the chairmen of the regional courts – on the implementation of accelerated procedures and harsher penalties for economic crimes.[328] Over seven hundred preliminary prosecutions were triggered during the first two weeks of the Commission's life. Magistrate courts (*kolegia*) received 4 030 cases. Hidden goods valued at 27.5 million zloty were uncovered in stores.[329] Later, this level of activity diminished somewhat but the success rate was nevertheless high: by October, almost eight thousand case proceedings had been initiated in magistrates' courts, and goods valued at 41 million zloty had been found hidden in the stores.[330]

It was not by chance that state propaganda focused on the stores as the culprits for shortages: was that not, after all, where the goods were hidden? Were the stores not the main source of supply for the black market? It was an easy explanation, and easily swallowed by much of society; it stood to reason – otherwise, why were the shelves empty and the lines in front of the stores so long?

---

326 T. Kuczyńska, *Walka ze spekulacja*, "Tygodnik Solidarność", no. 27, October 2, 1981.
327 AAN, URM, 32/119, fol. 2–3.
328 AAN, KC PZPR, WA, LI/116, fol. 288.
329 AAN, URM, 32/119, fol. 2–3.
330 *Ibid.*, fol. 7–9.

The systemic problems were all blamed on this last, and most visible, link of the distribution chain. "The sales staff caught red-handed offer all kinds of different excuses: they had saved the goods for themselves, they had forgotten, it had been an accident. They lie through their teeth [...]. Priority sales for families, friends, as a token of gratitude, and for many other reasons, have become common practice."[331] The goods found at the back of the store and ostentatiously put back on the store counter significantly improved the image of the authorities, at the time represented by the policeman, the PIH employee, and the "public inspector".

It has to be said that entirely blameless store employees were far and few between but the goods found at the back of stores constituted only a small percentage of the whole trade. More important was the need to create a clearly defined enemy. The saleswoman, the store manager, the stock manager were more suitable for that role than an enigmatic black marketeer that citizens were unable to put a name or a face to. A new anti-speculation law that penalized hiding or "intercepting" goods pointed at potential profiteers. Store managers, until then not known for voicing their opinions, in the new political and economic situation loudly declared that the goal of the new law was to divide society and focus attention on the tail-end of the distribution process instead of finding the real source of the problem. The Federation of Consumers was against the new law, the store staff's unions threatened to strike. Solidarity agreed that the concealment of goods was a crime; however, it was against accelerated court proceedings.[332] Store employees were fighting a losing battle. Even the reassuring words of the Minister of Interior Trade Zygmunt Łakomiec that the "practice of goods concealment by sales people in the nationalized sector was a marginal phenomenon" did not fall on sympathetic ears.[333] The frustrated customers had to be right. But when police arrived at the scene in response to a phone call from a customer, the store manager was often able to convince the functionaries they had more urgent business elsewhere.[334]

There were also critical voices directed at the anti-speculation operations and the new law. The ostentatious pursuit of black marketeers, always presented on TV in the same way – functionaries meet, discussion of action plan, marching orders issued, trucks with police and civilian inspectors leave, followed by the crackdown on some marketplace and a parade of the arrested profiteers, complete

---

331 S. Kopka, *Uwaga – czarny rynek*, "Zagadnienia Wykroczeń" 1981, no. 6, pp. 52–53.

332 M. Mazurek, *Społeczeństwo kolejki. O doświadczeniach niedoboru 1945–1989*, Warszawa 2010, pp. 99, 100; K. Świątecka, *Pozoracje*, "Tygodnik Kulturalny" 1981/50.

333 W. Łuka, *Nalot*, PiŻ, 1981/33.

334 M. Mazurek, *Społeczeństwo kolejki...*, pp. 100–101.

with a pile of the goods found beside them – was perceived as a flashy substitute for the nose-to-the-grindstone, effective daily toil on the part of the authorities. "One would have thought," wrote *Życie Literackie*, "that once the authorities have chosen to chase those loudly and clearly labeled 'PROFITEERS' and Public Enemy Number One and decided to wipe them out at all cost, then any day now we should be noticing a dramatic improvement in supply, and that there would be no-one on the street offering a can of coffee for [the exorbitant price of] three hundred zloty. This is nonsense! The black marketeers will survive – because the repressions directed against them are carried out for their propaganda effect; the penalties are, so far, negligible".[335] At times, earnest pronouncements were also made about the positive features of the black market – such as that it was delivering articles at balanced prices that were not available elsewhere and, in doing so, was plugging the inflation gap more effectively than the state – such pronouncements were, however, quite sporadic. People commonly noticed that the anti-speculation operations led only to the development of more sophisticated strategies. The black market transactions had now gone underground and moved to private apartments or workplaces. The once common crowds of dealers disappeared from the marketplaces; instead there were individuals to be seen hanging around and taking orders for home deliveries (at new, higher prices!).[336]

The new anti-speculation law, drafted hastily by the government, proved highly controversial. It had been prepared without consulting society, the unions, or lawyers. The law called for increasing the repressive measures; it also identified and penalized new kinds of crimes such as trading rationing stamps – which criminalized a wide range of underprivileged social groups – and delivering to stores money and invoices only, unaccompanied by goods. For black marketeers caught red-handed, the law introduced accelerated legal proceedings with immediate confiscation of the object of crime and any money found on the culprit. Little wonder that the braver souls among the journalists specializing in legal issues savaged the new law. The validity of fighting the effects rather than the causes was questioned. There were fears that the accelerated proceedings would violate human rights by increasing the likelihood of legal errors. "It does not seem necessary," wrote Jacek Ambroziak and Krzysztof Kauba in *Tygodnik Solidarność*, "to create new crimes when the existing criminal code already covers fully all eventualities. All that is lacking is that the bodies appointed to fight the

335 S.M. Jankowski, *Wielkie polowanie?*, "Życie Literackie", no. 36 , September 6, 1981.
336 AAN, URM, 32/112, fol. 28.

speculation, in particular the police and the National Trade Inspectorate PIH, act quick and effectively."[337]

The anti-speculation endeavors of the authorities were viewed critically not only in the media debates but also in discussions in the Sejm. Tadeusz Skóra, the Deputy Minister of Justice, who was engaged in the activities of the Extraordinary Commission, pointed out that even in the usually compliant parliament, "the law faced enormous obstacles".[338] Even if not enormous, the obstacles were certainly symptomatic. Not surprisingly, the MPs questioned the very name of the "Extraordinary Commission", which evoked associations with Felix Dzerzhinsky, a Polish revolutionary, who during 1917–1926 was in charge of the un-coincidentally similarly named, an All-Russia Extraordinary Commission for Combating Counter-revolution and Sabotage, or the Cheka, an organization which became notorious for its ruthlessness and mass terror.

Ultimately, the name "Central Commission for Combating Fraud" (Centralna Komisja do Walki ze Spekulacja) was accepted. The Commission's mandate was to organize and co-ordinate operations aimed at combating speculation in the country (voivodship and local commissions were responsible for specific administrative units or towns). The full-time employment offered to inspectors with police experience gave rise to many doubts. The government representatives rejected the suggestion of entrusting the inspection tasks to the PIH.[339] During the second reading, five MPs questioned the need for new legislation, arguing that achieving market balance could eliminate the black market altogether. However the majority of the Commission members not only accepted the validity of the bill but also agreed to move away from mitigating the criminal code and instead move towards tightening sanctions for speculation crimes and introducing the simplified proceedings.[340] Felicjanna Lesińska, a parliamentary commentator and MP summed it up: "We hope that anti-speculation action will make essentials more easily available for every Polish family, every citizen, and also that people who are physically weak, the elderly and those who don't have time to stand in line will be able to buy them. It is of paramount importance that Polish women, exhausted by everyday labor experience improvements in supply."[341]

337 J. Ambroziak, K. Kauba, *Ustawa o zwalczaniu spekulacji*, "Tygodnik Solidarność", no. 22, August 28, 1981; see: S. Podemski, *Spekulacja i prawo*, "Polityka", no. 33, August 15, 1981.

338 AAN, KC PZPR, WA, LI/116, fol. 288.

339 *Prace nad projektem ustawy antyspekulacyjnej*, TL, no. 207, September 4, 1981.

340 *Przeciwko spekulacji – środki nadzwyczajne*, TL, no. 213, September 11, 1981.

341 *Sprawozdanie stenograficzne z 16 posiedzenia Sejmu PRL 8 kadencji w dniu 16 września 1981*, col. 133.

On September 25, 1981, Halina Minkisiewicz-Latecka made a last-ditch stand, when the bill was already before the Sejm, to stop the implementation of accelerated proceedings. "As a lawyer," she declared, "I cannot agree with the expediency of introducing the anti-speculation law or with many of its provisions. Speculation is an evil and stifles the feeble organism of our economic and social life. However, repressive measures should be last on the list of means to diminish this damaging phenomenon. Only deep economic reform, with due regard for the laws of supply and demand, correctly set prices and improved supply can eliminate or marginalize the phenomenon of speculation [...]. The bill as presented [...] proposes increased repression, the abolition of supervision of prosecution, limited defense rights, and, most importantly, it proposes the country-wide introduction of accelerated proceedings. There is to be no inquiry, and no investigation. During the proceedings, the accused would not be officially charged and the immediate hearing of the case would deprive the accused of the possibility of preparing a defense and choosing defense counsel.

The accelerated procedure is not conducive to uncovering the truth and undermines the constitutional right to a defense. It also contravenes the international human rights convention ratified by Poland in 1977."[342]

The motion to abandon the provisions for an accelerated procedure was defeated. Moments later, voting took place on the whole bill and it was of course passed, although, it must be noted, with a significant number of votes against (11) and abstentions (12). Even in the revolutionary conditions of 1981, the fact that there were not only any votes against the motion, but indeed as many as eleven, was unprecedented.[343]

The law on combating speculation[344] was expected to remain in force until the end of 1982. It detailed and penalized all manifestations of the black market. New crimes such as selling rationed articles, ration-coupon fraud, the hiding or interception of goods in transit between a manufacturer or warehouse and a retail outlet joined the existing list of specific, punishable offences (Items 221–225 of the criminal code and items 132, 133, 135 of the code of misdemeanors). Felonies were punishable with up to five-year imprisonment and/or a fine (even in excess of 100 thousand zloty). The black marketeer could expect confiscation of the object of the crime and of money (if the authorities had a reasonable basis for linking it with black market operations). The police and the National

342 *Ibid.*, col. 134–135.

343 *Ibid.*, col.137–138.

344 Dz. U. 1981, no. 24, item 124.

Trade Inspectorate (PIH) conducted most investigations and were authorized to "support the charges" before the Court of the First Instance. The accelerated procedure could be applied to both felonies and misdemeanors.

In comparison to the previous anti-speculation legislation, the creation of an institution that was to deal with speculation in an integrated way was a novelty. Although the new law was quite general, it was fleshed out by the decree of the Council of Ministers of October 12, 1981 "concerning particular tasks, the composition, and mode of operation of the commission for combating fraud" (Dz. U. 1981, No. 25, Item 133), which was much more detailed. There was now a chance that the war on speculation would enter a new phase.

3.5.3 The Front Line of the War on Speculation: The Central Commission

At the turn of the 1940s and 1950s, the Central Commission had enormous powers; it could prosecute, pass judgments and administer sentences. Its 1980s successor had similar powers but adopted more of a softly-softly approach. Although its main statutory tasks included the combating of speculation and prevention of its growth, identification of the black marketeers' modus operandi, and the initiation and improvement of methods of control, in practice, the powers of the new governing bodies, especially those the Central Commission, were much wider. The Commission did not have labour camps at its disposal; nevertheless, due to its special position in the state structure, it could exert considerable influence on both the executive organs (ministries, regional administration, etc.) and legislation or modify the scale of the repressive measures taken.

Unlike its predecessors, the Central Commission for Combating Fraud (Centralna Komisja do Walki ze Spekulacją, CKWS), was not subordinate to the national councils or the State Council but answered directly to the government, its headquarters located conveniently in the building of the Office of the Council of Ministers (URM). It was the Prime Minister who nominated the Central Commission's members. From February 1981 to November 1985, the Polish Prime Minister was General Wojciech Jaruzelski, and the fact that he was a military man had implications for the composition of the Commission, its way of functioning and even the terms used in the official correspondence. Statutorily, one of the deputy Prime Ministers was at the helm of the Commission[345] but the real power throughout its existence was in the hands of its deputy chairman, Colonel

345 Stanisław Mach, Jerzy Ozdowski, Zenon Komender (the longest term, from August 1982 to November 1985), and Józef Kozioł. The greatest personnel changes in CKWS

Władysław Trzaska. As a deputy director of the Office for Combating Economic Crimes at Militia Headquarters (Biuro do Walki z Przestępstwami Gospodarczymi KG MO), he knew this business well. Other deputy chairmen: General Józef Beim (Chief of the State Police, Komendant Główny MO), General Marian Ryba (Main Inspector of Control at URM), and, from November 1985, Tadeusz Skóra, first deputy minister of justice contributed significantly to the Commission's work. According to the ordinance of October 12, 1981 the deputy secretaries of state in the Ministry of Administration, Ministry of Environment, Ministry of Finance, Ministry of Internal Trade and Services, Ministry of Agriculture and Food, Ministry of Justice, Ministry of Internal Affairs, and the Chief Inspector of the PIH, all became members of the CKWS. The chairman could also invite representatives of other bodies to participate in the Commission's work (especially in its meetings) – these included the Supreme Audit Office (NIK), the State Council Chancellery (Kancelaria Rady Państwa), the Office of the Prosecutor General, national economic associations (Samopomoc Chłopska and Społem), trade unions (since 1982, the only one remaining was the All-Poland Alliance of Trade Unions, Ogólnopolskie Porozumienie Związków Zawodowych, OPZZ) and social organizations.[346] With the changing political reality, the invitation to participate in the Commission's work was gradually extended to representatives of the Patriotic Movement of National Revival (Patriotyczny Ruch Odrodzenia Narodowego, PRON), the Executive Board of the League of Polish Women, and the Consumers' Federation.

The representatives of these organizations gained de facto status as CKWS permanent members and participated regularly in the meetings organized at the Office of Council of Ministers. Beside an annual "national anti-speculation conference", with the participation of all voivodship and regional commissions, smaller meetings were often organized (five in 1981, 25 in 1982, 23 in 1983, and 16 in 1984). The meetings were a platform not only for fiery discussions and

---

took place after Zbigniew Messner's government was constituted in the fall of 1985; AAN, URM, 32/85, fol. 2–3.

346 Forty-nine voivodship commissions had a similar structure: a deputy voivod as chairman, and two deputy chairmen (one continuously in office). Representatives of the Voivodship Police Command Center, (KW MO), the National Trade Inspectorate (PIH), the National Price Commission (PKC) and "employees of relevant departments in the voivod's office" were also members of the Commission. Voivodship Commissions employed 730 officials and activists while 1 715 local commissions (at the lowest level of state administration) employed 1 773 persons. (October 1985); AAN, URM, 1.5/43, fol. 289.

the swapping of experiences but also for gathering information and issuing instructions to the individual ministries and institutions and for exercising control over their execution. During every meeting the Commission officially accepted the reports from a number of voivodships. The headquarters often voiced legitimate objections about the effectiveness of their local counterparts.

Following the protests in August and September 1981, the first months of the Commission's activity were a period of building structures and perfecting rules. The scrutiny of the media and the presence of Solidarity members at regional meetings prevented the Commission from spreading its wings. Headquarters urged the executive organs to concentrate on "organized speculation" with a special focus on particular articles (cigarettes, alcohol, coffee, sweets) by following their route from manufacturer and warehouse to consumer. Social, youth, and coop organizations were encouraged to participate actively in the operations.[347]

Martial Law invigorated the commissions. The Solidarity Trade Union ceased to be a threat. The rigorous legal measures implemented on December 13, 1981 (such as the introduction of summary legal proceedings) simplified all procedures and the "social activists", marginalized earlier, could again exercise their strong influence. The anti-speculation operations fit perfectly with propaganda slogans promising "stabilization" and emphasizing the need to "bring back order". The deputy ministers who were also members of the Central Commission (CKWS) now had a brief to organize active anti-speculation teams throughout their departments and to raise the topic of combating speculation in all their dealings with the "region". The emphasis was on invigorating departmental inspections, which had hitherto been ineffective. The goal was to alleviate the burden on the police, who "during the days and weeks busied themselves with activities connected with the implementation of Martial Law."[348]

It soon became clear that neither the summary procedures nor the curfew, the limiting of freedom of movement, road blocks, suspended phone communication or the "militarization of supply"[349] were able to curb the black market. After several turbulent days, the second economy players resumed their previous ways of operating in often new, clandestine ways. The black marketeers continued

347 *Ibid.*

348 AAN, URM, 32/6, fol. 3.

349 The initial suspension of sales included articles officially designated as "strategic", such as blankets, sleeping bags, mattresses, bedding, batteries, precious metals and articles made thereof, paper and luxury articles (furs, leather, clothes, rugs). The supply of clothes was under rigorous supervision. Sales of gold, furs, high end rugs and printing paper were suspended for the longest period.

to hone their strategies. The vicious circle began to turn even faster. The ever more sophisticated black market strategies forced the authorities to engage ever greater forces "on the frontline of the war on speculation" and to prosecute and punish ostentatiously people who had "made millions on speculation".[350] A steep price hike in February 1982 weakened the demand for goods only for a short time, particularly as halfway through the year, individual income rose significantly. Higher prices did not automatically translate into well-supplied stores. The incidence of shortages began to grow rapidly, reaching a level of 739 billion zloty. In the previous year, 278 billion zloty had seemed an inconceivably large amount, but the drastic price hike of February 1982 changed radically the price relations.[351]

The authorities soon realized how misguided the intention to continue the application of the anti-speculation law (and the activities of the Commission) only until the end of 1982. They instantly set about mending the error of their ways. On April 20, 1982, the topic of extending the period of application of the law was on the agenda of the Second National Anti-Speculation Conference (II Krajowa Narada Antyspekulacyjna). Tadeusz Skóra, the Deputy Minister of Justice (and at the same time a member of the CKWS) instructed his legal department in his sector to initiate the appropriate steps.[352] The voivodship commissions were required to send in comments and proposals.

In line with the zeitgeist, most of the resolutions presented by the voivodship commissions proposed the implementation of increased repressive measures and fines, and the introduction of a lower threshold for "qualifying speculation", and opted for an unlimited period for the application of the law. Selling meat from private slaughter (*ubój gospodarczy*) and exchanging goods between nationalized enterprises were also subject to provisions of the anti-speculation law. It also became clear that the demands of headquarters surpassed the capabilities of the regional commissions, which were often lost in the jungle of regulations (Katowice suggested compiling a glossary of the phrases used in the decree).[353] We cannot be certain whether the radical proposals coming from regional Poland genuinely reflected the prevalent point of view or were merely paying lip service in order to satisfy officials in Warsaw, whereas actions on the ground in the provinces suggested the existence of a more liberal approach (see next chapter). Only Białystok – a peripheral, rural region, with a high percentage of

350 AAN, URM, 32/113, fol. 24.
351 AAN, IRWiU, 317, fol. 54, pp. 56–57.
352 AAN, URM, 32/23, fol. 18.
353 Ibid., fol. 54.

Russian Orthodox population – was courageous enough to express any doubts. "We must consider the question of whether the voivodship and regional commissions for combating speculation created by this decree should continue with their operations. In the current setup, there are too many public inspection organs operating at the regional level and their activities overlap (commissions of public inspection, Federation of Consumers, housing development committees, anti-speculation commissions in workplaces). This extensive system of public inspection makes the voivodship and regional commissions redundant. We propose that the tasks of the voivodship commissions be handed over to the police and the National Trade Inspectorate (PIH), which both have the greatest responsibility for the war on speculation. Only specialized organs with wide legal powers should be focusing on this matter.'[354]

Very few members of the official media had the courage to express similar opinions (one that did was Stanisław Podemski in *Polityka*).[355] Most of the national and regional newspapers published triumphalist stories about winning the war on speculation. The evaluation and assessment of the work of the commissions was based, among others, on the number of references to their activities in the press (there was even a separate section on press coverage in the commission reports). This was only one of the elements of the propaganda campaign aimed at highlighting public support for the anti-speculation activities of the authorities. Another was the meetings with "representatives of teams of workers", during which the "workers demanded harsher penalties for black marketeers, parasites, and people guilty of wasting public property. According to the workers, the courts treated the accused too leniently and the mass media did not reveal their full names. Workers who had participated directly in the militia raids on marketplaces expressed similar opinions."[356]

The law on combating speculation was amended on October 9, 1982.[357] The amendment took care of minor defects in the 1981 law. It took account of the changes in the rationing system implemented in 1982, and set the level of "qualifying speculation" at 200 thousand zloty, as well as defined in more detail what constituted the "interception" of goods on their way to retail stores, which was the most damaging offence of all. But the most important was item 10

---

354 AAN, URM, 32/23, fol. 25–26.

355 S. Podemski, *Spekulacje wokół spekulacji*, "Polityka", no. 38/August 28, 1982.

356 AAN, URM, 32/119, fol. 156.

357 Act of 9 October 1982 amending the combating of speculation, Dz.U. 1982, no. 33, item 218; Z. Niewola, *Z aktualnej problematyki walki ze spekulacją*, "Ideologia i Polityka" 1982, no. 11.

of the amendment. It effectively removed the proviso that the law would apply "until December 31, 1982". The Party commentator remarked that the amendment made "this legal act into an instrument that now permitted an effective, long-term fight against speculation abuses."[358] Indeed, the decree was ultimately not repealed until July 5, 1990.

No piece of legislation, and especially one that aims to increase repression, can bring back a balanced market. Although store shelves slowly filled with kasha and sugar throughout the 1980s, meat, chocolate, and gas continued nevertheless to be rationed. The 1982 decree on sobriety education made it significantly more difficult to buy alcohol. Income growth outpacing growth in supply during most of the 1980s overheated the market with "hot" money, especially where consumer durables were concerned. As a result finding a refrigerator or TV set to buy bordered on the miraculous. Contrary to the declarations of the official propaganda, which applauded the normalized political and economic situation, the number of "speculation crimes" grew consistently. There were 14 934 such crimes (17.4% of all economic crimes) in 1982, and 24 171 (18.5%) in 1985.[359] The differences were not only quantitative but also qualitative. At the start of their existence, the anti-speculation commissions dealt mostly with the retail trading of meat, vodka, jam, or socks but soon it became clear that anything could be the object of black market trade – cars, gas, refrigerators, books, pianos, and even credit facilities for the newly married and special store coupons for veterans.[360] By the end of its term, the Commission had to face truly advanced technology – unofficial importers mostly from the Far East flooded the Polish market with electronic equipment, including computers.The most important objects of the black market trade are presented in the monograph chapters; here we would like to focus on the bureaucratic aspect of the black market operations. The primary strategy continued to be the diversion of goods from the official distribution channels. Traditionally, the most common was "speculation of goods bought in nationalized trade outlets" (Item 221 of the Criminal Code; in 1981 – 56.9% of all black market cases, in 1985 – 47.2%). During most of the 1980s, alcohol sales constituted some 60% of all black market cases under prosecution. Most of the offenders were small-scale dealers who could not count on big returns and who treated black market transactions as a way of supplementing their hunger wages

358 AAN, URM, 32/2, fol. 5.
359 Ibid.
360 AAN, URM, 32/117, fol. 80.

or pensions. This began to change in the middle of the decade when industrial articles started to play a more important role in the black market.[361]

The analysis of the rationing system conducted at the beginning of 1983 predicted that coupons, or stamps, for some products (meat, chocolate) would be abolished by 1985.[362] Reality did not meet expectation, however: coupons for sugar were abolished on November 1, 1985, but for chocolate – only in March 1988, for gas – not until January 1989, and for meat – only on August 1, 1989. This delay left enough time for often sophisticated techniques for breaking and bypassing the rules of the rationing system to be developed. The availability of the product and its price, usually much lower within the rationing system than on the free market, played a very important role. The number of detected rationing system violations (punishable according to the decree of September 25, 1981) grew continuously. In 1981, they constituted 1.3% of all speculation crimes, and in 1985 – 29.1%; the number kept growing. In 1986, when the experiment with free market sales of meat from private slaughter began, the majority of scams applied to gas rationing. At the same time, the improved supply of basic food products resulted in smaller numbers of cases that involved concealing goods from buyers in stores (from 24.8% in 1982 down to 6.9% in 1985).

The percentage of crimes involving the interception of goods on their way from manufacturer or warehouse to retail store (the store would receive only the invoice and the money) stayed at a similar level (6.7% in 1981 and 11.3% in 1985). Such undertakings were the most risky and usually required cooperation between the employees of manufacturers, warehouses, transportation companies, and retail outlets. They were risky but brought in big profits; for example, the value of the intercepted goods (furniture, rugs, and household items) in half of the cases detected in 1984 exceeded 200 thousand zloty.[363]

Since 1986 this section of the black market had also been in downturn mode, which probably was related not only to the increased repression but also to the growing hard currency sales of consumer durables in the system of internal export and the growing trade of articles brought privately (legally or not) from abroad. The wider opening of the border was also responsible for the increase, from the middle of the decade, in "speculative accumulation of goods" – by 15%

361 Ibid., fol. 121.

362 AAN, IRWiU, 318, fol. 34.

363 AAN, URM, 32/116, fol. 29. In 1984 the average wage in industry (in tangible output) was 18 300 zloty, in 1985 – 20 000 zloty, in 1986 – around 24 000, and in 1987 – around 29 000 zloty; *Rocznik statystyczny 1988*, Warszawa 1988, p. 157.

in 1986 alone. People stored not only food products but also industrial articles destined for unofficial export, such as silver, tools, sporting equipment, etc., or those coming from abroad: clothing and electronics.[364]

If anti-speculation operations were to meet the expectations raised by government propaganda, they had to have an audience. Big, spectacular operations involving thousands of people provided just that. Even if in individual places the results were paltry, when added together on a national scale they looked quite impressive. In 1984 alone, in addition to local actions there took place a number of nationwide operations – twelve code-named Rynek(Market), seven Benzyna (Gas) and one operation against book dealers (as well as Operation Sector, directed against private enterprise) took place nationwide. Special attention was paid to acknowledging the participation of *social forces*, for example in 1984; 29 thousand civilian activists and over 24 thousand members of the Police Volunteer Reserve (ORMO) took part in anti-speculation operations.[365]

In the end, the community teams had little impact, even less than the often criticized internal inspections within particular trade branches,[366] but they (especially the workers' brigades) were always the government's pets. On the one hand, from the ideological and class-oriented point of view, the workers were recognized as the healthy core of the nation. On the other, for decades the authorities had been paying special attention to supplying workers adequately with necessary goods and now considered them especially vulnerable to the operations of the black market. Already in the fall of 1981, the commissions were ordered to "identify (based on the existing situation) sites in the voivodship with the largest concentration of workers and low income population where the black market is especially strong. [...] In those places, extensive controls with the use of necessary auxiliary means have to be planned. The concentration of such

364 AAN, URM, 32/117, fol. 5.

365 AAN, URM, 32/116, fol. 27.

366 The results in May 1986 are typical. In that year, the professional inspection institutions (PIH, PKC, and the State Inspectorate for Purchase and Processing of Agricultural Articles [Państwowa Inspekcja Skupu i Przetwórstwa Artykułów Rolnych, PISiPAR]) detected almost 38% of all speculation cases, their branch sections detected 18% and "mixed teams with the participation of public activists" – 13.6%; AAN, URM, 32/180, fol. 263. Branch inspections, especially in trade, were criticized for their seeming inability to detect shortcomings identified immediately by an external inspection. AAN, the Central Custom Office, Główny Urząd Ceł (GUC), 16/153, fol. 5. This was not an isolated opinion.

operations will allow the streamlining of the existing resources, which are now at the disposal of various institutions."[367]

A militia inspection at the Różycki Bazaar in Warsaw, a traditional haunt on the black-market map of Warsaw, 28 January 1982; photo from the archives of the Polish Press Agency (PAP).

367 AAN, URM, 32/112, fol. 8–10.

The true "concentration of operations" started after the imposition of Martial Law when Solidarity members no longer posed a threat to the decisions of the commissions. "The program for stabilizing social discipline and public safety in 1982", approved by Wojciech Jaruzelski on February 21, 1982, envisaged the further development of wide social control.[368] "It is not enough to create an institution," Jerzy Ozdowski, deputy prime minister argued during the Anti-Speculation Meeting in April 1982, "no matter how effective an official or how efficient an inspector, they are not enough. We need to create a social atmosphere hostile towards black market and able to eradicate all symptoms of this social malady."[369] Characteristically, the politicians were the ones who wanted to include the activists in control operations while the representatives of social organizations held a more pragmatic view. At the same meeting Andrzej Nałęcz-Jawecki (later editor-in-chief of the consumers' weekly *Veto*) proposed setting up "tiger brigades" (after a popular French TV series), efficient and mobile units consisting of professionals (police and National Trade Inspectorate). "But maybe let's call them 'lynx' or something." he reflected, "since there are no tigers in Poland." Catching the perpetrator red-handed was the most important because it allowed the application of summary measures.[370]

The views of the Military Council on National Salvation (Wojskowa Rada Ocalenia Narodowego, WRON) prevailed. Its members argued that the fight against social pathologies, including the black market, had "to be conducted in a consistent and coordinated way and should involve the social element [ordinary citizens], particularly the working class".[371] On September 11, 1982, the WRON approved the document "On the broad inclusion of the working class in the direct fight against speculation." The following day, the document landed on the desks of the directors of voivodship commissions with the order to mobilize "workers' brigades". Since the procedures were left unspecified, the simplest solutions were embraced. For example in Piotrków Trybunalski, the voivod set up brigades consisting of men that he selected personally, mainly the tried and tested activists of the former Main Council of Trade Unions (CRZZ). In Poznań and Wałbrzych, specific factories were singled out to provide recruits.[372] The decisions of the factory management tended to be guided by the consideration of maintaining

368 *Ibid.*, fol. 26.
369 AAN, URM, 32/113, fol. 20.
370 *Ibid.*, fol. 37–38.
371 AAN, URM, 32/178, fol. 1.
372 *Ibid.*, fol. 12, 32; A. Gawlik, *Robotnicy w brygadach tygrysa*, "Sprawy i Ludzie" 1982, no. 30.

efficient production; thus, contrary to the guidelines, the selected recruits were often white-collar rather than the ideologically correct working class.

By the end of 1982, more than 16 thousands workers had joined 1 750 brigades. It is not possible to assess how many of them thought of this job as meaningful. It seems that, as often happens in volunteer-based actions, the enthusiasm was short-lived and was quickly followed by weariness and mere going through the motions and by various forms of evasion. Moreover, even the most dedicated activists were not immune to feeling the pinch. Inspections, followed by having to appear in court as witnesses were time-consuming and hardly lucrative, especially as the activists were employed on a piecework basis.[373] Additionally, the specifics of a given location made all the difference. In small towns there were "various informal connections, within social groups and families" that limited, or even made it entirely impossible to carry out "appropriate inspections and suppression operations."[374] The geography of activist involvement in anti-speculation operations depended on the degree of urbanization and industrialization. By the end of 1982, almost seven thousand people had participated in inspections in the Gdańsk voivodship, and some three thousand each in the Katowice and Warsaw voivodships. No wonder that, in the predominantly rural Biała Podlaska and Lublin voivodships, with their closely-knit communities, there had been but 35 and 75 participants respectively. A voice from the conservative Bydgoszcz voivodship (with 175 activists fielded) expressed the general sentiment plainly: "Let workers stick to producing consumer goods and let the organizations set up to fight the black marketeers do their job."[375]

Organs of inspection tend to be susceptible to corruption; the workers' brigades were no exception. Frequently, the "workers' inspection" turned out to be a sham or cases of bribery would come to light.[376] Halfway through the decade, such problems were significant enough to force the commission to conduct large-scale operations (for example Operation Rynek) without involving social forces but rely instead only on the professionals and the police (MO).[377]

It is difficult to assess the degree of antipathy of members of workers brigades and other community inspection units towards private enterprise and the intelligentsia. The bias against the latter was clearly visible during bookstore checks when the booksellers had to face the same accusations as salespersons

---

373 AAN, URM, 32/178, fol. 18.

374 AAN, URM, 32/150, fol. 70.

375 *Ibid.*, fol. 32–34.

376 *Ibid.*, fol. 66, 69–70, 82–83, 95, 98–99. *Ibid.*,1.4/60, fol. 7.

377 AAN, URM, 32/118, fol. 118.

at butcher's stores. An example from the Silesian town of Ozimek followed a familiar pattern: "an inspection by two workers and a policeman found that in the warehouse at the back of the store there were dictionaries and multi-volume works set aside for schools and subscribers. The manager was sent home and a search conducted; several books by Tolstoy were seized (a multi-volume set). In the evening, the manager was arrested. The following day she was in court facing a fast-track trial. The judge decided that the case should be dismissed and sent it back to be investigated under the normal procedure."[378]

The above quote shows some of the characteristics of the justice system in the 1980s in general and in particular in the context of speculation cases. The judges found themselves between Scylla and Charybdis: orders from above demanding increased repression, and the common sense of everyday practice, which demonstrated plainly that many of the accused had broken the law not because they wanted to get rich but because they were under economic duress. The reality was more complicated than the rules and laws provided for. "A judge often comes across," Ryszard Bolecki, a Supreme Court judge, said in April 1985, "instances of petty offences, coming face to face with poverty. Because in the times that we live in, we don't hide that we have poor people in this country. There is the law, which must be adhered to [...] but the truth of the matter is that judges do have some conscience too."[379] Only rarely, however, were they able to take advantage of the (theoretical) independence of their judicial power and dismiss smaller cases without further ado, for example by finding a compromise or settling for a lesser evil. But there were also those judges who were only too happy to follow religiously the orders from above.

Speculation, which the authorities considered one of the greatest threats to the existence of the state, had to be dealt with severely. By December 1980, the Prosecutor General had ordered that all speculation proceedings be concluded within one month and not three, as had previously been the case. However, until the fall of 1981, the penal emphasis was on economic repression. In comparison with the years 1978 to 1980, the immediate custodial sentences were softened (93.2% of cases were conditionally suspended). By the fall of 1981, the era of liberalization had slowly come to an end. In September, the Ministry of Justice appealed to judges asking for "more consistency", reminding them of Article 426 of the criminal code, which allowed confiscation of property and also Article

378 AAN, URM, 32/36, fol. 11, 20.
379 AAN, URM, 32/74, fol. 27.

412, which allowed confiscation of the proceeds of crime.[380] The fines were now increased or combined with prison sentences. The real change, however, came with Martial Law.[381]

After December 13, 1981, law enforcement naturally focused on cases of "breaking the social order in a manner leading to anarchy". Next in line was speculation. The authorities declared: "Today, the situation requires tough penalties for crimes of speculation and the frequent imposition of immediate custodial sentences".[382] In January 1982 alone, 830 people were convicted under articles 221– 225 of the criminal code and the anti-speculation law (in 1981, on average 389 people had been convicted monthly! – 622 of them under the accelerated procedures.[383] Magistrates' courts, which until then had treated the black marketeers leniently, were now put under the microscope. At the end of February 1982, the magistrates' courts received instructions to give priority to cases of speculation (second only to misconduct under the Martial Law decree), to pass tougher sentences and to maintain "full readiness to examine cases under the accelerated procedures, as well as to conduct effective investigations under the normal procedures."[384] The problem of the magistrates' courts remained unsolved; in 1983 they were still persisting in their reluctance to pass custodial sentences. In the first half of the year there were 106 arrests, of which 80 took place in Warsaw![385]

All these efforts were only partially effective, particularly in smaller towns, where "society failed to condemn unequivocally the perpetrators".[386] Although in 1982 and 1983, the number of people accused of speculation and the number of convictions were higher than in 1981, the percentage of immediate custodial sentences, which were supposed to demonstrate the authorities' determination and consistence, remained at a similar level (table 1). According to the Prosecutor General's Office, in 1982 the "repressions used by the courts often do not meet social expectations. This applies to custodial sentences, the majority of which have been suspended and to the fines which are being set at a level disproportionate to the wealth and profits of the accused."[387]

---

380 AAN, URM, 32/112, fol. 67, 70.
381 AAN, URM, 32/14, fol. 20, 22.
382 AAN, URM, 32/113.
383 AAN, URM, 32/14, fol. 23.
384 AAN, URM, 32/113, fol. 6, 23.
385 AAN, URM, 32/47, fol. 11.
386 AAN, URM, 32/47, fol. 11.
387 AAN, KC PZPR, WA, LI/118, fol. 156.

Table 1. Convictions for speculation in years 1981–1986

Year	Proven crimes of speculation	Arrests for speculation	Sentences for speculation	Of these, immediate custodial sentence
1981	5 729	102	4 655	4.2%
1982	14 934	391	9 983	4.1%
1983	14 723	337	7 076	4.9%
1984	20 829	628	11 619	5.7%
1985	24 171	998	12 594	9.8%
1986	17 683	549	8 167	14.1%

Source: AAN, URM, 32/2, fol. 13

The war on speculation offered a practical proof of the Stalinist theory that class war intensifies in step with the progress of the building of socialism. Martial Law was abolished in July 1983, restrictive measures loosened, and border controls relaxed but penalties for crimes of speculation remained strict. Tightening the repressive measures and perfecting the tools for their implementation became for the Ministry of Justice its main concern in 1983 and 1984.[388] In mid-1983, the Ministry embarked on briefing the judges of all the voivodship courts – in individual and group meetings – on the importance of arriving at "appropriate findings".[389] The Ministry seemed to have much faith in the effectiveness of this approach – soon it began to insist that the chief voivodship judges submit detailed monthly reports on the number of convictions, type of proceedings and details of charges and sentencing.[390]

In the following year, the Ministry of Justice and the Central Commission continued to criticize the leniency of the courts, complaining about the low number of immediate custodial sentences, and the excessive number, over 60 percent, of suspended sentences. Both institutions were dissatisfied with the liberal treatment of qualifying speculation. Of the 270 cases processed in the first half of 1984, no more than every fifth black marketeer was sentenced without suspension. The Ministry also took a dim view of the judicial reluctance to confiscate property – in

388 AAN, URM, 32/74, fol. 12.
389 AAN, URM, 32/47, fol. 74–75.
390 AAN, URM, 32/186, fol. 15–17.

279 cases, confiscation was ordered in only two cases. In 1984 there were fifteen confiscation orders, half of them passed by the court in Konin.[391]

The regional differences in the approach to crimes of speculation crimes were another tender spot for the justice system and a quick remedy was nowhere to be found. The highest percentage of immediate custodial sentences was noted in 1984 (up to September) in the Legnica (13%), Zamość (10.2%), and Kraków (10.1%) voivodships. In the Opole voivodship it was only 1.2%, in the Siedlce voivodship – 1.3%, in the Sieradz voivodship – 1.4%, and in Konin, Łomża and Rzeszów voivodships, immediate custodial sentences were not used at all. In Katowice, Leszno, Olsztyn or Opole not a single "qualifying black marketeer" had been identified.[392] Fines in excess of 50 000 zloty were imposed only in 21 (out of 49) voivodships, most of them in Koszalin voivodship (26.3% of all fines), Wałbrzych (20%) and Suwałki (18.2%), and were applied the least in the voivodships of Lublin (2.4%), Bielsko-Biała (3.4%), and Szczecin (3.8%). "In the Warsaw district where there is the greatest threat of black market crimes occurring, no fine in the aforementioned range was imposed."[393]

In these circumstances, the Ministry of Justice came to view the homogenous distribution of penalties as its main task for 1985,[394] naturally, by achieving equilibrium at the level of uniformly higher rather than lower sentences. It began by reviewing the more lenient sentences. In the first quarter of 1985 alone, the Ministry conducted 86 extraordinary reviews of black market cases – half the number of annual reviews in previous years – increasing the penalties imposed in almost all of them.[395] The decree of May 10, 1985 on special criminal liability[396] further narrowed the judges' room for maneuver in speculation cases. The new law significantly limited the option of suspended imprisonment, removing it completely in cases of qualifying speculation. The fine could not now be less than twice the value of the object of speculation; the application of the accelerated procedures was widened, and an administrative summary procedure was

391 AAN, URM, 32/63, fol. 12, 15, 93.

392 *Ibid.*, fol. 64.

393 *Ibid.*, k. 64–65. The authorities were happy to see the effects of implementing the accelerated procedures. In 1984, 852 sentences were passed under these procedures, 64.2% more than in 1983; AAN, URM, 32/116, fol. 24.

394 AAN, URM, 32/74, fol. 12.

395 *Ibid.*, fol. 13.

396 Dz.U. 1985, no. 23, item 101. The decree was in force between July 1, 1985 and April 30, 1988.

introduced – without any trial at all. Additional sanctions became obligatory such as advertising the sentence in the press.

The new blueprint changed the game. While in the first half of 1985, there had been 442 accelerated sentences, in the third quarter of 1985 the number went up to 663 (and with another 710 implemented by means of the administrative summary procedure).[397] In mid-November 1985, Prime Minister Zbigniew Messner received reports that since the implementation of the decree of May 10 "almost 26.0% of the profiteers are tried under the accelerated procedures and almost 30.0% under the summary administrative procedure, that is, without a trial".[398] This reflected the authorities' point of view on the "necessity for tough sentences for the most dangerous perpetrators of speculation crimes, including immediate custodial sentences and fines as well as wide range of additional penalties to help profiteers realize that the crimes were not worthwhile."[399] This trend continued in 1986. Almost 60% of all cases were tried in under either the accelerated or summary administrative procedures.[400]

While repression escalated, the social structure of the black market remained unchanged, with the majority of participants driven to involvement by poverty. Although in September 1981 Stanisław Zaczkowski, the Chief of Police, had referred to the black marketeers as the "margin of society" and "the unemployed",[401] a review of three hundred cases from the first half of 1981 showed a different picture. 61% of all those convicted for speculation were women, and 46% – people older than 50. In 59% of cases the scene of the crime – particularly where sales of alcohol were concerned – was a private apartment.[402] In September 1984, Deputy Minister of Justice Tadeusz Skóra admitted that while half of convicted black marketeers were involved in trading, the other half included "small fry, pensioners, elder women caught at the market places".[403] In 1986, this breakdown stayed the same – 40% of the people convicted on speculation charges were employed in nationalized workplaces, with 15% of them in management. At 30%, pensioners constituted the second largest group, and the unemployed – 18.5%, the majority dependent on their spouses. Women constituted 39% of all convicted, and the

397 AAN, URM, 32/122, fol. 233.
398 *Ibid.*, fol. 260.
399 AAN, URM, 32/117, fol. 33.
400 AAN, URM, 32/118, fol. 7.
401 AAN, URM, 32/112, fol. 91.
402 AAN, URM, 32/186, fol. 1.
403 AAN, URM, 32/63, fol. 20. See: J. Klimek, *Spekulant na etacie*, "Gazeta Prawnicza" 1983, no. 10.

over-40s – 64%. What made this group of criminals exceptional was the fact that 87% had no prior convictions.[404]

Even if not blind, Justice was certainly ruthless; this proved to be the last straw for those opposed to the repressive policies and the war on speculation and brought forth a barrage of criticism. The futility of the anti-speculation operations was frequently pointed out. "It is easy to see," Józef Popkiewicz wrote in *Polityka* in the spring of 1984, "that it is the unbalanced market that breeds speculation and not the other way around [...]. Is it then possible to defeat or at least diminish the size of the black market without obliterating its permanent source? The answer is a resounding 'No!'"[405] The message between the lines was that the government should focus on balancing the market rather than on hounding small traders.

A strong reaction first to the passing and then implementation of the law of May 10, 1985 marked the beginning of the process of the gradual reclaiming of pluralistic public space. "They say," wrote Stanisław Podemski, "that you can't make an omelet without breaking eggs and that the war on speculation comes at high cost. This is not acceptable. Human beings are not to be broken like eggs."[406] The last straw was the aforementioned case, in June 1985, of a saddler from Przemyśl who for a small mark-up organized deliveries of bread to the nearby Stubno where there was no bakery. Despite the fact that the man had a written permission from the authorities and enjoyed the enthusiastic approval of Stubno's residents, he was arrested, charged with speculation, and in October 1985, sentenced to two years in jail, albeit suspended. His punishment also included confiscation of all his savings and a huge fine: 250 thousand zloty. What particularly incited response from the media was the comment that, had he been caught after May 10 – when the new law was passed – he would have had to serve his prison term *and* pay a much higher fine (double the value of the object of his crime).[407] This realization triggered a stormy discussion in the media. "University professors and cleaning ladies, farmers and workers [...] wrote letters to the editors defending

404 AAN, URM, 32/105, fol. 70.

405 J. Popkiewicz, *Nierównowaga i spekulacja*, "Polityka" no. 21, May 24, 1984.

406 S. Podemski, *Niech nie lecą wióry*, "Polityka" no. 18, May 4, 1985. See also: W. Markiewicz, *Sklep nieczynny z powodu aresztowania personelu*, "Polityka" no. 26, June 29, 1985.

407 *Szczęście w nieszczęściu*, "Polityka"nr 48 z 30 XI 1985; *Szlachetny spekulant*, "Polityka" no. 8, February 22, 1986.

the saddler. In the end the Minister of Justice reluctantly allowed an extraordinary appeal in favor of the accused."[408]

Mandatory press announcements of the sentences passed – intended as an additional punishment and a deterrent to others – backfired, bringing ridicule to the anti-speculation campaign: announcements about convictions for selling toys or herring made them appear absurd and futile. "Speculation is the lowest form of entrepreneurship, which has been known for thousands of years," wrote Daniel Passent in early 1986. "No-one has ever been able to eradicate it if the circumstances for it were favorable." The authorities should be happy that "despite educating people for two generations that hard work is the only source of wealth, the idea of buying cheap and selling high has not been completely eradicated. The obnoxious appetite for profit and for growing rich continues to lift its head despite years of scrubbing our morals with a tough brush, sometimes a prison one."[409]

Something also began to stir on the other side of the barricade. "One can observe a certain fatigue, weariness or demobilization in the area of fighting speculation," commented Deputy Chief of Lublin Police (MO), Colonel Andrzej Koczwarski, in early 1986. "There are some people, including police officers, who would like to take a back seat and get some rest."[410] A year later, even representatives of the Prosecutor General called for prudence in cases such as food ration coupon fraud committed by "farmers employed outside agriculture (*chłoporobotnicy*)".[411]

The discrepancy between theory and practice in the "war on speculation" and the economic, political, and social realities in Poland became increasingly clear in the second half of the 1980s. On the one hand state propaganda kept talking about economic reform, the US dollar was becoming the de facto main currency, and state travel agencies were organizing trips that were "tourist" in name only but in reality had a purely business character. On the other hand, the repressive measures employed against the black marketeers were quasi-Stalinist. Thanks to the amnesty bill of July 17, 1986, most political prisoners were let out of jail but the prison doors remained shut for even the most insignificant, small-scale profiteers – the amnesty did not cover economic crimes.

---

408 S. Podemski, *Sędziowie i kary*, "Polityka" no. 7, February 14, 1987. In early 1987, the Supreme Court discontinued the proceedings against the saddler and reminded the public that the criminal code had precedence over the decree of May 10, 1985.

409 D. Passent, *Karp z gwizdkiem*, "Polityka" no 6, February 8, 1986.

410 AAN, URM, 32/117, 179.

411 AAN, URM, 32/105, fol. 25.

It is difficult to say if the anti-speculations legacy troubled the new administration. It certainly did nothing to enhance the image of the government. The situation of 1954, when the Special Commission had been simultaneously praised and pushed out of the game now repeated itself. Now, on the one hand, the CKWS received high accolades (for example during the cabinet meeting on May 12, 1986 or on many occasions in parliament in May and June of 1986); but on the other hand, beginning in 1987, its activity visibly slowed down and the frequency of the meetings of the Central Commission and the regional branches decreased.[412]

On October 23, 1987, the Polish parliament passed a bill on the scope of the activities of chief and central administrative bodies and the CKWS was no longer among them. Since the anti-speculation decree was still in force, there was a need to create a substitute organization. The tasks of the CKWS were allocated to the Committee of the Council of Ministers for Compliance with the Law, Public Order and Discipline (Komitet RM ds Przestrzegania Prawa, Porządku Publicznego i Dyscypliny Społecznej). On the basis of the CKWS and the "Sektor" Central Coordinating Team (Centralny Zespół Koordynacyjny), the Central Team Coordinating the Internal Market Protection (Centralny Zespół Koordynujący Ochronę Rynku Wewnętrznego) was created. The plan was to set up Voivodship Teams Coordinating Internal Market Protection (with 29 positions for secretaries of the voivodship commissions). The Central Team, just as the CKWS had, was to synchronize anti-speculation operations, as well as analyze and evaluate the phenomenon of the black market. Colonel Zbigniew Nowicki (Deputy Chief of Police) was designated as its new chairman; his deputies were Piotr Ostaszewski, director of the PIH and Colonel Wacław Skoczylas, Director of the Office for Combating Economic Crime at Police Headquarters (Biuro do Walki z Przestępstwami Gospodarczymi KG MO).[413]

The dismantling of the CKWS proceeded much more smoothly than its operations ever had. On October 27, the voivods and mayors of Warsaw, Kraków and Łódź received a telex informing them of the liquidation of the voivodship and local commissions. A thank-you note on behalf of the Prime Minister to the activists participating in anti-speculation operations rounded off the message. Any authorization issued in the past to inspectors by the commissions was to be withdrawn "in a controlled manner".[414] The solemn farewell Party organized

412 AAN, URM, 32/2, fol. 10–12.
413 AAN, URM, 1.5/43, fol. 325–327.
414 AAN, URM, 32/2, fol. 50–51.

on November 4, 1987 at the Office of the Council of Ministers was brief. After the handing out of the medals, the reading of the laudatory letters and the final speech delivered by Józef Kozioł, the ex-chairman of CKWS, guests – a fact duly recorded![415] – were offered fruit juice.

This was a symbolic end of an era. The pace of the Central Coordinating Team (Centralny Zepół Koordynujący) slowed down significantly. We can only wonder whether the authorities came to deliberately allow a certain leeway for unofficial dealings, which inevitably accompanied market shortages, or whether, perhaps, the weakening government ran out of strength or will to act. While in 1987 as many as 5 607 people had been sentenced for speculation crimes (including 1 801 under the accelerated procedure and 1 565 under the administrative summary procedure), convictions slowed down to 3 682 in 1988 and even lower, to 2 120, in 1989 – fewer than at the end of the 1970s![416]

The disappearance of black market issues from the headlines marked the true end of the war on speculation. Even *Trybuna Ludu*, the official daily newspaper of the Polish United Workers' Party (PZPR) and one of its main propaganda outlets, hitherto passionately committed to the anti-speculation battle, had breathed its last in this war. On December 1, 1988 the newspaper published what sounded like a symbolic farewell: "We should have no illusions that repression is capable of eradicating speculation. The black market thrives on an unbalanced market. It can be destroyed only by increasing supply to equal demand."[417] A month later, with the new economic laws passed in December 1988, a new era began – also for the black market.

---

415 *Ibid.*, fol. 68–71.

416 *Rocznik statystyczny 1988*, Warszawa 1988, pp. 504–505; *Rocznik statystyczny 1991*, Warszawa 1991, p. 80.

417 Z. Krzyżanowska, *Między "pierwszym" a "drugim obiegiem"*, TL, no. 279, December 1, 1988.

4. The (Historical) Geography of the Black Market in the Polish People's Republic

4.1 General Remarks

This chapter does not aspire to present detailed characteristics of the centers of illicit distilling, illegal slaughter, smuggling, or of the hard currency trade. It aims rather to demonstrate correlations between black market phenomena and the geographical and historical context. There is no doubt, for example, that the partitions of Poland or the border changes and mass migrations after Second World War to this day continue to influence the political, social, economic and cultural situation in Poland.[418]

The geographical and historical determinants of the second economy were already in evidence immediately after the war. It was already clear in January 1948 that the local representative powers of the Special Commission for Combating Fraud and Corruption had to stand up against specific, at times endemic, phenomena. The Kraków and Bielsko sections of the Commission had to deal with smuggling, Kielce – with illegal leather tanning, Szczecin – also with contraband but mostly with looting.[419] The capital of Poland, Warsaw, was traditionally considered the center and the seedbed of all "speculation operations".

The post-partition legacy was also apparent. For example in 1957 when operations began against "economic criminals" who were also Party members, the greatest challenges arose in the regions where different historical traditions met. While in the Upper Silesia part of the Katowice voivodship, there were few, if any, problems in the former Polish Kingdom – created in 1815 by the Congress of Vienna and informally known as Congress Poland – the task was much more onerous. "In Częstochowa," it was reported in 1957, "where the economic underground is particularly extensive, the comrades are dealing with the largest number of cases. Especially when it comes to trade, there are several instances that are serious and difficult to tackle because of the connections between the people

418 See: M. Janicki, W. Władyka, *Dwie Polski*, "Polityka" no. 44/November 3, 2007; J. Raciborski, *Zachowania wyborcze Polaków 1989–2006*, in: *Wymiary życia społecznego. Polska na przełomie XX i XXI wieku*, ed. M. Marody, Warszawa 2007, pp. 344–372.

419 AAN, KS, 82, fol. 4.

involved, such as family ties. This is one reason why nobody was expelled from the Party in Częstochowa this year."[420]

There was also a reason why (until the 1980s) illegal alcohol production thrived in the lands formerly under Russian and Austrian partition and in the territories where a high percentage of population had originated from those areas. And, at least during the first decade after the war, regional differences were also reflected in different approaches to what was considered the store of value of choice, especially in conservative, rural areas. Peasants in the former Polish Kingdom preferred gold tsarist roubles, whereas in the former Galicia, they favored Austrian ducats and gold dollars.

The deliberate and autonomous actions of the voivods and the PUWP's local secretaries had a significant influence on the historic regional differences and divisions, especially during the initial phase of the rationing system in 1981.[421]

Individual administrative units conducted their own rationing policy "under the pressure of trade unions and voivodship committees, or following the initiatives of voivods, or generally under some kind of pressure."[422] Even in neighboring voivodships the same goods (coffee, cigarettes, alcohol, clothing, or fats) could be available on the market or under strict rationing. In accordance with the law of communicating vessels, goods trickled from the regions where they were available to the regions where their sale was limited.[423]

The national system of rationing included, even in its most restrictive phase at the turn of 1981 and 1982, only a portion of market goods, which left the regional decision makers with substantial room for maneuver. Already in April 1982, it had become clear that the "country is a mosaic of rationing and trade particularisms."[424] Inspections of the efficiency in implementing the rationing rules conducted in 48 voivodships found some irregularities in half of them. In parallel

420 AAN, KC PZPR, 237/XXXII–7, fol. 131.

421 Sometimes it led to creating coalitions, which Mieczysław F. Rakowski called "local deals". These were confederacies of several voivodships, with the strongest one as a leader. The first secretaries and voivods formed a "Public Safety Committee". "They help each other, they advise each other on how to by-pass the regulation coming from Warsaw, they foster surplus exchange between the voivodships, they help each outer out with the resources, etc. [...]. Preventing the economic crash is their most important goal"; M.F. Rakowski, *Rzeczpospolita na progu lat osiemdziesiątych*, Warszawa 1981, p. 82.

422 AAN, URM, 32/112, fol. 60, 114.

423 *Ibid.*

424 AAN, URM, 32/113, fol. 48.

with sales based on centrally issued ration coupons, there developed autonomous regional distribution of goods in exchange for vouchers, ID documents, and tax receipts. The heads of town and community councils often chose to grant "special allocations". The latter usually involved additional (frequently quite substantial) amounts of alcohol awarded "not only for weddings and baptism celebrations but also nameday parties, anniversaries and other undocumented occasions." Until the end of the 1980s, knowledge of the complicated rationing geography was an important part of black market strategies.[425]

4.2 Center – Periphery

The main dividing line on the black market map did not run along the old or current administrative borders but rather along the boundaries separating the big cities – the "centers" – from the "periphery", small towns and rural areas. The opposition between center and periphery is usually explored in cultural discourse but it is also of significance in economic discourse. In post-war Poland, the center and periphery represented two quite different worlds.

4.2.1 Center – Big Cities

A big city provided a wonderful backdrop for devising black market strategies. Industry and other state institutions were like bottomless coffers from which both the private sector and the "state" swindlers helped themselves by the handful. The following excerpt refers to Warsaw but it is also representative of Kraków, Katowice, Łódź or Gdańsk: "Warsaw industry produces many attractive articles, providing opportunities for theft. Various manufactories operating under the disguise of craft have their headquarters in Warsaw. Most of the time, they are doomed to rely on stolen materials for supplies. Various enterprises, for example publishing houses, in many instances ignore strict rules of financial discipline. If one adds to this a widespread practice of contract projects and an abundance of private subcontractors, it all creates even more opportunities for fraud and misuse."[426]

In 1957 in *Szpilki* magazine no. 35, the well-known cartoonist Karol Ferster published a telling caricature: a petty-bourgeois couple apply for a permit to open a store; handing their application to the clerk, they remark, "We are about to open a store in an area where there are no nationalized outlets. Where are we supposed to get our supplies from?" For contemporaries, the context was

425 *Ibid.*, fol. 20–23, 80; AAN, URM, 32/117, fol. 79–80.

426 AAN, KC PZPR, 237/VII-245, fol. 108–109.

immediately understandable. In 1957, the network of private traders comprised 26 thousand stores, twice as many as in the previous year; however, stores kept opening not in the outskirts and small towns where demand was great but mostly in downtown areas of big cities. In the free market system, merchants find the centers attractive, because this is where the wealthy clientele lives. In communist Poland, it was the concentration of nationalized trade in the big cities that drew the private merchants there. "Some private stores engage in the illegal practice of buying from nationalized stores large quantities of goods in short supply on the official market in order to sell them on the black market. With the increased speculation in private trade, the prices of goods from small private manufacturers are rising."[427] Year 1957 brought a veritable revolution: the number of private eateries grew fivefold. It was easier for the authorities to influence their location by granting (or withholding) liquor license but still the majority of the new restaurants opened in the central districts of the biggest cities.[428] State or coop trade constituted one of the most crucial sources of supply for private merchants (official and unofficial) until the late 1980s.

The big cities offered not only more business opportunities, but also a clientele more wised-up to the then current trends. These arrived first in Warsaw, the Tri-City (Gdańsk, Gdynia, and Sopot), Wrocław and Kraków. For this reason, demand in the big cities was the most sophisticated and developed, and their residents had the money to buy goods. Trade in the big cities, including the black market, differed from the traditional, often pre-industrial ways of conducting transactions in rural areas. It was not limited to group of acquaintances and often used modern methods of marketing such as press advertisements.

Big city public space facilitated the "modernization" of the second economy by delineating permanent, easily recognizable areas of black market activity. Traditionally these were located in large market places or long established market halls.[429] This was the case in Łódź, Kraków, and Wrocław[430] but especially in Warsaw, where the Różycki Bazaar, the Rembertów Marketplace or (in the 1980s)

427 AAN, URM, 22/115, fol. 2.

428 *Ibid.*

429 In November 1981, the chief of the Central Commission for Combating Fraud stated: "Speculation concentrates in big cities especially in large bazaars and market halls"; AAN, URM, 32/119, fol. 26.

430 Wrocław's most famous marketplace was at Nankier Square. See: HIM, Pressearchiv, P 6221, Item 6856/54, The Free Market and the Black Market in Wrocław, August 10, 1954; Z. Antosiewicz, *Prosperity placu Nankiera*, "Tygodnik Demokratyczny" 1956, no. 20.

and the Skra marketplace on the fields of an athletic club had cross-regional or national significance.[431]

Transport centers such as railroad stations were also black market hubs. One such, from the 1960s to the 1980s, was Katowice. "The crowd swirled right in front of my eyes," Romuald Teyszerski described the Katowice railroad station in 1968. "The foreign traders sat impassively against the walls, while Poles were excitedly rummaging in the piles of polo shirts, sweaters and non-iron shirts. The vendors – Hungarians, Czechs, citizens of Yugoslavia, and Austrians – were experts on the topic of current prices [...]. My friends later told me this was a normal sight. Katowice is a central hub for incoming traffic 'from the West' (this is where foreign tourists often start their visit to Poland) and with the arrival of each train, the trading begins. It's important to sell quickly, to get rid of the goods, to make money quickly and venture into Poland. The travelers come here having been told by their friends that this is the place for trading. And to do that, they don't even have to leave the station building."[432]

Every big city also had a well-known site where the illegal hard currency trading took place. In Warsaw, this was initially the area around the Hotel Polonia, near the corner of Marszałkowska Street and Aleje Jerozolimskie. Later, the area near Jasna, Traugutta, and Kredytowa Streets, where the banks were located, became known for hard currency black market deals.[433] In Kraków, Rynek Główny (the Main Market) and adjacent streets became the location of choice for the moneychangers' (known as *cinkciarze*[434]). In Gdynia it was Świętojańska Street (and to a lesser extent, all the other streets leading to the port), in Szczecin – the Piast Café and Kaskada restaurant,[435] in Wrocław – the restaurant in the Hotel Metropol, among other places.[436] The hard currency black market in Lublin was located between the PKO bank on Tysiąclecie Avenue and the market place across the street (on Ruska Street). "A dream location for the money dealers;" a journalist commented in 1988, "there, they had everything in one place – an official bank, underground passage, black marketeers, and a real market."[437]

---

431 See: J. Kurczewski, M. Cichowski, K. Wiliński, *Wielkie bazary warszawskie. Środowisko społeczne, kultura i problem społeczny*, Warszawa 2010.

432 R. Teyszerski, *Złote jajo po polsku*, "Kierunki", no. 36/September 8, 1968.

433 About Warsaw: J. Kochanowski, *"Niepewne czasy, pewny dolar". Szkic do obrazu warszawskiego czarnego rynku walutowego*, PH, 100, 2009/1, pp. 29–46.

434 APKr, KW PZPR, 293, fol. 214, 223.

435 J. Wołoszańska, *Nie tylko przez pryzmat prawa*, ŻW, April 22, 1971.

436 HIM, Pressearchiv, P 6221, Item 4942/58, Black market in Poland.

437 J. Nieporowski, *Raj dla cinkciarzy*, "Tygodnik Kulturalny", no. 14/October 3, 1988.

The money dealing spots moved around, depending on the meandering of the official hard currency policies. In early 1970s, Pewex stores became the location of choice for the money dealers. The immediately recognizable moneychangers were a permanent fixture of the big city landscape in communist Poland.

Warsaw was undoubtedly the most important black market center in the Polish People's Republic. The Warsaw dealers who sold gold, US dollars, alcohol and other products in short supply on the official market, effectively took advantage of their experience gained during the Second World War. They were indeed efficient, as one can conclude from the fact that 11.4% of all black market crimes investigated by the Special Commission in 1946 and 22.7% in 1947 were committed in Warsaw.[438] The Polish capital became a city with a high exposure to crime. In the early 1960s, the national crime rate in Poland was 130 incidents per 10 000 people. In Warsaw it was 211 (only Szczecin voivodship beat the record). It was also in Warsaw that the highest rate of crime against public property and black market offenses were reported. While the national average rate in crimes involving public property was 30 per 10 000 people, in Warsaw it was 50. For black market offenses, the national average was 2.2 cases per 10 000 people; in Warsaw – it was 7.3.[439] Warsaw was a big city and it was easy to engage in illegal trade there "without attracting any unwanted attention", even when this required international contacts. "In Warsaw," it was reported in 1964, "there are groups of active hard currency dealers (*waluciarze*) who have extensive connections with various international groups and maintain trade relations with economic swindlers, who buy from them foreign hard currency and gold using stolen money."[440] In 1976, seventy five percent of the 220 cases of "professional speculation" (Item 221, Clause 4 of the Criminal Code) were committed in the Warsaw voivodship, as was the highest number, that is – 820 of all speculation crimes (Items 221–225 of the Criminal Code); Katowice voivodship was in second place with 379 incidents, and Łódź voivodship was third with 274.[441]

Warsaw had the greatest number of private stores: in the early 1960s – there were 621 stores per 1.2 million city residents and 915 stores per 2.4 million Warsaw voivodship residents. In comparison, in the Katowice voivodship with a population of 3.4 million, there were 726 private stores. At the same time in Warsaw

438 AAN, KS, 10, fol. 175.

439 APW, KWar. PZPR, 30/XVIII-7, vol. 1, fol. 163–164.

440 *Ibid.*, fol. 164.

441 W. Krasucka, *Spekulacja (wybrane zagadnienia)*, "Studia Kryminologiczne, Kryminalistyczne i Penitencjarne" 10, 1979, p. 157.

and vicinity, there were to be found 30% of all artisan shops in Poland.[442] In 1969, in Warsaw and vicinity, there were some 40 thousand artisan shops, industrial plants, trade and service outlets – a similar number as those of Łódź, Kraków, and Wrocław put together. Almost half of the private export production came from Warsaw. One third of Polish "private millionaire businesses" (some 700) was located here.[443]

The private sector was an important but not the only factor influencing the shape and size of the Warsaw black market. Warsaw was the center of the cultural, scientific, economic, and political life of the country. Many Warsaw residents had at their disposal a substantial amount of illegally acquired cash. They needed to invest it discreetly. At the same time international diplomatic and trade representatives stationed in Warsaw and most of the foreign media correspondents also resided there. Already in the 1940s, foreign embassies had partially covered their operational costs with Polish money purchased on the black market. Their staff, including the diplomats, undertook their own illegal trading and smuggling operations (more in chapter 8). At that time, the only Polish international airport hosting intercontinental flights was located in Warsaw. As a result, not only did western patterns of consumption spread faster in the Polish capital city, but also western currencies flooded the local market.

As the capital of Poland, Warsaw was a "hotbed of all kinds of speculation."[444] In other Polish cities it was their history, geography, and economy that determined the characteristics of the black market. Port cities will be discussed in the next sub-chapter. Kraków based its black market on tourist traffic, Poznań on International Fair visitors.[445] Particular circumstances, especially historical ones, could strongly influence local black market prosperity. For example, Radom became in the 1950s one of the richest cities in Poland, although this was not officially acknowledged.

Radom owed its fame to its tradition of leatherworking going back to the Middle Ages. In the mid-1950s, the output of Radom tanneries was half of what they had been producing before the Second World War, and it barely covered the needs of the state-owned shoe factories. At the same time, 120 private shoemaker's shops were registered in Radom and vicinity. In 1957, they manufactured 56 thousand pairs of shoes, using 15 thousand square meters of soft leather and about 20 tons of hard leather. The official allowance covered one third of the needs (six thousand

442 APW, KWar. PZPR, 30/XVIII–7, vol. 1, fol. 163–164.
443 APW, KWar. PZPR, 30/XVIII–3, vol. 3, fol. 58.
444 AAN, URM, 32/74, fol. 19.
445 Archiwum Państwowe w Poznaniu, 1071, Prezydium WRN, 7122/X/79, fol. 114, 146.

square meters of soft leather and six tons of hard leather). The remaining leather came from three thousand illegal tanneries located in various places in the city and its vicinity. The unofficial tanning shops based their production also on that of state-owned factories, which were the source of otherwise unavailable tannins and strictly rationed raw leather. Substantial profits[446] both from stealing and production were invested primarily on the black market. Unofficial businesses requiring a special supply base influenced the development of illegal alcohol production and trade.[447] As a result of show trials in 1960 and 1961, which ended with some leather swindlers being sentenced to death[448] (albeit the sentences were not carried out), the black market in Radom gradually grew poorer and lost its luster.[449] Even in the 1970s, when the city became the voivodship capital, Radom's second economy had nothing special to offer.

It can be said that Radom belonged somewhere in between the center and the periphery. In the early 1960s, a *Polityka* journalist wrote: "A city that is big, grey, and ugly. The streets are crowded but the crowds are sluggish, spiritless, gray. It is a cross between a big industrial center and a small county town".[450] A "big city" characteristic was the fact that the more significant cases of illegal trading did end up in court. But Radom's "small town" ambiance was apparent from the fact that its second economy sailed under the radar for such a long time in theory only; in fact, the authorities kept their eyes more or less shut to its existence quite deliberately and not entirely disinterestedly.

4.2.2 Periphery: Municipal and District Poland

Writing about the Soviet Union in the 1940s, the American historian Julie Hessler noted: "At the local level, the repression of the unofficial economy was combined

446 According to the report of the PUWP commission from 1958, Radom residents' income in 1957 was 1 294 million zl and expenditure – 1633 million zl. Only local expenditure and savings in local banks were included in the report!; AAN, KC PZPR, XI/281, fol. 25–26.

447 *Ibid.*

448 J. Brodacz, *Mali ludzie – wielkie interesy. Afera skórzana w Radomiu*, "Polityka" no. 45/ November 5, 1960; S. Kozicki, *Radom czy Dedowo*, "Polityka" no. 1/January 5, 1963; C.T. Zwolski, *Historia miasta Radomia. Kronika*, Radom 2005; P. Chojnacki, K. Madej, *Przypadki prokuratora*, "Biuletyn Instytutu Pamięci Narodowej" 2005, no. 1–2, p. 116.

449 When in late January 1965, the authorities in the Kielce voivodship liquidated groups of "hard currency criminals", the largest number of arrests were in Radom; AIPN, MSW II, 4370, 34.

450 S. Kozicki, *Radom czy Dedowo*, "Polityka" no. 1/January 5, 1963.

with grudging toleration; police, prosecutors, market administrators, and financial agencies treated private exchange at the bazaar as an inevitable, though in many cases illegal, part of economic life."[451] There is no doubt that the further away the regions were from the decision-making political center, the more its population reliant on agriculture for their income, the lower the number of inhabitants per square kilometer, and the more conservative its social structures, the more liberal its authorities tended to be towards spontaneous economic activities of citizens. Often the official liberalism was associated with corruption, or informal, sometimes family-based, obligations and relations. Not infrequently, some altogether pragmatic reasons were behind official support for black market "tycoons".[452] The periphery (referred to as "greenfield" in the Polish People's Republic) was usually underprivileged in comparison with the big cities, and with smaller but industrialized cities,[453] as far as supplies were concerned. Local decision makers accepted a wider margin of economic freedom as a way of filling in the gaps in supply. The official trade coordinator in the Siedlce voivodship was characteristically sympathetic, when in 1981 he commented on the arrest of a black marketeer in the small town Żelechów: the "speculator was selling meat and meat products to the population. The police and my employer intervened. However, I must say that the reaction of the community, the buyers, was the very opposite. They did not want him punished severely, they did not want him destroyed – because he [was] the only meat supplier in the town and community."[454] In the years that followed, such reports became commonplace.[455]

---

451 J. Hessler, *A postwar Perestroika? Toward a history of private enterprise in the USSR*, "Slavic Review" no. 57, 1998, no. 3, p. 522.

452 *Ibid.*, p. 540.

453 For example, in 1970, the average deliveries in Kielce voivodship were 19.3 kg, but in the industrialized city of Starachowice – 38.5 kg; in the Rzeszów voivodship – 20.2 kg but in the city of Mielec where airplane factories were located – 56.6 kg. In the Warsaw voivodship deliveries reached on average 41.4 kg but in the city of Warsaw – 81 kg of meat and deli products. In subsequent years, the proportion did not vary greatly. In mid-1976, the average deliveries in the Warsaw voivodship came to 96 kg per person annually; in Łódź voivodship to 85.3 kg and in the Katowice voivodship to 75.5 kg (the three voivodships received two thirds of the deliveries of all best quality meat). At the same time, the deliveries for the less industralized Łomża and Zamość voivodships amounted to some 19.5 kg each. J. Kochanowski, *"...jesteśmy już przyzwyczajeni". Prolegomena do społeczno-modernizacyjnych kulis "problemu mięsnego" w PRL*, PH, 96, 2005/4, p. 603.

454 AAN, URM, 32/112, fol. 76.

455 AAN, URM, 32/64, fol. 34.

In small, closed communities, where people were interdependent and bound to deal with one another on a regular basis, the "patron-client" relationship was paramount. This situation led to the development of efficient social networks with a tight-knit structure, which successfully buffered any intervention from outside, with the help of the relationships that local entrepreneurs, state and private, legal and illegal, had with the local power elite. It was a tall order to infiltrate and fight such local arrangements, as can be illustrated by the efforts undertaken by the Central Team for Combating Fraud and Corruption (Zespół Centralny do Walki z Nadużyciami i Korupcją), created in 1957 (introduced in the previous chapter). In the big cities, sections of the unofficial economy were connected mostly by business links and they were easy to identify and expunge. In local communities, the family connections and client links were much less clear but more durable and, resistant to external influence. The local cliques were tightly knit, loyal and included lower level Party activists, salespeople and inspectors but also Party functionaries, policemen or prosecutors who, if need be, could hide incriminating documents in the deepest drawers. For example in the Upper Silesia town of Mysłowice in 1957, a local Team for Combating Fraud "excluded the chief prosecutor and his deputy from the Party for drunkenness and links with private enterprise. After they had been kicked out, it came to light that this chief prosecutor was having a villa built for him in Dąbrówka, and prisoners were building it for him. One has to wonder how he could have ever been able to prosecute crimes and abuses…"[456]

One can reasonably conclude that, as social trust in the economic capabilities of the state diminished in the late 1970s, the informal – and most certainly unlawful – economic activity that was of benefit to the local community gained the tacit acceptance of local authorities. This was clear from the way that they tended to adapt orders from the headquarters to local circumstances, and carry them out only when big city functionaries were really paying attention. But even then, the actions were often feigned. A report from September 1981 noted: "In villages and subdivisions the battle against speculation is so far highly unsatisfactory. We may say there are blind spots on the map of our fight against speculation. The specific relations among people in the rural areas, the nepotism in distributing the goods, the warning systems in place and the low frequency of inspections all allow the local black marketeers to get away with their operations."[457]

---

456 AAN, KC PZPR, 237/XXXII-7, fol. 12.

457 AAN, URM, 32/112, 31. The Solidarity revolution of 1980 and 1981 exposed social networks in provincial Poland. The most typical were informal ties existing at community level between different branches of local government and economic agencies.

In the following years, the blind spots were only superficially identified and certainly not removed. Of course, anti-speculation commissions were also set up in the peripheral areas, with meetings taking place and official reports submitted, but the results were usually modest. The regional-level, internal inspections of individual institutions such as the Peasants' Self-Help Cooperative (Samopomoc Chłopska) were often a pro forma, ritualized activity. Even if the inspections actually took place, they usually included local functionaries who were prone to not notice the shortcomings – which an external commission would uncover immediately on arrival.[458]

As a consequence, the number of speculation cases brought before the provincial courts was small. According to the police and judicial data, 90% (in 1982), and 76.5% (in 1983) of all speculation crimes occurred in the cities. Warsaw reacted with irritation to the regional prosecution statistics. For example in September 1983, in the Suwałki voivodship the courts did not hear a single speculation case, and in Białystok – only one. During the same period, Warsaw courts delivered 105 verdicts. Six months later, in March 1984, Polish courts sentenced 618 citizens for speculation crimes. In the Suwałki voivodship, as usual, no one was sentenced for speculation at all; in the Legnica, Zielona Góra, Tarnobrzeg, Łomża, Sieradz, Skierniewice, Opole, Kielce, Bielsko-Biała, Elbląg, Konin, Koszalin, Krosno, Piotrków, Płock, Tarnobrzeg, Nowy Sącz, and Olsztyn voivodships – between 2 and 10 people were sentenced. In the Katowice voivodship there were 69 sentences, and in Warsaw voivodship – 123.[459]

The head of the local authority (*naczelnik gminy*) was always blamed for tolerating the existence of such ties. Thanks to the networks, "tried and trusted" interest groups appeared in the community and informal structures are born. "They are like private entities within institutions or workplaces. In extreme cases, if aided by the community leader, they turn into family clans. Family clans usually operate rural trade." *Ibid.*

458 AAN, URM, 32/171, fol. 116.

459 AAN, URM, 32/186, fol. 15–17; *ibid*, 32/121, fol. 60. An anecdote told by Col. Wacław Skoczylas, the Director of the Office for Combating Economic Fraud at Police Headquarters (KG MO) in November 1986, shed some light on these results: "Two or three years ago, I had a conversation with one of the First Secretaries of the Voivoidship Committees. [...] I discussed with him the issue of arresting 60 drivers from a transportation enterprise. Why did I talk to the First Secretary? Because this was about making a political decision – about arresting 60 drivers in a company employing 70 drivers in total putting the transport system in the whole voivodship into chaos. This wise First Secretary – and very wise indeed he was, and he taught me a lot! – said to me: "To arrest 60 drivers means 60 temporary widows, at least 60 or maybe even

It was clear to many that the reality of the black market outside the big cities did not look rosy. By the second part of 1981, it was already apparent that the black marketeers were intercepting almost all means of productions in rural areas – tractors, farming equipment, building materials, coal, insecticides, "even pitchforks and rubber boots".[460] To a significant extent, it was the residents of the big cities who subsidized the black market prices of those items by purchasing food products in short supply, mostly meat, which flowed to the cities via independent channels.

4.3 The North versus the South

In the mid-1980s, as part of the step-up of the battle against the hard currency black market, the chief of the Police Headquarters department in charge of economic crime conducted "disciplinary talks regarding the unsatisfactory results of combating this type of crime with the chief of departments for combating economic crime in the following voivodship headquarters: Białystok, Biała Podlaska, Konin, Bydgoszcz, Ciechanów, Chełm, Częstochowa, Gorzów Wielkopolski, Kalisz, Koszalin, Krosno, Piła, Sieradz, Skierniewice, and Zamość."[461] All the conversations were conducted over the phone but in two cases, in Kraków and Gdańsk, at the opposite ends of the country, he showed up personally. This was not surprising – it was the mountainous region in the South and the coast in the North that were the black market hubs of socialist Poland. This was a result of the geographical and historical factors that influenced social behavior (economical, political, etc.), and could be best observed in Zakopane and on the coast, and especially in the Tri-city.[462]

120 orphans. No chance, comrade Skoczylas! You go and arrest the Director!" *Ibid.*, 32/99, fol. 39–40.

460 AAN, URM, 32/112, fol. 31. In the subsequent years (and probably until the end of the Polish People's Republic) not much changed. *Ibid.*, 32/114, fol. 50; *ibid.*, 32/115, fol. 39.

461 AIPN, KG MO, 35/554, fol. 49.

462 I will focus here on the well-researched 1960s and 1970s. I wrote about the second economy in Podhale in the following articles: *Zakopiański kapitalizm*, "Gazeta Wyborcza", December 18–19, 2004, *Socjalizm na halach, czyli "Patologia stosunków społeczno-ekonomicznych i politycznych w Zakopanem" (1972)*, PH, 98, 2007/1, pp. 71–96.

4.3.1 The South: It Is Impossible to Bring Socialism to the Polish Highlands!

Of all the Polish post-war land borders, only the section of the southern border running east from, Racibórz could pride itself on going back to the Middle Ages. The residents of this mountain borderland identified themselves not in terms of politics but rather of geography and culture and "more important than borders was kinship, in pursuit of which all the residents of the Carpathian region visited each other regardless of the obstructions posed by territorial administration. Being a *góral*, a highlander, mattered more than being a Pole or a Romanian. This tradition was so engrained that border patrols were quite unable to keep their compatriots under control."[463] Mountain societies all over the world (and the Polish highlanders are no exception) live in conservative social structures where the dominant role is held by the "big family" and the authorities and their law enforcement are approached in a utilitarian manner. Well aware of their inability to control the highlanders, the authorities tended to allow them quite a bit of leeway. A Radio Free Europe report from 1961 got it right when observing that the "highlanders' prosperity is usually derived from overt violations of legal regulations".[464]

Difficult geographical and climate conditions that hindered any possibilities for productive agriculture or industry forced the *górals* to develop specific survival strategies. One such was social mobility, manifested in emigration and seasonal work migrations. Emigration from the Podhale region to North America (between 1870 and 1930 approximately 42 thousand people left this region) had a significant impact on local strategies. From the US or Canada, the emigrants sent money and parcels with western products, which made post-war Podhale a center for trading fashionable western clothing.[465] The emigrants already settled

---

463 M. Prandota, *Koński interes*, "Tygodnik Kulturalny", no. 22/1983.

464 HIM, Pressearchiv, P 6221, RFE-Research, Item No 2823, September 3, 1961, "Gorale" (the highlanders) – the privileged class in Poland.

465 In the spring of 1958 a refugee from Poland confessed to a Radio Free Europe representative: "For those who sell clothes, Podhale, and the vicinities of Nowy Targ and Nowy Sącz are still the best sources of supply. The cheapest second-hand items are in Nowy Targ and even professional traders go there to buy a bargain second-hand coat or other clothes. Fashionable Warsaw families who wear foreign outfits or who plan their budgets well, buy their clothes once or twice a year in Nowy Sącz or Zakopane when they go there for vacation"; HIM, Pressearchiv, P 6211, RFE-Research, Item 1660/58, Warsaw flea market does booming business.

in the West provided support for their compatriots from the region who were also looking for opportunities to earn money overseas (especially after 1956, when it became easier to leave Poland). Only 223 people left Zakopane for the US and Canada; in 1967 and in 1971, the number rose sixfold. After working overseas for one year, a Podhale woman brought home on average $3.5 000, a man – between 5 and 7 000. We can safely assume that the returning seasonal workers pumped annually into Zakopane and Podhale economy several million dollars.

Tradition going back a long time and easily available raw materials made Nowy Targ the center of a (mostly illegal) fur industry. According to Radio Free Europe: the "financial elite of the highlanders [...] is created by furriers [...]. There are many furrier workshops in Podhale and apart from an official workshop, every furrier has several other concealed in different shacks."[466] When in the 1960s, demand for the products of Podhale furriers increased significantly, thanks also to the winter Olympics in Grenoble, where the stylish sheepskin coats from Zakopane were a big hit, the highlanders started to bring in sheep even from faraway regions of Poland. In the past, a similar long-distance trade had existed in horses, which the highlanders bought in the Suwałki voivodship in the North, among others, in order to smuggle them into Czechoslovakia.

Already in the 19th century, the highlanders had recognized smuggling as an effective survival strategy, which they often considered a profession. Smuggling maintained its position as a significant source of income during most of the 20th century, adapting with ease to outside circumstances such as fluctuating demand and a rise in tourism. In its1959 report on economic crime, the Supreme Audit Office (Najwyższa Izba Kontroli) paid special attention to the "smuggling on the southern border, in which the highlander population engages on a professional level."[467] In the first post-war decade, smuggling routes traditionally led to Slovakia, with Slovakian zippers brought in covering the entire Polish nationwide

---

466 *Ibid.*, Item No 2823, September 3, 1961. Until the 1980s, the Podhale "furrier industry" was a favorite topic of "anti-speculation" journalism; see: G. Wall, *Kwiatki do kożucha*, "Walka Młodych" August , 1971; A. Kulicka, *Rekiny w baranicach*, "Polityka" no. 44/ November 4, 1978; A.R. Szymański, *Kożuch z meliny*, "Fakty" December 1, 1984.

467 *Informacja o przestępczości gospodarczej w 1959 r.*, Warszawa 1960 (NIK, Wydział ds. Nadużyć Gospodarczych, copy in author's possession), p. 19. See: A. Buńda, *Pogranicze mniej formalne czyli nielegalne przekraczanie granic na Podhalu*, in: *Góry i góralszczyzna w dziejach i kulturze pogranicza polsko-słowackiego (Podhale, Spisz, Orawa, Gorce, Pieniny). Historia*, ed. J.M. Roszkowski, R. Kowalski, Nowy Targ 2005, pp. 127–134.

demand for this product. In the next decade, the routes extended to reach Italy and Yugoslavia.[468]

Tourism discovered Zakopane and the Podhale region in the 1870s, becoming an important engine of change. In a few decades, Zakopane was turned into the best known resort in Poland, a center of high culture, and a magnet for the intellectual elite. After the Second World War, Zakopane was able to maintain its position and consolidate it, especially after the events of 1956, when accelerated modernization boosted demand for recreational activities. When the state was unable to meet this demand, the private sector seized the opportunity and quickly outdid, usually in an unofficial manner, the sluggish state infrastructure, overloaded with regulations. In Zakopane, private money reserves were put to good use and invested in the development of a tourist empire, practically independent from the state and extremely profitable. The privatization of the state in the winter capital of Poland went so far that, in the words of a statement of the Party commission dispatched to Zakopane in 1972, "the state in Zakopane was put in a position much worse than it would have been in capitalism; it was sidelined to the position of not even janitor but to that of an unpaid crossing guard or street sweeper."[469]

From the 1960s onward, each year some 2.5 million tourists visited Zakopane and nearby villages; they all required food, shelter, transportation, and entertainment and successfully supported if not forced the development of local black market strategies. Investment in tourist infrastructure yielded between 20% and 35% profit on accommodation and 50% on catering. Under favorable conditions, the capital invested could be recovered within two to five years. In the 1960s, organized groups of private builders had already descended on Zakopane. They pressurized the highlanders, often aided and abetted by city officials, to sell their land, which the entrepreneurs later re-sold at much higher prices. The same groups tried to control the market for construction services. The building boom entailed a thriving development of the black market for building materials. They were often imported from distant regions of the country or even smuggled from abroad, from Czechoslovakia, Hungary or Yugoslavia.

In the early 1970s, illegal craft studios that manufactured souvenirs (local members of the intelligentsia commonly did some outwork to supplement their income) had a revenue perhaps as much as ten times higher than the profits

468 See chapter 9.

469 Large fragments of the report were published in: *Socjalizm na halach...*, pp. 80–96, p. 89; original: AAN, KC PZPR, XI/564, fol. 212–279.

(some 37 million zloty) of the 700 registered private enterprises. The necessity to provide food for the tourists led to the development of usually illegal strategies of acquiring products that were hard to get (such as meat) and boosted the illegal distilling and sale of alcohol. "There are streets in Zakopane," the 1972 Party report continued, "where in every second house, there is an illegal joint selling alcohol (it seems Zakopane has the highest alcohol consumption rate in the country, because, as the locals put it, 'It's an exceptionally good place to have a drink.'"[470]

The real gold mine, however, was the hard currency trade. According to estimates, Zakopane residents and its 180 local "professional" hard currency dealers, as well as some 250 dealers visiting from different parts of Poland and another 450 dealers from abroad were jointly able to turn over 16 million dollars in total annually. In a year, foreign tourists left between two and three million dollars in the town. Of some 400 000 foreigners annually, only 10% (including the 40 000 from the capitalist states) availed themselves of the accommodation provided by the state; the overwhelming majority opted for private rooms or houses where they paid the rent in hard currency (or goods) at an exchange rate favorable for both parties. In the late 1950s, when the borders regulations between the member countries of the Soviet Bloc countries were relaxed to a certain extent, Zakopane became a vacation favorite for tourists from Czechoslovakia, Hungary and the GDR. There, they could find vacation options different from those offered by standard holiday resorts and free from state control.[471] In the summer of 1970, the acclaimed opposition writer and journalist Stefan Kisielewski commented on the tourist situation in Zakopane: "there is a lot of Germans from the GDR, Czechs, Hungarians, even Russians. I don't know how they can afford it here [...], they must have their own calculations, if they come here in such numbers."[472]

Podhale took advantage of the heavy traffic at the main southern border crossing. In 1968, for example, some 900 000 people crossed the border at Łysa Polana.[473] High demand in Poland for Soviet Bloc currencies,[474] favorable exchange rates, and easy access made this region an attractive destination for Soviet Bloc citizens. In the 1970s, the Thursday market in Nowy Targ turned into a

---

470 *Socjalizm na halach...*, p. 81.

471 For example in 1971, the Hungarians opened a winter bus route between Budapest and Zakopane, in the summer extended to Kraków (via Zakopane); AAN, Główny Komitet Kultury Fizycznej I Turystyki (GKKFiT), 16/93, fol. 6.

472 S. Kisielewski, *Dzienniki*, Warszawa 1998, p. 427.

473 APKr, KW PZPR, 293, fol. 244, 257.

474 See chapter dedicated to hard currencies and gold.

currency exchange hub thanks to some 30 000 Czechs, Slovaks, Hungarians, Bulgarians, Yugoslavia citizens, and GDR Germans who visited in high season. The visitors brought money, exchanged it at the black market rate and went shopping (for food, textiles, auto parts, sport equipment, and radio and TV sets) at very attractive prices.[475]

The Party commission report from 1972 offered a relatively reliable estimate of the profits of the Zakopane second economy. The annual revenue that flowed to Zakopane from vacation rentals, food industry, transportation, trade (including hard currency), and prostitution reached the dizzy heights of over one billion zloty – the equivalent of state investment in the infrastructure of Zakopane in the entire decade of the 1960s! The magnitude of this income stream certainly had an impact on local government structures – an important part of this quasi-capitalist machine. The informal groups that had formed around particular interests and were actively involved in their implementation had a key role in Podhale. The financial means at their disposal were such that the problem tended to be not "how can we afford to bribe him?" but rather "why won't he take the bribe?" These groups effectively corrupted members of the Party apparatus, city clerks, tax collectors, and police and prosecution officials. As a result, the Party and state authority was "delivered through direct contacts between the first secretary of the PUWP Municipal Committee and the directors of the enterprises and managers of various institutions and agencies." This "directorial group" was the proper, or indeed the ultimate authority. Having spent several years in the Party apparatus, lower-level administration employees would move on to lucrative posts such as resort managers. The distinction between the state and private ownership as well as between legal and illegal operations became even more blurred.

Unfortunately, no academic analysis of the "underground" Zakopane of the 1970s and 1980s exists. We can safely assume that the attempts of the authorities, mostly in the 1970s, to force the owners of private rentals to use the state agencies and to obey the building by-laws altered only minimally the existing structure of power. What they certainly did achieve was to trigger new accommodative strategies. In December 1975, a report on implementing the government's resolution suggested that the "dynamic increase in tourist numbers […] calls for a program that would reign in this phenomenon and foster conditions to control it fully."[476] There is also a paucity of primary sources recording "the war on speculation"

475 W. Markiewicz, *Przyjedź pan w lipcu…*, ŻW, no. 101/ April 20, 1976; see: T. Robak, *Miasto przy przystanku*, "Polityka" no. 62 / October 14, 1972.

476 AAN, GKKFiT, 11/45, fol. 66.

waged in the Nowy Sącz voivodship in the 1980s.[477] However, careful scrutiny of the contemporary Podhale and Zakopane can teach us a thing or two about how old practices can be adapted to new circumstances.[478]

4.3.2 The North: "The Land Fills Your Belly, the Sea Fills Your Pockets"[479]

In socialist Poland, this aphorism was true also in the context of the black market. The size of the second economy on the Baltic coast was comparable with the Podhale region's black market, even though the objects of trade and the local environment were different. Port cities tend to evolve characteristic economic, cultural, and social structures. In comparison with traditional, conservative, highland communities – culturally homogenous and static, the populations of port cities are usually dynamic, open to the outside world, and creative, as well as multicultural and multi-ethnic.[480] They are more open to modernization. New models of behavior that come in from the outside thick and fast are absorbed with ease. While emigration is often a part of highlanders' experience, coastal communities are open to the reverse phenomenon – immigration. The characteristics of port cities influence their social structure and the behavior of their residents. Pre-modern bonds (such as in the extended families of the highlanders) are less important than the modern factors that exist outside a family, work or place of residence.

---

477 AAN, URM, 32/22.

478 For New Year's Eve 2007/2008, Zakopane had the capacity to host 50–100 000 visitors, of which, however, only 22 000 beds were available as legal tourist accommodation. The others slept in beds that belonged to the gray market; http://www.turinfo.pl/p/ak_id,22478,,zakopane,w_zakopanem,tatry,sylwester,noclegi,miejsca_noclegowe,dziennik_polski.html (March 8, 2014). Supply follows demand often in the shape of building without permits. A regional weekly wrote about the illegal construction of a 62-room hotel. Official decisions ordering demolition were rarely respected; "Tygodnik Podhalański" April 9, 2005; February 3, 2007.

479 On this topic I wrote also in: *"Ziemia żywi, morze bogaci". Strategie czarnorynkowe w polskich miastach portowych 1945–1989*, in: *Morze nasze i nie nasze. Zbiór studiów*, ed. P. Kurpiewski, T. Stegner, Gdańsk 2011, pp. 229–240.

480 See: I. Jakimowicz-Ostrowska, *Mniejszości narodowe w Gdyni w latach 1944–2005*, Gdynia 2008; *Tożsamość kulturowa. Szkice o mniejszościach narodowych na Pomorzu Gdańskim. Series 2*, ed. A. Chodubski, A.K. Waśkiewicz, Gdańsk 2002; *W starej i nowej ojczyźnie. Mniejszości narodowe w Gdańsku po II wojnie światowej*, ed. I. Hałagida, Gdańsk 1997.

Initially, Gdynia stood out among the port cities of post-war Poland. Less destroyed than Gdańsk, subject to fewer restrictions than Szczecin, which for many years after the war was more of a Soviet than a Polish port, Gdynia was able to retain some of its pre-war residents, including the entrepreneurs. Soon, it became a Polish window to the world. This happened thanks to the private and coop owned businesses, whose participation in total trade was initially greater than that of the state owned enterprises. Already in the 1940s, trade in Gdynia had re-attained its pre-war level. Because of the importance of foreign trade to the Polish economy, the authorities looked favorably on the operations of Gdynia's private sector. In Gdynia, it had existed longer than anywhere else in Poland. There is no doubt, even if it is difficult to find conclusive source evidence, that the uninterrupted long-term settlement and ability to maintain the pre-war tradition of creativity and entrepreneurship had an impact on the behavior of Gdynia's inhabitants, and their willingness to engage in black market activities.

Newcomers searching for work in Gdynia during the interwar period, even those unfamiliar with port cities, instantly adapted to what the city had to offer; by the end of the 1930s, a high proportion of them identified with Gdynia.[481] A similar phenomenon was apparent in Szczecin, Świnoujście and Gdańsk, where after 1945, the population was almost entirely displaced by new settlers, attracted by the proximity of the sea, with the opportunities and advantages that it provided. According to estimates from early 1984, "during the interwar period and especially after the war, large population cohorts arrived in the Gdańsk voivodship from various regions of Poland […].The newcomers usually settled in greater Gdańsk. They were often young, dynamic, and looking for a new and easier way of life as well as demanding rapid social and professional advancement. These large migrations fundamentally changed the population structure in the voivodship. People between the ages of 15 to 25 constitute more than 30% of people of working age, and 50% of all employed have post-primary education […]. The numerous residents employed in international transportation, fishing, and foreign trade enjoy the additional lucrative proceeds of price differentials and currency parity. These people have substantial financial reserves and accept the petty bourgeois system of values, treating money as a fetish, and are under the influence of social-democratic and clerical ideology."[482]

---

481 In 1936, there were 31% of Gdynia residents under the age of thirty, 17% owned a business, and 33% were employed in industry and crafts.

482 AAN, KC PZPR, WA, LI/3, fol. 4. See: M. Gulda, *Struktura i ruchliwość społeczna Trójmiasta w świadomości jego mieszkańców. Studium socjologiczne*, Gdańsk 1980; I. Sobczak, *Obraz demograficzny województw nadmorskich Polski w latach 1946–1990.*

The factor that spurred on the black market in Polish port cities was not so much tourism, as was the case with Zakopane, but a multi-layered "seafaring" factor. The opening of the ports in Gdynia and Gdańsk in mid-July 1945, and later also in Szczecin, set in motion an unofficial flow of goods and money that even Stalinism could not stop. The port cities opened up a crack in the Iron Curtain wider than usually appreciated (and certainly wider than anywhere else in Poland). Regardless of the international situation, Polish ships sailed west and Western ships entered Polish ports. Until 1952, Western seamen, often from the Netherlands, worked on Polish fishing vessels. During Stalinism, the Polish fishing fleet had at its disposal permanent bases in the ports of Western Europe, for example in Ostend and Cuxhaven. Ship operators from Gdynia or Szczecin tried at all costs to maintain permanent trade connections with capitalist countries and create new ones (for example in 1953, between Szczecin and the Finnish ports). The first Polish Baltic ferry, Gdynia–Trelleborg, began to operate in April 1946. A real boom in passenger and freight traffic began at the turn of the 1960s and the 1970s. The new ferry connections with the Scandinavian countries were crucial in the development of black market phenomena, in which not only Poles but also Germans, Danes, Swedes or Finns were involved.[483] The Polish marine navy was often ironically referred to as "merchandise" rather than "merchant", but crews from other countries did not refrain from smuggling, either.[484]

Ships were capacious enough to conceal even a very large amount of contraband and the perspicacity of the custom officers often could not keep up with the ingenuity of the crew members. To start with, there were not enough customs officers, and at first, their equipment was modest, or non-existent. For example in late 1946, the Polish customs on the Baltic coast did not have a single motor boat[485] or enough time to inspect each ship thoroughly. Sometimes the contraband was picked up outside of a port, in the open sea with the help of fishing or leisure

Wybrane liczby i tendencje rozwoju, Gdańsk 1992; I. Sobczak, *Procesy demograficzne w województwie gdańskim w latach 1945–1965*, Gdańsk 1970.

483 On the development of sea transport and communication, see: W.G. Strąk, *Kronika Polski na morzu 1918–1989*, Warszawa–Olsztyn 1996; see also: R. Górniak, *Most promowy między Polską i Szwecją*, Wiadomości Celne (WC), 1973, no. 8, pp. 19–21.

484 HIM, Pressearchiv, P 6211, Item 3691/58, Soviet goods smuggled into Poland. In the late 1950s, there were cases of entire ship crews, complete with the captain, conducting smuggling operations. For instance, the entire crew of the Curie Skłodowska "was discharged […] for smuggling pepper and selling it in Rotterdam port." AAN, KC PZPR, 327/XXXII-8, fol. 47.

485 AAN, URM, 5/639, fol. 2–4, 7.

boats.[486] The smuggling network comprised seafarers, fishermen, longshoremen and – surprisingly frequently – also custom officers, whose official wages were never very high, which gave them an incentive to augment them by extramural activities.

Port warehouses were vulnerable to theft. All attractive items such as textiles, wool, plastics, alcohol, cigarettes, citrus fruits, canned food, leather, non-ferrous metals, and auto parts went missing on a daily basis. In the late 1950s, in Gdynia alone, ten thousand cases of theft were recorded annually.[487] Local port authorities and local police were not keen to intervene and tended to turn a blind eye. On the one hand, longshoremen all over the world considered theft a part of their rightfully earned wages,[488] on the other – "brazen accumulation of wealth by seamen in a relatively short time creates a glaring disparity in the material circumstances of different strata of the working class". For the authorities to give the longshoremen a chance to make extra money constituted a peculiar form of bonus, and contributed to maintaining social peace.[489] The introduction of containers limited the opportunities for theft but did not eliminate them.

While theft was by nature a crime of opportunity, trading by seafarers was a goal-oriented activity geared towards achieving the highest gains possible. It required flexibility and a good knowledge of the market, as well as efficient co-operation of the crew.[490] Good reconnaissance and preparation could yield truly enormous profits. The crew of the cargo ship *Kopalnia Wirek* proved this when they brought a ton of garlic from Spain. On selling it, for an outlay of one dollar – at that time worth 100 zloty on the black market – they gained 3 100 zloty.[491] Gold smuggling was also lucrative during the post-war period. However, the precious-metals branch of the second economy required not only large-scale capital investment but also entailed high risk, so the majority of seamen and fishermen limited their operations to smuggling goods, focusing on what sold well at any particular time. In the 1950s and 1960s, artificial jewelry was the bestseller;

486 AIPN, 01521/784, Stanisław Banaszek, Marian Czerepiński, *Przestępstwa przemytnicze i zasady ich zwalczania*, Warszawa 1969, Wydawnictwo WOP, pp. 95–96.

487 AAN, MS, 558, fol. 169.

488 E. Smithies, *The Black Economy in England since 1914*, Dublin 1984, pp. 78, 132.

489 AAN, MS, 558, fol. 173.

490 "In legal importation by seafarers, collective forms such as shared money or shared profits, often take precedence. The myth of Polish individualism has been shaken". J. Koźliński, K.W. Olszewski, *Dwie stopy na złotym wybrzeżu*, "Kierunki", no. 36/ September 8, 1957.

491 AAN, KC PZPR, XII/1795, fol. 56.

between 1956 and 1960 – beauty products, especially lipstick, were popular. Between 1955 and 1966, watches were in high demand and between 1960 and 1965 – clothing (for example nylon raincoats).[492] Smuggling on a mass scale of electronic watches and mini calculators came into vogue in the early 1970s. The goods – from gold and watches to wigs and chewing gum – were supplied by specialized firms usually managed by Polish emigrants and located in ports of Western Europe such as Hamburg, Kiel or Rotterdam.[493]

Although customs duties on private imports diminished their profitability, some of the time the seafarers declared part of the incoming cargo to the customs; this usually occurred when they expected the duties to be not too high and the profits to be worthwhile, or when the size of the cargo made a clandestine transfer ashore unviable. However, most of the goods were probably undeclared to the customs and remained concealed. We do not have reliable tools to gauge the proportion of goods that remained undeclared, but a comparison of Central Customs Office (GUC) data with the volume of wholesale purchases of foreign articles by the state institutions provides an insight (see Table 2).

The regulations, from the late 1950s onward increasingly liberal, made operations easier. "A special instruction says," a journalist from *Trybuna Ludu* commented in 1960, "that it is only forbidden to purchase goods from people who are intoxicated or show visible signs of mental illness, and the third clause says the delivered goods must not bear any indication of having been stolen."[494] Transactions of up to six thousand zloty in value could be carried out anonymously. For higher amounts, the wholesalers had to show their ID, but this was not a problem, because "in port cities there was an army of touts and patsies willing – for a fee – to 'lend' their ID to help close a transaction. Wholesale depot managers are fully aware of this practice but they ignore it because they get paid and receive bonuses only if the official targets have been met."[495] It is important to emphasize that

492 *Uwagi dotyczące rozmiarów i metod przemytu w ruchu morskim*, WC, 1970, no. 1, pp. 14–15. Brokerage between foreign ports increased profits. For example in 1967, the crew of the Boruta bought nylon raincoats on the Kiel Canal and sold them in Klaipeda, with the hard currency proceeds buying goods in high demand in Poland, such as gold; "Biuletyn Szkoleniowy" GUC, no. 37, July 1967, pp. 43–44.

493 B. Piastowicz, *Marynarz wciąż się bawi*, "Biuletyn Szkoleniowy" GUC, no. 41, April 1969, pp. 1–6. Seafarers often delivered hard currency to middlemen and addresses where the goods were to be sent; J. Olszewski, *Waluciarze i przemytnicy*, TL, no. 129/ May 9, 1971.

494 *O przemycie portowym bez osłonek*, TL, no. 250/September 8, 1960.

495 *Ibid.*

we are only able to consider articles that had gone through the commercial and bureaucratic apparatus of the state. It is difficult to estimate the volume sold via private channels outside of any control apparatus, both in Poland[496] and abroad. We can assume that the crews of Polish ships met a large part of the demand for chewing gum in Czechoslovakia (in the late 1950s) and for wigs and jeans in the Soviet Union (a decade later).

Table 2. Foreign goods from private imports 1959–1961

Year	Article	Purchased by *komis* stores		Duty paid	
		Number	Value in zloty	Number	Value in zloty
1959	Fountain pens	13 347	1 775 910	70	9 800
1960	Fountain pens	5 999	479 920	138	11 040
1959	Watches	6 735	11 448 100	1	1 700
1960	Watches	12 158	15 825 250	5	7 500
1959	Nylons	9 291	1 319 460	373	52 966
1960	Nylons	19 430	1 578 307	1 089	108 900

Source: AAN, NIK II, 19/46, fol. 36.

Before the crisis of 1981 emptied all the shelves in Polish stores, private import arriving through Baltic ports had played a supplementary role on the Polish market, delivering articles commonly considered as luxury goods. However, after the state channels of distribution had failed completely, it became one of the most important sources of supply (for example of cosmetics). In mid-1981, the situation was so catastrophic that on July 15, the customs import duties on the majority of goods were abolished. The decision of the Gdańsk and Szczecin voivods to relieve state-owned warehouses of the obligation to prove the identity of suppliers of foreign articles gave a new impetus to private importers. Before the tax authorities realized that as a result of the new regulations the state treasury was suffering great losses, the private importers managed to make fortunes in Szczecin and the Tri-City. Just in the period August 1 to November 20, 1981,

496 A copious supply of foreign articles on the Baltic coast lowered their prices in comparison to the rest of Poland. "A shop owner from the coast who does not have his own car (and there are not many of them) takes a taxi, if he wants to go to Lublin, Rzeszów or Zamość. There, he can sell to a state-owned store for 24 zloty the Kiwi shoe polish, which is in abundance on the coast, where it can be bought for 16 zloty a box." J. Koźliński, K.W. Olszewski, *Dwie stopy na złotym wybrzeżu*, "Kierunki", no. 36/September 8, 1957.

state institutions in Szczecin bought cosmetics worth 300 million zloty and in the Tri-City – over 180 million zloty. A later investigation showed that private merchants had imported a staggering volume of goods. For example an "unemployed" man from Rumia near the port of Gdynia imported from Sweden 9 600 kg of washing machine detergent and 2 300 kg of soap; a bartender on a Polish ferry bought, also in Sweden and in October 1981 alone, 2 750 liters of shampoo. The calculation showed that at least 200 thousand dollars must have left Szczecin in order to buy cosmetics alone.[497]

Naturally, the goods arriving in Polish ports through private channels had been purchased for hard currency, whether illegal or not. Since the government recognized the fact that a Polish wage would not go far even in the humblest canteens of exotic ports all over the world, Polish merchant seafarers received a hard currency allowance on top of their wages. These allowances were, however, only a drop in the ocean of need. For example in 1964, seafarers were paid a "hard currency supplement" of 1 369 000 dollars. Some of this they could, and did, spend in state-run dollar stores, such as the Baltona chain; after this "official" shopping, a healthy surplus of 1 080 000 dollars still remained in the pockets of merchant seafarers and fishermen. In the same year, various warehouses – officially! – bought from seafarers goods worth 465 million zloty (285 million in Szczecin, and the rest in the Tri-City). This was four times as much as seafarers' dollar earnings even if calculated at the black market exchange rate – much higher than the official one.[498] What accounted for the difference was the smuggling out of goods or – even more frequently, since it was easier to accomplish – of hard currency.[499] Strategies to acquire hard currency had been developing on the Baltic coast since 1945. They were driven by the huge differential between the

497 AAN, URM, 32/113, fol. 249; *ibid.*, 21/185, fol. 1–2.

498 S. Sumiga, *Szkodzą dobremu imieniu ogółu*, "Tygodnik Morski" 1965, no. 7. In Szczecin in 1962, the value of total purchases of foreign goods amounted to 140 million. At the same time, foreign currency earnings of seafarers and fishermen in Szczecin were only 11 million "foreign exchange zloty" (the so-called *złoty dewizowy*, a unit used as an artificial currency for calculation purposes only); B. Karski, *Przemyt w majestacie prawa*, PiŻ, 1963, no. 14.

499 In 1950, the Customs Office in Gdynia initiated 29 proceedings in hard currency smuggling cases, in 1965 – 195, in 1970 – 217, and in 1975 – 405. E. Graban, *Niektóre aspekty powstania i funkcjonowania Urzędu Celnego w Gdyni*, in: *Korzenie Gdyni*, part 4: *Mała stabilizacja. Materiały z konferencji historycznej 22 września 2004 r.*, Gdynia 2004, p. 29.

official and black market exchange rates[500] that persisted in post-war Poland and deterred visitors and seafarers from using banks and official hard currency agencies, where the rates offered were quite unattractive. In September 1945 (according to the data from November 1946) of the twenty institutions operating from Szczecin to Gdańsk and authorized to buy hard currency, twelve did not record any transaction due to a "lack of any offers". Similarly, the majority of the hard currency recovered for the state by the Treasury Protection Brigades (Brygady Ochrony Skarbowej) came from confiscations from currency dealers rather than purchases.[501] Prostitution, which targeted foreign visitors, also brought in large quantities of foreign money. According to police records, in the early 1970s more than 1 220 prostitutes were registered in the Tri-City, of which 700 in Gdańsk alone.[502] It is difficult to estimate the number of currency traders (the previously mentioned *cinkciarze*) that operated in restaurants and hotels in the Tri-City, Szczecin and Świnoujście.[503] One thing is certain: the demand for hard currency on the Baltic coast vastly exceeded the quantities of dollars, marks or crowns that the dealers and the prostitutes could supply. The goods taken to Lublin or Przemyśl were sold there for hard currency, the currency obtained then "imported" back to the coast. According to police records, the hard currency gangs of the coast had "their agents everywhere in Poland – in Warsaw, Kraków, Wrocław, in Silesia, and in the Sub-Carpathian region. They [bought] dollars there and [took] them back to the Baltic coast."[504]

The infamous "December 1970" brought protests, sparked mainly on the coast in Gdańsk, Gdynia and Szczecin by a sudden increase in the price of food and other everyday items. The riots were extinguished by the Polish People's Army and the police (MO), with at least 42 people killed and more than 1 000 wounded. In the wake of the riots, the authorities examined thoroughly all aspects of political and social life in the Gdańsk voivodship.[505] The analysis showed the mechanism by which black market phenomena influenced the behavior of the local

500 For example, in the fall of 1946, the US dollar officially cost 100 zl while on the black market its price was between 900 and 1 000. The British pound cost, respectively, 397 and approx.1 500, the Swedish crown – 25 and 150 zloty.

501 AAN, URM, 5/639, fol. 2–4.

502 J. Oleksiewicz, *"Miłość" w portowym mieście*, "Express Poznański", 1973, no. 217; AAN, KC PZPR, XII/1795, fol. 57.

503 According to police sources, in 1971, approx. 500 currency traders operated in the Tri-City J. Olszewski, *Waluciarze i przemytnicy*, TL, no. 129/May 9, 1971.

504 *Ibid.*

505 AAN, KC PZPR, XII/1795, fol. 1–59.

population. In Zakopane the profits were usually invested in tourist infrastructure, on the Baltic coast in private (legal or otherwise) production and trade. As a result, in the 1960s, the private sector on the Baltic coast was much more dynamic than the state sector, for obvious reasons: wages paid by private manufacturers, artisans and merchants were much higher.[506] Most of the artisan workshops in Poland were in private ownership. In the Gdańsk voivodship, especially in the Tri-City, the private sector was dominant in trade (50% of all outlets) and catering (60% of outlets). In private manufacturing, the fastest growing branches of industry were those based on new technologies, such as the chemical sector.[507] This can be attributed to the regional connections with the West, closer than elsewhere in Poland, and to the importation of raw materials and equipment by seamen.[508] Already in the late 1960s, almost a quarter of private industrial and artisan production was exported, mostly to the capitalist countries, which shows how innovative Gdańsk businessmen were. In 1970 alone, private exports grew by 240%.[509]

While residents of the Podhale region, afraid of entrusting their money to the state, had for a long time preferred to put their money under the proverbial mattress, the financial elite in the Tri-City commonly used modern savings instruments. High-rate term accounts and "automobile saving accounts" constituted only 10% of all bank accounts but accumulated half of all deposits in the Gdańsk voivodship (over three billion zloty). The fastest growing accounts (threefold growth between 1965 and 1970) were the anonymous saving accounts, used as safe currency in large-scale transactions. "It seems that many deposits on those accounts come from hidden, untaxed income from private enterprise and illegal machinations. Such accounts make black market trading much easier."[510]

A large proportion of the profits acquired from illegal hard currency smuggling as well as legal private enterprise operations (all, as the tax authorities claimed,

---

506 *Ibid.*, fol. 46.

507 *Ibid.*, fol. 53.

508 Between July 1 and December 31, 197, the Customs Office in Gdynia examined duty-paid goods brought in by seafarers on 13 ships. Customs officers paid particular attention to articles destined for the private services and production markets: 387 sets of false eyelashes, 3.2 kg fake nails, 253.4 kg artificial leather, 62.4 kg plastic foil, 2567.12 kg artificial fur, 4 935.23 kg Crimplene, 705.97 kg of laminate, and 391.2 kg of jersey fabric. The 1 418.3 kg of wigs found were probably destined for "re-export" to the Soviet Union; AAN, GUC, 30/78, k. 1–14. Cf. Archiwum Państwowe w Gdańsku, Oddział w Gdyni, Komitet Miejski PZPR w Gdyni, 325/307, fol. 55–68.

509 AAN, KC PZPR, XII/1795, k. 54.

510 *Ibid.*, fol. 50.

deeply rooted in the grey market) was invested in residential construction for own need, as in the Podhale region. Private investors financed 26% of all residential dwellings built between 1956 and 1969; these "utilized, probably not always legally, a quarter of building materials and potential."[511] In 1969, the usable floor area of an average apartment built by the state was 42.6m^2 and of those built privately – 93m^2. In the same year, 30% of private single-family houses and 70% of private apartments were constructed in large cities; this was "in blatant contrast to the 'dwelling hunger' among employees of the nationalized economy, especially the workers."[512]

The authors of the analysis were probably right in saying that "there exists a close link and interdependency [...] of criminal phenomena involving hard currency. Seafarers are exposed to regular contacts with the 'western way of living', the existence of substantial private wealth on the Baltic coast, and the demoralizing influence that this way of life has [...] on certain groups of young people, especially workers on the lowest wages. This influence manifests itself by involving some of them in this kind of life for example as currency traders, which elicits among some workers strong feelings of hatred towards the world of wealth and resentment towards the authorities who tolerate such a state of affairs. These factors all played some role in the December events [of 1970]."[513]

4.4 East–West

The 1980s were the twilight of the golden era of trading by seafarers. The economic crisis and Martial Law diminished both sea traffic and the volume of foreign trade. More seamen than ever before were waiting to be signed up, and once they got the job, were anxious to keep it. Mariners lost their privileged position as monopolists. Large volumes of goods now arrived in Poland directly from Turkey, India and the Far East, brought in by private tourist importers, usually by air. Seafarers now focused on the, often arcane, trading operations between foreign ports, and continued to be a conduit of bringing hard currency to Poland.[514] Amateur outsiders filled in the gap in the market vacated by the seafarers, and smuggled goods including alcohol, bed linen, and food as well as various knick-knacks on

511 *Ibid.*, fol. 55.

512 *Ibid.*

513 *Ibid.*, fol. 57.

514 M. Olszewski, *Przestępczość celna i graniczna dewizowa w 1987 r.*, WC, 1988, no. 41, p. 23. Seafarers continued to engage in smuggling. On May 26, 1986, for example, 900 linear meters of Madeira cotton were found (in the captain's cabin!) aboard the Gorce, arriving from Holland; AAN, KC PZPR, WA, 541, 1985, fol. 3v.

ferries arriving from Sweden, Denmark and Finland. In the mid-1980s, travel agencies began to organize short ferry trips to Scandinavian countries, without even bothering to conceal their commercial goal.[515] A similar process of "domesticating" the cross-border black market took place on the western and eastern borders of the country, along, respectively, the Oder and the Bug rivers.

While the southern and northern borders of Poland largely retained their pre-war shape, the eastern and western borders had been completely re-drawn after the war; this had political, social, and economic consequences. The rivers Oder, Lusatian Neisse and Bug now flowed through, and divided, previously cohesive territories. After the end of the war, the more complicated the everyday relations between communities on either side of the rivers (as in the divided cities on the Oder and the Neisse[516]) became, the more the practical aspects of life dominated the political imponderables. Despite being in different countries, the riverside communities (more so in the west than in the east) remained parts of a self-regulating system for some time after the war.[517] This phenomenon was reinforced by the presence of the remaining original local population unwilling to accept the political and geographical changes. Forced and voluntary mass-scale migrations effectively prolonged the chaos (which facilitated black market operations) and made impossible any efforts to control effectively the new borders. Corruption thrived along the Oder and the Bug rivers. While in the east it was often triggered simply by the will to survive – and to bribe guards or ticket collectors could shorten a lengthy journey or improve its conditions – in the west, the usual incentive was an opportunity to make big money. Industrial products,

---

515 AAN, KC PZPR, LII/127, fol. 29.

516 For example in Zgorzelec/Görlitz, the gasworks remained on the Polish side and the power and water plants – on the German side. Słubice (the former Frankfurt-an-der-Oder suburb of Dammvorstadt), where the first bank opened as early as 1945 but the pharmacy not until 1952,was a town completely dependent on Frankfurt-an-der-Oder, today known as Frankfurt (Oder). In Gubin, the gasworks, slaughterhouse, and railroad station were on the German side, Guben. The water supply of Świnoujście (formerly Swinemünde) came from the German side. See: D. Jajeśniak-Quast, K. Stokłosa, *Geteilte Städte an Oder und Neiße. Frankfurt (Oder) – Słubice, Guben–Gubin und Görlitz–Zgorzelec 1945–1995*, Berlin 2000; K. Stokłosa, *Grenzstädte in Ostmitteleuropa. Guben und Gubin 1945 bis 1995*, Berlin 2003; J. Kochanowski, *Zanim powstała NRD. Polska wobec radzieckiej strefy okupacyjnej Niemiec 1945–1949*, Wrocław 2008.

517 J. Kochanowski, *"Naczynia połączone". Nieoficjalne kontakty ekonomiczne pomiędzy obywatelami radzieckiej strefy okupacyjnej/NRD i Polski w latach 1945–1989*, in: *RFN-NRD-PRL. Zbliżenia*, ed. K. Ruchniewicz, D. Wojtaszyn, Wrocław 2014, pp. 107–117.

cars, currencies, and gold were smuggled out of Germany; large amounts of food, especially fats, not to mention people, were smuggled from Poland.

During the chaotic post-war years, even state institutions, including the Ministry of Public Security, participated in black market operations.[518] The Chief of the Polish Military Mission in Berlin, Jakub Prawin, reported in late January 1946: "In Berlin there are numerous Poles, who are involved in loitering and speculation on black markets; there are even incidents of robbery. A certain German black marketeer came to me complaining that he had been robbed by a Pole, who was wearing the uniform of a captain. People arrive, even for business trips, without visas, sometimes without passports."[519]

The stiffening of the passport regulations in 1946 limited illegal travel from the interior of the country but did not mean much for the borderland residents who could always find a weak spot even along the best-guarded border. Geographical conditions facilitated illegal border crossing; low morale and modest wages made the guards more open to accepting bribes.[520] Polish and German railroad workers successfully smuggled goods (and people).[521] They also took business advantage of the transports of displaced Germans, where supervision was haphazard.[522] As long as the divided border cities were dependent on each other and German workers worked in Polish factories and mines, the smuggling thrived.[523]

---

518 J. Kochanowski, *W polskiej niewoli. Niemieccy jeńcy wojenni w Polsce 1945–1950*, Warszawa 2001, p. 53.

519 Ministry of Foreign Affairs Archive (Archiwum Ministerstwa Spraw Zagranicznych, AMSZ), z. 6, w. 42, vol. 671, PMW, Report no. 2, January 27, 1946, fol. 17. See: *Polska – Niemcy Wschodnie 1945–1990. Wybór dokumentów*, ed. J. Kochanowski, K. Ziemer, vol. 1: *Polska wobec radzieckiej strefy okupacyjnej Niemiec: maj 1945 – październik 1949*, ed. J. Kochanowski, doc. ed. A. Krajewski, M. Mazurek, Warszawa 2006, pp. 90–91. At least up until the end of 1945, despite the robust passport regulations in force at the time, corrupt border guards allowed to cross the border anyone, who had any kind of permit or authorization issued by any number of, not always official, institutions (such as for example the "Warsaw Cafe" in Wałbrzych, the Polish Western Union in Toruń or the Polish Red Cross in Chełmno); K. Stokłosa, Grenzstädte […], p. 51; AAN, MZO, 132, Polska Misja Repatriacyjna w Berlinie do MAP, 13 XII 1945 (see: *Polska – Niemcy Wschodnie* […], vol. 1, pp. 78–81).

520 AMSZ, z. 6, w. 42, vol. 668, fol. 6 (see: *Polska – Niemcy Wschodnie* […], vol. 1, pp. 115–116).

521 Archiwum Państwowe w Szczecinie, Oddział w Gorzowie Wielkopolskim, Urząd Celny Kostrzyn, 6.

522 AMSZ, z. 6, w. 42, vol. 671, PMW, fol. 64.

523 Wrocław State Archive (Archiwum Państwowe we Wrocławiu, APWr), Voivodship Committee of the Polish Workers' Party (Komitet Wojewódzki Polskiej Partii

The high demand for animal fat in Germany, which local production could not meet, forced the Polish "exporters" to bring them even from remote places in Poland. For example, in mid-1947, in Zgorzelec and other border towns, packages with pork fat began to arrive, sent by mail from the Lublin region, and were later smuggled across the border. It was a profitable business: "In exchange for two kg of fat, the smugglers could buy a decent radio."[524] This practice reached such proportions that on June 30, 1948, the Polish Workers Party (PPR) committee issued a special circular: "The smuggler is the enemy of our heroic Nation! A smuggler is a spy! […] The well-being of our Democratic State and the security of our borders demand that we decry and destroy all smugglers and their helpers. Not one gram of fat will be allowed to leave our People's State."[525] Central authorities used the exhortation to fight the smuggling as one of the pretexts to close the border even for the petty border traffic. Although in the 1960s, the border on the Oder-Neisse was not entirely devoid of activity, and tourism (especially from the GDR to Poland) was growing slowly but steadily, it was only in January 1972 that the real turning point came.[526]

Traffic on the new eastern border came to a standstill even earlier than on the western border. From 1944 to 1946, there were still wide gaps in that border, which allowed into Poland, beside those coming as part of the official resettlement program, approximately 200 thousand additional people. These were Home Army soldiers who wanted to keep a low profile or peasants from Eastern Galicia and Volhynia running away from Ukrainian terror, as well as those from the Vilnius Region that did not want to wait any longer for official repatriation. It was much more difficult to cross this border in subsequent years, whether lawfully or otherwise. Black market phenomena similar to those at the Oder-Neisse border could not develop along the Bug, because on neither sides of the border with the Soviet Union did people have much to offer in the way of goods to be traded. The migrant population on both sides of the river focused their efforts rather on survival than on illegal, profitable transactions. They either wanted to sell personal belongings that they could not take to Poland, stock up on their food supply, and hide from border guards and robbers items not allowed across

Robotniczej, KW PPR), 196, Sprawozdanie Komitetu Powiatowego PPR Zgorzelec na miesiąc luty 1948 (see: *Polska – Niemcy Wschodnie* […], vol. 1, pp. 339–340).

524 AAN, Central Inspectorate of Treasury Protection (Główny Inspektorat Ochrony Skarbowej, GIOS), 117, unpag.

525 APWr, KW PPR, 162, fol. 95 (see: *Polska – Niemcy Wschodnie* […], vol. 1, pp. 339–340.

526 L. Koćwin, *Polityczne determinanty polsko-wschodnioniemieckich stosunków przygranicznych 1949–1990*, Wrocław 1993, pp. 20–29.

the border, or make sure that at least they took their religious objects with them when they set off to leave home.[527] Those who were returning from the interior of the Soviet Union did not usually have any personal possessions and required immediate assistance. The main phase of resettlement from the Soviet Union to Poland, as well as in the reverse direction, ended in late 1946 and thereafter "the friendship border" was friendly only in name. For the average citizen it was as difficult to get across as the Iron Curtain.[528]

Certainly, the eastern border of Poland was sealed better than the border on the Oder-Neisse. Even in the early 1950s, reports of successful smuggling operations and numerous clandestine escapes across the western border were quite frequent.[529] The Polish, German and Soviet boat crews sailing along the Oder largely eliminated the imbalance of supply to the two banks of the river. For example in the fall of 1951, "the citizen Maria Cyprys from Golszewice, in the county of Niemodlin, killed a hog weighing approximately 100 kg, handed the meat to the crew of a river boat run by German citizens on the Oder and in return received four tons of coal and a substantial supply of clothing fabric."[530]

Facing hunger brought on by the natural disasters of 1946 and 1947 – a severe winter and spring flooding, residents on both sides of the Bug realized there were hidden gateways also on the eastern border. In the spring of 1947, reports started circulating about "Soviet citizens [buying out grain], particularly in the Lublin, Kielce, and Łódź voivodships. For example, in the Lublin voivodship in Lubartów, Biała Podlaska, Kraśnik, Łęczna, and Włodawa, unknown Russian

527 Numerous examples in: *Przesiedlenie ludności polskiej z Kresów Wschodnich do Polski 1944–1947*, ed. S. Ciesielski, introd. W. Borodziej, S. Ciesielski, J. Kochanowski, Warszawa 1999. On the, often very dramatic, instances of transporting religious objects see: T. Kukiz, *Madonny Kresowe i inne obrazy sakralne z Kresów w diecezjach Polski*, Warszawa 2002 (and other works by this author).

528 On border closing, see: D. Stola, *Zamknięcie Polski. Zniesienie swobody wyjazdu i uszczelnienie granic w latach 40. i 50*, in: *PRL – trwanie i zmiana*, ed. D. Stola, M. Zaremba, Warszawa 2003, pp. 159–186.

529 Archiwum Instytutu Pamięci Narodowej, Oddział we Wrocławiu, Komenda Wojewódzka MO we Wrocławiu, 053/312, Sprawozdanie PUBP w Zgorzelcu za grudzień 1950 r.; *ibid.*, 053/216. Conducted in mid-1957, the "Counter-intelligence examination of the state border between Poland and the GDR" showed it could be easily "broken along its whole length"; *Polska – Niemcy Wschodnie 1945–1990. Wybór dokumentów*, ed. J. Kochanowski, K. Ziemer, vol. 3: *Lata 1956–1957*, ed. M. Górny, M.J. Hartwich, Warszawa 2008, pp. 369–384.

530 Trade Unions Archive (Archiwum Związków Zawodowych, AZZ), Wydział Ekonomiczny, 5/8.

speaking individuals arrived at the market place and bought all the grain – outbidding everybody else. On May 13, similar individuals purchased grain in Chełm Lubelski, paying 15 thousand zloty for 100 kg of rye and 20 thousand zloty for [100 kg] of wheat."[531]

The railroad, especially the transit connection between Germany and the Soviet Union, allowed for significant improvements in black market operations on the eastern and western borders. While Soviet ships entering Gdynia or Szczecin played an important role in maritime contraband traffic, it was railroad transport, mainly military, that had the same function on land. At the turn of the 1940s and 1950s, Soviet citizens, usually in uniform, constituted the majority of people crossing both the border on the Oder and that on the Bug. Convoys of supplies travelled both ways. They contained installations disassembled in Germany, war loot, war reparations, and demobilized as well as freshly conscripted soldiers.[532] Every time that the train stopped, its crew wasted no time in bonding with the locals. Kutno was an important east–west junction. "After the lecture [...], some of Kutno's residents came over to tell me about their town," Maria Dąbrowska noted in her diary on February 10, 1948. "Kutno is a center for trading German loot brought by Soviet military personnel. For pork fat, vodka, and spirits one can get radios, bicycles, silk, etc. They told me that they have a saying: 'Who knows not Kutno, knows not life.'"[533] As far as the experience of life based on illegal trade went, other towns on this route, including Warsaw, were not far behind Kutno.

Soviet convoys were always more difficult to inspect than all others, and, from 1947, arrest of their personnel became forbidden even if it had been established that smuggling had taken place. There is little wonder that there was always a place for contraband in a Soviet train's storage area.[534] Despite an agreement signed in the late 1950, which gave the Polish authorities more opportunities for inspection, the results were meager. A customs official from Rzepin remembered how "transit passenger and freight trains from the GDR to the Soviet Union and in the reverse direction were manned on the Frankfurt (Oder) – Brest (Brześć) route by GDR

531 AAN, GIOS, vol. 117.

532 In October and November 1952, eighty-two thousand entries and hundred and six thousand exits of Soviet citizens were noted in passport-free traffic. The mobility of Polish citizens was several dozen times less; D. Stola, *Zamknięcie* [...], p. 168.

533 M. Dąbrowska, *Dzienniki powojenne*, vol. 1: *1945–1949*, ed. T. Drewnowski, Warszawa 1997, p. 190.

534 "Smugglers," it was reported in 1950, "make hiding places in service cars, in steam engines and cargo cars. They bring from the city tens of kilos of goods set aside for smuggling and place them in the familiar hiding spots." AAN, GIOS, 123, fol. 223.

railroad employees. The crews engaged in large-scale smuggling on trains in both directions."[535] It is difficult to trust claims that smuggling operations decreased after Polish crews had replaced the German ones on transit trains. Such operations became rather more professional while cross-border private traffic, increasing after 1956, deprived the railroad workers of their monopoly position. There is no doubt that trains from the West continued for a long time to play a pivotal role in transporting "high value" contraband such as gold, watches, and currency. In the instructions for custom officials issued in 1958, the examples of hiding places for contraband to look out for were based on French or German rolling stock.[536] Some of the hiding places, especially those containing gold ruble coins, a favorite store of value for Soviet savers, were probably only searched once the train had reached the Soviet side of the border, and not any sooner.

The turning point came in 1956 when, thanks to the political thaw, former Polish citizens living in the Soviet Union could be resettled back home; by 1959, almost 250 000 people had returned to Poland. The Poles going home were aware they would have to rebuild their life from scratch and so tried to bring along any goods that would easily sell in Poland. In the Soviet Union, they bought radios, motorcycles, or even cars.[537] For the people released from labor camps and for the exiles, often not short of money but lacking lacking opportunities to invest it, the authorities arranged ad-hoc solutions. "Everywhere in railroad stations," Barbara Skarga remembered from her journey across the Soviet Union on a train full of former deportees, "we encounter hastily set up jewelry kiosks. We are allowed to take everything to Poland with us without paying any customs duty but we are not allowed to take rubles out. Any rubles that we have on us, we have to spend on something. Those who had cashed in a substantial number of bonds buy silver: rings, powder boxes, or cigarette cases. They are often in bad taste but the metal is of high quality."[538] Customs exemptions for personal effects facilitated the use of the repatriation process as a way of bringing in substantial

---

535 *Ibid.*; J. Kubzdyl, *Walczyłem z przemytem kolejowym*, WC, 1985, no. 37, p. 24.

536 *Album skrytek przemytniczych*, Warszawa 1958. For example, at the turn of 1964 and 1965, a group approximately 30-strong hid gold on a train and smuggled it between Paris and Moscow (they smuggled to West Germany 16 000 dollars, which they used to buy 457 twenty-dollar coins); AIPN, MSW II, 4370, fol. 26–27. See: J. Kubzdyl, *Walczyłem z przemytem…*; *Przemyt w ruchu osobowym*, WC, 1970, no. 1, pp. 23–24.

537 M. Ruchniewicz, *Repatriacja ludności polskiej z ZSRR w latach 1955–59*, Warszawa 2000, p. 265. For literary rendition see: M. Ławrynowicz, *Diabeł na dzwonnicy*, Warszawa 1998.

538 B. Skarga, *Po wyzwoleniu… (1944–1956)*, Kraków 2008, p. 294.

amounts of contraband, which often belonged to a different "investor" and not the actual re-settler. Those returning from the West used a similar strategy.[539] After 1956, tourists and visitors could cross the eastern border more easily and successful black market dealing was part-and-parcel of their trips. A real breakthrough came two decades later.

When, in the late 1940s, the borders were sealed, the volume of the small-scale black market operations conducted by railroad workers across the borders on the Oder and the Bug was not significant for the second economy of the borderlands. The image of the black market both in the South and that in the North began to change radically soon after 1956; the former – thanks to the local tourism and stable settlements on both sides of the border, whereas the latter benefited from the sea factor. However, the eastern and the western border areas required time and an external impulse to change. In the case of the western border, this happened quite abruptly on January 1, 1972 when the passage between Poland and the GDR opened for passport-free and visa-free traffic. Much has been written about this decision and its political consequences on both sides of the Oder-Neisse.[540] It allows us to focus here on the transformation of the borderland black market image. Naturally, residents living close to the bridges on the Oder and the Neisse rivers became the beneficiaries of the new situation. Until October 1980, when the border was closed again, they made up between a third to a half of all those visiting the neighboring country.

The sleepy towns on the Polish side of the border such as Zgorzelec, Słubice, Gubin, and Kostrzyn, all of a sudden found themselves much closer to Berlin or Dresden than to Warsaw or Poznań. In 1972, Hanna Krall wrote, "Słubice and Gubin became part of Europe literally overnight."[541] And overnight, Poles discovered the contents of the stores in the GDR. Mass buying alerted the government in East Berlin and forced it to introduce stricter customs inspections. In response to pressure from the GDR authorities, the Polish authorities limited the mark exchange allowance to 200 per month (by the regulation issued by the Governor of the Polish

---

539 HIM, Pressearchiv P 0141, RFE-Research, Item 914/57, Discontented Polish repatriates from France and USSR.

540 L. Koćwin, *Polityczne determinanty* […]; D. Jajeśniak-Quast, K. Stokłosa, *Geteilte Städte* […]; C. Osękowski, *Otwarta granica między NRD a Polską w latach siedemdziesiątych. Wymiar polityczny, gospodarczy i społeczny*, in: *Przyjaźń nakazana? Stosunki między NRD i Polską w latach 1949–1990*, ed. B. Kerski, A. Kotula, K. Wóycicki, Szczecin 2003.

541 H. Krall, *My patrzymy na Europę*, "Polityka", no. 38/September16, 1972.

National Bank on December 21, 1972).[542] Of course, this decision influenced the local black market situation. Border officials tended to treat more favorably the residents of border towns who frequently crossed the Oder–Neisse line. "Cottage manufacturers" from even remote regions of the country immediately took advantage of such leniency and began to hire Zgorzelec or Słubice residents, many of whom worked in the GDR, to carry small amounts of goods across the border. In the mid-1970s, "smuggling communities" developed in the border towns.[543]

Limiting the mark allowance for the Poles (from April 1974, to only 100 marks per three months) increased trafficking to the GDR of Polish goods in high demand on the other side of the border and made illegal money exchange flourish. GDR nationals were selling their currency because the unofficial transactions offered better rates but also because incompetent bureaucrats on both sides of the border made official exchange difficult. "In Słubice," a *Polityka* journalist wrote in 1977, "we observed how a mark exchange kiosk functions. A pleasant girl would mostly shake her head when asked by Germans whether they could exchange marks for zloty. This was not possible without official paperwork from their bank but very few people in the GDR were aware of this. Later, we saw the very same people offering their marks to exchange for zloty in various other places."[544]

There is no doubt that a significant number of the unofficial currency transactions were not spontaneous but planned well in advance, and expertly organized and executed,[545] since it was the currency trade rather than, say, shoe smuggling that yielded the real profit. People quickly realized that there was a healthy margin in buying GDR marks for western marks at locations close to West Berlin.[546]

---

542 See: M. Mazurek, *Antropologia niedoboru w NRD i PRL 1971–1989*, Wrocław 2010, pp. 30–60; J. Kochanowski, *Groźba nad NRD*, "Karta" 1999, no. 28, pp. 132–135; *Polskie dokumenty dyplomatyczne 1972*, ed. W. Borodziej and P. Długołęcki, Warszawa 2005, pp. 609–610, 634–635. See: K. Lenk, *Von Salamiwürsten und Salamanderschuhen. Schmuggel zwischen der DDR und der Volksrepublik Polen in den 1970er und 1980er Jahren*, Diplomarbeit an der Fakultät für Kulturwissenschaften, Europa-Universität Viadrina, Frankfurt/Oder 2006 (with thanks to Prof. Philipp Ther for allowing me to use the manuscript).

543 *Łańcuszek*, WC, 1975, no. 17, p. 20.

544 A. Paszyński, M. Turski, *Granica bez kompleksów*, "Polityka", no. 22/May28, 1977.

545 *Polityka i dyplomacja polska wobec Niemiec*, vol 2: *1971–1990*, ed. M. Tomala, Warszawa 2006, pp. 105–108; H. Kożuchowski, *Wymiana przygraniczna*, in: *Rozwój społeczno-ekonomiczny obszarów przygranicznych*, ed. B. Winiarski, M. Musiał, M. Klamut, Wrocław 1979, p. 239.

546 AIPN, 01521/2035, Jacek Oleś, *Przemyt wartości dewizowych, Akademia Spraw Wewnętrznych, Instytut Kryminalistyki i Kryminologii*, Warszawa 1978, pp. 65–70.

With East German marks, those that knew the right people could also buy gold, which in Poland gave the best return on the initial investment. At first, it was the Polish Roma living along the western border who specialized in such transactions, since many of them had relatives either in the GDR or in West Germany. In May 1972, an entire Roma family was arrested for involvement in large-scale gold smuggling.[547] Six months later, another Roma family attracted the attention of the authorities by selling gold coins in Jubiler stores. The investigation proved how easy the business was: over the course of a few months, seven million zloty had been officially exchanged for eastern marks. Later, in the GDR, 1 233 South African Krugerrands – 42.1 kg of gold! – had been purchased from people arriving from West Germany or West Berlin.[548] Soon, there mushroomed specialized "enterprises" that were illegally purchasing GDR marks, and to lesser degree other Soviet Bloc currencies, with which they bought hard currencies and gold in the GDR. One consignment of currency alone, which arrived in Poland from Berlin in the summer of 1975, included 593 580 000 GDR marks.[549]

Smaller or larger smuggling operations were only part, not even the most important, of the borderland landscape. The banks of the border rivers complemented each other in a much more prosaic way: guests from Poland enthused about East German products while visitors from the GDR were impressed with what Polish artisans had to offer. These craftsmen, who operated both legally and illegally, flocked every week to the border towns and sold to those arriving from across the Oder–Neisse border all kinds of bric-à-brac such as plastic toys, fashionable clothing and underwear and such sought-after symbols of Western pop culture as toys and various gadgets with logos of popular bands or singers.[550] The suspension by the GDR authorities (from October 30, 1980) of the agreement allowing passport-free and visa-free cross border traffic seriously disrupted the grey economy status quo that had developed for the past decade between the two societies. Martial Law, declared in Poland on December 13, 1981, put up another very effective obstacle to the cross-border trade. From then on, Polish contract workers employed in the GDR were the primary unofficial traders. For many, a job in a German factory or on a construction site was merely a source of capital used for trading; and it was this trading that constituted their main source

547 S. Kot, *Samochód pełen złota*, PiŻ, 1974, no. 42.

548 J. Arturowicz, *"Złoty" gang*, "Express Poznański", no. 294/December 15–16, 1973.

549 M. Buchowski, *Wielki pieniądz*, "Trybuna Odrzańska", no 274/1, 1976.

550 A. Mozołowski, *Skoczyć na małe piwko*, "Polityka", no. 21/May 22, 1976. In 1974, Polish artisans and merchants supplied the residents of the GRD borderlands with soccer trinkets popular during the World Cup in West Germany; *ibid*.

of income. While in 1983, the official GDR mark's exchange rate was 17 zloty and the black market rate was the very attractive 60–80 zloty, it was overshadowed by the rates achieved through trading specific goods: the "chocolate" rate was 200, the "shoe" rate – 250, the "pepper" rate – 250, and the "baking powder" rate – over 300 zloty to the mark. The further away from the border, the higher the return was. Merchants from far and wide already positioned at the border swarmed onto trains, trying to buy the smuggled goods for as little as possible. And the closer to the border, the more liberal in their approach were the local authorities. According to a high-ranking police official from Gorzów Wielkopolski, a town close to the border, in mid-1983, trading operations conducted by Poles employed in the GDR had "stirred up controversy" but they were also advantageous for the state by "enriching the market with goods and replenishing the state treasury with hard currency." He proposed to regularize the practice by introducing regulated prices or giving the state purchasing rights.[551]

The privileged position of Polish workers in the GDR gradually weakened during the 1980s, along with the liberalization of passport regulations. The ultimate blow came with new rules that allowed Poles to retain their passports between trips (from early 1989). From that moment on, instead of being the destination of trading trips, the GDR became merely a transit route to West Berlin – now the source of *real* profit. "The departures take place," it was reported in mid-March 1989, "usually at weekends. On those days, dozens of buses of tourist groups organized by Orbis, Gromada, Turysta or other foreign travel agencies, as well as hundreds of private cars, pass through the border crossings at Świecko and Kołbaskowo."[552] The first official hard-currency exchange kiosk at the Świecko crossing opened on March 16, 1989, followed soon by others opening along the western border.

Transit traffic also revived the black market on the eastern border. Unofficial trade with the Soviet Union (more in chapter 9) had always been very profitable.

---

551 W. Przybyłowicz, *Kontrabanda*, "Polityka", no. 26/June 25, 1983. "Every Friday at 2:10 am an express train from Leipzig enters the railway station in Wrocław. One can buy everything on this train: coffee, chocolate, a moped, a washing machine, kitchen mixers, vacuum cleaners, tights, spices and many other articles unavailable on our market." W. Faściszewski, *Przemytnik*, "Sprawy i Ludzie" 1984, no. 4.

552 AAN, KC PZPR, 95/12B, GUC, fol. 30–32. Se: U. Weber, *Der Polenmarkt in Berlin. Zur Rekonstruktion eines kulturellen Kontakts im Prozess der politischen Transformation Mittel- und Osteuropas*, Neuried 2002; M. Irek, *Der Schmugglerzug Warschau–Berlin–Warschau. Materialien einer Feldforschung*, Berlin 1998.

It did not require sophisticated strategies. In the Soviet Union, public demand for anything with a passing resemblance to a Western product was even greater than in Poland but the supply was much lower. Many Poles became the middlemen who transferred to the East not only technologies but also consumer trends. The majority of those crossing the eastern border – relatives visiting their families, participants in organized trips, including the so-called "friendship trains", functionaries protected by passports issued for the purposes of conducting their duties, contract workers employed on construction sites, students and scholars – took advantage of the situation. They all carried with them wigs, blouses, underwear, coats, jeans, and plastic bags with the mandatory English logo. Coming back, they brought gold, currency (cheaper in the Soviet Union than in Poland), household items, furs, and coffee. Choosing the right goods was not difficult. Figuring out how to enter the Soviet Union was, however, a challenge. Individual trips, such as those to the GDR, were not possible. One could only visit the USSR on a business trip, with a private invitation or as part of an organized trip. Other than those, there was only one trouble-free way of entering the country: on a transit journey to somewhere else.

In the latter part of the 1970s, trips to other Soviet Bloc countries reached a mass scale. From 1977, nothing more than the appropriate stamp in one's ID document was required for such journeys but this lenient approach did not apply to the Soviet Union. Trips to Turkey, Greece or the Middle East also became easier than before. Soon, travelers enthusiastically tested the thousand-year old principle that profits increase in proportion to the number of countries visited. Even those with less time or money to invest in such business ventures, or those who were simply less entrepreneurial, could still carry on a lucrative trade by simply getting on the train to Lvov. They could take advantage of the brief change-over of electric locomotives just before the train got to the city (some even went as far as to use the emergency brake or bribe the railroad workers to stop for longer) to sell the goods quickly and return to Poland without ever reaching the supposed "country of destination". Some would make a quick stop in Lvov to sell goods in demand in the Soviet Union and buy articles that could be later easily sold on in Hungary, Romania, Yugoslavia, Greece, Turkey or the Middle Eastern states. Lvov, thanks to its advantageous geographical location since the Middle Ages famous as a thriving business hub, quickly became an important center of illegal trade; soon, the term "Lvov transit" entered the smuggling, and diplomatic, lexicon. On the other side of the border, the city of Przemyśl also gained a new significance. In the 1970s and

1980s, it featured prominently in the reports on trafficking on the eastern border delivered to the Ministry of Internal Affairs.[553]

Martial Law did not interrupt these extremely profitable operations for long. Unlike Czechs, Slovaks and East Germans who usually shared their authorities' adverse opinion of Polish traders, not only did the social players east of Poland accept such operations but were keen to cooperate. It is not surprising that by mid-1983, Lvov had regained its position as a center of "concentrated smuggling of goods and trading of hard currencies."[554] The "Lvov transit", which had played an important role until the late 1980s, now gradually began to lose its significance in favor of the traditional trading exchange; all the more so, since with the beginning of *perestroika*, the borders opened wider for travelers, both those arriving and departing. The growing demand for outwardly visible social status symbols such as clothing was as difficult to meet as before. After the introduction of new regulations at the turn of 1986 and 1987, cross-border traffic quickly began to grow. For example in Belarus the number of visitors from Poland increased sixfold in 1988 in comparison to the previous year. In 1989, the number of "destination" arrivals in the USSR grew by 100%, and of transit arrivals – by 200%. Poland consolidated its position as the nation whose citizens visited the USSR most frequently. And vice-versa: Poland became a primary destination for Soviet citizens.[555]

This affected the black market landscape mostly on the eastern side of the border. Naturally, travelers from Belarus and Ukraine were in evidence in the market places in Przemyśl, Siedlce and Białystok but were not as numerous as the Poles frequenting the Ukrainian or Belorussian *baracholkas*. During 1987–1988, Polish trading developed sufficiently[556] to force the authorities of the border Soviet republics to set up bazaars to accommodate it, for example in Vilnius, Zasław near Minsk, Brześć/Brest and Grodno. The last of these was renowned "in all of the Soviet Union. Soviet citizens traveled to this market from as far away as Siberia and the Asian republics to shop and sell their own goods there."[557] The bazaars did not last long and soon closed down. The authorities justified the decision on

553 AIPN, Biuro Paszportów MSW, 21052; AIPN, KG MO, 35/185, fol. 20–21, 170. K. Stipsicy, *Schmuggeln nach Plan*, "Die Zeit", no. 37/September 9, 1983; R. Geremek, *Pokój, przyjaźń, dieńgi*, "Życie", June 3–4, 2000.

554 AMSZ, Consular Department (Departament Konsularny, DK), 22/87, w. 10.

555 AMSZ, DK, 29/97, w. 20.

556 In the late 1980s, the profitability of trading operations in the East equaled transactions conducted in the West; M. Bednarski, *Drugi obieg gospodarczy. Przesłanki, mechanizmy i skutki w Polsce lat* osiemdziesiątych, Warszawa 1992, pp. 138–139.

557 AMSZ, DK, 29/97, w. 20.

the basis that criminal "elements" had been gathering around the market where the illegal goods sold and the local police had not been able to control them. Official *komis* stores, which bought goods from Polish tourists, replaced the bazaars.[558] The restrictions deterred neither the Poles nor the inhabitants of Lvov, Vilnius, and Grodno who soon privatized the commerce with visitors from the West and established private, unofficial *komis* stores.[559]

The year 1989 was a turning point for black market geography including the East–West axis, where the changes seemed to be the most profound. The transformation triggered by the "autumn of the peoples" removed some of the old political barriers, and widened the range of needs and aspirations without blurring the differences in the standards of living. In 1990, with the unification and currency union of the two German states, the West reached the Oder–Neisse. In the same year, for the USSR (and its successor states), it was Poland that now became the "West". The Russian market place in Warsaw replaced the Polish market place in Berlin. On the one hand, smuggling (traditionally most important on the East–West route) became professionalized and criminalized, on the other – to a large extent, it reverted to its old function as the medium of unofficial exchange between border communities that played a very important role in the Polish-German, Polish-Ukrainian, Belorussian and Russian borderlands. This, however, belongs to a different era.

558 AMSZ, DK, 21/93, w. 5.

559 *Spekulatiwnaja gorjaczka: istoki i łabirinty*, in: *Tenewaja ekonomika*, Moskwa 1991, p. 91.

5. Meat

"What did you have for dinner tonight"?

"Meat!" X or Y answers, beaming delightedly. "There was no meat today..." – the tone is plaintive, pessimistic, reproachful. "I am off to get some meat!" is uttered in tones of excitement and anticipation; "I have got some meat!" is pronounced with a triumphant grin. "They had no meat in the store..." is full of bitter disappointment. Human thoughts and words revolve around meat, as do the people themselves almost literally so. Meat is the subject of group psychosis; it is the trigger for violent swings from cheerful expectation to morose resignation. Omnipotent meat, the realm of fantasy and gossip [...]."[560]

The above excerpt from October 1948 could have been equally well written in 1951, or any of the years 1959, 1963, 1970, 1976, 1980, or 1989. There is no doubt that meat – or rather the enduring shortage thereof – was the most common topic of conversation both in private homes and in government offices throughout the entire era of the Polish People's Republic. Since individual, private farmers were the main producers of meat in Poland and the state wanted to play the role of the monopoly distributor of this Polish staple food, meat became the most common object of illegal trade and created thereby an important link between the periphery and the center, the city and the countryside, the state and the private domain. That is why we shall look not only at unofficial meat trade strategies but also their social, economic and political context.

5.1 "Meat Is Problem Number One":[561] But Why?

It would be a simplification to say that all the post-war political upheavals were triggered by meat shortages but public opinion certainly perceived it that way. Meat was the prism through which society viewed the authorities. If we accept political jokes as the most common expression of public opinion, the fact that meat was the most popular topic of jokes between late 1940s and late 1980s is quite revealing.[562] By the turn of the 1940s and 1950s, meat supply had reached

560 J. Kawalec, *"Spadochronowe" zakupy*, "Echo Dnia", no. 298/October 30, 1948.

561 AAN, KC PZPR, 237/XXXI–243, fol. 223. PH, 96, 2005, z. 4, pp. 587–605.

562 See: Ł. Kamiński, A. Małkiewicz, K. Ruchniewicz, *Opór społeczny w Europie Środkowej w latach 1948–1953 na przykładzie Polski, NRD i Czechosłowacji. Wstępny raport z badań*, Wrocław 2004, pp. 285–290; T. Szarota, *Śmiech zakazany – kawał (dowcip) polityczny jako informacja o postrzeganiu peerelowskiej rzeczywistości*, "Polska

a high position on the list of unsolved problems both at central and regional government level. One of the indicators was the frequency with which the topic of meat turned up in the documents of the Politburo, where it started to feature in the late 1940s, gained a permanent place during the catastrophic collapse of the market in the summer and fall of 1951 and kept that position until 1989.[563]

While society considered the incompetence and misguided economic policies of the authorities the main reason for the chronic meat shortages, the actual causes were more complex. We need to look at meat as one of the crucial indicators of social prestige and financial status. The correlation has been well established[564] between industrialization-cum-urbanization and changes in consumption patterns, accompanied by increased consumption of high-protein, high-quality food products. In *The Making of the English Working Class*, E. P. Thompson pointed out that meat could certainly serve as a sensitive measure of the material standard of living, since it was one of the first products purchased with real income growth.[565]

Meat consumption patterns depended on historical, economic, and social factors but we can safely assume that in Europe of the time, the further east and south you went, the more meatless the average diet was. While in the 1930s in Great Britain and Switzerland people consumed on average 66 kg of meat per year, and in Germany 48–52 kg, in Poland (shortly before the Second World War) the annual average was just 21.6 kg. In pre-war Poland, 45% of the population did not reach this average (the lowest consumption was some two kg per year), roughly 25% exceeded it (for example in Poznań, the average consumption was 61 kg, and in Krakow – 53 kg) and one percent of Poles consumed as much as 100 kg of meat per year.[566] The differences were significant in the post-war period, a

---

1944/45–1989. Studia i Materiały" 5, 2001, pp. 209–236; about "meat jokes" see: D. Jarosz i M. Pasztor, *Afera mięsna: fakty i konteksty*, Toruń 2004, pp. 196–200.

563 The "meat problem" was discussed at the session of KC PZPR Politburo for the last time on November 7, 1989; AAN, KC PZPR, 2162, fol. 67.

564 M. Pohorille, *Preferencje konsumentów a postulowany wzorzec spożycia*, Warszawa 1978, pp. 178–179; H.-J. Teuteberg, *The general relationship between diet and industrialization*, in: *European diet from pre-industrial to modern times*, ed. E. and R. Forster, New York 1975, pp. 61–109.

565 E.P. Thompson, *The Making of the English Working Class*, New York 1964, quoted from H.P. Müller, *Die "feinen Unterschiede", wo es keine geben sollte. Anmerkungen zum Verhältnis von Arbeiteraristokratie und Luxus*, in: *"Luxus und Konsum" – eine historische Annäherung*, Münster–New York–München 2003, p. 209.

566 *Mały rocznik statystyczny 1938*, Warszawa 1938, pp. 147, 149–151; W. Szewczyk, *Spożycie żywności w Polsce w okresie międzywojennym (na tle dochodów i wydatków*

time when the former lower classes now enjoying new political, economic, and social circumstances, wanted at all costs to reach the pre-war consumption model of the middle class.[567]

After the Second World War, Polish society had to re-establish consumption patterns from the ground up. The war not only starved everyone equally but it also equalized the chances of all social groups. Pauperization affected all, but the situation of the ruling classes soon began to improve, and polices of full employment and wage increases quickly eliminated the income differentials between white- and blue-collar employees.[568] Although, for the next few years, real income was lower than it had been before 1939, it was sufficient to subsist on relatively cheap, subsidized food. Low food prices were expected to ease the harshness of post-war living, endear the poorer part of the population to the new authorities, provide conditions for a high birth rate, and facilitate industrialization.[569]

During the era of reconstruction of the state between 1946 and 1950, meat consumption in Poland grew on average by 5.2 kg annually, between 1950 and 1970 – by 0.8 kg, and in the first part of Gierek's decade, at the time considered abundant and prosperous – by 3.5 kg.[570] Propaganda provided a boost for consumption, with its exhortations to give to every citizen "according to his needs" – the prerequisite stipulation for a socialist state, and repeatedly stressing the biological, material, and cultural equality of all citizens. Society accepted the egalitarian approach but the attempts of the authorities to instill a vague definition of a "socialist model of consumption" were destined to end in failure. Models of consumption, social needs and aspirations are never the sum of the perceptions of the authorities, but tend to rely on, often long-engrained, social customs and

---

na konsumpcję), Warszawa 1991, pp. 144, 150; J. Żarnowski, *Polska 1918–1939. Praca – technika – społeczeństwo*, Warszawa 1999, pp. 150, 252.

567 W. Szymański, *Ceny a konsumpcja i produkcja żywności*, Warszawa 1979, p. 177.

568 L. Beskid, *Ekonomiczne uwarunkowania rozwoju konsumpcji*, in: *Badania nad wzorami konsumpcji*, ed. J. Szczepański, Wrocław–Warszawa–Kraków 1977, pp. 99–100; S. Jankowski, *Warunki bytu ludności*, in: *Gospodarka Polski Ludowej 1944–1955*, ed. J. Kaliński, Z. Landau, vol. 2, Warszawa 1976, p. 66.

569 W. Michna, W. Sztarbałło, K. Prędecka, A. Dyka, *Modele spożycia żywności (w aspekcie polityki wyżywienia na lata 1986–1990)*, Warszawa 1986, p. 5.

570 Z. Lewandowska, *Model konsumpcji w Polsce w okresie industrializacji socjalistycznej*, Warszawa 1979, pp. 75–76. In 1950, meat consumption in Czechoslovakia represented 90%, in Hungary 71%, and in the GDR 60% of meat consumption in Poland. In the next twenty years, the proportions reversed; *ibid.*, p. 79.

habits, shaped by living conditions, cultural tradition, copy-cat behavior and other factors.[571]

Contrary to the popular perception that the peasant model of consumption was a feature of the ruralization of post-war Polish cities, it was not the case that peasants who migrated to the cities imposed their village diet on the city dwellers. In fact, the opposite was true. It was the rural migrants who adopted the petty bourgeois model of consumption, with its higher proportion of meat. The lower middle class became the standard-setting group for the workers and peasants – first for those who moved to the cities, then for those living on farms but employed outside agriculture, and finally for rural residents living solely from farming.[572]

With robust consumption, social tensions rose quickly every time that state production faltered. From the late 1950s, people began to pay attention to the quality of food; aspirations of a growing section of society moved beyond a plateful of potatoes or cabbage accompanied by pork scratchings. As mentioned earlier, increased demand for meat is an integral part of modernization. Indeed, the generation born during the post-war demographic boom was growing up – and this entailed an increased requirement for high-calorie foods – at a time when the modernization process was accelerating rapidly. The number of city dwellers employed in industry and services rose; the general level of education increased. Women were now more active professionally which meant they spent less time on household chores. As it did in the West, expenditure on grain products, potatoes, eggs, sugar, and animal fat decreased but there was an increased demand for meat products, especially those of high quality. The appetite however remained unsatisfied.[573] The growth in production, especially of meat, lagged behind the growth in population. Since the population in the cities was increasing the fastest, the amount of meat per capita for city inhabitants systematically decreased. For example in comparison with 1958, in the years 1960, 1963, and 1964 meat supply decreased by more than 8 kg.[574] Increased demand for high quality meat

---

571 M. Pohorille, *Konsumpcja*, in: *Systemy wartości a wzory konsumpcji społeczeństwa polskiego*, Warszawa 1980, p. 111.

572 J. Szczepański, *Zagadnienia konstruowania i realizacji modelu i wzorów konsumpcji socjalistycznej*, in: *Badania nad wzorami konsumpcji* […], pp. 61–62.

573 L. Beskid, *Ekonomiczne* …, pp. 187, 195; E. Kieżel, *Podstawy programowania spożycia żywności*, Katowice 1985, pp. 51, 122–123; Z. Żekoński, *Wstępne informacje o strukturze żywienia ludności miast*, OBOP, Warszawa 1960 (I used a copy stored in ODZP TVP, 1847/7). See: D. Jarosz, M. Pasztor, *Afera mięsna* […], pp. 158–162.

574 AZZ, Wydział Ekonomiczny, 204/43, October 1, 1965.

coincided with a significant increase in the export of such products. It never rose to the excessive levels claimed by urban myth (in fact, it never exceeded 12% of national consumption); it was, however, not the quantity but the quality of the exported meat that mattered. Poland exported the highest quality meat, which was also the most sought-after, and often unavailable on the local market. In 1955, 99% of the national production of canned ham was sold abroad; twenty years later, this had risen to 74.3%. This was one of the reasons for the singular supply conundrum: in 1965, ham, which on average constituted 23% of carcass meat, made up only 1.1% of the official market in meat.[575]

Furthermore, the standards of labor-saving services such as restaurants and of products such as processed fast foods were not keeping up with social change, which allowed more women – since it was women who were in charge of the logistics of putting food on the plate in the-then Poland – to work or study than had been the case before the war. Moreover, the quality of food on offer in the Polish catering system that consisted of workplace cafeterias and a few restaurants was not very enticing. Thus, most Poles took their meals at home and the Polish woman remained in the kitchen – with the stereotype of a good wife that serves a two-course cooked lunch every day alive and well. In only 1.5% of urban households and 0.2% of rural households were home meals not on offer. Dinner was served at home each day in 88% of city households and in 93% of homes in rural areas.[576] As refrigerators were in short supply, this meant bulk grocery shopping daily, which in turn put much pressure on the market places.[577]

Attempts undertaken in the early 1960s to ease the housewife's burden with such brand-new, labor-saving measures as frozen foods and the sale of meat in pre-packaged portions as well as canned foods and deli products were not successful. Poland did not have the appropriate technology for the mass production

575 AAN, KC PZPR, 237/V/598, fol. 33; W. Szymański, *Ceny a konsumpcja* [...], p. 257.

576 E. Kieżel, *Podstawy programowania spożycia* [...], p. 61; A. Wiśniewski, *Czasochłonność żywienia w gospodarstwach domowych*, in: *Diagnoza zmian w strukturze konsumpcji (na przykładzie gospodarstw domowych)*, Katowice 1990, p. 117; A. Wiśniewski, *Warunki i sposoby realizacji funkcji żywieniowej gospodarstw domowych w Polsce w końcu lat osiemdziesiątych*, in: *Konsumpcja w gospodarstwach domowych lat osiemdziesiątych*, ed. T. Pałaszewska-Reindl, Katowice 1992, p. 34.

577 Before long, refrigerators became more popular, making it possible to store food for longer periods. For example in 1975, a reporter on *Polityka* observed: "after standing in line for a long time you usually buy more. There is a reason why refrigerators with big freezers are now disappearing from the stores whereas before they were not so popular""; Z. Szeliga, *Mięso – kłopoty i perspektywy*, "Polityka", no. 11/March 15, 1975.

of packaging and there were problems with distribution. Moreover, society resisted such novelties and chose to rely on traditional catering preferences. Despite the adverse opinion of dieticians, pork remained the most popular meat: in 1960–1961, it constituted 69% of meat consumption; during 1974–1975, it never fell below 66.2%. However, between 1950 and 1976 poultry production grew sevenfold and beef production increased four times but the old favorite, pork, only by two thirds.[578] The reason was that the natural environment in Polish rural areas and the type of fodder available were more conducive to cattle rearing than pig farming and thus the consumption of beef and dairy products prevailed, regardless of the fact that given a choice, Poles would have preferred pork chops and ham on the plate. Meat was much less labor-intensive than other foodstuffs, which were not any easier to buy. Not only that: its price remained competitive.[579]

Society perceived the efficient supply of affordable meat as a basic public good, part of the status quo, based on a consensus with the authorities. The latter were ready to maintain stable food prices even at the expense of massive and ever-growing subsidies. In 1975, government subsidies of food in Poland amounted to 168 billion zloty, and by 1978, they were up to 270 billion. In 1977, a farmer was paid 41 zloty for one kilogram of livestock while a kilogram of pork shoulder cost 42 zloty![580] In the late 1980s, subsidies absorbed almost 30% of the budget. This social policy led to a paradoxical situation: in 1988, the value of retail sales in the meat industry was 618.2 billion zloty, whereas the value of livestock in state purchase prices was 1 298.7 billion zloty. In the middle of 1989, in order to maintain the price of cured and deli meat, the government had to subsidize it by 211.4%, pork – by 220.7%, and beef – by 276.8%.[581]

As a result, meat consumption rose faster than people's income. What was even worse, both indicators grew more quickly than production. For example between 1970 and 1974, meat supply increased by 78.5% and the payroll budget by 114%, which rapidly increased demand (the prices stayed the same!).[582] It was not possible to turn people's attention to highly processed food products, because their quality was poor and their quantities insufficient. Gomułka's and

578 *Polityka i organizacja żywienia ludności*, ed. W. Kamiński, Warszawa 1980, p. 70.

579 K. Hofman, *Konsumpcja żywności w Polsce. Aspekty ekonomiczne, społeczne i żywieniowe*, Warszawa 1989, pp. 103, 139; B. Kowrygo, E. Rosiak, *Spożycie żywności przez ludność rolniczą w świetle danych Instytutu Ekonomiki Rolnej*, in : *Model konsumpcji żywności w Polsce w środowisku wiejskim*, Warszawa 1981, p. 99.

580 W. Szymański, *Ceny a konsumpcja* [...], p. 304.

581 AAN, KC PZPR, 2149, fol. 161.

582 W. Szymański, *Ceny a konsumpcja* [...], pp. 251, 256.

Gierek's administrations undertook such attempts without much success. Finally, the emphasis on food consumption in general and meat in particular became so pronounced that it began to re-direct government policy. The authorities were making desperate decisions such as, in the 1970s, incurring massive debt for the importation of animal feed, introducing "commercial stores" in 1976 or forcing workplaces to run animal husbandry on the side.

Ultimately, the government resorted to drastic measures such as sudden price hikes (in 1953, 1959, 1967, 1970, 1976, 1980, and 1982). They usually had in common two characteristics: they sparked social protests (in two of these instances, in 1970 and in 1976, as result of protests, the hikes were reversed), and they had no permanent economic effects. Even the price increase of early 1982, the most radical in the history of the directed Polish post-war economy, had only limited results. On the one hand, the authorities did not dare to raise prices to the level of profitability; on the other, meat was such an attractive product that people continued to buy it even at the higher prices and at the expense of reducing demand for other products. Consumers opted to use their savings if it allowed them to maintain their level of consumption (known as the "bolt effect"). This mechanism of the minimal effectiveness of increasing meat prices was usually explained in terms of "minimal meat price elasticity of demand". One could say that in the case of meat, the reverse was also true: the "income elasticity" was high: the higher real income, the greater was expenditure on food, especially on meat. When in the early 1970s, the incomes in the lowest bracket began to grow significantly, Poles started to spend a larger portion of their money on meat. This was a vicious circle, which only the reforms of 1989–1990 would be able to break.[583]

Polish agriculture, subject to continuous economic experiments, was not able to rise to the challenge of the growing demand for food. Agricultural policy in the times of the Polish People's Republic was an area of "constant clashes between political and social goals on the one side and the effectiveness of production goals on the other."[584] While the authorities had to acknowledge the social demand for ever-larger pieces of meat on the plate, private agriculture (the largest supplier of meat) continued to constitute an ideological and economic burden that was difficult to bear. Comments by the-then agriculture minister Kazimierz

583 *Mechanizmy ekonomiczne kształtowania spożycia. Kryzys, próba reform, kierunki zmian*, ed. L. Żabiński, Katowice 1991, p. 44; E. Kieżel, *Podstawy programowania spożycia* [...], p. 55.

584 S. Golinowska, *Decyzje centrum o kształtowaniu rzeczowej struktury spożycia*, Warszawa 1989, p. 105.

Barcikowski, noted down by Mieczysław Rakowski (on January 12, 1973), illustrate very well the see-saw fluctuations in agricultural policy: "Agriculture always develops very well in our country when the Party feels weak. This was the case in 1948. The moment we begin to "believe in our strength" – as we did in 1949 – we immediately go after the peasant's money, and as a result, production decreases. Later, when we are again weak, as in 1956, agriculture begins to thrive again. And so forth. Right now the comrades from the Finance Ministry again propose to invade the peasant's pocket."[585]

In the year 1958 alone, private agriculture received approximately the same funding as the state and coop sectors put together. It is not surprising that 1958 was one of the very few years when the demand for meat was met.[586] The equilibrium did not endure; expenditure on private agriculture fell to 30% (in the late 1960s), while the financial burden rose; this effectively held the peasants back from long-term investment in their farms.[587] The story repeated itself in the 1970s, when, after several fat years (including increasing state purchase prices and the abolition of compulsory deliveries), agricultural funding was cut again and more money was allocated to industry.[588] As a result, Polish farms were so underfunded that in the early1980s, their resources were estimated to be no more than half of their actual requirements for fertilizer, insecticide, land amelioration etc.[589] This affected the volume of production and increased vulnerability to weather fluctuations. Poor potato harvests caused by drought or excessive rain resulted in a collapse of animal husbandry from which it took years to recover. The correlation between bad weather (in 1947, 1951, 1959, 1962, 1964, 1969, 1974–1975, and 1979–1980) and the collapse of the meat market and political upheavals is evident.[590]

When dealing with individual farmers, the authorities had to be careful not to upset the delicate balance. Polish peasants remained capitalists at heart and followed the laws of the market. If they did perceive what the state had to offer – for example, the official state purchase price, credits offered, or supply – as being sufficiently to their advantage, farmers would try to increase production and sell

585 M.F. Rakowski, *Dzienniki polityczne 1972–1975*, Warszawa 2002, p. 89.
586 S. Golinowska, *Decyzje centrum* [...], pp. 84, 116.
587 B. Gulbicka, *Dochody, spożycie i akumulacja w indywidualnych gospodarstwach chłopskich w Polsce Ludowej*, Warszawa 1986, pp. 83, 92.
588 W. Michna, W. Sztarbałło, K. Prędecka, A. Dyka, *Modele spożycia żywności* [...], pp. 6–8.
589 B. Gulbicka, *Dochody, spożycie i akumulacja* [...], pp. 10, 13.
590 S. Golinowska, *Decyzje centrum* [...], p. 117.

more to the state. In a process of denaturation of consumption, they would do so even at the expense of their self-sufficiency. In the topsy-turvy Polish economy, they knew very well that at neighborhood stores they could buy cheese, bread or sausage at prices lower than their own production cost! However, when state purchase prices remained stable and the cost of the means of production was going up (or the means of production were in short supply), nothing could force the peasant to continue or increase production and sell the products to the state, especially when the unofficial market guaranteed much better prices.

In the 1970s, shortages of animal feed crushed animal husbandry in Poland and, by the same token, the daily diet. In 1976, a journalist on the weekly *Polityka* hit the nail on the head when he noted that the "battle for animal feed in the countryside is fiercer than the battle for meat in the cities."[591] In the end, specialized farms dependent on feed supply and geared towards mass production gave up on animal husbandry. Small farmers, who grew a little bit of this and a little bit of that, were in a better situation. The problem was that their limited production could not ensure a balanced market.

State meat supply did not meet consumer demand. The authorities prioritized meat deliveries to large agglomerations and large working-class centers, leaving the so-called green areas to their own devices; this entailed the de facto legalization of the black market. Rationing had a similar effect. It stopped the process of the denaturation of farms and reduced radically the opportunities for buying meat for sections of society used to higher consumption and able to pay for it. Until rationing was abolished, and the free market introduced, the only solution that remained was to use the services of the ubiquitous "veal woman" or intensify efforts to acquire more ration coupons.[592]

5.2 Meat on the Black Market: Between Repression and Consent

In its *Report on Economic Crime in 1959*, the Supreme Audit Office (NIK) wrote, without beating about the bush, that shortages on the meat market translated

591 A.K. Wróblewski, *Świni banknotami nie nakarmi. Sztufada zamiast schabowego*, in: *Czarna księga cenzury PRL*, part 2, Londyn 1978, p. 460.

592 R. Milic-Czerniak, *Adaptacja konsumentów do warunków kryzysu ekonomiczno-społecznego w pierwszej połowie lat osiemdziesiątych*, in: *Warunki i sposób życia – zachowania przystosowawcze w kryzysie*, ed. L. Beskid, Warszawa 1989, pp. 115–116; *Umowa o kartki*, ed. J. Kurczewski, Warszawa 2004.

immediately into increased activity of the "criminal elements"[593] in society. Those activities were wide-ranging – from illegal slaughter, meat speculation, and under-the-counter sales to theft and the often large-scale fraud in state-owned processing plants. These strategies were a response to state policies and, in turn, immediately elicited further reaction from the state. The next chapter presents the mechanisms of this mutual interaction.

5.2.1 "The Great Battle for Meat": 1944–1950

The beginning of the illegal meat trade goes back to the interwar period. During the economic crisis in the early 1930s, the average consumer, and thus the small butcher, began to look for cheaper sources of meat. Since meat delivered to the cities had to be inspected – naturally, for a fee, as a way of bypassing this onerous obligation, large-scale smuggling developed. Meat could, for example, be delivered without inspection in cheap food mail packages or by "railroad workers for their own needs and for other railroad workers and for trading also by railroad pensioners and widows, by persons who did not sell meat but brought it for their own families, for school children, as gifts for friends or business partners. Meat and cold cuts were smuggled through city tollgates in buses and trucks, which city authorities had no authority to stop, and traveled to Krakow in horse drawn wagons. Pedestrians also transported meat; for instance, women who sold milk concealed meat in milk cans."[594] This description of the smuggling of meat into Krakow applied equally well to other cities.

During the German occupation, the illegal meat trade was an activity with mass participation of professional players. After the war, these did not give up their profitable pursuit but now found themselves having to negotiate the obstacles put before them by the new authorities, who did not want to lose control over this strategic product. The Polish authorities, keen to maintain low prices and keep the system of the ration coupons afloat, embarked on regulation of animal husbandry and imposed compulsory meat deliveries to state outlets (on August 22, 1944 and February 9, 1945). The new system allowed for a relatively wide margin of free market operations, although merchants and artisans had to buy farm animals through official channels. Initially, state supervision was limited to counteracting the raising of prices above the official level, to enforcing public health

593 *Informacja o przestępczości gospodarczej w 1959 r.*, Warszawa 1960 (NIK, Wydział ds. Nadużyć Gospodarczych, copy in the author's possession), p. 40.

594 R. Radzyński, *Produkcja, handel i spożycie mięsa w Krakowie*, Kraków 1934, pp. 33–34, 45.

standards and the introduction in February 1946 of meat-free days in restaurants and canteens. Penalties for violating the regulations were not, however, severe.

There were also other reasons why the authorities did not want to push too hard. Excessively repressive measures could have encouraged further professionalized black market strategies and, after the abolition in July 1946 (for propaganda purposes) of benefits in kind, there was a danger that they might spark off deep social dissatisfaction. And, perhaps, the authorities had misgivings about tangling with the meat industry, since – as reported in mid-1946 – it was the domain of the "most brutal human elements, of low ethical standard" which promoted the "most negative and dishonest trading practices and methods of competition."[595] Moreover, small merchants, wholesalers, and other traders often had connections with local power elites.[596]

For quite prosaic reasons, it was not possible to eliminate quickly and effectively the private middlemen, without whom meat shortages would have been much greater. As a result, the "battle for meat" was one of the last stages of the "war on trade". It began with the authorities dealing with the last link of the distribution chain by imposing, from mid-1948, restrictive inspections on butchers. The retail prices imposed were the same as or barely higher than the cost of the carcasses. No businessman in his right mind will sell without making a profit or, worse still, at a loss. Inevitably, the butchers resorted to illegal slaughter and under-the-counter sales, where they could get a higher price at all times. This in turn gave the authorities, usually represented by the Special Commission, an efficient propaganda weapon.[597]

In July 1948, the announcement heralding a change of agricultural policy triggered the eruption of "kolkhoz" panic. Drunkenness and religious fervor intensified; there were rumors about impending war or even the end of the world, which was supposed to arrive on August 15 of that year. "Just in case", people started hoarding pork fat and sugar.[598] The proceedings of the August session of the Central Committee of the Polish Workers Party (which lasted from August 31 to September 3, 1948) was a telling preview of the methods which the Party would soon use to deal with both the "right-wing nationalist deviation" and such freedoms as remained, including economic freedom. In early September 1948,

595 AAN, Akta Józefa Wojtyny, 18, fol. 6–7.

596 AAN, Komisarz Rządowy do Spraw Organizacji Gospodarki Mięsnej, fol. 3–4, 6–7.

597 AAN, KS, 5, fol. 122.

598 D. Jarosz, M. Pasztor, *W krzywym zwierciadle. Polityka władz komunistycznych w Polsce w świetle plotek i pogłosek z lat 1949–1956*, Warszawa 1995, pp. 29–30; "Głos Ludu", no. 256/September 15, 1948.

"meat fever" erupted. Citizens waited in long lines in front of the still-private butcher shops. Housewives had no qualms about paying over the odds for a piece of fatty bacon, an indispensable ingredient of a Polish meal at the time, even though it was considerably more expensive than leaner meat. Private restaurants also stocked meat regardless of the price, so that on "days when meat sale is prohibited they were able to offer their favored clients a pork chop of impressive size."[599] The authorities reacted immediately and lists of corrupt butchers and restaurant owners punished by the Special Commission started to appear in the press.[600] *Let's Slap Down the Wreckers!* exhorted the daily *Express Ilustrowany* in Łódź on September 17, a day after a large anti-speculation operation had been conducted nationwide in Poland by the Special Commission, the police, and "worker activists".[601] For the targeted culprits, this was a painful blow. In Poznań, "Agapit Czyżak, the owner of a restaurant on Mylna Street, paid a 30 thousand zloty fine for serving two pork chops on a meat-free day."[602]

At the same time, the authorities zeroed in on the market places, where there were allegedly two buyers competing for every animal brought by peasants, which drove the price to absurd heights.[603] This enabled the authorities to widen the battlefront and strike at the private middlemen, who were much more effective than the state and coop purchasing agencies. The advantage that these private operators had is easy to explain. They had broad experience, often from

599 "Polska Zbrojna", no. 254, September 15, 1948. "On meatless days poultry and game are allowed," Aleksander Janta-Połczyński remembered from his visit to Poland in 1948. "On such days one can find on a restaurant menu, for example, a roast boar, pork or chicken schnitzel. I asked: what is this schnitzel made from? It's all made with veal, of course, they answered." A. Janta-Połczyński, *Wracam z Polski 1948*, Paryż 1949, p. 20.

600 "Gazeta Robotnicza", no. 253/September 13, 1948; "Dziennik Zachodni", no. 256/September 14, 948; "Gazeta Zachodnia" (Poznań), no. 314/September 16, 1948.

601 "Express Ilustrowany", no. 257/September 17, 1948; see: "Kurier Codzienny", no. 257/September 18, 1948.

602 *Kontrakcja Rządu i klasy robotniczej łamie dywersję spekulantów na rynku żywnościowym*, "Trybuna Robotnicza" (Katowice), no. 244/September 20, 1948.

603 "Kurier Codzienny", no. 254/September 15, 1948; "Rzeczpospolita", no. 268/September 28, 1948; see: *Kupcy podbijają ceny. Na targu bydlęcym w Rawie Mazowieckiej*, ŻW, no. 258/September 18, 1948; *Reorganizacja rynku mięsnego warunkiem skutecznego zwalczania spekulacji*, *ibid.*, no. 259/September 19, 1948; *W Siemiatyczach* [...], "Wieczór", no. 260/September 20, 1948; *Nadszedł czas walki*, "Słowo Polskie" (Wrocław), no. 258/September 18, 1948; *Walka z paskarzami rozpoczęta*, "Głos Pomorza" (Toruń), no. 260/September 2, 1948.

before the War; they were familiar with the local area and enjoyed the trust of the peasants. They also knew how to avoid inspections and had at their disposal the, usually illegal, distribution channels in the cities.[604] While the authorities advised leniency towards the farmers, because harsh repression was considered a "political error", merchants or restaurant owners could be punished mercilessly: not just fined but sent to labor camps. While in mid-1948, the average prison sentence amounted to no more than a few months, by the fall of that year, black marketeers were being sent to camps in Mielęcin or Chrusty with a sentence that was increasingly often as much as two years. The newspapers meticulously reported the harsh punishments, as a deterrent to others.[605]

The official propaganda was skewed to imply that it was the black marketeers who were the perpetrators, whereas the government was doing no more than fighting back. There was to be left no doubt who the winners were, with headlines such as: *After Deflecting the Attack* (*Trybuna Robotnicza*, September 23, 1948) or *Broken Offensive* (*Wrocławski Kurier Ilustrowany*, September 26, 1948). The goal of the propaganda was to demonstrate the caring nature of the government, portrayed as being concerned with the contents of the average citizen's cooking pot, and to imply a causative link between the new "meat stabilization" with the new political developments. In December 1948, the amalgamation of the Polish Workers Party (PPR) and Polish Socialist Party (PPS) took place. The two combined to form the Polish United Workers' Party (PZPR), which would remain in power until 1989. The "return to normalcy" promised during the Party Congress materialized on December 20, when the momentous decision to abolish rationing (from January 1, 1949) was made.[606]

The authorities achieved their first propaganda goal: proving that there was a link between pacifying the black marketeers and achieving market equilibrium. Now, the time came to comprehensively eliminate the enemy and substitute coop stores for the private stores.[607] In early 1949, the authorities were not denying they would be on the offensive this time around. For the time being, harassment continued, as the newspapers published ever-longer lists of those punished for illegal slaughter and trade. There was a new emphasis on denouncing black market sales of meat coming from sick or dead animals and much coverage space was

---

604 "Głos Ludu", no. 258/September 18, 1948.

605 AAN, KS, 11, fol. 84; "Gazeta Zachodnia", no. 258/September 20, 1948; "Głos Ludu", no. 268/September 28, 1948.

606 M. Jastrząb, *Puste półki. Problem zaopatrywania ludności w artykuły powszechnego użytku w Polsce w latach 1949–1956*, Warszawa 2004, p. 130.

607 "Robotnik", no. 319/November 19, 1948.

given to "butchers' scheming to prove that meat sales ought to be concentrated to a greater extent in the hands of the nationalized sector. Only then, when this had become a reality, would buyers be able to purchase meat easily and it would cease to be an object of speculation."[608]

These actions prepared the ground for the government's ultimate offensive. By December 7, 1948, the Economic Committee of the Council of Ministers (KERM) had decided on a new animal husbandry policy. "Operation H" was to stimulate animal production on small private farms and on large state and coop enterprises. Large funds, in excess of 6.2 billion (old) zloty, were allocated for the purpose.[609] On January 28, 1949, the Council of Ministers passed the motion and launched Operation H in public. The Council, according to *Kurier Polski*, "announced a new and great economic battle which we have to win just as we had won other battles: on bread, on trade, on surpassing production plan targets. On February 1, the great battle for meat begins!"[610]

Operation H began in an ominous way: on February 1, in an outside session in Żyrardów, the Warsaw District Court summarily sentenced the butcher Tadeusz Syrociński, accused of hiding 84 kg of pork fat, not only to confiscation of his store and deli meat shop as well as revocation of his professional license but also to the draconian –and unprecedented – seven years in prison.[611] From then on, the media coverage of "meat news" fell into two categories: either it focused on the successful government operations that, it was hoped, would be welcomed by peasants (such as governmental aid to newly opened state purchasing stations), or else it highlighted details of the battle with the nefarious black marketeers. Their operations, the public was told, "weigh heavily on the meat trade and impede supplying inhabitants of cities in accordance with the plan and which harm meat production. In order to win the battle for animal husbandry, we need to implement repressive measures against the speculator elements who engage in illegal slaughter and carcass trade. The inspections should be stepped up and the swindlers severely punished."[612]

---

608 "Express Ilustrowany", no. 15/January 16, 1949; "Kurier Codzienny" (Warszawa), no. 4/January 5, 1949.

609 "Kurier Polski", no. 29/January 30, 1949.

610 *Ibid.*

611 "Rzeczpospolita", no. 32/February 2, 1949.

612 "Słowo Polskie" (Wrocław), no. 46/February 16, 1949; see: "Dziennik Zachodni", no. 46/February16, 1949; "Express Poznański", no. 47/February 18, 1949.

In the countryside, the authorities carried out surveillance of travelers and market places as well as other sites where animals were traditionally sold.[613] Frequent inspections of butcher's stores and restaurants took place in cities and they usually resulted in the closing down of the raided establishments. For example in Kutno, store inspections lasted for three days (from February 10 to 12). The lists of butchers found guilty got longer again and, in line with the (in Polish, rhyming) saying that "hiding veal gets you straight to Mielęcin" (labor camp), sentences to labor-camp terms prevailed.[614] The authorities wanted to kill two birds with one stone: eliminating private buyers could force the peasants to "sell legally and locally, and by doing that contribute to fulfilling obligations in accordance with the plan."[615]

This was not easy. Private merchants immediately responded by developing further effective strategies.[616] Peasants were generally reluctant to establish any contact with the authorities, since they knew that even to register the sale of a pig or a calf would rebound on them with a tax, collected directly at the purchasing station. Ever since 1949, the authorities feared the consequences of tampering with meat production and tended to treat leniently peasants,[617] who were well aware of this. This is clear from the fact that there were cases of a farmer taking the blame for a butcher or other merchant, who would in fact pay the fine.[618] The anonymous letters arriving at the police (MO) and the Security Office (UB) or Special Commission (KS) offices, which were probably the trigger for most of the "slaughter" cases, reveal the intricate, interconnected network that hindered the punishment of violators. The following unsigned missive, from 1954, is equally

---

613 During a big inspection conducted before Easter 1949 (April 8 to 12) it turned out that on the first day alone and only in Gdańsk DOKP, 926 kg of meat was confiscated and approximately 50 people were arrested. The result was that smugglers developed new, shrewder strategies. For example, meat was mailed in packages (before Easter the number of such packages in Łódź alone rose from one to eight thousand daily) or transported via remote routes. "Głos Wybrzeża", no. 105/April 16–18, 1949; AAN, KS, 11, fol. 110.

614 "Express Ilustrowany", no. 43/February13, 1949; ibid., no. 64/March 6, 1949; "Głos Kutnowski", no. 44/February15, 1949; "Życie Częstochowy", no. 45/February15, 1949.

615 AAN, KS, 11, fol. 98.

616 The Warsaw Delegation of the Special Commission reported in September 1949: "What mostly happens during inspections is that meat is confiscated; the dealers are much harder to catch". *Ibid.*, Odprawa przewodniczących Delegatur KS, September 29, 1949, fol. 127.

617 *Ibid.*, fol 118.

618 *Ibid.*, fol. 127.

representative of periods earlier and later than the time it was penned: "in the village of Gulczewo, [citizen X] is engaged in selling meat and kielbasa. He kills cows and pigs, sells a lot, kills two animals every week and has been selling for over seven years. He got rich from selling meat, re-built his house and he gives nothing to the State. Yesterday in Kręgi Stare he bought a hog weighing 160 kg from this cobbler Skoczeń. He has no fear trading because he gets along well with the sołtys [head of the village], he invites him over and gives him scraps of meat so the sołtys doesn't make a fuss. When the police from Somianki arrive in the village, they don't even stop at Skoczeń's house, and why is that? So I am turning to the security authorities, please start the investigation because [citizen X] is a wrecker of the State." (NB, the Polish original was ungrammatical and misspelt.)[619]

In December 1949, the battle against illegal slaughter and meat sales entered a new phase, with "Operation U" [in Polish: *ubój* – slaughter], whereas "Operation Z" [in Polish: *zboże* – grain] was set up to tackle illegal milling. The recommended penalty for illegal slaughter and meat trading was a minimum of 18 months of labor camp.[620] Whereas, preceding the Operations, in 1946 and 1947, no-one had been sentenced to labor camp for illegal slaughter, and in 1948 – the measure had represented just over six percent of sentences, with 314 people punished in that way, in 1949 labor camp sentences jumped to 23.2% of sentences, with 2 119 issued.[621] In early 1950, Operation U intensified. After analyzing the defensive strategies of butchers, peasants and merchants (for example the right to slaughter for their own consumption), in late February 1950 the authorities issued a special circular which set out explicitly the circumstances in which slaughter could take place and meat be distributed and sold. It was now easier to catch peasants involved in criminal activity and send them to labor camp. However, by the spring, the authorities were already recommending that the repression ease and proceedings discontinue.[622] By 1950, the government felt sufficiently strong in the driving seat that, on July 24, Operation H ended.

619 AAN, KS, 1503, fol. 46.

620 AAN, KS, 11, fol. 166.

621 *Komisja Specjalna do Walki z Nadużyciami i Szkodnictwem Gospodarczym 1945–1954*, ed. D. Jarosz, T. Wolsza, Warszawa 1995, p. 104.

622 AAN, KS, 4, fol. 2–4, 6.

5.2.2 "State Ribs Will Taste Better..." 1950–1956

The authorities declared victory too early. The meat supply had not improved and the meat black marketeers continued their operations. Contrary to expectations, the government's actions prompted the appearance of new illegal merchants: butchers who, having been ousted from their shops, traveled from village to village, offering their services. The scale of illegal slaughter can be estimated by noting the discrepancy between the official numbers of purchases of cattle by head and the purchase of rawhides. According to the State Commission for Economic Planning, between January and July 1951, the state bought 404 857 cows and 559 799 cow rawhides, as well as 1 250 247 calves and 1 993 086 calfskins.[623] Clearly, a proportion of the carcasses must have been spirited away.

During the 1950s, an entire network of middlemen was involved in the illegal meat trade. Zbigniew Kiulin, Illnesses caused by meat: TAPEWORM, *"Szpilki", no. 35, 2 September 1951.*

623 M. Jastrząb, *Puste półki...*, pp. 82–83.

By 1950, there were recurrent waves of hunger panic. In the following year, largely due to post-war burdens, the state supply system collapsed; this much was most painfully evident within the sensitive meat industry sector. State purchases kept decreasing; in August 1951, the amount of meat the state bought from the farmers did not reach even half of the level achieved in the previous year. People openly voiced their dissatisfaction. A strike broke out in Żyrardów. The lines in front of the, mostly state-owned, butcher stores would begin to form in the evening for the next morning's opening. In a butcher's on Puławska Street in Warsaw (on August 23), the crowd was heard chanting: "Stalin! Bierut! Meat!" – a daring juxtaposition for the era.[624] The authorities had no option other than to reinstate the ration coupons, now euphemistically called "meat-and-fat vouchers".[625] A street poet expressed his feeling about how effective they were:

> What's there to say,
> Why bother to yell.
> They won't let us die,
> So we gotta stay alive.
>
> It'd be all simple and plain –
> The Grim Reaper would win the day…
> But the meat stamp gets in the way,
> Won't let Death take you away.
>
> And just when you're almost done,
> It fights Death with some spam.
> For the meat stamp
> Does little to nourish,
> But it just won't let you perish.[626]

Naturally, it followed that both the illegal trade and the ostentatious fight against it intensified.[627] In stores, railway stations and at market places inspections

---

624 APW, KWar. PZPR, July 3–43, vol. 1, fol. 187.

625 *Centrum władzy. Protokoły posiedzeń kierownictwa PZPR. Wybór z lat 1949–1970*, ed. A. Dudek, A. Kochański, K. Persak, Warszawa 2000, pp. 96–98; M. Jastrząb, *Puste półki…*, pp. 161–207.

626 ODZP TVP, 1050/1, letter from October 18, 1951.

627 The anonymous letter sent by a farmer from Biłgoraj to a Fala 49 radio program on August 31, 1951 shows what the authorities were up against: "Dear Fala 49, how can we catch these profiteers? If a worker doesn't buy under the counter even as little as 10g of meat or fat, then he won't get to eat meat or fat at all since it's unavailable in the coop stores. If I could buy at the coop at least one kg of some fat once a week for a family of five […], I myself would denounce at least three profiteers. But if I did

became more frequent, and women smuggling meat in milk cans were arrested, just as they used to be during the German occupation. Once again, merchants arrested and punished by the Special Commission became the news of the day.[628] The war on the meat front continued. In a circular distributed in early December 1951, the Ministry of Public Security (MBP) announced: "The fight against illegal slaughter, speculative trading of meat and cattle and all other forms of hostile activities is one of the main conditions of successful contracts, crucial for meat supply [...] The County Office of Public Security (PUBP), the County Police Headquarters (PKMO) and in particular the community divisions of the police must engage in the fight against the enemy in this field."[629]

The main goal of the operation was to secure the implementation of obligatory deliveries of livestock for slaughter, which were re-instated by the Act of February 15, 1952. President Bolesław Bierut personally censored a flyer prepared for that occasion by the Central Committee of the Polish United Workers' Party (KC PZPR) and the General Committee of the United People's Party (ZSL).[630] He was the author of the invocation "Citizen peasants!" and added several anti-speculation phrases to the body of the text (such as the need to "subdue the profiteers getting fat at the expense of the working people" on account of "speculation").[631] Introducing the obligatory deliveries was one of the preparatory stages for Operation R, with the "R" standing for the (simultaneous) "regulation of prices and wages" – euphemism for steep price hikes – and abolition of food coupons, as well as legalizing private, albeit regulated, trade in farm product surpluses that was meant to provide competition for the black market. The changes were to be implemented on January 3, 1953. The authorities assumed that even though the official prices would be higher than those on the black market, the superior quality of the product would compensate for the difference. They expected "state ribs" to taste better since the peasants who sold meat illegally, usually kept behind a portion of pork fat for their own use, whereas the authorities calculated the "price of meat with fat included". The "legal" meat would be available in smaller quantities, whereas the farmers sold meat in volume.[632]

---

turn in a profiteer, then all that I and my family would have to eat would be potatoes without even any butter...."; *ibid.*, Biuletyn 29, September 6, 1951.

628 APW, KWar. PZPR, July 30; 43, vol. 1, fol. 199, 240.

629 AIPN, Ministry of Public Security (Ministerstwo Bezpieczeństwa Publicznego,) 699, fol. 165.

630 "Polish United Workers Party and United People's Party to all peasants, small and medium landholders".

631 AAN, Bolesław Bierut Archive, 254/IV–16.

632 AAN, KC PZPR, 237/V/151, fol. 6.

Individual peasants could seek a permit for legal commercial slaughter. It was common practice to make repeated use of a single issued permit, and the meat found its way to the black market, as the cartoon by Jerzy Srokowski illustrates; "Szpilki", no. 35, 2 September 1951.

rys. Jerzy Srokowski

Niektórzy chłopi biją większą ilość świń na jedno zezwolenie.

— Po co bijecie tyle świń?
— Dla rodziny.
— ?
— Dla tej rodziny, która co tydzień przyjeżdża po towar.

"The process of creating free a market," the authorities predicted, "should reveal the following trends: on the one hand, the disappearance of speculation risk should result in decreased demand for meat. On the other – additional demand for meat should arise among the categories of population that today do not have access to the black market and do not have time to stand in lines."[633] Such a mechanism might have worked with a larger margin of political freedom. However, in 1953 it was not feasible: the budding free market blueprint was marred

633 *Ibid.*, fol. 3.

by the numerous restrictions on the peasants, which made it unacceptable. In order to sell meat officially, farmers were expected to first provide all their obligatory deliveries and slaughter the animals in state-owned or coop slaughterhouses. They could then sell meat in designated places only, exclusively in "retail portions" of up to five kilos each. Transporting larger amounts of meat without an appropriate certificate was forbidden.[634]

The poor harvests of 1952 and 1953 aggravated the already difficult situation, while official policies did nothing to inspire experimental ingenuity among peasants. The money paid for compulsory deliveries often covered only half of the cost of production (which in 1953 alone caused the farmers a massive loss of between three and five billion zloty) and, together with high land tax, effectively eroded the farmers' economy. Peasants did nothing to up production even when they were able to, because they worried about the rising costs of services and other financial burdens.[635] Unsurprisingly, they distributed legally only a portion of the surplus, while the remaining part they tried to sell, even if not at higher prices, certainly outside of the state-regulated market. It is difficult to estimate the size of the unofficial deals between the cities and the rural areas; however, its sheer existence had to be painful for the authorities, which is why, on November 29, 1954, the government issued a circular urging citizens to intensify the fight against the illegal trade in animals for slaughter with a view to profiteering and to tighten the discipline of compulsory deliveries.[636]

The circular failed to have the expected effect. By the second half of 1955, the first signs of a political thaw encouraged the peasants to sabotage the compulsory deliveries. In August 1955, they delivered to state outlets only 63% of the stipulated quantities of meat and milk, and in Lublin, Kielce, Białystok, and Koszalin voivodships – no more than 40%. In spite of the official supervision of the meat trade implemented as a countermeasure, in September 1955, compulsory deliveries fell to 48.4% of the required amount.[637] Criminal sanctions also proved fairly ineffective in the face of that great enemy of communism – the weather: a severe winter impeded deliveries; soon after, the spring flooding had the same effect.[638] Reports arriving in Warsaw from all over the country were similar to the

634 *Ibid.*, fol. 16.

635 L. Próchniak, *Kolektywizacja rolnictwa w regionie łódzkim*, Łódź 2003, p. 141.

636 A. Kochański, *Polska 1944–1991. Informator historyczny*, vol. 1: *Podział administracyjny, ważniejsze akty prawne, decyzje i enuncjacje państwowe (1944–1956)*, Warszawa 1996, p. 550.

637 AAN, KC PZPR, 237/XII-240, fol. 27, 41.

638 AAN, MHW, 78, fol. 38.

one sent from Łódź in mid-March 1956: "The butcher and dairy stores are under great pressure. Meat, cured meats and fats all sell out in an hour or two, and the lines are interminable. There is a mood of dissatisfaction and anxiety among the customers. The workers express their discontent during official meetings, in letters sent to various institutions, and so on."[639] Soon, the workers' discontent would spill out onto the streets.

5.2.3 "In Gomułka's Times, There Are Only Crumbs…": 1956–1970

Immediately following Polish Thaw in October 1956 butchers, who after 1948 had been forced to close their stores and shops, took advantage of the new green light for the private sector. The number of butcher stores grew again from 479 in 1955 to 863 in 1956, and 2 525 in 1957.[640] This partially relieved the pressure on the authorities, especially those at the provincial level, of supply problems and this in turn improved somewhat the public mood. Indeed, the improvement merited bending the law a little. By early 1957, the Minister of Justice informed Prime Minister Józef Cyrankiewicz that in regional Poland, official consent for the further development of crafts had been misunderstood – "in the sense that the leading role of the State is unnecessary, including in the meat trade, and that the monopoly of state institutions in this sector of the economy should be limited in favor of private butcher shops."[641] The National Council presidia widely authorized private butchers to purchase meat and livestock directly from farmers. As for the farmers, they compared the profit from state deliveries and private sales with that to be derived from selling meat to the group of illegal middlemen that had quickly re-emerged – and increasingly chose the latter option, especially since the risk was minimal. By the turn of 1956 and 1957, the situation on the market resembled that of the fall of 1948. There were instances when the law enforcement agencies sided with meat profiteers; for example in Limanów, at the instigation of black marketeers, the county police assaulted the official purchase agents.[642] In the Kraków voivodship in early January 1957, "according to estimates, black marketeers bought amounts of livestock that would be enough for a week's provisions for all of Kraków and Nowa Huta."[643] The situation was similar everywhere in Poland.

639 *Ibid.*, fol. 45.
640 AAN, MS, 3084, fol. 26.
641 AAN, MS, 3091, fol. 6.
642 *Ibid.*, fol. 7.
643 *Ibid.*

The regulations issued in early 1957 that limited the economic freedom of private butchers were not effective, nor were attempts to bring their operations to the attention of the police (MO) and National Trade Inspectorate (PIH). The old distribution networks were quick to re-emerge, and new ones would soon appear, and adapt themselves to the new circumstances. The authorities were not eager to impose drastic measures, as they were fully aware that in times of chaos, a full plate food is a good guarantee of peace. Some of the regional decisions have been mentioned earlier. The central government conducted a policy of appeasing the citizens by raising wages and maintaining lower prices, including those of meat. Economists, Czesław Bobrowski to name one, fully aware of the dire economic consequences of such a policy, tried to convince the decision makers that it was imperative to raise prices. To no avail. "The longer the lines for meat," argued Prime Minister Józef Cyrankiewicz, "the easier it will be for citizens to accept new prices."[644] The authorities were hoist by their own petard: society got used to low prices, and to increased consumption. In 1955, the annual average public-sector wages could buy 41 kg of beef, 32 kg of pork, 41 kg of plain sausage, 19 kg of ham, and 31 kg of pork fat. Three years later the figures were, respectively, 56, 44, 56, 26, and 54 kg.[645]

In 1958, probably for the first time since the Second World War, a supply of meat sufficient to meet demand was recorded. It was also the last time. In 1958, the authorities changed their economic policy and initiated the next phase of intensive industrialization – at the expense of agriculture. Rumors – not entirely baseless – of collectivization, returned and immediately put a stop to farmers' investment in production. It did not help that coincidentally in 1958, a poor potato harvest had an adverse effect on cattle and pig farming. The awakened appetites were not satisfied in 1959: the deepening problems with meat brought a wave of discontent in the summer of that year. Elements of nostalgia for what, with the hindsight, now seemed like the "good ol' times" under Bierut and the "right and just" rationing system began to appear in the letters arriving at Polish Radio. The title of this subsection comes from that correspondence.[646]

On October 20, 1959, Mieczysław Rakowski noted in his diary: "The Party has been gripped by meat fever. The shortage of meat has revealed all the other weaknesses in the system. Let's put it in plain words: we have an economic crisis."[647] At this troubled time, the government reverted to the tried and tested

644 C. Bobrowski, *Wspomnienia ze stulecia*, Lublin 1985, p. 256.

645 AAN, KC PZPR, 1692, fol. 11.

646 ODZP TVP, 1050/29, Biuletyn listów no. 47/September 12, 1959.

647 M.F. Rakowski, *Dzienniki polityczne 1958–1962*, Warszawa 1998, p. 145.

remedies of the past: hikes in the price of meat (on average by some 20%; yet for the cheapest kinds of cured meat purchased mostly by workers, the rise was in excess of 35%)[648] and renewed, intense onslaught on the black marketeers, again blamed as partially responsible for the higher prices. Just as a decade earlier, this strategy was supposed to convince farmers to sell the livestock to the state just as it had been – and with no better results.

The first item on the agenda of the Politburo session on October 3, 1959 was the meat price hikes, the second – the fight against meat speculation. The Politburo accepted the Prime Minister's ordinance of October 1, 1959, which established special Inspectorates for Fighting the Abuses in the Meat Economy at Police Headquarters (KG MO) and Voivodship Police Headquarters (KW MO), not only in Warsaw and Łódź but also down to county level. The new institution destined to deal with crime in all sectors of meat industry (state purchase, processing, and trade) was to be under the special care of Voivodship Committees of the Polish United Workers' Party, which were also responsible for hiring appropriate civil personnel (National Trade Inspectorate, PIH, Supreme Audit Office, and NIK).[649] A hastily organized press campaign resembled that from the turn of 1948 and 1949, and was aimed at convincing society that it was the peasants and black marketeers who were to blame for the shortages.[650]

The propaganda campaign created the backdrop for the Third Session of the Central Committee of the Polish United Workers' Party, dedicated mostly to meat problems. Party First Secretary Władysław Gomułka, who chaired the session, came up with a blindingly obvious assessment of the situation: "The crux of the problem is that the demand for meat is greater than the supply."[651] More importantly, these were the causes of the shortages that he listed: increased purchasing power, population growth, an incorrect relationship between the price of meat and that of other products, declining animal husbandry, and the increased

648 AAN, KC PZPR, 1693, Politburo session, September 15, 1959, fol. 504.

649 AAN, KC PZPR, V/63, Poliburo session, October 3, 1959, fol. 102. The ordinance of the Minister of Internal Affairs from October 8, 1959 established the mandate of the inspectorates in Police and Voivod Police Headquarters. On December 5, 1959 the Prime Minister appointed inspectors in city and county police headquarters; A. Kochański, *Polska 1944–1991. Informator historyczny*, vol. 2: *Ważniejsze akty prawne, decyzje i enuncjacje państwowe (1957–1970)*, Warszawa 2000, pp. 180, 188.

650 For example: "Kurier Polski", no. 241/October 12, 1959.

651 W. Gomułka, *Aktualne trudności na rynku mięsnym i środki niezbędne dla ich przezwyciężenia*. Presentation at the Third Session of the PUWP CC on October 17, 1959, Warszawa 1959, p. 10.

number of animals slaughtered by farmers. The Session called for the raising of meat prices and an increase in the production of meat substitutes, the introduction of a more restrictive policy towards farmers and, finally, for the waging of a "decisive war against economic crimes".[652]

The police had their work cut out for the next few months. In October 1959, Police Headquarters (KG MO) specified what should be on its radar: purchases of livestock for reasons other than farming by people who did not own farms, slaughter or sales of livestock sooner than three months from the date of purchase (undue haste taken to be indicative of speculation), meat deliveries to the market by farmers not complying with their delivery obligation, sales of "home-made" cured meats and meat from slaughter without official permission, meat inspections in places other than designated and in pieces weighing more than five kilograms.[653] The police were expected to show interest in market places, flea markets and crowd gatherings, and instructed to inspect access roads, main roads, and bus and railroad stations. Both uniformed and undercover agents were required to identify individuals involved in illegal trade, conduct conversations with well-known black marketeers and organize around them a network of secret "informers in order to provide a constant flow of information on the illegal meat trade."[654] In the cities, the police were instructed to keep an eye on those who bought meat in stores with the intention of re-selling it, and on those who offered for sale meat brought from the countryside. In order to identify the latter, local police had to watch anyone who regularly delivered "milk and dairy products each morning in order to establish if they were at the same time distributing meat from illegal slaughter."[655] Police had also to check whether illegal "booze dives" – known as *melinas* – were engaged in meat trade as a side line. Special attention had to be paid to slaughterhouse and meat processing plants employees who stole meat from their place of work; such cases were to be handled by specialist investigative police units.

In late November 1959, the Ministry of Internal Trade joined the crackdown against the black marketeers by confirming an absolute ban on selling meat and cured meats from private slaughter and by hindering strategies used by farmers such as repeated use of permits for individual slaughter and sale. The local councils, responsible for granting and issuing permits, could now reject the application

652 *Ibid.*, pp. 69–83.
653 AIPN, KG MO, 35/3422.
654 *Ibid.*
655 *Ibid.*

if the permit seeker had been previously convicted for meat speculation.[656] There were many such applicants – by the end of February 1960, the police (MO) had embarked on 13 153 meat-related investigations, most of them in the Bydgoszcz, Katowice, Kielce, Kraków, Poznań, and Warsaw Voivodships.

By late 1960, the inspectorates had launched 24 705 investigations and pressed charges in 21 052 cases. The pace slowed down significantly in the following year. The inspectorates engaged National Trade Inspectorate (PIH) and Supreme Audit Office (NIK) employees only temporarily, and they soon had to return to their previous duties. In 1961, the inspectorates at county and city level were dissolved and in police headquarters, including the voivodship level, a mere 202 functionaries were allocated to these specific tasks. Most of them perceived this as a professional degradation and used any pretext to switch jobs. Those who remained tended to be less skilled and many became corrupt in the course of their duty. In 1961, the number of investigations fell to 7 113 (down by 71.2%) and only in 2 829 cases (down by 86.6%) were charges pressed.[657]

Table 3. Fraud in the meat economy: September 1959 – February 1960

Perpetrator Category	Total	Arrests
Meat traders	4 694	626
Animal traders	3 202	595
Meat plant employees	2 553	524
State purchase station employees	1 233	341
Retail store employees	1 063	131
Other	2 571	207

Source: Information on economic crime in 1959, Warszawa 1960 (Supreme Audit Office, NIK, Economic Fraud Department (Wydział ds. Nadużyć Gospodarczych); copy in the author's possession).

Subsequently, the numbers probably decreased further; it is not possible to find any trace of the inspectorates' activity in the following years, even though they existed on paper until 1970.

None of this meant that the market was stable. On the contrary – 1962 brought another deep slump in meat supply and a wave of new ideas about limiting its

656 *Ibid.*
657 AZZ, CRZZ Wydział Socjalny, 204/29, 204/36, unpag.

consumption, including restricting the number of meat dishes in restaurants and increasing the number serving only vegetarian fare.[658] The severe winter of 1962/1963, followed by a summer drought, exacerbated the problems and led the authorities to implement radical saving programs.[659] "Standing in line is a part of everyday life," Mieczysław Rakowski noted in his diary on December 2, 1963. "Hundreds and millions of people chase after meat and deli cuts. We have not had such difficulties in a long time."[660] The authorities were taking note of meat issues and becoming more sensitive about the topic. There had already been plans in 1961 and 1962 to create a National Inspectorate for the Meat Economy (Państwowa Inspekcja Gospodarki Mięsnej) with a brief to supervise all aspects of the meat trade, from state purchase to retail, thus complementing the police inspectorates.[661] A Meat Inspectorate was finally created in August 1964, without doubt as a side effect of the "meat affair", a scandal which – in a different economic and political environment – would have not ended as it did: with the death penalty for Stanisław Wawrzecki.[662]

An analysis of acts of fraud committed in the meat industry and presentation of methods used to combat them is not one of my main goals. However, scams in the industry significantly influenced how the authorities viewed the meat problem, part of which was the traditional meat black market. The grand operation against the profiteers did nothing to fill the butcher stores with stock. "Many people conclude," the authorities reported from Warsaw in July 1964, "that even though the swindlers have been arrested, there is no improvement in the

658 AZZ, CRZZ Social Department (Wydział Socjalny), 204/30, Conclusions concerning limiting meat consumption in public catering, October 2, 1962.

659 AZZ, CRZZ Social Department, 204/33, Market evaluation 1962–1963, June 25, 1963. The resolution of the Economic Committee of the Council of Ministers (KERM) from August 10, 1963 restricted the deliveries of bulk meat fat for voivodships. Consequently, the Ministry of Internal Trade (MHW) asked the chairmen of the presidiums of the Voivodship National Councils (WRN) to save the maximum amount of meat at the expense of cured and processed meat and make restaurants and other public catering outlets "serve fish, herring and vegetarian dishes". Meat-free Mondays should be observed unconditionally; *ibid.*, MHW to the chairmen of WRN presidiums, August 20, 1963. The authorities considered replacing meat with soya in cured meats. AAN, KC PZPR, 1730, Note on changes in meat and meat products supply, December 16, 1963, fol. 96.

660 M.F. Rakowski, *Dzienniki polityczne 1963–1966*, Warszawa 1999, p. 97.

661 AZZ, CRZZ Wydział Socjalny, 204/29.

662 See: D. Jarosz, M. Pasztor, *Afera mięsna…*

provision of meat."[663] As a result, the authorities sought unconventional administrative and technological solutions,[664] while at the same time increasing repressive measures, especially against farmers. In the Central Archives of Modern Records in Warsaw there can be found Władysław Gomułka's notes from 1964, among them, his "Note on banning the slaughter of calves and on increasing the number of cattle in individual farms" that Gomułka wrote after reading a, less than uplifting, report on "Production reserves of medium and large peasant farms."[665] His emphasis was not so much on the development of animal farming but rather on the prosecution of illegal slaughter. Gomułka advocated steep fines (of between one and two thousand zloty) and suggested that "to be more effective, we can reward those who report illegal slaughter with 100 zloty per calf, with the reward payable once the fine had been levied. Transferring the fines wholly or in part to the Community National Council (GRN) should be considered in order to encourage the combat of the illegal slaughter of calves."[666] Gomułka recommended the introduction of a national ban on private trading in veal in order to limit the slaughter of calves, thereby providing a boost to livestock husbandry. Each case of illegal slaughter would be punished with steep fines and confiscation of meat. "In order to encourage the prosecution of illegal veal trading, the police should receive a reward each time that they confiscate veal."[667] Let us bear in mind that these words were not written by a local party apparatchik but by the First Secretary of the Polish United Workers' Party!

But even the most innovative ideas could not repair the market. Random inspections of stores conducted on the orders of Prime Minister Józef Cyrankiewicz in the cities and towns of the Warsaw, Łódź, Kielce, and Poznań voivodships in September 1965 yielded depressing results. The stores had insufficient stock; meat and processed-food shortages were chronic.[668] Withdrawing some meat

---

663 APW, KWar. PZPR, 30/VII–43, t. 24, Special Information, July 10, 1964.

664 See: D. Jarosz, M. Pasztor, *Z badań nad stosunkiem władz Polski Ludowej do niedoborów mięsa*, "Roczniki Dziejów Społecznych i Gospodarczych" 65, 2005, pp. 229–266.

665 AAN, KC PZPR, 237/V/917, fol. 43–47.

666 *Ibid.*, fol. 46.

667 *Ibid.*, fol. 47. Indeed, in 1964 the slaughter of calves was banned, which led to bizarre situations: "Agricultural services, ORMO patrols, the police, and Party activists blocked the roads on market days trying to prevent veal 'leaks'. Often disturbances would occur, with the protesters using pitch forks and stakes. More cases were brought before the courts against those who had assaulted the functionaries than those slaughtering calves illegally." The ban was abolished in 1971; M. Mońko, *Zedrzeć skórkę incognito*, "Polityka", No. 8/February 22, 1986.

668 AZZ, CRZZ Wydział Ekonomiczny, 204/43.

from supplies earmarked for export did not radically change the situation. The year 1966 was a little better but the next big slump was just around the corner. On September 6, 1967, the Minister of Agriculture Mieczysław Jagielski "emphasized that, in comparison with the actual capacity, plans concerning the internal needs and the export of agricultural produce are pure fiction." This naturally had impact on the growth of illegal trade, particularly in smaller cities, where the official distribution of meat practically ceased to function.[669]

Rumors resurfaced of the government plans to increase prices. In fact the authorities had been considering this option for some time, as a way of temporarily limiting demand for meat but kept postponing the unpopular decision. They decided to try and implement it at the worst possible moment, in the fall of 1967, when due to the shortages, the public mood was on the verge of explosion.[670] On October 24, 1967, the Politburo supported a 16% price hike.[671] It came into force in late November and caused a wave of discontent and protest, even short-lived strikes. In the end, the authorities managed to pacify the public; it is possible that the anti-Semitic campaign, unleashed at the turn of 1967 and 1968, was partly intended to divert public reaction to the price rises. There was however, another effect of raising prices, which the Party strategists had in fact been aware of. They raised retail prices but not the state purchase prices. Once again, the peasants turned out to be capitalists: instead of selling to the state, they opted for the black market.[672]

State purchase prices went up only on January 1, 1970. The peasants responded with mass deliveries, which in several voivodships closed down the delivery stations for several days.[673] The price increase could not eliminate the abysmally inadequate supply of animal feed, coal and fertilizer, nor counter the effects of the long and severe winter of 1969/1970. By April 1970, the Ministry of Agriculture began to spin a dark forecast for the second half of the year.[674] The predictions included problems with provisions, an increase of illegal slaughter and general fraud in the meat sector. The grim outlook probably prompted the accelerated setting up of the National Inspectorate of Purchasing and Processing Agricultural Products (Państwowa Inspekcja Skupu i Przetwórstwa Artykułów Rolnych, PISiPAR) that was to replace two existing Inspectorates, which dealt specifically

669 AIPN, 0296/66, vol. 2, fol. 1–2.

670 M. Zaremba, *Gdzie jest mięso. Donosy o nastrojach Polaków z przełomu 1967 i 1968 r.*, "Polityka", No. 8/February 21, 1998.

671 AAN, KC PZPR, 1738, fol. 190.

672 J. Krok-Paszkowski, *Podatek od mięsa*, "Kultura", Paris 1968, No. 1/243–2/224, p. 128.

673 AAN, URM, 5.3/11, fol. 38.

674 AAN, URM, 5.3/12, fol. 5, 12–13.

with grain and meat. The authorities did not hide their desire to strengthen the "meat division", until then only loosely connected with the prosecuting authorities and city councils, which operated only in seven voivodships. The Inspectorate (PISiPAR) was finally created by the Act of June 30, 1970 (Journal of Laws, no. 16, Art. 137), its authority enhanced at national level with increased powers and appropriate tools.[675]

The bleak forecast turned out to be correct. In late 1970, store shelves emptied, free-market prices went up again,[676] and the authorities got ready to impose a new price hike. It had not been long since the last one, and the public mood was so fragile that even members of the Party establishment worried about the fallout. By late November 1970, Artur Starewicz predicted that a price rise would "start a deep and fast-spread political crisis"[677] – little could he know how fast. In no more than a month, a new team came to power.

5.2.4 "When There Are Pigs, There Will Be Smart Ideas…":[678] 1971–1980

A day after the December price rise had been announced, one Krystyna Dębińska from Żory wrote to a radio station: "The price hike has hit us like a bolt out of the blue. We've been plunged into a horrible predicament. We used to have meat and choice cuts on Sundays and on special occasions. From now on, we will be having meat at best three times a year: for Christmas, Easter and maybe on May the First [the International Workers' Day]."[679] A year later, she would have been able to feel much more optimistic. As mentioned earlier, consumption, including meat, rose rapidly in the early years of the decade. Higher state purchasing prices altered patterns of consumption: the peasants now slaughtered their animals less often for their own consumption, preferring instead to buy meat at the butcher's store. Rudimentary market laws proved to be working and helped arrive at an outcome that Gomułka had tried to achieve by repression: in 1971, the number

675 AAN, URM, 5.3/13, fol. 27; *ibid.*, 5.3/14, fol. 523--525, 528. It turned out that the security measures in the meat industry had been tightened only on paper. Between 1965 and 1968 alone, twelve major affairs were exposed. Meat plants managers-in-chief of were involved in nine of these, and their deputies – in all of them. Major frauds were also uncovered in plants where criminal gangs had previously been liquidated." AAN, KC PZPR, 237/XII–448, fol. 7.

676 APW, Warsaw Voivodship Committee of PUWP, 60/VIII–31, vol. 1, fol. 48–51.

677 M.F. Rakowski, *Dzienniki polityczne 1969–1971*, Warszawa 2001, pp. 263–264.

678 AAN, URM, 5.3/86, fol. 96.

679 ODZP TVP, 1231/2, Biuletyn 1971, 1(560), Commentary on recent events.

of animal hides purchased by the state – a clear indicator of private slaughter – began to decrease. Comrade Wiesław's dreams were finally materializing – farmers' main objective was now livestock husbandry.[680]

However, consumption kept growing quickly – too quickly! – and often on credit, to boot. An economic collapse became a matter of time. A supply crisis was first experienced in the middle of 1973 and led immediately to a renewed proliferation of illegal strategies. "In the cities, door-to-door illegal sales of meat and 'neighborly' deliveries to work places are commonplace. In the first six months of this year, state purchases of cowhide grew by 33%, and pigskin by 21% while sales of calfskin are still going strong – all this points to the growing presence of illegal operations."[681]

A temporary improvement in supply fooled the decision makers. "When I was recently talking with Jaroszewicz," Mieczysław Rakowski noted on June 18, 1974, "and told him that people were grumbling about meat shortages, I heard from him there would be no more meat. He said that people would complain at first but then calm down."[682] The supplies kept getting worse yet Poles showed no signs of calming down. The first meltdown came in February 1975, when stores began to resemble those of the final, ravenous years of the previous decade.[683] It certainly influenced the public mood. According to polls conducted by the Center of Public Opinion Research (OBOP) in 1974, 34% of the population rated the level of provision in grocery stores as good. A year later, less than half could find any poultry, fish or liverwurst to buy in the neighborhood store, and only 4% of the respondents were able to buy boneless beef or ham.[684] Despite the prevailing "propaganda of success" (according to the plan accepted in October 1974 at the 15th Plenary Session of the Central Committee of the Polish United Workers' Party, annual meat consumption was expected to grow to 90 kg per capita by 1990), it was becoming increasingly clear that the demand would not be met, especially if prices remained as they were. A re-run of the hard-to-forget 1960s was just around the corner. The less chance there was to buy meat in official stores, the more often people turned to illegal sources.[685]

---

680 AAN, URM, 5.3/30, fol. 258–259; *Rynek mięsny*, "Polityka", No. 37/ September 9, 1972.

681 APKr, KW PZPR, 319, fol. 174.

682 M.F. Rakowski, *Dzienniki polityczne 1972–1975...*, pp. 258–259.

683 Z. Szeliga, *Mięso – kłopoty i perspektywy*, "Polityka", No. 11/March 15, 1975.

684 M. Zaremba, *"Bigosowy socjalizm". Dekada Gierka*, in: *Polacy wobec PRL. Strategie przystosowawcze*, ed. G. Miernik, Kielce 2003, p. 198.

685 AAN, KC PZPR, WO, 3067, vol. 56, fol. 44.

The black market distribution assumed such proportions that on October 8, 1975 the government embarked on a battle against the unofficial trade in agricultural produce. Meat was the only item specifically identified in the document.[686] As in the fall of 1959, the state was guaranteed a pre-emptive right to buy livestock. The authorities were to identify individuals selling theirs – legally or otherwise – on the free market as well as all those who did not fulfill their contract agreements or sabotaged their state deliveries (although deliveries to state outlets had not been compulsory since 1972). City and county officials were expected to talk to such people "explaining the economic and social damage caused by this kind of action, urging them to fulfill their duties to the state, and forbidding further illegal activities." If this approach did not work, the officials could refer the case to the "appropriate agencies", which included PISiPAR, police, and the prosecutor's office.

The onus was now on the Minister of the Interior Affairs to urge the police to put some vigor into the fight against illegal trade and make use of existing legislation (such as the Public Health Regulations, already in force since the 1940s); however, no discrete institution was set up for the purpose, as had been the case in 1959. The operation did not bring spectacular results, accompanied as it was by significant public (and one can guess also institutional) resistance. In any event, a mere year later, after the price hikes announced in 1976 were abandoned, the local officials at *gmina* (lowest administrative) level were again required to give verbal warnings to farmers who were not fulfilling their contracts with the state. Permits for private slaughter were to be refused. This time, however, the officials were expected to create special teams that would combat illegal trading and control distribution and transportation.[687]

By all accounts, the relevant authorities were just as reluctant to implement these recommendations as they were to force through the Politburo's orders to limit the amount of meat in the catering industry, with an emphasis on "low meat-content dishes" (and preferably no meat content at all), to introduce a second meat-free day a week,[688] and to make it compulsory for industrial enterprises to set up their own livestock fattening houses.[689] Neither any of these initiatives nor the fast-track research on krill-processing and adaptation of "other sea organisms"[690] for human consumption did anything to improve the outlook for meat stores; on

686 AAN, KC PZPR, 1786, fol. 576–587.

687 AAN, KC PZPR, 1792, The Minister of Internal Trade and Services to voivods and city mayors, July 1976, fol. 446.

688 *Ibid.*

689 AAN, KC PZPR, XI/834, k. 162–165.

690 AAN, KC PZPR, 1794, k. 4.

the contrary, they contributed directly to further expansion of the black market, further upping the illegal prices. In July 1977, in the Nowy Sącz voivodship there were complaints that free-market prices had gone up by almost a third in comparison with the previous year.[691] A year later, a Nowy Targ resident sent a missive to the Politburo: "There are illegal dives in our city where you can buy choice cuts of meat for 120–140 zł (sausage) and ham at 300 zl per kilogram, but I ask you, who can afford that? Only furriers and doctors, and nobody else".[692] All sectors of illegal meat production showed signs of recovery. In 1977, the Department of Professional Development at the Ministry of Internal Affairs published (for internal purposes only) reference materials on "meat"[693] crimes, and the Institute of Crime Problems in Warsaw conducted research on fraud in the meat industry.

In the "commercial stores", which opened in 1976, choice cuts of meat were offered at much higher prices. The stores were intended to facilitate the process of realigning market prices. The authorities were also seriously considering allowing farmers to set independent prices of the meat distributed legally (until then, they had been able to raise prices by no more than 40%). This move was aimed at reducing the profitability of black market transactions, usually conducted in poor hygienic conditions but, above all, it was expected "to educate buyers about the actual costs of meat production".[694] It took a decade to achieve this goal. In the years that followed, the meat market changed in ways that the planners of the Gierek era could not have imagined.

5.2.5 "They Slaughter a Pig, Because They Have to Eat ...": 1980–1989

The year 1979 was not good for Polish agriculture but the following year proved to be catastrophic, the worst since the Second World War. Agricultural production fell by 10.7%. The grain harvest stayed at the same level as in the previous, weak year but the sugar beet harvest was smaller by a third and that of potatoes shrank to half its former size; this had an immediate impact on animal husbandry. In the second half of 1980, the authorities imported a significant amount of animal feed but this move was not enough to prevent the catastrophe. Shortage of animal feed had a short-lived, positive impact on butcher stores meat supplies

691 AAN, KC PZPR, WO, 3202.

692 AAN, KC PZPR, XI/1064, k. 156.

693 W. Dąbrowski, T. Jakubczyk, *Nielegalny obrót zwierzętami rzeźnymi i artykułami rolno-spożywczymi. Wybrane zagadnienia*, Warszawa 1977.

694 AAN, KC PZPR, XIA/476, fol. 21–22.

when, in the fall of 1980, peasants started selling off their livestock. State purchasing stations and cold storage groaned with meat and the processing plants could not keep up.[695] It was a harbinger of problems in the very near future.

The crash came in the first months of 1981. In that year, the state bought 42.6% fewer pigs, 42.4% less cattle, and 27.1% less grain than in the previous year.[696] "I only want to say this," Radom deputy voivode, Wawrzyniec Pietruszka, announced during the First National Anti-Speculation Meeting on September 15, 1981, "the state purchase of meat in Radom voivodship has fallen to a level unprecedented in the history of the voivodship. We are now buying twenty or forty pieces daily whereas we used to buy 2 000 or 2 500; on average, 1 500 items a day."[697] The crash was felt acutely in the eastern part of Poland, where most individual farms were small. Their owners significantly limited animal farming and, on account of the shortages, put aside for their own use a larger part of their production than before. Another factor was that in eastern Poland, the black market tradition of illegal meat trade was the strongest.[698]

In the summer of 1981, the situation became even more disastrous. On August 13, General Wojciech Jaruzelski asked the Prime Minister of the Soviet government, Nikolai Tichonov, for 30 000 tons of meat in exchange for potatoes; the Minister of Internal Trade withdrew the regulations introduced much earlier by President Bierut, which allowed legal trade in meat from private slaughter.[699] The authorities were fully aware of their utter inability to control the market in the situation when to even be able to buy food on ration coupons bordered on the miraculous and the countryside had been denied the coupons altogether. "We can do nothing to eliminate the unofficial meat trade," the Deputy Prime Minister, Stanisław Mach, admitted in September 1981. "When a nephew visits his uncle, they kill a pig and he takes it to town. I don't see any sense in taking action against such situations. We are not able to do this and such cases are not worth prosecuting, we won't get anywhere. It's just not worth it. If he brings the meat to the city, than at least he won't be buying it there. It works out the same. We should approach the issue in a

695 AAN, KC PZPR, WO, 3448, fol. 4 (Legnica), 16 (Radom), 23 (Bielsko-Biała), 27 (Koszalin), 34 (Częstochowa).

696 B. Gulbicka, *Dochody, spożycie i akumulacja…*, p. 208.

697 AAN, URM, 32/112, fol. 47.

698 AAN, KC PZPR, XI/756, fol. 23; see: E. Fiala, *Gdzie jest mięso?*, TL, No. 223/September 23, 1981.

699 A. Kochański, *Polska 1944–1991. Informator historyczny*, vol. 3: *Ważniejsze akty prawne, decyzje i enuncjacje państwowe (1971–1991)*, part 1: *1971–1982*, Warszawa 2005, p. 506.

flexible way. The same way we approach the question of slaughter of livestock by neighboring farmers. Two neighbors share a slaughtered pig. They slaughter a pig because they have to eat."[700]

Soon, however, the official voices ceased to be as liberal as that. It became clear that the officially acknowledged "breaking of the economic bond between the city and the countryside" applied primarily to state channels. The farmers effectively took advantage of the situation and were selling their products illegally. The opening of the price scissors benefited the countryside (in 1981, average earnings from selling agricultural products rose by 67%, while prices of industrial articles only by 27%). It was advantageous for farmers to sell meat and potatoes outside of the official channels and to purchase farming equipment in the same way.[701] Selling was easy – city residents were coming directly to the farms, as had happened during the German occupation, and paid the inflated price without batting an eyelid.

Illegal mobile meat shop. Warsaw, 2 September 1981. Photo: Polish Press Agency (PAP).

700 AAN, URM, 32/112, fol. 118–119.

701 D.T. Grala, *Reformy gospodarcze w PRL (1982–1989). Próba uratowania socjalizmu*, Warszawa 2005, p. 76. See: AAN, The Institute of Internal Market and Services, 317, Market Development under Insufficient Supply and Rationing 1980–1984, Warszawa, December 1983, fol. 34.

For the city and the countryside, direct mutual cooperation was vital, bypassing state institutions. City dwellers did not feel like decreasing their consumption as radically as the imposed rations implied,[702] preferring to dip into their savings instead, if need be. As a result, between 1980 and 1981, the standard of living did not decline in line with the whole economy. While in 1980 the national income fell by 6%, consumption actually rose by 1%, and in 1981, with a fall in the national income in excess of 10%, consumption declined only by 5%.[703] For the increasingly demanding peasants, the offer put on the table by the state was less than satisfactory. For example in 1982, although the prices that the state paid farmers for agricultural products did rise, the increase was only half that of the rise in the prices of consumer goods and farming equipment (56.9% and 112.4% respectively) that the peasants were obliged to keep buying. In the following years, the ratio worsened further.[704] Participation in black market operations became all the more profitable.

In 1981, the meat black market entered its golden era. Never before had it boasted such mass participation, using such an abundance of strategies, with such a universal acquiescence in its complex modus operandi, applied both by individuals and by institutional players (and the latter did not always side with the authorities). The government was unable even to estimate the size of the unofficial meat trade and admitted helplessly: "It is not possible to establish the actual amount of meat [...] brought to the market from illegal slaughter or as a result of various economic schemes outside of the rationing and distribution system."[705] It was estimated that between 30 and 70% of all bulk meat was sold in ways that were more or less illegal. Even when an animal was delivered to a state purchasing station, this was no guarantee that all the meat would end up in a butcher's store. "Complicated economic operations in the meat industry," according to the Meat Industry Center (Centrala Przemysłu Mięsnego), "begin with state contracts and purchase, through meat processing and up to the final sale of a ready product, and at each stage, there are opportunities for abuse."[706]

702 In urban agglomerations, rationing drastically decreased the size of annual deliveries per person: in Warsaw from 109.9 kg (1980) to 54.5 kg (1986), in Katowice from 98.9 to 55.5, in Łódź from 88.7 to 54.1, and in Gdańsk from 65.6 to 49 kg.

703 L. Beskid, *Ekonomiczny i społeczny wymiar przemian warunków życia w latach 1980–1985*, in: *Warunki i sposób życia...*, p. 20.

704 B. Gulbicka, *Konsumpcja w indywidualnych gospodarstwach chłopskich w latach 1980–1984: report*, Warszawa 1986, p. 3.

705 AAN, URM, 32/64, fol. 11–12, 17; *ibid.*, 32/75, fol. 24.

706 See: A. Wolin, *Nie tylko pięć miliardów*, "Rzeczpospolita" January 29, 1982.

5.2.5.1 Meat Industry or (Creative) Relapse into Crime

Once in a state purchasing station, pigs and cows often mysteriously vanished, in reality immediately bought "under the table" by unofficial agents, owners of private butcher's shops or franchised restaurants and guesthouses.[707] Traditionally, the meat industry remained the source of supply for the unofficial market. The meat industry continued to be an arena of repeat crime – "often before one investigation ends, the next one has to be opened in the same plant."[708] The panoply of old illegal strategies ranging from sophisticated scams generating surplus to petty thefts was now extended by some new strategies, often based on the "creative" interpretation of existing regulations.

Meat and meat products "leaked" from all kinds of plants, big processing plants operating under the Meat Industry Center (Centrala Przemyslu Mięsnego) and small enterprises, which belonged to the Warsaw Consumer Cooperative (WSS Społem), Farmers Self-Help Cooperative (Samopomoc Chłopska), Community Cooperatives (Gminna Spółdzielnia), State Agriculture Farms (PGR) and the Agricultural Cooperative (RSP). It was an open secret that the scale of the abuses was greater in the peripheries than in central Poland, where it had the backup of community networks and the very setting of the plants – these were usually located in former craft shops in residential areas, often adjacent to apartment houses – shielded the local meat industry from official intervention.[709]

In early 1982, according to the Meat Industry Center there were two kinds of "meat" crimes: "group crime operations involving employees of various departments (purchase, production, distribution, and security) in a meat plant working together with the goal of creating unrecorded surplus to sell with the help of people operating outside of the industry," and individual theft committed by meat plant employees who helped themselves to "various amounts of meat and meat products."[710] The first method was wholesale – it supplied the black market with often industrial quantities of fresh and cured meat. For example, in late 1981 and early 1982, meat plant workers in Szczecin in cooperation with

707 AAN, URM, 32/23, fol. 70; *Przestępstwo zaczyna się w punkcie skupu. Z kapitanem mgr. inż. Krystynem Pochlidem z Biura do Walki z Przestępstwami Gospodarczymi Komendy Głównej MO rozmawia Sławomir Orłowski*, "Express Wieczorny" September 21–23, 1984.

708 *Zamknięte koło malwersacji mięsnych*, TL, November 14, 1980.

709 AAN, KC PZPR, XIA/1459, fol. 328; *W masarniach… chudną*, TL, August 5, 1982.

710 AAN, URM, 32/10, fol. 4.

PKS bus drivers carted away 3.5 tons of meat and 6.4 tons of offal.[711] In 1986, in processing plants in Chrzanów and Bytom, 1.6 tons of meat and meat products was discovered ready to be "disappeared".[712] There were also "targeted" thefts usually of "de-completed half-carcasses" which involved trimming off the most valuable cuts of meat. One such scam was uncovered in the Katowice Meat Plant, where the inspectors reported that "in the post-slaughter warehouse a notebook was found, in which warehouse employees entered an accurate record of the number and category of cuts diverted for their own purposes. It transpired from the notes that between April and June 1981, they had cut 12 360 carcasses, which constituted approximately 11.9% of the total number of half-carcasses acquired from slaughter. The daily number of cuts varied between 17 and 242, while daily slaughter varied between 500 and 550 animals."[713]

The employees of meat plants could easily treat meat obtained in this manner as "added value" that could be sold through unofficial channels or exchanged for other goods or services. They did not have to worry about their own everyday supply; they received special allowances, which had increased since 1981 thanks to the recent collective agreements. According to the agreements, all meat industry employees, from couriers to directors, were entitled to receive or buy approximately 15 kg of meat per month each. However, the inspection conducted at the turn of 1981 and 1982 by the Ministry of Finance, the Central Commission for Combating Fraud (CKWS) and the National Inspectorate of Purchasing and Processing of Agricultural Products (PISiPAR) revealed that only one (in the Poznań voivodship) in twenty six plants complied with the regulations. In all the others, the employees received as much as up to 42 kg of meat and meat products, usually the best cuts, monthly. This was quite legal and based on management decisions, taken under pressure from the unions, including Solidarity. There were 146 000 authorized employees and retirees in the meat industry but numerous outsiders took advantage of buying meat in factory stores, among them employees of institutions working closely with the meat industry or persons of "vague status, who bought meat following a verbal or written recommendation of the director".[714] For example, in the Żerań factory there were at least 250 such people, and in Wrocław the PISiPAR employees also had similar privileges.

711 *Mięso w nielegalnym obrocie*, TL, April 17–18, 1982.

712 AAN, KC PZPR, XIA/1459, fol. 328.

713 AAN, URM, 32/6, PISiPAR, fol. 40.

714 *Hojne deputaty w zakładach mięsnych*, ŻW, 12 III 1982; *Nadużycia w przemyśle mięsnym*, "Rzeczpospolita" March 12, 1982; AAN, URM, 32/113, fol. 76.

According to the Prosecutor General's Office, in 1981, in factory stores in Kalisz, Poznań, Płock, Tarnobrzeg, Wrocław, Jelenia Góra and Warsaw voivodships alone at least 330 tons of meat and its products and over 20 tons of fats had been sold in quantities above the guaranteed allowance. It is difficult to say how widespread this phenomenon was and what the decision process was for granting special allowances for weddings, baptisms, and other family celebrations. Often, the allowance was just a pretext for a legal meat transfer out of the factory.[715] Attempts undertaken in mid-1982 to decrease the meat allowances of the industry's employees' met with understandable and effective resistance.

By virtue of dealing with scarce and valuable goods, meat plants found themselves in a highly privileged position in comparison with other branches of industry and services. Their management teams often took advantage of the situation and, contrary to the law and with workers' approval, engaged in barter transactions with other enterprises.[716] This was possible as part of good relationships with other industrial entities, and with the help of an imaginative interpretation of the State Enterprise Act of September 25, 1981 as well as of the government decision to allow enterprises to purchase and sell market goods "on the basis of freely arranged sales agreements." The fact that the Act did not include the rationed articles in the transactions was rarely acknowledged and prosecutors generally did not support police intervention in such cases.[717] The prosecutors were also usually indulgent in instances where the law had self-evidently been broken, such as in the case of the Powiśle Social Services Agricultural Conglomerate in Czernin, where between January 1 and March 31, 1984 the management bought and slaughtered 3 138 animals weighing 322 488 kg and sold the meat outside the rationing system to its own employees (83 tons) but also to the Gdańsk Shipyard, the Malinowo Gardening Company near Tczew or the Żywiec Brewery.[718]

State and cooperative agriculture producers were often more concerned with satisfying the needs of employees and local residents than complying with the demands of the government. To achieve this goal, they took advantage of the regulations that referred, on public health grounds, to selective slaughter of weak or injured animals. Meat obtained in this way did not have to be delivered to state purchasing stations. Sometimes, however, it was healthy animals

---

715 AAN, URM, 32/17, fol. 80.

716 For example, in late 1981 Meat Plants in the Służewiec district of Warsaw exchanged 768 kg of kielbasa for alcohol with the Warsaw Spirits Plant; AAN, URM, 32/17, fol. 141.

717 AAN, URM, 32/182, fol. 66.

718 AAN, URM, 32/191, fol. 104–105.

that were earmarked for employees' own consumption, and the ones selected on health grounds were sold to the state. The case of the Agricultural Cooperative in Borowiec in Wielkopolska was fairly typical. In 1981, the Coop "directed to the slaughterhouse 1 412 pigs weighing 151.5 tons and 198 cattle weighing 50.7 tons for its own needs. Healthy animals were selected for slaughter to meet employees' own needs and the animals to be slaughtered compulsorily were sent to the Meat Plant in Ostrów Wielkopolski. Aside from that, while the rationing rules were in effect, 74 pigs and two cows were sold to the Orbis Travel Agency in Warsaw, LOT Airlines in Warsaw, the Furniture Factory in Wrocław, the Forest Service in Taczanów, and to others. With such a large volume of slaughter for its own consumption and sales to other agencies, the Agricultural Cooperative Conglomerate (RKS) under inspection fulfilled only 87.8% of the quota under its livestock delivery agreement with the Meat Plant in Krotoszyn and only 28% of its hog quota."[719] In 1981 alone, the cooperatives sold 1 440 cows and 8 504 pigs to various state businesses and institutions, among them the National Bank of Poland. Its Central Hard Currency Department in Warsaw purchased four "cows with a cumulative live weight of 1 732 kg for 56 zloty per kilo. After slaughtering the cows in the Nowy Dwór slaughterhouse, on October 19, 1981 the meat was delivered to Warsaw by the coop's transportation and sold to NPB employees, five kilograms per person at 130 zloty per kilo."[720]

After the introduction of Martial Law, the scheme was practiced perhaps less ostentatiously but probably on a similar scale. In August 1984 it was estimated that the State Agriculture Farms (PGR) and Agricultural Cooperative (RSP) reserved for their own needs between 30 and 40% of all livestock.[721] Between 1983 and 1984 alone, in "nationalized agriculture units" at least 22 679 animals (3 993 cows and 18 686 pigs, in total 2 730 tons in weight) were slaughtered and "meat and its products were sold in significant amounts outside the rationing system to state farm employees, local residents, restaurants and resort managers."[722]

This widespread privatization of the state took place with the tacit consent not only of plant management teams but also of local political elites, for whom it was a way of preventing social tensions and reinforcing client networks.[723] This situation created two categories of people – those with access to this kind of distribution channels and those without. The first tried to entrench themselves in

719 AAN, URM, 32/119, fol. 79.
720 AAN, URM, 32/113, fol. 58.
721 AAN, URM, 32/62, fol. 8.
722 AAN, URM, 32/75, fol. 108.
723 *Ibid.*

their comfortable positions and defended them ferociously. The second engaged in futile protests and tried to develop individual strategies for looking for direct access to meat in the countryside. As a fallback position, they could also rely on the "veal woman"…

5.2.5.2 "The Veal Woman": A Retrospective Portrait

"They treated me like I was some kind of minister," the peasant woman from a village near Radzymin, who used to deliver meat to Professor Władysław Bartoszewski and other members of the Warsaw elite, reminisced fondly in conversation with this author in 2004.[724] Today, it is the ubiquitous "veal woman" – with her characteristic headscarf, and laden with big baskets and bundles – that springs to mind as a symbolic image of the days, now happily in the past, when Poland experienced food shortages that were alleviated only through a symbiosis of the country and the city. The veal woman paid regular, often prescheduled visits to city apartments and offices and sold veal, unavailable elsewhere. The complexity of the situation deserves a closer look, also from a historical perspective. Direct vending as a solution to the meat supply problem was based on practices of transfer and distribution going back not only to the times of the German occupation but even to the First World War. Additionally, the mass migration from rural areas to the cities, which began in the late 1940s, resulted in a whole network of private dependencies and new distribution channels, quite informal and extremely difficult to examine. All big cities in Poland had their own "meat and dairy supply hinterland". Near Warsaw, the most absorbent market in the country, initially the most important were Karczew (during the War already known as "Prosiakowo", Piglet Town[725]), Nowa Iwiczna (aka the "capital of illegal slaughter" in the late 1940s),[726] and the neighborhoods of Radzymin, Wołomin and Wyszków. In early 1949, every second adult resident of Rybienko and Jadów and every fourth of the Radzymin county was said to be engaged in illegal slaughter.[727] The production capacity of local barns and pigsties soon became insufficient to satisfy the growing demand but people were constantly

724 Wacława Grzelak's testimony, Stary Kraszew, February 22, 2004, in the author's possession.

725 In the fall of 1948 there were still 34 butcher stores, approximately 170 livestock merchants and 11 legal enterprises rendering slaughter waste into industrial fat in this village with the population of 5 000; "Głos Ludu", No. 276/October 6, 1948.

726 ŻW, No. 307/November 7, 1948.

727 TL, No. 50/February 20, 1949.

expanding the supply networks. For example in the early 1950s, illegal butchers from Karczew were bringing pigs from Mińsk, Łuków, and even Kozienice counties from where they were shipped down the Vistula.[728] In the 1980s, thanks to the developing transportation system, everyday provisions for Warsaw came from as far away as Siedlce, Ostrołęka and Radom.[729] The Warsaw market had a great absorptive capacity, as is clear from the fact that in 1985, in the Warsaw voivodship 120 times more calf hides were bought by the state than live animals (the actual numbers were 36 775 and 300 respectively). Incidentally, the number of hides was four times higher than the calf head-count in the voivodship.[730]

In the big cities, the transfer of meat from rural areas was of great significance.[731] During the first post-war decade, the narrow-gauge commuter railway was used more often than the regular trains. Since the turn of the 19th and the 20th centuries, the narrow gauge railroad had helped to supply the cities with food and, to large extent, determined the type of agriculture along its route. The passengers of commuter trains were not chance travelers but often a tightly-knit group. Frequent train stops, the slow pace and the mostly cooperative, locally based crew provided relative security for the illegal traders.

The atmosphere in regular trains, where inspections were easier to carry, was less trade-friendly. To avoid transporting meat on trains, traders instead posted it by mail or enlisted the help of railroad workers, who knew how to avoid the inspectors, or of the military who did not allow them to touch their luggage.[732] Often dealers reached for proven methods of hiding contraband, tested during the First World War, such as putting it in milk cans or faking pregnancy – using the latter method, women from Wyszków carried several kilos of veal at a time.[733]

The more experienced meat dealers tried to use the bus service (PKS), which replaced the narrow-gauge railroad, gradually withdrawn from service from the

---

728 AAN, KS, 1500.

729 Zwoleń, Białobrzegi, Skaryszew, Przytyk, and Jedlińsk (among others) constituted a meat hinterland for Radom; "Życie Radomskie", No. 75/March 17, 1949.

730 M. Mońko, *Zedrzeć skórkę incognito*, "Polityka", No. 8/February 22, 1986.

731 The examples apply mostly to Warsaw. The strategies used in other big cities did not differ significantly. On Poznań see: M. Czech, *Przedwojenny smak*, in: *Prywaciarze 1945–89*, ed. A. Knyt, A. Wancerz-Gluza, Warszawa 2001, pp. 97–98.

732 APW, KWar. PZPR, 30/VIII–12, vol 1, fol. 14; *Szlakiem handlu pokątnego. "Małkinia" - 20.50*, ŻW, No. 265/September 26, 1948.

733 *Dziś rozmawiamy z kpt. A. Skomskim z Komendy Wojewódzkiej MO w Warszawie o mięsie w bańkach i sztuczkach z klasą*, "Sztandar Młodych", No. 252/October 22, 1959; "Dziennik Polski" London, No. 157/July 23, 1960.

beginning of the 1950s, or random private cars, especially company cars, which were rarely inspected by police. The buses were a convenient option, because the traders had the opportunity of getting off before the stop where the inspection was expected. "The so-called blockades we use in our operations," the authorities reported in September 1984, "prompt the dealers to get off the bus at an earlier stop or at a request stop, in order to avoid searches."[734]

Public transportation did not guarantee safety but it was cheap. One could almost say that the state subsidized the black market by providing cheap transportation. However, only small dealers used public transport; those who dealt in quantity had to rely on cars.[735] Several dozen kilograms of goods could be taken by train or by bus, but by car you could transport several hundred. For example in March 1984, police from Wyszków found 217 kg of pork in a Fiat arriving from Warsaw. In June, they discovered 179 kg of veal.[736] The "motorized" trade allowed shorter transit times and improved sanitary conditions. "There are those," wrote Marek Przybylik in 1984, "who come in cars equipped with refrigerators where meat is neatly packaged according to the wishes of the clients, exactly to order."[737]

Although many urban families retain vivid, and now entertaining, memories of the complex and ingenious operations of the 1980 meat smuggling from the countryside to their doorstep,[738] these operations were in reality quite amateurish and did no more than meet the immediate needs of family members and a few friends. Usually, attempts to make serious money from the trade probably ended in a way similar to the experiences of a Warsaw taxi driver in the mid-980s, who in the village Kosów Lacki in Podlasie bought some 150 kg of meat products to sell for profit. "I paid 125 500 zloty from my own pocket for these fresh, mouth-watering tidbits. Later that evening, we went on our way back to Warsaw. We felt apprehensive, since at that time the police were quite aggressive in dealing with such activities and often stopped cars for inspection. We got home without any trouble. The goods stayed at my place. Next morning, I went to Filona Street to Staszek's workplace. There I sold some of the cold cuts for about 30 000 zloty. For another 20 000, I sold meat among my friends but I still had over 60 kg left. And it was Sunday. What was I supposed to do?! I visited a few

---

734 AAN, URM, 32/64, fol. 46.

735 Wacława Grzelak's testimony, Stary Kraszew, February 22, 2004, in the author's possession.

736 AAN, URM, 32/64, fol. 190.

737 M. Przybylik, *Słonina i schab spod serca…*, "Polityka", No. 49/December 6, 1984.

738 See: J. Wachowicz-Makowska, *Panienka z PRL-u*, Warszawa 2007, pp. 197–198. Literary rendition in: J. Niemczuk, *Plaga*, Warszawa 1990.

restaurants. No luck... We stopped at the auto market in Bemowo and chatted with some grill owners, then visited the flea market on Księcia Janusza Street. All to no avail. They either had enough of their own stuff or they wanted invoices. All fired up (me especially), we set off to the village of Marki. The owner of a roadside pub, Under the Roses, bought 12 kg of kielbasa from us at 800 zloty per kilo; he then called a motel. They wanted 20 kg. When we turned up with 46 kg, they were a bit surprised but in the end took it all. I was so relieved. We barely broke even. And what a hassle! I decided to stay away from the meat business in the future, unless as a middleman or a driver."[739]

Bearing in mind the perishable nature of the product in question, the reliability of the supplier was of utmost importance in the meat trade. Both state propaganda and urban myths referred darkly to cases of selling dog meat as veal; these were not always far-fetched. This alone was one good reason why tried and tested distribution networks were long-lived and the contact details of a reliable and honest "veal woman" – valuable information, carefully protected and passed on only to a chosen few. The reverse was also true: the supplier wanted a stable network of solvent customers to whom they could deliver repeat orders on a fixed day and at fixed place. "Special orders" were possible but their price was usually higher. Out of necessity, the women traders set out on weekdays,[740] when most of their, usually also female, customers were at work. Thus the image that lives on in the collective memory is of a "veal woman", who would visit an office, an institute or a hospital, surreptitiously weighing out the portions of veal or pork in some den at the back. "I was taking meat to the hospital in Spartańska Street [in Warsaw]. Doctors and nurses ran to get meat as soon as they saw me. When the director saw that I had veal, he chased me away and threatened to call the police if he saw me there again. He threw me out but did me no harm. I did not go there regularly but there were other people who had a place in a basement where they portioned the veal."[741]

---

739 L. Wand, *Z własnego życia*, "Gazeta Wyborcza" Supplement October 10, 1997.

740 Most travel dates had to be correlated with the days of farmers' markets, where the animals were usually bought. Convoys from Dobre near Mińsk Mazowiecki took off on Tuesdays (after the Monday market) and from Radzymin on Thursdays (after the Wednesday market); testimonies in the author's possession.

741 Wacława Grzelak's testimony, Stary Kraszew, February 22, 2004, in the author's possession. The "veal woman's" visit to the State Medical Publishing House (PZWL) is worth mentioning: "At PZWL a "veal woman" used to show up on specific days. She had her own spot: a wide windowsill right next to the main entrance, slightly shielded by a wall, and when she busied herself there, she also put up a curtain. Everyone took equal advantage of the services of the "veal woman"– from cleaning ladies and

In the mid-1980s, in a Warsaw downtown area, Świętokrzyska Street, where private stores and numerous state institutions were located, the police identified approximately fifty regular traders but were well aware that the real number was at least double that.[742] These tended to be "retailers"; the wholesalers would hang around market places, particularly the one at Polna Street, which "mostly served select customers from the embassies and the cultural elite."[743] "We know from our investigation", a policeman reported to the Central Commission for Combating Fraud (CKWS), "that, near Polna marketplace, a profiteer sells illegal meat from two calves three times a week. We can assume that with good organization, he can turn over 200 calves a year. The profit from selling the meat of a single calf is 6–9 000 zloty, depending on the season. After taking into consideration the additional profit from the anonymous sale of the offal and calfskins in the GS-Farmers Self-Help at between 600 and 700 zloty per item, the trader's profit can exceed one million zloty a year. Trading for hard currency has been recorded."[744] Undoubtedly, the state stores were also an important distribution place for meat brought from the countryside.[745]

---

cloakroom attendants to the directors and Party functionaries. I often met our Party executive secretary and we exchanged comments about the current delivery ("a wonderful veal shoulder", "beautiful bacon"). During the Solidarity period, our PZWL "veal woman" wore two buttons pinned to her dress or coat – one with the face of Pope John Paul II, the other with the Solidarity logo. After the imposition of Martial Law, she took them off but she gladly accepted underground leaflets to emphasize that, ideologically, she was one of us"; J. Wachowicz-Makowska, *Panienka…*, p. 197.

742 AAN, URM, 32/64, fol. 43–44.

743 *Ibid.*, fol. 43.

744 *Ibid.*, fol. 46. By late 1980, at the Polna marketplace there was no shortage of clients willing to pay between two dollars fifty and three dollars for a kilo of veal; A. Kołodziejski, *Cielęcina… za dolary. Czy nie można opanować czarnego rynku żywnościowego?*, TL, No. 298/December 15, 1980. Market halls and bazaars were traditionally a place where effective black market strategies in trading meat were developed. In 1948, before Christmas, a newspaper described the market hall on Koszykowa Street in Warsaw in the following way: "A fellow walks around and takes orders from numerous lady clients. One can order everything there, even quarters of a calf or a pig. Of course, at a much higher price… After taking an order, the dealer sends the customer to a vegetable booth, where the transaction is executed. Several minutes later the customer, clutching the precious package, sneaks out of the market hall. At the "small Karcelak" marketplace at Grójecka Street […], the customer pays cash and the meat is delivered a little later, from a private apartment or some kiosk"; "Express Wieczorny", No. 349/December 18, 1948.

745 AAN, URM, 32/64, fol. 46.

From the late 1940s, if not earlier, janitors had been playing an important role in the unofficial distribution of meat. They were usually born in small villages, where they still had relatives and friends. Their job was to look after an apartment block, and so they had regular contact with the residents without raising suspicions, and they knew their preferences well. "Wyglądała, the janitor, always had some meat for sale," the Polish writer Maria Dąbrowska wrote in her diary on March 22, 1949.[746] The role of janitors in meat distribution did not disappear when they became "building caretakers" in high-rise buildings. For example in February 1984, a profiteer was arrested "in a trash chamber in a building at 6 Grzybowski Square as he was engaged in the processing of 21 kg of meat into kiełbasa, using a meat grinder. He was aided and abetted by the caretaker's husband."[747]

Private customers were not the only clients of the itinerant farmers. In 1981 especially, many workplaces had the tacit agreement of management and the enthusiastic approval of the personnel, supported by the unions, which often organized "provisions operations", to taking advantage of provisions arriving from farmers' stables and pigsties. For example, in late November 1981, police in Rychtal near Kalisz stopped a "bus, which belonged to Creativity the Invalids' Coop (Spółdzielnia Inwalidów "Twórczość"). It was reported that the bus was carrying the half-carcasses of twelve pigs with a total weight of 1 847 kg. During the investigation it was established that the pigs had been purchased from individual farmers at 200 zloty per kilo of live weight. The persons transporting the meat were delegated by the workers of the above mentioned Coop."[748] This was not an isolated case.

Often in the transactions between workplaces and farmers no money changed hands; they were instead based on barter – factory cars transported to the villages their products, such as cement or coal and returned with a load of meat or potatoes. For example in 1981, a brewery in Brzesko received 1 500 chickens in return for regular deliveries of beer to villages. The Fixture Plant in Kraków exchanged radiators with farmers for 83 sheep.[749]

This phenomenon was so widespread and universally accepted that it made the large-scale anti-speculation operations (with the code names "Rynek" and "Mięso") and periodical inspections at market places and means of transportation (especially before the holidays), largely ineffective. For example, in the last quarter of 1984 including the Christmas period, the inspections conducted in Warsaw, Łódź,

746 M. Dąbrowska, *Dzienniki powojenne*, vol. 1: *1945–1949*, ed. T. Drewnowski, Warszawa 1997, p. 413.

747 AAN, URM, 32/64, fol. 46.

748 AAN, URM, 32/119, fol. 39.

749 *Owce za kaloryfery, czyli nielegalny obrót mięsem*, TL, no. 292 /December 12/13, 1981.

Gdańsk, Lublin, and Wrocław and in the mainly rural voivodships of Skierniewice, Siedlce, Ostrołęka, Radom, Płock, and Ciechanów revealed illegal slaughter and meat trading worth 22 million zloty. Criminal investigations were instigated against 73 people.[750] The black marketeers immediately found loopholes in the existing regulations. "It is difficult for our policemen to arrest a suspect at the point of being engaged in an act of illegal trading," Andrzej Szymanowski, in charge of economic crime in Warsaw Police Headquarters, commented in September 1984. "They are often recognized and closely watched by criminals. And it is not easy to obtain proof from the suspect or testimony from a witness, either, since they don't want to lose an additional source of meat supply."[751] Some meat dealers took care to legitimize their activities, for example by obtaining permits allowing them to sell products from internal export including meat and deli cuts.[752]

The black marketeers used different defense strategies when they were finally arrested. For example, each time that a pensioner from Wołomin was caught selling meat, which happened repeatedly, she "creates a situation where emergency paramedics don't allow her arrest, which in turn makes it impossible to use accelerated summary proceedings."[753] In consequence, the most common punishment for the "veal woman" was a fine. She regarded the amount part of her opportunity cost and in no time at all made up for it in sales.[754]

5.2. 5.3 "Legalize the Illegal Just a Little": 1984–1989

Paradoxically, the dynamic growth of the meat black market in the first half of the 1980s contributed to its legalization. First of all, it proved there was sufficient meat in Poland and if society were to accept it being priced higher, no rationing would be necessary. After analyzing the black market mechanisms, Polish economists were again hopeful that the market could be balanced. While in late 1981 the ratio of black market to retail prices was 4:1, after the steep price hikes in the early part of the following year, it went down to only 1.3:1 and this remained the average until mid-decade. Of course, a lot depended on the range of products

750 AAN, URM, 32/75, CKWS session on counteracting irregularities in the meat industry, May 2, 1985, fol. 107–109. For example in Płock viovodship in the first eight months of 1984 only six proceedings in illegal slaughter cases were initiated; *ibid.*, 32/64, fol. 195.

751 AAN, URM, 32/64, fol. 47.

752 *Ibid.*, fol. 44.

753 *Ibid.*, fol. 46.

754 *Ibid.*, fol. 157; Wacława Grzelak's testimony, Stary Kraszew, February 22, 2004, in the author's possession.

available and the circumstances prevailing locally; prices tended to be higher in big cities and in industrial areas. In rural voivodships such as Zamość, Koszalin, Zielona Góra, and Olsztyn, free market prices were very close to official prices and sometimes, as in Olsztyn – even lower, and, the "rationing coupon crimes" in consequence almost non-existent.[755]

Significantly, it was representatives of the Voivodship Commission for Combating Speculation, from rural voivodships such as Ostrołęka, Skierniewice, Ciechanów, Płock and Radom, that proposed the reinstatement of legal meat trading in marketplaces. The chairman of the parliamentary Internal Market Commission (Komisja Rynku Wewnętrznego) and soon to be a minister, Jerzy Jóźwiak, voiced this idea during a meeting on September 27, 1984, declaring, "personally I would prefer to give some thought to this other meat market, which has many features of a legal market, as to how we could, ahem… take control of it…"[756]

What was postulated was not revolutionizing the distribution but only partial legalization of the status quo and control over at least some of the meat sold via unofficial channels. The idea did not fly – mostly due to fears that loosening the rigors introduced in August 1981 would not so much constrict the black market as rather reduce official deliveries to state purchasing stations and, in effect, reduce the supply to state-owned stores. Such fears were real – a significant part of the Polish population had gotten used to the security of life with a ration coupon in hand and did not want to give it up. Especially when wage increases kept ahead of official meat prices: between 1982 and 1986 wages grew on average by 207.2% while prices rose by 148.2%.[757]

In the spring of 1985, a well-known journalist, Krystyna Zielińska, who later became a deputy chief of the parliamentary Commission for the Internal Market, during a radio broadcast proposed an "experiment" to be conducted in one or two voivodships to "return to the question of marketplaces and legalize the illegal trade just a little", since it was so "widespread".[758] The solution that she raised was also being discussed in the Ministry of Internal Trade and Services but the debate did not set the wheels in motion. The Ministry was worried that, once the

---

755 *Ceny mięsa na czarnym rynku*, "Życie Gospodarcze", May 9, 1982; AAN, KC PZPR, 2015, Prerequisites of abandoning rationed sales of meat, June 1987; see: W. Starzyńska, *Rynek żywności w warunkach niedoboru. Studium statystyczno-ekonometryczne*, Łódź 1990.

756 AAN, URM, 32/64, fol. 66.

757 *Ibid.*, fol. 81–83; AAN, URM, 32/75, fol. 114–115.

758 AAN, URM, 32/75, fol. 15.

rigid regulations were relaxed, ordinary citizens would not be able to buy their rations because restaurant owners and artisans would snap up all meat. In early May 1985, referring to meat prices, Deputy Prime Minister, Zenon Komender, admitted openly, "If we raised the price, we would be able to abolish rationing. We keep the rationing coupons so we can guarantee eight kilos for the miners, four for the hard physical workers, and two kilos for the rest of us. The point is that if we decide [...] in favor of the free market [...], the next day there will be terrible outcry, above all in Łódź, Katowice, Warsaw, and Gdańsk. So, we have to remind all those who propose an easy departure from rationing what would happen if people did not have that certainty..."[759] The authorities decided to revisit the issue in the second quarter of 1986.

In the event, this happened much sooner. In the fall of 1985, the Polish parliament, the Sejm, took on the question of re-instating marketplace trading and the issue hit the headlines.[760] Finally, in February 1986, in three voivodships, followed by another four in March, (Warsaw, Leszno, Tarnobrzeg, then Łódź, Katowice, Bielsko, and Siedlce) the "experimental marketplace sale of meat" was introduced, planned to take effect from August 1986. The goal was to take over as much black market meat as possible and "to draw preliminary conclusions about conditions and about the future prospect of revoking the rationing."[761] Without a doubt, getting people used to high prices was also high on the agenda.

Apparently, some meat black marketeers, especially those who had cars and could trade wholesale, did switch to the new modus operandi, which they, however, approached as always with a twist, selling meat also outside of the marketplaces and sourcing meat from non-designated voivodships.[762] This posed yet another dilemma for the authorities. "Until the experiment started in the seven voivodships, nothing was in doubt," members complained during the CKWS meeting in April 1986. "Now there are doubts. As things stand, we should regard the sale of meat from private slaughter also in those seven voivodships but outside of the marketplaces as harmful to the public. Those responsible should be prosecuted."[763]

759 *Ibid.*, fol. 27.

760 A. Mozołowski, *Na kartki i na targu*, "Polityka", No. 48/November 30, 1985.

761 AAN, URM, 32/183, fol. 25. The "experiment" introduced was based on a regulation of the Minister of Internal Trade and Services of January 2, 1986 ("Monitor Polski" No. 1, item 3 and No. 8 item 59); see: AAN, MHWiU, 17/2.

762 According to official data, 51.7 tons of meat was sold in the free market system in three voivodships in February 1986 and in March (already in seven voivodships) – 257.6 tons; AAN, URM, 32/183, fol. 25.

763 AAN, URM, 32/88, fol. 34–35.

Although the authorities did not entirely give up on the idea of prosecuting the "veal woman", at the same time the worsening supply and growing inflation forced them not only to extend marketplace meat vending to all the other voivodships but also to embark on mapping out methods of abandoning rationing. In late 1986, a new, cross-industry commission presented the first draft of a paper on "Conditions for Abandoning Rationing of Meat and Meat Products". The next draft, from June 1987,[764] appeared on July 28, at the discussion forum of the Politburo. Despite the ordinance of the Tenth Congress of the Polish United Workers' Party of June 1986 anticipating the end of rationing by 1990, there were suggestions to introduce it earlier, in 1988. The year 1989 was expected to be challenging in terms of meat supply. There were fears that – since incomes, although high, failed to put food on the table – social tensions might rise higher and would be difficult to appease with yet another price hike. "Market self-regulation" was deemed more rational.[765]

Out of the three possible strategies, the government experts rejected the safest option: abolishing rationing accompanied by a small price increase of 8–10%. They also vetoed the most radical option – the introduction of free market, with supply and prices completely unregulated. The authorities chose the path that, while unlikely to result in a resounding victory, ought at least to minimize losses: to reach market equilibrium by continuing to drip-feed appropriate official price rises. The manual market regulation was to be maintained, in the expectation that central "direction of bulk meat coming from central state purchasing" would preserve the status quo for a while.

With a "positive news offensive", the government Press Bureau launched a propaganda strategy in which marketplaces and bazaars, until recently considered the lair of speculators, were painted as effective bulwarks of the free market. The emphasis was on showing that although the market stalls were groaning with meat, the prices were high. To fight the assumption that the free trade relied on flogging meat from pickup trucks and station wagons, the new propaganda images were to show "nationalized, and occasionally also non-nationalized, stores where meat was sold at contract prices (*ceny umowne*)" and "highlight the glaring discrepancy in the hygienic conditions between the state stores and marketplaces."[766]

764 AAN, MHWiU, 10/8, fol. 1–42.
765 AAN, KC PZPR, 2015, fol. 97.
766 *Ibid.*

The Politburo and the government accepted the plan in September 1987 and, for the time being, the matter was put to rest. In the tense political situation of 1988 and 1989, the authorities were wary of taking any decisive steps on the meat minefield. In the spring of 1989, the situation grew paradoxical to the point of schizophrenic. On the one hand, there was unrestricted economic freedom, Polish citizens were allowed to keep their passports at home (rather than, as before, having to hand them in immediately on return from abroad, which let the state monitor closely their international comings and goings) and were free to use hard currency. On the other hand, the bulk meat trade was still being steered manually so that, as the explanation went, mass catering such as that in schools and hospitals and rationed supply would not suffer. The only concession, in 1988, was that artisans were now allowed to purchase livestock at contract prices and to sell meat production outside of the rationing.[767]

The cross-industry commission persevered, every so often releasing a new version of "Conditions for Abandoning Rationing".[768] The material presented in January 1989 made no bones about the fact that the days of ration coupons were numbered and they would end soon enough, best of all, with effect from March 1, since there were no guarantees that implementation at a later date would be any easier. However, nobody wanted to make any unpopular decisions during the momentous Round Table Talks, which took place in Warsaw from February 6, to April 5, 1989, and in which the government initiated discussions with the banned trade union Solidarity and other opposition groups in an attempt to defuse growing social unrest. And so, all voivods continued to receive their non-negotiable quotas of "bulk meat" for distribution.

The ambitious decisions of the Economy and Social Policy Team (Zespół Gospodarki i Polityki Społecznej) at the Round Table Talks intended to improve market supply and the standard of living and bring about the necessary abolition of the rationing of goods and deregulating market prices turned out to be more difficult to put into practice than changes in the Constitution and calling an election. As soon as the agreements had been signed, the Ministry of Internal Market started backpedaling, suggesting that it would perhaps be wiser to rephrase the statement that the improvements "would take place *in* 1989" to "would take place *from* 1989". The voivods continued to be bombarded with official letters urging increased "discipline in comprehensive and timely current account-keeping for

767 AAN, Ministry of the Internal Market (Ministerstwo Rynku Wewnętrznego, MRW), 6/1, fol. 5.

768 AAN, MRW, 6/4 and 6/1.

rationed meat sales".[769] It is ironic that in order to feed the election commissions, over 86 tons of meat had to be found outside of the rationing system.[770]

Immediately following the elections in 1989, there was still no-one eager to take any radical steps. The situation became a virtual stalemate: with inflation accelerating rapidly, the hot money put more and more pressure on the increasingly depleted market. Farmers also bided their time, resignedly waiting for the promised free market that would bring higher prices for their produce. As they did in 1981, they preferred to sabotage the compulsory state deliveries and favored alternative distribution channels. In July 1989, this led to a situation that those living in the cities were unable to buy meat with their coupons and were forced to use the free market.

As if nothing had happened, the coupons for August 1989 were nevertheless issued as usual. These were, however, soon destined to remain forever in home archives – as the poignant memento of the eight years of rationing that Poland had lived through. On July 27, with little prior discussion, the Politburo approved the government motion to deregulate meat sales and introduce a free market. From August 1, "any restrictions on the purchase and trade of meat, meat products and livestock" were abolished.[771] Two days later, the Council of Ministers rubber-stamped the decision with Official Act Number 109.[772] This was the end of rationing. It was also the beginning of the end of the – half-a-century long – Polish meat psychosis.

769 AAN, MRW, 6/2, fol. 59v.
770 *Ibid.*, fol. 69.
771 AAN, KC PZPR, 2149, fol. 185.
772 "Monitor Polski" no. 24, item 185.

6. Alcohol

The excessive alcohol consumption in communist Poland has been a topic of extensive research. We therefore need not dwell on the social and cultural context of the phenomenon and focus instead on its most important black market aspects such as illegal alcohol production and unofficial distribution of state-produced alcohol.[773]

In communist Poland's second economy, alcohol vied for top position with meat and the US dollar. Without a doubt, however, it was alcohol that had the longest tradition on the black market. Polish peasants became adept at breaking the state spirit monopoly as early as the 19th century. High alcohol consumption was traditional in their way of life, the ingredients necessary for alcohol production, such as grain and potatoes, were within easy reach and their natural habitat was less easy to keep under official supervision than the cities. No wonder that when the monopolist state encountered financial problems and tried to reach deeper into the wallets of Polish alcohol drinkers, they reacted by developing effective defense strategies.

Ubiquitous moonshine distillation began in the Polish territories at the outbreak of the First World War, with the introduction of prohibition in the Russian Empire. Alcohol production was banned and most of the supply destroyed. German and Austrian occupation of the Kingdom of Poland made little difference, since the new occupiers did not resume local alcohol distillation and rigidly controlled both production and consumption. Unsurprisingly, illegal breweries began to pop up like mushrooms.[774]

Experience acquired during the First World War was put to good use after the end of hostilities, when alcohol production failed to keep up with demand and the majority of the pauperized population could not afford the alcohol produced by the state monopoly, and worth 10% of state revenue. This situation led to a proliferation of illegal breweries. In 1919, it was estimated that there were 20 000

773 See the substantial bibliography in the almost 700-page work by K. Kosiński, *Historia pijaństwa w czasach PRL. Polityka – obyczaje – szara strefa – patologie*, Warszawa 2008. About the alcohol black market: *ibid.*, pp. 525–578; B. Sygit, *Nielegalny wyrób spirytusu*, Warszawa 1987; B. Sygit, *Potajemne gorzelnictwo (przed, w okresie reglamentacji i obecnie). Studium z dziedziny kryminologii i polityki kryminalnej*, Bydgoszcz 1996; S. Galarski, *Kryminologiczne i prawne aspekty nielegalnego gorzelnictwa*, Warszawa 1976.

774 B. Sygit, *Nielegalny…*, pp. 12–14.

industrial-scale, illegal distilleries (more than the legal ones!) in the territory of the former Kingdom of Poland alone.[775] The illegal production of alcohol decreased in the middle of the 1920s when the economic situation improved, only to increase again during the Great Depression. The pauperized rural population was the least able to afford the "monopoly" vodka, the price of which was many multiples of that of moonshine. Naturally, for the connoisseur, the quality and flavor of home-distilled *bimber*, as moonshine was known during the war and continued to be referred to thereafter, were not on a par with the officially produced liquor but what counted first and foremost for the rural drinker were its price and potency. In the first half of the 1930s, the authorities ruthlessly combated illegal distillation, each year closing down between three and five thousand such distilleries, mostly in central Poland and in the Eastern borderlands.

In the latter part of the 1930s, *bimber* production fell in step with the improving economy but during the Second World War, especially in the territory of the General Government, it acquired the status of a "national industry". Alcohol became both a substitute currency and a basic remedy to help one survive the horrors of the occupation.[776] As Kazimierz Brandys remarked in 1945, "alcohol did not hinder the fight and every German defeat was celebrated with an ocean of spirits."[777] The loosening of social and moral norms, the weakening of social discipline, and the absence of firm authority and social control that had prevailed during the war all contributed to the increased consumption of alcohol. Moonshine, until then drunk mostly in the countryside, became common also in the cities and was by no means shunned by the middle class. The demand was so enormous that huge moonshine centers appeared in the vicinities of big cities, such as Legionowo and Jabłonna near Warsaw. The distilleries and distribution networks operated very effectively and *bimber* became one of the less laudable icons of the time of the German occupation. At the same time, however, since the Germans had monopolized both alcohol production and its profits, making moonshine was a *sui generis* patriotic act.

---

775 *Ibid.*, p. 22.

776 S. Buryła, *Wojna i alkohol. Zaproszenie do tematu*, in: *Wojna. Doświadczenie i zapis. Nowe źródła, problemy, metody badawcze*, ed. S. Buryła, P. Rodak, Kraków 2006, pp. 205–230. See: K. Janicki, *Pijana wojna. Alkohol podczas II wojny światowej*, Warszawa 2012.

777 K. Brandys, *Wódka, bimber i Frank*, "Przekrój" 1945, no. 28, as cited in: J. Jaworska, *Cywilizacja "Przekroju". Misja obyczajowa w magazynie ilustrowanym*, Warszawa 2008, pp. 155–156.

The "heroic" period of moonshine production was over as soon as the German occupation ended but what did stay with the Poles was a deep conviction that illegal production of alcohol did not constitute a crime. The habit of drinking moonshine or indeed moonshine dependency also survived the war. Official production could not satisfy the demand exacerbated by the trials and tribulations of the war and, just as had been the case after the previous world war, many could not afford the expensive officially produced alcohol, revenue from which made a significant contribution to the state budget. Last but not least, all those who had benefited from moonshine – producers, middlemen, and distributors – had no intention of foregoing any opportunity of a healthy profit. The circumstances were perfect for business: the state was weak, there was no shortage of drinkers, and the production and distribution infrastructure was in place. Little wonder that the *bimber* industry made a smooth transition to peacetime and maintained a, sometimes stronger sometimes weaker, presence during the post-war period. Indeed *bimber* is not entirely absent from the Polish economy even today.

The price of monopoly alcohol regulated the level of the illegal distillation. The state justified the high price with seemingly contradictory reasons – the well-being of the state budget and the battle against the scourge of alcoholism. Limiting the accessibility of alcohol (by introducing a minimum age to buy it, decreasing the number of sales outlets and shortening their opening hours) were the measures deployed to the latter end. However, their effectiveness was questionable since they immediately triggered the development of illegal channels of alcohol distribution, usually through *melinas*, as the drinking dens were called. The phenomenon of these speak-easies was closer to the standard definition of the black market than illegal distillation; they were often run to satisfy the illegal brewers' own drinking requirements and with no market transaction involved. Thus, for a considerable period, the *melinas* did no more than recycle – at a higher price – alcohol bought in state stores. It was the introduction of rationing in 1981 that led to the modification of the existing strategies and the development of sophisticated new ones – from producing fake coupons, through intercepting alcohol from official production or shipment, to re-distributing vodka purchased in the "internal export stores" – that is to say, stores where purchases could only be made by those with a handful of greenbacks.

For the record, let's not forget that it was not only in the internal Polish market that the social players competed with the state but also in the international trade. While the Żytnia and Wyborowa brands of vodka were too expensive for the average Polish consumer, they were very attractively priced from the point of view of a foreign, and particularly Western, buyer. Polish sailors, tourists, and athletes (not to mention Polish diplomats and other officials) did a good job of transferring alcohol abroad on a mass scale, especially to the Scandinavian countries, where the mark-up was the most gratifying.[778]

6.1 A National Hobby: Illegal Alcohol Production

6.1.1 The Clandestine Distilleries: Moonshine and the Authorities

Illegal alcohol production is at all times a painful blow to any state budget. And so it proved for the post-war, socialist Poland that came into being on July 22, 1944. As early as December 12, 1944, the first Act on combating this practice was issued. Concise, no more than a single sentence, it provided stringent sanctions for illegal alcohol production.[779] The new law did not change much, what with the inadequate alcohol supply in official stores and the agencies created to investigate economic crimes merely going through the motions. The Treasury Revenue Protection Department (Ochrona Skarbowa) had no appropriate apparatus at its disposal, and as for the policemen of the recently established "Citizen's Militia" (MO), as the police were called, they themselves were commonly suspected of excessive consumption of moonshine. All the more so since – after the war, and particularly in rural areas – the police were recruited mostly from the locals, and not eager to make enemies among their neighbors in the closely-knit communities.

In early October 1945, the government approached the Polish People's Party (PSL), the Polish Socialist Party (PPS), and Wici the Rural Youth Association with the suggestion of cooperation "in the field of combating moonshine". The Propaganda Minister was ordered to "develop a propaganda campaign for fighting *bimber*" and the Minister of Justice was told to order the courts to deal with moonshine cases as a priority.[780] The results however, were less than satisfactory – in 1945, no more than 7 100 distilleries were shut down, in spite the fact that illegal alcohol production was common and conducted openly.[781]

---

778 A. Markiewicz, *Przemyt napojów alkoholowych w porcie morskim*, WC, 1974, no. 12, pp. 24–26; W. Brzeziński, *Przemyt na barkach, ibid.*, 1974, no. 15; *Wpadki, ibid.*, 1990, no. 51.

779 "Anyone who distils alcohol beverages from grain, potatoes, sugar beets, sugar, molasses, and other resources without a permit shall be subject to a penalty of up to five years' imprisonment and a fine of between 10 000 and 500 000 zloty", Journal of Laws, 1944, no. 15 item 85.

780 AAN, URM, 5/613, fol. 2–3.

781 AAN, MS, 558, fol. 147.

Stanisław Cieloch, Spirits Séance, *"Szpilki", no. 30, 25 September 1945.*

In 1946, mostly thanks to input from paid informers, almost 28 000 distilleries were uncovered. The number looked impressive but in practical terms the operations failed to achieve radical eradication of illegal distillation, which continued to flourish. The penalties meted out were no more than symbolic (the Special Commission sent ninety three *bimber* distillers to the camps), the demand for moonshine was enormous (in 1946, the state monopoly satisfied barely half of the demand) and the low price of grain made individual production highly profitable. One indication of the scale of the phenomenon was the fact that in 1946, sales of yeast, an ingredient used in distilling, re-attained the pre-war level despite the decreased population and lower consumption of bread.[782]

On January 26, 1947, Maria Dąbrowska wrote in her diary after watching the film *Forbidden Songs* (Zakazane Piosenki), the popular post-war musical that mocked the Germans: "The songs have been changed [...]. Instead of 'Axe, hoe, down the *bimber*', the actors sing 'Axe, hoe, ball, glass' (because *bimber* is

782 AAN, URM, 5/229, GIOS report for August 25 – September 24, 1946, fol. 57.

now banned)".[783] The year 1947 indeed did not look good for the illegal alcohol producers. Not only did the Polish Spirit Monopoly (Polski Monopol Spirytusowy, Polmos) now become more competitive, expanding in 1947 to cover the whole country with a network of sales outlets but weather anomalies caused the free market price of agricultural products to rise – which included the ingredients used to make moonshine, and the legal system clamped down on the illegal distiller with radically more severe penalties. The Special Commission now took an active part in combating the illegal alcohol production and took over the *bimber* cases from the courts. The Commission was now also better equipped – on April 11, the Treasury Criminal Law was passed (Journal of Laws, no. 32, item 140). This specified in greater detail crimes against the state monopoly.

Although fewer illicit distilleries (some 20 300) were exposed in 1947 than in the previous year, the sanctions were now drastically steeper – 1 016 *bimber* manufacturers ended up in labor camps and they constituted almost a quarter (23.4%) of all new prisoners.

Table 5. Number of detected illegal distilleries and labor camp sentences for illegal alcohol production in years 1947–1954.

	1947	**1948**	**1949**	**1951**	**1952**	**1954**
Detected cases of illegal distilling	20 338	14 615	5 842	2 601	2 563	1 796
Labor camp sentences	1 016	509	1 278	1 260	1 401	250

Source: K. Kosiński, Historia pijaństwa w czasach PRL. Polityka – obyczaje – szara strefa – patologie, Warszawa 2008, pp. 527, 532 (The years 1950 and 1953 have been omitted due to incomplete data).

The fight against illegal alcohol production began slowly to lose its momentum in 1951 when the police took over the duties of the experienced but now defunct Treasury Revenue Protection Department (Ochrona Skarbowa). The year 1953

783 M. Dąbrowska, *Dzienniki powojenne*, vol. 1: *1945–1949*, ed. T. Drewnowski, Warszawa 1997, p. 122.

brought important changes with the Act of June 24 (Journal of Laws, no. 34, item 143) on the production and processing of spirits – the first attempt in post-war Poland to regulate all legal issues surrounding the illegal production of alcohol and marked the end of a fiscal penal approach in favor of administrative penalties.[784] Even though the number of labor camp sentences for illegal distilling, at 1 127 in 1953, was still high, the authorities decided the problem was fizzling out and the police stopped recording individual cases.

The decline proved short-lived. In 1955, the two factors that had always encouraged illegal alcohol production re-appeared simultaneously: the price of alcohol went up and, with slacker sentencing, courage became cheaper. Although illicit distilling did not reach the level of the late 1940s, the number of alcohol-related criminal offences such as *bimber* production and large-scale theft from state distilleries went up, even in hitherto relatively quiet regions such as the Poznań and Bydgoszcz voivodships.. The moonshine trade re-entered the market in the big cities.[785]

The problem hit home after the authorities added up the profits of the official spirit industry for the first quarter of 1958. It turned out that Poles had bought 3.6 million liters fewer, calculated in pure alcohol, in comparison with corresponding period of the previous year. Initially, this was taken as a positive outcome of the fight against alcoholism; soon, however, a more rational explanation had to be considered, particularly since in the same period sales of sugar and yeast, especially in rural areas, had grown significantly, for example by 60% in the Warsaw and 40% in the Kielce voivodships respectively.[786]

It is now difficult to establish whether the wave of anti-*bimber* coverage that swept through the Polish press from the early spring of 1958 was part of an orchestrated campaign. The news items identical in respect of facts, people, and places – a fact which, since they were not always supplied by the press agencies, could point to their origin in government briefing – that appeared in newspapers in different parts of the country seem to favor such a hypothesis. The war on illegal distilling was a perfect fit with the crackdown on the economic underground, which began in the middle of 1957. The law and the law-makers were commonly accused of being too lenient towards the self-appointed distillers. Over 25% of all cases were dropped straight away by the prosecutors, and those that ended up in front of a judge usually ended either in a suspended sentence, a small fine or a few months of suspended prison sentence. The light sentences were often

---

784 B. Sygit, *Nielegalny...*, pp. 35–36.

785 AAN, MS, 558, k. 150.

786 *Spadek sprzedaży alkoholu*,"Sztandar Młodych", no. 118, 1958/May19,; J. Horodecka, *Bimber wyżej*, ŻW, no. 233, 1958/September 28/29.

due to the perpetrators pointing their finger as the guilty party at the elderly, single mothers, and the disabled, who could always count on the leniency of the judges.[787]

In July 1958, police bonuses introduced in 1957 for uncovering illegal distilleries doubled. Policemen who found the whole "works" – the full apparatus, moonshine mash, and moonshine, complete with the perpetrator – could expect a reward of between 500 and 1 000 zloty and 25–50 zloty for each liter of pure alcohol.[788] In the summer of 1958 at Police Headquarters, representatives of the Prosecutor General's Office and the Ministry of Finance met with local police chiefs from the voivodships where illegal distillation was the most prevalent (Białystok, Lublin, Łódź, Rzeszów, and Warsaw). The conclusion was unanimous: tougher sanctions.[789]

The press changed the mood music to match: the focus was now on "public" expectations of the government and the Sejm, its tardiness gently criticized, to take care of the problem urgently.[790] The authorities rose to the challenge and in the spring of 1959, the newspapers featured a steady flow of coverage on the progress of the new law upping the penalties for the illegal distillers. The headlines said it all: *Illegal distilling will not be worth it* (in *Trybuna Ludu*), *Pogrom of bimber producers imminent* (in *Słowo Powszechne*). The draft of the bill received the "full support of all MPs",[791] as it did in parliament.

The Act of April 22, 1959 on combating the illicit production of spirits[792] was to remain in force, with small changes, for over forty-two years, until April 26, 2001! The secret of its longevity was in the permanency of the phenomenon of illegal distilling as well as in the detailed presentation of the regulations and the severity of the sanctions provided. The fines stipulated were high enough to feel painful even when applied at the turn of the 1970s and the 1980s. The production of *bimber* even in the smallest quantity for personal use carried a penalty of up to three years in prison and a fine of upwards of five thousand zloty. Where "significant quantities" were involved, the distiller was subject to a prison term of between two and five years and a fine of not less than 30 000 zloty. The offender no longer

787 D. Słoń, *Bimbrownie i walka z nimi Milicji Obywatelskiej*, "Słowo Powszechne", no 113/May 13, 1958; R. Młodar, *Bimber*, PiŻ, nos. 26, 27 /1957.
788 J. Horodecka, *Bimber wyżej*, ŻW, no. 233/September 28/29, 1958.
789 *Uwaga – bimber. MO proponuje zaostrzyć sankcje*, TL, no. 199/August 18, 1958.
790 *Prosimy o chwilę uwagi*, "Słowo Powszechne", no. 216/September 16, 1958.
791 TL, no. 97/1959.
792 Journal of Laws 1959, no. 27, item 169.

needed to be arrested red-handed. The possession or storage of the even the simplest moonshine production apparatus was a punishable offence under the Act.

The authorities were keen to prove that the new law was not mere tokenism. Soon after it had entered into force on June 1, 1959, the papers were filled with news of harsh prison sentences and high fines for illicit alcohol producers. Whereas a few months earlier, the tone assumed in the press coverage was portentous, now the matter had become a fait accompli (*Illicit distilling is not profitable any more*[793]). Indeed, the number of detected distilleries began to decrease and in 1961, only 1 002 cases of illicit alcohol production were uncovered by the authorities. "The current year," a journalist on *Polityka* wrote in spring of 1963, "will be one of the last in which we write about moonshine. Soon enough, it will have become mere folklore, a funny story about an individual case or two but no longer a topic. *Bimber* as a problem and as a scourge of society will safely descend to its grave."[794]

These hopes did not materialize. The alcohol price hike in the fall of 1963 immediately thinned out the customers of the official alcohol stores and triggered increased demand for the raw materials and paraphernalia involved in its production such as sugar, yeast, big kettles, and glass pipes. The number of detected distilleries increased from 1 153 in 1963 to 1 549 in the following year and stayed at that level for several years. The next price hike, in 1969, coincided with the deep economic crisis that was responsible for renewed interest in independent alcohol production. In 1969, the authorities detected 1 847 distilleries, and in 1970 another 2 908, and in 1971 as many as 5 378.[795] The significant escalation in 1971 was a result of the operation to "restore public order", undertaken by the new Minister of Interior Affairs, Franciszek Szlachcic. The operation was intended to remind Poles that the Ministry of Finance would reward the reporting of clandestine distilleries to the authorities. The average reward was 3 000 zloty but it could go as high as 15 000 zloty.[796]

Somewhat paradoxically, illicit alcohol production was a much bigger, and certainly more visible, problem in the first – prosperous – half of the decade than in the second, when the crisis came knocking at the door. This was mostly due to high prices of alcohol so, when in the second half of the decade, they became relatively lower, the wave of illicit alcohol production receded and stabilized at

793 "Express Wieczorny", no. 148/June 22, 1959.

794 A.K. Wróblewski, *Bimber*, "Polityka", no. 23/June 8, 1963.

795 K. Kosiński, *Historia pijaństwa…*, p. 532.

796 *Nagrody za ujawnienie nielegalnych gorzelni*, TL, no. 260/September 17, 1971; "Kurier Polski", no. 225/September 26, 1971.

the level of the mid-1960s. For example in 1977, when vodka was at its cheapest, the number of detected distilleries in comparison with the previous year fell by 1 300 (from 2 878 to 1 568).

All the more shocking was the size of the moonshine boom triggered by the 1981 crisis, declining production, rationing and partial prohibition during Martial Law. Whereas in 1981, 1 435 cases of illegal distilling had been recorded (most of them in the last quarter of the year, after the introduction of rationing), in the following year there were ten times as many – 14 067. Despite the increased detection rate (and accelerated sentencing) due to the strict requirements imposed by Martial Law, only a small number of illicit distilleries were uncovered. According to the probably very conservative estimates of the time, there were approximately 150 000 distilleries in Poland during the period of rationing.[797]

The easing of alcohol rationing in July 1982 (free market sales at higher prices were authorized) and its withdrawal in March 1983 only temporarily diminished the demand for moonshine. After a temporary decrease in 1983 (9 696 detected distilleries), drinking habits accompanied by prevalent alcoholism as well as continuous price hikes of legal alcohol and its limited availability, especially as a result of the Act of October 26, 1982 on education in sobriety and counteracting alcoholism, caused the statistics to spike (14 817 distilleries exposed in 1984 and 15 262 in 1985).

There is no doubt that the lifting of Martial Law in July 1983 and revocation of the harsh regulations that allowed summary sentencing once more fanned enthusiasm for illegal distilling. The great majority of illicit distillery production from the early 1980s was for distillers' own needs, which resulted in relatively mild sentences. For example, from January to November 1984, in the Krakow voivodship 357 cases of illegal distilling were discovered and as many legal proceedings were brought but in only four cases were the accused held on remand.[798]

The sheer scale of illegal distilling worried not only the police and the Finance Ministry but also the state employees responsible for introducing and later ending the alcohol rationing system. Illegal alcohol production turned out to be one of the most important reasons to postpone the abolition of the rationing of sugar which some decision makers were concerned would be mostly used for moonshine production – a conclusion based on the fact that the ratio between the price of one kg of sugar and 0.5 l of "official" alcohol was 1:12 (and had gone

797 K. Kauba, *Za wcześnie na toast*, "Tygodnik Kulturalny" March 3, 1985.
798 Z. Krzysztofiak, *Pędzą wszyscy*, "Polityka", no. 2/January 12, 1985.

down to 1:7 a decade earlier).[799] Against such pessimism, there were also voices of reason: "For those who were making moonshine 15 or 10 years ago and still do so today," the deputy chair of the National Price Commission (PKC), Antoni Gryniewicz, argued in January 1985, "there is no such thing as the 'correct' relation between the price of vodka and the price of sugar. I think we are demonizing the moonshine problem in Poland, even on such scale as it is occurring currently. Let me quote Police Headquarter estimates of how much moonshine is produced in Poland today. These estimates are based on research, on reports from inspectors, on the convictions. These estimates are that it is approximately 40 million liters [...]. How many more moonshiners could we have, well – how many? Double the number? I don't think so, but let's assume pessimistically that there might be 50% more. What would it mean? Another 20 000 tons of sugar..."[800] A number of that order was irrelevant to the stability of Polish economy.

Indeed, abolishing the rationing of sugar (on November 1, 1985) did not bring about any *bimber* revolution, unless we consider as significant the fact that the number of distilleries detected halved (to 7 134) in 1986. This was mostly due to the gradually stabilizing economy and the fact that the profitability of moonshine production was decreasing due to the rise in the price of sugar following the abolition of rationing and above all – the harsher sanctions. The Act of May 10, 1985 (mentioned earlier, see chapter 3.5.3) played a deterrent role, since it created a situation where even indirect contact with illegal distilling could end in a prison sentence.

While the repressive measures certainly shrank the amount of illicit distilling (4 789 distilleries in 1987 and 3 418 in 1988), they frequently bordered on the absurd. It was easy to arrive at a decision which, while consistent with the rule of law, simultaneously made a mockery of the whole idea of war on illegal distillation. In late 1985, the story of a pensioner from Katowice riveted the public. A man with no previous criminal record, he was arrested for helping a neighbor suffering from back pain to move a jar of moonshine mash from the floor to the table, for which he was charged as an accomplice. When during the investigation he artlessly admitted that in the previous several months he had given his

---

799 Demand for sugar was, indeed, enormous. In 1982, at its highest, the black market price of 1 kg of sugar was several times higher than the official one (it reached 200 zloty); unrationed artificial honey, glucose and jam were also bought in high quantities; AAN, URM, 32/114, Third National Anti-Speculation Meeting (Krajowa Narada Antyspekulacyjna), January 27, 1983, fol. 53; *ibid.*, 32/115, Fourth National Anti-Speculation Meeting, January 26, 1984, fol. 42.

800 AAN, URM, 32/69, CKWS session on rationing questions, January10, 1985, fol. 42–43.

neighbor two kilos of sugar while being fully aware of its purpose, the pensioner was additionally charged with illegal alcohol production, and sentenced to eight months in prison (without suspension) and a 50 000 zloty fine.[801]

It is ironic that after 1989, illicit distilling did indeed become, as Andrzej Krzysztof Wróblewski predicted it would, "exotic" – but not due to the activities of the government or increased social awareness but thanks to cheap alcohol smuggled in from abroad. One could say that the moonshine industry was beaten at its own game.

6.1.2 "He Has a Drinking Habit but Not a Lot of Money":[802] Determinants, Technology, Geography

Shortage of alcohol was a leading factor in the development of the black market trade only during the first few years after the war (between 1945 and 1947) and the first half of the 1980s, mainly when alcohol rationing was in force (between 1981 and 1983). The decisive factor was the high price of the monopoly alcohol; kept high since its sales accounted for a significant percentage of state revenue, rarely falling below 10% and usually hovering between 11 and 15.5% (with the record year in 1985).[803] The authorities showed great determination in fighting the moonshiners who, in turn, were very good in devising strategies to outsmart the state. Only after 1989 would this vicious circle be broken.

Research on illegal distillation in Poland indicates that the phenomenon disappears when average monthly pay is sufficient to buy between 60 and 70 bottles of vodka. In communist Poland this rate was no more than approximately 30 bottles! In 1970, the average monthly salary could buy 30 bottles, in 1974 it barely increased, to just 31, and in 1978 it nudged up to a mere 33 but after the price hike in December 1981, an average Pole's monthly pay was the equivalent of no more than 22 bottles. In communist Poland, vodka was twice as expensive as it had been in pre-war Poland and was one of the most expensive in Europe.[804] The illegal distilling industry grew with each hike in the price of alcohol (in 1953, 1957, 1961, 1963, 1969, 1974, 1978, 1980, and annually throughout the 1980s).

801 J. Dziadul, *Pożytki z bimbrownika*, "Polityka", no. 50/December 14, 1985.

802 R. Młodar, *Bimber*, PiŻ, 1957, no. 26/27.

803 K. Kosiński, *Historia pijaństwa…*, pp. 44–48.

804 P. Kapuściński, *Ile wódki wypić musimy i ani setki więcej*, "Tygodnik Solidarność", no. 27 /October 2, 1981; AAN, IPP, 65, Alcohol related crimes in the alcohol rationing system, fol. 11, 16–17; M. Bednarski, *Drugi obieg gospodarczy. Przesłanki, mechanizmy i skutki w Polsce lat osiemdziesiątych*, Warszawa 1992, p. 91; B. Sygit, *Nielegalny…*, p. 17.

The rate of growth depended on the level of prices and income, the general state of the economy, the level of social satisfaction, and the strictness of legal sanctions. Without a doubt, such correlation was systematic, and until the final days of communist Poland, the government applied the principle of keeping the "price of moonshine at a safe distance from the price of monopoly alcohol".[805]

Moonshine distilling was an excellent business from an economic point of view. During most of the post-war period it was common in rural areas where the distillers had the basic resources such as potatoes, grain, and flour to hand, often on their own farm. Labor was cheap, particularly in the case of a family business. Even when sugar became the basic feedstock for moonshine, the increases in its cost were neutralized by, among others, higher productivity. As a result, the cost of production of moonshine was a fraction of that of the production of the monopoly vodka, in spite of the advantages of the economies of scale that the state had. Other factors such as the financial circumstances of the customers or general insecurity also shaped the retail price of *bimber*. "We always aim for the middle ground," a professional moonshine distiller from Sobolewo near Ryki explained, talking to a journalist in 1957. "The higher the price of vodka, the higher the level of this middle ground gets. It works like this: it takes one kilo of sugar, give or take a few grams, to make one liter of moonshine. Which means that one liter costs me 15 zloty. How much does one liter of [monopoly] vodka cost? Seventy zloty. So, my figures work like this: I have to earn quite a lot, because otherwise why bother to go into this business, why bother to take such risk… But I can't ask for *too* much, or else I'd lose the customers. So I have to charge much more than 15 zloty but much less than 70."[806] And, so, in 1957, the moonshine price fluctuated between 40 and 50 zloty a liter.

The cost calculation applied also to production for personal use. We need to understand that "personal use" meant something quite different in Warsaw or Krakow and in the rural areas – where one liter of alcohol per person at wedding or baptism parties was the norm. Since such celebrations were usually very well attended, the savings to the host from buying moonshine were considerable.

There was a fine line between the professionals and amateurs in illicit alcohol production; in the 1980s, the latter remained as sole winners. The post-war period however, belonged to the professionals, who distilled alcohol often on a very large scale, with – one suspects – the tacit approval of local authorities. For

---

805 A.K. Wróblewski, *Bimber*, "Polityka", no. 23/June 8, 1963; K. Kosiński, *Historia pijaństwa…*, p. 390.

806 R. Młodar, *Bimber*, PiŻ, nos. 26, 27/1957.

instance, in Ciechomin near Łuków, the administrator of the Cooperative Jedność, which was well established during the German occupation, after the war ended, transformed it into a large distilling enterprise, which not only produced but also sold moonshine.[807] There is little doubt that this initiative was closely connected with the construction of the Soviet airport nearby, which must have provided steady custom.

Wholesale production proper depended on well-organized and secure sales, guaranteed by big cities. In the post-war period, often very large illicit distilleries were frequently discovered in the suburbs. For example, on July 17, 1945 at Powiśle Street in Krakow, the inspectors from Central Office for Combating Speculation and War Usury (Główny Urząd do Zwalczania Spekulacji i Lichwy Wojennej) found a "complete set of equipment for distilling moonshine [...], a warehouse with semi-finished and finished product, as well as tax bands and labels of foreign and Polish brands of vodka. The tax band templates lay beside the tax bands [...]. The moonshine factory was located in a two-bedroom apartment. Tax bands and documents related to the distillery occupied one of the rooms [...]. The other contained bottled vodka [...]. In the third room, which was used by the female workers of the distillery, empty bottles were found. In the kitchen there was a massive oven with filter tubes. In the basement ...], another oven with filter tubes running to the janitor's lodge [...]. In the janitor's lodge we found a boiler with starter mash of approximately 500 liters, a distilling oven with a manometer, and electric ventilators."[808] The owner of the distillery was nowhere to be found.

This impressive setup is a good example of a phenomenon typical of the post-war period. Large, well-equipped distilleries produced alcohol of relatively decent quality that could pass for not only Polish but also foreign liquor.[809] Moreover, it was rare for the elusive entrepreneur, who usually remained in the shadow of the cottage industry, to be apprehended. It was striking that distilleries surprisingly often kept re-appearing in apartments or homesteads where the owners or tenants were clearly unable to afford the expensive professional distilling equipment.[810] We can safely assume that they were sub-contractors using equipment owned by the investor. In Legionowo near Warsaw there were entire

807 *Spółdzielnia czy bimbrownia*, "Sztandar Ludu", no. 281/November 7, 1945.

808 AAN, URM, 5/31, fol. 16.

809 For example at the turn of 1945 and 1946, products of well-known brands (Belgian "Hulstkamp" among others) appeared in Warsaw. The authorities considered them as "produced from moonshine by secret bottling plants" AAN, MAP, 14, fol. 7.

810 AAN, KS, 2965.

“firms” producing distilling equipment, which helped maintain the high quality of production and the quick launch of a new distillery, should the existing one be seized by the authorities.

Militia raid an illegal brewery in the vicinity of Warsaw, November 1946; photo from the archives of the Polish Press Agency (PAP).

For example, the distillery (it would be an understatement to call it a moonshine plant) uncovered in October 1946 in Legionowo specialized in the purification of moonshine distilled at home by farmers from nearby villages (some of whom delivered weekly between 150 and 200 liters). In an hour, the plant was able to distill 10 liters of 95-proof spirit. The middlemen bought the entire processed amount at between 300 and 360 zloty, and transported it two or three times a week, sometimes in vehicles that belonged to the Ministry of Health, to Warsaw where they sold it for between 400 and 420 zloty.[811]

811 AAN, KS, 1509. To a large degree the operations were made possible by the corruption of the local authorities. According to one of the employees of the distillery, the police station in Legionowo knew about the distillation. The owner of the illegal still, citizen Pios told me that policemen came to his house and he had to give them a bribe of 7 000 zloty.” *ibid.*

Thanks to the private networks of stores and restaurants distribution did not pose any problems. The owners of restaurants and stores, especially fruit and vegetable stores where "carrots are sold at the front, *bimber* at the back"[812] on the one hand, naturally, sought maximum profits and were willing to take a risk, but on the other, sold *bimber* simply because there was demand for it, since legal alcohol was in short supply. The owner of a café at Wolska Street in Warsaw when arrested on July 21, 1945 and told she was not allowed to sell moonshine, asked rhetorically, "What else is there to sell?"[813] In mid-October 1945, the Polish Spirit Monopoly (Polski Monopol Spirytusowy, PMS) complained to the Ministry of Treasury that a large number of private stores "of all kinds" were selling moonshine and imitation monopoly alcohol.[814] By the middle of the next year "almost all cafes or similar gastronomic enterprises, and also many grocery stores sold illegal alcoholic drinks, packaged and available for on-site consumption. The illegal sale of alcoholic drinks in marketplaces from stands and booths or directly on the street [was] a common occurrence."[815]

This was an open and universally accepted practice and those who sold illicit alcohol were often protected. The incident in Warsaw on November 3, 1945, extreme as it was, nevertheless reflected well the prevailing sentiments toward trading bootleg alcohol. On that day, the Central Inspectorate of Treasury Protection (Główny Inspektorat Ochrony Skarbowej, GIOS) together with the police (MO) and Security Office (UB) conducted inspections of all restaurants in Warsaw. "I gave the Investigation Office (Urząd Śledczy) orders to shut down," wrote a GIOS official, "one of the illegally operating restaurants at 15 Litewska Street, which sold *bimber* and left its fate to the decision of citizen Prime Minister. After the search, the restaurant owner incited a Polish Army unit, stationed at 14 Litewska Street, to attack the police. This resulted in a shootout and assault on several policemen, who were then disarmed by the completely drunk above mentioned unit."[816]

However, the increased repressive measures on the one hand and the improved supply of legal alcohol on the other forced moonshine distillers to change their strategies. Production ceased to be run openly. By the end of 1946, the

812 R. Burzyński, *O knajpach i samobójcach*, "Przekrój" 1945, no. 26, as cited in: J. Jaworska, *Cywilizacja "Przekroju"*..., p. 154.

813 AAN, KS, 2965.

814 AAN, MAP, 14, fol. 1.

815 AAN, GIOS, fol. 14.

816 AAN, URM, 5/229, fol. 3.

illicit distilleries were moved from suburbs to the "most remote villages, and into forests and swamps, which due to poor security and difficult driving conditions are hard for the Police and Treasury Protection (Ochrona Skarbowa) to reach. The clandestine distilling is moving from outbuildings into fields and abandoned bunkers and is changing its operating hours to night-time."[817] By the late 1940s, remote distillery locations had become the norm.[818] In the cities, a decisive blow for alcohol distribution networks came with the wiping out of the majority of private stores and restaurants by the "battle for trade" and putting the existing ones under even stricter supervision. As a consequence, until the early 1980s, the alcohol black market concentrated in the cities in *melinas*, where mostly monopoly vodka was sold.

Of course none of this means that alcohol was no longer distilled in the cities. However, it was done amateurishly and chiefly for personal use. Throughout the 1950s, 1960s and 1970s, *bimber* distilleries were usually mentioned in the press in the context of rural areas or small towns. Newspaper stories, all very much alike, mainly focused on anti-moonshine police operations and the problems that the police functionaries faced. "The larger-scale production flees from the usual locations to places where a policeman will not go either by chance or on suspicion, because he is reluctant to venture into some backwoods. One needs a customized horse-drawn cart to get through, to carry boilers and the starter mash there; firewood can be cut in the forest nearby and, a few days' worth of corked and bottled moonshine is brought back."[819]

817 *Ibid.*, fol. 86.

818 AAN, KC PZPR, 237/VII–2679, fol. 92.

819 A.K. Wróblewski, *Bimber*, "Polityka", no. 23/June 8, 1963; see: Z. Szopiński, *Lekarstwo na ischias*, "Tygodnik Kulturalny", no. 39 /September 27, 1970.

The official campaign launched in 1957 to fight alcoholism by raising the price of alcohol and closing a proportion of retail alcohol shops resulted in no time at all in a boost to illegal alcohol brewing. Szymon Kobyliński, We have completely eradicated alcoholism in our district, *"Szpilki", no. 4, 7 December 1958 (courtesy of the author's family).*

In some regions such production was well in excess of the needs of "family" consumption. Unfortunately, we do not know much about the distribution channels of this surplus. Probably only a small portion was delivered to the cities, where since the early 1950s, different demand and consumption models had developed. The greater part of the product was distributed locally, and local residents had easy access to the source of moonshine, also on a wholesale basis.

"Before," a resident of Garwolin confided to a journalist in 1970, "you could ask anybody and they would show you [where to find it]. Now people are on guard. If they don't know you they won't sell it to you. But if you go with a local guy, you can buy as much as you want."[820] It is also hard to determine how commonplace the middlemen were who specialized solely in alcohol distribution. It seems however, that the modus operandi of a peasant woman in a village near Sieradz was the rule rather than the exception: "Zenobia picked up the cans herself and carried them on a motorbike or in her son-in-law's Škoda. She took any amount, paid a thousand per liter and sold it for 400 more [...]. At Zenobia's, [alcohol] was available day and night, unlike at the store in [the local village of] Fajum. There was enough moonshine for any occasion or none. For baptisms, weddings, pig slaughter, for a rainy day, and a funeral. People came to Zenobia's from near and far and never returned home with empty cans."[821]

When moonshine producers or distributors were caught by the authorities, it was usually as a result of denunciation rather than any sophisticated police operations. "Almost all the cases that landed in court," a journalist evaluated the situation in 1975, "are the result of a denunciation by neighbors. The distiller or the illegal dealer needs to remain on good terms with their neighbors. As soon as they fall out, the police get a tip off."[822] That a culprit would be found guilty was not, however, a foregone conclusion. The rural code of ethics which allowed the denouncing of neighbors did not allow one to testify against them in court.[823]

Another commonly practiced strategy involved, as already mentioned, the sole breadwinners in the family or the elderly volunteering to take the blame. "Usually it is grandmas and grandpas who plead guilty," a policeman from Sobolewo near Ryki explained in 1970. "That's a real plague. The old granny who is pushing eighty stands in front of the judge and starts sobbing. What can the judge do? It usually ends with a suspended sentence."[824]

Policemen operating in rural areas did not have an easy job, repeatedly finding themselves between a rock and a hard place when dealing at the same time with the demands of their superiors and of the local public. It is clear that chiefs of local police stations had to compromise, which often involved striking a fine balance. One of their strategies was to bust illegal distilleries, taking the credit

820 Z. Szopiński, *Lekarstwo na ischias....*

821 R. Kubiak, *Wielki zacier*, "Tygodnik Kulturalny", no. 11/March 15, 1987.

822 J. Majkut, *Konkurenci przemysłu spirytusowego*, "Słowo Powszechne" April 1, 1975.

823 R. Młodar, *Bimber*, PiŻ, 1957, no. 26/27.

824 Z. Jagielski, *Dosyć zmowy milczenia*, TL, 1970, no. 332; see: Z. Szopiński, *Lekarstwo na ischias...*; J. Konieczna, *Śladami bimbrownictwa*, TL, February 5, 1974.

due but neglect to gather the evidence, which made it impossible to initiate the legal procedures and move the matter along any further.[825] It is difficult, however, to say how common such a phenomenon was.

The burden of keeping an eye on *bimber* was not evenly spread among the local police forces. For a long time, illicit distillation was concentrated in parts of Poland "where there is poverty, poor soil, and scattered farms – in Poland B".[826] These were also the areas with the lowest social standards and the lowest acceptance of the authorities as well as the longest tradition of making moonshine (going back to the time of the German occupation). Among the regions where the distillers prevailed were therefore the lands of the former Russian and Austrian partition, including the vicinity of Warsaw, as well as the regions of Białystok, Kielce, Łódź, Lublin, Krakow (where, near the city of Nowy Sącz, the famous plum vodka was distilled), and Rzeszów. The illegal distilling of alcohol was rarely found in the area of the former Prussian partition.

Illegal brewery, late 1970s. Photo: Andrzej Baturo, FORUM Polish Photography Agency.

825 TL, no. 213/August1, 1958.
826 A.K. Wróblewski, *Bimber*, "Polityka", no. 23/June 8, 1963.

Just because in a particular area there did not happen to be many distilleries, this by no means meant that there was no demand for moonshine. By late 1945, there were cases of transporting *bimber* from Warsaw and vicinity all the way to Katowice and Bielsko.[827] Returnees from the Eastern Borderlands and migrants from central Poland quickly transplanted their distilling traditions to these Recovered Territories but for a long time were unable to match the expansion levels of the Krakow or Kielce region (not to mention Białystok where between 1955 and 1958, almost a quarter of all distilleries in Poland were uncovered). In 1958, of the total number of 2 451 *bimber* investigations, 536 were conducted in the Białystok voivodship, 524 in the Warsaw voivodship, 411 in the Lublin voivodship, and 211 in the Łódź voivodship. At the same time there was only one investigation in the Gdańsk voivodship, five in Koszalin, four in Olsztyn, two in Szczecin, and three in the Zielona Góra voivodships.[828]

As mentioned before, at the turn of the 1940s and 1950s, moonshine production predominated in rural Poland, where 78% to 82% of all the cases prosecuted were uncovered.[829] Reports on distilleries or moonshine sales in the cities were sporadic.[830] After a small distillery had been raided in the Praga district of Warsaw, a journalist from *Kurier Polski* commented, "Warsaw *bimber* lovers have lost one of the very few sources for purchasing moonshine [in the capital]."[831] A decade later, he would have probably not been able to put it like this. The social, economic and cultural changes taking place in the 1950s and the 1960s affected also clandestine distilling. Industrialization and urbanization together with mass migrations blurred both the lines between the regions and between rural and urban areas. This had a knock-on effect on patterns of consumption including that of *bimber*.

Already during the moonshine boom in the early part of the Gierek era, progressive "urbanization" of the bootleg distilling had been in evidence. Now, city residents more and more often got involved in *bimber* production; initially these were mostly workers, and occasionally clerks supplementing their wages.[832] Technological changes, in particular the now widespread use of sugar as

827 AAN, KS, 2953.

828 D. Słoń, *Geografia bimbru*, "Słowo Powszechne", no. 112/May 12, 1958; see: B. Sygit, *Nielegalny...*, pp. 26–27.

829 B. Sygit, *Nielegalny...*, p. 29.

830 AAN, KC PZPR, 237/XXXI–243, fol. 164.

831 "Kurier Polski", October 11, 1965.

832 J. Olszewski, *Bimber*, TL, no. 270/September 27, 1971; E. Bryl, *Babcia robi interesy*, "Tygodnik Kulturalny", no. 45/November 6, 1977.

the main ingredient, led to a moonshine comeback in the cities. Starter prepared from potatoes or flour required large amounts of ingredients; the "production cycle was long and complex, the pulp fermenting in barrels stank horribly and could give away the location of the distillery."[833] In contrast, sugar-based technology allowed one to prepare small, "domestic-use" quantities of the starter (as in the Grunwald recipe: 1 kg of sugar, 4 l of water, 100 g of yeast), and the production process was easy and did not require sophisticated equipment. A small stove, cold running water and a modified kettle were all that was necessary.

A real breakthrough came in the fall of 1981, together with the introduction of alcohol rationing and Martial Law. There were important geographical and social changes. *Bimber* production spread quickly in areas where earlier it had been almost non-existent, such as the Opole region, where the rise in distilling was statistically the greatest, as it was from a low base. It again became a city-based phenomenon. Beginning in 1982, the majority of those sentenced for illegal distilling were city dwellers.[834] The moonshine-producer identikit was changing rapidly. Whereas in the early months of rationing, it had been mostly workers[835] who had been involved in distilling moonshine in the cities, Martial Law turned it into an activity of the intelligentsia. The "distilling fad" among the intelligentsia was only partly due shortage of liquor. Socio-cultural factors played an important, if not more important role. Intelligentsia had much spare time, with few opportunities to fill it up, and a liking for socializing. Moreover, to brew *bimber* was a form of political, "oppositionist" statement. "Distilling is fashionable mostly among members of the intelligentsia. A teacher and an engineer swap recipes, taste samples together, and hone the equipment. At family or friends' gatherings, it's not the herring [...], the apple pie or home-made liqueurs that the hosts are praised for. It's the *bimber*!"[836] While garages or boiler rooms had been the typical sites for illicit distilling, now it was not uncommon to carry out the production in the workplace, even if this happened to be a university, or especially a science lab.[837]

This fad did not last long. Homemade distilling by the intelligentsia did not disappear altogether but after alcohol rationing ended in spring 1983, it ceased

833 J. Olszewski, *Bimber*, TL, no. 270/September 27, 1971.
834 AAN, URM, 32/182, k. 7; AAN, IPP, 65, fol. 28, 30–31.
835 "Since they introduced the rationing coupons," Praga resident chips in, "I haven't once bought monopoly alcohol. For five bills [I buy] a sack of sugar from Wedel; problem solved! I've asked my next door neighbor and he says there is no stench of bimber"; D. and A. Wroniszewscy, *O lesie, dlaczego tak kochamy ciebie*, PiŻ, 1984, no. 51.
836 Z. Krzysztofiak, *Pędzą wszyscy*, "Polityka", no. 2/January 12, 1985.
837 B. Sygit, *Nielegalny...*, pp. 32–33.

to play any cultural, not to mention iconic, role. Especially now that an extensive network of booze stores made it possible to buy liquor any time of the day and night to one's heart's content.

6.2 "Buy a Bottle, Mister!" Illegal Trading in Legal Alcohol

The state monopolist was between the devil and the deep blue sea: the budget demanded maximization of alcohol revenue but the scourge of alcoholism, which led to quantifiable losses, pointed to curtailing the sales. With that aim in mind, and in view of the minimal effectiveness of the anti-alcohol campaigns, the authorities resorted to increasingly strict measures. Until the mid-1950s, the inter-war legislation remained in force, slightly modified and adjusted for the requirements of the new reality by acts such as the Act of 1950 on securing socialist discipline at work (Ustawa o zabezpieczeniu socjalistycznej dyscypliny pracy). The second part of the decade brought two anti-alcohol Acts[838] that limited alcohol sales and/or consumption opportunities in the workplace, in working men's hostels, and in community centers. Municipal councils were given the authority to limit the numbers of outlets, their opening hours and the volume of supply. Councils were also authorized to introduce local prohibition, for example on paydays or state holidays such as May 1 or July 22. From 1966, only those over 18 were officially allowed to buy alcohol and cigarettes. The 1970s brought on the one hand a significant increase in alcohol consumption, on the other – more restrictions and a decreased number of outlets (by the Council of Ministers' resolutions from May 5, 1972 and August 10, 1978). The legal crowning of the fight with alcoholism was the Act of October 26, 1982 on upbringing in sobriety and the prevention of alcoholism (Journal of Laws, no. 35, item 230).[839] The most unpalatable change for consumers was undoubtedly the ban on selling alcohol, both in stores and in restaurants, between 6 am and 1 pm.

When confronted with changing social behavior related to alcohol, such as increased consumption and drinking in the workplace, all the new bans and

838 They were titled identically: Act on Preventing Alcoholism, April 24, 1956, Dz.U. no. 12, item 32 and December 10, 1959, Dz.U. no. 69, item 434; see more: K. Kosiński, *Historia pijaństwa...*, pp. 268–275.

839 Public and the Catholic Church initiatives are also worth mentioning. Before Christmas 1980, Polish Primate Stefan Wyszyński issued an order to Warsaw Archdiocese priests to "refuse funeral services to those conducting illegal sales of alcohol, and to pass by in their Christmas visits those involved in alcohol trading"; "Słowo Powszechne" December 23, 1980.

regulations led to further development of the bootleg trade. The commercial relationship between the state monopoly and consumers was invaded by an additional agent – a go-between, who charged commission for the risk taken. "Each legal outlet that has been closed down," the Ministry of Justice warned in 1957, "is immediately replaced by illegal mobile vending points at marketplaces and bazaars, as well as in private apartments."[840] The illicit dealing in legally manufactured spirits took different forms – from selling alcohol in public places that customers were usually very familiar with, such as squares, and marketplaces, or in the *melinas* where the underworld could buy liquor to go; some of these places also offered on-site consumption as well as sex or profiteering. Initially limited, the range of services available in due course often expanded with new business propositions.[841]

In the early post-war years, unlicensed private stores, restaurants, and eateries commonly sold monopoly alcohol. "The battle for trade" drove also this practice onto the streets and in to marketplaces but most of all into private apartments. Booze dives selling "state" alcohol, which included wine and beer, were mostly an urban phenomenon; while until the 1980s most of those convicted of illegal distilling lived in rural areas, those who were apprehended in those *melinas* lived in the cities.[842] In the cities there were different consumption patterns, with more financial resources available to numerous potential customers, and easy access and smaller risk.

The workers were definitely the best customers. Booze dives, initially called *potajemka* or *bunker*, popped up around "excavators, cranes, bulldozers [...], where there is a sign: structure 'X' or 'Y' under construction [...]. They thrive when surrounded by makeshift, bunkhouse workers' hostels, among the sounds of rubber boots thumping on the sticky clay."[843] But they also did quite well in the vicinity of already established factory plants. For example in the mid-1960s in Warsaw, most of the approximately 400 *melinas* identified by police were located

840 AAN, MS, 558, fol. 154.

841 J.W. Wójcik, *Meliny i ich klienci*, "Gazeta Prawnicza" 1985, no. 4.

842 Each campaign directed against illegal distilling, also in provincial Poland, inevitably led to increasing the number of booze dens. In the third quarter of 1958, the authorities detected 149 bootleg dens in Warsaw voivodship; a year later, having embarked on an anti-moonshine operation – 205; *Bimbrowni – mniej, melin pijackich – więcej*, "Głos Pracy", no. 284/November 27, 1959.

843 E. Klonowicz, *"Sasanki" przeszkadzają budować*, "Słowo Powszechne", no. 38/February 15, 1965.

in industrial districts – Wola, Żoliborz, Praga North, and Praga South.[844] When dealing with regular customers, the booze dive owner was willing to wait for payment until the next payday or accept in lieu products and materials stolen from the workplace. Alcohol bought in these illegal places was often bought with money acquired by selling "public property".[845]

Sometimes *melinas* operated inside workplaces, and were usually run by doorkeepers, janitors or the technical staff, who adapted their methods of trading to the local circumstances and needs. *Bimber* manufacturers, who played an important role in unofficial everyday life, were appreciated and often protected by the employees of the plants. When one of the janitors at the Warsaw Gardening Cooperative was caught selling liquor and the manager decided to fire him, all the employees including the blue and white collar workers, and even the managers protested vehemently against this decision. There is no doubt they were all customers of the janitor.[846]

Poor suburbs and city districts populated by workers who liked their drink were often *melina* hubs. In the greater Warsaw area in the 1960s, there were to be found in Czerniaków, Powiśle, Targówek, Wawrzyszew, Rembertów and in the neighborhoods of marketplaces.[847] "The police are aware of these sensitive areas," a Warsaw newspaper wrote in 1959, "where as many as 12 *melinas*, in which "grandmas", "aunties", and "uncles" conduct prohibited trading, can operate within 100 meters of one another."[848] Representatives of social groups other than the working class, including the intelligentsia, were also at times driven to using the services of a *melina* in situations such as alcohol running out during a party or an unexpected guest turning up. Anonymous polls quoted by Jerzy W. Wójcik in the mid-1980s, conducted among 422 people with higher education concluded that almost 55% had had contact with *melinas*.[849] This did not mean that illicit dives were easily accessible even if their addresses were an open secret – to minimize risk, they tended to stick to their trusted regular clientele and their doors were closed to strangers and random callers.

---

844 B. Szykuła, *Meliny i ich klienci*, "Głos Pracy", no. 139/June 12, 1967.

845 M. Regent, *Z zagadnień spekulacji (Uwagi na tle orzecznictwa sądów okręgu kieleckiego)*, "Nowe Prawo" 1956, no. 10, pp. 118–119; AAN, URM, 32/112, First National Anti-Speculation Meeting, September 15, 1981, fol. 30.

846 J.W. Wójcik, *Meliny i ich klienci*, "Gazeta Prawnicza" 1985, no. 4.

847 *"Waciowa" wreszcie wpadła, ale inni nadal rozpijają*, "Kurier Polski", no. 71/March 25, 1963.

848 "Express Wieczorny", no. 83/March 3, 1959.

849 J.W. Wójcik, *Meliny i ich klienci*, "Gazeta Prawnicza" 1985, no. 4.

Naturally, law enforcement agencies took an interest in all illicit liquor vending dens. The police were usually able to identify their location, often not so much with the help of their clients, which did also happen, but from disgruntled neighbors, not pleased with nightlong drinking sessions and late-night visits. Nevertheless, it was more difficult to shut down a *melina* or to arrest its owner than to close down an illicit distillery. The price of alcohol in these dens was often much higher than in stores but the customers did not feel cheated; on the contrary, they defended booze den keepers if they got into trouble. On the one hand, group solidarity and the code of ethics that prescribed the solving of conflicts without involving the authorities were important. On the other hand, pragmatic considerations played the most crucial role: although the client had to pay more, only a *melina* guaranteed access to alcohol twenty four hours a day, seven days a week and credit purchase for cash or barter. For many, the closing down of a *melina* would have been synonymous, at least temporarily, with losing unlimited access to alcohol.[850] A closure operation provided the police with a logistical problem: possession of even a large amount of monopoly alcohol, unlike possession of *bimber*, was not a criminal act. The policemen had to gather clear evidence in order to prove that illegal trade had taken place, and catch the perpetrators red-handed – a tall order, as well as find documentary evidence of the sales – again, unlikely, with cash sales being the norm.[851]

Understandably, illicit liquor vendors developed defensive strategies similar to those practiced by currency dealers. In their own apartments, they kept only a small amount of alcohol – often in opened bottles, to imply personal consumption. Wholesale amounts were stored elsewhere, in a basement or in a neighbors' apartment. Those who operated outside of *melinas* stored alcohol in their cars. This was, however, a risky practice especially in the 1980s, when a car could be confiscated as a "tool of crime", together with its contents. It was safer to trade in alcohol at home, since there was no legal provision for evicting *melina* owners.[852]

As a result, only a small percentage of these operators could be effectively brought to court,[853] and the sentences were usually mild – a fine of a couple of

850 W. Krasucka, *Spekulacja (wybrane zagadnienia)*, "Studia Kryminologiczne, Kryminalistyczne i Penitencjarne" 10, 1979, p. 163; "Express Wieczorny", no. 83/March 3, 1959.

851 M. Regent, *Z zagadnień spekulacji…*, pp. 118–119.

852 See: A. Cubała, *Melina na czterech kółkach*, PiŻ, 1986, no. 5 (Suwałki); J.W. Wójcik, *Meliny i ich klienci*, "Gazeta Prawnicza" 1985, no. 4.

853 For example in 1962 in Warsaw, police knew about the existence of approximately 300 alcohol dives but were able to "bring the investigation to a point of pressing

hundred zloty and a sentence of a few months in jail, mostly suspended. The average fine in the late 1960s was 500 zloty, a negligible amount that could be easily made on a single good day or a Saturday night.[854] The reasons for such leniency were both economic and social. Since the dealers were selling, albeit on a margin, monopoly alcohol, produced by state-owned factories, the Treasury incurred no financial losses. As early as February 1946, the Ministry of Public Administration instructed the voivods that vigorous combating of illegal sales of monopoly vodka was "harmful for the state Treasury" because it limited the trade in monopoly articles, which were "heavily taxed." "Temporary" leniency was advocated.[855]

No similar recommendations for the later period can be found but there can be no doubt that *melina* owners enjoyed mild treatment by the authorities. A *Polityka* journalist pointed this out in the mid-1980s, asking why "those who distil are punished severely while *melina* owners are treated leniently. No serious sentences are reported in the press, there are no immediate custodial sentences [...]. Smart people know that moonshine is rarely available in these dens, where monopoly and Pewex vodka rule." He drew the correct conclusion that, with the favorable dollar exchange rate, it was worth the dealers' while not only to resell monopoly spirits bought in ordinary stores but also brands bought exclusively for dollars and other hard currency in the also state-run Pewex stores, allowing not only a higher profit margin *for* the *melina* owners but also boosting earnings in the tills of state monopoly and Pewex stores: clearly, a win-win situation, at least from aneconomic point of view.[856] Yet again, the social dimension of the problem encouraged leniency by the judges. Until the 1980s, the vast majority of *melina* owners were women, often older, burdened with child-rearing costs and rarely able to count on even the slightest support from their partners.[857] Selling illegal alcohol was often a means of survival.

---

charges (by the prosecutor) only in 91 cases"; *"Waciowa" wreszcie wpadła, ale inni nadal rozpijają*, "Kurier Polski", no. 71/March 25, 1963.

854 "Express Wieczorny", no. 83/March 3, 1959.

855 AAN, MZO, 338, The Ministry of Public Administration to the voivods and mayors of Warsaw and Łódź, February 26, 1946, fol. 1. However, two months later, in the localities where state stores had been opened, the authorities ordered that there be published in the press a special warning regarding the prosecution and punishment of all those who sold alcoholic beverages without a license; *ibid.*, fol. 4.

856 J. Dziadul, *Pożytki z bimbrownika*, "Polityka", no. 50/December 14, 1985.

857 K. Kosiński, *Historia pijaństwa...*, pp. 558–561; APW, 30/XVIII–7, vol. 1, Report on the implementation the Voivodship Committee of PUWP resolution on

It is not surprising that closed down *melinas* tended to reappear quickly or be replaced by new ones. In 1966 in Warsaw, 119 such places were taken out but soon thereafter, another 250 new ones sprung up. Of those 119, thirty-five were shut down a second time, nine – a third time, and three – a fourth time.[858] Opening a new venture of this kind did not require great effort; it was enough to buy a few bottles of vodka or cheap wine in a liquor store and resell them with a mark-up (albeit the known dealers were charged at a premium at the stores as part of an informal deal struck with the store sellers). This entire system, which had been built over many decades, finally collapsed in 1981.

6.3 Excursus: The 1980s

In early 1981, the situation on the official alcohol market still did not appear too bad – in comparison with the previous year, the supply had shrunk by only 4.1% and the disappearance of alcohol from store shelves was due to massive hoarding and market chaos rather than a genuine shortage. The latter arrived in the second quarter of 1981, when alcohol deliveries shrank by a quarter. In the next three months they dropped to no more than 71.8% of the 1980 level.[859] Simultaneously, alcohol established itself firmly as a commonly accepted substitute currency and object of hoarding as well as being a store of value. The rationing of alcohol, gradually introduced from June 1981, was adopted in all Poland in October 1981. Since the rationing was implemented at the discretion of local authorities, the rules were not immediately identical in all regions, the available product range varied, and at best a consumer could count on one liter of spirits per month. After standardizing the regulations in January 1982, the ration went down to not more than half a liter.[860] These developments created a congenial environment for the now exceedingly lucrative illicit alcohol trade.

providing safety and order in the city, December 1963, fol. 90. For examples from Warsaw in the 1960s, see: B. Szykuła, *Meliny i ich klienci*, "Głos Pracy", no. 139/June 12, 1967.

858 B. Szykuła, *Meliny i ich klienci*, "Głos Pracy", no. 139/June 12, 1967.

859 P. Kapuściński, *Ile wódki wypić musimy i ani setki więcej*, "Tygodnik Solidarność", no. 27/October 2, 1981.

860 AAN, IPP, 65, fol. 5–7.

Illegal brewery in Czarna Białostocka, eastern Poland. Photo: Mariusz Olkowski, FORUM Polish Photography Agency.

Melina owners disappeared from the media and police reports to be replaced by "alcohol profiteers". This was not just a semantic change but above all quantitative. Police Headquarters, which was monitoring the illegal alcohol market, emphasized that the introduction of rationing had radically decreased the number of small alcohol dealers, who now faced a challenge in purchasing alcohol in the first place and secondly in having to justify the possession of large amounts of alcohol.[861] Before the introduction of rationing "one could possibly explain that the large quantity of alcohol was the result of long hours spent in lines", with sob stories about the whole family taking numerous turns in line, until it all added up.[862] From October 1981, this defense was no longer admissible. New trading strategies had to be devised, and new channels of supply and distribution charted. Wholesalers, who had capital, contacts, and operational capacity, were more likely to succeed than small-time dealers. They soon worked out a whole range of ways of acquiring liquor – from creatively taking advantage of state producers, through stealing and ration coupons scams to purchases in Pewex stores. Their risk was higher but their potential profits could be, and often were, considerable.

861 *Ibid.*, fol. 27.

862 *Spekulacja wódką i spirytusem*, TL, no. 2/January 4, 982.

For example in late 1981, a team of seven speculators from Poznań sold 20 000 bottles of vodka, making some 4.5 million zloty in the process.[863] In the following years, this impressive amount proved to be far from a record!

The simplest method was getting alcohol at source, from a state distillery. As was the case with the meat plants mentioned earlier, under pressure from the unions and often with the acquiescence of local authorities, Polmos (Polish Spirits Monopoly) factories pursued their own distribution policy. They bartered products with other factories, and sold directly to institutions and private individuals.[864] In 1981 alone, at least 270 000 bottles of spirits and 380 000 bottles of vodka "dematerialized" en route to clients.[865] The practice continued when Martial Law was introduced. By then, however, the government had a number of new, different regulations at its disposal. In early February 1982, both employees' spirits allowances and sales outside the official retail network were robustly curtailed. As a result, in 1982, the alcohol industry became one of the few branches of food industry where the employees could not expect allowances.[866]

It was possible to limit the quasi-legal alcohol trade with legislation but not to eliminate other channels for the flow of alcohol out of the distilleries. Despite the fact that by 1982, Polmos had conducted a staff review, replacing some of its security employees and giving everybody a 20 percent pay rise – intended as a disincentive to theft, throughout the decade fraud in distilleries was as common as it was in meat plants. Polmos employees tended to generate a strategic production surplus, by such means as applying the upper limits of permitted losses and the so-called production atrophy. Stealing alcohol at bottling stations or in transportation was also common.[867]

During alcohol transportation, breakage allowances were commonly used to the utmost. In May 1984, General Edwin Rozłubirski shrewdly pointed out that there were ten times fewer breakages during the transportation of vinegar or methylated spirits than in alcohol shipments. Crucially, the retail outlets masked

---

863 *Ibid.*

864 AAN, URM, 32/45, fol. 90; see: *ibid.*, 32/190, fol. 13.

865 *Spekulacja w "Polmosie"*, TL, no. 215/September 10, 1982. During the first four months of rationing, one of the Warsaw alcohol plants sold 50 000 bottles of spirit and vodka outside the rationing system. The buyers, usually restaurant franchise owners, were selling the alcohol often outside the premises, and always at a much higher price. In Łódź in late 1981, another single plant bought and sold 2 250 bottles of alcohol; AAN, URM, 32/113, fol. 29; *ibid.*, 32/15, fol. 22.

866 AAN, URM, 32/45, fol. 91–92.

867 AAN, URM, 32/57, fol. 95.

theft as breakage in order to avoid investigation. In 1983, in railroad transport there were alcohol "breakages" to the value of 729 million zloty.

Theoretically, instances of theft were considerably less frequent (in 1983, 50 million zlotys' worth of alcohol "disappeared" in railroad transportation; for comparison – 20 million zlotys' worth of cars and bicycles, and 26 million zlotys' worth of sugar vanished from transportation during the same period).[868]

Kasztel club in Warsaw, the storehouse. The haul during a raid in November 1981 included 2 500 bottles of vodka. Photo: Polish Press Agency (PAP).

The methods of stealing were often quite sophisticated. For example in 1983 in Lublin, a group of drivers delivering alcohol to Pewex stores "invented a method of opening and closing [bottles] without damaging the aluminum caps, which allowed them to remove alcohol from the bottles, replace it with water and then deliver them to the recipient with the said content." The culprits were never identified.[859] The stolen alcohol was sold to small-scale *melina* owners and savvy wholesalers among whom were liquor store employees and managers of restaurants – either state-owned or private; these clients had the best opportunities for

868 AAN, URM, 32/57, fol. 10–12, 70.

869 AAN, URM, 32/104, fol. 67.

further distribution. To take one example, in 1982 the owner of a restaurant franchise in Księży Dwór near Działdowo turned into cash more than 43 000 bottles of vodka, with a massive profit of 9 million zloty. The agents of two Poznań bars, Dobosz and Osiedle, made four million zloty by selling 20 000 bottles through other outlets. Reports about the sales of bottles of alcohol in their thousands were the order of the day.[870]

State monopoly stores had strategies of their own, albeit not always foolproof, that allowed them to generate profit from legally obtained supply. The retailers had little faith in the viability of complete control of the rationing system, especially since the complicated rules for the barter of rationed goods such as coffee or chocolate for alcohol rendered any supervision impossible.[871] In early 1982, in one of the stores in the Warsaw district of Mokotów, 6 934 bottles of vodka were sold without ration coupons; another outlet, in Kutno, sold outside of the rationing system approximately 16 000 bottles between July 1981 and July 1982 (at a profit of 3 million zloty).[872]

There were numerous attempts to obfuscate the unlawful operations by using counterfeit coupons or re-using alcohol coupons that had already been used. Time and time again, bogus coupons were discovered in the stores in such large quantities that it was impossible to put this down to accidental mistakes or the inattentiveness of staff members. Just in one Grocers' Cooperative store in Szczecin, as many as 3 320 fake coupons were found, in another store, Farmers Self-Help – 615, and in the state spirit monopoly store in Inowrocław – 1 091. Several months later, thousands of counterfeit alcohol coupon stubs surfaced in stores in Upper and Lower Silesia.[873] Forged alcohol coupons were widespread in all Poland.[874]

Equally profitable and certainly less risky was a creative interpretation of the edict that authorized state administration officials to grant special alcohol allowances on account of birth and wedding celebrations as well as funerals. A common strategy was to submit in the registry office "documents referring to a planned marriage for no other reason but to acquire a permit to purchase a large amount of alcohol for the wedding reception. As soon as the document has been obtained, the couple would change their mind and the wedding was off."[875] The

870 AAN, URM, 32/114, fol. 104; AAN, KC PZPR, WA, LI/118, fol. 155–156.
871 AAN, URM, 32/114, fol. 53.
872 AAN, URM, 1.4/21, fol. 43; *ibid.*, 32/119, fol. 187.
873 AAN, URM, 1.4./21, fol. 36–37; *ibid.*, 32/180, fol. 3, 18.
874 AAN, IPP, 65, fol. 27; AAN, URM, 32/13, fol. 22.
875 AAN, URM, 32/119, fol. 25.

certificates were also forged on a mass scale or used on multiple occasions by different people.[876] In that way, with shrewd forward planning, one could acquire significant amounts of liquor and make a tidy profit. In February 1982, it was reported from Siedlce that three representatives of, as the dispatch strenuously emphasized, "private initiative" – the owner of a concrete making business, of a private cab, and of a repair work shop – were suspected of "buying alcohol with forged certificates and selling it at black market prices. The authorities seized a typewriter, stamps, and a set of print fonts used to forge the certificates authorizing the purchase of alcohol for a wedding reception. It was established that the culprits had bought more than 1 500 bottles and made 750 000 zloty."[877]

The black market price of alcohol was so high and the dollar price in the hard-currency-only Pewex stores so low that it was worthwhile buying vodka, especially the cheaper brands, in Pewex and selling it on through unofficial channels with a satisfactory profit margin. By late 1981, large amounts of Pewex alcohol had entered the free market. Pewex vodka or cognac was commonly traded in monopoly stores, restaurants, and dining cars,[878] as well as being routinely available in *melinas*. Not only was alcohol available in Pewex stores without any ration coupons but it could also be bought as soon as the store opened: early in the morning rather than from 1 pm, as was the case with other stores. No wonder that Pewex remained the supply destination of choice for alcohol dealers even after the abolition of rationing.

The abolition of alcohol rationing in the spring of 1983 only minimally diminished the volume of the illegal liquor trade. Rationing coupons and certificate fraud became a thing of the past. With high prices and poor supply, all the above mentioned strategies for generating surplus remained in use. The abolition of alcohol rationing coincided with the introduction of sales restrictions, combining to create a perfect base for rebuilding the traditional system of underground alcohol dives. The majority of those waiting in line in front of a state monopoly liquor store before it opened at 1 pm every weekday were female owners of the *melinas*.

Unsurprisingly, until the second half of the 1980s, alcohol was the uncontested winner in the black market statistics. Even in 1987, as much as 60 percent of illegal trade involved spirits. The potential profits were sufficiently rewarding that even the stepping up of repression at the turn of 1984 and 1985, in particular the

876 AAN, URM, 32/113, fol. 275.

877 AAN, URM, 32/119, fol. 73.

878 J.W. Wójcik, *Meliny i ich klienci*, "Gazeta Prawnicza" 1985, no. 4.

Act of May 10, 1985, the introduction of higher fines and the potentially longer custodial sentences did nothing to curb the thriving black market in alcohol.

"Indeed, there are still fines of five thousand each," the Supreme Court Judge Ryszard Bodecki said in April 1985. "As I was just saying to the Minister, yesterday we had the case of a retired vodka dealer. It is mainly pensioners who trade in vodka. No one is researching this phenomenon. One can say that 90% of them are pensioners, so let's just fine them 5 000 for the hell of it...The Minister insists on a 50 000 zloty fine. The man's pension is 7 900 zloty, he is old and sick but he's been trading bootleg for a long time. So, to be blunt, we did up the ante and applied the 50 000 zloty fine. Throughout the proceedings he kept crying and we could not communicate with him at all. But here is the interesting thing. After the sentencing, we told him – after all, he is an elderly man – that there was a possibilty of paying in installments. His face brightened and he said 'God bless you, Judge'. I said nothing but what I'm trying to say here is that, clearly, the 50 000 did not pose a problem for him."[879]

Judge Bodecki unwittingly touched upon the changes taking place in the social profile of the illicit alcohol trade, partly due to the eventful start to the 1980s. In 1986, the law enforcement agencies reported 2 927 cases of alcohol speculation, of which 75% were in the cities. Among the 2 267 convicted offenders, 1 226 (49.6%) were women, 1 088 (47.9%) – pensioners and retirees, 373 (16.4%) unemployed, 352 persons with previous convictions, 1 318 (58.1%) were above the age of 49, and 698 (30.7%) in the 30–49 age group.[880] These statistics show that the stereotypical image of the illicit alcohol trader as a pensioner was no longer accurate. Quite a number of these operators were capable of turning over vast quantities of alcohol. The record was perhaps set by a female janitor from Przemyśl who between January 1984 and June 1986 bought and sold with spectacular profit (9 million zloty!) at least 58 400 bottles of vodka and wine.

Just like the money changers, the *melina* owners were creative and flexible; having adjusted well to the state retail strategies, they did not shy away from attempts to monopolize the local market. When in the mid-1980s, a night alcohol store opened in one of the big cities, the authorities received numerous letters of complaint. After some investigation, the police established that they were written by local bootleg dealers who wanted to squash the competition. When a night store opened in Warsaw, the nearby *melina* began to sell alcohol with the same

879 AAN, URM, 32/74, fol. 25.
880 AAN, URM, 32/104, fol. 97.

20% surcharge.[881] Whereas, however, the state store was closed between 6 am and 1 pm, the illicit dens operated at all hours and were able to dictate the prices.

On July 19, 1990 (Journal of Laws, no. 73, item 431), the regulations of the Act of October 26, 1982 were abolished with the effect of restricting alcohol sales and putting paid to the majority of *melinas*. It was only the small-fry retailers, however, who were eliminated from the black market. The sharks continued to do well and, together with gas, liquor became one of the pillars of the grey zone retail commerce in the era of transformation. Interestingly, in today's capitalist Poland *bimber* has not yet become history – despite the distillation of moonshine by private individuals remaining illegal, it continues to be widely produced today. Some distil their own *bimber*, because they cannot afford store alcohol. Others, as they did in the early 1980s, enjoy the activity as a hobby. Moonshine has come to be an attraction on even the most sophisticated tables.

881 AAN, URM, 32/104, fol. 47–48.

7. Gasoline

Automobiles and, as a result, the fuel that they ran on were probably the leading commodities traded on the black market in the Soviet Bloc countries. The mass prevalence of the automobile as a private means of transportation did not arrive there until decades later than in the capitalist world; this delayed gratification only reinforced the symbolic status of car ownership. Unlike in the West, where the automotive industry had long been considered the motor of the economy, and where a brand-new car was available for less than the average annual wage, in the countries behind the Iron Curtain it was a truly onerous endeavor to buy a vehicle and the coveted goal considerably more expensive, often involving a multiple of the Western price. Prospective buyers had to commit themselves to long-time money-saving, often taking a second job and making numerous sacrifices. In the Eastern bloc shortage economy, the automobile was not a commodity that was universally accessible. "To buy a car in Eastern Europe," wrote the British journalist Roger Boyes, "you need the patience of a Franciscan monk, a pocket full of dollars or the sixth sense of a horse trader. Sometimes – all three."[882]

In the Soviet Bloc countries, the government aspired to a tight grip on the carefully managed automotive market. The commodity was allocated on the basic of a complex system of formal and informal rationing aided by priority lists, car coupons and individual allocations based on a person's merit, rank, status or connections. To be able to buy a car was a privilege, a reward, a gratuity, and at times a form of bribery. Those whom the authorities considered useful, or those high in the pecking order, could expect to lay their hands on a four-wheeler of their own relatively swiftly. The vast majority of all others, just as eager to get behind the wheel, not only had to make pre-payments greatly in advance but also wait patiently, not infrequently for a number of years. Unsurprisingly, from the Elbe to Vladivostok, social strategies focused on ways of by-passing the line for cars or whittling down the wait. One common practice was to buy coupons allocated to other people – at a hefty mark-up – bought off dealers who had harassed the lucky recipients of the said coupons to trade them in. Another method was to intercept allocations for privileged groups such as the handicapped and

882 R. Boyes, *The Hard Road to Market. Gorbachev, the Underworld, and the Rebirth of Capitalism*, London 1990, p. 128. See: L. H. Siegelbaum, *Car for Comrades. The Life of the Soviet Automobile*, Ithaca–London 2008; *The Socialist Car: Automobility in the Eastern Bloc*, ed. L. H. Siegelbaum, Ithaca–London 2011.

farmers.[883] Those who were in a hurry, who could afford it, and who cared about quality could bring a car from abroad, or buy it from the state for hard currency or for zloty on the free market.[884] What all these methods had in common was that none was cheap; often, as a result, the "financial effort put into buying a car was so strenuous that it subsequently forced the driver to save on the running costs of the vehicle."[885]

Thus, the dream car often remained idle rather than hitting the road. Many owners used their car only sporadically, content purely with the ownership of the vehicle; the proverbial "Sunday driver", with his less than assured driving skills, was a common sight on the poorly marked and signposted roads of communist Poland and other Soviet Bloc countries. For a significant number of the owners such rationed use was understandably not an optimal solution. Paradoxically,

---

883 D. O'Hearn, *The Consumer Second Economy. Size and Effects*, "Soviet Studies" 32, 1980, no. 2, pp. 218–234; Z. Kapitány, J. Kornai, J. Szabó, *Reproduction of shortage on the Hungarian car market*, "Soviet Studies" 36, 1984, no. 2, pp. 236–256. *The socialist car...* (especially Valentina Fava on Czechoslovakia, pp. 17–29, Mariusz Jastrząb on communist Poland, pp. 30–46, and György Péteri on Hungary, pp, 47–68). In the 1970s, in the Polish People's Republic car coupon made possible the quick purchase of a car at the wholesale price. The difference with the retail price formed therefore a handsome bonus. See: *Rynek motoryzacyjny*, ed. Z. Krasiński, Warszawa 1980, p. 85. On the Polish system of allocation (and especially breaking its rules) see: J. Nawrot, *Talonowy biznes*, PiŻ, 1982, no. 10; J. Nawrot, *Pamiętnik młodego asystenta*, *ibid.*, no. 12.

884 D. O'Hearn, *The Consumer Second Economy...*, p. 220; Z. Kapitány, J. Kornai, J. Szabó, *Reproduction of Shortage...*, p. 239; S. Wolle, Die heile Welt der Diktatur. Alltag und Herrschaft in der DDR *1971–1989*, Berlin 1998, pp. 312–315. In Poland such institutions as PHZ, Pol-Mot, Pewex, and Motoimpex sold commodities for hard currencies. Since the 1960s, marketplaces (such as *giełda*, the popular public auction) sprung up in larger towns and cities. On these markets, car went for some 30 to 50 percent above wholesale prices; *Rynek motoryzacyjny...*, pp. 86–87. Since the mid-1960s, the number of cars brought privately from abroad grew systematically: 1 110 cars in 1962, 2 314 in 1965, 5 587 in 1968, 6 198 in 1969. After raising customs duties in March 1970, only 558 vehicles were privately imported in the following year. In March 1972, with the tariffs lowered, their numbers quickly went up again, reaching 3 532 vehicles in 1973 and 4 011 in 1974. In 1979, as many as 12 050 automobiles were brought from abroad. At the turn of the 1960s and the 1970s, the most popular western brand was Volkswagen, followed by Fiat, Ford, Opel, BMW, Mercedes, NSU, Simca, Volvo, Peugeot, Austin, Citroen, and Morris; AAN, GUC, 23/397, Kompendium statystyczne administracji celnej 1946–1974, fol. 121–126; *Rynek motoryzacyjny...*, p. 45.

885 J. Urban, *Z głowy na szosę*, "Polityka", no. 46/November 18, 1976.

while the communist shortage economy, on the one hand, made owning a car difficult, on the other hand it provided easy access to illegal gas, for which the state held the monopoly. The nationalized economy was wasteful and well known for its absurd rules and regulations. The illusory inspections and large numbers of eager participants, both as vendors and buyers, often led to a situation where fraud was practically inevitable. Due to its economic and physical characteristics, gasoline was the commodity par excellence for illicit trade: no gasoline substitute was available nor could it be produced by homegrown methods, as was the case with other black-market products that had been siphoned off from state supplies. Gasoline was relatively easy to obtain while frauds were difficult to detect.

A peculiar characteristic of the black market and gasoline was that both parties to the transaction could notch up a tangible profit. The fuel could usually be acquired relatively easily from official sources, since the gasoline "surpluses" artificially created by the employees of the state monopoly to enable themselves to commit fraud were quite considerable, demand was limited due to insignificant private car ownership. Under the circumstances, the black market price of gas was half the official price. As the fluctuations in the price of gas in Poland during the 1980s demonstrated, however, such favorable pricing could and did change rapidly according to the circumstances. The private demand for fuel, prompted by the rapidly growing number of vehicles and citizens developing a liking for the freedom of movement they provided, expanded so much that when gas supply collapsed, drivers were willing to pay multiples of the official price without batting an eyelid. The alternative was unpalatable to the prevailing pragmatic approach: pay more for gas – or travel on the overcrowded public transportation.

There is no doubt that a black market for fuel existed in all the Soviet Bloc countries. Its size and type depended on the accessibility of gas, the number of people who owned cars, and the official price of gas, as well as social determinants: prosperity, level of acceptance for black market practices, etc. Unquestionably Poland was similar to the Soviet Union where in the mid-1970s one third of private vehicles ran on state gas. Where the distances were greater and people earned less, between 60 and 70% (but as much as 86.5% in Omsk in 1971) of gas found its way to private gas tanks from illicit sources. In places where the citizens did not have great distances to drive and society was more prosperous, such as the Baltic Republics, this rate hovered between 18 and 38%.[886] However, when in the mid-1980s state deliveries of fuel were not able to keep up with a growing

886 D. O'Hearn, *The Consumer Second Economy...*, p. 221; M.V. Alexeev, *The Underground Market for Gasoline in the USSR*, "Comparative Economic Studies" 30, 1988, no. 2, p. 53.

automobile sector, the number of people taking advantage of the illegal supply grew radically. Of all the Soviet Bloc countries the problems with fuel were the most drastic in Poland in the 1980s. Polish strategies for bypassing the state monopoly were therefore the most developed and sophisticated.

7.1 Driving on Bootleg: From the 1950s to the 1970s

Immediately after the Second World War, the only private vehicles in Poland were survivors from pre-war times or those released from army surpluses. Nevertheless, automobiles were so few and far between that the *Statistical Year Book* from 1949, in the section entitled *Transportation and Communication* did not list private cars at all. In 1951, the Polish government factory launched the Warszawa trademark autos but the numbers rolling off the production line made barely a dent in the existing demand. In 1955, there were only 20 500 vehicles in private hands – a drop in the ocean in a country, the population of which in the last census (1950) exceeded 25 million. With such insignificant numbers, the gas flowing from official to private gas tanks – which indubitably must have been going on – remained overshadowed by the large volume of other black market offences and remained unrecorded. This changed in 1956 when the political thaw left its mark also in the automobile sector. This was due to evolving models of consumption, with car ownership becoming socially acceptable rather than a remaining a suspect sign of "conspicuous consumption"; moreover, the development of private enterprise was combined with increasing prosperity. In Radom, to take but one example, between early 1957 and May 1958, the number of private vehicles doubled.[887] The demand for cars triggered a black market in permits authorizing the purchase of a car.[888]

Demand for cheap gas grew as a consequence, and gas thefts soon followed, albeit on a small scale in comparison to other crimes within the state transportation system. In 1956, gas thefts were estimated to have reached a value of 70 million zloty whereas there were 200 million worth of thefts of ferried goods, 170 million worth of tools and illegal transportation of people also took place.[889] However, it was gas theft that proved to be an increasingly prominent phenomenon – so widespread, in fact, that it became a running joke with the nation

887 AAN, KC PZPR, XI/281, fol. 26.

888 AAN, KC PZPR, 237/XXXII-7, fol. 30; *ibid.*, 237/XXXII–27, fol. 186.

889 *Szara strefa Października. „Notatka" o nielegalnych dochodach w Polsce 1956–1957* (*The October 1956 grey zone. A "note" on illegal income in Poland 1956–1957*), ed. J. Kochanowski, PH, 95, 2004, z. 1, p. 87.

resigned to the 'new normal': "Do you drive on the right or on the left in Poland?" "Neither. You drive on bootleg". Satirical magazines were not averse to ridiculing the situation.[890]

"Do you drive on the right or on the left in Poland?" "Neither. You drive on bootleg", Zbigniew Kiulin, "Szpilki", no. 7, 15 February 1959.

890 See Z. Kiulin's joke, on similar lines, in the satirical magazine "Szpilki", no.7, 1959/ February 7. Nota bene, by 1959 the number of private autos increased threefold in comparison to 1956 – from 24 700 to 78 600!

Without a doubt, large numbers of vehicles were driven on bootleg gas. In May 1965, Police Headquarters, the Oil Products Market, and the National Councils' presidia estimated that in 1964, private vehicles used approximately 284 400 tons of fuel in spite of the fact that gas stations had sold only 124 400 tons to drivers. The remaining 160 000 tons came from state gas tanks.[891] It was not very difficult to obtain gas illegally – the allowances in state transportation were inflated and state inspectors were not interested in putting a lot of effort in monitoring transport. Drivers, dispatchers, and security co-existed on transport bases in mutually beneficial, symbiotic relationships.

Corruption was so widespread that in workplaces where the fuel management rules were strictly observed, workers occasionally mutinied and drivers quit, looking for bosses prepared to turn a blind eye.[892] The substitute solutions offered to drivers proved unattractive. State enterprises provided a bonus of an amount of up to 85% of the value of the theoretically saved fuel. This was more than the driver could get by selling gas illegally (*na lewo*) or by striking an agreement with employees of the Centrala Produktów Naftowych (CPN), the state enterprise that comprised all petrol stations in Poland. The following confession made in the 1980s by a driver illustrates very well the motivation of many others also in the earlier years: "Why are we engaging in wheeler-dealing? If I manage to save gas systematically, for each liter they will pay me 85% of the value but there are strings attached. In three months they will cut my allowance. Meanwhile the vehicle is getting older. It uses more gas. So I use more than my allowance. And for that they deduct 100% of the price from my wages. I can't afford to be subsidizing the state business."[893]

Thus, the drivers commonly recorded in their logs heavier loads than they had transported in reality, so as to justify higher fuel consumption. For example in 1962, in the Katowice voivodship, according to drivers' logs, a shipment authorized by the Ministry of Construction comprised 26 million tons of goods whereas in reality there was not more than 3.8 million tons – a staggeringly bold discrepancy. The drivers tweaked the engines and logged much longer routes than the ones actually covered. This led to a situation similar to that in the mid-1970s in the Voivodship Car Transportation Enterprise in Bydgoszcz where the trucks would have had to have driven with an average speed of 200 km/h in order to cover the distance recorded in the drivers' logbooks.[894] It was

891 AAN, KC PZPR, 237/V–615, fol. 104.

892 A. Teneta, *Na jałowym biegu*, "Polityka", no. 3/January 18, 1976.

893 A.J. Socha, *Kurs na lewo*, "Tygodnik Kulturalny", no. 19/May 11, 1986.

894 D. Frey, *Ciemna liczba*, "Tygodnik Demokratyczny" May 15, 1977.

impossible to check how many kilometers the drivers really had covered – of the 20 000 vehicles inspected in 1964, 7 028 had no odometers or their odometers were broken. In one of the firms in Gorzów, 72 out of 74 vehicles had tweaked odometers.[895] The specialists counted thirty methods of "adjusting" an odometer – from basic to quite sophisticated.[896] Tachographs registering all the actions of vehicles and drivers became more popular only at the turn of the 1970s and the 1980s, impeding the lucrative trade. But even the most elaborate equipment was never an obstacle to the determined drivers.

Every year thousands of tons of the "saved" fuel ended up in private gas tanks. The operation took place mostly in the garages – of which there were more than ten thousand in transport bases, on construction sites, in factories, mines, and on State Agriculture Farms (PGR). The practice was not very convenient for the state-employed drivers who had to look for clients and transfer fuel to their tanks. Drivers preferred to buy fuel at CPN gas stations, of which there were 1 300 in Poland in the 1970s, and supplement their income in this, much easier way. This method, used from the 1950s until the 1980s, was not exactly a black market operation, since the object of the trade was not the fuel but the documents confirming its purchase. Nevertheless, it merits a mention.

The drivers kept a running tally of the fuel saved. They would pull up at the gas station where they had struck up a "special" relationship with the manager and get from him "receipts for a larger amount of gas than they had actually purchased. For example the driver would buy 20 liters of gas and the manager would give him a receipt for 120. The fictitious number of liters appeared only in the top copy of the receipt given to the driver. The manager of the gas station kept the copy […], on which there was the actual amount of gas sold in the transaction."[897] Sometimes, the manager would write a receipt without selling any gas, which conjured up for him an instantaneous surplus. He would get rid of it by selling fuel to regular customers, for the official price but without providing any receipts. The gas station employee would typically be rewarded with a third of the value of the gas saved by the driver, who in turn had to share his profit with his partners at the workplace.[898]

This practice was relatively safe. The accounts at the CPN station balanced and corresponded to the amount of gas remaining, and the state enterprise managers

895 AAN, KC PZPR, 237/V–615, fol. 104–105.

896 A. Teneta, *Na jałowym biegu*, "Polityka", no. 3/January 18, 1976.

897 Report on economic crime in *1959*, Warsaw 1960 (Supreme Audit Office, NIK, Department of Economic Fraud, copy in author's possesion), p. 58.

898 *Ibid.*; Z. Branach, *Przecieka nie tylko benzyna*, "Życie Literackie" 1982, no. 40.

rarely questioned the receipts submitted by the drivers for reimbursement, and not just because they also participated in the profits of the operation. More important was the fear that a disgruntled employee could walk out; factory managers could not afford to miss their production targets – and this was likely with reduced worker numbers. Even if the internal inspection did find irregularities, which was rarely the case, the usual sanctions were no more than a warning or a reprimand.[899] The scale of the frauds transpired only when the police investigated the receipts. From mid-1958 to mid-1959, a manager of a CPN station in Katowice issued 1 330 fictitious receipts for 570 000 zloty (for 120 000 liters of gas in total); between 1962 and 1963, another gas station manager, in Praszka, sold 1 700 receipts to the total value of 944 000 zloty to 387 drivers from 91 companies. Gas station attendants from Gdynia and Lębork clocked up deals to the tune of 700 000 zloty. It transpired that the ratio of profit division was almost identical with the ratio of prosecuted gas station workers to state company drivers – the investigation conducted between 1963 and 1965 included 349 CPN workers and 861 "nationalized enterprise drivers"[900] – was this no more than a coincidence?

Whereas in the 1950s and the 1960s the CPN employees and drivers involved in the deals had known one another, if only because they had been based in the same locality, and the relationship had been built on trust, the next decade brought a radical change. The practice, until then local in character, began to function "on a mass and national scale with partners who did not know each other."[901] In large part, this was a consequence of the automobile revolution of the Gierek era coinciding with the international oil crisis and a local recession. In the 1970s, Poland finally crossed over the great divide between the "motorcycle civilization"[902] and the age of the automobile, when four wheels of one own finally "stopped being at odds with the acceptable socialist lifestyle."[903] Regardless of the government's intentions, in the first half of the decade the number of privately owned automobiles grew on average by 100 000, and in the second half – by

899 S.M. Jankowski, *"Swoje chłopy" przy beczce z benzyną*, "Życie Literackie" March 9, 1980.

900 AAN, KC PZPR, 237/V–615, fol. 103.

901 S.M. Jankowski, *"Swoje chłopy" przy beczce z benzyną*, "Życie Literackie" March 9, 1980.

902 While in the West cars were much more numerous than motorcycles, there were 6.82 motorcycles to every car in Poland in 1961. In 1972 this ratio was still high – 2.84 motorcycles per car – but falling systematically; Z. Krasiński, H. Mruk, P. Rzepczyński, *Handel i usługi na tle rozwoju motoryzacji indywidualnej*, Warszawa 1977, p. 18.

903 AAN, KC PZPR, XIA/465, fol. 174.

almost 300 000 per annum (with the increases in 1977 of 1 505, in 1998 of 1 791 000, and in 1979 of 2 069 400).[904]

The awakened appetites were brutally dampened by the international oil crisis, which arrived in Poland with some delay. In January 1974, gas and diesel prices went up significantly, 75% and 22% respectively. The reaction of the market was as immediate as it was typical. Whereas in 1973 deliveries for private customers had increased by 20%, in 1974 they shrank by 6%. The trend remained constant – while between 1970 and 1973 the pace of fuel deliveries to the market was related to the expanding number of automobiles, between 1974 and 1976, the growth in supply was half the rate of that of private vehicles. Initially, this was attributed to more rational gas usage and a larger number of more economic, low engine capacity cars. As time went on, it was the "leaks" from the nationalized sector that came to be blamed for the situation.[905]

As mentioned before, in the 1970s, the "leaks" became a national phenomenon, occurring regularly in places where before they had been sporadic. Characteristically, the incidence of these "gas leaks" replicated the rate of decreasing purchases at gas stations. In the Krakow voivodship, several months after the price hike, although the number of cars had increased by a few thousand during the period, the sales of 78-octane gas, fell by a quarter, and diesel sales fell by two thirds. Only the sales of 94-octane gas – on which very few cars in nationalized sector were running – remained stable.[906]

The fall in diesel sales was due to the fact that farmers and those who used it for heating had found alternative sources of supply. For example, in preparation for the winter of 1973, the residents of Zakopane purchased 34 000 liters of diesel during October alone. A year later they bought only 3 000. Private farmers were significant consumers of diesel. Between 1971 and 1979, the number of private tractors rose eight times, from 30 000 to 250 000. During the same period, diesel sales tripled from 94 000 to 255 000 tons. "In the vicinity of large entities such as the Farmers' Cooperative Association (Spółdzielnia Kółek Rolniczych, SKR) and the National Machinery Center (Państwowy Ośrodek Maszynowy, POM), no-one buys diesel at CPN gas stations. The transaction takes place directly between the heavy vehicle driver and the buyer."[907] However, estimated "leaks" of 350 000 liters of diesel annually seem understated.[908]

904 *Rynek motoryzacyjny…*, p. 45.
905 AAN, KC PZPR, XIA/476, fol. 26–28.
906 A. Teneta, *Na jałowym biegu*, "Polityka", no. 3/January 18, 1976.
907 Z. Branach, *Przecieka nie tylko benzyna*, "Życie Literackie" 1982, no. 40.
908 *Ibid.*

The strategies used by gas station managers also changed. On the one hand, they continued cooperation with the drivers, based on double account keeping as outlined earlier. However, the practice became increasingly risky and perhaps insufficiently profitable. With the growing demand for fuel, a much more financially rewarding option now was to cooperate with gas warehouse wholesalers from warehouses and treatment plants owned by CPN instead of with retailers from gas stations. "Leaks" from such sources had occurred earlier but only in the 1970s did they reach a significant scale. The best-known was the case of the Oil Products Management Enterprise (Zakład Gospodarki Produktami Naftowymi) in Mościska near Warsaw, where – manipulating the permitted wastage limits – from July 1977 to May 1979 the employees were able to "save" for illicit dealing approximately 1.6 million liters of gas, which was then cashed in in 16 CPN gas stations in Warsaw and its vicinity.[909] As often happens, the discovery of one fraud had the knock-on effect of an avalanche of inspections, which resulted in 32 investigations, the identification of 600 suspects and 180 arrests. It turned out that a large-scale, illegal flow of fuel was occurring throughout the entire country, with the greatest number of cases uncovered in the Białystok voivodship, in the vicinity of Ciechanów, and in the Warsaw, Krakow, and Tarnów voivodships, replicating – interestingly, and perhaps not incidentally – the "moonshine geography" outlined earlier.[910] And, just as it turned out to be for the illicit alcohol trade, the following decade was critical also for the black market in fuel. State-owned transportation bases and CPN stations became the equivalent of *melinas* and, seeking compensation for the increasingly risky endeavor, charged increasingly high commission.

7.2 "The As-good-as Private Pump": The 1980s

In the late 1970s Polish refineries processed approximately 17 million tons of oil annually. Most of it, some 13 million tons, was imported from the Soviet Union, and 3.5 million tons came from the so-called "second payment area", while only 400 000 tons were from Polish resources. As a result of the economic crisis, first deliveries from the capitalist countries shrank tenfold, then local production fell by 200% (hopes for "big-time oil" in Karlin failed to materialize), and imports from

909 I. Czaplarska, *Benzynowy gang, czyli okazja czyni złodzieja*, TL, no. 303/December 22, 1983.

910 S.M. Jankowski, *"Swoje chłopy" przy beczce z benzyną*, "Życie Literackie" March 9, 1980. Towards the end of the 1970s, the annual fuel market reached 1.5 mln tons, of which some 200 000 was traded on the black market; AAN, URM, 32/84, fol. 27–28.

the Soviet Union diminished. While in 1979 Poland had at its disposal 17.1 million tons of oil, in 1980 it had only 15.8, in 1981 – 13.8, and in 1982 –13.3 million. Although every year several hundred thousand new automobiles appeared on Polish roads, the amount of gas sold on the official market remained unchanged. "The car sector grew", a Warsaw gas station employee explained in mid-1983, "folks got used to driving cars, and then… no more gas! So they try to cheat whenever they can."[911] In the fall of 1981, the topic of the fuel trade and consumption swamped the anti-speculation official reports and until 1989 occupied a prominent position next to meat and alcohol. New strategies were added to the old tried and tested ones, particularly after the introduction of the fuel rationing system.

Poles experienced serious problems with fuel supplies in mid-1981, and in the following year the situation got even worse. Until then, driving a car remained the only luxury that did not require ration coupons, a luxury that was systematically curtailed due to some the gas stations earmarked exclusively for privileged customers. This was compounded by the ban on selling gas pumped directly into canisters and on selling more than 10 to maximum 20 liters at a time, by selling gas on odd or even dates only and according to the last digits of the driver's license plate. Overcoming these obstacles had important practical implications: those who had a tankful of gas were able, for example, to "drive to the countryside and buy from a farmer more meat than the modest amount possible with food coupons, which also required a lot of time wasted standing in long lines. It is better to sit in a car waiting for gas than to stand in line for meat."[912]

Those with fat enough wallets did not have to wait in line at all. In March 1981, the authorities ended the practice of reimbursing state drivers based on gas receipts from CPN gas stations, which obliterated the two-decade old, successful cooperation. Now, the basis for reimbursement became the mileage, or rather the kilometer count. State drivers, however, were able to sell the surplus to private clients, who now came in person and paid three or as many as five times the regular price. Some drivers of state-owned vehicles radically accelerated the whole process. Allowed to buy gas at designated stations, as soon as they had filled up their own tanks, they transferred the contents to a private customer's gas tank. Some of the cab drivers that enjoyed similar privileges gave up cab driving altogether and focused on re-selling gas, as this was now a much better business.[913] "When it comes to gas, 1981 was the best year," a driver of a company

911 M. Kwiatkowski, *Kto rano. wstaje…*, "Polityka", no. 29/July 16, 1983.

912 A.K. Wróblewski, *Ostatni luksus*, "Polityka", no. 47/November 21, 1981.

913 S. Drozdowski, *Tajne kanały czarnego rynku*, "Słowo Powszechne", September 8, 1981; AAN, KC PZPR, WA, LI/116, fol. 112; AAN, URM, 32/119, fol. 21.

Fiat125 reminisced in 1983. "We didn't even have to do any driving. People paid through the nose for a 20-liter canister."[914] Selling gas to foreigners was particularly profitable. On the main routes one could get as much as 30 Deutschmarks for a 20-liter canister.[915]

Kasztel club in Warsaw, the storehouse. The haul during the raid in November 1981 included 1 500 litres of petrol. Photo: Polish Press Agency (PAP).

The stolen or "spirited away" gas competed with the CPN product. In November 1981 it was officially reported that "fuel is re-sold, at steep prices, from barrels or canisters brought directly in horse-drawn wagons and cars parked not far from the gas station."[916]

914 *Jak za zboże*, "Polityka", no. 29/July 16, 1983.
915 S. Drozdowski, *Tajne kanały czarnego rynku*, "Słowo Powszechne", September 8, 1981.
916 AAN, URM, 32/5, fol. 14.

Gas stations had a special place in the topography of the fuel gray zone. Since their employees naturally had a privileged position in the pecking order of the unofficial gas trade, gas stations became the hub of all black market gas operations. The vast majority of automobile drivers went there first when they wanted to acquire extra, or indeed any, amount of gas. In mid-1983, CPN director Marian Bartoszewicz admitted, "Clients are so insistent that almost all our employees give in to the temptation of making an illicit profit."[917] The state inspectors were aware of the situation and subjected all gas stations to rigorous supervision. For example, among the twenty-one anti-speculation operations conducted in 1983 on a "mass and nationwide scale", four were code-named "Gas". Another fifteen operations – designated more generally "Market" – nevertheless, also involved tank inspections. On just a single day, March 29, 1983, frauds were uncovered in 78% of the 368 gas stations inspected. As the result, in the first six months of 1983, of the 5 800 employees of 1 300 CPN stations, 1 002 were fired and 3 335 disciplined. In the following year, 3 271 gas station managers were penalized, 1 161 fired, and 550 cases of criminal proceedings were launched. Between January and September 1985, every gas station underwent five inspections on average; as a result, 229 managers had their contracts terminated and 1 723 were sanctioned.[918] The profits were considerable,[919] however, and even the increased invigilation inspired the perpetrators to employ more sophisticated strategies rather than abandon the illegal gas trade altogether.

Initially the strategies did not have to be very sophisticated. The regulations restricting gas sales by customer profile, in force until early 1982, were easy to bypass, since to catch a gas station employee red-handed would have required an inspector to stay put by the pump for long periods at a time – clearly not a viable solution. In March 1982, new rules were introduced, stipulating that the manager had to stamp a car insurance document and log each transaction for every individual sale. These rules did little to improve the situation: in mid-1982, they were abused in every second gas station inspected.[920]

Customers got creative in devising new methods of filling up their gas tanks, especially after the mid-1983 exacerbation of the fuel crisis; the Main Energy

917 AAN, URM, 32/42, fol. 8.

918 AAN, URM, 32/120, fol. 3; *ibid.*, 32/84, fol. 90–91.

919 In 1983, the additional annual income of gas station managers derived from illicit gas sales was (probably under-) estimated at 2.5 billion zloty in total, thus some 430 000 zloty per individual – approximately 350% of his official earnings; Z. Szułczyński, *Przecieki*, "Express Wieczorny", December 9–11, 1983.

920 *Jak paruje benzyna*, TL, no. 177/July 26, 1982.

Inspectorate (Główny Inspektorat Gospodarki Energetycznej, GIGE), usually quite generous in allotting additional gas allowances, switched to a more frugal policy. One ingenious method was to treat car insurance documents with wax so that the CPN stamps could be easily removed. Another was to insure defunct vehicles that had long been off the road. It was estimated that thirty percent of insurance documents were forged or extorted.[921] Generally, however, car owners tried to strike a hush-hush ongoing deal with the managers of gas stations, with backhanders for selling additional amount of gas. This mutually profitable arrangement was difficult for the authorities to uncover.[922]

Unsurprisingly, the situation at the pump seemed to fly in the face of the basic rules of an economy in crisis. Officially, in the first half of 1983, gas stations in Poland sold 145 500 tons of fuel monthly; during the same period, the National Insurance Company (Powszechny Zakład Ubezpieczeń, PZU) issued authorization for 161 500 tons. The actual monthly consumption was estimated to be higher still.[923] The discrepancy was obfuscated by large-scale frauds in CPN depot stations, by state drivers redistributing their fuel "saved" illegally, and by the leaks from the so-called garage stations. In the 1980s, I witnessed tanker truck drivers sharing fuel on the roadside while transporting it from a depot in Emilianów near Radzymin. They were just the retailers. The true wholesalers were the employees of CPN depots, who by bypassing the waste directives and mixing various kinds of fuel were able to put aside hundreds of tons. Frauds were uncovered in depots and transfer stations in Koluszki, Toruń, Nowa Sól, Działdowo, Międzyrzecz, and Płock. In Płock alone, 32 employees – out of 37! – were brought to court for stealing at least 600 tons of fuel and several dozen tons of diesel.[924] Their usual modus operandi was to take the fuel they had managed to "save" to CPN stations, where they split the profit equally with CPN management and staff. At other times, the gas station managers paid a backhander to an employee of the District Office of Weights and Measures for the service rendered: while authorizing the pump accuracy, he "would wind back the meter by however many thousand liters the customer required. The manager was then able to sell illegal gas without having to worry that a sudden inspection would find more fuel at the pumps than stated in the invoices."[925]

921 M. Kwiatkowski, *Kto rano. wstaje…*, "Polityka", no. 29/July 16, 1983.
922 *Smutek szejka*, "Polityka", no. 13/March 31, 1984.
923 Z. Szułczyński, *Przecieki*, "Express Wieczorny" December 9–11, 1983.
924 *Ibid.*; M. Henzler, *Skąd wycieka*, "Polityka", no. 29/July 16, 1983.
925 M. Henzler, *Skąd wycieka*, "Polityka", no. 29/July 16, 1983.

In April 1984, after new gas rationing rules had been introduced, it became indispensable for stations to have surplus gas. Now, the customer had to leave his rationing coupon at the gas station; in theory, these could be compared with the readings on the pump meters, thereby helping to eliminate illicit "leaks". The method was not a success. The coupons of the state owned companies ("units of nationalized economy") became the weak link. Left unused, they legitimized an unofficial gas surplus, which was later sold off by station managers. This practice continued until the abolition of gas rationing.[926]

Although the authorities were far from surprised by the emergence of a black market involving forged and extorted gas coupons, which indeed they had anticipated, the reality surpassed their expectations. The social players turned out to be much more creative with scams involving gas coupons than they had been with meat and alcohol coupons. Gas station managers, just like meat and alcohol stores employees, entered into their accounts the same coupons – again and again – generating a substantial unlawful profit. Soon after the introduction of gas coupons, forged authorization cards for state companies (mentioned earlier) started popping up everywhere in Poland. Most of the counterfeit documents were poorly executed but some were of high quality. In 1984, an entrepreneurial Polish woman residing in West Berlin ordered ten thousand fake gas authorization cards, which looked like the originals.[927] Polish-made imitations were often executed so skillfully that they could be only identified under ultraviolet lamps. From 1985, Polish gas stations began to use such lamps routinely.[928] Whereas formerly break-ins to city or district offices resulted in meat and alcohol coupons going missing, now it was gas coupons that became the main object of the thieves' interest. By September 1984, some 7 300 cards authorizing gas purchases worth 152 million zloty had vanished from PZU offices.[929]

PZU employees, in expectation of chaos similar to that which had accompanied the distribution of ration coupons for other products, reached for a tried and tested method: "dead souls" (or rather "phantom engines"). With help from colleagues in the communications department, they assigned gas coupons to vehicles that were no longer in use, no longer registered in other voivodships or simply non-existent. When in 1986, Police Headquarters in Wrocław introduced

926 "Drivers leave unused coupons", Słupsk voivode, Borys Drobko, admitted in January 1985, "with gas stations managers who use them to cover fuel shortages caused by illegal sales"; AAN, URM, 32/116, fol. 156.

927 AAN, URM, 32/66, fol. 37; *ibid.*, 32/122, fol. 136–137.

928 AAN, URM, 32/84, fol. 14.

929 AAN, URM, 32/66, fol. 101.

computers to compare lists of registered cars and gas cards, it transpired that ten thousand cards had been issued for non-existent vehicles.[930] The police expert in economic crime had no doubts that this practice was prevalent in all Polish voivodships.

Poles continued to discover new ways of puncturing the state rationing system. Cars running on diesel fuel became popular since it was available on the free market. A car owner who had managed to misrepresent his diesel-powered vehicle, fraudulently, as a gas-guzzler and register it as such, was able to drive at almost no cost at all, after selling his allotted gas on the black market, especially if he bought his diesel there as well. Such cases were, however, far and few throughout the country (in late 1984, no more than 700 were reported). Taxi drivers – of whom there were 80 000 in the mid-1980s – were another abundant source of gas coupons. Despite the fact that in Warsaw alone as many as 9 000 cabs operated – very many more than in any other European capital at the time – it was not an easy task to hail one. The apparent mystery was simple to explain: a taxi driver received a daily allowance of ten liters of gas, against a private driver's allocation of no more than 30–45 liters a month. No wonder that carrying passengers ceased to be a profitable activity for Warsaw cabbies, who could make a good enough living just by selling the gas to gas station managers, or else sell them gas coupons, which they then used to sell gas at a higher price.[931] As calculated by the Deputy Chief of the Central Commission for Combating Speculation, Colonel Władysław Trzaska, a cab driver who actually did work could still make a very satisfactory profit of up to 50 000 zloty just by selling gas.[932] Cabbies did not put their business operations on hold even when leaving the country for spells abroad as migrant workers – a common Polish pursuit during the decade. Their families continued to receive gas coupons and put them to the same use as ever. For example in Wrocław in 1985, 1 500 taxi drivers out of 4 000 went abroad, often for several months at a time.[933] All attempts by the authorities to strip them of their taxi licenses or withdraw their gas allowances proved futile.[934]

Although the authorities were to some extent able to curb the "leaks" from CPN stations, the gas containers in some 16 700 garage stations were more difficult to keep under control. This mattered; particularly if we keep in mind that approximately 70 % of all fuel in Poland (89% of diesel and 33% of gas) was distributed

930 AAN, URM, 32/105, fol. 35.
931 AAN, URM, 32/116, fol. 70; *ibid.*, 32/95, fol. 25.
932 AAN, URM, 32/84, fol. 38.
933 AAN, URM, 32/95, fol. 3; *ibid.*, 32/123, fol. 102–103.
934 AAN, URM, 32/95, fol. 50.

via those garage stations. They were located on factory premises and serviced the plant's own vehicles. It was easier to strike deals in an environment where a gas surplus was easy to both generate and conceal. An "understanding" among the employees did not have to be the result of deliberate and sophisticated operations. As was to be expected, fuel shortfalls or surpluses often materialized by accident – since the equipment was dramatically outdated and the style of management usually chaotic and sloppy. I met a man who in the early 1980s quit his job in the Opoczno Farmers' Cooperative Association (Spółdzielnia Kółek Rolniczych, SKR) because he did not want to be having to keep going through the process of explaining to his bosses the reasons for the surpluses of many thousand liters of gas.[935] But for anybody keen to lay his hands on some black-market gas, this was a dream-come-true environment. According to the director of the National Trade Inspectorate (PIH) Piotr Ostaszewski, in more than 90% of garage stations "nothing works, one can steal without any consequences, the pumps are not working, because it's not possible to fix them, the accounting is not updated, and so on."[936]

Despite the fact that this statement was made in late 1984, the garage stations came under scrutiny only in 1986. The Inspection Office of the Council of Ministers examined 495 stations. In 79% of these it found stocktaking irregularities and in 48% – discrepancies between the amount of incoming and outgoing fuel. If one were to take at face value the curious world reflected in the documentation, those with their hands on the wheel would have had to either be driving like racing drivers or else moving along at a snail's pace. Moreover, some appeared capable of performing supernatural feats such as filling up their tanks with more gas then their capacity permitted or – in some extreme cases – driving on no fuel whatsoever, with one driver apparently setting the record of "driving on empty" at 2 462 km.[937] Between January and September 1986, 1 722 legal proceedings against garage stations employees were initiated. At the Council of Ministers, an inter-ministerial department was set up, with the mandate to target garage station fraud. The team, led by the deputy secretary of state in the Ministry of Chemical and Light Industry Stanisław Kłos, considered mass-scale inspections and tinting the fuel to facilitate the identification of its origin; the implementation of IT systems in 12 000 gas stations was another option on the table. In the end, however, cutting gas station gas allocations proved the only viable solution.[938]

935 From testimony by Przemysław Nowak, Opoczno, March 26, 2010; in author's possession; AAN, URM, 32/99, fol. 14.

936 AAN, URM, 32/66, fol. 27.

937 AAN, URM, 32/99, fol. 14–15, 77–79.

938 *Ibid.*, fol. 66–69, 222–225, 230–234.

Any radical changes were simply impossible to implement. The garage stations were a crucial element of the economy in the Polish peripheries, tightly connected with local social networks. There was no interest in changing the status quo. Someone ironically pointed out that the stations epitomized the worker–peasant alliance. Without the transfers of thousands of tons of fuel from the leaky state and coop distribution centers to the tanks of tractors and combine harvesters (conservatively estimated as some 100 000 tons of diesel annually)[939] that took place in the stations, the food supply would have been even worse than it already was. As things stood, not only did the average peasant obtain fuel at half price (in 1984, one liter cost 30 zloty at a gas station and 15 zloty on the black market)[940] but also had it delivered to his own backyard.[941] The fuel sector of the black market had every reason to be one of the most enduring.

The official debates on how best to deal with the thorny issue of fuel went on for just as long as the attempts to cut through the Gordian Knot of meat supply. With gas, there was even less room to maneuver, one good reason being that all fuel had to be imported. The proposals to sell it at an economically viable "commercial price", as it was referred to, that would allow gas to be bought outside of the rationing system were abandoned by 1983 and triggered social, political ("gas for the rich") and economic protests, which resulted in private entrepreneurs raising prices, with even hitherto-uncorrupted gas station managers "enticed to speculate".[942] At a meeting in November 1986 of the Central Anti-Speculation Commission (Centralna Komisja do Walki ze Spekulacją, CKWS), the representative of the Chief Energy Inspectorate (GIGE), Jerzy Banasiuk, pointed out that, once "commercial" gas was introduced, Poland would have no fewer than three different fuel prices: the official price requiring coupons, the commercial price – a euphemism for high-priced, and the black market price, somewhere between the two.[943]

Yet a solution had to be found since the black market had become ubiquitous, revealing a consensus that high prices were acceptable; moreover, the rigid system of quarterly rationing forced drivers who were planning longer trips to hoard gas. "Comrades," Colonel Władysław Trzaska warned members of the CKWS in October 1985, "Our homes are sitting on a bomb. Literally so. Our attics, basements, and storage rooms are full of gas. Especially now that people are buying gas for the fourth quarter […] and they don't have anywhere to store it.

939 AAN, URM, 32/42, fol. 7.
940 AAN, URM, 32/66, fol. 26.
941 A.J. Socha, *Kurs na lewo*, "Tygodnik Kulturalny", no. 19/May 11, 1986.
942 AAN, URM, 32/42, fol. 38; *ibid.*, 32/66, fol. 42.
943 AAN, URM, 32/99, fol. 51.

I have seen them storing it in milk cans, demijohns, plastic containers, and even ordinary jugs."[944]

The authorities dared only to take a first tentative step in that direction in mid-1988. On July 1, in sixty-four designated stations, gas was sold without coupons at high commercial prices; 260 and 300 zloty per liter. "This makes no difference for the average Pole," commented Jerzy Baczyński, "who will now be able to buy fuel officially for the price that, until now, he has been paying on the black market."[945] This would have been the case, if the "coupon-free" gas had been easily available. The commercial gas stations were few and far between – on average, 1.3 per voivodship and two in Warsaw – and customers had already begun to form lines for the "coupon-free" gas by June 29.[946] At sixty-four in total, the paltry number of commercial gas stations was no competition for regular gas stations, where, in any case, the unofficial price of gas surpassed the commercial price and reached as much as 350 zloty per liter. "Faced with the choice between hours-long standing in line to buy gas for 300 zloty a liter or sticking to the tried and tested "devil you know "– a deal with a gas station manager and paying 350 or 400 zloty, many drivers pick the second option."[947]

It was not until January 1, 1989 that ration coupons for fuel were abolished, albeit only for Polish nationals. There were no shortages of gas through the winter, as people drove less. However, in the spring, problems returned, when drivers hit the roads in their masses. State pumps could not keep up with the demand. The shortages were painful and yet again, rationing began to look like an attractive option; gas station employees refreshed their strategies from the recent past.[948] Until the early 1990s, the authorities persevered in their efforts to calm down the market in gas. However, even once the pumps had become fully privatized, shady dealings in gas did not disappear completely, but merely – as they had always done – evolved.

---

944 AAN, URM, 32/84, fol. 38–39.

945 J. Baczyński, *Przelewanie z pustego*, "Polityka", no. 28/July 9, 1988.

946 W. Markiewicz, *Ludzie są wyposzczeni, ibid.*

947 J. Baczyński, *Przelewanie z pustego, ibid.*

948 P. Tarnowski, *Kartki były lepsze*, "Polityka", no. 18/ May 6, 1989.

8. Dollar and Gold[949]

8.1 Dollar and Gold: A Panacea for Tough Times

There are good reasons why gold and the dollar have been treated together in this chapter. What they had in common was not just that they were both used as stores of value and referred to by Polish economists by the collective name "hard currency assets"[950] but also that both merited the equal and special attention of the law enforcement agencies.[951]

Gold and hard currency in general, and US dollars in particular, played a special role in the social, economic and political life of post-war Poland, providing a panacea during the hard times which the 20th century brought to the country in abundance. Two world wars, frequent changes of the political system involving the moving of borders, economic crises, (hyper)inflation, and the absurdities of the communist economy made Poles only too acutely aware of how fragile human life was and how unreliable any investment, be it bank savings, stocks and shares, or even real estate. With the outbreak of the First World War, coins made from precious metals disappeared immediately from circulation. Those lucky enough to have any hid them well and spent sparingly, to protect themselves from the fast-growing inflation that was eviscerating paper money. Another side effect of the First World War was to bring the USA and its currency to Europe. The US dollar challenged the supremacy of the British pound in a number of countries, including the Second Polish Republic, coming to the fore. The hard currency bonds issued by the Polish Ministry of Treasury in the 1930s were denominated in US dollars.

In the interwar period, gold continued to be a "symbol of wealth, happiness and power; it was the lever of industry, trade, and art that brought beauty into everyday life; the dream of the poor, the measure of all values, blood that pulsated throughout the economic organism of the world, the only true currency since

949 I wrote about this in the articles: *Zysk i strach. Z dziejów peerelowskiej "gorączki złota"*, in: *Od Piłsudskiego do Wałęsy. Studia z dziejów Polski w XX wieku*, ed. K. Persak et al, Warszawa 2008, pp. 276–290; and *"Niepewne czasy, pewny dolar". Szkic do obrazu warszawskiego czarnego rynku walutowego*, PH, 100, 2009/1, pp. 29–46.

950 Such as "foreign legal tender, documents confirming funds and precious metals (gold, platinum)", AAN, IPP, 123, Note on researching hard currency and smuggling crimes, 1977, fol. 4.

951 K. Madej, *Wszyscy byli przemytnikami. Obraz przestępczości przemytniczej i dewizowej w latach 1956–1970*, "Pamięć i Sprawiedliwość" 2008, no. 2, p. 124.

time immemorial."[952] The lower classes such as peasants and petite bourgeoisie had never had much trust in the banks and put their savings in gold items and coins as much as possible. What was different was that, unlike before, besides gold rubles, marks, and Austrian crowns they could now invest in American twenty-dollar pieces.

Hard currency and gold really came into their own during the Second World War – a time when to lose all one's possessions in an instant was not only possible but indeed common. Under such precarious circumstances all stores of value such as hard currency, gold and diamonds that were easy to hide and easy to carry about one's person gained tremendous importance. Those who owned such valuables had a greater chance of survival. Many Holocaust survivors owed their life to being able to pay in hard currency or gold for a hiding place "on the Aryan side".[953]

The war and the German occupation brought an unprecedented boom to the gold and hard currency black market. This was when the very term "hard dollars" – referring to coins made of precious metal – originated, as opposed to "soft dollars" – paper money. During the German occupation, most major financial transactions in Poland were conducted in hard currency. Wartime diary entries often began with quoting the dollar exchange rate for the day.[954] Even though anyone trading in hard currency or gold faced a high risk of being sent to a concentration camp or the possibility of a death sentence, there was no shortage of those eager to act as buyers, sellers, or middlemen. It is difficult to assess how many Poles from different social backgrounds survived the war thanks to the black market in hard currency and gold. We do not know much about the details of such transactions, the scale of profit and turnover or whether the occupiers or any foreigners were involved. This side of the everyday history of the Second World War still awaits its historian.

Paradoxically, the social and economic changes brought about by the war effectively democratized the US dollar and the precious metal. During the German occupation the dollar and gold trade entered the streets, alleys, eateries, and private apartments with a new status that was to endure for the next fifty years. With unprecedented frequency, dollars and gold found their way to the countryside – whether in exchange for food delivered to the cities, or received in payment

---

952 M.K. Wołowski, *Złoto*, Warszawa 1933, p. 5.

953 L. Landau, *Kronika lat wojny i okupacji*, vol. 2: *Grudzień 1942 – czerwiec 1943*, Warszawa 1962, p. 164.

954 *Ibid.*, vol. 1–3, Warszawa 1962–1963; F. Wyszyński, *Dzienniki z lat 1941–1944*, ed. J. Grabowski, Z.R. Grabowski, Warszawa 2007.

for hiding Jews or shelter offered to refugees from the Warsaw uprising. A large part of the expenses of the Polish Government Delegation to the Home Country (Delegatura Rządu RP na Kraj) and the Home Army (AK) were covered with hard currency and gold bullion sent from London.

After the war, both American dollars and the yellow metal continued as the only durable assets universally accepted not just in Poland but everywhere in the rapidly changing world. In February 1965, General Charles de Gaulle demanded, albeit unsuccessfully, that the French economy return to the gold standard. "There cannot be any other criterion, any other standard than gold. Oh yes! Gold which never changes its nature, which can be shaped into bars, ingots or coins, which has no nationality and which is eternally and universally accepted as the unalterable fiduciary value par excellence."[955] In 1966, at least 16 000 tons of gold were stored in private hoards – 1.5 times as much as in the US reserves; this was two thirds of all the globally accounted-for metal. Thirty years later, half of global gold production was being used as value storage.[956] Each significant incident of economic turbulence such as the oil crises in 1973 and 1974, the gas price hike in 1978, political upheavals such as the Iranian Revolution in 1979 and the war in Afghanistan in 1980 immediately resulted in gold soaring, with little trust in the authorities that themselves were busy swapping paper money for gold bars and bullion.[957]

Gold is considered insurance for a rainy day in countries that are poor and unstable, and less so – in those that are affluent and peaceful. Yet even the residents of such prosperous European countries as France and Italy, enjoying a sound economy, have been known to keep their savings in gold coins and ingots. Even in those societies, however, the "yellow devil" tended to be a pursuit of the poor, misers and the less educated – peasants rather than city dwellers, workers rather than engineers.[958] In countries where demand for the precious metal was high but local production small or non-existent, the state often introduced a rationing system to restrict the trade and instituted a monopoly in the export and import of gold. This usually led to smuggling, at times quite sophisticated, which

---

955 P.L. Bernstein, *The Power of Gold: The History of an Obsession,* Wiley 2000, p. 364; see: R.T. Naylor, *The Underworld of Gold,*"Crime, Law and Social Change" 25, 1996/3, pp.191–241.

956 H. Cywiński, *Złoto. Skąd pochodzi, dokąd idzie?,* Warszawa 1987, p. 129; R.T. Naylor, *The Underworld of Gold...*, p. 195.

957 P.L. Bernstein, *Historia złota...*, pp. 393–395.

958 A.W. Anikin, *The Yellow Devil,* Progress Publishers 1978, p. 74; see: T. Green, *The World of Gold Today,* London 1973.

resulted in higher gold prices. In the early 1970s, in Egypt and India an ounce of gold cost 20 to 30 dollars more than in Great Britain; inevitably, such profitable arbitrage opportunities led to extensive smuggling that no official restrictions could curb.[959] Post-war Poland was another good example of this syndrome.

Gold's unique position had been established over thousands of years but it was the American dollar that – after the end of the Second World War – triumphantly became the global reserve currency and the dominant means of exchange not only of official but also black markets round the world.[960] The greenback was more than a universally accepted unit of value; it acquired a symbolic meaning and became an icon of freedom and prosperity. In 1948, a Polish worker donated as his contribution for the construction of the Party House in Warsaw the "one dollar he had received from relatives from abroad, the first and the only dollar he had ever had."[961] Poignantly, he gave away his most valuable possession.

The US dollar was not the only hard currency that mattered on the black market. Which currency dominated the illegal trade in a given country depended on many factors, such as in what currency the government conducted its accounts with foreign trade partners and which was its reserve hard currency of choice. Local history and tradition also played a part. For example, in Cuba, the US dollar was the one and only foreign currency; the West German mark ruled in the GDR, and the Turkish lira in Bulgaria, whereas in Yugoslavia the US dollar and the West German mark shared second currency status. In Poland, the greenback ruled supreme both throughout official economy and on the black market.[962]

---

959 A.W. Anikin, *Yellow Devil…*, p. 71.

960 On the post-war history of the dollar, see: W. Morawski *Zarys powszechnej historii pieniądza i bankowości*, Warszawa 2002, pp. 179–191; R. Sédillot, *All the Monies of the World – a Chronicle of Currency Values*; *Moralna i niemoralna historia pieniądza*, transl. K. Szeżyńska-Maćkowiak, Warszawa 2002, pp. 228–232. In 1995, more than half of the 375 billion dollars remaining outside the banks circulated outside of the US borders; A. Mourmouras, S.H. Russell, *Smuggling, Currency Substitution and Unofficial Dolarization: A Crime-theoretic Approach*, "IMF Working Paper" 00/176, October 2000, http://www.imf.org/external/pubs/ft/wp/2000/wp00176.pdf (March 10, 2014).

961 "Robotnik" 1948, no. 133; I am grateful to Andrzej Skalimowski for bringing my attention to this case.

962 R. Boyes, *The Hard Road to Market, Gorbachev, the Underworld, and the Rebirth of Capitalism*, London 1990, pp. 49–54. See: P.A. Wingender, *Westdevisen und Devisenschwarzmärkte in sozialistischen Planwirtschaften*, Stuttgart–New York 1989. On Yugoslavia: J.W. Dawson, S.W. Millsaps, M.C. Strazicich, *Trend Breaks and Non-stationarity in the Yugoslav Black Market for Dollars, 1974–1987*, "Applied Economics"

In post-war Poland, the dollar and the yellow metal began their black-market career level pegging as stores of value. Gradually, they parted ways. Hidden in the attic or buried in the backyard, gold remained a rainy-day reserve until the last days of communist Poland. Hard currency was a long-term, safe investment and, increasingly, a form of working capital, which not only enabled more sophisticated consumption but also helped generate profits. At the turn of the 1970s and the 1980s, a fully-fledged, dual-currency system took hold in Poland. "In the 1970s, all children growing up in the People's Republic of Poland knew very well from early childhood that money came in two kinds – the real money and Polish money."[963]

The authorities, that during the post-war period had experienced a painful shortage of "real" money, tried to acquire it by means fair and foul, happy to pass on the cost of their actions to citizens. As always, Poles refused to play ball, instead developing highly effective defense strategies. Polish society and those in power continued to play the dollar and gold game until 1989. As with any long-term game plan, there had been turning points, changes of rules, periods of respite and of increased effort, as well as occasions of turning a blind eye to the enemy's unfair play. In the end, it was the authorities that lost miserably.

8.2 Power, Dollar, Gold

8.2.1 1945–1950–1956

While visiting Soviet Union in 1929, a Warsaw journalist, Mieczysław Weinryb, experienced an unpleasant surprise involving hard currency as soon as he got to the border. "The customs officer asks how much cash I have and specifically if I have any rubles. Apparently, one cannot bring them into Russia. At the same I have to show how much foreign currency I have with me. This information is then written down on a special receipt and everything is meticulously itemized. This receipt is a treasure I must not part with until I go back home. After the search has been conducted comes the surprise. There is a special cashier's counter, a branch of the State Bank, where all foreign currency must be exchanged

39, 2007/1, pp. 43–51; on Cuba: E. Facio, A.R. Roschelle, M.I. Toro-Morn, *See You in Havana!*, "Peace Review" 13, 2001/1, pp. 121–127; M. Jastrząb, *Kilka uwag o funkcjach walut obcych w rzeczywistości Polski Ludowej*, in: *Społeczeństwo PRL. Historia. Kultura. Pamięć*, vol. 1: *Historia*, ed. S. Jankowiak, D. Skotarczak, I. Skórzyńska, Poznań 2011, pp. 143–153.

963 W. Orliński, *Dzieci Pewexu. Muzeum narodowe kultury masowej*, "Gazeta Wyborcza" December 20, 2000.

into rubles. Only now do I understand why the checking of currency was so scrupulous. The cashier exchanges my dollars at the official rate – very painful for the visitor, who receives a mere 1.9 rubles to a dollar, while at home for a dollar you get five rubles. [...] The foreigner experiences this as a great injustice."[964] This was a feeling shared by all Western travelers to the Soviet Union. Useful tips on ways of bypassing the official currency obstacles quickly spread on the Polish grapevine, reported by those that had taken a trip to the east. Recommended (by such as Henryk Szoszkies) methods were either to smuggle into Russia rubles bought in Poland or to buy some on the Soviet black market (as advocated by Zygmunt Nowakowski).[965]

The tone of such reports was reminiscent of travelers' tales describing adventures in "primitive" countries; the account invariably ended with self-satisfied declarations to the effect that "This would have been unthinkable in Poland".[966] Yet, less than two decades later the same mechanisms became part of Polish reality. In post-war Poland, the trade in foreign exchange assets, as hard currency and gold were referred to in official parlance, had been taken over by the restrictive state monopoly long before the new political system entrenched itself. A local resident or a visitor could sell foreign currency only to the state, and then at a low, arbitrarily determined rate, but he could not buy it legally or in unlimited quantity. Only the state was empowered to administer such valuable assets and rationed them out rarely and only to its trusted agents.

In its announcement of June 20, 1945, the Treasury Minister recalled the pre-war laws (from April 26, 1936 and September 2, 1939) passed by the Polish President, which banned all trade and export of "foreign means of payment". Breaking those rules carried a penalty of five years in prison and a fine of 200 000 zloty. In extreme cases, if a "perpetrator turned such crimes into regular practice", he could be sentenced to life imprisonment. The amount of the fine did not have

964 As cited in: *Spojrzenie na Rosję*, ed. J. Kochanowski, Warszawa 1994, pp. 15–16.

965 *Ibid.*, pp. 20, 57.

966 A Polish engineer, Jan Błeszyński, who worked in the Soviet Union at the turn of the 1920s and 1930s had this to say about *torgsins*, state-run hard currency stores, where gold was also accepted in payment: "This institution could operate only in the Soviet Union, with the backdrop of apathy, slavery, and lack of social energy evident in the Russian population. If communism were established for example in France or even here, people would destroy such stores, as they would be considered a slap in the face for citizens condemned to suffering while exposed to the tantalizing sight of tasty products they were unable to buy"; *ibid.*, p. 33.

a ceiling.[967] It was, however, easier to issue an ordinance than to implement it. Whereas people were highly motivated to get involved in black market transactions, the law enforcement bodies were modest in size (in 1945 only GIOS actively participated in the operations), and the state itself benefited from the illegal market. If we are to believe Leon Chajn, by 1945 the state Treasury was itself supplementing its modest supply of hard currency on the black market.[968] In late November 1945, the Treasury Minister ordered that the illegal currency market be monitored closely; it certainly proved a useful barometer of the economic situation.[969] Bank employees and state officials able to travel abroad commonly participated in illegal operations.[970]

The district around the Hotel Polonia, the only Warsaw hotel to have survived intact, which immediately after the war provided premises for the majority of embassies, became the nerve centre of illegal trading of hard currency and gold. Stanisław Łuckiewicz, In New York: Damn it, not a single dollar in my pocket, even though my uncle is hanging around outside the Polonia in Warsaw, *"Szpilki", no. 16 z 16 IV 1946.*

967 AAN, URM, 5/30, fol. 46.
968 L. Chajn, *Kiedy Lublin był Warszawą*, Warszawa 1964, p. 144.
969 AAN, GIOS, 121, unpag.
970 AAN, URM, 5/637, fol. 1.

The low official hard currency exchange rate (black market rates could be ten times higher) upped the living expenses of foreign diplomats in Poland. It was probably their complaints that, in mid-1946, led the Prime Minister, Edward Osóbka-Morawski, to intercede with the Treasury, asking it to "rationalize" the official dollar rate, at least for the representatives of foreign states. The tax authorities were adamant. All they did was turn a blind eye when the diplomats availed themselves of the black market. Polish representatives abroad behaved similarly.[971] This was not an isolated case of hard-currency pragmatism. When in the fall of 1946 the black-market exchange rate reached an exorbitant 1 000 zloty to the dollar, the Treasury eased the repressions against the currency black market, which lowered the rate and "brought a positive psychological influence to bear on the stalling of speculation tendencies."[972]

The liberalization did not last long. In mid-1947, the "battle for trade", which pushed affected merchants and artisans into investing their savings in durable stores of value, emboldened the police, the Special Commission and GIOS functionaries to intensify operations directed against the currency black market. The absence of conclusive evidence was no longer an obstacle to sentencing a black marketeer to several months in a labor camp. Often a mere suspicion, lack of permanent employment, or a policeman's hunch sufficed. "Although the body search did not reveal the presence of any foreign currency on the suspects," a report stated on May 8, 1947 after a round-up of money changers operating in front of the Hotel Polonia in Warsaw, " it revealed only 3 600 zloty on Mr. Lipiński and 3 042 zloty on Mr. Jarzębowski. Nevertheless, the testimony of the witness Orłowski combined with the fact that the suspects do not have a permanent job bring us to the conclusion that they are middlemen who solicit in the foreign currency trade."[973] Antoni Szymański was arrested during the police raid organized in the same location five days later; "After checking with the Investigative Office, it turned out he already had a record as a suspect in foreign currency trading. [...] Considering the facts that suspect Szymański was arrested during a roundup at

971 A. Bliss-Lane, *Widziałem Polskę zdradzoną*, Warszawa 1984, p. 91; AAN, URM, 5/638, Edward Osóbka-Morawski's correspondence with MS, September 1946, fol. 1–3. Most European countries acted in a similar manner directly after the war. Often, the gap between the official and black market price was even larger. For example in the Soviet Union the official dollar exchange rate was 5.30 rubles whereas the black-market rate – approximately 80, while in Austria 10 and approx. 70 schilling, and in Germany 2.50 and up to 200 marks respectively.

972 AAN, URM, 5/229, fol. 89.

973 AAN, KS, 2651.

the money changers' haunt, that on two previous occasions he had been recorded by the Investigative Department as being suspected of trading foreign currency, and that he has admitted in his testimony to not being in employment, the Warsaw Delegation of the Special Commission has come to the conclusion that he is a "konik", or a "waluciarz" [illegal currency dealer] and as such he is socially and economically a destructive type."[974]

Whereas in 1946, 106 persons had been sent to the Special Commission camps for trading foreign currency, in 1947 the number grew to 180, in 1948 – it reached 189, and in 1949 – 196 people suffered a similar fate.[975] Increasingly harsh repression, which threatened a common black marketeer with a sentence of between three to six months of labor camp, even when based on circumstantial evidence, led to the development of adaptive strategies such as equipping standard jackets with additional pockets, upping the level of conspiracy, and storing the money or gold with friends, or fellow employees, who were not subject to suspicion.[976]

Truly tough times for the hard-currency black market came in the fall of 1950. The Act of October 28, 1950 (Journal of Laws no. 50, item 459) on changing the monetary system, prepared and enacted in secrecy, became the basis for a savage currency revaluation and deprived the population of two thirds of their savings stored at home, mostly in cash. The trauma was so deep that until the last days of communist Poland the smallest rumor of any possibility of a currency revaluation immediately triggered defensive strategies: depositing money in banks and searching high and low for reliable stores of value, also on the black market. Putting Polish zloty at par with the ruble and setting the new official dollar exchange rate at four zloty – which allegedly strengthened the zloty – did nothing to inspire trust in the new national currency.

With the Act of October 28, 1950 (Journal of Laws no. 50, item 460), the second of the hard currency laws, the government not only banned all illegal trading in hard currency and precious metals but also prohibited the possession of any foreign currency and precious metals, the latter in "utility form", or scrap metal.[977]

---

974 *Ibid.*

975 *Komisja Specjalna do Walki z Nadużyciami i Szkodnictwem Gospodarczym 1945–1954*, ed. D. Jarosz, T. Wolsza, Warszawa 1995, pp. 9, 104.

976 AAN, KS, 2657, 2651.

977 The "utility" criteria were specified in some detail: "For example a broken wedding band or chain [...] but not [...] incomplete parts of a pocket watch, fragments of rings, bands, etc."; *Komunikat Narodowego Banku Polskiego w sprawie obowiązku sprzedaży walut obcych, monet złotych oraz złota i platyny*, "Trybuna Ludu" November 2, 1950.

Hard currency, gold and platinum had to be either sold to the state at a ridiculously low price or deposited with the state. Possession of gold bullion or bars carried a punishment of up to 15 years in jail; trading could trigger a death sentence.[978] Nevertheless, apparently only a relatively small number of Polish citizens obediently sold their precious belongings for a fraction of their real value, as instructed. Most gold and paper dollars or rubles remained buried or otherwise hidden.[979] By the third day of the new law being in force, Ministry of Public Security agents reported: "due to the currency revaluation, black marketeers [...] refrained from trading in gold bullion but focused instead on divesting themselves of "soft" foreign currencies. On a mass scale, however, they began to melt scrap gold and gold coins no longer in circulation and quickly began production of rings in order to retain the gold. [...] Also jewelers are secretly melting gold and engaging in the production of rings and bands. There are rumors that the owners of gold coins currently still in circulation will keep them hidden."[980] Another agent mentioned a "conversation with private enterprise traders from the Różycki Market" and reported that "they all have "soft" dollars that they will be selling in order to buy gold pieces, which they intend to bury in the ground."[981]

It is not surprising that the authorities had little faith that the provisions of the law were going to be effective. By November 2, 1950 the Minister of Public Safety, Stanisław Radkiewicz, issued Order No. 050 calling for show trials of money traders as a "deterrent, and to curb the unbridled hard-currency criminals".[982] The penalties became indeed tougher; beside fines and imprisonment, they included forced banishment from big cities, especially the capital of Poland, Warsaw. The essence of instilling terror in the population relies not in inflicting penalties on those who knowingly violate the law of the land but rather on sending to jail innocent people, often quite unaware that they had committed any unlawful act – *pour décourager les autres*. The Special Commission documents recorded many cases in which individuals were sentenced for possession, often accidental, of small quantities of dollars. A good example was the case of

978 *Ibid.*

979 AIPN, 01521/2035, Jacek Oleś, Smuggling of Currency Assets, the Academy of Internal Affairs, Institute of Criminology, Warszawa 1978, p. 25; A. Jezierski, C. Leszczyńska, *Historia gospodarcza Polski*, Warszawa 1999, p. 537.

980 AIPN, The Ministry of Public Security, the Minister's Office, 1572/553, fol. 249–250.

981 *Ibid.*

982 A. Kochański, *Polska 1944–1991. Informator historyczny*, vol. 1: *Podział administracyjny, ważniejsze akty prawne, decyzje i enuncjacje państwowe (1944–1956)*, Warszawa 1996, p. 353.

Katarzyna Mościcka from Zacisze near Warsaw. At her trial on December 20, 1950 the court proved that the accused "had in her possession without the authorization of the Currency Commission one dollar bill, which she had received in 1947 from Zofia Gawarecka in exchange for a chicken." Ms. Gawarecka was charged with "putting into circulation, at an unspecified time in 1947 and contrary to existing regulations, one US dollar by giving it to Mościcka in return for the chicken."[983] In July 1951, a woman from the small village of Ciepielin near Pułtusk was charged by the Special Commission with "failing, by February 9, 1951 [...] and against the laws in force, to re-sell to the National Bank of Poland two US dollars which had been in her possession since mid-January 1951 and which she had at that time received in a parcel from abroad." Another person put on trial in this case was a friend of the accused, who had received from her the two dollars and failed to deliver them to the Bank within seven days.[984]

Despite the new, strict law on hard currency of March 28, 1952 (Journal of Laws 1952, no. 21, item133), which specified two- to ten-year prison sentences for currency traders and life sentence for "professional" dealers, the black market in foreign currencies and gold remained active. As ever, Poles learned to accommodate themselves to the restrictive rules and find ways of bypassing them. When they were caught, usually due to a neighborhood snitch, they often used legal loopholes[985] to protect the assets and the family members who had been arrested or appealed the sentence at the State Council. After, in October 1953, the female owner of a private restaurant was charged with possession of and speculative trading in dollars and jewelry, and sentenced to a fine, a prison term and a five-year exile from Warsaw, her husband wrote to the President of the State Council, Aleksander Zawadzki: "The jewelry and the money constituted the fruit of thirty years of hard work and were collected with the goal of securing our

983 AAN, KS, 2651. Mościcka was sentenced to pay a 1 500 zloty fine or two months of prison. Gawarecka – to a 60 zloty fine or one week of prison.

984 AAN, KS, 2673.

985 The Act of 1950 forbade the ownership of hard currencies and precious metals but it penalized exclusively the legal owner. Supplementary Acts of 1952 allowed the possession of hard currency (legally owned, of course), providing this was authorized by the state. Defense lawyers interpreted this law as releasing a "person accepting foreign currencies for the purposes of storage" from the obligatory confirmation of legal ownership. Some, a clerk at the Ministry of Justice commented, use the defense line stating their innocence even when currencies are illegally owned as they claimed there is no 'trading in currency assets' since they do not share the ownership; AAN, MS, 3019, fol. 83.

livelihood in our old age. Some of the jewelry was my wife's daughter's property. The instinct to accumulate valuables is a result and leftover of the past political system with its living conditions under which a person could at any moment face poverty. This instinct is very strong and not everyone is able to cut free from its influence especially if that someone spent most of her life under the hostile political regime of the past, having to struggle for survival [...] The present verdict will only serve to break up a family, which in the socialist system is the fundamental unit of the social fabric and remains under the protection of the state. This sentence demonstrates that a human being who has erred and redeemed her faults is, nevertheless, dispensable – and should be isolated from her family and society. To whom is my wife a threat, and who will benefit if, for five years, she will have been removed from Warsaw like a leper? I have heard on the radio about such methods, but they were used in America, where blacks are put in ghettoes and re-settled outside of the cities."[986] The husband's judicious eloquence did the trick. According to the notes of December 11, 1953, following his appeal, it was ruled that "there was no case to answer".

Professional money dealers were not deterred by show trials.[987] Some were in fact sentenced to capital punishment but, as a rule, this was not carried out. The case of Adam Sawicki is instructive. In 1952, he received the death sentence but it was soon changed to a life sentence, and with consecutive amnesties decreased to 12, and subsequently to eight years of prison. In fact, the currency dealer left prison a mere five years after the initial verdict, in January 1957.[988] Stanisław M. Korowicz explained such a turn of events matter-of-factly: "In the six months that followed the money reform, several profiteers were caught and subjected to a show trial in order to intimidate everybody. As a result, only a minimal amount of dollars and pounds were exchanged in banks and the rest disappeared, for a while, from the black market. And so people began to marvel at a new political and economic phenomenon: a political regime in need of dollars and pounds. [...] Government agents knew very well that there were a lot of dollars in Poland. In the end, show trials for currency dealers faded away, and profiteers were no longer threatened in the press. The regime, in various indirect ways, began to purchase the valuable dollars and pounds on the black market."[989] We do not

---

986 AAN, KS, 1325, fol. 49.

987 *Funty i dolary stałym pieniądzem w Polsce. Procesy przeciw "waluciarzom" dla zastraszenia publiczności*, "Dziennik Polski" (London), no. 286/November 29, 1952.

988 APW, KWar. PZPR, 30/XVIII-7, vol. 1, fol. 60–61.

989 S.M. Korowicz, *W Polsce pod sowieckim jarzmem*, London 1955, pp. 235–236.

have a reliable source to corroborate this version of events; we cannot, however, dismiss it out of hand.

8.2.2 1956–1981

Those who were able to keep their hard currency and gold safely hidden until the fall of 1956 could then breathe easy. By early November 1956, the Minister of Finance issued an ordinance, and soon thereafter the parliament passed the Act (Journal of Laws 1956, no. 50, item 223) rescinding the ban on the possession of hard currency, gold, and platinum. Poles were now allowed to withdraw from the bank "hard currency assets" that they had deposited after October 1950 and were allowed to take outside of Poland and bring back precious stones and articles made from precious metals. A ban on private trading in hard currency and precious metal scrap was upheld. On November 9, 1956, during a press conference given by the Ministry of Finance, it became clear that the relaxation of the rules was intended to "release stored hard currency in order to improve the supply of resources and equipment for small manufacturing industry and fertilizers, insecticides, building materials and machinery for farmers. [...] Allowing those in possession of hard currency in order to pay for having a house built, to invest in a small manufacturing enterprise, or in increased agricultural production, etc. should encourage such activity and should result in bringing more goods on to the national market."[990] All hard currency operations were taken over by Bank PKO (Polska Kasa Opieki), which since the late 1920s had already been facilitating similar transactions between Poles at home and abroad. PKO clients could use the money officially sent to their accounts from abroad to purchase from the Bank industrial goods and food, unavailable on the local market.[991]

This was a time of prosperity for the hard currency and gold black market. The authorities were weakened and confused and the law enforcement agencies operated without conviction. There was no shortage, however, of factors to encourage illegal currency dealing. The borders opened wider, both for tourists and emigrants; those who were about to leave Poland were eager to buy hard currency, while repatriates from the West and from the Soviet Union brought with them US dollars acquired at a lower price than in Poland, which they were eager

990 TL, November 10, 1956.

991 Stefan Atlas wrote in 1960: "The Bank was established in order to enable Poles living abroad to help their relatives in Poland; it allows the beneficiaries to choose from a wide range of products and delivers much needed hard currency to the state"; S. Atlas, *Paragraf zero – raz jeszcze*, TL, no. 145/ May 26, 1960.

to sell. Consumption patterns were changing and the private sector, which on the one hand needed equipment and resources from the West, and on the other needed to store the profits, was growing. Suddenly, courage got cheaper – those who had previously been afraid to even own gold bullion were now happy to act on the principle of "uncertain times, certain dollar" and began to invest their savings in the American currency.[992] The times certainly *were* uncertain, and the demand so great that in 1957, the US-dollar black market exchange rate reached 220 zloty, twice as much as a year earlier. Treasury authorities drove the demand even higher when in early 1957 they began to scrutinize the sources of income of individuals suddenly flaunting "significant monetary assets". As predicted by Stefan Bobrowski, the better-off Poles stopped building villas and buying cars but instead put their savings in hard currency and gold, the increased demand soon taking the black market price higher.[993]

As a result of the state of the market and the intentional operations of the government, from the beginning of 1958 the dollar exchange rate began to fall – in other words, the Polish currency became stronger. By the end of the decade, the greenback had stabilized at around 90 zloty. This was due partly to the increased supply of American banknotes, brought into Poland by the ever-growing numbers of visitors arriving from the West, as well as Poles resident abroad sending cash to their relatives in Poland, both the sender and recipient well aware of the value of such tangible support. On the other hand, dollar demand had diminished. Those going abroad still needed hard currency; however, the wave of, mostly Jewish, emigration subsided, and tourist trips abroad were not as easy to arrange as in 1957. The use of dollars on the internal Polish market also lessened somewhat. In December 1957, Bank PKO, the only legal intermediary between foreign agencies and private individuals in possession of hard currency backed away from supplying artisans with imported materials, such as polyethylene. And vigorous persecution of economic crimes also brought some, if modest, results.[994]

---

992 HIM, Pressearchiv, P 612, Item 5169/57, Dollars brought from the USSR. The black-market rate for gold. In the first six months of 1957, 35% more hard currency crime was recorded in Warsaw than in a comparable period in 1956; APW, KWar. PZPR, 30/XVIII–7, vol. 1, fol. 35.

993 W. Teliga, *Czy złotówka staje się droższa*, "Słowo Powszechne" March 12, 1958.

994 In 1958, law enforcement dealt with 3 524 hard currency cases, in 1959 with 1 781 and in 1960 with 1 201; AAN, NIK, 18/33, Note on economic crime in 1960, Warszawa 1961, p. 21.

Currency dealers customarily took advantage of provincial visitors to the capital, who were unfamiliar with the current foreign exchange rates and who had dollars that they had been sent by their family in the USA or Canada. Jerzy Zaruba, Currency dealers in front of the PKO bank, *1960. Photo: Warsaw Museum of Caricature, sign. 9928.*

Nevertheless, the gradually developing system of internal export and the differences between the official and black market dollar exchange rate kept the illegal currency trade in good shape. From 1957 the official dollar rate, now at 4 zloty, was applied exclusively in settling Poland's international accounts. This exchange rate had very little in common with the different exchange rates applicable within the country itself. At the official exchange rate offered by banks, tourists visiting Poland received 24 zloty for one dollar. But only first-time visitors or those completely clueless bothered to stock up on all the zloty they required from official sources. Most were well aware that they could get four times as many zloty for their foreign banknotes on the black market! The authorities were just as aware of the exchange-rate discrepancies that worked to their disadvantage and evolved ways of tempting the flow of dollars towards the government outlets, with the law treating "hard currency natives" – as Poles receiving dollar consignments from relatives abroad were known – more leniently. The money they had been sent was exchanged at the comparatively generous rate of 72 zloty. They also were able to obtain in branches of PKO dollar checks, allowing them to buy foreign goods or spend them in special PKO stores. These, however, were poorly supplied, especially in the 1950s; moreover, they were only to be found in the capital, where initially hard currency operations were exclusively performed. Visitors from outside of Warsaw, often confused by the complicated procedures, were easily persuaded to sell their checks for a few zloty more than the official going rate. "Much effort has been wasted," complained *Kierunki* journalists in 1957, "campaigning for a network of stores where citizens can buy attractive goods using hard currency. Not everybody can afford peregrinations to PKO stores from remote Polish cities. It is much easier to sell the dollar checks to a random dealer who will then transfer them abroad, than wait for weeks for attractive goods at the PKO stores. And thus the repeal of the inane, anti-democratic law prohibiting possession of foreign currency benefits only black market dealers and smugglers."[995]

Since complete and effective eradication of the black market was deemed to be not feasible, the authorities aimed their efforts at re-directing at least part of the stream of foreign currency flowing into the black market to the Treasury. On June 18, 1958, the Minister of Finance issued a new regulation, which was implemented swiftly – barely a month later; it allowed "hard currency natives" to open non- interest-bearing, hard currency accounts in a number of banks. The account holders were allowed to make unlimited deposits and spend unlimited quantities on goods within the "internal export" system. All other withdrawals required special authorization. A year later, another regulation (MP 1959, no. 60, item 295) made it possible to buy goods in Bank PKO stores using undocumented hard currency.

The introduction, in 1960, of PKO dollar coupons was a truly revolutionary step. The coupons were not a currency sensu stricto but rather an auxiliary means of settlement effective only within Poland. The foreign currency that Polish citizens received from abroad and the apportionment of their wages earned abroad while employed on state contracts were paid out to them not in bank transfers or foreign banknotes but in PKO dollar coupons. On the black market they were worth only slightly less than US dollars, because – importantly – trading in them was not restricted. If one wanted to buy or sell dollar coupons – unlike in the case of dollars – one could advertise one's intention in a newspaper ad. In time, well-understood codes of communication developed: a small ad offering

995 J. Koźliński, K.W. Olszewski, *Dwie stopy na złotym wybrzeżu*, "Kierunki", no. 36/ September 8, 1957.

a coupon transaction was understood to refer potentially also to trading hard currency.[996]

With its many loopholes, PKO-coupon circulation was a system that provided black marketeers with numerous opportunities for quasi-legal operations, which greatly frustrated law enforcement efforts. If we are to believe the press, the situation "threw the Police Station in Walicón Street [in Warsaw] into a blind rage"; under the circumstances, they were reduced to observing and analyzing the money changers' modus operandi and once in a while staged, mostly unsuccessful, roundups.[997] The law enforcement forces counted on the new criminal law passed on April 13, 1960 (Journal of Laws 1960, no. 21, item 123, in force from June 30, 1960) and largely dedicated to hard currency crimes. The new law raised fines, with a new maximum of one million zloty – an unimaginable amount at the time;[998] it did not pander to the wishes of the police who would have preferred to see longer prison sentences and left the maximum term at three years in jail. Following the tried and tested practice of demonstrating the effectiveness of any new law in action, the authorities instantly launched show trials of money dealers. On July 26, 1960, for the crime of purchasing a $100 bill, a Warsaw currency dealer was fined 40 000 zloty – more than two years' average salary! – and given the option of eight months of prison instead.[999] In spite of the toughened sanctions, the money changers exploited expertly numerous loopholes such as the absence of restrictions on transactions involving PKO dollar coupons. As a result, fighting hard currency crimes was an exercise in futility, with the press incessantly urging more effective law enforcement. It was not the PKO coupons but hard currency that shaped the image of the foreign money black market. From the late 1950s to the early 1970s, one of the most important driving forces behind this black market sector was the illegal import of luxury articles such as clothing and watches but above all gold, where the stakes were at their highest. This was one type of contraband that could always rely on solvent customers and was immune to the vagaries of fashion. In the seemingly stable 1960s there was

996 A system of similar codes probably existed in all the Soviet Bloc countries. For example in the GDR, an advertisement for "blue tiles" (*blaue Fliesen*) meant an offer of selling or buying West German marks (hundred-mark bills were blue); S. Sommer, *Das große Lexikon des DDR-Alltags*, Berlin 2002, pp. 47–48.

997 S. Atlas, *Paragraf zero – raz jeszcze*, TL, no. 145/May 26, 1960.

998 L. Hochberg, *Przestępstwa dewizowe w nowej ustawie karnej skarbowej*, "Państwo i Prawo" 1960, no. 8/9, pp. 303–309.

999 ŻW, no. 178/July 27, 1960.

no shortage of buyers among private businessmen, professionals and assorted shady operators.

Stefan Brzozowski, The speculator's last currency deal, *circa 1960.*
Photo: Warsaw Museum of Caricature, sign. 3616.

During the Gomulka era, the newspapers never ceased to report how yet another "gold gang" had been exposed, typically buying hard currency, transferring it abroad and bringing back the precious metal. The government's perennial dilemma was whether to support the existing anti-speculation laws or favor sound economic considerations such as the profit principle. Firstly, the state had a monopoly in hard currency and gold transactions, and besides, smuggling and illegal currency trading and hoarding were against the law. Secondly, gold bullion and bars hidden in attics and buried in backyards played the useful role of partially eliminating the monetary overhang, which would have otherwise flooded the poorly supplied food and general goods market, leading to inflation. Moreover, the state itself needed gold and private individuals were as good a source of supply as any. This consideration alone caused the government to tread gently when it came to repressive measures. The upshot was that the official approach towards citizens' activities in the field of currency and precious metals was bipolar and irrational. On the one hand, customs officials and police did their job of prosecuting smugglers and investigating currency smuggling gangs. On the other, institutions authorized by the state to buy precious metals such as Veritas, Ars Christiana, and above all the state-owned Jubiler[1000] were busy buying gold so as not to antagonize sellers unduly by being excessively inquisitive about its provenance; managers' eyes were firmly on the business goals and satisfaction of their customers. Introduced in 1957, the regulations pertaining to the purchase of goods by the state were much more liberal in the case of gold and platinum, than food and industrial articles. The gold purchase price was set at a level (164 zloty per gram) sufficiently high to make smuggling the precious metal to Poland in order to sell it to the state a worthwhile pursuit. The authorities chose to overlook the fact that only a small portion of the gold purchased by state institutions from citizens was of the "utility" kind – that it that is to say, jewelry and watches. Most of it was gold bullion gold bars, which must have entered Poland as contraband.[1001]

In 1961, the state purchase of "goods of foreign origin" became subject to new regulations. With goods worth more than six thousand zloty, sellers were now obliged to show their ID, with all the particulars duly recorded, as well as a customs receipt to prove that the goods had entered the country legally. When it came to such popular petty contraband as razors, sweaters or cognac, both buyers and sellers mostly ignored the new regulations by immediately developing

1000 All institutions had to re-sell precious metals to the Polish Mint, where their further fate was decided.

1001 *Alicja w krainie towaru*, TL, December 16, 1960.

defensive strategies; selling gold was, however, more complicated. In spite of Deputy Prime Minister Eugeniusz Szyr urging that the rule should also apply to gold, this was initially rejected by the Ministry of Internal Trade, clearly governed by different objectives. The requirement to present personal identification documents at the time of purchase was temporarily abandoned whereas the purchase price of gold by state institutions was lowered to 115 zloty per gram. The effects of this move soon followed. Whereas in 1960, authorized institutions had purchased 1 997 kg of gold to the value of 322 million zloty, in 1961 they bought only 138 kg for a total of 152 million zloty; of this amount, 942 kg was purchased in the first half of the year and only 196 kg in the second.[1002] Gold drifted away to the black market, which offered higher prices. The growth of the illegal market forced the repressive state apparatus to enhance and professionalize its anti-profiteering operations. Tellingly, in 1962, Police Headquarters published a manual, featuring photographs of gold bullion from all over the world.[1003] On September 26, 1963 the Criminal Chamber of the Supreme Court adopted the resolution that the "unauthorized purchase of foreign gold coins used in payment of foreign bills constitutes a trade in hard currency executed as a purchase-sale transaction as defined in item 45 paragraph 1 of the Fiscal Offences Act of April 13 1960."[1004]

The calls of economists advocating a more flexible state policy in regard to precious metals were brushed aside. This did not mean the decision makers stopped paying attention to gold. To the contrary, some of the motions suggested at the time now appear shocking. On November 8, 1966, at a meeting of the representatives of various government departments including the Police and the Prosecutor's Office, the chairman of the State Price Commission Janusz Strzemiński proposed, in all seriousness, that – since Poles were able and willing to pay a great deal for "hard-currency gold" – in order to meet demand, the State Mint should embark on the production of coins of defunct states such as replica tsarist rubles or Austro-Hungarian ducats. In the event, common sense prevailed and the motion was not approved.[1005]

1002 AAN, Supreme Audit Office II, 19/46, fol. 59–60.

1003 *Album złotych monet*, eds I. Skolimowski, S. Tarko, Warszawa 1962.

1004 A. Kochański, *Polska 1944–1991. Informator historyczny*, vol. 2: *Ważniejsze akty prawne, decyzje i enuncjacje państwowe (1957–1970)*, Warszawa 2000, p. 365.

1005 AIPN, KG MO, 35/1927, fol. 3–4. This idea was discussed again on the NBP's initiative in July 1969. Once more it was decided that the "benefits of the operation would not outbalance the negative political and social repercussions". The production of collector's coins such as the pre-war 10-zloty piece with Boleslaw I the Brave was accepted as a feasible alternative; AAN, National Bank of Poland (Narodowy Bank Polski), 8/7, Minutes of Ministry of Finance Council meeting, July 19, 1969, fol. 234.

The official purchase price of gold did not go up until 1969, differentiating between scrap, at 140 zloty per gram, and undamaged coins – at 200 zloty per gram. In 1971, the customs duty on gold, until then – at between 25 and 120 zloty per gram – prohibitively high, decreased to between 5 and 10 zloty. A year later, the regulations yet again became lax: those selling precious metals to "nationalized entities" were no longer required to show their ID. This led to increased purchases of gold by the state: in 1972, a ton more than in the previous year. Citizens of Yugoslavia sniffed out a good business opportunity and, taking advantage of freedom to travel, flooded the Polish market with Austrian ducats (which until 1972 had been cheaper on the black market than on the official one).[1006] The rigid official prices did not reflect the global price of gold, which skyrocketed in 1973. The black market, always flexible, was once again in a privileged position. In 1973, despite the rising price, the Polish state bought a mere 81 kg of gold (only a year earlier, in 1972, it acquired as much as 1 476 kg). History repeated itself during the next global gold boom at the turn of the 1970s and the 1980s. The Polish state remained commercially defensive until 1989 and in this field also conceded to the black market.

Some of the gold found in October 1983 at the house of a manager of a shop in Kutno charged with speculation offences. Photo: Polish Press Agency (PAP).

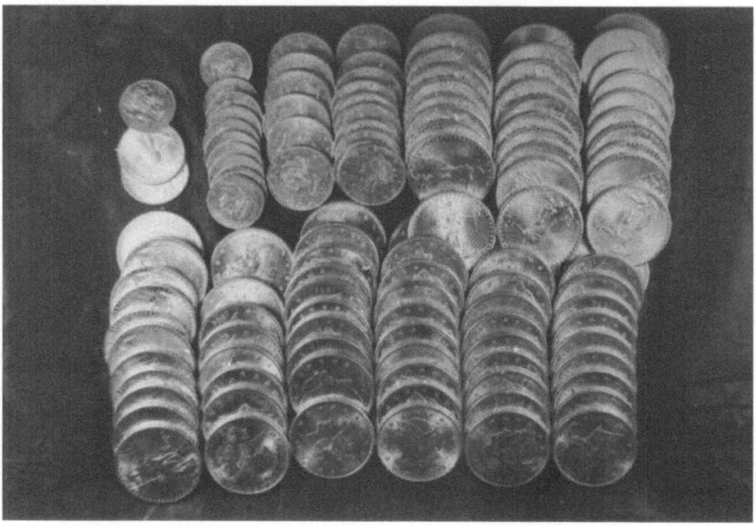

1006 AIPN, 01521/2035, Jacek Oleś, Smuggling of currency value, The Academy of Internal Affairs, Institute of Criminology, Warszawa 1978, pp. 39–40.

The liberalization in the gold trade evident in the early 1970s had an impact on the dollar trade. At the end of the Gomułka era, the Ministry of Finance regulation of April 4, 1970 (MP 1970, no. 11, item 95) introduced private, interest-bearing hard currency accounts. These came in two kinds. In Account A, Poles were able to deposit foreign funds of documented origin; they could withdraw them at will and take them out of the country. There was no obligation to document a legitimate origin of foreign funds deposited in the Account B, also interest-bearing; these, however, could be used solely for purchases in the internal export market. Three years after the date of the original deposit, the funds would automatically acquire legitimate status. In 1970, 4.9 million dollars were held in 7 000 private accounts; barely two years later, in 1972, the deposits had increased dramatically to 24 million dollars held in 37 000 accounts, and in 1975 – they shot up to 125 million dollars held in as many as 245 000 accounts.[1007]

It is difficult to establish beyond doubt whether the large operations against hard currency and gold dealers organized by the Ministry of Internal Affairs (MSW) in the fall of 1971 were part of the government's general hard currency policy. They were probably unconnected with the Fiscal Offences Act of October 26, 1971 (Journal of Laws 1971, no. 28, item 260). Had the operations been part of standard communist propaganda-in-action that usually accompanied the implementation of a new law, they would most likely have been conducted immediately after the law came into force on January 1, 1972, especially since it provided a much more detailed classification of hard currency crimes and violation than previous legislation had and included harsher sanctions. The operations were probably merely a law-enforcement blitz typical of the new political era, an attempt to demonstrate the determination of the new political team to eradicate the "pathologies of social life". In August 1971, the Minister of Interior Affairs, Franciszek Szlachcic, approved "Guidelines for the Operation of the Department of Interior Affairs for the Benefit of Public Safety and Order." In the same month, the operation optimistically named "Order" began. It was directed primarily against currency and gold dealers, smugglers and pimps. The "W" office in the Ministry of Internal Affairs (MSW) was put in charge of the "surveillance of the correspondence of people who receive substantial amount of hard currency"; in practice, this involved opening, often at random, large numbers of private letters often sent by post by and to people quite unconnected with any illegal activity. In the period August 14 to 28, 1971, 32 610 police officials, 6 560 members of

1007 M. Bednarski, *Drugi obieg gospodarczy. Przesłanki, mechanizmy i skutki w Polsce lat osiemdziesiątych*, Warszawa 1992, p. 119.

the Volunteer Reserve Militia (ORMO), 4 500 MSW and Police Headquarters employees and "public activists" (2 242 persons) took part in the operation. By early October, 4 559 people had been arrested and over 47 000 cases had been sent to police courts. On September 17, 1971 "Operation Rubin" began. It was directed against currency changers and gold dealers operating in Gdańsk, Katowice, Krakow, Łódź, Szczecin, Warsaw and Wrocław. Several days later "Operation Korona" was launched, aimed at money changers and prostitutes working in Warsaw's best hotels. Following that, Gdańsk, Bydgoszcz, Katowice, Wrocław, Łódź, Kraków, Szczecin were targeted.[1008]

The wave of large-scale actions against the black market quickly receded, with no similar action replays taking place for the rest of the Gierek era but of course investigation and prosecution of "hard-currency smuggling gangs" continued. Krzysztof Madej got it right with his comment: "This approach was part of the bigger picture of the Gierek team approach to phenomena perceived as pathological and unwelcome. Instead of radical repression or show trials, the authorities preferred to monitor the undesirable phenomena or, using today's terminology, to "manage" them."[1009] This became especially true when the government's new legislation concerning hard currencies turned black market currency dealers into an important institution performing a sui generis service for the benefit of the state. In early October 1976, a Ministry of Finance resolution (MP 1976, no. 38, item 173) did away with accounts B, leaving only accounts A. This move proved extremely effective – by 1979, the deposits in these accounts grew to 438 million dollars.[1010] Not only did Poles empty their drawers and other domestic hidey-holes of dollars and marks but also bought additional hard currency on the black market in order to maximize their deposits into these legitimate bank accounts, which were treated as investment. The bank offered a relatively high interest, which considerably increased the return on deposits, since the black-market dollar exchange rate kept rising.[1011] One could support oneself nicely just by living off this interest if the deposit was large enough. Even the interest on smaller savings represented a significant supplement to a family budget. Another reason that made account A immensely attractive was the fact

1008 AIPN, 0296/113, vol. 3, fol. 7–8, 30, 45, 77, 100, 123, 153, 156–157; *ibid.*, 0296/114, vol. 1, fol. 2, 4, 45, 60, 82. See: F. Szlachcic, *Gorzki smak władzy. Wspomnienia*, Warszawa 1990, pp. 182–184.

1009 K. Madej, *Wszyscy byli przemytnikami…*, p. 139.

1010 D. Stola, *Kraj bez wyjścia? Migracje z Polski 1949–1989*, Warszawa 2010, p. 301.

1011 In 1974, the black-market average dollar exchange rate was 91 zloty, in 1975 – 105.5 zloty, in 1976 – 127 zloty, in 1977 – 141 zloty, in 1978 – between 133 and 138 zloty.

that it was useful in facilitating trips abroad. Let us not forget that this was still a time when travelling outside of Poland, particularly to a Western country, could by no means be taken for granted and required elaborate strategies – such as for example having to obtain a formal invitation from an identifiable foreign citizen, the paperwork verified by a foreign consulate. Another method was to apply for an allocation of hard currency by the state, which was far from generous or indeed adequate to meet the cost of staying however briefly in a Western country. In contrast, hard-currency account holders were entitled to a passport that could be used to travelling outside of the Soviet Bloc countries without the necessity to resort to such elaborate maneuvers. Each trip to the West and occasionally even a sojourn in the East offered opportunities to acquire foreign money, which could then be brought back to Poland. "The increase in the numbers of citizens making trips abroad using their own hard currency", the chief of the Przemyśl police noted in his report to headquarters in Warsaw in November 1978, "is related to the increasing numbers of hard-currency account holders. These accounts are opened with dollars that the holders bring from capitalist countries or which they buy while visiting Bulgaria, Yugoslavia, Romania, and Hungary. From our reconnaissance it is clear that the majority of trips based on hard currency are not of a tourist character but they serve rather as an opportunity to conduct all kinds of trade and smuggling transactions. In contrast to previous years, instead of gold and attractive goods, today's "tourists" bring home foreign currency – mostly dollars. Some citizens use foreign currency brought back to Poland to augment their deposits in their foreign currency accounts or to open new ones. The accounts make it possible for them to organize trips abroad in subsequent years."[1012]

This diminished interest in bringing back from abroad attractive Western goods with the goal of reselling them at home at a profit was largely due to the reform of the hard-currency stores. On January 1, 1974 the Internal Export Company (Przedsiębiorstwo Exportu Wewnętrznego, Pewex) began its operations. Pewex took over from Bank PKO "internal export trading" and rapidly expanded into a dense network of stores, which offered attractive goods at prices often lower than in the West. For the Polish state it was more profitable to sell products made in Poland in Pewex (which thus hardly merited the term "export ") – in1977 sales of such goods made up 60 percent of the stores' revenue. It was more profitable than selling goods genuinely imported from abroad, and in particular Western goods, to obtain which the centralized economy had

1012 AIPN, MSW II, 21052, fol. 12–13.

to waste precious reserves of hard currency. Besides, it was easier to "export" Polish goods internally within the country to a hard currency store than to the demanding West, where they were often found to be substandard or otherwise failed to meet Western expectations. The government developed a system of incentives for buyers. The price of the two most important articles on sale at Pewex – cars and Polish alcohol – when calculated at the black market hard currency exchange rate was somewhat lower than the price of that same alcohol in regular stores and the price of new cars on the free market. The same was true of the price of apartments and farming equipment. Pewex revenue grew fast allowing the state treasury to replenish its coffers. No wonder that – faced with the reality that illicitly obtained money ended up as a legitimate deposit in a foreign currency bank account or was used for legal Pewex purchases – even the courts were inclined to be lenient towards those facing criminal charges involving hard currency.[1013]

Nevertheless, the dual currency system was a source of numerous economic, social, and political concerns for the Polish authorities in the second part of the 1970s. Increasing numbers of Western tourists visiting Poland bought Polish currency from state outlets in no more than the obligatory minimum quantity of dollars, which was hardly surprising. Bearing in mind the derisory official exchange rate of 31zl, they were able to complete their currency exchange at a much better rate on the black market. In 1971, unofficial transfers of hard currency from foreign visitors were estimated at ten million dollars. In 1977 the estimate swelled to 120 million dollars while the state officially purchased 23% fewer. Thanks to the unofficial rate of exchange, foreigners were able to buy – for, in their perception, next to nothing – leather goods, silver, and clothes with the zloty purchased from money dealers (estimated at eight billion zloty). The authorities worried not only about foreign tourists draining the increasingly depleted Polish market but also about the "transfer of the national income to the capitalist countries, with no recompense whatsoever."[1014]

The progressive "dollarization" of Poland gradually undermined trust in the national currency. Worse than that: it also made jobs remunerated in zloty unattractive. In the second part of the 1970s, the average net wage calculated at the black market exchange rate was approximately $35 per month, or $420 annually. To be in possession of dollars became a criterion of social class. Privileged

1013 G. Kurkiewicz, *"Change money"… czyli dolary dla operatywnych*, "Czas" 1978, no. 41; R. Czerniawski, *Gra w zielone*, PiŻ, 1983, no. 15.

1014 AAN, KC PZPR, XIA/511, fol. 12.

holders of hard currency bank accounts traveled abroad and shopped at Pewex. The rest had only Polish zlotys in their wallets and shopped in regular stores, where the choice was limited. For someone upwardly mobile socially, to break the law by availing themselves of the black market seemed a small transgression that could open the door to the exclusive dollar group.[1015] In the column written for the Warsaw magazine *Kultura* that the writer Bohdan Czeszko sent in weekly from the small town provincial town where he lived, he told the following story: "The ultimate example of extreme aversion to our native currency is the attitude of a certain farmer. One day, this reasonable fellow brought potatoes to sell in the market. This was just a typical small town market that takes place once or maybe twice a week. [...] The farmer had an extraordinarily cunning plan for selling his potatoes. He would only part with the product in exchange for hard currency. Specifically, he was happy to accept US dollars and West German marks, charging $2.50 for a sack of potatoes. You can see that not only was he familiar with the black-market dollar rate but was an honest merchant to boot, since the price was nothing if not eminently reasonable.

And he would have likely been willing to go even lower, had the transaction actually taken place. But it didn't. People fell about laughing. Asked what had inspired this absurd idea, the farmer explained that he was having a house built but construction materials where only available via the internal export system – so he had decided to 'internally export' his own product."[1016]

Not all the dollar-less pariahs were as desperate as this provincial farmer. The majority were simply bitter or mad as hell, and kept complaining. In the fall of 1978, the Department of Planning and Economic Analysis at the Central Committee prepared a package of remedial measures, which included tightening foreign exchange controls for non-residents, and lowering the internal-export and black-market price ratio to 90 zloty to a dollar in 1979 and down to 70 zloty in 1980; to look at it in a different way, this simply meant higher prices in the Pewex and Baltona stores. Another measure was to maintain the hard-currency stores only in big cities and in hotels for foreign visitors. By 1980, all domestic articles in short supply on the domestic market were to be withdrawn from internal export stores.[1017] The striking workers on the Baltic coast were in agreement with most of those proposals, as could be seen from their demands in August

1015 *Ibid.* fol. 13.
1016 AAN, KC PZPR, XIA/472, fol. 33.
1017 AAN, KC PZPR, XIA/511, fol. 18–21.

1980.[1018] Ironically, all that the revolution they ignited achieved was to accelerate the dollarization of Poland.

8.2.3 1981–1989

The changes in hard currency policy in the preceding quarter of a century had been evolutionary rather than revolutionary. Even the dollar exchange rate did not change much, and in 1980 it was on average 125 zloty. However, the 1980s had its share of extremities, from quasi-Stalinist restrictions to extreme liberalism. Historical analogies come to mind. For example, 1981 was reminiscent of 1957. The government and its agencies were weak and confused. The gates to the West opened wider: in 1981 Poles traveled to other Soviet Bloc countries half as often (from 6 157 000 trips in 1980 the number dwindled to 2 984 000 in 1981) but twice as frequently to capitalist countries (from 695 000 to 1 248 000). Most trips had commercial goals – the travelers were planning to work or engage in lucrative trading. Increasing amounts of hot money in the wallets of Polish citizens (just as in 1957) and rapidly growing shortages made selling foreign goods unusually profitable. It paid to bring gold home – always an attractive investment, as well as any other marketable goods. The authorities turned a blind eye to the private imports, which in 1981, according to the estimates, was worth 310 million dollars.[1019]

In 1981, just as it had done a quarter of a century earlier, the dollar exchange rate went crazy – in May it was 200 zloty, and by early December it had shot up to 500 zloty. When Martial Law was imposed on December 13, there were many desperate enough to be prepared to pay as much as 1 000 zloty for a dollar. The panic was short-lived but in the following weeks the rate oscillated between 800 and 900 zloty, to again halve in 1982 (to 360–400 zloty). The restrictions imposed on hard-currency bank accounts worked in favor of the black market.[1020] By October 1982, withdrawals were only possible if paid out in dollar coupons rather than actual hard currency, and the onerous limitations remained in force

1018 *Postulaty 1970–71 i 1980. Materiały źródłowe do dziejów wystąpień pracowniczych w latach 1970–1971 i 1980 (Gdańsk i Szczecin)*, ed. B. Chmiel, E. Kaczyńska, Warszawa 1998, pp. 185, 186, 194, 202, 206, 209.

1019 W. J. Kostrzewa, *Devisenschwarzmarkt in Polen. Seine Eigenschaften, sein Modell und seine Bedeutung für die polnische Wirtschaft*, Kiel 1987, pp. 24–25. According to the estimates of the World Currency Yearbook (1984, p. 871), in 1980 alone, and just from Great Britain, three tons of gold were transferred to Poland, *ibid.*, p. 29. In 1981 this amount was probably much larger.

1020 AAN, URM, 32/6, fol. 5.

for some time. Trips abroad ended and, with them, the trade in goods brought from abroad. Large hikes of food prices in February 1982 led to many of those with savings in hard currency selling their store of value in order to put food on the table; this supported the black market and at the same time lowered the dollar rate.

For the first few months after the imposition of Martial Law, the law enforcement agencies paid little attention to the black market, preoccupied as they were with other plentiful problems. Rather, they went through the motions, mostly to appease public opinion particularly in large factories where workers protested against the speculative trade in goods purchased within the internal export system.[1021] The hard currency black market re-appeared on the government's radar in mid-1983, after Martial Law had been lifted and cross-border traffic again given a green light, resulting in increased export-import activities by Polish citizens.[1022] The regulation issued by the Minister of Finance and the chairman of the National Bank of Poland on November 30, 1984 (MP 1984, no 27, item182) , with effect from January 1, 1985, which abolished all restrictions on the use of foreign currencies deposited in A accounts " (with documented origin), provided a massive boost for the hard-currency black market. Nevertheless, funds of undocumented origin could be deposited in account N; from there – after only a year – they would graduate to account A status.

The interest paid on hard-currency accounts was sufficiently high to cushion the effects of the high inflation that was devouring all savings denominated in Polish zloty. Unsurprisingly, as much as two billion dollars had been parked in individual hard-currency accounts by 1987. This helped the state alleviate some of its hard-currency problems but it had nevertheless to find a compromise between the existing law and socio-economic reality. This frequently resulted in paradoxical situations. In spite of being subject to the law and censorship, in the mid-1980s, the consumers' weekly *Veto* as well as automobile and computer magazines carried information on the current black market currency exchange rates.[1023] The state bank was buying from the citizens gold coins and bars that clearly must have been smuggled from abroad and paid for them with hard currency calculated at a fair exchange rate; the sellers could deposit the proceeds

1021 AAN, URM, 32/114, fol. 73.

1022 AAN, URM, 32/171, fol. 137. According to estimates, 40 million dollars left Poland for Turkey and 100 million dollars left for West Germany with the goal of importing goods, W.J. Kostrzewa, *Devisenschwarzmarkt in Polen…*, p. 25.

1023 M. Gruszczyński, M. Stokłosa, *Efektywność nieoficjalnego rynku walutowego w Polsce w latach 1982–1989*, "Bank i Kredyt" 37, 2006, p. 39.

legally in their account A – today, the process would be described as money-laundering, with the state and its institutions colluding with the citizens.[1024] Ostensibly, the government frowned upon Polish travelers abroad engaging in trade activities – yet, apparently incongruously, it also instructed them on how to avoid the repressive measures of the customs agencies of the Soviet Union, Hungary, Bulgaria, and other Soviet Bloc countries – which, if applied successfully, would have been detrimental to the interest of the Polish Treasury. Ultimately, the government was obliged to engage in a price war with the black market and; in 1984, in a singular acknowledgement of free market mechanisms, Pewex was obliged to drop the price of VHS cassettes in order to compete successfully with private importers.[1025]

Simultaneously, the government maintained that hard-currency trade based on high exchange rates had a negative effect on the "process of shaping social perceptions and behavior. It [increased] negative attitudes towards working in Poland and undermined trust in the national currency. Simultaneously it [created] a cult of the dollar and glamorized the status of a job in the West."[1026] The police continued the crusade against currency smuggling; by mid-1986 it had identified "693 sites and locations where illegal hard currency transactions [were] conducted" and "3 582 individuals conducting illegal trade in public places".[1027] The operation continued in 1987, with the clear-up rate for currency smuggling offences increasing by 128.6%; the result was used to justify extending the "operations for 1988."[1028]

Police operations dealt with the tip of the iceberg and were unable to halt the pro-active approach and initiatives in relation to matters of foreign currency of Polish citizens, who gradually abandoned the national currency for the US dollar. Whereas 1976, savings in foreign currency constituted a mere 7.8% of those in Polish zloty, in 1980 this had increased to 16.6%, in 1983 – to 45.1%, and in 1986 – to 78.7%. By 1987, Poles had abandoned all hope of any re-animation of the communist economy, as is evident in the fact that dollar deposits shot up to a massive 137.2% of those in zloty, only to triple a year later, to 319.4%.[1029] For a young person, the only way of saving enough to buy quickly even the smallest

1024 W.J. Kostrzewa, *Devisenschwarzmarkt in Polen...*, pp. 29–30; *W Warszawie płacą dolarami*, "Veto" 1985, nr 41.

1025 W.J. Kostrzewa, *Devisenschwarzmarkt in Polen...*, pp. 24–25.

1026 AIPN, KG MO, 35/554, fol. 40.

1027 *Ibid.*, fol. 46, 50.

1028 *Ibid.*, fol. 82–83.

1029 M. Bednarski, *Drugi obieg gospodarczy...*, p. 120.

apartment was to earn the money abroad. With the high black-market dollar rate in relation to Polish wages – in 1981, the average monthly wage could buy a paltry 35 dollars; by 1988, this had dwindled to a pitiful 22 dollars – it became a way of life to make money "over there" and spend it "over here".[1030] In addition, the foreign currency deposited in the bank yielded healthy interest and such savings enabled the holder to shop in Pewex stores rather than in the depressingly grey, and usually quite bare, regular stores. Whereas in 1982 internal export turnover had been 366.3 million dollars, by 1988 it had grown to 700 million dollars, approximately a quarter of all retail sales in the country. All private transactions that involved purchasing a larger item such as a car or an apartment were conducted in hard currency. In newspaper small ads and real estate sections the rubric, "Will rent/sell to a person returning from abroad" became common. This was a coded message, which indicated that the advertiser was interested solely in a hard currency transaction.

The authorities recognized the necessity of finding a way out of this preposterous situation. In May 1987, the National Bank of Poland (NBP) proposed intervention in the dollar market in order to lower the absurdly high black market exchange rate, which had outpaced both price increases and income growth.[1031] The proposal included long-term strategies such as bringing down inflation, improving the supply of up-to-date consumer goods and doing away with or curtailing of hard-currency rationing. Immediate measures were also proposed, such as the purchase of dollar coupons by state institutions at a price close to the black-market level, the introduction of zloty-denominated credit lines using hard currency as collateral, selling foreign currency to Polish tourists at a "balanced rate" (but with a "tourist surcharge") and, above all, allowing internal export prices to find their market level. Prices in Pewex stores – especially for goods made in Poland such as alcohol or cars – were calculated so as to be relatively low compared to elsewhere, even though the dollars to be spent there had to be bought on the black market. In turn, the coffee or wool purchased in Pewex was sold at a profit on the black market. Thus, Pewex generated demand for hard currency and powered the black economy; the dollars spent there kept in business many an illegal currency dealer…

1030 See: D. Stola, *Kraj bez wyjścia?…*

1031 *Propozycje działań zmierzających do zmniejszenia czarnorynkowego kursu walut obcych*, NBP, Warszawa, May 1987 (I am grateful to Grzegorz Sołtysiak for sharing this material).

In the fall of 1987, eleven branches of the National Bank of Poland in the largest cities embarked on the purchase of dollar coupons at prices close to the market rate. In no time at all, money changers demonstrated the superiority of the private-enterprise economy over the communist one. In order to be able to sell dollar coupons, state institutions first had to buy them. As for the money changers, they had no problem at all carrying out both operations regardless of the time of the day, amount or currency involved. "Their small, pocket banks, portable currency exchange offices [...] win the competition [...] up front", a journalist observed in the spring of 1988. "If the state bank paid 980 zloty for a coupon, the dealers would offer 1 030 zloty. If the bank quoted 1 150, they would topped it with 1 200. When finally the bank raised the price to 1 300, they immediately offered 1 350 zloty. No wonder that people would rather sell to the money changers. The public sell them anything going – coupons, dollars, marks, rubles, and forints. And anything they need, they buy from the dealers, too. Where else?"[1032]

A year later, new opportunities arose. The rigid and restrictive hard currency law was one of the main obstacles in enforcing the Act on Economic Freedom, passed on December 23, 1988. In the new Hard Currency Act of February 15, 1989, (Journal of Laws 1989, no. 6, item 33) the most important provision for the business-oriented citizens was item 10, which stated: "Having obtaining a currency permit and in accordance with the stipulations set out by the Chairman of the NBP, Polish citizens may conduct and manage economic activity involving the purchase, sale, and brokerage of hard currency assets." First off the block was a businessman by the name of Aleksander Gawronik, who had prior experience in the hard-currency black market and had collaborated with the secret services. Despite the existence of a complicated verification procedure, Gawronik was able to start his business a mere couple of days after the new law had been implemented on March 13, 1989, (MP 1989, no. 6, item 35). It is anybody's guess whether it was his business experience or his special connections in the secret services that enabled Gawronik to launch his new lucrative business before all competition.

1032 J. Niepcrowski, *Raj dla cinkciarzy*, "Tygodnik Kulturalny", no. 14/April 3, 1988; see: J.S. Jóźwiak, *Cinkciarz prezesa*, *ibid.*, no. 29/July 17, 1988.

Advertisement for the Foreign Currency Exchange in Aleje Jerozolimskie in Warsaw, December 1989. Photo: Aleksander Jałosiński, FORUM Polish Photography Agency.

The first private Bureau de Change in post-war Poland opened its doors to the public near the border crossing in Świecko on March 16, 1989, at 12.01 am. The first customer appeared barely 15 minutes later – a border guard from East Germany. A 100 DM bill in hand, he put the functioning of Polish capitalist enterprise to an empirical test.[1033] It worked perfectly! In the first few months, the NBP issued some two thousand permits to run money exchange businesses. They were springing up everywhere: in banks, in the branches of the Orbis travel agency, in

1033 P. Pytlakowski, *Krótki spacer Gawronika*, "Polityka", no. 46/November 19, 2005.

Pewex and Baltona stores, and in travel agencies but first and foremost they were being set up by, according to Paweł Tarnowski, "individual citizens with cash and business talents, who came to the conclusion this was the best way to multiply their already considerable wealth (with the initial capital to launch such a business estimated at tens of millions of zloty)."[1034] There can be no doubt that many of those investors had amassed the necessary financial resources changing money in front of state banks and Pewex stores. The hard currency chapter of the Polish black market culminated in March 1990, with the regulation issued by the chairman of the NBP (MP 1989, no 15, item 119) which authorized the circulation of gold bullion, bars and gold scrap; soon, the price of Krugerrands and twenty-dollar gold coins became part of the staple information on boards at money exchange kiosks.

8.3 The Greenback Game: Mechanisms and Players

The illegal trade in hard currency and gold was a complex and multilayered phenomenon, as enduring as it was universal. Invariably, it was powered by fear and greed. This chapter attempts to present – without any prospect of exhausting the topic – the players in this game, their motivation and ways of operating.

8.3.1 Motivation

During the Second World War, some had sold the gold and valuables that they had stockpiled earlier in order to survive, while others engaged in buying, thus creating great fortunes.[1035] Gold, jewelry, precious stones, and hard currency were relatively easy to hide and escape with, even during such a cataclysm as the Warsaw Uprising. "It was becoming apparent," the historian Kazimierz Wyka, who lived near Krakow, noted about refugees from Warsaw, "that in crafty hidey-holes in their shoes, clothes or inside toothbrushes, they had salvaged from the burnt city unexpectedly large quantities of dollars. The hard currency trade revived."[1036]

1034 P. Tarnowski, *Rok dolara*, "Polityka", no. 51/52/December 23–30, 1989.

1035 Post-war finds testify to the extent of the storage of value. For example in early May 1947, four people found approximately 35 kg of gold in a destroyed building at Nowy Swiat 64, which they shared among themselves. Once the Special Commission had been put in charge of recovering hidden treasures, in March 1948 it hauled in 2 269 five ruble coins, 1 112 ten ruble coins, 84 fifteen ruble coins, and eight coins to the value of 7.50 rubles, two twenty-dollar coins and several dozen assorted gold items; AAN, KS, 808. These were not isolated cases (see: AAN, KS, 2656).

1036 K. Wyka, *Życie na niby*, Kraków 2010, p. 256.

Gold dollar and ruble coins helped to rebuild post-war life in Poland. They were used as capital to open a store or a workshop, to start a business and to renovate a house or an apartment. A pharmacist, Michał Albrecht, during his testimony in January 1948 to the Special Commission stated that when he was "running away from Warsaw during the Uprising he took with him $5 000, a $1 000 of which he exchanged into zloty in 1945 when he opened the pharmacy on Targowa Street, and that in 1946 and in 1947 he was selling and buying dollars according to his needs. He explained that when he did not have the money to buy a supply of pharmaceuticals, he would sell some dollars on the black market to get the funds necessary but when he had cash on his hands and nothing else to spend it on at the time, he would buy dollars."[1037]

After the war ended, a large number of private entrepreneurs engaged in similar activity. In 1946, officials at the Main Inspectorate of Treasury Protection (Główny Inspektorat Ochrony Skarbowej, GIOS) identified as the most important black market – besides "emigrants of Jewish nationality" – millers, manufacturers of milling equipment, restaurant owners, jewelers, and "criminal elements from among the functionaries of nationalized industry and trade."[1038] The more worrisome the international situation became during 1946 and 1947 and the more the "battle for trade" jeopardized the future of business, the more private citizens turned to honing their strategies for hoarding stores of value. Between 1948 and 1949, when the government's economic endeavors left no illusion about the intentions of the state, private manufacturers and merchants began to buy greater amounts of hard currency and gold, which in accordance with the laws of supply and demand caused their prices to rise.[1039]

This form of investment continued in the first part of the 1950s. The revaluation of the national currency in October 1950 proved an extremely traumatic experience for citizens. The fear of having to relive the upheaval stayed with Poles until the last days of communist Poland and often motivated their actions. Rumors about a forthcoming money reform cropped up repeatedly – always creating a panic, deepening a distrust of the domestic currency and spurring Poles to invest their savings in foreign currency or gold. The Six-year Plan and the war in Korea not only impoverished Polish society, but also brought inflation and rapidly devalued the national currency. Those who had more courage and more

1037 AAN, KS, 2651.

1038 AAN, URM, 5/637, GIOS do PRM, March 6, 1947, fol. 6.

1039 AAN, KS, 2651. The rise in black-market gold and currencies was the most marked in Warsaw; this siphoned off dollars from other cities. AAN, KS, 1289, Documentation in the case against Abraham Danziger.

money immediately swapped their Polish zloty for more enduring valuables. Those who had run out of national banknotes but had been prudent enough to bury dollars, pounds or rubles in their backyard, every so often sold some of their strategic hoard to make ends meet.

Undoubtedly, until 1956/1957 this phenomenon appeared on a modest scale and stayed mostly underground. Especially in big cities where enforcement was rigorous, the black market went deeper underground. Apparently, in smaller towns and rural areas, hard currency and gold operations were conducted more openly. In August 1952, a helpful anonymous zealot, signing off only as "Honest Citizen", reported to the local authorities in Zamość that every miller in the region was engaged in trying to "save as rapidly as possible not zlotys but dollars in large denominations or gold bullion and willing to pay generously."[1040] Hoarding gold had been traditional among the Polish peasantry and not even Stalinism was able to eradicate it. In the area of the former Russian partition, the farmers tended to recycle the proceeds of sales of grain, vegetables, and meat into gold rubles. In the fall, they would buy the popular five-ruble coin, commonly referred to as the "piggy", and – after food supplies had dwindled through the winter – sell it the following spring.[1041]

Beginning with the fall of 1956, such operations became relatively safe and thus commonplace. Whether a small storeowner or an experienced black-market swindler with cosy connections in governmental echelons of power, their preferred method for the preservation of capital was the same: bury a jar with golden rubles, dollars or Austrian ducats in the backyard. "There he stands behind the till of his small local store, a jar full of candy on the counter, dreaming about gold filling up his stocking – gold that neither water nor fire nor the financial department will take away."[1042] This little vignette epitomized the petty-bourgeois gold

1040 ODZP TVP, Newsletter of Radio Committee Letter Office, 1050/3, no. 75, September 30, 1952.

1041 HIM, Pressearchiv, P 6211, Item 8798/56. Foreign exchange trade flourished. The case of a family doctor from Tuliszków near Konin shows that hoarding valuables was ingrained and socially acceptable in provincial Poland. In August 1977, he was arrested for buying scrap gold and 1 279 dollars, as well as taking part in other, much larger transactions. Soon, the prosecutor office and Voivodship Party committee received letters signed by hundreds of Tuliszków community residents demanding the release of the doctor. The letters emphasized that he was an "honest and diligent" citizen, indispensable to the community. In the local church, a mass was celebrated for a "positive outcome" of the doctor's case; AAN, KC PZPR, WO, 3095, fol. 5.

1042 J. Tetter, *Wolność, złoto i hazard*, "Tygodnik Morski" 1967, no. 19. Not much had changed by the end of the 1970s. "Part of smuggled gold goes literally 'into the

hoarding in 1967. In 1964, a raid on just some of the perpetrators in the "meat affair" uncovered 17 285 dollars in gold dollar pieces and another 15 000 in bills, 1 500 gold rubles, 2 000 gold crowns, 22 gold ducats, 1.7 kg of gold bars and a substantial amount of gold items "of value yet to be established."[1043] The volume of gold accumulated in communist Poland is hard to estimate but it is reasonable to assume that the practice must have been widespread through social groups other than storekeepers and criminals.[1044]

Whenever political or market conditions worsened, nervous gold and currency hoarders became more active. The waves of panic that kept erupting on the market due to international crises and the fear of war (the Berlin crisis in 1961, Cuban missile crisis in 1962, Warsaw Pact invasion of Czechoslovakia in August 1968) and recurrent rumors about currency revaluation (notably in September and October 1963, January 1968, and October and November 1969) not only prompted runs on stores, denuding them completely of pasta, sugar and canned goods but also resulted in a soaring black-market dollar price and increased demand for gold.[1045] The 1968 political crisis, which came to be known simply as "March 1968" or the "March events", was characteristic in that regard. The events of March 1968 put black-market activities on hold until April. During that period, the demand for hard currency and gold soared. Due to scarce supply, the price soon followed the upward path. Dollar bills rose accordingly: bills of small denominations up to 125 zloty and in larger denominations up to 132 zloty for a dollar; the price of 100g gold bars exceeded 20 000 zloty. […] Between mid-August and mid-October, the hard currency trade diminished. Small denomination dollar bills rose to 131 zloty and larger ones to 134–135 zloty per dollar; gold bars

ground' as a 'rainy day' backup. The owner often lives frugally and sometimes dies before divulging his secret to anyone. Recently, employees of one of the voivodship police headquarters seized 12 kg of smuggled gold buried by a vegetable stall owner"; A. Kłodzińska, *Wyprawa po złote runo*, ŻW, January 25, 1979.

1043 AAN, KC PZPR, 237/XIV–305, fol. 45.

1044 AAN, IPP, 123, fol. 8v. Professionals such as lawyers, physicians, and dentists commonly used gold as a store of value. See: J. Niczyporowicz, *Ballada do żółtego kruszcu*, PiŻ, 1978, no. 17.

1045 AAN, KC PZPR, XI/775, April 1970, fol. 25–26; AIPN, 0296/66, vol. 2, Notes on public mood, fol. 67, 84, 92. Another indication was the growing volume of gold seized at the border. In 1968, custom officials found 93.5 kg gold bullion, bars, and jewelry, but in 1969 – almost 162 kg; AIPN, 01521/876, vol. 1, Bogdan Chybowski, Nielegalny skup dewiz (Taktyka ujawniania i zwalczania). Departament Szkolenia i Doskonalenia Zawodowego MSW, Warszawa 1973, p. 11.

from 170 to 180 dollars, thus from 23 600 to 24 500 zloty. In gold transactions, Polish cash was rarely used."[1046]

The government policy towards private entrepreneurs – the main buyers of dollars and gold – had a significant effect on the going market rate. The restrictions implemented in 1969 that lasted until the early 1970s, which included increasing taxes, limiting state sector cooperation, and media propaganda accusing entrepreneurs of "unjust enrichment", temporarily impoverished private business owners. As a result, the price of valuables fell. Between December 1970 and June 1971, the dollar went from 127 down to 97 zloty, a 100g gold bar from 23 000 to 19 000 zloty, and a twenty dollar coin from 8 200 to 6 800 zloty. In consequence, the state jewelry enterprise Jubiler increased its purchase of gold by several times.[1047] When the green light for private initiative was again given, coinciding with symptoms of the national crisis becoming more visible, the demand for gold rose rapidly. A similar mechanism could be observed in the following decade.

Apart from the internal economic factors, the Polish gold market was also affected by the fluctuations in international markets. From 260 dollars per ounce in 1979, gold shot up to 850 dollars in late 1980. In Poland, the black market price of gold grew much more slowly, which made bringing the precious metal to Poland gradually less profitable and there were instances of trade reversal, with gold bars and bullion taken to the West.[1048] However, when, in the second half of the 1980s, gold went down on the global market, while the monetary overhang and thus the possibility of price hikes in Poland increased, gold once more began to pour into the country in quantity. Interestingly, it was largely paid for with the proceeds of the illegal export of silver, a natural resource abundant in Poland, hence cheap – whereas in the West its price was rising rapidly.[1049]

Polish migration, temporary and permanent, was of vital importance in shaping the black market in hard currency and gold. This was particularly noticeable immediately after the war. The returnees were bringing back to their homeland foreign money and gold; those leaving, whether legally or not, tried to take valuables with them. Refugees from Poland, both Poles and Jews, exchanged their possessions for gold and money, which were to help make their new life easier. Those who were already abroad and had no intention of coming back but had left behind some belongings, exchanged them for valuables that were easy to

1046 AIPN, KG MO, 35/1740.
1047 AIPN, MSW II, 1149, fol. 1–3, 6–7.
1048 AIPN, MSW II, 10780, fol. 40–41.
1049 AIPN, KG MO, 35/554, fol. 25.

smuggle out of the country.[1050] The scale of the transfers can be gathered from a note referring to the UNRRA camp for Displaced Persons (DPs), which was published in the Special Bulletin of the Polish Military Mission to Germany in April 1946. The majority of those in the camp were Jewish refugees from Poland. "Jews are complaining about the stricter recent checks at all the border crossing points. The border guards confiscate something from every single person. This "something" ranges from $1 000 to $2 000 in cash or items of jewelry of similar value. [...] The camp residents are in possession of huge amounts of foreign currency, as is evident from the fact that last week, in the Russian zone near Szczecin, NKVD officials confiscated from Hersz Mandelbach from Łódź $11 200. He had made this fortune by smuggling saccharine."[1051] As could be expected, rumors that "emigration of the Jewish population" was soon to be suspended and a "group of emigrants would be returning to Poland from Austria and Czechoslovakia" contributed to the short-lived decline in gold and hard currency price in August and September 1946.[1052]

This mechanism was repeated with each subsequent wave of emigration from Poland – Jews between 1956 and 1957, and again between 1967 and 1968, Germans between the 1950s and the 1970s, and the mass exodus in the 1980s. Studies to date have focused more on the political circumstances of emigration from Poland,[1053] rather than the mechanisms that facilitated the financial aspects of the move such as prospective émigrés selling their assets in order to transfer their value into hard currency or gold (not to mention the legal and illegal transport of personal effects) – which await future research. There is no doubt that both

1050 AAN, URM, 5/229, fol. 61. A similar strategy was implemented during forced migrations such as the resettlement of the Germans. Since they were not allowed to leave the country with hard currency and precious metals, they tried to hide them. In 1946 the Polish authorities issued guidance to border crossings on the hiding places most frequently used by the resettling Germans (such as buckets, suitcases, strollers, toys and pipes); Archiwum Państwowe w Gdańsku, Oddział w Gdyni, Dyrekcja Ceł, 91/123.

1051 AMSZ, z. 6, w. 42, vol. 668, fol. 7, 8; *Polska – Niemcy Wschodnie 1945–1990. Wybór dokumentów*, ed. J. Kochanowski, K. Ziemer, vol. 1: *Polska wobec radzieckiej strefy okupacyjnej Niemiec: maj 1945 – październik 1949*, ed. J. Kochanowski, A. Krajewski, M. Mazurek, Warszawa 2006, pp. 115–116.

1052 AAN, URM, 5/229, fol. 63. Since gold jewelry could be legally taken out of Poland, gold coins were often made into rings or bracelets; *ibid.*, fol. 90.

1053 See: D. Stola, *Kraj bez wyjścia?...*

gold and hard currency played an important role,[1054] and that the emigrants provided a solid base for gold and currency cross-border trade operations. MBP/MSW officials responsible for the prosecution of currency smuggling pointed to the significant participation in this type of crime by the Jewish population in Poland and abroad. Indeed, by the end of the 1960s Jewish-sounding surnames kept appearing in investigation and court reports. It is hard to determine if this over-representation genuinely reflected the fact that a large number of emigrants settled in Germany, Austria or Belgium were actively participating in illegal trade with the homeland, or whether the focus of the interest reflected the bias of the state agencies. The fact remains that soon after 1968, names stereotypically considered Jewish disappeared from the reports on currency smuggling. As a matter of fact it was not ethnicity or nationality that was most important, since the police had representatives of many countries documented in their files, but the expected profit. Contrary to popular opinion, currency smuggling was not an easy way to make a living.

8.3.2 Transfer

By the late 1950s, dollars and gold had assumed distinctively separate functions in Poland. Dollars became a form of working capital, often assembled with an investment in mind (for example in international trade) or used to finance consumption while gold maintained its role as a long-term investment to be deployed only in emergencies. One thing had not changed – a potential Polish investor had to purchase gold abroad and bring it back, usually having to pay for it in hard currency. These were indeed large-scale operations: according to police estimates, between 1945 and 1971, an influx from abroad of 273 million dollars and of approximately 40 tons of gold penetrated the area of the economy not under state control.[1055] A large proportion of the gold arriving in Poland had been obtained in Germany, Italy, and Austria and paid for with smuggled currency, which, according to the Prosecutor General, was the domain of both "accidental criminals" and "professional hard currency dealers and smugglers".[1056]

1054 HIM, Pressearchiv, P 612, RFE-Research, Item 5169/57, Dollars brought from the USSR: The pricing of black-market gold. *ibid.*, P 6211, RFE-Research, Item 5594/57, History of the dollar black market in Poland. Just a single issue of the "Biuletyn Szkoleniowy" GUC (no. 37/July 1967) provides many examples of individuals emigrating to West Germany, Israel, and France smuggling out of Poland hard currencies and gold bullion and jewelry.

1055 K. Madej, *Wszyscy byli przemytnikami…*, p. 127.

1056 AAN, KC PZPR, WA, LI/18, fol. 10.

Smuggling watches in walnuts, pre-1958; photo from a private collection.

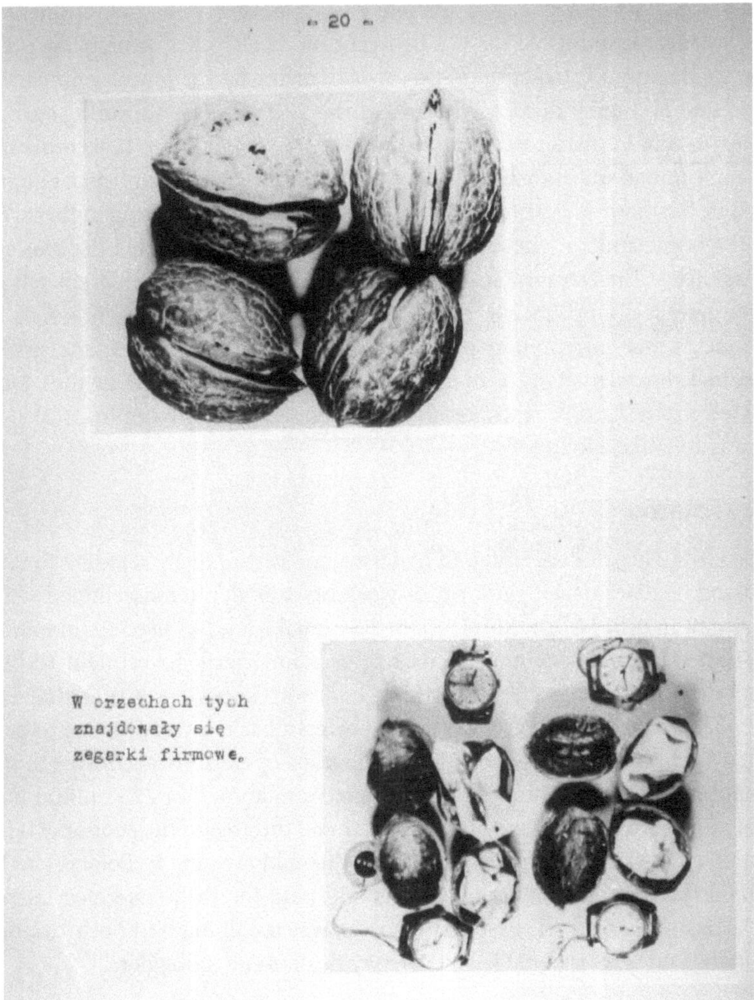

Those who used their trip abroad to smuggle items at their own risk – whether as tourists, visiting family, or doing business – could be classified as being in the first category. The mass scale of the phenomenon put a large amount of goods on the market, including hard currency and gold. The retailer smugglers merit a chapter to themselves; here I would like to focus on the wholesale – large-scale business that significantly influenced the Polish black market. In the Gomułka and Gierek eras, the media regularly reported on the successes of the authorities in smashing "currency smuggling groups", portrayed as gangs of shady mafiosos. A group liquidated in the spring of 1971 was nicknamed "Red Inn"; its boss, Jan Kucharski, the owner of a café in Szaflary, was dubbed by the press the "Banker of Podhale".[1057] Most of the gangs, usually named after their most prominent figure (Oksztel, Laster, Głogowski, Smoliński, Mętlewicz, etc.), were networks that included officials higher in the pecking order, customs officers, private operators, railroad workers, and housewives who all shared an appetite for profit-yielding pursuits. "The 'gold gangs'," an *Odgłosy* journalist wrote in 1973, "have always operated, and continue to do so, through such incongruously diverse personal configurations, bringing together people so different in their social demeanor, mentality, knowledge, and position held, that nothing would surprise us any longer. Thousands of people follow the example of the legendary Midas and want to be surrounded with gold."[1058]

Membership of the gang was usually unstructured and determined by utilitarian factors. Profit from currency transactions was earned in addition to official wages, which it often exceeded many times over. Drivers and railroad workers provided safe transportation for smuggled goods; customs officials made sure there were no unpleasant surprises at the border. Store managers and craftsmen could, without attracting suspicion, store the hard currency and distribute the gold that had been smuggled in. From analysis of the social composition of gang members it is plain that they were more likely to wield a pen than a gun as their weapon of choice – this was often a white-collar crime. For example in February 1964, the Wrocław Security Service identified a group of hard currency criminals which, from the late 1950s, had been bringing illegally to Poland gold coins and bars as well as precious and synthetic stones. All the goods were bought with dollars and with the silver smuggled out of the country. Sixty people were arrested, and 19 were charged. Among them, four watchmakers, four Jubiler store managers, a toy store owner, three owners of a synthetic products factory, employees of the Polish Tourist and Sightseeing Society (PTTK), the Pharmacy Board, a pensioner, a waitress and four unemployed persons.[1059] The makeup of other groups was not very different.

1057 M. Osiadacz, *Bankier Podhala*, PiŻ, May 28, 1972; S.A. Siwek, *"Bankier Podhala" i spółka…*, "Słowo Powszechne", no 225/September 20, 1973.

1058 Z. Tarnowska, *Oczarowanie złotem*, "Odgłosy" 1973, no. 37; see: F. Graboś, *Dewizowe podziemie*, PiŻ, 1965, no. 18.

1059 AIPN, MSW II, 4368, fol. 109.

We know from court records that the gangs were impressively effective; their success relied on tight logistics and extensive knowledge of the market in Poland and abroad, where gangs often had a resident insider.[1060] For example, between 1960 and 1963, the Leonard Smoliński group[1061] "smuggled out of Poland more than 765 000 US dollars, 50 000 rubles, and 600 000 Polish zloty in cash, and also brought in illegally over 10 000 twenty-dollar gold coins, with a total weight of approximately 300 kg."[1062] In early 1976, the trial of ten large-scale hard currency and gold illegal traders began. One of the accused, Wiktor Mętlewicz, had between 1963 and 1973 traded in Warsaw and Vienna 502 million zloty of "currency assets"; another, Mieczysław Młynarczyk, had shifted approximately a billion zlotys' worth. He was accused of purchasing or acquiring for the purpose of re-sale 96 000 dollars, 113 920 gold twenty-dollar, 14 000 5-ruble coins, and 2 245 kg of gold bars. "From this amount, however" – as the indictment pointed out in all fairness, "one should deduct the 80 kg of gold that had been smuggled in, although it was subsequently smuggled back abroad due to the rapid gold price hike in the West."[1063] Such cases provide some indication of the size of the transactions made by specific groups but not of the nationwide scale of the gold black market. In 1972, some 10 million dollars were estimated to be smuggled out of Poland annually and exchanged abroad for 2.5 tons of gold and approximately one ton of artificial gems and similar goods[1064] but we shall never know how accurate those estimates were.

1060 "Visitors from Warsaw," the writer Marek Nowakowski reminisced, "stayed in Budapest for months at a time, networking, buying forints and swapping them for dollars, and even along the way picking up a little, notoriously difficult, Hungarian…; M. Nowakowski, *Moja Warszawa. Powidoki*, Warszawa 2010, pp. 131–132.

1061 On March 27, 1965 in Warsaw, Smoliński was sentenced to nine years in prison and 12 of his closest collaborators were also found guilty. Their educational and employment backgrounds are interesting. The boss had completed only three grades of vocational school, three persons graduated from secondary schools, nine – from primary school, with or without a certificate. The group included a manager of a shoe kiosk, a driver, railroad employees, a blue-collar worker from the League of Nature Conservation, two locksmiths, a nurse, and four unemployed persons; AIPN, MSW II, 4370, fol. 123–125.

1062 AAN, KC PZPR, 237/XIV–305, fol. 45.

1063 B. Seidler, *Krach wyznawców Midasa*, "Życie Literackie" February 4, 1976; B. Wróblewski, *Złotogłowi. Największe złoto Polski Ludowej*, "Gazeta Wyborcza" (supplement "Ale Historia"), September 28, 2012.

1064 AAN, GUC, 2/18, fol. 221.

The practice of smuggling rubles and zloty out of the country requires additional clarification. The secret of its success lay in the grassroots creative approach prevalent in the socialist states including Poland: the officially non-convertible rubles, forints and korunas were not only treated as convertible but indeed backed by gold. In Vienna, it was more profitable to buy gold ducats paying with Hungarian forints (often called Carpathian dollars), Czechoslovakian korunas or Soviet rubles than to buy them with US dollars smuggled out of Poland. Occasionally, Poles would sell dollars in order to buy the currencies of Soviet Bloc countries', then smuggle these out to Vienna, Trieste, Hamburg, or West Berlin.[1065] No wonder that on the black market, socialist state currencies were valued almost as highly as US dollars or West German marks.

Until the late 1950s, smuggling was the domain of diplomats on official trips abroad, sailors, and railroad workers who took advantage of the opportunities provided by their professional circumstances. After 1956, when the borders restrictions were eased, the situation changed. In the 1960s and the 1970s, smuggling became a mass pursuit; Polish illegal traders ventured as far afield as the Middle and Far East and America, now with varied means of transportation such as private cars and airplanes at their disposal. The job of customs officials became more onerous. The customs trade newspaper commented on the ruses of aircraft passengers: "Gold products smuggled in [to Poland] – mostly rings and chains – are hidden in hollowed-out citrus fruit, shoe heels and inside women's wigs. […] One well-known Warsaw entertainer returning from a tour of the Soviet Union used a sizeable fake microphone to smuggle in a substantial number of gold objects."[1066] Those who stuck to traditional travel by trains and bus developed tricks to surprise even the most experienced customs officer. A dental technician from Łódź, Jerzy Paszkowski, had an original idea: between 1959 and 1964, he smuggled into France 38 thousand dollars in hollowed-out kiełbasa and brought back approximately 30 kilos of gold. On other occasions, powdered gold traveled to Poland in seemingly factory-sealed coffee or cocoa cans. Upon arrival, the gold powder was separated and melted into bars – not a very complicated task.[1067]

Poles took advantage both of the well-established practice of smuggling across the "green border" – crossing the border at random, unguarded places

---

1065 AIPN, 01521/2035, Jacek Oleś, *Przemyt wartości dewizowych*, Academy of Internal Affairs, Institute of Criminology, Warszawa 1978, pp. 45, 54–56.

1066 J. Kulak, *O przemycie w Urzędzie Celnym Port Lotniczy w Warszawie – uwag kilka*, WC, 1974, no. 15, p. 13.

1067 AIPN, MSW II, 4369; F. Graboś, *Dewizowe podziemie*, PiŻ, 1965, no. 18, fol. 233.

in the countryside (a specialty of the Podhale region, with its many miles of mountainous borderland) – as well as through mass tourist travel, assuming correctly that backpackers would not be subjected to thorough checks at the border. With the gold smuggled in from Turkey and southern Europe the trick was for the traveler returning, for example, from Italy, with jewelry that he intended to take illegally across the border, to pass the goods on to someone about to cross the border into Poland, someone who had traveled into Czechoslovakia no further than the narrow strip of the designated mass tourist zone, where there were no opportunities to buy gold. The customs checks for such tourists were much less thorough. This method was probably used on numerous occasions – until June 27, 1970, when, at a border crossing in Łysa Polana, customs officials searching four tourists who had been no further than the "convention zone" happened on 1.8 kg of gold jewelry worth 433 000 zloty.[1068]

The most effective smuggling method for currency assets was to use as mules people who traveled frequently, or, best of all diplomats, who were protected by their prestige and professional immunity. In the first group were Polish athletes who engaged in contraband activities on a mass scale. In the mid-1960s, the javelin thrower Janusz Sidło and Władysław Komar, later an Olympic shot-put medalist, were charged with smuggling. "According to the Ministry of Internal Affairs," the Prosecutor General wrote to Prime Minister Józef Cyrankiewicz in March 1965, "this type of fraud is quite common and prosecuting all those guilty of such abuses could lead to the breaking up of the track and field national team and those of other athletic disciplines."[1069] Since to bring to justice members of national sports teams – household names in Poland and abroad – would have had negative repercussions, the prosecution of famous athletes was swept under the carpet.[1070] However, the cases of less popular athletes who ostentatiously engaged in currency smuggling usually landed up in front of a judge. In 1971, the Army Prosecutor's Office charged athletes of the Warsaw Legia team with smuggling hard currency out of the country and bringing back gold, which they later sold to "owners of private crafts shops."[1071] Members of the Duplicate Bridge Union were involved in smuggling on a mass scale, and between 1968 and 1972 brought to Poland more than 76 kg of gold.[1072] In 1973, verdicts were handed down in

1068 J. Koczorowski, *O wynikach zwalczania przemytu w 1971 roku*, WC, 1972, no. 6, p. 25.
1069 AAN, URM, 1.2/1, fol. 18.
1070 *Ibid.*, fol. 20.
1071 APW, KWar. PZPR, 30/XVIII-7, vol. 1, fol. 445.
1072 *Byli reprezentanci w brydżu sportowym przed sądem*, "Głos Wielkopolski" October 17, 1973; *Brydżowy nokaut*, "Wieczór Wybrzeża" July 30, 1973; J. Kołodziejski, *Nokaut*

the "ski gang" case; Stefania Biegun, a cross-country skier who had represented Poland three times in the Olympics, was found guilty.[1073]

The transfer of hard currency and gold by diplomatic routes was also thriving. In 1962 it turned out that Ministry of Foreign Affairs couriers and employees of Department I (Intelligence) of the Ministry of Internal Affairs, by taking advantage of the diplomatic bag, had spirited out of Poland at least 160 000 dollars and brought back, also via diplomatic mail, 4 000 twenty-dollar gold coins, gold bars and other valuables. "Our employees," the Ministry of Internal Affairs commented, "and those of the Ministry of Foreign Affairs' admit their guilt. They blame the climate prevailing at the MFA. They add that almost all MFA employees who travel abroad and/or are stationed abroad have been involved in illegal trade, even those who occupy top positions in Poland and abroad."[1074] Foreign diplomats were not far behind. From the late 1940s until the late 1980s, there were persistent reports about the mass-scale involvement of foreign diplomats in the trading of hard currency and gold. There was no particular pattern – all employees of foreign embassies were implicated, Italian as much as Iranian, Finnish as much as Brazilian or Mexican.[1075]

Until the late 1980s, the foreign agencies covered a significant part of their costs by selling their currencies on the black market. Every so often, especially when hard currency was in short supply, the issue would appear on the radar of the Polish authorities. In the late 1970s, foreign embassies and Polish branches of foreign companies complained that the legally exchanged currencies did not cover the wages of even their Polish employees. And thus the Warsaw black market received annually no fewer than 5 million dollars.[1076] At the same time, diplomats residing in Warsaw made full use of their diplomatic immunity and exemption from border controls by using their privileges for their own black market operations. These were the rule rather than the exception, and the very scale of the trade makes it noteworthy. Conchita Partillo, employed at the Mexican embassy during her posting in Warsaw "personally and with the help of

---

brydżowy, PiŻ, 1973, no. 17; J. Kołodziejski, *Przemytnicy i kibice*, PiŻ, 1973, no. 34; K. Jagiełło, *Wszystkiego za mało*, "Literatura" 1973, no 40.

1073 Stefania Biegun was found guilty of smuggling 25 kg of gold in bars, more than 300 gold coins, 4 kg of jewelry, 47 kg of silver, and approximately 53 000 dollars; TL, no. 100/April 11, 1973; ŻW, April 12, 1973.

1074 AIPN, MSW II, 97, fol. 1.

1075 AIPN, MSW II, 4369, fol. 120–121; *ibid.*, 4370, fol. 89.

1076 AAN, KC PZPR, XIA/511, fol. 9–10.

other employees" brought to Warsaw 165 kg in gold bars and 2.4 kg in gold ruble coins.[1077] In 1949, a Polish employee at the Brazilian embassy offered to act as a go-between in selling hard currency on the black market. Soon this local business turned into a fully blown international enterprise that involved a network of diplomatic outposts and which no longer required any Polish middlemen. Brazilian diplomats "brought [to Poland] large quantities of gold, sold it for dollars, then smuggled the dollars out to use them to buy gold."[1078]

It was not only diplomats who shaped the cosmopolitan image of the Polish black market in gold. Rank-and-file citizens from the East and the West were willing to take the risk, acutely aware of the potentially handsome profits. Danes found it worthwhile to smuggle into Poland the gold that had been stolen at Copenhagen's Kastrup airport between 1971 and 1972.[1079] Between 1968 and 1970, a representative of the French branch of General Electric, one Jean Teophile Girardot, brought to Poland approximately 35 kg of gold bars and seven thousand gold 10-ruble coins. He smuggled out of Poland 170 000 dollars.[1080] The citizens of Yugoslavia became very adept at channeling gold to Poland. Czechs, Slovaks, and Hungarians followed suit. Budapest's Keleti railroad station was considered an important European center of illicit gold and hard currency trading. "This is where the European routes cross. Organized groups of dealers work there. Foreigners coming to Hungary from Yugoslavia and Italy exchange gold products for hard currency. Others pay hard currency for gold. Yet others exchange Soviet Bloc currencies for forints."[1081]

We touch here upon the geographic aspect of communist Poland's "gold rush". Italy and the Soviet Union were the traditional sources of gold jewelry. Gold coins and bars were usually bought in Hamburg or Amsterdam, if to be transported by sea, and Vienna or West Berlin, if destined as overland contraband. In all those cities there were companies mostly run by Jewish refugees from Poland (a fact emphasized in Polish police reports in the 1960s) that specialized in supplying goods sought after on the Polish market, in particular – gold. There were

1077 APW, KWar. PZPR, 30/VII–43, vol. 49, fol. 68–69.

1078 B. Seidler, *Krach wyznawców Midasa*, "Życie Literackie" February 4, 1976.

1079 B. Kołodziejski, *"Złote ptaki" z Kopenhagi*, "Dziennik Łódzki" February 28, 1973; B. Kołodziejski, *Tragarz z lotniska Kastrup*, "Kurier Szczeciński" March 21, 1973.

1080 M. Bekajło, *Doigrałeś się amatorze*, "Życie Literackie" 1971, no. 23; APW, KWar. PZPR, 30/VII–43, vol. 49, fol. 68–69.

1081 K. Świątecka, *Waluciarze*, "Perspektywy" 1977, no. 49.

rumors that a significant number of gold $20 coins were manufactured locally with a reduced content of the precious metal.[1082]

Travelers were always on the lookout for new, effective methods of smuggling but also for new markets, where they could profitably sell Polish products, often not very attractive by international standards, in order to spend the proceeds on buying gold. In the 1970s Poles zeroed in on Egypt, Turkey and the Middle East. "Those countries," a journalist of the Main Customs Office magazine wrote in 1974, "eager to vacuum up all kinds of goods, are the focus of attention for many Polish tourists. The customs clearance of almost every Orbis group traveling there begins to resemble an Eastern bazaar even before leaving Warsaw International Airport. During the customs inspection, the counters quickly pile up with sewing machines, tape recorders, crystal vases, glass products, irons, fans, coil heaters, paintbrushes, beauty products and many other goods. Every tourist has one main goal – to bring as much gold back home as possible. For many of them this end justifies the means even though they risk losing all their undocumented hard currency. Citizens of Middle Eastern countries behave in a similar fashion. They not only try to smuggle valuable goods out of Poland but have recently also been striking deals with our citizens who give them dollars in advance to buy particular articles."[1083]

For commercially gifted and inventive individuals, the world was their oyster. By the late 1970s, Poles had discovered that in Cuba, gold jewelry, and American and Mexican coins – bought, naturally, on the black market – were relatively cheap.[1084] Importantly, Poland was often not the final destination but simply a transit point between the Soviet Union and the West. Groups of Polish smugglers, at times aided by trading partners in Austria and West Germany, masterminded the logistics – spiriting away to the East tsarist 5- and 10-ruble pieces, the favorite store of value for Soviet hoarders. Dollar bills and platinum – much cheaper in the Soviet Union – kept arriving in Poland, to be transferred to France, Austria, or Germany. The operation required substantial capital and in-depth preparation but merited the effort. Certainly, all the organized groups that found themselves facing the Polish justice system at the turn of the 1950s and 1960s were charged

1082 J. Tetter, *Wolność, złoto i hazard*, "Tygodnik Morski" 1967, no. 19. In the mid-1960s the price of an American 20-dollar gold coin in Swiss banks oscillated between 42 and 44 dollars, while in Poland the going rate was 54 dollars. The profit of 25% was a given; AIPN, MSW II, 4369, fol. 120.

1083 J. Kulak, *O przemycie w Urzędzie Celnym Port Lotniczy w Warszawie – uwag kilka*, WC, 1974, no. 15, p. 12.

1084 AAN, KC PZPR, WO, 541, fol. 50–52.

with smuggling thousands of gold coins, kilograms of platinum and tens of thousands of dollars in cash.[1085]

It was not, however, the big boss of the smuggling gang who would remain in the collective memory as a symbol of the hard currency black market but rather the nameless money changers – without them this whole enterprise could not have existed.

8.3.3 Money Changers: A Portrait Study

"In the mid-1950s," Jan Nieporowski wrote in 1988, "the rivulets of dollars seeping through the concrete barriers put up by bureaucrats converged into a single, rapidly flowing river, full of whirlpools frothing with scum but worth millions. It was a strange river, partly running on the surface but with stretches flowing underground, one shore somewhat regulated and the other still wild. Decision makers, policemen, and bankers were bustling all along its course. But the most important were the indestructible money changers."[1086]

The term "cinkciarz" is not new; it came into mainstream Polish usage in the 1960s, when Polish currency dealers endeavored to accost in broken English the growing numbers of visitors arriving in Poland from the West with offers to buy and sell dollars, pounds, and marks. The opening gambit in English did not usually live up to its promise; "change money" were usually the only two English words the dealers knew.[1087] The phrase "change money" was initially polonized as the onomatopoeic *cinksiarz* or *cynkciarz*[1088] and by the early 1970s had evolved into the current form *cinkciarz*. Regardless of the name, for half a century these one-man, peripatetic banks were a fixture in the social, economic, and cultural landscape of Polish cities.[1089] To sketch a collective portrait of this underground

1085 Kurier Polski", no 260/November 3, 1959; *ibid.*, no. 156/July 2/3, 1960; *ibid.*, no. 79/ April 3, 1962; AAN, KC PZPR, WA, 275, fol. 35.

1086 J. Nieporowski, *Raj dla cinkciarzy*, "Tygodnik Kulturalny", no. 14/April 3, 1988.

1087 By 1957, the term had appeared in a Gdynia Security Service report, AIPN Gd. 0046/158/2, fol. 170.

1088 T. Kur, *Gorzki smak miodu*, PiŻ, 1968, no. 7; M. Brzeszczot, *Konie, koniki i białe kołnierzyki*, PiŻ, 1971, no. 10.

1089 This was mostly an urban phenomenon; its presence in resort towns such as Zakopane and Sopot was the exception rather than the rule. According to police estimates from 1985, of the 3 939 persons suspected of dealing in hard currency, 89.8% (3 537) lived in cities; of which 40% (1 471) – in larger cities with at least 200 000 inhabitants; AIPN, KG MO, 35/554. In Zakopane, in early 1970s, there were approximately 180 local black-market currency dealers and 250 from other regions of the country, while

contingent is more difficult than may appear at first glance. The rules of the black market game were the reverse of those in the theatre – the more important the actor, the more he kept to the back of the stage, with the bit-part actors hogging the limelight.

None of this of course meant that the walk-ons and extras were any the less interesting. After the Second World War, which effectively tore down the old social barriers and conventions, the moneychangers became a colorful and diverse group. Alceo Valcini, who in 1945 and 1946 resided in the Hotel Polonia – at the time Warsaw's most prestigious hotel and home to diplomatic missions, in spite of being located in the midst of the post-war black market bustle, reminisced that on the black market one could meet "an intellectual, a teacher, professionals and young thugs […] ex-students, former servants and common criminals; all those whom war had displaced from regular walks of life and who, with patience and cunning, were making a splendid job of remaining afloat."[1090] Attempts to return to the old ways of life were often wrecked on the rocks of post-war reality. The official wages of workers and the intelligentsia were insufficient to survive on whereas illegal trading guaranteed a much higher standard of living. In the pioneer period immediately after the war the risks were negligible and thus the currency black market was a natural transition for those who had honed their skills during the German occupation but it also quickly attracted new blood.

The majority of these money changers, who plied their trade more or less in the open, were sub-contractors who operated with capital supplied by dealers higher in the black-market hierarchy. They worked on commission and sometimes dealt in significant amounts of money.

As mentioned before their main clients were merchants and craftsmen who invested their profits in gold and hard currency. Private stores were often the clandestine money exchange counters. While trading *bimber* was a natural side line for restaurant and food kiosk owners, jewelers took over the trade in gold

---

in Szczecin there were some 300, and in Krakow – 370; J. Wołoszańska, *Nie tylko przez pryzmat prawa*, ŻW, April 22, 1971; APKr, KW PZPR, 293, Posiedzenie egzekutywy, October 14, 1969, fol. 247.

1090 Cf.: A. Valcini, *Ballo all'hotel"Polonia"*, Edizioni del Moretto, Brescia 1983. In her diaries, Maria Dąbrowska mentions the Kelles-Krauz family, who made a living in Radom by "manufacturing soap and selling UNRRA gifts and hard currencies". "In the morning," Dąbrowska noted on November 12, 1945, "the other Krauz daughter arrived; she sells hard currencies. […] She is the one who wears the trousers in the family and makes the most money." M. Dąbrowska, *Dzienniki powojenne*, vol. 1: *1945–1949*, ed. T. Drewnowski, Warszawa 1997, p. 85.

and hard currency. Jan Łada, the owner of two jewelry stores on Warsaw's most prestigious thoroughfare, Marszałkowska Street, engaged "from 1945 until February 1949 in illegal, large-scale hard currency trading. He networked closely with numerous well-known hard currency dealers, conducting transactions worth on average two to three hundred dollars. He bought foreign currencies from well-known dealers and others who were not hard currency professionals."[1091]

In the first half of the 1950s the money dealers' modus operandi evolved out of necessity. The traditional markets, located in well-known places where the distinctive figures of touts (*koniki*) offered, *sotto voce*, transactions in foreign money and gold, disappeared. Now, the dealers were operating clandestinely but they were easy to find. In mid-1956, an emigrant from Poland reported on Radio Free Europe: "In comparison with the early post-war years, the situation has changed: no longer are there specific areas where one can find money dealers and do business. One does have to know where to look but anyone with their head screwed on straight can still find them."[1092] "Cafés, archways, stores", recalled another visitor from Poland, "served as [the dealers'] meeting places." In the morning, usually at around 11 am, a handful of those with the most authority would gather to coordinate the exchange rate. [...] In Warsaw, the daily rate was set under the clock at the suburban commuter train station (EKD) at Nowogrodzka Street, where "come 11 am, there were always some individuals moving through the crowd and nervously exchanging opinions on the current value of the dollar, only to disappear quickly in different directions."[1093]

The transactions were usually not conducted directly but via a contact "box". This was a third person whom the buyer approached for the goods after paying the amount due. Sometimes it was a woman with a stroller, who, if the need arose, could plausibly explain that a stranger must have planted a roll of bills under her baby's blanket. Sometimes a store was used as the box, since this was a place where this was unlikely to arouse suspicion. Only rarely would deals be struck in private apartments. That was too high-risk for all those involved.[1094] The post-October 1956 political thaw "re-opened the gates to the dealers' paradise. They could once more carry cash about their person and meet in the open."[1095]

1091 AAN, KS, 1303. On other jewelry stores see *ibid.*, 1274, 2646.

1092 HIM, Pressearchiv, P 6211, RFE-Research, Item 87/56, Foreign exchange trade flourished.

1093 *Ibid.*, Item 5594/57, History of the Polish black market in dollars.

1094 *Ibid.*

1095 *Ibid.*

Boom time for the hard currency dealers had arrived, and was to continue for another three decades. It was favored by variable exchange rates, the temporary weakening of the political regime and the easing of the repression, the development of the internal export system and the introduction of PKO coupons, as well as less strict border controls, which meant a greater influx of foreign visitors and more Poles traveling outside of the country. The enduring prosperity shaped in a natural way the image of the black market milieu and influenced the development of its hierarchical structure with its distinct division of tasks and roles, idiosyncratic language, customs, behavior and rituals, and its characteristic methods of operation and defense strategies.[1096]

The big shots stayed in the shadows. The "bankers", "merchants" (in the Warsaw terminology) or "organizers" (as they were called in Krakow) were often big-time businessmen operating with sums of money that, for that era and political system, were truly staggering: thousands of dollars and gold by the kilogram. It was they who coordinated the rules of the black market game and to a large degree controlled its course. "Their working day," a *Życie Warszawy* reporter wrote in 1971, "begins early in the morning with numerous phone calls followed by 'office' time at a café [...]. There, they clinch the deals and deal with their minions – the money changers and touts. They focus on wholesale deals; petty cash is of no interest to them."[1097] The dollars, marks and pounds these black market would-be tycoons bought in bulk were simply the operating capital used in a wide range of foreign trade transactions, such as the import of gold and synthetic precious stones[1098] or consumer articles unavailable in Poland.

Most of the operations were of course unrecorded and their scale could only be estimated from such unreliable and speculative sources as investigation files.

1096 AIPN, 01521/2035, J. Oleś, *Przemyt wartości dewizowych...*, p. 60.

1097 A. Kłodzińska, *Waluciarze*, ŻW, April 10–12, 1971.

1098 Why did the smuggling of synthetic gemstones to Poland take off? From October 1967, the state jeweler Jubiler was permitted to buy and sell second-hand jewelry and watches, fetching a much higher price per weight of precious metals than for minted coins. It made sense to melt down the gold bullion brought to Poland illegally and turn it into pieces of jewelry such as rings – and these often required stones. A four-ducat coin yielded four rings. Even after adding the cost of the synthetic stone and labor, and providing the hallmark, in the early 1970s the profit was as much as 9 000 zloty. A Krugerrand provided enough gold for ten rings, with a potential profit of 12 000 zloty; AIPN, 01521/2035, J. Oleś, *Przemyt wartości dewizowych...*, pp. 51–53. In 1973, the police closed down 37 illegal jewelry manufactories; AIPN, KG MO, 35/289, Biuletyn Instruktażowo-szkoleniowy no. 6, Biuro do Walki z Przestępstwami Gospodarczymi KG MO, Warszawa, February 1974.

The authorities were out to prove the crime was being committed but the usual suspects were determined to frustrate these efforts. Even if we assume that the indictment data were only estimates, they are nevertheless impressive in the context of the economic reality of the time. The five-year turnover of Henryk Płoski, "the prince of Warsaw money dealers" put on trial in 1966, was allegedly some eight million zloty including 54 000 dollars in cash, 62 000 dollars' worth of gold and 5 kg of gold bars.[1099] Wiktor Mętlewicz and Mieczysław Młynarczyk who came before the court in 1976 have already been mentioned.

Among the leading lights of the Warsaw black market were such colorful figures as Andrzej Rzeszotarski aka "Count Lolo" or "Uncle", who was an engineer by profession and a *bon vivant* by inclination; rumor had it that he was in cahoots with those in the high echelons of power.[1100] A typical black-market "banker" posed as a Mr. Average and tried to keep a low profile so as not to attract the attention of the authorities. Tomasz Szczypułkowski, arrested in 1973 and sentenced in 1976 to 12 years in prison, worked as a teacher in a secondary technical school and his wife was an usher. Bolesław Krasucki, a waiter also on trial at the same time (who received a six year sentence), between 1960 and 1973 handled 389 kg of gold, 1 850 $20 coins, 820 5-ruble, and 410 10-ruble coins, and 100 Austrian ducats, together valued at 57 000 dollars.[1101] Piotr Ambroziewicz commented in 1976: "It is ludicrous to attempt to depict the score-settling between Polish black-market currency marketeers as some kind of professional gun-slinging gangsters in action. Rubout is a noisy business that stinks to high heaven and this is a business that is very hush-hush."[1102]

These "bankers" managed both the rank-and-file traders who worked on the streets and the middlemen, the "studs" (*ogiery*) and "hacks" (*szkapy*) buying hard currency both from regular suppliers – who had access to foreigners through prostitutes, cabdrivers, waiters, or hotel doormen – and from random sellers. If the average tout (*konik*) was usually a small-time dealer, the "stud" was a semi-wholesaler who operated with much larger sums of money.[1103]

1099 *Książę warszawskich waluciarzy przyznaje się do winy*, "Kurier Polski", no. 208/ September 3–4, 1966.

1100 AIPN, MSW II, 4370, fol. 222–224. On Rzeszotarski see J. Karaszkiewicz, *Słodkie lata*, "Gazeta Wyborcza" May 15, 1998; J. Głowacki, *Z głowy*, Warszawa 2004, pp. 29–31.

1101 "Dziennik Polski" (London), no 151/August 12, 1976; P. Ambroziewicz, *Historia wzlotu i upadku Bolka-kelnera*, PiŻ, December 26, 1976.

1102 P. Ambroziewicz, *Historia wzlotu i upadku Bolka-kelnera*, PiŻ, December 26, 1976.

1103 HIM, Pressearchiv, P 6211, RFE-Research, Item 2794/60, Illegal currency transactions flourished in Poland.

The low-ranking money changers could be seen on city streets, in ports, in hotels, restaurants, train stations, on international trains, outside of banks and Pewex stores. Some became dealers by chance; others were "pros", able to size up their clients at a glance, browbeat them into accepting the price offered and clinch the deal there and then. Warsaw currency dealers were not very different to those in Krakow, Poznań or Gdańsk; they could all tell straight away who was likely to have hard currency or dollar coupons to sell. They only offered 80 zloty to a dollar and upwards – the going rate at the turn of the 1950s and 1960s – to clued-up city dwellers; the out-of-towners and country bumpkins would at best get half that.[1104]

In the money changer and client relationship there quickly developed a code of behavior that both sides easily got the hang of. "The sale is the most interesting part," Radio Free Europe commented, presenting scenes from the Warsaw black market of 1950/1960, "Our interviewee accosted a tout and asked about 'paper'. It is a bad idea to ask for dollars – it would scare the dealer away or else make him think that he was dealing with a greenhorn and up the price. If his client is fluent in black market vernacular, the money changer concludes that his client is a 'badass' who won't be easily bamboozled. The client settled for 99 zloty a dollar and was then told to go to a nearby café [...] and wait. As a security precaution, the dealer never carries hard currency. Meanwhile a 'tout' or a 'bitch' [a woman brought along to provide a cover] runs to the 'banker' to buy the required cash, paying a price that reflects for how much the 'hack' had sold the currency to the 'uncle' beforehand, which was more or less three to four points below 99 zloty (one point equaling one zloty), so that the 'touts' can make some money too. The 'tout' accompanied by the bitch' can then deliver the dollars without raising suspicion. The transaction is conducted in secret."[1105]

This author has no wish to idealize the dealers. The money changers rarely focused exclusively on money deals; they would never say no to any profitable business coming their way.[1106] Some would not shy away from cheating

1104 Sometimes the transactions were very advantageous. From a member of the Glen Miller Orchestra visiting the Polish capital , a Warsaw tout managed to buy a sizeable number of dollar bills at 27 zloty each – a rate that was three zloty more than the official rate at the bank; HIM, Pressearchiv, P 612, Item 5169/57, Dollars brought from USSR. The black market rate for gold.

1105 HIM, Pressarchiv, P 6211, RFE-Research, Item 2794/60, Illegal currency transactions flourished in Poland.

1106 See: P. Wojasz, *Niebieski ptak. Absurdy peerelowskiej rzeczywistości we wspomnieniach byłego cinkciarza,* Chorzów 2011.

by slipping in fake money in the last phase of the transaction (in the 1980s in Warsaw, Aleksander Gawronik – who went on to become a controversial businessman and politician, serving as senator during 1993–1997 – was cheated out of 100 000 dollars in one fell swoop[1107]) or by using sophisticated social engineering tricks. In the early 1970s, after a large transaction, one of the Warsaw money changers had a habit of flashing a court officer's ID and announcing: "I am arresting you for trading hard currency". Begging for mercy, the customer would usually be only too content to be allowed to walk away without – needless to say – his money. Another *cinkciarz*, in an effort to get rid of 5 000 counterfeit dollars that someone had conned him into accepting earlier, ordered a bishop's cassock from a tailor and, thus attired, passed himself off as a bona fide trustworthy trader. At other times he would gain credibility by dressing as a railroad worker or miner.[1108]

Karol Ferster, I buy dollars, *circa 1970. Photo: Warsaw Museum of Caricature, sign. 1247.*

1107 P. Mączyński, L. Kostrzewski, *Przed mafią pistolet by mnie nie ochronił. Wywiad z Gawronikiem*, "Gazeta Wyborcza" June 29, 2009. On ways of cheating clients see: AIPN, 01521/876, vol. 1, Bogdan Chybowski, *Nielegalny skup dewiz (Taktyka ujawniania zwalczania)*. Departament Szkolenia i Doskonalenia Zawodowego MSW, Warszawa 1973, pp. 86–89.

1108 "Express Wieczorny" March 11, 1973.

It is difficult to establish today what form, if any, "corporate inspections" took in the money dealers' world. Until the 1970s, while the money changer community was still small and compact, its members shared a certain *esprit de corps* and closed ranks against those who blatantly broke the accepted rules of the game. Certainly, one reason for radical exclusion and a ban on carrying on with the trade – or, in extreme cases, physical "elimination" of the undesirable individual – would be close contacts with the police and Security Service.[1109]

The money changers continuously developed and perfected this internal defense mechanism. It was very effective and uniformed police forces usually made no attempt to confront the hard currency underground. In the early 1970s, a police analyst observed that the money changers "do not acknowledge the presence of police. They keep a safe distance. When ordered to halt, they don't; if chased, they run. Once the police are gone, they go back to their trading spot. The only police officers to command their respect are the *dewizówka* [hard currency department]."[1110] But even for those specialized police units, the dealers were a tough nut to crack. Despite the fact that the police were well aware of the identity of the "bankers" and "touts" working the streets, arrests, not to mention court sentences, rarely followed. The law enforcement and justice system were often helpless in the face of hard currency black market defense strategies such as multi-level networking, the rule of not carrying money about one's person, money-laundering (usually via a bank account in a bank conveniently close to the transactions taking place) but above all extreme vigilance. The dealers were at all times on high alert, ending a transaction abruptly at the slightest whiff of suspicion. Often, the money changers were as *au fait* as any law graduate with the intricacies of the law, especially those pertinent to hard currency policies. "Unless they catch someone red-handed, they can't do much," a currency dealer from Gdańsk confided to a journalist in the early 1970s. "And catching them is not that easy. *Dewizówka* guys [the police unit designated for dealing with hard currency offences – JK) know almost all the dealers and often organize raids in the places where we work but we have our ways. We often have the doorman on our side and when something is up, he'll tip us off. At that point anyone who has any compromising evidence will quickly hide it in an abandoned coat hanging for that purpose in the cloakroom and all is cool. At other times, we just pass the

---

1109 K.W. Dębicki, *Komu zielone, komu…*, "Tygodnik Morski" 1973, no 38; *Na nasze konto. Rozmowa Wojciecha Koczanowicza z naczelnikiem wydziału w Biurze do Walki z Przestępstwami Gospodarczymi KG MO mjr. Janem Stępniem*, "Sztandar Młodych" October 5, 1979.

1110 AIPN, 01521/876, vol. 1, B. Chybowski, *Nielegalny skup dewiz…*, p. 80.

dollars or pounds on to friends of ours sitting at the next table, who are not in the *dewizówka*'s black books."[1111] In Krakow, pretzel sellers and store managers cooperated with the money dealers.[1112]

No wonder that the repeated operations undertaken every so often against the hard currency black marketeers brought meager results. Between April 4, 1961 and April 30, 1962, although 253 dealers were apprehended in the Warsaw hard-currency hub around Jasna, Mazowiecka, Traugutta, and Świętokrzyska streets, only 20 investigations were embarked on, with just 13 people arrested. The low effectiveness of the police raids is apparent from the existence of repeat offenders: 15 people were arrested five times, eight people seven times, and one record breaker was arrested 13 times.[1113] Between 1965 and 1969, in the Krakow voivodship including Zakopane, the police uncovered 2 781 hard currency offences, 52% of which had been committed at border crossings. However, only 51 cases against 89 individuals in total ended up in the county courts, including 22 cases (against 53 people) in Krakow itself. In 43 cases those found guilty received sentences of between two months to three years of prison and fines of 1 000 – 200 000 zloty.[1114] Occasionally, the authorities tried to implement non-standard solutions. In the early 1970s in Łódź, when dealing with the *cinkciarze*, the police resorted to harassment and intimidation, with arrests on charges of disorderly conduct and fines running into a few thousand zloty. Whenever the police were able to make an arrest at the time of an actual transaction taking place, the case was passed on to the Finance Department where the sanctions applied were much more severe.[1115]

Police and media reports made no secret of the fact that operations against money dealers were limited in their effectiveness; the culprits would pay the fines and serve prison sentences, only to return to their previous occupation with new ideas on improving the defense strategies, sometimes acquired in prison. It had been reported in Warsaw in 1962 that the "profiteers used very specific conspiracy techniques such as ways of alerting one another or

---

1111 K.W. Dębicki, *Komu zielone, komu…*, "Tygodnik Morski" 1973, no. 38. A common ploy was to use a "pocket" – which was a "briefcase stored by a friendly cloakroom or restroom attendant". When the need arose, this supply of emergency cash could be accessed rapidly; the main rule was that a dealer should carry no more than a minimum amount of cash; R. Czerniawski, *Gra w zielone*, PiŻ, 1983, no. 15.

1112 "Gazeta Krakowska", no. 26/January 31, 1973.

1113 APW, KWar. PZPR, 30/VII–43, vol. 1, fol. 306–307.

1114 APKr, KW PZPR, 293, fol. 247.

1115 *Nie ma miejsca dla dolarowych "koników" przed łódzkim PeKaO*, "Express Wieczorny", no. 147/June 24, 1970.

organizing counter-espionage."[1116] Following the anti-money dealer operations in the fall of 1971, the media reported: "The *cinkciarze* have turned their cars into taxis. They have now more opportunities to carry out hard currency exchange. Restaurant staff are surprised that the police have not revoked the cab permits, aware as they have been of the money changers' questionable past."[1117]

The money changers' attachment to their occupation is easy to explain. Nowhere else could they make financial gains of a similar order having, as they often did, little education and no qualifications. According to police estimates, in a month a professional money changer bought approximately 600 dollars' worth of hard currency and with that outlay made between 15 and 20 000 zloty – almost ten times more than the average wage! If he was a shrewd operator and had a smattering of foreign languages, he could expect to achieve as much as 150 000 zloty a month – a no-brainer.[1118] Best of all, the hours were flexible; there was the risk of going to prison, true… but this went with the territory and had been taken into account. No wonder that when in 1970 the authorities yet again attempted to encourage "social parasites" (as the official classification had it) – of which there were estimated to be some 12 000 in Warsaw alone – to consider taking up lawful employment, the interviews with these candidates for self-reform followed the familiar, less-than-promising pattern: "P.M., hard currency and foreign pharmaceuticals dealer; prior convictions. When asked by the Commission panel in what capacity and where he would like to work, he replied: 'I can be a counter-intelligence agent in space'". "J.T., a well-known hard currency dealer, criminal record includes numerous prior arrests. He told the Commission that he would be willing to take up any job with wages of at least 6 000 a month [an optimistic, or more likely cheeky target, bearing in mind that the average monthly wage at the time was 2 235 zloty! – comment by JK]. He has primary education and no skills."[1119]

Much as the authorities might sanction or attempt to re-socialize black market currency dealers, their attitude to this group remained ambiguous. It is difficult to establish whether officials also used the black market to buy and sell hard currency, whether institutionally or in their personal capacity, as they had in the 1940s and 1950s. In October 1969, the Chief of the Office for Combating Economic Crime Janusz Neldner, – interestingly – felt obliged to emphasize, "We are not purchasing any hard currency and gold for the Ministry of Internal

1116 APW, KWar. PZPR, 30/VII–43, vol. 1, fol. 306–307.
1117 AIPN, 0296/114, vol. 1, fol. 2, 9.
1118 AIPN, 01521/876, vol. 1, B. Chybowski, *Nielegalny skup dewiz…*, p. 76.
1119 APW, KWar. PZPR, 30/XVIII–7, vol. 1, fol. 400–405.

Affairs, nor for the Ministry of Finance, or the NPB."[1120] We have no data to either confirm or negate the veracity of this statement. Certainly, functionaries at the Ministry of Internal Affairs had plenty of opportunity to make such purchases on their own account during the Zalew affair or as part of secret operations (such as Operation Iron).[1121] One can assume, however, that – aware of their own ineffectiveness in fighting the money changers, yet recognizing the pro-state aspect of the dealers' activities – the authorities resigned themselves to mere surveillance. By virtue of their positioning, *cinkciarze* were a good source of information on foreigners who were of interest to intelligence, as well as on private entrepreneurs and, in the 1980s, also on the democratic opposition – supported financially by foreign institutions – whose members sold some of their foreign currency on the black market.

It is impossible to come to any definitive conclusion on the effectiveness of government surveillance. In 1985, the authorities boasted that they had attracted 5.7% more collaborators than in the previous year but at the same time complained about the rigid protocols limiting the range of their operations.[1122] However, in the mid-1980s it was intelligence that provided more than 88% of the "grounds for initiating an investigation". Anonymous letters and citizens' reports were responsible for only 2.8%.[1123] The reason for such low civic participation in squealing on dealers was simple: Polish society was de facto dual-currency and no amount of legislation could alter the status quo or diminish mass participation in currency exchange transactions. By the 1970s, the tight-knit group of money changers with loyalty-based gang mentality was a thing of the past. Previously, cabdrivers, waiters, and bartenders had commonly assisted in illicit hard currency operations, but now the circle of occasional participants encompassed new groups such as students or even school pupils.[1124] The development of tourism encouraged people in all walks of life to engage independently in hard currency operations.

1120 APKr, KW PZPR, 293, fol. 217.

1121 K. Madej, *Wszyscy byli przemytnikami…*; J. Morawski, *Złota afera*, Warszawa 2007; *Raport z działalności Komisji powołanej dla wyjaśnienia charakteru operacji kryptonim "Żelazo"*, ed. P. Gontarczyk, "Glaukopis" 7–8, 2007, pp. 233–271.

1122 AIPN, KG MO, 35/554, fol. 45–47. There is no doubt that former police and security service employees were part of the group. In 1969 in Krakow there were at least five among local money dealers ("which does hinder surveillance"), and four ex-functionaries "broke off criminal involvement with touts after preventive/repressive actions had been directed against them"; APKr, KW PZPR, 293, fol. 250.

1123 AIPN, KG MO, 35/554.

1124 *Na nasze konto…*, "Sztandar Młodych" October 5, 1979.

By the 1980s, all these new social players who had joined the hard currency game caused the money changers to complain about the "bunglers" spoiling their business. A bartender in one of the most elegant hotels in Warsaw told me at that time that he was one of the last links in the hard currency chain. A hard currency foreigner was usually first offered the "change money" service when still onboard the airplane or at the border and by the time he found himself at the hotel bar he would have been similarly accosted at the airport, train station, in a cab, at the hotel's reception, and by the hotel porter. In June 1985, Warsaw police were not surprised to arrest an 80-year old who was exchanging money and were not unduly surprised to find on this unlikely culprit approximately 14 000 dollars, 5 000 schillings, 500 West German marks, more than two million zloty, several dozen gold coins and two gold bars.[1125]

The money changers' milieu continued to evolve, as attested by a 1985 police report on their social composition. Police had taken a close interest in 3 939 individuals who were engaged in illicit currency exchange. The vast majority, 2 726, were in permanent employment (the question remains whether this was their genuine status quo or merely a fake stamp in their ID document), 515 (13.1%) were retired or receiving welfare benefits, slightly fewer than 14% did not work at all and were not at school or in any other educational institution. The stereotypical image of a *cinkciarz*, prevalent in the post-1989 Polish cinema, was of a flashy young man in a skimpy jacket. This image is misleading. Although police data did not record the sartorial habits of the dealers, dwelling instead on the social structure of the group, these did not correspond with the swanky, youthful perp profile. Over 27% (1 062) of the sample were women, 20% (792) were over 50 years old, just over half (50.4%/, 1 992) were between 40 and 49 and only 17% (675) were in the 25 to 29 age group.[1126]

1125 AAN, URM, 32/172, fol. 49.

1126 AIPN, KG MO, 35/554, k. 45–47. We do not have reliable data allowing comparisons with earlier periods. Some insight was provided by a 1969 survey of 78 Krakow touts, their number unchanged since the late 1950s. Of these, 74.3% – including 10 retirees – had no jobs; the others worked periodically. A majority (47) had completed secondary education, with or without a certificate, and another 27 – primary education, with or without a certificate; there are no gender data, the inference being that the touts were all males. APKr, KW PZPR, 293, fol. 249–250. According to the handbook for MSW and MO functionaries, published in 1973, money dealers were usually "in their prime, between 19 and 40, with primary or incomplete secondary education. Approximately 60% do not work, others perform odd jobs"; AIPN, 01521/876, vol. 1, B. Chybowski, *Nielegalny skup dewiz…*, pp. 77–78.

Illegal currency dealers in front of the NBP at Powstańców Warszawy Square in Warsaw, February 1990. Photo: Krzysztof Wójcik, FORUM Polish Photography Agency.

Although the late 1980s saw a spectacular boom for money changers working on the street, it was also their swan song. Their epic hard currency journey had continued successfully after Polish banks began to trade in the PKO coupons in 1987. However, the introduction of internal convertibility of the zloty in March 1989 was the beginning of the end; it marked the arrival of licensed money exchange counters, known as *kantors*. Some dealers perceived this development as a business opportunity and legalized their operations, moving from the street to behind the till in a *kantor*. Others, perhaps the majority, decided to continue their old practices, reasoning correctly that the legal *kantor* currency dealer would have to pay taxes. "And I won't," a Warsaw money dealer told a journalist, "They will have to deal with bureaucracy and I won't. They will have the daily rate and I will have my hourly rate, they will have an hourly rate and I will do it by the minute. Walkie-talkies will get more expensive."[1127] Although in the first few days after the opening of the first-ever money exchange counter, the newspapers

1127 *Nie pójdą na zieloną trawkę*, PiŻ, 1989, no. 2.

confidently forecast the "end of the fair-weather season for the money dealers[1128]", for a while they still managed to stay on top of their game: on April 5, 1989 they offered to buy dollars from the public at a much higher rate than the banks; this move effectively paralyzed the sale of US dollars in three Warsaw branches of the PKO bank.[1129]

In the second half of 1989, the rapidly growing inflation which soon billowed into hyper-inflation kept all those involved in currency exchange, whether legal or not, extremely busy. Those who had excess zlotys immediately exchanged them into hard currency which, unlike the national currency, kept its value, and spent it gradually as required to buy back zlotys needed for day-to-day expenses. In the new free market economy with a freshly deregulated banking sector that allowed public and private ownership, the money changers may have been quickly becoming a relic but they were refusing to leave the stage in a quick and orderly manner. "One can always bump into them," a journalist from *Gazeta Bankowa* wrote as late as 1993, "usually in the same spots where they have been standing for years, in front of a bank or hanging around in the marketplace. They are natural competition for the money exchange counters. They allegedly offer better deals, '*I will sell cheaper, will pay better*', but those who engage in a transaction with these characters often risk incurring a serious loss, since they are hardly model citizens. The money dealers do offer a better – but only slightly so – deal than that to be had at the official counters. Illegal dealers don't have any overheads such as rent, or wages. Many of their clients, who for years had conducted transactions on the street, prefer to avoid coming under the spotlight of the brightly lit places. Another group of clients are visitors from the East who cannot legally take advantage of money exchange counters."[1130] Gradually *cinkciarze* were losing their client base; now, for the majority of customers a minimal difference in the price offered or paid was less important than the comfort and safety of the transaction to be conducted. And so the familiar *cinkciarze* disappeared from the streets. They stayed in the collective memory and became as much a notorious icon of communist Poland as an empty butcher's store. The first online exchange portal opened in 2012 under the name *cinkciarz.pl.*

1128 Kurier Polski" March 21, 1989.

1129 *Czarny wtorek na walutowym rynku*, ŻW, no. 260/November 8, 1989; see: M. Smogorzewski, *Nim bank się ocknie – cinkciarz zarobi*, "Gazeta Wyborcza" July 4, 1989.

1130 A. Zeibel, *Zielone okienka*, "Gazeta Bankowa" December 10, 1993.

9. The Tourist Trade in Communist Poland[1131]

9.1 Trading Tourism:[1132] Introduction

"Friends of mine often go on trips abroad by car. I asked them once where they'd been that summer. 'Bulgaria,' the husband said. 'No, Romania,' the wife put him straight. He was not at all sure where he had been. What he *was* sure about was how the prices in that country related to prices in Poland. He boasted that he had never spent a cent on a trip abroad."[1133]

This anecdote illustrates very well one of the most enduring and ubiquitous black market phenomena. The tourist trade – which at a stroke broke the state monopoly of foreign trade, and made a mockery of customs, tax, and hard currency regulations – reached a mass scale in the second half of the 1950s when the borders became less impermeable and lasted, albeit only by a few years, beyond the fall of the communist system in 1989. This phenomenon was more complex than it seemed: its range and scale were broader, the group of participants – larger, and the motivation behind their involvement diverse.[1134]

Shortages were a permanent feature of the economies of the Soviet Bloc; some argued that they were a systemic flaw rather than merely a matter of malfunctioning. They were painful for the citizens, who developed endemic accommodative and defensive strategies, similar in all the countries behind the Iron Curtain. Local strategies alone were not sufficient to allow consumers to fulfil all their needs, which by the early 1950s had expanded beyond basic necessities. The end

---

1131 See: Jerzy Kochanowski, *Pionierzy wolnego rynku? Nieoficjalna wymiana handlowa między społeczeństwami krajów socjalistycznych. Lata 70. i 80.*, in: *Bocznymi drogami. Nieoficjalne kontakty społeczeństw socjalistycznych 1956–1989*, eds. W. Borodziej, J. Kochanowski, Warszawa 2010, pp. 109–144; Jerzy Kochanowski, *"Jesteśmy za biedni, aby urlop spędzać w kraju". Masowa turystyka i nielegalny handel w latach sześćdziesiątych XX w. Perspektywa polska*, "Roczniki Dziejów Społecznych i Gospodarczych" 68, 2008, pp. 125–150.

1132 W. Dymitrów introduced the term in "Życie Warszawy" in 1968.

1133 *Kapiści*, "Dziennik Ludowy", no. 244/October 12, 1962.

1134 It should be emphasized that by the early 1960s, tourist commerce had become an object of interest for Polish sociologists; see: J. Węgleński, *Wyniki badań nad handlem uprawianym przez uczestników wycieczek zagranicznych*, Ośrodek Badania Opinii Publicznej, Warszawa 1964; *Społeczeństwo polskie w badaniach ankietowych Ośrodka Badania Opinii Publicznej przy Polskim Radio i TV: lata 1958–1964. Przegląd zebranych materiałów*, ed. A. Siciński, Warszawa 1966.

of Stalinism accelerated the modernization process in the Soviet Bloc countries; citizens were now eager to make up for lost time and yearned to see the outside world, where they soon discovered – and came to crave – an astounding choice of consumer goods that they had never seen before, in the process developing aspirational needs for products beyond the drab, grey and often poor-quality basics that socialism had on offer.[1135] Anything at all, as long as it was foreign, and this showed at a glance, became all the rage, bestowing on its proud new owner kudos, sex appeal and brownie points in the social pecking order.[1136] Copycat mechanisms were uncritically and slavishly obeyed: every male craved Levi's jeans, every woman – Max Factor cosmetics or a fashionable Italian synthetic-fiber raincoat. This was before the Chinese mass production of fake designer labels and so every product purchased was authentic. What to a Westerner represented a few hours' wages, to a Pole was often a matter of weeks or months of squirreling every cent away to acquire the coveted item, worth paying any price for! At least until the late 1980s, colorful chocolate and soap wrapping and "Western" beer bottles were often cherished elements of house decoration, whereas a plastic carrier bag proudly displaying the name of any Western chain store or boutique was an item of envy per se.[1137] This feverish pursuit was the order of the day in the Eastern Bloc, whether in Warsaw, Bucharest, Prague or Moscow, much to the chagrin of the authorities, who frowned on such decadent tastes; the craze for all things Western also highlighted the inadequacies of domestic supply and the

1135 J. Misala, *Nieoficjalna wymiana handlowa obywateli polskich z zagranicą*, Warszawa 1989, p. 4; K. Karcz, *Efekt naśladowania zewnętrznych wzorców konsumpcji jako czynnik utrudniający sterowanie spożyciem indywidualnym*, in: *Narzędzia polityki gospodarczej i społecznej w procesie kształtowania konsumpcji. Ogólnopolska konferencja naukowo-dydaktyczna Katedr i Instytutów Obrotu Towarowego i Usług Uczelni Ekonomicznych, Ustroń, September 1987*, vol. 1, Katowice 1987, pp. 201–205.

1136 In 1958 a visitor from Poland recounted to a member of Radio Free Europe staff: "What do people want in today's Poland? Well, practically anything that comes from the West, especially from the US. It has to be a brand name product, though. Poles are very good at recognizing counterfeit products. Fake American cigarettes, which have no problem selling in Spain and Northern Africa, Parker pens manufactured in Italy […] – in Poland these fakes are exposed within a couple of weeks and people stop buying them"; HIM, Pressearchiv, P6211, RFE-Research, Item 3691/58, Soviet goods smuggled into Poland. On Varsovians aspiring to the Western "new look" see: B. Brzostek, *Za progiem. Codzienność w przestrzeni publicznej Warszawy lat 1955–1970*, Warszawa 2007, pp. 260–277.

1137 L. Chelcea, *The Culture of Shortage during State Socialism. Consumption Practices in a Romanian Village in the 1980s*, "Cultural Studies" 16, 2002, no. 1, p. 35.

quality of its products. Of course, the products that the people wanted had to come from the West so, when in the second part of the 1950s travelling abroad at last became feasible, Poles and other Eastern Bloc citizens were quick to spot its trade potential for improving their everyday life. During the next three decades they systematically modified and perfected strategies of using foreign travel as a means of meeting their own and others' domestic demand.[1138]

The communist authorities, who by the turn of the 1950s and the 1960s had become fully aware of their citizens' expectations, dealt with this pent-up consumer frustration by paying lip-service to providing "citizen satisfaction", while a tourist trip abroad acquired a political significance. However, leaders in Moscow, Warsaw, Prague and East Berlin were not keen to facilitate the desperately hankered-after trips to the West. Only the citizens of Yugoslavia, perceived as a half-way house to the West, enjoyed the freedom of traveling outside of the Iron Curtain[1139] – to the envy of all other citizens in the Soviet Bloc, who had to settle for being able to travel to other Soviet Bloc countries as part of the state-sanctioned "new consumerism". This was a gift with strings attached and opportunities to travel tended to be seasoned with more than a pinch of ideology: "Tourism to other socialist countries has been granted a high social and ideological status, thanks to its significance in the broader humanist sphere. This aspect is particularly relevant in the case of tourist exchange between socialist countries. The emergence of the socialist bloc has created a new, formerly unknown kind of international relations. In conjunction with the political and military alliance and economic integration, there has arisen a wider platform of cooperative realization of ideological and educational tasks resulting from the identical political and ideological objectives of individual communist parties."[1140]

As it turned out, however, as far as tourism was concerned, the apparent coincidence of objectives was illusory. Whether state-owned or co-op, travel agencies were not charities – they strived for profit or at the very least aimed to minimize their losses. From the mid-1960s, in Hungary, Czechoslovakia, Romania, Bulgaria, and other Soviet Bloc states, the authorities were keen to promote growth in incoming tourism from the capitalist states and to develop their own tourism to

1138 See: A. Wessely, *Traveling People, Traveling Objects*, "Cultural Studies" 16, 2002, no. 1, pp. 5–6.

1139 See: P.J. Patterson, *Dangerous Liaisons: Soviet-bloc Tourists and the Yugoslav Good Life in the 1960s and 1970s*, in: *The Business of Tourism: Place, Faith, and History*, ed. Ph. Scranton, J.F. Davidson, Philadelphia 2006, pp. 186–212.

1140 AAN, GKKFiT, 11/67, fol. 3–4.

other countries of the Warsaw Pact.[1141] Local tourists were only granted a very modest allowance of hard or indeed socialist currency to take with them, which inevitably led them to embark on various novel and ingenious methods of making money once they found themselves abroad. Holidays in one's own country were cheaper, but not always satisfactory even when partially funded by the state. For an enterprising Pole, thanks to the ample arbitrage opportunities due to an unbalanced market and the different range of prices and shortages in socialist countries, a much more expensive trip abroad could not only cover the cost of travel but even generate a profit.

9.2 The 1950s and the 1960s: "We Are Too Poor to Vacation in Our Own Country..."

After 1956 Poles increasingly traveled to the West and frequently used their private trips to conduct illicit trade.[1142] However, their westward excursions represented only a fraction of the volume of tourist traffic to the socialist countries, encouraged by ideological factors which also had an impact on bilateral tourist agreements. Although in theory every Pole was entitled to a passport, in practice it was not a foregone conclusion that one would be issued automatically and applicants were scrutinized for possible reasons for refusal. Moreover, after the trip, the passport had again to be surrendered to the authorities and the potential traveler had to reapply for each successive prospective trip abroad, his movements thus easy for the authorities to monitor and keep track of. Since 1959 it had been easier to get a passport for a socialist destination especially when "passport inserts" made traveling to some of these countries much easier. The first bilateral agreement, signed in 1955 with Czechoslovakia, allowed relatively problem-free trips to border zones. With these cheap passes, citizens of Poland and Czechoslovakia could visit the neighboring country twice a year for a maximum of six days and exchange a fixed number of korunas and zloty. Between 1957 and 1958, tourism across Poland's southern border became a mass phenomenon. The

1141 This was also true about Poland, where according to the official data from 1963 the revenue from Western tourism (not including black-market hard currency exchange) exceeded the cost – unlike Polish tourism to socialist states, which had to be subsidized by the Polish state; *Rocznik statystyczny 1970*, Warszawa 1970, p. 491.

1142 See: P. Sowiński, *Wakacje w Polsce Ludowej. Polityka władz i ruch turystyczny (1945–1989)*, Warszawa 2005; P. Sowiński, *Merchand adventures komunizmu. Handlowe podróże Polaków na Zachód w latach 1956–1970*, in: *Od Piłsudskiego do Wałęsy. Studia z dziejów Polski w XX wieku*, ed. K. Persak et al, Warszawa 2008, pp. 291–306.

agreement signed on August 24, 1960 by Poland and Czechoslovakia waived visa requirements for private travel.

In the early 1960s, other countries of the Bloc also embarked on similar tourist swaps. On October 19, 1961, Poland and East Germany signed an agreement to increase tourist flows between the countries, introducing the concept of "holiday traffic", which came into force on January 1, 1963. Despite the fact that East Berlin implemented the new regulations quite strictly, the headcount across the Oder-Neisse border (especially from East Germany to Poland) rose systematically. In July 1964, tourist traffic visa requirements were waived between Hungary and Poland, as a consequence of Hungarian social policy initiated in 1964.[1143] By the mid-1960s travel to Hungary, East Germany, Czechoslovakia, the Soviet Union, Bulgaria, Romania and Yugoslavia had become commonplace for Poles. As had cross-border black-market trade.[1144]

*Table 6. Tourist traffic from and to Poland**

Years	**Tourist trips abroad by Poles (in thousands)**			**Foreign tourists to Poland (in thousands)**		
	Total	Socialist countries	Capitalist countries	Total	Socialist countries	Capitalist countries
1956	256.7	242.7	14.0	78.2	64.1	14.1
1958	163.8	117.5	46.3	123.1	81.2	41.9
1960	216.4	175.0	41.4	184.0	130	53.9
1962	446.5	395.4	51.0	405.3	350.1	55.3
1964	577.3	505.8	71.5	586.9	500.7	86.1
1966	949.0	858.3	90.7	1 280	1 064	215.8
1968	728.1	635.7	92.3	1 712	1 487	225.7

1143 The change was indeed significant. Whereas in 1963, 569 775 Hungarian tourists had gone abroad and 921 021 foreign tourists had arrived in Hungary, in 1964 the numbers were respectively 1 485 712 and 1 799 932; T. Dessewffy, *Speculators and travellers: The Political Construction of the Tourist in the Kàdàr Regime*, "Cultural Studies" 16, 2002, no. 1, pp. 44–62, p. 50.

1144 In 1960, the Soviet Bloc customs service published a magazine in Russian and German ("Socialisticzeskij Tamozennyj Kontrol" / "Sozialistische Zollkontrolle"), devoted in large part to tourist commerce and smuggling.

Years	Tourist trips abroad by Poles (in thousands)			Foreign tourists to Poland (in thousands)		
	Total	Socialist countries	Capitalist countries	Total	Socialist countries	Capitalist countries
1970	871.3	757.2	114.1	1 888	1 610	279.3
1972	10 600	10 391	208.5	8 399	7 964	374.7
1974	8 287	8 007	280	7 893	7 221	672.1
1976	10 512	10 110	402	9 623	8 839	784.0
1978	11 141	10 602	539	10 695	9 712	983.0
1980	6 852	6 157	695	7 080	6 205	875.0
1981	4 282	2 984	1 248	2 172	1 594	578.0
1982	995	678	317	1 404	1 016	388.0
1984	3 289	2 550	739	2 997	2 235	761.9
1986	4 313	3 356	956	3 851	3 105	745.9
1988	6 924	5 259	1 665	6 196	5 092	1 104
1989	19 313	–	–	8 233	6 645	1 588

Source: P. Sowiński. Wakacje w Polsce Ludowej. Polityka władz i ruch turystyczny (1945–1989). Warszawa 2005, pp. 285–288.
**The table shows the number of border crossings, which was not identical to the number of participants in trans-border crossing.*

Whereas at the turn of the 1950s and the 1960s, food consumption in Poland had been more or less on a par with that of other countries, when it came to industrial consumption, an abyss separated Poland not only from the capitalist but also the other socialist countries (especially Czechoslovakia).[1145] "In terms of industrial goods, our market is insatiable. [...] Unfortunately there is a shortage of almost everything in Poland: artificial-fiber sponges, chewing gum, nylon socks, and

1145 V. Holešovský, *Personal Consumption in Czechoslovakia, Hungary and Poland, 1950–1960: A Comparison*, "Slavic Review" 24, 1965, pp. 622–635; M. Rogowiec, B. Tylec, *Kierunki przemian konsumpcji w latach 1960–1973 w wybranych krajach RWPG*, Warszawa 1977.

costume jewelry."[1146] The next decade brought quantitative but not qualitative changes. The only source of higher quality goods was abroad where prices were much lower than in Poland. "Professional" smugglers and sailors supplied wares such as nylon raincoats and watches manufactured in the West, often on a mass scale, since they had capital at their disposal. Tourists delivered the rest.

Alcohol was one of the principal goods smuggled out to the West. It was traded also by tourists on elitist group trips organised by Orbis. Ryszard Winiarski, Tourist Sales, *1962. Photo: Warsaw Museum of Caricature, sign. 6109.*

There are no data to establish whether illegal tourist commerce was the domain of people traveling individually or in organized groups. It is reasonable to surmise that decisive factors were geographic ease of access as well as individual logistical skills and business acumen. For example the mass-scale tourist trade in the Poland-Czechoslovakia border zone was a specialty of group tours organized by workplaces and travel agencies, usually involving day trips based on exchanging the maximum currency quota and targeting the nearest town that had a large number of stores. The results of an opinion poll conducted in 1962 left no doubt that, in the general perception, the main reason for the trips was to make a quick buck and this was bitterly resented by those not involved in the trade: "The numbers of trader group trips to Czechoslovakia need to be cut down. These are day trips that the same individuals go on repeatedly. The same surnames keep

1146 J. Hibner, *Uwaga – przemyt!*, PiŻ, 1957, no. 15.

cropping up on the lists." "Only back-packers traveling on foot should be allowed in the Tatra Mountains. The 'Polish locust' travels by bus for a three-day trip and for the entire three days swarms the stores and engages in backstreet trading. Trips like that are nothing to do with tourism. It is hard to find a Pole in the Tatra Mountains but there are hundreds of them in the local stores. I could not buy a single biro in the border zone because my fellow Poles had bought them all out by the hundred."[1147]

Similarly, Slovaks and Czechs did not need any encouragement to buy Polish cured meat, chocolate, cigarettes and vodka. Another respondent in the poll observed that it was unfair to blame Poles for "teaching Czechoslovak citizens to smuggle and profiteer. I was not the one accosting the hosts with goods for sale but the other way around. Everywhere I went, I was hassled for cigarettes, alcohol, and German watches. Staff in the mountain lodge were just as bad."[1148] Czechoslovaks engaged in trade on the other side of the border, taking advantage of the Polish legislation permitting sales to the state of goods up to the value of 6 000 zloty without having to show any custom receipts. Thanks to this loophole, in 1958 alone stores in Podhale received goods worth 1.2 million zloty.[1149] High-value items changed hands in private. It is difficult to say whether the case of the Prague resident Miroslav Honcu was an isolated one. Starting in 1961, he progressed from buying contraband goods from Poles in the border zone to setting up a full-blown underground Polish-Czechoslovak foreign trade office. Once a fortnight, together with his partner, another Czech, he would illegally cross the border in the Karkonosze Mountains, and smuggle into Poland fake fur and costume jewelry. He subsequently distributed goods all over the country through a network of his Polish friends. In Poland, he stocked up mainly on American cigarettes for the return journey. His luck held until November 1967.[1150]

1147 AAN, GKKFiT, 16/83, Józef Krynicki, Evaluation of polls conducted among conventional zone tourists Poland–Czechoslovakia, (ed. R. Łazarek), January 1963, fol. 203, 204.

1148 *Ibid.*, fol. 165.

1149 E. Orkiszewski, *Turystyka, podróże, lecz nie tylko…*, "Tygodnik Demokratyczny" 1958, no. 31.

1150 WC, 1972, no. 6, pp. 16–19. Czechoslovak citizens' trading contacts extended deep into Poland. At the turn of 1964 and 1965, the Czechoslovak security service asked its Polish equivalent for help in checking up on the Warsaw contacts of a group of "Czech citizens who use the tourist traffic between the CSRS and the PRL to conduct criminal activity, transporting to Poland by train large amounts of counterfeit fur fabric"; AIPN, MSW II, 1913, fol. 110–118.

The chapter on the geography of the black market referred to the tradition of smuggling amongst the highlanders living along Poland's southern border. It is interesting to examine the effect that the expansion of mass travel had on the development of smuggling techniques and strategies. When, in the second half of the 1950s, tourism became a mass phenomenon in Poland, it radically altered local smuggling methods and transformed old, accustomed social roles. "In old Poland [pre-1939 – JK] we were busy smuggling," a highlander declared in early 1960s, "and we still do today – but now we use the lowland mugs from Warsaw or Łódź to do it for us."[1151] The findings of the border authorities bore this out. Whereas in 1959, Border Defense Troops had arrested 865 smugglers crossing the southern border illegally, only 171 were stopped in 1960, and a paltry 139 in 1966. Fewer arrests did not mean that the number of smuggling operations had decreased but rather that goods were now carried across the border under the legitimate guise of tourism.[1152] The traffic helped smugglers make contacts abroad and organize the transport logistics, setting up complex cross-border delivery channels (these were also used in particular during the illicit trading of farm animals, usually horses.) Potential buyers would arrive in Poland as tourists, pick the animals to be bought, make a down payment or pay the full price outright and wait for delivery. A Pole would then cross the border "legally, with a pass or a passport. Once in Czechoslovakia or Austria, he would buy goods and return to Poland illegally or pass the contraband on to a person waiting for him at the border while he entered the country legally, now without any suspicious baggage."[1153] Large amounts of goods such as gold and textiles from Italy smuggled from capitalist states were dispersed in the border zone via a larger group of carriers who brought the contraband into Poland relatively safely in the guise of tourists.[1154]

The development of both private and official tourist infrastructure facilitated contacts and provided a convenient and relatively safe forum for trade. On both sides of the border, whether in the Tatra or Karkonosze Mountains, mountain shelters, tourist lodges and hotels were hotbeds of commercial activity. To give one example, as early as the 1950s, the manager of a PTTK (Polish Tourist

---

1151 HIM, Pressearchiv, P 6221, RFE-Research, Item 2823/61, 3 IX 1961, The highlanders – the privileged class in Poland. Tourists were allegedly paid 500 zloty (half of the average monthly wage) to transport 20 kg of goods across the border; *ibid.*

1152 AIPN, 01521/784, Stanisław Banaszek, Marian Czerepiński, *Przestępstwa przemytnicze i zasady ich zwalczania*, Warszawa 1969, WOP, p. 59.

1153 *Ibid.*, pp. 102, 105.

1154 A. Kłodzińska, *Waluciarze*, ŻW, April 10–12, 1971; J. Koczorowski, *O wynikach zwalczania przemytu w 1971 roku*, WC, 1972, no. 6.

and Sightseeing Society) tourist lodge in Podhale set up a distribution channel supplied by smugglers at one end with a private textile manufacturer in Łódź receiving the goods at the other end; the enterprise flourished, shifting Czech zippers and press-studs wholesale.[1155]

Józef Kaczmarczyk, New design for a tourist bus for Polish group excursions abroad. *On the windows – details of the goods most frequently traded by Polish tourists abroad in the 1960s: vodka, underwear, radios, sweaters, bedspreads. "Szpilki" 1962, no. 40.*

While in the Polish-Czechoslovak border zone the old smuggling strategies were being modified only slightly, trips to more remote destinations required new methods. Individual tourists traveled in groups, for greater safety and to make the border crossing process easier. Since goods carried had to be declared at the border in writing, those traveling with many items for sale entered some of them in the custom declaration forms of those of their traveling companions who had no contraband. This method of tackling the border was used for trips to Romania, Bulgaria, Hungary, and from there onward to Yugoslavia, Austria, Italy, and the return leg of the journey.[1156] In Bulgaria and Romania, where Poles began to arrive in increasing numbers in the early 1960s and where the greatest percentage

1155 AIPN, 01521/784, S. Banaszek, M. Czerepiński, *Przestępstwa przemytnicze i zasady ich zwalczania…*, p. 81.
1156 *Ibid.*, p. 83.

of Polish tourists participated in all kinds of commerce, the locals were interested not only in articles manufactured in Poland[1157] but also in those imported by Poles from Austria and Italy, such as watches. After 1965 tourists traveling individually to Hungary – on trips that were usually self-financed through trading conducted en route – replaced the former organized group excursions. "As a result, instead of pursuing appropriate tourist goals, in individual cases the travelers' undesirable endeavors came to the fore."[1158]

The commercial activities of Polish tourists were motivated by striving to acquire goods unavailable in Poland, recoup their travel expenses and of course gain as much profit as possible but they were also legitimized by the fact that Romanians, Bulgars, Czechoslovaks, Yugoslavs, Hungarians and citizens of East Germany acted in just the same way. It is difficult to establish credibly to what extent these were the grass-roots commercial initiatives of individual citizens or whether they were indirectly inspired by the respective governments, themselves short of foreign reserves, as a way of enabling their citizens to travel abroad without the burden of having to supply them with other socialist currencies. In 1968, the financial authorities of Czechoslovakia announced that they would permit each individual traveler to "exchange no more than 200 zloty, regardless of the duration of their stay in Poland. This encourages engaging in illegal trade."[1159] Certainly, in the Polish perception, Czech and Slovak tourists complied by "refusing to take checks denominated in zloty and opting to take goods instead of Polish money. Those they sell here, and pay with goods for private board and lodging."[1160]

In the mid-1960s this began to pose quite a problem, especially since the number of Soviet Bloc tourists visiting Poland grew more quickly than the traffic in the opposite direction. For example in 1967 the number of inbound trips grew, year on year, by 25% (1 330 807) surpassing the number of Polish trips by

---

1157 By the early 1960s, everybody knew what was selling well in Bulgaria. J. Węgleński's research confirms this: "When buying bedspreads at the Sukiennice stalls in Krakow, the questionnaire's respondent had no need to ponder his choices, since the sales clerk asked him, 'For the Soviet Union or Bulgaria?' and went on to offer two bedspreads of precisely the kind that was sought after in Bulgaria"; J. Węgleński, *Wyniki badania…*, p. 14. On Polish commercial tourist trips to Bulgaria and Romania, see: *Kapiści*, "Dziennik Ludowy" no. 244/October 12, 1962; W. Strzelecka, *Szczypta dziegciu w beczce miodu*, TL, no. 65/March 6, 1962.

1158 AAN, GKKFiT, 16/92, fol. 6.

1159 AAN, GKKFiT, 16/84, fol. 135.

1160 E. Orkiszewski, *Turystyka, podróże, lecz nie tylko…*, "Tygodnik Demokratyczny" 1958, no. 31.

495 681 – a massive 59%! Revenues, however, failed to keep up. Between 1966 and 1967 arrivals from Czechoslovakia alone (including border zone traffic) increased by 29% (342 174 and 443 975) and the revenue remained on a par: 2.92 million and 2.9 million zloty dewizowy –a convertible zloty, nominally worth 0.222168 grams of gold. Zloty dewizowy was a currency unit used until 1982 for accounting purposes in foreign trade conducted by the state. Similarly, Hungarians officially spent much less in Poland than Poles did in Hungary (in 1968 – 21.09 and 185.5 zloty dewizowy per capita). "This proves that the sale of goods brought from abroad or illegal currency exchange remains [their] major source of finance for their stay in Poland."[1161]

In Bulgaria, there was great demand for textiles sold by Polish tourists, such as plush; this provided the basis for the pun that Jerzy Srokowski used in 1969 in his cartoon 'On our holiday in Bulgaria we have made plush-or-minus 10 000 zloty'. Jerzy Srokowski, Plush-minus, *1969. Photo: Warsaw Museum of Caricature, sign. 7255.*

The first of the unofficial "tourist customs wars" between the socialist countries took place in 1968. The GKKFiT (Central Committee of Physical Culture and Tourism) approached the Polish government with a proposal to tighten customs checks for individual tourists from Bulgaria, Czechoslovakia, East Germany, and Hungary "in order to counteract the import of goods destined for sale in Poland

1161 AAN, GKKFiT, 16/93, fol. 190.

and intended to recoup travel costs."[1162] For its part, the government tried to curb the travel aspirations of its citizens, decreasing the foreign currency allowance and imposing limits on the number of Polish zloty permitted to be taken out of the country; moreover, each citizen was allowed to only one trip annually. For trips in the border zone the daily exchange was limited to 80 zloty.[1163] The restrictions did not appear to reduce the number of trips to Poland nor make a dent in the bilateral illicit trade. On the contrary, as always, they seemed to inspire Polish tourists in particular to be more effective and look for new trading routes. In 1970, due to stringent currency limits and the rising price of Hungarian tourist services, a two-week vacation on Lake Balaton, an old Polish cheap favorite, became a thousand zloty more expensive than a comparable stay in Bulgaria or Romania. Poles soon readjusted to the circumstances, re-directing their illegal trade to the shores of the Black Sea.[1164]

In the 1960s, both foreign travel and black-market commerce became commonplace and taken for granted. As Maciej Krasicki put it in 1967, "Exonerated from moral ambivalence, smuggling has become the measure of ingenuity and intelligence. Smuggling and common theft can no longer be treated on a par without risking social uproar."[1165] The communist party cell in a Warsaw enterprise "refused to condemn its secretary when caught red-handed smuggling into the Soviet Union goods worth several thousand zloty. Party members argued that 'everybody does it' and that the authorities 'should not penalize the guy who's already suffered a loss'. Moreover, with the support of the director of the enterprise, the secretary was expected to be re-elected to his post."[1166] Commercial activity made trips abroad possible for growing numbers of people of lesser means and those lower down the social ladder and traditionally less mobile.[1167]

1162 *Ibid.* In January 1969, the Polish authorities began to insist that Hungarian visitors have enough money to cover the cost of their stay in Poland; there was a provision to deny entry to tourists without any Polish currency.

1163 It proved to be effective to an extent. In 1967 the deficit fell to 77.5 million, in 1968 – to 22.1 million, in 1969 – to 14.3 million zloty dewizowy; AAN, GKKFiT, 16/3, fol. 44.

1164 *Rocznik statystyczny 1975*, Warszawa 1975, p. 496.

1165 M. Krasicki, *Przemyt turystyczny*, "Polityka", no. 38/September 23, 1967.

1166 K. Madej, *Wszyscy byli przemytnikami. Obraz przestępczości przemytniczej i dewizowej w latach 1956–1970*, "Pamięć i Sprawiedliwość" 2008, no. 2, pp. 123–124.

1167 It is difficult to say how representative such statements were but those who supervised the foreign tourist traffic pointed out that members of the intelligentsia were involved less frequently with trading; AAN, GKKFiT, 16/10, fol. 68, 101.

Already in the mid-1960s, many Poles claimed, not entirely as a joke, "We are too poor to take our vacation in our own country".[1168] For many of the travelers, trips abroad were a source of relatively high, tax-free income, only part of which was put aside to pay for the next trip.[1169] Due to the large number of participants and the sheer expanse of the geographic area involved, we can only guess at the scale of this surplus. There had evolved a network of trade connections encompassing all the European socialist states which extended out to the West and even beyond the European sub-continent. Sometimes smuggling had all the hallmarks of a professional activity that required managerial skills, an understanding of the markets and at times a touch of creative flair. In the late 1960s, the media reported on the business activities of sailors' wives who, with leisure time and capital on their hands, were no longer content merely to sell goods smuggled in by their husbands and embarked on cross-border operations of their own. "One of the wives was buying fishnet stockings in Hungary, dyeing them dark colors in Gdańsk and then selling them on in Moscow, turning 11 forints into 15 roubles."[1170] It was an excellent exchange rate.

The media gave nicknames to the well-traveled routes, eg the "lamb road" to Bulgaria or the "cosmetics and clothing road" to Romania; similarly, it was common knowledge that crystal glass and hard currency went to Yugoslavia and linen to Hungary. The collective sharing of knowledge established which product was best sold where, for how much and to whom and this information was disseminated by word of mouth. In the later decades of the 1950s, such activities involved literally millions of people.In the late 1960s, the greater part of tourist trading consisted of simple barter, the exchange of goods for other goods or selling goods for money only to buy other goods. These transactions were conducted on a square in Budapest, a beach on the Black Sea or in a mountain lodge in the Tatra Mountains. But, even within this type of exchange, specialization evolved. Mass-scale tourist traffic, now also across the Iron Curtain, led to professional market penetration, as well as evaluation of the scale of local shortages, needs and the opportunities and profits to be had, resulting in new trade strategies independent of state institutions. The profitable exchange of socialist currencies such as Hungarian forints, Czechoslovak korunas, and Soviet rubles in the West led in the late 1960s to the emergence of an unofficial socialist currency-and-goods market, where rates of exchange were set according to

1168 G. Gałuszczyńska, *O ludziach, metodach i sposobach myślenia*, PiŻ, 1966, no. 6.

1169 W. Nowierski, *Komisy nie powinny być "centralą skupu" przemycanych towarów*, "Express Wieczorny", no. 271/November 15, 1961.

1170 T. Kur, *Czas orki i podorywek*, PiŻ, 1970, no. 10.

international circumstances.[1171] The expected profit determined the attractiveness for tourist of a particular country and a choice of strategies (such as whether rubles should be sent to Frankfurt am Main or perhaps swapped in Budapest for forints that could then be used to buy gold bars and bullion in Vienna.[1172]

By then, the socialist authorities had already missed the boat for a decisive battle against the tourist trade. In just a single decade, Poles, Hungarians, and Romanians were able to build a lasting foundation upon which mass-scale cooperation would be based in the 1970s and '80s.

9.3 The 1970s: "Who Are the Smugglers? Every Single Person that Travels Abroad!"[1173]

With these words, the journalist Wojciech Markiewicz referred not just to Poles but also all those representatives of the entire socialist bloc, who, every Thursday during the tourist season, transformed Nowy Targ in southern Poland into the largest marketplace in Europe. Never before had so many Poles, Czechs, Hungarians, and Romanians traveled abroad and they were not willing to give up the privilege lightly.[1174] They did not have to. Allowing citizens to have relatively free movement within the Soviet Bloc was one of the main ways of defusing social unrest. For a Hungarian, a trip to the Polish mountain resort of Zakopane, or for a Pole – to the beaches of Varna, helped to appease the yearning to ski in the Alps or sunbathe on the French Riviera. The pent-up demand for foreign travel became apparent after the introduction of free tourist travel between Poland and East Germany on January 1, 1972. By the end of the year every fourth statistical Pole and every third East German citizen had visited their neighboring state.[1175]

Whenever politically and economically feasible, the authorities simplified the travel regulations. By the end of the 1970s, many Soviet Bloc citizens needed

1171 A significant example was the correlation between the Czechoslovak koruna exchange rate in Poland and the turbulence of the Prague Spring events, during which there was a "high demand for Czech korunas from Austria and West Germany (undoubtedly a result of mass commercial tourism from these countries to Czechoslovakia) which as a knock-on effect resulted in a rising Czechoslovak koruna exchange rate in Poland that took place mainly near the southern border"; AIPN, KG MO, 35/1740, fol. 2.

1172 AIPN, 01521/2035, J. Oleś, *Przemyt wartości dewizowych...*, pp. 65–70.

1173 W. Markiewicz, *Przyjedź pan w lipcu...*, ŻW, no. 101/April 20, 1976.

1174 The dynamic expansion of foreign travel in Poland is telling: while 2.7% of the (statistical) population ventured outside of the country in 1970, five years later the percentage rose to 25; AAN, GKKFiT, 11/58, fol. 4.

1175 For more, see chapter 4.4.

only their ID card to visit a fraternal state. The reasons were both ideological and pragmatic. With cross-border traffic expanding dynamically, the formerly complex system of passports, passport inserts and visas was inefficient and time-consuming. In November 1975, the Polish Ministry of Internal Affairs put forward a proposal to change the regulations for travel to socialist countries in Europe and replace the multiple passport inserts with an ID card with an appropriate permanent stamp. The full implementation of the new regulation was possible only after overcoming the reluctance of the main opponent, Czechoslovakia.[1176] The final agreement was signed on July 20, 1977. From then on, Poles were allowed to travel from the Elbe in the west to Vladivostok in the east with no more than the appropriate stamp in their ID card.

Poland's growing crisis made other socialist countries reluctant to follow in its footsteps in relaxing travel restrictions. Governments in East Berlin and Prague feared that the authorities in Warsaw would try to ease the country's painful shortages by encouraging tourist commerce. It was hardly coincidental that on June 24, 1976 – simultaneous with the announcement of price hikes in Poland – Czechoslovakia banned all private export of food, clothing and shoes, clearly fearing that with tourists from north of their borders vacuuming up industrial quantities of these goods, Poland's shortages would soon spill over into their own country. At the same time the East German customs service introduced "rationed export of selected food products". The restrictions were ostensibly aimed at citizens of all countries but there can be no doubt that they were introduced specifically to curb Polish appetites.[1177] In July 1976, the Czechoslovak customs began to check Polish travelers thoroughly on their way back from Turkey and the Middle East, looking in particular for undeclared gold. Poles traveling to Turkey were also stopped and had their goods confiscated. There were even cases of automobile confiscation.[1178] The Polish side soon began to give as good as it got. From June 1977, the Polish customs also started to implement rigidly their own stringent regulations.[1179]

Such were the administrative responses to the commercialization of tourist trade, which expanded dynamically in the 1970s changing both in quantity and

1176 AAN, GKKFiT, 18/5, fol. 1–2, 4, 9; *ibid.*, 18/54, fol. 10.

1177 AAN, GUC, 31/1, fol. 85, 125–126.

1178 *Ibid.*, fol. 58–59.

1179 AAN, Główny Komitet Turystyki (Main Tourism Committee, GKT), 10/100, fol. 181. In border zones the authorities regularly monitored categories of goods sought by foreigners to such an extent that they stripped entire stocks of retail supplies. The results were often surprising. In 1976, East German citizens "imported" from Poland approximately 6 800 fan heaters per month; AAN, GUC, 31/1, fol. 155–157.

quality. In comparison with the 1960s, the number and type of participants multiplied dramatically, and tourists now ventured considerably further afield, with financial gain as their prevailing goal, responding instantly to the changing needs of the market and to any new administrative obstacles.

In the mid-1970s, an official dispatch of the Central Customs Office estimated that not more than 20 percent of travelers were genuine sight-seeing tourists. Rather than referring to the "tourist season", it resignedly acknowledged the existence of a "commercial tourist season", taking it for granted that the term "professional tourism" was self-explanatory.[1180] Those prosecuted for smuggling were increasingly people with higher education and the involvement of entire families ceased to raise eyebrows.[1181] Małgorzata Mazurek describes a typical case. In the early 1980s, a man from Bydgoszcz secured a temporary contract in the Soviet Union. This put him in a position to earn money by bringing back as contraband attractive goods, difficult to obtain in Poland. The opportunity meant a revolution in the family's way of life. The younger generation spotted the commercial opening and rose to the occasion. Now, the daughter, Jola, busied herself sewing fake "Levi's", and organizing their export to the Soviet Union, while her parents took over the child care of the grandchildren and helped to sell the contraband from the USSR in Bydgoszcz marketplaces.[1182]

Similar scenarios became commonplace throughout the 1970s. In Soviet, East German, Czechoslovak, and Hungarian customs reports listing Polish citizens who had broken custom regulations between 1976 and 1980, what stands out is the high percentage of women. The geographic dispersal of those apprehended in the act is also striking: they came from all over Poland, including small towns

---

1180 M. Pietraszek, *O niektórych problemach w ruchu osobowym*, WC, 1974, no. 12, p. 16; A. Wantuch, *Przestępczość celna i graniczna dewizowa w latach 1970–1973, ibid.*, no 15, p. 7. Dariusz Stola tried to estimate the number of participants in tourist trading. He cautiously assumed that 30%–50% of tourists on group tours, 10%–20% of individual travelers, and 5–10% of athletes traveling to sports events were involved in tourist commerce. In the 1970s, this would have translated into "one to 2.3 million people during the particularly active year 1976–1978, and in less active years such as 1973 and 1980, somewhere between 800 000 and 1.5 million annually. If we take into consideration the increase in trading trips in the late 1970s, the number was likely to have been in excess of three million each year"; D. Stola, *Kraj bez wyjścia?*, p. 292.

1181 *Na nasze konto…*, "Sztandar Młodych" October 5, 1979; J. Kulak, *O przemycie w Urzędzie Celnym Port Lotniczy w Warszawie – uwag kilka*, WC, 1974, no. 15, p. 13; P. Worsnip, *Die Polen schmuggeln jetzt Devisen*, "Oberhessische Presse", no. 93/April 21, 1978.

1182 M. Mazurek, *Społeczeństwo kolejki. O doświadczeniach niedoboru 1945–1989*, Warszawa 2010, pp. 55–56.

and villages.[1183] Cross-border illicit commercial activities were no longer a way of supplementing a home budget but had become a main source of income. Writing in 1977 about Keleti railroad station in Budapest, a Polish journalist observed, "From every train arriving from Poland there spill out two or three hundred dealers. They make no attempt to pretend they have come to do some sight-seeing. They are quite brazen about having arrived in order to trade. Sophisticated ladies mingle with underage prostitutes, high-ranking gentlemen with callow youths. [...] They all have permanent lodgings close to the Keleti station, and their own pitches at the marketplace where they sell their specialized goods. Many of them approach this occupation professionally as their main source of income. They come regularly, on the same days of the week."[1184]

Cross-border travel swelled into a mass phenomenon and became so diversified that Polish consular and custom authorities lost the ability to control it effectively. In late 1972 it was not unusual for up to 2 000 passengers to board a train to Budapest – several times more than the permitted number. This rendered any effective supervision impossible.[1185] At the end of the decade, the Polish consul in Moscow reported, "The diverse forms of tourism between Poland and the Soviet Union, the decentralization of travel and the continuously growing numbers of travelers make any kind of complex evaluation of the tourist phenomenon by the Polish consular agencies in the USSR impossible."[1186] Similar complaints were pouring in from Budapest, Sofia, Prague, and East Berlin.

The sheer volume of tourist traffic made it easier to dodge getting caught. The repeat-business traffickers to Hungary learned to return to Poland via Czechoslovakia and East Germany, on the way destroying the compulsory border-crossing cards that had to be filled out at each border so as to enable the authorities to monitor their route. They got back into the country by crossing the East German-Polish border at Görlitz / Zgorzelec or Frankfurt (Oder) / Słubice, and got away with showing only their ID, which would have raised suspicions anywhere else but at these extremely busy crossings.[1187] After 1972, the institutionalization of smuggling became noticeable not only, as covered briefly in Chapter 4, on the western border of Poland – where smuggling groups appeared in towns on the Polish side of the border, and engaged local people often employed in East Germany[1188]

1183 AAN, GUC, 23/76, 24/103, 24/108, 24/110, 24/125, 24/130, 24/137, 32/1.

1184 *Komu majtki, komu krem*, "Słowo Powszechne" August 3, 1977.

1185 M. Pietraszek, *O niektórych problemach w ruchu osobowym*, WC, 1974, no. 12, p. 16.

1186 AMSZ, DK, 6/83, w. 59.

1187 AIPN, Biuro Paszportów MSW, 21052.

1188 *Łańcuszek*, WC, 1975, no. 17, p. 20.

– but also on other cross-border routes. A cottage industry developed, in which the investor would provide the travelers with goods, tickets, and other necessities, subsequently cashing in on the transactions or the goods brought back. A Polish trafficker, an engineer by profession, who worked the route to Romania, explained to a German reporter how it all worked. During transit of the Soviet Union, in the vicinity of Gorodok, the last larger town on the way to Lvov, someone would activate the train's emergency brake. Local Ukrainian dealers would already be waiting for the Poles in cars at the station, ready to spirit them away for a bout of brisk trading. Denim jeans brought from Poland would be swapped for goods in high demand in Romania. When the delayed train finally made it to Lvov, 30 km further on, the Polish traders – delivered to Lvov station by the Ukrainian accomplices – would already be waiting, ready to re-board the train.

They would then continue to Bucharest, where they traded the contraband acquired in the USSR for jeans sold by Romanian Roma. On the way back, Romanian customs officers, plied with Kent cigarettes, which in Romania functioned as hard currency,[1189] turned a blind eye to the luggage-laden travelers. More trading would take place in Lvov, selling, for example, jeans in order to buy gold. Back in Warsaw, the spoils of the sojourn were handed over to the "capo di tutti capi". Such a trip, repeated two or three times a month ensured a decent standard of living. The introduction of Martial Law in Poland in December 1981 put an end to such enterprise and the Polish engineer was obliged to live off a "meager salary, hoping that the travel regulations would soon be liberalized again."[1190] Many others shared his hopes.

The above case study encapsulates neatly a number of factors typical of the tourist trade of the 1970s, which Polish traders developed and perfected in the subsequent decade. They would go on to gain a professional edge, expanding their geographic horizons and "go native" in the foreign trading outposts of their choice. Whereas in the 1960s an average Polish tourist seldom visited countries outside the European part of the Communist Bloc, in the 1970s capitalist European countries such as Greece, Finland, and Sweden became the new normal, joining traditional destinations such as Austria, Italy and France. For the growing numbers of Polish tourist traffickers with a vehicle of their own, who now also covered Turkey and the Middle East, this expansion meant adjusting their trading strategies when passing through socialist states. A stopover in Lvov was popular:

1189 On this phenomenon see: M. Kuczewski, *Rumunia. Koniec złotej epoki*, Warszawa 2008, pp. 66–73.

1190 K. Stipsicy, *Schmuggeln nach Plan*, "Die Zeit", no. 37/September 9, 1983; see: AIPN, Biuro Paszportów MSW, 21052.

goods in demand in the Soviet Union such as jeans, wigs, and clothing in general were sold and articles purchased that sold well in Turkey, including sports equipment and tools. The city of Lvov soon became a notable hub of illegal trading and the new term "Lvov transit" entered smuggling as well as diplomatic jargon. Other smugglers undertook multiple trips to Hungary and Romania, where they had prearranged to store goods to be sold in Turkey.[1191] Increasingly more complex and profitable, in the 1980s, these operations escalated to a truly mass scale.

Trading relations between socialist countries were becoming specialized. Poland continued to be a source of clothing, shoes, objects made out of crystal and food products (although by the mid-decade it could no longer be taken for granted that "any product from these categories" would find a buyer[1192]) but the objectives of the transactions changed. The proceeds from selling goods abroad were increasingly used to purchase currency; throughout the 1970s, hard currency played an increasingly important role in Poland. It made sense also to buy currencies of other socialist states, where the US dollar exchange rate against the domestic legal tender was usually lower than in Poland: American dollars bought with Hungarian forint, Czechoslovak koruna or East German marks were considerably cheaper than when acquired with Polish zloty. As a result, a black market in socialist currencies rapidly developed.[1193] Poles now brought dollars or marks from Hungary, Bulgaria, Romania, and East Germany.[1194]

This black market was also stimulated by another factor: gold remained the ultimate means of storing value. The yellow metal could be bought at attractive prices in Vienna or in Trieste not only with the greenbacks smuggled out of Poland but also for Hungarian forints, Czechoslovak korunas or Bulgarian lev. The traffickers' modus operandi was flexible and depended on the circumstances. For a while it was profitable to smuggle rubles into Hungary and swap them for forints, which were then spent on gold bullion in Vienna.[1195]

On the one hand, the black market created a huge demand for socialist currencies in Poland, causing their prices to rise; on the other hand, it made visiting Poland more profitable for other Soviet Bloc citizens. During the 1970s, thanks

1191 AIPN, Biuro Paszportów MSW, 21052, fol. 2–5.
1192 J. Kulak, *O przemycie w Urzędzie Celnym Port Lotniczy w Warszawie – uwag kilka*, WC, 1974, no. 15, p. 12.
1193 K. Świątecka, *Waluciarze*, "Perspektywy" 1977, no. 49.
1194 AAN, KC PZPR, XIA/511, 1978, fol. 1–21. By at the turn of the 1960s and 1970s, hard currencies were brought in from the Soviet Union, usually obtained by Soviet currency dealers from Finnish tourists. A. Panow, *Farcowszcziki*, London 1971, p. 91.
1195 AIPN, 01521/2035, J. Oleś, *Przemyt wartości dewizowych…*, pp. 43–46, 54–56.

to the as many as 30 000 Czechs, Slovaks, Hungarians, Bulgars, Yugoslavs, and East Germans that descended on the Polish city of Nowy Targ each Thursday, the weekly market turned into one gigantic Bureau de Change. The visitors sold their own home currency at a black market rate that they found very advantageous when shopping in Poland for locally produced goods such as food, textiles, auto parts, sport and audio equipment.[1196] The socialist currencies had entered Poland illegally and – just as illegally – they were subsequently once more taken abroad by Poles.[1197] In the 1970s, black market individual trade became an acknowledged, and probably the principal, forum for relations between socialist societies. Yet, despite the large-scale turnover of goods and people, these bonds were not strong. For Poles, the closest links that they had established were in Budapest – by the 1970s the "traditional smuggling and transit center, the junction where the interests of criminals organizing international contraband from the Arab countries, Yugoslavia, Austria, Italy, and West Germany converged".[1198] Poles accounted for no more than a fraction of those groups, in which they did not have a dominant role; they acted, rather, as middlemen and small retailers, albeit enjoying support among the local criminals".[1199]

At the turn of 1978 and 1979, two journalists – one from Poland and the other from Hungary – provided an interesting insight into this underworld. Swapping their country of origin for the duration of the experiment, they posed as dealers, the Hungarian playing the role of a Pole trading in Budapest, and the Pole impersonating a Hungarian dealer in Katowice. Their observations revealed remarkable similarities in the behavior of both trader cohorts. The active players, whether buyers or vendors, who operated in the railroad stations of the two cities, were only interested in profit; their trade and all their marketing strategies, including the sourcing of contacts, were at all times based on the timeless principle: sell

1196 As frequently pointed out in 1978, between 1971 and 1976 the amounts spent by the statistical foreign tourist (including the Soviet Bloc) halved, despite the rising prices of tourist services. As an example, in 1977, in the Nowy Sacz voivodship 7 000 Hungarians bought Polish currency in a state bank, even though as many as some 600 000 tourists from that country had visited the region; J. Maziarski, *Turystyczne dewizy*, "Polityka", no.16/April 22, 1978.

1197 AAN, GKT, 10/100, fol. 152.

1198 *Ibid.*

1199 *Ibid.* See: *Ujawniono i zlikwidowano*, TL, no. 229/September 29, 1979; *Koniec przemytniczo-dewizowego biznesu*, TL, February 7–8, 1981. See: *Komu majtki, komu krem*, "Słowo Powszechne" August 3, 1977; K. Świątecka, *Waluciarze*, "Perspektywy" 1977, no. 49; P. Worsnip, *Die Polen schmuggeln jetzt Devisen,* "Oberhessische Presse", no. 93/ April 21, 1978.

high, buy low. The price was all that mattered.[1200] We can safely assume that this Polish-Hungarian illicit trade scene was no exception within the Warsaw Pact.

9.4 The 1980s: "The Phoenicians Are on the Move!"

Whereas the 1970s had brought rapid, if still evolving, development of the tourist trade in socialist countries, the 1980s were truly revolutionary. At the beginning of the decade, the awakened social and consumption aspirations of Soviet Bloc citizens encountered formidable economic and political barriers; the events of August 1980 – a memorable month that made an indelible mark on the history of the country, with its workers' strikes on the coast that led to political agreements with the government – had repercussions beyond the borders of Poland. The markers of that decade were defined also for tourist trading, by political events such as the introduction of Martial Law in Poland and the coming to power of Mikhail Gorbachev, the architect of the *perestroika* that was to culminate in the demise of the Soviet Union. The decade ended with the momentous year 1989, which changed fundamentally the political map and economy of the region. In Poland, a breakthrough for tourism was a harbinger of the political transformations to come. From 1989, Poles could keep their passports at home. This may seem trivial to a Westerner, who naturally takes for granted taking possession of his or her passport as an identity document that should at all times remain with its rightful bearer. Yet, in socialist Poland, this precious document was deemed the property of the state and was only ever released for the specified period of travel, to be returned promptly to the appropriate administrative office – which effectively precluded unauthorized travel abroad. With the dawn of new freedom, it came as no surprise that in 1989 three times as many Poles went abroad as had done so in the previous year – 6 924 000 in 1988 and 19 313 000 in 1989. The changes were not only quantitative but also qualitative. Whereas at the beginning of the decade the government had had to deal with the issue of tourist trading, by the end of the 1980s it was faced with a huge, highly specialized commercial activity that involved considerable capital and increasingly extended beyond the borders not only of the Soviet Bloc but of Europe as well.[1201]

1200 K. Horváth, *Jak się nie podoba mogę zawołać policję!*, "Kultura", no. 4/January 28, 1979; M. Listkiewicz, *Cipu jest?*, *ibid.*; see: H. Jankowski, *Okazyjnie od Polaków*, "Polityka", no. 3/January 20, 1979.

1201 M. Irek, *Der Schmugglerzug Warschau–Berlin–Warschau. Materialien einer Feldforschung*, Berlin 1998, pp. 8–9.

In the summer of 1980 the Polish authorities introduced "Smuggler" – an electronic system intended to "collect data on violations of customs and currency border regulations"[1202] that reflected symbolically the extent of the changes in cross-border activities since the 1970s. Initially, in the following few years, the scope of observation was limited as the economic and political crisis mounting in Poland in the second half of the 1970s prompted the neighboring countries to introduce restrictive customs regulations. However, the events triggered by the strikes in the Polish cities on the Baltic coast in August 1980 brought about decisive, systemic restrictions on travel. The East German authorities were the first to react, on October 30, 1980 in a unilateral decision suspending passport- and visa-free traffic across the Poland-GDR border, although individual Polish tourists continued to be free to cross if equipped with official invitations – a document executed in a consulate by a named individual or business guaranteeing to take care of the Pole in question. At the same time the East German government launched a propaganda campaign aimed at discouraging trips to Poland by its own citizens.

Of the other socialist states, only Czechoslovakia unilaterally suspended, on December 4, 1981, free travel. Earlier, anxious to avoid being infected with the "Polish virus" of social disorder and afraid that the Poles who no longer had shopping access to the GDR would now swamp Czechoslovak stores, Prague looked for other ways of shutting the borders. In the fall of 1980, the Czechoslovak authorities imposed limits on currency exchange with Poland. Both sides pledged to undertake efforts aimed at limiting the "transportation of goods for black market purposes".[1203] Prague, following in the footsteps of East Berlin, discouraged its own citizens from visiting Poland. The official Czechoslovak propaganda created an atmosphere of fear, intended to keep potential travelers out of Poland where they were told they would be confronted with strikes, and unable to buy food or gas – all actually not far from the truth.[1204] In December 1980, the government implemented, and proceeded to enforce strictly, unusually harsh customs regulations. State enterprises were no longer allowed to fund business

1202 AIPN, MSW II, Passport Bureau, Ministry of Internal Affairs (Biuro Paszportów MSW), 104/778, Central Custom Office (GUC) to Voivodship Police Headquarters (KW MO), March 17, 1981.

1203 AMSZ, Departament Polityczny, 32/83, bundle 1, Notes on talks between Polish and Czechoslovak delegation on passenger traffic between October 30, 1980 and November 6, 1980.

1204 AMSZ, DK, 22/87, bundle11, Consulate General of the Polish People's Republic in Ostrava, report for 1981.

trips to Poland and all advertising of trips to Poland ceased. Meanwhile Czechs were encouraged to visit other socialist countries instead – so successfully that travel agencies could not keep up with the demand for travel to the Soviet Union, Hungary, Bulgaria, East Germany or Romania. As a result, in the summer of 1981, only 5% of the expected tourists from Czechoslovakia arrived in Poland.[1205]

Similarly, other countries of the Bloc found ways to gradually reduce tourism to and from Poland. The Hungarian authorities drastically cut funding for foreign exchange with Poland, the resultant cash shortages curtailing not only the numbers of individual tourists but also those using state travel agencies.[1206] Although the propaganda in Hungary was not as aggressive as in Czechoslovakia, East Germany and the Soviet Union, it nevertheless discouraged many Hungarians from choosing Poland as their destination. The rising cost of living was another contributory factor in discouraging Hungarians from traveling in general. In 1981 there was a 74.8% fall in the number of tourist arrivals in Poland from Hungary in compared with 1979 and a 68.2% fall in comparison with 1980.[1207] The Soviet authorities initially limited organized travel (in 1980, as many as 57 "friendship trains" arrived in the USSR from Poland whereas in 1981 – only two[1208]) and between May and June 1981, individual trips to and from Poland were limited by the cautious rationing of invitations and permits for visiting Poland. Transit regulations were observed with unprecedented scrutiny, which limited Polish citizens' visits to the Balkans.[1209] The only country to receive more Poles in 1981 than before was Romania. This can be attributed not so much to the liberalism of its authorities as to the sums owed by Romania to Poland, which were settled through the medium of tourist services. Like other socialist countries, Romania limited access to its own currency thus reducing the number of visitors from Poland.[1210]

The imposition of Martial Law in Poland on December 13, 1981 effectively stopped Polish cross-border traffic. If from the Polish government's perspective,

---

1205 AAN, GKT, 10/53, fol. 119–120; AMSZ, DK, 22/87, bundle 12, Polish Embassy in Czechoslovakia, Consular Department, report for 1981.

1206 AAN, GKT, 10/100, fol. 8.

1207 AAN, GKT, 10/102, fol. 58–59.

1208 AMSZ, DK, 19/91, bundle 20, Consulate General of the Polish People's Republic in Kiev to the Ministry of Foreign Affairs, June 13, 1983; AAN, GKT, 10/100, fol. 35.

1209 AMSZ, 19/91, bundle 20, Consulate General of the Polish People's Republic in Kiev to the Ministry of Foreign Affairs, April 15, 1983; AMSZ, DK, 22/87, bundle 7, Polish Consulate General in Kiev , report for 1981.

1210 AAN, GKT, 10/100, fol. 39.

military rule had closed the borders with the socialist countries only temporarily, for Berlin, Prague and Moscow the measures provided a convenient pretext for cutting off travel to and from Poland for the foreseeable future; little wonder then that the Polish authorities undertook relatively quickly measures to reinstate tourist exchanges with the socialist countries, both as relief for its citizens from the rigors of Martial Law and to provide Poles access to well-stocked stores at a time of hardship. "In view of the fact that travel to the capitalist states has stopped," the argument went, "widening the possibilities for travel to the socialist countries [...] will be a factor in calming the mood in Poland and will help citizens to satisfy their social needs."[1211] The measure was intended to drain some of the savings accumulated by society and at the same time to protect the almost completely depleted Polish internal market. The Polish authorities planned to ease the pressure on the consumer market in Poland by shifting the onus of satisfying demand on to the better-supplied socialist countries and "allowing tourists to bring back goods in short supply in Poland." This aim was both deliberate and explicit.[1212]

In the assessment of the Polish Passport Bureau, by May 1982 there was no obstacle to the resumption of individual travel to the socialist countries, especially in view of the fact that none of the bilateral agreements had been formally rescinded but had been merely unilaterally suspended. However, the socialist partner countries voiced strong opposition; they were fearful that traveling Poles would bring with them democratic ferment and that Polish shopping sprees would destabilize their own fragile domestic markets. None of the fraternal socialist states countries was therefore in a hurry to reinstate the formerly liberal border regulations. The Soviet authorities allowed only organized tourism controlled by political, social, and professional organizations.[1213] Czechoslovak border control at times went as far as breaking international law by refusing entry to travelers with valid passports and invitations.[1214] Traffic across the Oder and the Neisse rivers was maintained only by a trickle of Polish workers employed in East Germany. Hungary, increasingly more interested in attracting tourists from the West, was no longer interested in hosting large number of visitors from the impecunious East. In an interview with *Der Spiegel*, the Hungarian Secretary for Tourism stated firmly: "Hungary does not subscribe to socialist tourism".[1215]

1211 *Ibid.*, fol. 10.

1212 *Ibid.*; AAN, GKT, 10/26, fol. 68.

1213 AMSZ, DK, 22/87, bundle 10, Consular Department of the Polish Embassy in Moscow, report for 1982; *ibid.*, bundle 8, Consulate General in Leningrad, report for 1982.

1214 AMSZ, 19/81, bundle 19, Report "Ruch osobowy z CSRS", June 27, 1982.

1215 AAN, GKT, 10/103, fol. 104.

For East German, Czechoslovak and Hungarian citizens, the attractiveness of Poland also waned. Before 1981, it had relied not so much on the beauty of the landscape and gourmet cuisine but on providing vacationing that was relatively free of state interference and, above all offered profitable shopping. Now that the Polish retail market was virtually exhausted – and attractive goods such as cosmetics, audio equipment and shoes were nowhere to be found, not to mention the now much stricter customs control – the commercial appeal of travel to Poland declined rapidly.[1216] In fact, 1982 was the first and only year since the late 1950s in which the problem of illicit trading did not loom large in Polish police and consular reports.

The problem was indeed insignificant but it did not go away completely. Combined with the economic crisis in Poland, restrictions on cross-border traffic inspired new strategies in individual cross-border trade in socialist states. Just as in the free market economy, the profit motive proved capable of over-riding all obstacles, with the players zeroing in on the right object and opportunity to make a trade – the reduction in the flow of illicitly imported goods combined with the increased risk helped to raise profit margins. Among the articles smuggled from Poland by Czechoslovak citizens between November 1982 and April 1983 and listed in Central Customs Office (GUC) reports, there were audio/TV equipment and miscellaneous items such as glasses, leather belts, and Christmas decorations but also Polish zloty, Czechoslovak koruna, and hard currency.[1217] In the absence of reliable sources we can only speculate that a large proportion of the articles for sale had not been purchased in official stores but acquired through private networks.

Under Martial Law, the character of cross-border trade changed. Given that the internal market in Poland was in a catastrophic state, it made more commercial sense to smuggle in goods rather than currency. Until the lifting of Martial Law in 1983 when tourism began to flourish again, cross-border trade was the domain of Polish contract workers, especially those employed in East Germany. For a considerable number of guest workers, a job in the GDR was above all a source of capital to finance the trading that was their staple income. The profits were enormous (see chapter 4.4) and Poles working in the GDR were developing highly specialized security strategies, among them – "partnerships" which increased the safety of the transactions, with accomplices hiding the goods in transit on trains or bribing railroad employees. Such strategies were so effective that in 1987 the number of identified smuggling cases where the perpetrators

1216 AAN, GKT, 10/55, fol. 64–66.
1217 AIPN, MSW II, 104/265, fol. 1–12.

could not be apprehended rose to 63.6%. The losses might be great but the advantages of working in East Germany – even greater.[1218]

It is relatively easy to assess the volume of trade by looking at turnover and profit or even at the severity of legal sanctions; it is more difficult to assess the level of commercial penetration of markets abroad, including those of the socialist countries, or of the steering and stimulating of demand, which led to the creation of shared areas of business activity and niche markets. Contract workers were in an ideal position for such a commercial assault: they had spent a considerable amount of time in the country in question; meeting the locals daily and were able to build informal relations, often based on economic need, with the local community.[1219] When in the first half of the 1980s the smuggling of Polish silver to East Germany suddenly became the trade *du jour*, mixed groups of Poles and East Germans who specialized in such transactions sprang up almost overnight.[1220]

It was not only Poles working long-term in socialist countries that were able to bond with local communities. For a while there had been other groups of Poles that had economic ties with Budapest, East Berlin, and Lvov. As long as travel was relatively easy, these ties remained fairly loose; however, as soon as, in December 1981, the borders were closed, Polish drifters living, often illegally, in socialist states were forced by circumstances to cooperate more closely with local communities. Out of choice, they settled in locations that promised business opportunities without excessive exposure to risk.

At the beginning of the 1980s, a group of some 60 or 70 such Poles lived in Budapest, divided into the "Keleti people" – so known as they tended to congregate on the square near the Keleti railway station in Budapest, where trains from Poland arrived – and the "city people". The former operated among Polish tourists, the latter had connections with local criminal gangs.[1221] With time, the geography of such "free trade zones" in socialist states changed. On the one hand, their location depended upon evolving trading strategies and trade routes; on the other,

1218 M. Olszewski, *Przestępczość celna i graniczna dewizowa w 1987 r.*, WC, 1988, no. 41, p. 22. Import policies targeted specific products. In the late 1980s, Simson motorbikes were popular; the customs in Zgorzelec often came across more than 200 per day; WC, 1989, no. 45, p. 14.

1219 For literary rendition see: H. Sekulski, *Przebitka*, Olsztyn 2001.

1220 AIPN, KG MO, 35/154, fol. 17–18. For a kilogram of silver, the vendor would be paid more than 6 000 marks net, which at the black market rate yielded between 250 and 350 000 zloty. The Polish black market price of gold was at the time approximately 80 000 zloty per kilo.

1221 *Rzucają cień na polskich turystów*, ŻW, no. 139/June 28, 1982.

there was a growing conflict between the aspiration to consumption of society and official regulations. Although in the second half of the 1980s the liberalization of travel regulations resulted in literally millions of people joining the trade routes, the freedom of movement was nevertheless limited by the requirement for tourists to carry "currency books" that were an official record of all legally acquired socialist currency in their possession. Moreover, rather than notes or coins, state-owned tourist agencies sold tourists talons or vouchers nominated in a specific currency. For those tourists who wanted to get their hands on foreign cash it was not unusual to apply for a transit visa to, say, Bulgaria or Turkey. Having got one, they would linger for months or sometimes years in Hungary, not bothering to proceed to their destination, busy organizing trading trips to the neighboring countries. Thus the Poles who lived in the town of Szolnok on the river Tisza operated as middlemen in the bulk trade in coffee, buying it in Vienna for $3.50 per kilo and reselling in the city of Timisoara in Romania for twice as much. The profit was several hundred dollars per transaction. The average salary in Poland averaged between $22 and $32 per month (at the black market exchange rate). This was a no-brainer. Hungarians rated Polish middlemen as good customers who rented rooms, frequented local restaurants and used local transport. Their illegal presence was tolerated as long as they refrained from trading in currency.[1222]

Highest in the pecking order of Polish currency black marketeers in the socialist countries were the dealers who lived in a Bucharest hotel called Dunavea, situated close to the Bucharest North (Gara de Nord) train station – the largest in Romania, which played a crucial role in their illicit operations. By the second half of the 1980s, stores in Romania had even less to offer than those in Poland, and Polish trains in transit to Bulgaria became retail outlets on wheels. Once they had sold their contraband to Romanian peddlers, the passengers would end up with wallets full of Romanian lei, for which they had little use. This is where the Polish money changers stepped into action: faced with such a perfect captive market, they were able to exchange – at desultory rates – the tourists' lei for hard currency, which they went on to resell at a regular black market rate to Romanian money dealers.[1223]

1222 Janusz Nowakowski to the author, January 26, 2005.

1223 Janusz Nowakowski to the author, December 27, 2004. Polish money changers had been active in socialist countries since the 1970s. In Hungary, Romania, and Bulgaria they were under the surveillance of Polish agencies. "In Bulgaria alone," an MO functionary reported in 1979, "we have conducted 400 preventive interviews. We made arrests and confiscated illegally acquired goods"; *Na nasze konto…*, "Sztandar Młodych", October 5, 1979.

The cost of living continued to rise in all the countries of the Soviet Bloc, with signs of impending economic crisis visible even in such model socialist states as East Germany, Hungary and Czechoslovakia. Although the aspirations of consumer were leveling out within the Bloc and were increasingly influenced by Western standards, disparities in the supply and price of the desired goods remained and were enormous. Unofficial trade between the countries of the Warsaw Pact began to flourish again immediately after the lifting of Martial Law and, with it, the travel restrictions. Momentous political transformations in the socialist Bloc were favorable to commercial activity not generated by the state. Grass-roots cross-border trade spread and flourished – from the Adriatic to the Baltic, from the Elbe to Vladivostok.

In the latter half of the 1980s, Poland once again became a desirable destination on the economic map of the Bloc. Entry into the country was easy, official prices were low and, in non-official outlets, there was an abundance of attractive goods. The Polish authorities now acquiesced in the existence of numerous private producers (including many new Polonia* firms); this policy helped to make Poland an important supplier for the countries of the Bloc of goods known in the 19th century as "Nuremberg products" – accessories, toys, and clothing, which the key industries in Brno or Dresden were unable to manufacture at the time.

In the 1980s, Poland established for itself within the Soviet Bloc the position held in today's global economy by China. In the second half of the decade, the country extended its trading routes to India and the Far East – in the mid-1980s, Polish Airlines LOT opened new connections with Dubai, Singapore, Bangkok, and Taiwan – and so Poles also became middlemen for Asian products such as clothing and computers.[1224] A Polish journalist commented at the time, "A Polish trader can afford to sell cheap. It makes sense to an East German customer to buy

---

1224 M. Olszewski, *Przestępczość celna i graniczna dewizowa w 1987 r.*, WC, 1988, no. 41, p. 23. See: W. Markiewicz, *Nasz człowiek w Stambule*, "Polityka", no. 44/November 2, 1985; P. Waromski, *Pan Jasiek w Bangkoku*, "Polityka", no. 29/June 20, 1985; A. Person, *Złota trasa*, "Polityka", no. 13/March 28, 1987; *Dzień przemytnika*, "Kurier Polski", July 28–30, 1989. One could do business in Japan selling even classical music records; *Bazariada wykształciucha*, "Gazeta Wyborcza", July 11–12, 2009.

*"Polonia" is the Polish term for the Polish diaspora outside of the country. From 1979, foreign capital was allowed into Poland in order to be used for business start-ups in selected branches of production. Since the majority of these companies (of which by 1988 there were more than 700, with 80 000 employees) were set up by Polish emigrants, they were known as Polonia businesses, and produced clothes, cosmetics, and food.

goods that would cost him twice as much back home, as well as to pay over the odds for things that are unavailable in the GDR, such as Polish golden dress belts that are very popular with the fashion-conscious German women. Polish jeans that carry Western brand tags even though they are manufactured near Łódź also sell quickly. Equally, electronic watches made by Polonia firms are in high demand. […] And moreover, Polish traders can supply their clients with goods made to order."[1225]

As soon as the Polish borders opened to a wider public in 1983, the subject of tourist commerce returned to the headlines and again began to feature in police and diplomatic reports. The dealers now came in two varieties: the stick-in-the-mud ones, who continued to use the labor-intensive and not very profitable old smuggling methods, going back to the 1950s, and those who had evolved with the times and worked out new effective, foolproof ploys. The former relied on buying large amounts of cheap, basic products, thus risking attracting the attention of customs officers and likely confiscation of the goods. The latter had the foresight to invest in the safety and convenience of their operations – an approach that in spite of a higher capital outlay improved profit margins. One such operation, used in the mid-1980s, went as follows: Polish dealers would buy video cassette recorders in Poland – legally, with hard currency. There was no prohibition on goods such as these, purchased in state shops, being taken abroad, so the dealers now could – and did – take the VCRs quite legally, where – now entirely illegally – they would proceed to sell them in Budapest and Debrecen at a 100% profit.[1226] It also paid to bring hard currency to Hungary – again a perfectly legal operation, if superficially expensive, since in Poland Western currencies were twice as expensive. Nevertheless, once in Hungary, they could be sold on the black market, strategically to a known dealer. Forints acquired in such transactions were then used to buy luxury items that yielded significant profit when sold in Poland.[1227]

In the mid-1980s, the improved supplies in Polish stores and the deteriorating supplies in the stores in other countries of the Bloc, combined with price and currency exchange rates that were advantageous for foreigners, made Poland an attractive shopping destination. Visitors from Hungary, Bulgaria, Romania, Czechoslovakia, and Yugoslavia were well-informed about what was and what was not available on the Polish market; equally, they were aware of what would

1225 W. Faściszewski, *Przemytnik*, "Sprawy i Ludzie" 1984, no. 4.
1226 AIPN, KG MO, 35/185, fol. 206.
1227 J.S. Mac, *Znajomi z Dworca Wschodniego*, PiŻ, 1984, no. 17.

sell in their own country. Often, they made no effort to act like tourists.[1228] In the second half of the 1980s Hungarians, citizens of Yugoslavia and Czechoslovakia descended en masse on the cities of southern Poland, stripping store shelves bare, and frequently got as far as Warsaw. Each nationality had slightly different trading strategies. Hungarians were now came mostly with goods and brought their own currency less frequently than they had in the 1970s. "The experienced ones go to the 'dens', i.e. to the dealers that they already know, and barter goods for goods. By a conservative estimate, in Katowice alone there are several dozen such 'dens' where goods change hands efficiently and the "tourists" get straight back on the express train home the same day. They take with them anything and everything – anything they can lay their hands on. Shoes are very popular but only those of lesser quality, bought in sales, and the truly hideous items bought in private stores. They will pay top dollar for T-shirts with 'Made in France' labels produced in… Częstochowa."[1229]

The strategies of the Yugoslavs were more varied. Some brought to Poland goods such as cheap electronic watches that they had bought in Vienna; others brought hard currency, which they immediately sold to Polish money-dealers. They took back silver, Soviet Bloc currencies, which they sold on in Vienna and […] men's suits. Bytom, the Polish producer of men's suits calculated that in 1986 foreigners accounted for a quarter of its revenue, 100 out of 400 million zloty. Their most expensive suit, which at the black market exchange rate cost approximately twenty US dollars in Katowice, sold easily in Belgrade and Zagreb for a hundred.[1230]

Although higher in comparison with those in Hungary and Yugoslavia, retail prices in Poland were still attractive enough that visitors from those countries bought in Poland "everything they could: wool and ribbons, buttons and lingerie. They buy twenty and more item of underwear, blouses, and sweaters. […] Foreign tourists are also buying shoes, auto parts, electronic equipment, electric tools, and fabric."[1231] Comments such as this were common: "A Hungarian in Katowice or a Yugoslav citizen in Krakow is the mirror image of the Pole at the Keleti railroad station in Budapest. […] The sight of a Pole wearing a fox fur coat and a hat in the middle of summer at a Budapest marketplace is as common as that of a Hungarian laden with bags groaning with goods to be taken home."[1232] Indeed, this reciprocity of smuggling was reflected in the statistics. In 1987, more

---

1228 *Turyści zagraniczni na "handlowych szlakach" w Polsce*, TL, no. 170 /July 24, 1987.
1229 D. Tresenberg, *Przemyt lub słotę*, "Panorama", August 9, 1987.
1230 *Ibid.*, *Na zarobek do Polski*, "Polityka", no. 11/March 16, 1985.
1231 *Turyści zagraniczni na "handlowych szlakach" w Polsce*, TL, no. 170/July 24, 1987.
1232 D. Tresenberg, *Przemyt lub słotę*, "Panorama", August 9, 1987.

than half (51.7%) of customs and currency offences in Poland were committed by Poles, against 22.4% by foreigners; 25.9% were recorded as the work of unidentified perpetrators and it is impossible to fathom out how many of these may have been Polish. Nevertheless, compared with previous years, the percentage of Poles charged with such offences decreased, while the percentage of foreign nationals, and in particular those from other Soviet Bloc countries, rose. For example 1 015 Yugoslav citizens were charged with criminal offences (an increase of 24.5% compared with 1986), 301 Hungarians (59%), and 170 Czechoslovak citizens (67%) were also held criminally responsible.[1233] In 1987 the Hungarian customs authorities initiated 5 400 investigations against Poles – twice as many as in 1986.[1234]

Border crossing in Świeck – "Operation Barrier" designed to make smuggling goods out of Poland impossible, 9 April 1989. Photo: Polish Press Agency (PAP).

1233 M. Olszewski, *Przestępczość celna i graniczna dewizowa w 1987 r.*, WC, 1988, no. 41, p. 21.

1234 *Ibid.*, p. 22.

If Soviet Bloc citizens had come to the conclusion that "smuggling makes you rich", so had the socialist authorities, going increasingly after foreigners, especially those involved in large-scale operations. Thus, the Czechoslovak customs service paid close attention to smuggling taking place on the transit routes between Austria and Poland and repeatedly made a killing on the confiscated contraband.[1235] In the mid-1980s, customs officials in Bulgaria, Romania, Hungary and the Soviet Union – faced with increased transit traffic to Greece and Turkey and other destinations that involved higher value smuggled goods, gold, and currency – followed the Czechoslovak example. A wave of protest from hapless Polish would-be smugglers forced Poland's Ministry of Foreign Affairs to deal with the problem,[1236] especially since, as a knock-on effect, the state treasury had suffered significant losses as a consequence of having "lost the hard currency profits of our banks and Pewex stores as well as the loss of the tax revenue and customs charges due". The Polish authorities urged travelers to carefully read and fill out transit declaration forms as well as use bank wire transfers and direct air mail rather than risk carrying vulnerable items across the border.[1237]

In the 1980s, in a striking development, Soviet citizens joined in the unofficial trade across the Soviet Bloc's borders. Western consumerism and its style icons had reached the USSR, fueling demand for outward symbols of social status such as clothes and accessories, yet, until the end of the decade, opportunities for cross-border contacts for Soviet nationals were limited; this naturally enhanced the role of, mostly Polish, middlemen. It was much easier for Poles to establish trade contacts in Lvov, Grodno, Minsk and Moscow than in East Berlin and Prague, if only because Russian was a compulsory subject on the primary school national curriculum in Poland at the time and the language became the lingua franca of the Soviet Bloc. The transit routes running across the Soviet Ukraine to Hungary, Romania, the Balkans and Turkey were an important trade-booster for unofficial commerce.

The Soviet Union was a very attractive market for Polish tourists and in 1982 even the carefully vetted (for instance on the grounds of their Party

1235 According to the Polish consul in Ostrava in 1981, "In the previous year, in our consular region alone, the value of the confiscated property [5 532 675 korunas – JK], which should have become property of the State Treasury, would have covered all hard currency expenses of the Polish Consulate in Ostrava for five years"; AMSZ, DK, 25/84, bundle 10, Consulate General of Poland in Ostrava, report for 1980. See: *ibid.*, 22/87, bundle 3, Consulate General of Poland in Bratislava, report for 1983.

1236 AAN, GKT, 10/27, fol. 27, 47.

1237 *Ibid.*, fol. 28.

membership) participants of organized trips to the USSR engaged in illicit commercial activities.[1238] That same year, the Polish consul in Kiev suggested an in-depth analysis of previously used smuggling practices in order to "prevent a spontaneous rebirth of the 'Lvov transit' with all its negative characteristics and consequences."[1239] The consulate's concerns proved prescient, and within a year Lvov had reclaimed its commercial position. In 1983, according to the Soviet authorities, more than 430 000 Polish citizens in 75 740 cars transited the city. "[Ukrainian] comrades," the Polish consul in Kiev noted, "agree with us that crime and fraud especially that involving hard currency and custom violations are down to no more than a few thousand people, who have turned tourism into an excellent source of exceptionally high profits. They have contacts and partners in the Soviet Union and other socialist countries. The Visa and Registration Department (Oddział Wiz i Rejestracji, OWiR) in Lvov maintains that they had imposed sanctions on three to four times as many of their own citizens and that the penalties were tougher."[1240]

The clamp-down on black market participants failed to curb the illegal operations, particularly since the approach of the Soviet authorities was not consistent. On August 23, 1986 the Presidium of the Supreme Soviet of the USSR issued an Act enhancing legal measures against illegal profits, including those derived from trade. However, several days later the Council of Ministers of the USSR made a regulation making travel in and out of the country much easier. From January 1, 1987 the regulations were further relaxed (for example, the limit on the number of border crossings permitted per person was abolished). Needless to say, tourist numbers shot up. In 1986 more than 800 000 Poles crossed the Soviet borders - more than all other visitors from socialist countries combined, including 200 000 from the GDR, 120 000 from Hungary, 100 000 from Romania, 166 000 from Czechoslovakia, 70 000 from Bulgaria, 4 000 from Mongolia, and

1238 AMSZ, DK, 22/87, bundle 10, Consulate General in Minsk, report for 1982. Visitors from Poland showed a pragmatic approach to ideology. "The comrades from Lvov told us with profound disproval about smugglers and other law-breaking people who, when caught red-handed, showed their Party membership cards and professed their devotion to socialism and Polish-Soviet friendship in order to ensure more lenient treatment"; AMSZ, 19/91, bundle 20, Consulate General in Kiev to the Ministry of Foreign Affairs, July 20, 1984.

1239 AMSZ, DK, 22/87, bundle 7, Consulate-General in Kiev, report for 1982.

1240 AMSZ, 19/91, bundle 20, Polish Consulate-General in Kiev to the Ministry of Foreign Affairs, July 20, 1984.

2 500 from Cuba.[1241] In 1989, the number of visitors to the Soviet Union doubled and the number of transit travelers tripled.[1242]

Polish domination of the Soviet tourist routes was not only quantitative, but also qualitative. "Interestingly, back then in the 1980s," recalled one of the participants of trading trips to the USSR, "I never met *en route* Czechs or Hungarians, and traders from other socialist countries only rarely."[1243] The Poles were quick to find common commercial ground with the Ukrainians, Belarusians and Russians and soon diversified. Some concentrated on trading locally, and others focused on transit operations; there were also those who combined both strategies. Between 1987 and 1988, Polish trading operations developed to such extent that the authorities in the Soviet republics bordering Poland began to consider methods of legalizing the phenomenon and channeling it into official outlets. Initially, as mentioned in the chapter on the geography of the black market, there had been attempts to introduce free market principles, with organized marketplaces in Vilna, Zaslawye near Minsk, Brest and Grodno among others.[1244] These were soon closed down and replaced with official *komis* stores.[1245] This move did not prove to be a serious obstacle for the population of the trading cities, who soon developed individual commercial relations with the visitors from the West. "We should emphasize," the Polish consul in Minsk wrote in a dispatch, "that Polish trading tourists are not deterred by any obstacles or new regulations limiting the volume of goods brought to the country nor do they care about the attitude of the local administration. Recently, our tourists have been trading religious objects and anything else that will sell".[1246]

The new strategies, presented above, tried and tested by Polish "tourists" in Hungary in the 1980s, mentioned earlier, were quickly adopted by those traveling to and through the Soviet Union. Poles now planned their trips carefully and had a detailed business plan. Little was left to spontaneity and chance. Dealers who were after quick, big-time profit no longer engaged in time-consuming

---

1241 *Ibid.*, Consul General in Kiev, note on the meeting in the Consular Department of the Ukrainian Ministry of Foreign Affairs, August 20, 1987.

1242 AMSZ, DK, 29/97, bundle 20, Consular Department of the Polish Embassy in Moscow, report for 1989.

1243 R. Geremek, *Pokój, przyjaźń, dieńgi*, "Życie", June 3–4, 2000. See: M. Fish, L. Edwards, *Shadow trading by international tourists in the Soviet Union*, "Journal of Criminal Justice" 17, 1989, no. 5, pp. 417–421.

1244 AMSZ, DK, 29/97, bundle 20, Consulate-General in Minsk, report for 1989.

1245 AMSZ, DK, 21/93, bundle 5, Consular Agency in Lvov, report for 1987.

1246 AMSZ, DK, 29/97, bundle 20, Consulate-General in Minsk, report for 1989.

chain trading which involved tedious, risky, and often outright dangerous deals, buying and selling stuff in countries en route. From 1986, they no longer took to Turkey and Bulgaria small items to trade but instead carried hard currency legally bought in Polish banks and goods purchased legally at hard currency stores. Even when they did buy en route items for sale in the destination country, they were in modest quantities so as not to complicate the procedure of border crossing. "Four or five cars leave Poland for Bulgaria with travel vouchers valid for several days," Przemyśl policemen reported to Warsaw Headquarters. "Upon arrival, the visitors busy themselves establishing contacts with prospective local buyers. One or two from the group in possession of entry visas for Turkey (these can be obtained in the Turkish consulate [...] in Bulgaria or in Poland) go there in order to buy merchandise. After coming back from Turkey, they sell all the goods in Bulgaria. The average load per car is 300 pairs of pants and jackets. [...] In Turkey, the wholesale price for a pair of pants is five dollars; in Bulgaria they are sold, also wholesale, for 14 or 15 dollars a pair. All in all, the profit on selling in Bulgaria 300 pairs of pants and jackets brought from Turkey is 2 100 dollars."[1247]

Compared with average Polish wages, calculated at the black market exchange rate, these gains were enormous. All the same, this was no more than petty retail trade, with a small turnover and relatively small profits when compared with the operations of the true wholesalers. For example, during the course of a few months in 1989, one person was able to transport from Poland to the Soviet Union 304 desktop computers. In the same year, the Polish passengers on a single Black Sea cruise brought to the Soviet Union from Turkey 100 thousand pairs of jeans, 700 000 beauty products, 500 000 meters of fabric, 500 000 electronic watches, and four tons of chewing gum. The value of all these goods, probably only a fraction of what did reach Poland, was estimated by the Soviet customs service at 50 million rubles or 10 million dollars calculated at the black market exchange rate! By some estimates, in the late 1980s in the Lvov region alone, Polish citizens turned over goods worth a billion rubles.[1248]

These estimates, even if exaggerated, are impressive especially when we realize that they take into account only the initial gains. These would frequently

---

1247 AIPN, KG MO, 35/185, fol. 170. Sales in Romania were even more profitable. However, very restrictive border inspections made this route less attractive; *ibid*.

1248 *Spekulatiwnaja gorjaczka: istoki i łabirinty*, in: *Tenewaja ekonomika*, Moskva 1991, pp. 91–92.

be multiplied as a result of consecutive transactions.[1249] Not surprisingly in the late 1980s, the profitability of trading operations in the East matched those conducted in Western Europe. In the second part of 1988, the wholesalers brought from the Soviet Union gold (which had the best rate of return), hard currency, and rubles. The retailers, who usually operated only on the territory of the Soviet Union, stuck to merchandise-trading operations and beside currency and gold also brought to Poland caviar, cocoa, cameras, fishing rods, and color TV sets. In 1988 alone and just from Lithuania and Belorussia, Poles "imported" approximately 120 000 TV sets, which prompted the authorities in Minsk and Vilna to limit their sale and export.[1250]

The authorities in Prague and East Berlin reacted strongly to the trading operations of the Poles, and in the fall of 1988 forced Warsaw to wage a customs war on two fronts. The first took place at the border with Czechoslovakia, after the local authorities had on November 15, 1988 unexpectedly introduced a ban on exporting 366 categories of goods, ranging from car equipment to citrus fruit. Extremely rigorous customs inspections often assumed the form of "nationalist discrimination against Poles" and, as a rule, ended with a confiscation of goods that could not be appealed against. No receipts were issued.[1251] Although the East German customs implemented similar regulations on November 18, 1988, in contrast to their Czechoslovak counterparts, they at least provided statements acknowledging the confiscation.[1252] Representatives of both countries were summoned to the Polish Ministry of Foreign Affairs – an almost unprecedented move – which resulted in the situation changing for the

---

1249 Electronic watches are a good example here. A watch manufactured in the Far East would be purchased at a wholesale price of $2 and resold in the Soviet Union for 45 rubles ($9 to the ruble at the black market exchange rate). According to the Polish security agency, Poland found itself on the smuggling route for this type of contraband which was controlled by emigrants from the Soviet Union; AIPN, MSW II, 01304/529, December 1987, fol. 128–139.

1250 *Ibid.*; AMSZ, DK, 21/92, bundle 9, Consulate-General in Minsk, report for 1988; M. Bednarski, *Drugi obieg gospodarczy. Przesłanki, mechanizmy i skutki w Polsce lat osiemdziesiątych*, Warszawa 1992, pp. 138–139. Soviet rubles, easily exchanged for hard currency in port cities such as Gdańsk and Szczecin, were much sought after. Rubles were brought to Poland on a massive scale by Soviet citizens; AIPN, KG MO, 35/185, fol. 41.

1251 T. Urban, *Zollkrieg zwischen sozialistischen Brüdern*, "Süddeutsche Zeitung", no. 47/ February 25/26, 1989; AMSZ, DK, 21/92, bundle 8, Report of the Consular Dept. of the Polish Embassy in Prague, January 1, 1988 – December 31, 1988.

1252 T. Urban, *Zollkrieg zwischen…*, *ibid.*

worse: the border inspections became even more ruthless and grueling. Towards the end of November 1988, under the pretext of "protecting the internal market", Warsaw embarked on a counter-offensive, conducting thorough customs inspections of all Soviet Bloc (and Yugoslavia) citizens departing from Poland. By November 30, Polish custom officers had extracted 81.5 million zloty of export customs duty including 64.4 million zloty from Yugoslavian citizens, 2.5 million from Czechoslovaks, and 15.6 million from Hungarian citizens. Moreover, 5 526 travelers were denied entry into Poland, among them 3 026 from Czechoslovakia. This time, a Polish diplomat was summoned to the Hungarian Ministry of Foreign Affairs, with no discernible outcome.[1253] The conflict escalated in 1989 when it became possible for Polish citizens to travel with almost no restrictions and although the "peak tourist season usually occurred in the summer, it started as early as the beginning of the year. The liberalization of passport regulations brought immediate results, with millions of Poles traveling East and West."[1254] The main goal of the trips was to acquire hard currency, which would help survival in times of rapidly growing inflation, soon followed by hyperinflation. Entry to Austria and West Berlin no longer required a visa. Poles conducted supplementary transactions in transit countries, East Germany, Czechoslovakia and Hungary, where the length of a transit stay could no longer be limited.[1255]

1253 AAN, KC PZPR, LII/125, fol. 5–7.

1254 E. Pawełek, *Fenicjanie ruszyli*, ŻW, April 24, 1989. On trading operations of the Poles, see a series of articles: "Bazarowa odyseja Polaków '89" in "Gazeta Wyborcza": P. Głuchowski, M. Kowalski, *Wieszak umiera ze strachu* (July 6, 2009); P. Głuchowski, M. Kowalski *Katastrofa w złotym trójkącie* (July 7, 2009); P. Głuchowski, M. Kowalski, *Solidarność tanio* (July 8, 2009); W. Szabłowski, *Donos na własną rodzinę* (July 9, 2009); *Bazariada wykształciucha* (July 11–12, 2009).

1255 Thanks to cheap, state-subsidized train tickets within the Soviet Bloc, travel abroad was available also to those who did not own a car and had limited resources (changing in Bratislava for Vienna or in East Berlin for West Berlin did not pose any problems). For example, in summer 1982, a train ticket from Poznań to Berlin cost 2 000 zloty or one West German mark. No wonder the trains were overcrowded. On September 8, 1989 on the *Batory* train equipped with 956 seats there were 3 900 passengers; M. Hradil, *Podloudnictví: nevítaný host*, "Tribuna", 1989, no. 45. New transportation enterprises specializing in commercial transfers to Vienna and Berlin appeared in no time.

The "Polish market" in Berlin, 1989. German customs officers checking the luggage of a Polish trader. Photo: Andrzej Stach (courtesy of the author).

Polish flea markets on the Potsdamer Platz in West Berlin and around the Mexikoplatz in Vienna quickly became the largest black markets in Europe, with "traders from the East – to the shock of local residents – proving the better capitalists."[1256] However, the Polish trade invasion of Berlin and Vienna was nothing in comparison to the veritable burst of Polish commercial creativity displayed in the small town of Záhony at the border with Ukraine. An agreement between the Soviet Union and Hungary on limited cross-border traffic, signed in 1985 and implemented in early 1989, permitted residents of a 30 km radius zone on both sides of the border to visit the neighboring country using a special visa valid for one month. In a mere three months, 1.5 million out-of-towners visited, or rather overran, the borderlands in Hungary and turned Záhony into a

1256 *Największy supersam Europy*, WC, 1990, no. 49–50, p. 19. On Berlin "Polenmarkt" see: U. Weber, *Der Polenmarkt in Berlin. Zur Rekonstruktion eines kulturellen Kontakts im Prozess der politischen Transformation Mittel- und Osteuropas*, Neuried 2002; M. Irek, *Der Schmugglerzug...*

bustling Eastern bazaar.[1257] In no time at all, Poles also showed up, effectively redistributing among the Ukrainians goods the majority of which had come from other socialist countries.[1258]

This Polish commercial activity was, for many reasons, increasingly difficult to handle for the authorities in Prague, East Berlin, and Budapest. The Poles acted as middlemen in distributing the often highly subsidized goods extracted from the less and less affluent markets of the socialist countries. The costs to the East German or Czechoslovak economies were high, laying respective governments open to criticism from their own citizens, who blamed the foreigners for the rapidly emptying store shelves. The free-traveling and free-trading Poles brought with them news about the political transformations taking place in Poland, which further destabilized the places they visited. Thus, the anti-black market initiatives undertaken in early 1989 were not merely about the safeguarding of local markets but also aimed at the prevention of social unrest, and, were, ultimately about the communists staying in power. All the Soviet Bloc countries visited by Poles undertook massive propaganda campaigns directed against the "Polish peddlers".

As a new measure, in the border regions of the Soviet Union and in places on transit routes such as Lvov, it was only local residents who were now permitted to buy food products and industrial goods.[1259] In January 1989, in the East German town of Lubmin, a group of Polish traders was assaulted by local perpetrators; according to Polish authorities, this was a "showcase event staged in order to contain the growing phenomenon of illegal wheeling and dealing by Polish citizens."[1260] Germans had for a while voiced the opinion that Poles were buying out goods that they were "incapable of producing themselves", warning that such behavior would not be tolerated.[1261] The anti-Polish propaganda intensified in the days immediately after the fall of the Berlin Wall, when Polish "tourists" monopolized the headlines.[1262] In early February 1989, the Czechoslovak authorities banned the

---

1257 In 1988, 2.1 million people crossed the Hungarian-Soviet border, in 1989 more than 11.2; B. Cichocki, *Wschodnia granica zewnętrzna poszerzonej Unii Europejskiej*, "Prace Ośrodka Studiów Wschodnich" 14, 2004, p. 17.

1258 *Mafia der Armen*, "Der Spiegel", no. 39/September 25, 1989; *Bordering on Capitalism*, "The Economist" (US), July 1989.

1259 AMSZ, DK, 29/97, bundle 20, Polish Consular Agency in Lvov, report for 1989.

1260 AAN, KC PZPR, X/47, fol. 12.

1261 *In Ost-Berlin droht polnischen Händlern jetzt die Ausweisung*, "Die Welt", no. 182/ August 8, 1989.

1262 H. Haibach, *Ärger zwischen Polen und der DDR*, "Frankfurter Allgemeine Zeitung", no. 275/November 27, 1989.

export of practically everything, and at the same time upped the propaganda offensive against the Poles. The Czechoslovak tactics included concentrated acts of petty harassment, such as issuing parking tickets for cars displaying Polish license plates as well as confiscation of goods and cash; there were cases of the Czechoslovak police using physical violence against Polish tourists. Prague and Budapest, egged on by an Austria that was also inundated by Polish peddlers, stepped up restrictive measures against transit travelers. Instances of denying entry to Austria and applying the principle of shared responsibility were common.[1263]

There was, however, the other side of the coin. While Czechoslovak police and custom officials were battling Polish hawkers, every Sunday tens of thousands of people from all over Czechoslovakia would arrive in Ostrava, on the Czechoslovak side of the border "interested in the Polish commercial offer, buying in the market place above all goods unavailable at their own stores such as denim clothing, fashionable shoes, tape recorder cassettes, video equipment, and auto accessories. One could buy everything there, from keys to sheepskin coats."[1264] This demonstrated eloquently that all ideologically justified restrictions had to give way to the laws of the free market: supply and demand, profit and loss, and price and turnover. The creative tourism[1265] practiced in communist societies did much to oil the creaking cogs of the malfunctioning economic apparatus.

1263 AMSZ, DK, 29/97, bundle 18, Consular Dept. of the Polish Embassy in Prague, report for January 1, 1989; December 31, 1989; January 17, 1990; *ibid.*, Polish Consulate-General in Bratislava, report for 1989; *ibid.*, Polish Consulate-General in Ostrava, report for 1989; see: M. Hradil, *Podloudnictví: nevítaný host*, "Tribuna" 1989, no. 45. International agencies acknowledged the scale of the smuggling operations conducted by Poles. In June 1989 at a crossing between Czechoslovakia and Austria, customs officers arrested a taxi driver from Zakopane and a hair salon owner from Nowy Targ. The two men had attempted to smuggle into Austria 355 300 rubles, 255 000 forints, 5 990 lei, 30 000 Czech korunas, 6 120 wedding bands and 4.8 kilos of scrap gold; L. Mazan, *Obiecujący początek lata*, "Polityka", no. 26/July 1, 1989.

1264 *Grzywny i konfiskaty towaru polskim handlarzom w Ostrawie*, TL, no. 207/September 6, 1989.

1265 See: R. Boyes, *The Hard Road to Market: Gorbachev, the Underworld, and the Rebirth of Capitalism*, London 1990, p. 189.

Closing Remarks: Through the Back Door – or the Front?

In all the Soviet Bloc countries, a similar mechanism had been at work: political revolution, imposed from above and often coming from abroad, had abolished the free market and replaced it with a hand-steered, centrally planned economy, resulting in intrinsic consequences: shortages, followed by spontaneous social strategies devised to alleviate them. Even the most restrictive communist regimes such as North Korea, Cuba, and Romania in the 1980s were incapable of eradicating completely the capitalist mindset.[1266] The communist black markets displayed distinctive, sometimes unique characteristics that depended on the scale of shortages, historical experience (including the degree of lawlessness), social structure, political and national determinants, and the size of the country. The larger the state and the more diverse economically, geographically, socially, and ethnically, the more distinct were the internal commercial flows. This was the case in China[1267] and in the Soviet Union, where the most important internal commerce routes were circumscribed by the meridians. The European North was in charge of industrial products and contacts with the world, while the Asian South supplied Soviet Union markets with fruit and moreover had a vast surplus of manpower and more liberal Party personnel, who turned a blind eye to the illicit economic initiatives of its citizens.[1268]

However, in countries where the "desertification" effect of communism was apparent, from the River Elbe to Vladivostok and from Tirana to Murmansk, the basic social strategies were very similar. Residents of port cities effectively proved that the sea could fill their pockets. Farmers "privatized" large state and coop farms and initiated more or less official exchange with the cities, where unofficial artisan shops responded much more quickly to market demand than bureaucratic, state-owned factories. The production of counterfeit Western products would

1266 AIPN, 01521/784, Stanisław Banaszek, Marian Czerepiński, *Przestępstwa przemytnicze i zasady ich zwalczania*, Warszawa 1969, WOP, p. 29.

1267 A. Chan, J. Unger, *Grey and Black: The Hidden Economy of Rural China*, "Pacific Affairs" 55, 1982, no. 3, pp. 452–471, here p. 458.

1268 G. Grossman, *The Second Economy of the USSR*, in: *The Underground Economy in the United States and Abroad*, ed. V. Tanzi, Lexington–Massachusetts–Toronto 1982, pp. 254–255; H.E. Gramatzki, *Schattenwirtschaft*, in: H.G. Bütow, *Länderbericht Sowjetunion*, Bonn 1988, pp. 427–431, here p. 431.

not have been possible without state resources and equipment. The strategies of private legal entrepreneurs were even more elaborate. Workers in state factories supplemented their wages with petty theft and jobs on the side and took advantage of state owned equipment and resources. Drivers employed by the state commonly used state-owned trucks and buses as their own transportation and sold the gas they saved to private car owners. Administrative officials forged any and every document: reports, payroll lists, sales and purchase contracts, and official travel reimbursements. All used informal connections and contacts among family, friends, and acquaintances to obtain desired goods or services.[1269]

In the late 1980s, the size of the Soviet "second economy" was estimated at between 120 and 130 billion rubles, approximately 20% of the gross national income.[1270] In the countries of the Bloc considered by Moscow and Warsaw as affluent and prosperous, the results of the unofficial activities of their citizens were similar. For example in Hungary in the mid-1980s, approximately 10% of GNP was being generated in the grey zone,[1271] while in Czechoslovakia, stealing socialist, or communal, property constituted 20% of all crimes.[1272]

1269 K.M. Simis, *USSR. Secrets of a Corrupt Society*, London–Melbourne–Toronto 1982, pp. 103–104; A. Arp, *VEB – Vaters ehemaliger Betrieb. Privatunternehmer in der DDR*, Leipzig 2005; AAN, MS, 5489, Economic crime problems in Hungary (WRL), October 10, 1959, fol. 11–12; F.J.M. Feldbrugge, *The Soviet Second Economy in a Political and Legal Perspective*, in: *The Underground Economies: Tax Evasion and Information Distortion*, ed. E.L. Feige, Cambridge–New York–New Rochelle 1989, pp. 297–338; A.V. Ledeneva, *Russia's Economy of Favours: Blat, Networking and Informal Exchange*, Cambridge–New York 1998; B. Rumer, *The "Second" Agriculture in the USSR*, "Soviet Studies" 33, 1981, no. 4, pp. 560–572; *"Schwarzer Markt" in der CSR*, "Volkszeitung" March 19, 1958; HIM, Pressearchiv, T 6211, RFE-Research 29/53, Smuggling and Winning of Informants on the Elbe, March 20, 1953; *ibid.*, 7047/54, Great demand for American cigarettes and chewing gum on the Prague black market, August 13, 1954; *ibid.*, 8417/54, Illegal watch business in Prague, October 6, 1954; *ibid.*, 11480/54, Spot searches in Praque hotels, cafes and night spots, December 24, 1954; *ibid.*, 11183/56, Black market in Swiss watches, December 19, 1956.

1270 K.A. Ułybin, *Znakomaja neznakomka*, in: *Tenewaja ekonomika*, Moskva 1991, p. 21.

1271 I. Kemény, *The Unregistered Economy in Hungary*, "Soviet Studies" 34, 1982, no. 3, pp. 349–366; I. Kemény, *The Second Economy in Hungary*, in: *The Second Economy in Marxist States*, ed. M. Łoś, Houndmills–London 1990, pp. 50–68; E. Sik, *From the Second to the Informal Economy*, "Journal of Public Policy" 12, 1992, no. 1, pp. 153–175. See: I.R. Gábor, *The Second Economy and Socialism: the Hungarian Experience*, in: *The Underground Economies...*

1272 "Polityka", no. 26/June 25, 1987.

An evaluation of this half-a-century long black market ordeal of communist societies (and one which lasted even longer in the Soviet Union) is as difficult as the present attempt to define it. Undoubtedly, these unofficial strategies made it easier to live and indeed survive in Poland, Romania, the Soviet Union, Hungary and Czechoslovakia. The worker enjoyed a bigger pork chop on his plate, citizens were more stylish, and some of the charms of foreign lands could be sampled in reality and not merely in the imagination. All this did, however, carry a price tag.

The economic strategies developed by Soviet Bloc societies were a reaction to the actions of the state, which in the black market theatre was not only the director and censor but also, depending on the circumstances, an actor, stage designer, and prompter. While the authorities put much effort into combating the economic underground, they also grew dependent on it and replicated its modus operandi. Thanks to black market operations, society was able to solve some of its own problems that the state had ignored or was unable to tackle. The status quo forced upon both citizens and the authorities a "make-believe" life, in parallel with the real one – the pragmatic, some would say, hypocritical one, symbolically represented by the prosecutor in post-war Germany who wrote anti-speculation indictments on paper bought on the black market, a cup of contraband coffee next to his typewriter. This was a self-perpetrating systemic spiral; ordinary social players watched the behavior of the elites – from the local community's administrative chief to the Politburo – and felt largely justified in their own illicit endeavors. "I am quite convinced," observed Bolesław Karski in 1963, "that it would be possible to bring criminal charges of profiteering against many Poles with a reputation as pure as the driven snow and prove them guilty. After all, how many of us do not write with foreign pens, buy foreign refills or shave with foreign razors; and what about the many women who use Cutex lipstick […]. Often, those who can afford it, will have a glass of Martell cognac. Yet most of these products entered Poland illegally, as contraband. Since smuggling is a crime, it follows that to buy goods that come from smuggling has to be a crime too."[1273] State-owned travel agencies were fully aware that the majority of tourists participating in official organized trips abroad used them as a pretext for and as a means for illegal trade operations. There was a clear, unwritten agreement between a young person hired to work in a center of foreign trade and his superiors: the official salary would be low but there would be opportunities to travel. It was up to the employee to take advantage of these. Such informal packages applied equally to a company truck driver and the pilot of a government airplane.

1273 B. Karski, *Przemyt w majestacie prawa*, PiŻ, 1963, no. 14.

Factory management tended to turn a blind eye to employees doing a job on the side during working hours. An intricate system of vouchers, additional allocations and internal trade facilitated access to scarce and often rationed products at prices usually lower than the official ones or those of the black market. These policies were ostensibly meant to "attract employees and mitigate tension [...], maintain staff stability and improve team integration", yet in fact they brought about a spontaneous, grassroots re-privatization of "state property while maintaining the nominal status quo of its ownership."[1274] Needless to say, employees were much in favor of such rules of engagement and any attempt to tamper with them was met with angry protests, in which both unions and management took part. "There appears to be an idea prevalent among work crews", a report noted in 1984, "about what constitutes a good manager or a good trade unionist: it is someone who takes care of the workers by facilitating the purchase of everyday manufactured goods or food. There also persists a fallacy that there is another kind of management altogether, who gives priority to the regulations in force and is not willing to assist employees in a similar manner; this stance leads to dissatisfaction among the workers."[1275] Workers did not perceive such practices as speculative; if anything, they thought that it was easier for goods sold via the traditional process through retail stores to become objects of black market trade whereas informal "inter-factory exchange" was bound to reach directly those that it should.[1276] When in 1984, the Minister of Internal Trade and Services asked ninety seven trade unions to express their opinion on the issue of inter-factory barter, it turned out that "unions representing employees of enterprises producing non-market goods opted for keeping and strengthening a ban on the preferential sale of market articles, whereas unions representing the employees of the plants producing market goods were in favor of maintaining the current practices."[1277]

Factory management was primarily concerned with timely execution of the economic plan – the "plan" being a key concept in the planned socialist economy – since, if the preset targets were met, the managers would receive bonuses. Thus, management cared little about the quality of the work of private co-operators or the provenance of the resources and semi-finished products – in sourcing these or the raw materials indispensable in the production process, those in charge

1274 K. Nowakowski, *Niedobory w gospodarce a społeczeństwo i jednostka*, Katowice 1993, pp. 22–23.
1275 AAN, URM, 32/115, fol. 80–81.
1276 *Ibid.*
1277 AAN, URM, 32/184, fol. 65.

often sailed close to the wind of legitimacy. Soviet factories employed buyers known as *tolkachs*, who used all kinds of formal and informal connections to provide the necessary means of production. In one of his books, Roger Boyes describes a Moscow household appliance factory, where the main skill of three such specialists is their know-how in identifying those to bribe, intimidate or get drunk to get results. On an occasion, when the timely meeting of production targets depends on getting a crucial supply of copper wire, a *tolkach* triumphantly pulls off the necessary purchase on the black market, in the full knowledge that the wire has been stolen from another factory.[1278] It has to be said that the role of buyers employed by Polish factories was quite similar.

On both micro and macro scale, the state adapted itself to strategies evolved by society, acquiescing, for instance, in the "dollarization" of the Polish People's Republic in the full knowledge that the dollars and marks spent in the Pewex stores – much needed by the country's economy – came mostly from the black market. It is hard to disagree with the observation of the sociologist Zygmunt Bauman that a "centralized economy cannot survive without its illegal and ugly reverse side."[1279] One must then ask: did the black market undermine the socialist system or – on the contrary – did it strengthen and stabilize it?[1280] Undoubtedly, by bringing some flexibility and freedom to the rigid, centrally planned economy, the black market helped stabilize the system – but only in the short term. In the long run, the anarchic economic activities of citizens that went directly against the precepts of the ideology embraced by the state produced increasingly deeper cracks in the socialist edifice.

Real socialism would probably not have survived as long as it did without market mechanisms taking their course within the planned socialist economy. We should therefore perhaps view the illicit commercial activities as the relics of a healthy economy – re-introduced by the back door –that made it possible for entrepreneurship to survive. Was the black market the last stronghold of economic freedom of the individual, never conquered by the communist state? Journalists (such as Daniel Passent or Stanisław Podemski) and economists (Marek Bednarski and Kazimierz Rogoziński) drew attention to the characteristics of

---

1278 R. Boyes, *The Hard Road to Market. Gorbachev, the Underworld, and the Rebirth of Capitalism*, London 1990, p. 11.

1279 As cited in: H.E. Gramatzki, *Schattenwirtschaft…*, p. 428.

1280 See: C. Petrescu, *Entrepreneurial Tourism in Romania: A System-stabilizing Factor?*, in: *Schleichwege. Inoffizielle Begegnungen sozialistischer Staatsbürger zwischen 1956 und 1989*, edited by W. Borodziej, J. Kochanowski, J. von Puttkamer, Köln–Weimar–Wien 2010, pp. 115–133.

the individual businessmen who were operating illegally, such as their creativity, initiative and a free market mindset. In 1987, Kazimierz Rogoziński wrote: "In the most critical phase of the market crisis, between 1981 and 1983, the black market proved indispensable for two reasons: it offered goods unavailable in retail trade and created opportunities to barter rationed goods for others, not necessarily rationed. [...] The presence and the mechanisms of the black market," concluded the author, "perceived in the context of market ethics, give us reasons to be optimistic. Despite the lessened impact of material incentives, entrepreneurship among Poles is alive and well, it just needs to be put to good use."[1281]

Certainly, a significant number of Poles exhibited spontaneous, grass-roots inventiveness and mobility: working out business plans, estimating profit and loss, finding investment capital, and carrying out transactions across a variety of geographical locations. Whether consciously nor not, they built an "intermediate space" suspended between the two worlds, a space that broke free from the rigid, ideological framework. This was, however, only one side of the coin. Despite its insights into the specific contexts and determinants of the prevailing system, the black market nevertheless criminalized everyday life and encouraged breaking of the law. In 1964, "Trybuna Ludu" published a story about a teacher who was having a family house built and was determined to accomplish the project legally but who "had been unable to buy a gas central heating boiler from any legitimate source. At the time, this was a product that was easily available on the black market, and that was where all his neighbors had bought theirs. To keep his conscience clear, the teacher settled for a legally available coke boiler, even though his neighbors thought him peculiar."[1282] Regardless of whether this particular story was apocryphal, undoubtedly – besides those who relied on and took the black market for granted – there were others who, for a variety of reasons, did not take advantage of illicit sources, whether because they could not afford it, did not how to go about it, had too little money or simply did not want to take part in an illegal activity.

The black market was a drain on state supplies and resources, further exacerbating shortages; this led to more chaos in the less-than-perfect state distribution system and impeded it catering for the needs of the economically and socially underprivileged. The black market had never been a charity; its active players took

1281 K. Rogoziński, *Kryzys jako weryfikator w sferze rynku i konsumpcji*, in: *Narzędzia polityki gospodarczej i społecznej w procesie kształtowania konsumpcji. Ogólnopolska konferencja naukowo-dydaktyczna Katedr i Instytutów Obrotu Towarowego i Usług Uczelni Ekonomicznych, Ustroń, wrzesień 1987 r.*, vol. 1, Katowice 1987, pp. 159–161.

1282 B. Lewicki, *Przestępcy mimo woli*, TL, October 20, 1964.

full advantage of their privileged position by imposing monopoly prices, which only the richest could afford. There is no doubt the black market supported the wealthy and the risk takers, and excluded the majority of the poor and the less tough. What determined whether the unofficial price was acceptable was the household budget. Some items could be bought more expensively on the black market; others could be siphoned off from official distribution channels, using the tried-and-tested ruses. The latter option was of course preferable since it usually involved a complex system of "scratch my back and I'll scratch yours" rather than parting with excessive amounts of cash, and the voices demanding the equality of rationing were directed not only against the shortages but also against various black market activities that were beyond the financial reach of the masses. The response of the authorities was to introduce anti-market solutions such as rationing coupons – which, after a fashion, stabilized the system since both the coupons and cheap products in the stores were provided by the central government.

While the average consumers had very little leverage against the state distributor, on the black market they were totally disenfranchised, their only option was to vote with their feet and stay away. Dissatisfied clients of state stores or coops could at least resort to the provisions of consumer protection, and start by making a complaint in the ubiquitous "Customer Complaints and Feed-back Book", which every retail outlet was obliged to display; in practical terms, this usually meant that lip service had been paid to the letter of the law, but hardly ever led to any tangible outcome. The black market transactions did not offer even such, largely illusionary, guarantees. One could only blame oneself for having been duped into buying counterfeit dollars, rotten meat or lethal alcohol. The free market subjected the entire society in Poland and in other socialist countries to compulsory attendance at the "school of hard knocks", more akin to a "prison academy" where new inmates learn improved criminal techniques from old lags than to a business school. Nevertheless, the question remains what impact the demoralizing force of the socialist second economy had on social and economic behavior after 1989, when Poles took to capitalism with gusto.[1283]

One would not wish to go as far as condone the popular opinion, albeit unsupported by academic research, that the illicit, grass-roots economic activity helped to bring about a more rational distribution of resources and products within the inefficient, centrally-planned socialist economy. This perception led

1283 M. Tymiński, *Malwersacje w przedsiębiorstwach socjalistycznych (1950–1970)*, "Dzieje Najnowsze" 34, 2002, no. 4, pp. 97–98; see: L. Holmes, *The End of Communist Power Anti-corruption Campaigns and Legitimation Crisis*, Cambridge 1993.

directly to glorifying the black market as a form of social resistance, as indeed the black market during the German occupation had been perceived in the People's Republic of Poland. What is certain is that, prevalent and spontaneous as the illicit economic activities were, they demoralized citizens as well as undermining and ridiculing the structure of the state. Naturally, the primary goal of the black marketeers was profit and other side effects such as these were incidental. And the black market itself would not have arisen in the first place, had it not been for the shortage economy of the socialist system, from which it benefited and with which it co-existed in a symbiotic relationship. Shortly before 1989, when the writing was on the wall for the socialist economy, many Poles who under socialism had evolved a cosy modus operandi, based on dependable social connections, watched the developments of a new and unpredictable system with trepidation, unsure of how they would function in the new reality.

Although Edmund Mokrzycki's comments below apply to private enterprise in general, they also apply to the black market per se, as both sectors often intersected: "Contrary to popular opinion that saw private enterprise as a capitalist Trojan horse in a socialist stronghold, the sector was as integral a part of the socialist economy as the Vladimir Lenin Steelworks or the State Agriculture Farms (PGRs). The very first weeks of the transformation revealed the total dependency of the sector on the central distribution of goods and above all its symbiotic relationship with state industry and trade. For the sector, market mechanisms – to the extent that they had been indeed effectively implemented by the reforms – turned out to be lethal rather than beneficial."[1284] Roger Boyes poignantly observed that the year 1989 represented a revolution of consumers who wanted to join the "economic republic" that had previously been the preserve of the authorities and the hard currency elite.[1285] Without a doubt, the half-century long black market experience of socialist society helped raise economic awareness and as a result brought victory over the status quo. If one were to wonder by what route the black market Trojan horse had been led in, it was through neither the front nor the back door, but rather through a side gate. There is no need to erect monuments to the currency dealers and the 'veal women'; let us, all the same, preserve them as a fond memory.

1284 E. Mokrzycki, *Nowa klasa średnia*, "Studia Socjologiczne" 1994, no. 1, p. 46.
1285 R. Boyes, *The hard road to market…*, p. 4.

Bibliography

Archives

Archiwum Akt Nowych w Warszawie
(Central Archives of Modern Records in Warsaw)
Akta Józefa Wojtyny
Archiwum Bolesława Bieruta
Biuro Kontroli przy Prezydium KRN
Biuro Kontroli przy Radzie Państwa
Delegatura Rządu na Kraj
Główny Inspektorat Ochrony Skarbowej
Główny Komitet Kultury Fizycznej i Turystyki
Główny Komitet Turystyki
Główny Urząd Ceł
Instytut Problematyki Przestępczości
Instytut Rynku Wewnętrznego i Usług
Komisarz Rządowy do Spraw Organizacji Gospodarki Mięsnej
Komisja Specjalna do Walki z Nadużyciami i Szkodnictwem Gospodarczym
Komitet Centralny Polskiej Zjednoczonej Partii Robotniczej
Krajowa Rada Narodowa
Ministerstwo Administracji Państwowej
Ministerstwo Handlu Wewnętrznego
Ministerstwo Handlu Wewnętrznego i Usług
Ministerstwo Rynku Wewnętrznego
Ministerstwo Skarbu
Ministerstwo Sprawiedliwości
Ministerstwo Ziem Odzyskanych
Najwyższa Izba Kontroli
Narodowy Bank Polski
Urząd Rady Ministrów

Archiwum Instytutu Pamięci Narodowej w Warszawie
(Archive of the Institute of National Remembrance in Warsaw)
Ministerstwo Bezpieczeństwa Publicznego, Gabinet Ministra
Ministerstwo Spraw Wewnętrznych II
Komenda Główna MO
Biuro Paszportów MSW

Archiwum Instytutu Pamięci Narodowej, Oddział we Wrocławiu (Archive of the Institute of National Remembrance in Wrocław)
Komenda Wojewódzka MO we Wrocławiu

Archiwum Ministerstwa Spraw Zagranicznych (Archive of the Ministry of Foreign Affairs)
Departament Polityczny
Departament Konsularny
Zespół depesz

Archiwum Państwowe m.st. Warszawy (State Archive in Warsaw)
Komitet Warszawski PZPR
Starostwo Grodzkie Śródmiejsko-Warszawskie
Urząd Informacji i Propagandy
Warszawski Komitet Wojewódzki PZPR

Archiwum Państwowe w Gdańsku, Oddział w Gdyni (State Archive in Gdańsk, Gdynia Section)
Komitet Miejski PZPR w Gdyni
Dyrekcja Ceł

Archiwum Państwowe w Krakowie (State Archive in Krakow)
Komitet Wojewódzki PZPR

Archiwum Państwowe w Poznaniu (State Archive in Poznań)
Prezydium Wojewódzkiej Rady Narodowej

Archiwum Państwowe w Szczecinie, Oddział w Gorzowie Wielkopolskim (State Archive in Szczecin, Gorzów Wielkopolski Section)
Urząd Celny Kostrzyn

Archiwum Państwowe we Wrocławiu (State Archive in Wrocław)
Komitet Wojewódzki Polskiej Partii Robotniczej

Archiwum Związków Zawodowych (Trade Union Archive)
Wydział Ekonomiczny
Wydział Socjalny

Herder-Institut Marburg
Pressearchiv

Ośrodek Dokumentacji i Zbiorów Programowych TVP (Polish Television Documentation Center)
Biuletyny listów

Oral history

Radosław Grzelak (2002)
Wacława Grzelak (2004)
Katrin Gudmundsson (2006)
Przemysław Nowak (2010)
Janusz Nowakowski (2004–2005)
Janusz Primula (2006)

Press

„Czas" 1978
„Dziennik Ludowy" 1962
„Dziennik Łódzki" 1973
„Dziennik Polski" (Londyn) 1952, 1955, 1960, 1974, 1976
„Dziennik Zachodni" 1948, 1949
„Echo Dnia" 1948
„Express Ilustrowany" 1948, 1949
„Express Poznański" 1949, 1973
„Express Wieczorny" 1948, 1959, 1961, 1970, 1973, 1983, 1984
„Fakty" 1984
„Frankfurter Allgemeine Zeitung" 1989
„Gazeta Bankowa" 1993
„Gazeta Krakowska" 1973
„Gazeta Prawnicza" 1983, 1985
„Gazeta Robotnicza" 1948
„Gazeta Wyborcza" 1989, 1997, 1998, 2000, 2004, 2009, 2012
„Gazeta Zachodnia" 1948
„Głos Kutnowski" 1949
„Głos Ludu" 1948
„Głos Pomorza" 1948
„Głos Pracy" 1959, 1967
„Głos Wielkopolski" 1973
„Głos Wybrzeża" 1949
„Ideologia i Polityka" 1982
„Kierunki" 1957, 1968
„Kultura" (Paryż) 1957, 1968
„Kultura" (Warszawa) 1979
„Kurier Codzienny" 1948, 1949

„Kurier Polski" 1949, 1958, 1959, 1963, 1965, 1966, 1971, 1989
„Kurier Szczeciński" 1973
„Literatura" 1973
„Nowe Drogi" 1957, 1959
„Nowe Prawo" 1956
„Oberhessische Presse" 1978
„Odgłosy" 1973
„Odrodzenie" 1944
„Palestra" 1959, 1960
„Panorama" 1987
„Państwo i Prawo" 1960
„Perspektywy" 1970, 1977
„Polityka" 1957, 1960, 1963, 1967, 1972, 1973, 1975–1979, 1981–1989, 1998, 2005, 2007, 2010.
„Polska Zbrojna" 1948
„Prawo" 1953
„Prawo i Życie" 1957, 1959, 1960, 1963, 1965, 1966, 1968, 1970–1976, 1978, 1981–1984, 1986, 1989
„Rada Narodowa" 1958
„Robotnik" 1948
„Rzeczpospolita" (I) 1948, 1949
„Rzeczpospolita" (II) 1982
„Słowo Polskie" 1948, 1949
„Słowo Powszechne" 1957, 1958, 1965, 1973–1975, 1977, 1980, 1981
„Der Spiegel" 1989
„Sprawy i Ludzie" 1982, 1984
„Süddeutsche Zeitung" 1989
„Szpilki" 1945, 1959
„Sztandar Ludu" 1945
„Sztandar Młodych" 1959, 1974, 1979
„Tribuna" 1989
„Trybuna Ludu" 1949, 1950, 1956–1962, 1964, 1970, 1971, 1974, 1979–1983, 1987–1989
„Trybuna Odrzańska" 1976
„Trybuna Robotnicza" 1948
„Tygodnik Demokratyczny" 1957, 1958, 1977
„Tygodnik Kulturalny" 1970, 1977, 1981, 1983, 1985–1988
„Tygodnik Morski" 1965, 1967, 1973

„Tygodnik Podhalański" 2005, 2007
„Tygodnik Solidarność" 1981
„Veto" 1986
„Walka Młodych" 1971
„Die Welt" 1989
„Wiadomości Celne" 1970–1975, 1985, 1988–1990
„Wieczór" 1948
„Wieczór Wybrzeża" 1973
„Zagadnienia Wykroczeń" 1981
„Die Zeit" 1983
„Życie" 2000
„Życie Częstochowy" 1949
„Życie Gospodarcze" 1957, 1982, 1984
„Życie Literackie" 1971, 1976, 1980–1982
„Życie Radomskie" 1949
„Życie Warszawy" 1948, 1957–1960, 1971, 1973, 1976, 1979, 1981, 1982, 1989

Published sources

Album skrytek przemytniczych, Warszawa 1958.

Album złotych monet, oprac. I. Skolimowski, S. Tarko, Warszawa 1962.

Centrum władzy. Protokoły posiedzeń kierownictwa PZPR. Wybór z lat 1949–1970, oprac. A. Dudek, A. Kochański, K. Persak, Warszawa 2000.

Czarna księga cenzury PRL, part 2, London 1978.

Dziennik Ustaw 1919, 1944, 1945, 1947, 1950, 1953, 1956, 1957, 1959, 1960, 1965, 1970, 1971, 1981, 1982, 1985, 1989, 1990.

Gomułka W., *Aktualne trudności na rynku mięsnym i środki niezbędne dla ich przezwyciężenia. Referat wygłoszony na III Plenum KC PZPR w dniu 17 X 1959 r.*, Warszawa 1959.

Informacja o przestępczości gospodarczej w 1959 r., Warszawa 1960 (NIK, Wydział ds. Nadużyć Gospodarczych).

Komisja do Walki, ed. G. Sołtysiak, „Karta" 1991, no. 1, pp. 81–97.

Komisja Specjalna do Walki z Nadużyciami i Szkodnictwem Gospodarczym 1945–1954, compiled, intro., and ed. D. Jarosz, T. Wolsza, Warszawa 1995.

Mały rocznik statystyczny 1938, Warszawa 1938.

„Monitor Polski" 1958, 1959, 1970, 1974, 1976, 1984, 1989.

Polityka i dyplomacja polska wobec Niemiec, vol. 2: *1971–1990*, oprac. M. Tomala, Warszawa 2006.

Polska – Niemcy Wschodnie 1945–1990. Wybór dokumentów, red. J. Kochanowski, K. Ziemer, t. 1: *Polska wobec radzieckiej strefy okupacyjnej Niemiec: maj 1945 – październik 1949*, compiled, intro., and ed. J. Kochanowski, ed. A. Krajewski, M. Mazurek, Warszawa 2006.

Polska – Niemcy Wschodnie 1945–1990. Wybór dokumentów, red. J. Kochanowski, K. Ziemer, t. 3: *Lata 1956–1957*, intro., selected and ed. M. Górny, M.J. Hartwich, Warszawa 2008.

Polskie dokumenty dyplomatyczne 1972, ed. W. Borodziej, coed. P. Długołęcki, Warszawa 2005.

Postulaty 1970–71 i 1980. Materiały źródłowe do dziejów wystąpień pracowniczych w latach 1970–1971 i 1980 (Gdańsk i Szczecin), comp. and ed. B. Chmiel, E. Kaczyńska, Warszawa 1998.

Protokoły Posiedzeń Biura Politycznego KC PPR 1944–1945, ed. A. Kochański, Warszawa 1992.

Protokoły posiedzeń Prezydium Krajowej Rady Narodowej 1944–1947, comp. intro., and ed. J. Kochanowski, Warszawa 1995.

Przesiedlenie ludności polskiej z Kresów Wschodnich do Polski 1944–1947, selected and ed. S. Ciesielski, intro. W. Borodziej, S. Ciesielski, J. Kochanowski, Warszawa 1999.

Raport z działalności Komisji powołanej dla wyjaśnienia charakteru operacji kryptonim „Żelazo", ed. P. Gontarczyk, „Glaukopis" 7–8, 2007, pp. 233–271.

Rocznik statystyczny: 1958, 1970, 1972–1981, 1988, 1991.

Socjalizm na halach, czyli „Patologia stosunków społeczno-ekonomicznych i politycznych w Zakopanem" (1972), ed. J. Kochanowski, „Przegląd Historyczny" 98, 2007, pp. 71–96 .

Sprawozdanie stenograficzne Sejmu PRL (1979, 1981).

Szara strefa Października. „Notatka" o nielegalnych dochodach w Polsce 1956–1957, oprac. J. Kochanowski, „Przegląd Historyczny" 95, 2004, pp. 77–96.

Zapowiedź sierpniowego przełomu. Meldunki MSW o sytuacji w kraju w okresie 1 lipca – 16 sierpnia 1980 r., ed. K. Dubiński, „Zeszyty Historyczne" 2000, no. 133, pp. 69–164.

Memoirs, diaries, novels.

Bliss-Lane A., *Widziałem Polskę zdradzoną*, Warszawa 1984.

Bobrowski C., *Wspomnienia ze stulecia*, Lublin 1985.

Boyes R., *The Hard Road to Market: Gorbachev, the Underworld, and the Rebirth of Capitalism*, London 1990.

Chajn L., *Kiedy Lublin był Warszawą*, Warszawa 1964.

Dąbrowska M., *Dzienniki powojenne*, vol. 1: *1945–1949*, selected, intro., and footnotes T. Drewnowski, Warszawa 1997.

Domaniewski T., *Uśmiech z dalekich dróg. Opowiadania*, Warszawa 1973.

Franciszka Starowieyskiego opowieść o końcu świata czyli reforma rolna, recorded by K. Uniechowska, Warszawa 1994.

Głowacki J., *Z głowy*, Warszawa 2004.

Grynberg H., Kostański J., *Szmuglerzy*, Warszawa 2001.

Janta-Połczyński A., *Wracam z Polski 1948*, Paris 1949.

Kisielewski S., *Dzienniki*, Warszawa 1998.

Korowicz S.M., *W Polsce pod sowieckim jarzmem*, London 1955.

Kuczewski M., *Rumunia. Koniec złotej epoki*, Warszawa 2008.

Landau L., *Kronika lat wojny i okupacji*, vols. 1–3, Warszawa 1962–1963.

Lenzner J., *Brennende Kehle. Schwarzer Markt 1945–1948 oder: Der authentische Bericht eines Kenners der dunkelsten Schattenwirtschaft zwischen Stunde Null und Währungsreform von ihm selbst aufgezeichnet*, Bremen 1988.

Ławrynowicz M., *Diabeł na dzwonnicy*, Warszawa 1998.

Łuczak M., *Miś, czyli rzecz o Stanisławie Barei*, Warszawa 2000.

Morawski J., *Złota afera*, Warszawa 2007.

Niemczuk J., *Plaga*, Warszawa 1990.

Nowakowski M., *Moja Warszawa. Powidoki*, Warszawa 2010.

Panow A., *Farcowszcziki*, London 1971.

Prywaciarze 1945–89, ed. A. Knyt, A. Wancerz-Gluza, Warszawa 2001.

Rakowski M.F., *Dzienniki polityczne 1958–1962*, Warszawa 1998.

Rakowski M.F., *Dzienniki polityczne 1963–1966*, Warszawa 1999.

Rakowski M.F., *Dzienniki polityczne 1969–1971*, Warszawa 2001.

Rakowski M.F., *Dzienniki polityczne 1972–1975*, Warszawa 2002.

Rakowski M.F., *Dzienniki polityczne 1981–1983*, Warszawa 2004.

Rakowski M.F., *Rzeczpospolita na progu lat osiemdziesiątych*, Warszawa 1981.

Sandulescu J., *Hunger's Rogues: On the Black Market in Europe, 1948*, New York–London 1974.

Sekulski H., *Przebitka*, Olsztyn 2001.

Skarga B., *Po wyzwoleniu… (1944–1956)*, Kraków 2008.

Spojrzenie na Rosję, ed. J. Kochanowski, Warszawa 1994.

Szlachcic F., *Gorzki smak władzy. Wspomnienia*, Warszawa 1990.

Trees W., *Schmuggler, Zöllner und die Kaffeepanzer. Die wilden Nachkriegsjahren an der deutschen Westgrenze*, Aachen 2002.

Tyrmand L., *Zły* [multiple editions].

Valcini A., *Bal w hotelu „Polonia"*, trans. A. Dutka, Warszawa 1983.

Wachowicz-Makowska J., *Panienka z PRL-u*, Warszawa 2007.

Wojasz P., *Niebieski ptak. Absurdy peerelowskiej rzeczywistości we wspomnieniach byłego cinkciarza*, Chorzów 2011.

Wyka K., *Życie na niby*, Kraków 2010.

Wyszyński F., *Dzienniki z lat 1941–1944*, ed. J. Grabowski, Z.R. Grabowski, Warszawa 2007.

Monographs

Alexeev M.V., *The Underground Market for Gasoline in the USSR*, Comparative Economic Studies 30, Summer 1988, no. 2.

Anikin A.W., *Żółty demon*, trans. T. Aniszewski, Warszawa 1987.

Arp A., *VEB – Vaters ehemaliger Betrieb. Privatunternehmer in der DDR*, Leipzig 2005.

Battrick C., *Smuggling as a Form of Resistance in the Warsaw Ghetto*, Journal of Holocaust Education 4, 1995, no. 2, pp. 199–224.

Bednarski M., *Drugi obieg gospodarczy. Przesłanki, mechanizmy i skutki w Polsce lat osiemdziesiątych*, Warszawa 1992.

Bednarski M., *Gospodarka „drugiego obiegu" a kryzys lat osiemdziesiątych*, in: *Rzeczywistość polska i sposoby radzenia sobie z nią*, ed. M. Marody, A. Sułek, Warszawa 1987.

Bernstein P.L., *Historia złota. Dzieje obsesji*, trans. E. Ressel, Warszawa 2003.

Beskid L., *Ekonomiczne uwarunkowania rozwoju konsumpcji*, in: *Badania nad wzorami konsumpcji*, ed. J. Szczepański, Wrocław–Warszawa–Kraków 1977, pp. 81–227.

Beskid L., *Ekonomiczny i społeczny wymiar przemian warunków życia w latach 1980–1985*, in: *Warunki i sposób życia – zachowania przystosowawcze w kryzysie*, ed. L. Beskid, Warszawa 1989.

Beskid L., *Przemiany spożycia w gospodarstwach domowych w Polsce w latach siedemdziesiątych*, in: *Diagnozy społeczne w okresie narastającego kryzysu. Ekspertyzy Instytutu Podstawowych Problemów Marksizmu-Leninizmu*, ed. Z. Sufin, Warszawa 1981.

Boelcke W.A., *Der Schwarz-Markt 1945–1948. Vom Überleben nach dem Kriege*, Braunschweig 1986.

Bożyk P., *Marzenia i rzeczywistość czyli Anatomia polskiego kryzysu*, Warszawa 1983.

Brunnbauer U., *„Die sozialistische Lebensweise". Ideologie, Gesellschaft, Familie und Politik in Bulgarien (1944–1989)*, Köln–Weimar–Wien 2007.

Brzostek B., *Za progiem. Codzienność w przestrzeni publicznej Warszawy lat 1955–1970*, Warszawa 2007.

Bundgård Christensen C., *Den sorte børs. Fra besættelsen til efterkrigstid*, København 2010.

Bunda A., *Pogranicze mniej formalne czyli nielegalne przekraczanie granic na Podhalu*, in: *Góry i góralszczyzna w dziejach i kulturze pogranicza polsko-słowackiego (Podhale, Spisz, Orawa, Gorce, Pieniny). Historia*, ed. J.M. Roszkowski, R. Kowalski, Nowy Targ 2005, pp. 127–134.

Buryła S., *Wojna i alkohol. Zaproszenie do tematu*, in: *Wojna. Doświadczenie i zapis. Nowe źródła, problemy, metody badawcze*, ed. S. Buryła, P. Rodak, Kraków 2006, pp. 205–230.

Butterworth J., *The Theory of Price Control and Black Markets*, Hong Kong–Singapore–Sydney 1994.

Cegieła K., *Kartki na szczęście. Reglamentacja dóbr w Polsce Ludowej*, „Mówią Wieki" 2002, no. 4, pp. 23–29.

Chan A., Unger J., *Grey and black. The hidden economy of rural China*, Pacific Affairs" 55, 1982, no. 3, pp. 452–471.

Chelcea L., *The culture of shortage during state socialism. Consumption practices in a Romanian village in the 1980s*, „Cultural Studies" 16, 2002, no. 1, pp. 16–43.

Chojnacki P., Madej K., *Przypadki prokuratora*, „Biuletyn Instytutu Pamięci Narodowej" 2005, nos. 1–2, pp. 115–120.

Chugh R.L., Uppal J.S., *Black Economy in India*, New Delhi 1986.

Cywiński H., *Złoto. Skąd pochodzi, dokąd idzie?*, Warszawa 1987.

David M., *Le Marché noir*, Paris 1945.

Davydov A. Û., *Mešočniki i diktatura v Rossii 1917–1921*, Sankt Petersburg 2007.

Dawson J.W., Millsaps S.W., Strazicich M.C., *Trend Breaks and Non-stationarity in the Yugoslav Black Market for Dollars, 1974–1987*, Applied Economics 39, 2007, no. 1, pp. 43–51.

Dąbrowski W., Jakubczyk T., *Nielegalny obrót zwierzętami rzeźnymi i artykułami rolno-spożywczymi. Wybrane zagadnienia*, Warszawa 1977.

Debû-Bridel J., *Histoire du marché noir (1939–1947)*, Paris 1947.

Dessewffy T., *Speculators and Travellers: The Political Construction of the Tourist in the Kádár Regime*, Cultural Studies 16, 2002, no. 1, pp. 44–62.

Drobnomieszczaństwo w strukturze i świadomości społecznej, ed. Z. Zagórski, Wrocław 1988 (Acta Universitatis Wratislaviensis. Prace Filozoficzne. Socjologia, 2).

Działalność Delegatury Komisji Specjalnej do Walki z Nadużyciami i Szkodnictwem Gospodarczym w Szczecinie w latach 1945–1954. Materiały z konferencji naukowej odbytej w dniu 20.03.1998 r., ed. Z. Chmielewski, Szczecin 1998.

Encyklopedia historii gospodarczej Polski do 1945 roku, ed. A. Mączak et al., vols. 1–2, Warszawa 1981.

Engelking B., Leociak J., *Getto warszawskie. Przewodnik po nieistniejącym mieście*, Warszawa 2013.

Erker P., *Ernährungskrise und Nachkriegsgesellschaft. Bauern und Arbeiterschaft in Bayern 1943–1953*, Stuttgart 1990.

Facio E., Roschelle A.R., Toro-Morn M.I., *See You in Havana!*, Peace Review 13, 2001, no. 1, pp. 121–127.

Feldbrugge F.J.M., *The Soviet Second Economy in a Political and Legal Perspective*, in: *The Underground Economies: Tax Evasion and Information Distortion*, ed. E.L. Feige, Cambridge–New York–New Rochelle 1989, pp. 297–338.

Fiedorczyk P., *Komisja Specjalna do Walki z Nadużyciami i Szkodnictwem Gospodarczym 1945–1954. Studium historycznoprawne*, Białystok 2002.

Fish M., Edwards L., *Shadow Trading by International Tourists in the Soviet Union*, Journal of Criminal Justice 17, 1989, pp. 417–421.

Friszke A., *Kultura polityczna w PRL 1948–1989*, in: idem, *Przystosowanie i opór. Studia z dziejów PRL*, Warszawa 2007, pp. 394–413.

Fułek W., Stinzing-Wojnarowski R., *Kurort w cieniu PRL-u. Sopot 1945–1989*, Gdańsk 2007.

Galarski S., *Kryminologiczne i prawne aspekty nielegalnego gorzelnictwa*, Warszawa 1976.

Gliński P., *Ekonomiczne uwarunkowania stylu życia. Rodziny miejskie w Polsce w latach siedemdziesiątych*, Warszawa 1983, PhD thesis under Prof. A. Siciński, Instytut Filozofii i Socjologii PAN.

Gospodarka nieformalna. Uwarunkowania lokalne i systemowe, ed. K.Z. Sowa, Rzeszów 1990.

Górniok O., *Przestępstwa gospodarcze. Rozdział XXX Kodeksu Karnego*, Warszawa 1981.

Graban E., *Niektóre aspekty powstania i funkcjonowania Urzędu Celnego w Gdyni*, in: *Korzenie Gdyni*, part 4: *Mała stabilizacja. Materiały z konferencji historycznej 22 września 2004 r.*, Gdynia 2004.

Grala D.T., *Reformy gospodarcze w PRL (1982–1989). Próba uratowania socjalizmu*, Warszawa 2005.

Gramatzki H.-E., *Schattenwirtschaft*, in: H.G. Bütow, *Länderbericht Sowjetunion*, Bonn 1988, pp. 427–431.

Green T., *The World of Gold Today*, London 1973.

Grenard F., *La France du marché noir (1940–1949)*, Paris 2008.

Gries R., *Die Rationengesellschaft. Versorgungskampf und Vergleichsmentalität. Leipzig, München und Köln nach dem Kriege*, Münster 1991.

Griffiths O., *Need, Greed and Protest in Japan's Black Market, 1938–1949*, „Journal of Social History" 35, 2002, no. 4, pp. 825–858.

Grodek Z., *Zaopatrzenie kartkowe w okresie Rządu Tymczasowego (31 grudnia 1944 - czerwiec 1945)*, „Przegląd Historyczny" 60, 1969, pp. 684–698.

Grosse T., Grużewski J., Kozak M., Kula M., Meller M., Piasecki K., Piskorski P., Salak P., Woźniak M., Zalewski P., *Szarzy ludzie zaplątani w codzienności komunizmu*, „Przegląd Historyczny" 84, 1993, pp. 335–350.

Grossman G., *The Second Economy of the USSR*, in: *The Underground Economy in the United States and Abroad*, ed. V. Tanzi, Lexington–Massachusetts–Toronto 1982, pp. 245–269.

Grube F., Richter G., *Die Schwarzmarktzeit. Deutschland zwischen 1945 und 1948*, Hamburg 1979.

Gruszczyński M., Stokłosa M., *Efektywność nieoficjalnego rynku walutowego w Polsce w latach 1982–1989*, „Bank i Kredyt" 37, 2006, pp. 33–46.

Gulbicka B., *Dochody, spożycie i akumulacja w indywidualnych gospodarstwach chłopskich w Polsce Ludowej*, Warszawa 1986.

Haffner F., *Ist die Schattenwirtschaft ein Reformansatz? Das Verhältnis der Wirtschaftsreformen in Osteuropa zur Schattenwirtschaft*, „Vierteljahreshefte zur Wirtschaftsforschung" 1985, pp. 177–187.

Hankiss E., *The* Second society: *Is There an Alternative Social Model Emerging in Contemporary Hungary?*, „Social Research" 55, 1988, nos. 1–2, pp. 13–42.

Häusser A., Maugg G., *Hungerwinter. Deutschlands humanitäre Katastrophe 1946/47*, Berlin 2009.

Herrschaft und Eigen-Sinn in der Diktatur. Studien zur Gesellschaftsgeschichte der DDR, ed. T. Lindenberger, Köln–Weimar–Wien 1999.

Hessler J., *A Postwar Perestroika? Toward History of Private Enterprise in the USSR*, „Slavic Review" 57, 1998, nr 3, s. 516–542.

Hionidou V., *Black Market, Hyperinflation, and Hunger: Greece 1941–1944*, „Food & Foodways" 12, 2004, pp. 81–106.

Holešovský V., *Personal Consumption in Czechoslovakia, Hungary and Poland, 1950–1960: A Comparison*, „Slavic Review" 24, 1965, pp. 622–635.

Holmes L., *The End of Communist Power anti-corruption Campaigns and Legitimation Crisis*, Cambridge 1993.

Holzer E., *Schleichhändler vor Gericht. Der Schwarzmarkt in der Steiermark nach dem 2. Weltkrieg*, Graz 2007.

Hryciuk G., *Polacy we Lwowie 1939–1944. Życie codzienne*, Warszawa 2000.

Irek M., *Der Schmugglerzug Warschau–Berlin–Warschau. Materialien einer Feldforschung*, Berlin 1998.

Janicki K., *Pijana wojna. Alkohol podczas II wojny światowej*, Warszawa 2012.

Janicki T., *Czarny rynek w Poznaniu podczas II wojny światowej*, „Kronika Miasta Poznania" 2009, no. 3 (Okupacja II), pp. 94–116.

Jankowski S., *Warunki bytu ludności*, w: *Gospodarka Polski Ludowej 1944–1955*, ed. J. Kaliński, Z. Landau, vol. 2, Warszawa 1976.

Jarosz D., *Mieszkanie się należy... Studium z peerelowskich praktyk społecznych*, Warszawa 2010.

Jarosz D., *Peerelowskie lamenty mieszkaniowe*, w: *Od Piłsudskiego do Wałęsy. Studia z dziejów Polski w XX wieku*, eds. K. Persak et al, Warszawa 2008, pp. 307–320.

Jarosz D., Pasztor M., *Afera mięsna: fakty i konteksty*, Toruń 2004.

Jarosz D., Pasztor M., *W krzywym zwierciadle. Polityka władz komunistycznych w Polsce w świetle plotek i pogłosek z lat 1949–1956*, Warszawa 1995.

Jarosz D., Pasztor M., *Z badań nad stosunkiem władz Polski Ludowej do niedoborów mięsa*, „Roczniki Dziejów Społecznych i Gospodarczych" 65, 2005, pp. 229–266.

Jastrząb M., *Kilka uwag o funkcjach walut obcych w rzeczywistości Polski Ludowej*, in: *Społeczeństwo PRL. Historia. Kultura. Pamięć, vol. I: Historia*, ed. S. Jankowiak, D. Skotarczak, I. Skórzyńska, Poznań 2011, pp. 143–153.

Jastrząb M., *Puste półki. Problem zaopatrywania ludności w artykuły powszechnego użytku w Polsce w latach 1949–1956*, Warszawa 2004.

Jastrzębowski W., *Gospodarka niemiecka w Polsce 1939–1944*, Warszawa 1946.

Jaworek R., *Gospodarka nieformalna – czwarty sektor gospodarczy*, Warszawa 1984.

Jaworska J., *Cywilizacja „Przekroju". Misja obyczajowa w magazynie ilustrowanym*, Warszawa 2008.

Jezierski A., Leszczyńska C., *Historia gospodarcza Polski*, Warszawa 1999.

Kaiser R.G., *Cold Winter, Cold War*, New York 1974.

Kaliński J., *Bitwa o handel 1947–1948*, Warszawa 1970.

Kaliński J., *Gospodarka Polski w latach 1944–1989. Przemiany strukturalne*, Warszawa 1995.

Kaliński J., *Wpływ sytuacji rynkowej na warunki bytowe ludności. Lipiec 1946 – grudzień 1948 r.*, „Kwartalnik Historyczny" 76, 1969, no. 2, pp. 319–336.

Kamiński Ł., Małkiewicz A., Ruchniewicz K., *Opór społeczny w Europie Środkowej w latach 1948–1953 na przykładzie Polski, NRD i Czechosłowacji. Wstępny raport z badań*, Wrocław 2004.

Kapitány Z., Kornai J., Szabó J., *Reproduction of Shortage on the Hungarian Car Market*, „Soviet Studies" 36, 1984, no. 2, pp. 236–256.

Karcz K., *Efekt naśladowania zewnętrznych wzorców konsumpcji jako czynnik utrudniający sterowanie spożyciem indywidualnym*, w: *Narzędzia polityki gospodarczej i społecznej w procesie kształtowania konsumpcji. Ogólnopolska konferencja naukowo-dydaktyczna Katedr i Instytutów Obrotu Towarowego i Usług Uczelni Ekonomicznych, Ustroń*, September 1987, vol. 1, Katowice 1987.

Katsenelinboigen A., *Coloured Markets in the Soviet Union*, „Soviet Studies" 29, 1977, no. 1, pp. 62–85.

Kemény I., *The Unregistered Economy in Hungary*, „Soviet Studies" 34, 1982, no. 3, pp. 349–366.

Keshen J., *One for All or All for One: Government Controls, Black Marketing and the Limits of Patriotism, 1939–1947*, „Journal of Canadian Studies" 29, 1994, no. 4, pp. 111–143.

Klinkmüller E., Leptin G., *Terminologische Anmerkungen zum Begriff der Schattenwirtschaft*, w: *Beiträge zum Problem der Schattenwirtschaft*, ed. G. Hedtkamp, Berlin 1983.

Koch B., *Przestępstwa i wykroczenia dewizowe*, Warszawa 1975.

Kochanowski J., *„...jesteśmy już przyzwyczajeni". Prolegomena do społeczno-modernizacyjnych kulis „problemu mięsnego" w PRL*, „Przegląd Historyczny" 96, 2005, pp. 587–605.

Kochanowski J., *„Jesteśmy za biedni, aby urlop spędzać w kraju". Masowa turystyka i nielegalny handel w latach sześćdziesiątych XX w. Perspektywa polska*, „Roczniki Dziejów Społecznych i Gospodarczych" 68, 2008, pp. 125–150.

Kochanowski J., *Naczynia połączone, czyli polsko-czechosłowackie Schleichwege 1945–1989*, w: *Amicus Poloniae. Teksty ofiarowane Profesorowi Heinrichowi Kunstmannowi w osiemdziesiątą piątą rocznicę urodzin*, ed. K. Ruchniewicz, M. Zybura, Wrocław 2009, pp. 203–214.

Kochanowski J., *„Naczynia połączone". Nieoficjalne kontakty ekonomiczne pomiędzy obywatelami radzieckiej strefy okupacyjnej/NRD i Polski w latach*

1945–1989, w: *RFN–NRD–PRL. Zbliżenia*, ed. K. Ruchniewicz, D. Wojtaszyn, Wrocław 2014, pp. 107–117.

Kochanowski J., *„Niepewne czasy, pewny dolar". Szkic do obrazu warszawskiego czarnego rynku walutowego*, „Przegląd Historyczny" 100, 2009, pp. 29–46.

Kochanowski J., *Pionierzy wolnego rynku? Nieoficjalna wymiana handlowa między społeczeństwami krajów socjalistycznych. Lata 70. i 80.*, w: *Bocznymi drogami. Nieoficjalne kontakty społeczeństw socjalistycznych 1956–1989*, ed. W. Borodziej, J. Kochanowski, Warszawa 2010, pp. 109–144.

Kochanowski J., *W polskiej niewoli. Niemieccy jeńcy wojenni w Polsce 1945–1950*, Warszawa 2001.

Kochanowski, J., *„Ziemia żywi, morze bogaci". Strategie czarnorynkowe w polskich miastach portowych 1945–1989*, in: *Morze nasze i nie nasze. Zbiór studiów*, ed. P. Kurpiewski, T. Stegner, Gdańsk 2011, pp. 229–240.

Kochanowski J., *Zysk i strach. Z dziejów peerelowskiej „gorączki złota"*, in: *Od Piłsudskiego do Wałęsy. Studia z dziejów Polski w XX wieku*, eds. K. Persak et al, Warszawa 2008, pp. 276–290 .

Kochański A., *Polska 1944–1991. Informator historyczny*, vol. 1: *Podział administracyjny, ważniejsze akty prawne, decyzje i enuncjacje państwowe (1944–1956)*, Warszawa 1996.

Kochański A., *Polska 1944–1991. Informator historyczny*, vol. 2: *Ważniejsze akty prawne, decyzje i enuncjacje państwowe (1957–1970)*, Warszawa 2000.

Kochański A., *Polska 1944–1991. Informator historyczny*, vol. 3: *Ważniejsze akty prawne, decyzje i enuncjacje państwowe (1971–1991)*, part 1: *1971–1982*, part 2: *1983–1991*, Warszawa 2005.

Kohler E.D., *Inflation and Black Marketeering in the Rhenish Agricultural Economy 1919–1922*, „German Studies Review" 8, 1985, no. 1, pp. 43–64.

Korbonski A., *'The Second Economy' in Poland*, „Journal of International Affairs" 35, 1981, no. 1, pp. 1–13.

Kornai J., *Niedobór w gospodarce*, trans. U. Grzelońska, Z. Wiankowska, Warszawa 1985.

Kornai J., *The Socialist System: The Political Economy of Communism*, Princeton 1992.

Kosewski M., *Ludzie w sytuacjach pokusy i upokorzenia*, Warszawa 1985.

Kosiński K., *Historia pijaństwa w czasach PRL. Polityka – obyczaje – szara strefa – patologie*, Warszawa 2008.

Kostrzewa W.J., *Devisenschwarzmarkt in Polen. Seine Eigenschaften, sein Modell und seine Bedeutung für die polnische Wirtschaft*, Kiel 1987.

Kowalewski J., *Miasto portowe – obszar badawczy socjologii miasta czy socjologii morskiej?*, „Roczniki Socjologii Morskiej" 12, 2000, pp. 65–70.

Kożuchowski H., *Wymiana przygraniczna*, w: *Rozwój społeczno-ekonomiczny obszarów przygranicznych*, ed. B. Winiarski, M. Musiał, M. Klamut, Wrocław 1979.

Krasiński Z., Mruk H., Rzepczyński P., *Handel i usługi na tle rozwoju motoryzacji indywidualnej*, Warszawa 1977.

Krasucka W., *Spekulacja (wybrane zagadnienia)*, „Studia Kryminologiczne, Kryminalistyczne i Penitencjarne" 10, 1979.

Kumar A., *The black economy in India*, New Delhi 2002.

Kurczewski J., Cichowski M., Wiliński K., *Wielkie bazary warszawskie. Środowisko społeczne, kultura i problem społeczny*, Warszawa 2010.

Landau Z., *Selected Problems of Unofficial Economy in Poland*, in: *The Unofficial Economy: Consequences and Perspectives in Different Economic Systems*, ed. S. Alessandrini, B. Dallago, Gower 1987, pp. 175–179.

Lecouturier Y., *Le marché noir en Normandie (1939–1945)*, Rennes 2010.

Ledeneva A.V., *Russia's Economy of Favours: Blat, Networking and Informal Exchange*, Cambridge–New York 1998.

Lewandowska S., *Życie codzienne Wilna w latach II wojny światowej*, Warszawa 1997.

Lewandowska Z., *Model konsumpcji w Polsce w okresie industrializacji socjalistycznej*, Warszawa 1979.

Madej K., *Bezradność lub represja: władze wobec przestępczości gospodarczej w PRL (1956 - 1970)*, Warszawa 2010.

Madej K., *Milicja Obywatelska wobec przestępczości gospodarczej (1956-1970). Ewolucja struktur i jej uwarunkowania*, „Przegląd Historyczny" 98, 2007, pp. 49–70.

Madej K., *Siermiężna i dolarowa - korupcja w PRL w latach 1956–1980*, w: *PRL - trwanie i zmiana*, rd. D. Stola, M. Zaremba, Warszawa 2003, pp. 249–280.

Madej K., *Wszyscy byli przemytnikami. Obraz przestępczości przemytniczej i dewizowej w latach 1956–1970*, „Pamięć i Sprawiedliwość" 2008, no. 2, pp. 121–140 .

Mała encyklopedia prawa, Warszawa 1980.

Mariani R., *Borsari neri in Roma citta aperta*, Roma 1989.

Marody M., *Od społeczeństwa drugiego obiegu do społeczeństwa obywatelskiego*, „Studia Socjologiczne" 1999, no. 4 (155), pp. 35–51.

Mazower M., *Inside Hitler's Greece: The Experience of Occupation 1941–44*, New Haven–London 1993.

Mazurek M., *Antropologia niedoboru w NRD i PRL 1971–1989*, Wrocław 2010.

Mazurek M., *Społeczeństwo kolejki. O doświadczeniach niedoboru 1945–1989*, Warszawa 2010.

Michna W., Sztarbałło W., Prędecka K., Dyka A., *Modele spożycia żywności (w aspekcie polityki wyżywienia na lata 1986–1990)*, Warszawa 1986 .

Miry R., *Zwarte handel in levensmiddelen*, Brussel 1946.

Misala J., *Nieoficjalna wymiana handlowa obywateli polskich z zagranicą*, Warszawa 1989.

Models of Disequilibrium and Shortage in Centrally Planned Economies, ed. Ch. Davis, W. Charemza, London 1989.

Mokrzycki E., *Nowa klasa średnia*, „Studia Socjologiczne" 1994, no. 1.

Morawski W., *Zarys powszechnej historii pieniądza i bankowości*, Warszawa 2002.

Mörchen S., *Schwarzer Markt: Kriminalität, Ordnung und Moral in Bremen 1939–1949*, Frankfurt/Main 2011.

Mourmouras A., Russell S.H., *Smuggling, Currency Substitution and Unofficial Dollarization: A Crime-theoretic Approach*, „IMF-Working Paper" 00/176, 2000, http://www.imf.org/external/pubs/ft/wp/2000/wp00176.pdf.

Müller H.-P., *Die „feinen Unterschiede", wo es keine geben sollte. Anmerkungen zum Verhältnis von Arbeiteraristokratie und Luxus*, w: *„Luxus und Konsum" – eine historische Annäherung*, Münster–New York–München 2003.

Na pograniczu „nowej Europy". Polsko-ukraińskie sąsiedztwo, ed. M. Zowczak, Warszawa 2010 .

Narojek W., *Socjalistyczne „welfare state". Studium z psychologii społecznej Polski Ludowej*, Warszawa 1991.

Naylor R.T., *The Underworld of Gold*, „Crime, Law & Social Change" 25, 1996, no. 3, pp. 191–241.

Nowakowski K., *Niedobory w gospodarce a społeczeństwo i jednostka*, Katowice 1993.

O'Hearn D., *The Consumer Second Economy: Size and Effects*, „Soviet Studies" 32, 1980, no. 2, pp. 218–234.

Ökonomische Theorie der Rationierung, ed. M. Tietzel, München 1998.

Passenstein M., *Szmugiel w getcie warszawskim*, „Biuletyn Żydowskiego Instytutu Historycznego" 1958, no. 26.

Patterson P.J., *Dangerous Liaisons : Soviet-bloc Tourists and the Yugoslav Good Life in the 1960s and 1970s*, in: *The Business of Tourism: Place, Faith, and History*, ed. Ph. Scranton, J.F. Davidson, Philadelphia 2006, pp. 186–212.

Paxton J., Wroughton J., *Smuggling*, Basingstoke–London 1971.

Petrescu C., *Entrepreneurial Tourism in Romania : A System-stabilizing Factor?*, in: *„Schleichwege". Inoffizielle Begegnungen sozialistischer Staatsbürger zwischen 1956 und 1989*, eds. W. Borodziej, J. Kochanowski, J. von Puttkamer, Köln–Weimar–Wien 2010, pp. 115–133.

Pick D., *Fenomen „prywaciarza" w PRL. Warszawa w latach 1956–1970*, Warszawa 2003, PhD thesis written under prof. W. Borodziej, Instytut Historyczny UW (the author has a copy).

Pohorille M., *Preferencje konsumentów a postulowany wzorzec spożycia*, Warszawa 1978.

Polityka i organizacja żywienia ludności, ed. W. Kamiński, Warszawa 1980.

Próchniak L., *Kolektywizacja rolnictwa w regionie łódzkim*, Łódź 2003.

Puzškarëv V.S., *„Cernyj" rynok w SSSR v gody velikoj otecestvennoj wojny i ego vlijanie na sostojanie vnutrennego rynka strany*, „Ekonomičeskij Žurnal" 12, 2006, pp. 212–225.

Raciborski J., *Zachowania wyborcze Polaków 1989–2006*, in: *Wymiary życia społecznego. Polska na przełomie XX i XXI wieku*, ed. M. Marody, Warszawa 2007, pp. 344–372.

Radzyński R., *Produkcja, handel i spożycie mięsa w Krakowie*, Kraków 1934.

Ray S.K., *Economics of the Black Market*, Boulder (Colorado) 1981.

Robertson A.J., *The Bleak Midwinter: Britain and the Fuel Crisis 1947*, Manchester 1987.

Roesler J., *The Black Market in Post-war Berlin and the Methods Used to Counteract It*, "German History. The Journal of the German History Society" 7, 1989, no. 1, pp. 92–107.

Rogowiec M., Tylec B., *Kierunki przemian konsumpcji w latach 1960–1973 w wybranych krajach RWPG*, Warszawa 1977.

Rogoziński K., *Kryzys jako weryfikator w sferze rynku i konsumpcji*, in: *Narzędzia polityki gospodarczej i społecznej w procesie kształtowania konsumpcji. Ogólnopolska konferencja naukowo-dydaktyczna Katedr i Instytutów Obrotu Towarowego i Usług Uczelni Ekonomicznych, Ustroń*, September 1987, vol. 1, Katowice 1987, pp. 151–161.

Roodhouse M., *Black market Britain. 1939–1945*, Oxford 2013.

Ruchniewicz M., *Repatriacja ludności polskiej z ZSRR w latach 1955–59*, Warszawa 2000.

Ruffner K.C., *The Black Market in Postwar Berlin: Colonel Miller and an Army Scandal,* "Prologue Quarterly of the National Archives and Records Administration" 34, 2002, no. 3, pp. 170–183.

Rumer B., *The „second" agriculture in the USSR*, „Soviet Studies" 33, 1981, nr 4, s. 560–572.

Rynek motoryzacyjny, ed. Z. Krasiński, Warszawa 1980.

Sanders P., *Histoire du marché noir 1940–1946*, Paris 2001.

Schmölders G., *Die Zigarettenwährung*, w: *Sozialökomische Verhaltenforschung. Ausgewählte Aufsätze von Günter Schmölders*, ed. G. Brinkmann, B. Strümpel, H. Zimmermann, Berlin 1973, pp. 166–171.

Schneider F., Enste D.H., *The Shadow Economy: An International Survey*, Cambridge 2002.*The Second Economy in Marxists States*, ed. M. Łoś, Houndmills–London 1990.

Sédillot R., *Histoire des marchés noirs*, Paris 1985.

Sédillot R., *Moralna i niemoralna historia pieniądza*, trans. K. Szeżyńska-Maćkowiak, Warszawa 2002.

Sekściński B., *Ogniwo terroru. Delegatura Komisji do Walki z Nadużyciami i Szkodnictwem Gospodarczym w Lublinie,* Warszawa 2012.

Siegelbaum L. H., *Car for comrades. The Life of the Soviet Automobile,* Ithaca–London 2008.

Sik E., *From the Second to the Informal Economy*, "Journal of Public Policy" 12, 1992, no. 1, pp. 153–175.

Simis K.M., *USSR: Secrets of a Corrupt Society*, London–Melbourne–Toronto 1982.

Smithies E., *The Black Economy in England Since 1914*, Dublin 1984.

Smithies E., *Crime in Wartime: A social History of Crime in World War II*, London 1982.

Smolorz R.P. „*Verwaltung mit Rechtsbefugnissen im stalinistischen Polen. Die Spezialkommission zur Bekämpfung von Wirtschaftsschädigung und Wirtschaftsmissbrauch,* Regensburg 2004.

The Socialist Car: Automobility in the Eastern Bloc, ed. L. H. Siegelbaum, Ithaca–London 2011.

Sommer S., *Das große Lexikon des DDR-Alltags*, Berlin 2002.

Sowiński P., *Merchand adventures komunizmu. Handlowe podróże Polaków na Zachód w latach 1956–1970*, w: *Od Piłsudskiego do Wałęsy. Studia z dziejów Polski w XX wieku*, eds. K. Persak et al, Warszawa 2008, pp. 291–306.

Sowiński P., *Wakacje w Polsce Ludowej. Polityka władz i ruch turystyczny (1945–1989)*, Warszawa 2005.

Społeczeństwo polskie w drugiej połowie lat siedemdziesiątych. Raporty z badań, ed. Z. Sufin, Warszawa 1981.

Starzyńska W., *Rynek żywności w warunkach niedoboru. Studium statystyczno-ekonometryczne*, Łódź 1990.

Steege P., *Black Market, Cold War: Everyday Life in Berlin, 1946–1949*, New York 2007.

Stola D., *Kraj bez wyjścia? Migracje z Polski 1949–1989*, Warszawa 2010.

Stola D., *Zamknięcie Polski. Zniesienie swobody wyjazdu i uszczelnienie granic w latach 40. i 50*, w: *PRL – trwanie i zmiana*, ed. D. Stola, M. Zaremba, Warszawa 2003, pp. 159–186.

Strąk W.G., *Kronika Polski na morzu 1918–1989*, Warszawa–Olsztyn 1996.

Struye P., Jacquemyns G., *La Belgique sous l'occupation allemande (1940–1944)*, Brussels 1950.

Strzeżek A., *Od konsumpcji do konspiracji czyli warszawskie lokale gastronomiczne 1939–1944*, Warszawa 2012.

Sufin Z., *Tendencje w opiniach i postawach społeczeństwa polskiego w latach 1975–1976*, w: *Diagnozy społeczne w okresie narastającego kryzysu. Ekspertyzy Instytutu Podstawowych Problemów Marksizmu-Leninizmu*, ed. Z. Sufin, Warszawa 1981.

Sygit B., *Nielegalny wyrób spirytusu*, Warszawa 1987.

Sygit B., *Potajemne gorzelnictwo (przed, w okresie reglamentacji i obecnie). Studium z dziedziny kryminologii i polityki kryminalnej*, Bydgoszcz 1996.

Szarota T., *Okupowanej Warszawy dzień powszedni. Studium historyczne*, Warszawa 1988.

Szarota T., *Życie codzienne w stolicach okupowanej Europy. Szkice historyczne, kronika wydarzeń*, Warszawa 1995.

Szczepański J., *Zagadnienia konstruowania i realizacji modelu i wzorów konsumpcji socjalistycznej*, w: *Badania nad wzorami konsumpcji*, ed. J. Szczepański, Wrocław–Warszawa–Kraków 1977, pp. 15–80.

Szewczyk W., *Spożycie żywności w Polsce w okresie międzywojennym (na tle dochodów i wydatków na konsumpcję)*, Warszawa 1991.

Szuba L.S., *Komisja Specjalna do Walki z Nadużyciami i Szkodnictwem Gospodarczym i jej delegatura bydgoska (1945–1954)*, Toruń 2009.

Szymański W., *Ceny a konsumpcja i produkcja żywności*, Warszawa 1979.

Taylor L., *The Black Market in Occupied Northern France, 1940–4*, "Contemporary European History" 6, 1997, no. 2, pp. 153–176.

Tellenbach S., *The logic of development in socialist Poland*, "Social Forces" 57, 1978, no. 2, pp. 436–456.

Tenewaja ekonomika, Moskwa 1991.

Teuteberg H.-J., *The General Relationship Between Diet and Industrialization*, in: *European Diet from Pre-industrial to Modern Times*, eds. E. and R. Forster, New York 1975, pp. 61–109.

Thomadakis S., *Black Market, Inflation and Force in the Economy of Occupied Greece*, in: *Greece in the 1940s: A Nation in Crisis*, ed. J.O. Iatrides, Hanover (USA)–London 1981.

Tomczyk W., *Delegatura Komisji Specjalnej do Walki z Nadużyciami i Szkodnictwem Gospodarczym w Rzeszowie 1946–1954*, Rzeszów 2007, PhD thesis under prof. W. Bonusiak, http://www.pbc.rzeszow.pl/dlibra/docmetadata?id=959&from=publication.

Tomkiewicz R., *Olsztyńska Delegatura Komisji Specjalnej do Walki z Nadużyciami i Szkodnictwem Gospodarczym 1945–1954*, Olsztyn 1995.

Tymiński M., *Malwersacje w przedsiębiorstwach socjalistycznych (1950–1970)*, „Dzieje Najnowsze" 34, 2002, no. 4, pp. 97–113.

Umowa o kartki, ed. J. Kurczewski, Warszawa 2004.

The Uofficial Economy: Consequences and Perspectives in Different Economic Systems, eds. S. Alessandrini, B. Dallago, Aldershot 1987.

Unplanned Society: Poland during and after Communism, ed. J.R. Wedel, New York 1992 .

Veillon D., *Vivre et survivre en France 1939–1947*, Paris 1995.

Voglis P., *Surviving Hunger: Life in the Cities and Countryside during the Occupation*, in: *Surviving Hitler and Mussolini: Daily Life in Occupied Europe*, eds. R. Gildea, O. Wieviorka, A. Warring, Oxford–New York 2006, pp. 16–41.

Wagner M., *Die Schmugglergesellschaft. Informelle Ökonomien an der Ostgrenze der Europäischen Union. Eine Etnographie*, Bielefeld 2011.

Walczak M., *Walka ekonomiczna narodu polskiego 1939–1945*, Warszawa 1983.

Wasiak K., *Przygraniczna współpraca PRL–NRD w dziedzinie turystyki i sportu*, in: *Współpraca przygraniczna PRL–NRD*, eds. H. Szczegóła, K.H. Graefe, Zielona Góra–Drezno 1984.

Weber U., *Der Polenmarkt in Berlin. Zur Rekonstruktion eines kulturellen Kontakts im Prozess der politischen Transformation Mittel- und Osteuropas*, Neuried 2002.

Wedel J.R., *Prywatna Polska*, trans. S. Kowalski, intro. J. Kurczewski, Warszawa 2007.

Wessely A., *Traveling people, traveling objects*, "Cultural Studies" 16, 2002, no. 1, pp. 3–15.

Węgleński J., *Wyniki badań nad handlem uprawianym przez uczestników wycieczek zagranicznych*, Ośrodek Badania Opinii Publicznej, Warszawa 1964.

Wijk J., *Svarta börsen – samhällslojalitet i kris. Livsmedelsransoneringarna och den illegala handeln i Sverige 1940–1949*, Stockholm 1992.

Wildt M., *Der Traum vom Sattwerden. Hunger und Protest, Schwarzmarkt und Selbsthilfe in Hamburg 1945–1948*, Hamburg 1986.

Wingender P.A., *Westdevisen und Devisenschwarzmärkte in sozialistischen Planwirtschaften*, Stuttgart–New York 1989.

Wolle S., *Wspaniały świat dyktatury. Codzienność i władza w NRD 1971–1989*, trans. E. Kaźmierczak, W. Leder, Warszawa 2003.

Wołowski M.K., *Złoto*, Warszawa 1933.

Woźniak R.B., *Miasto portowe w zarysie socjologicznym*, www.portymorskie.pl/2001/19.pdf.

Woźniak R.B., *Socjologiczne procesy socjologii miasta portowego*, „Roczniki Socjologii Morskiej" 7, 1993, pp. 43–58.

Wyczański P., *Dwuwalutowość w gospodarce polskiej oraz metody i możliwości jej ograniczenia*, Warszawa 1989.

Zaćmiński A., *Przestępstwa polityczne w orzecznictwie Komisji Specjalnej do Walki z Nadużyciami i Szkodnictwem Gospodarczym 1950–1954*, „Pamięć i Sprawiedliwość" 2008, no. 1, pp. 321–343.

Zaremba M., *„Bigosowy socjalizm". Dekada Gierka*, in: *Polacy wobec PRL. Strategie przystosowawcze*, ed. G. Miernik, Kielce 2003, pp. 183–200.

Zaremba M., *Społeczeństwo polskie lat sześćdziesiątych – między „małą stabilizacją" a „małą destabilizacją"*, in: *Oblicza marca 1968*, eds. K. Rokicki, S. Stępień, Warszawa 2004, pp. 24–51.

Zaremba M., *Trzej jeźdźcy: strach przed głodem, drożyzną, chorobami zakaźnymi w Polsce 1944–1947*, in: *Gospodarka i społeczeństwo w czasach PRL-u (1944–1989)*, red. E. Kościk, T. Głowiński, Wrocław 2007, pp. 182–206.

Zaremba M., *Wielka trwoga. Polska 1945–1947. Ludowa reakcja na kryzys*, Kraków 2012.

Zatlin J.R., *Currency of Socialism: Money and Political Culture in East Germany*, Cambridge 2007.

Zee H.A. van der, *The Hunger Winter: Occupied Holland 1944–5*, London 1982.

Zierenberg M., *Stadt der Schieber. Der Berliner Schwarzmarkt 1939–1950*, Göttingen 2008.

Zweiniger-Bargielowska I., *Austerity in Britain: Rationing, Controls, and Consumption, 1939–1955*, Oxford–New York 2000.

Zwolski C.T., *Historia miasta Radomia. Kronika*, Radom 2005.

Żarnowski J., *Polska 1918–1939. Praca – technika – społeczeństwo*, Warszawa 1999.

Websites

http://www.filmpolski.pl/fp/index.php/124661.

http://www.tur-info.pl/p/ak_id,22478,,zakopane,w_zakopanem,tatry,sylwester,noclegi,miejsca_noclegowe,dziennik_polski.html.

World War II Rationing, www.u-s-history.com/pages/h1674.html.

Glossary

Abbreviation	Polish	English
AAN	Archiwum Akt Nowych w Warszawie	Central Archives of Modern Records in Warsaw
AIPN	Archiwum Instytutu Pamięci Narodowej w Warszawie	Archive of the Institute of National Remembrance in Warsaw
AK	Armia Krajowa	Home Army
AMSZ	Archiwum Ministerstwa Spraw Zagranicznych	Archive of the Ministry of Foreign Affairs
APKr	Archiwum Państwowe w Krakowie	State Archive in Krakow
APWr	Archiwum Państwowe we Wrocławiu	State Archive in Wrocław
APW	Archiwum Państwowe m.st. Warszawy	Warsaw State Archive
AZZ	Archiwum Związków Zawodowych	Trade Unions' Archive
BGK	Bank Gospodarstwa Krajowego	Home Economy Bank
BP MSW	Biuro Paszportów Ministerstwa Spraw Wewnętrznych	Passport Bureau of the Ministry of Internal Affairs
BP KC PZPR	Biuro Polityczne Komitetu Centralnego Polskiej Zjednoczonej Partii Robotniczej	Politburo of the PUWP
BRL	Bułgarska Republika Ludowa	Bulgarian People's Republic
CHZ	Centrala Handlu Zagranicznego	Foreign Trade Office
CKWS	Centralna Komisja do Walki ze Spekulacją	Central Commission for Combating Speculation
CPLiA	Centrala Przemysłu Ludowego i Artystycznego, Cepelia	Polish Art and Handicrafts Foundation

CPN	Centrala Produktów Naftowych	Office of Petroleum Products
CRS	Centrala Rolnicza Spółdzielni Samopomoc Chłopska	Farmers' Mutual Aid Cooperatives Central Office
CRZZ	Centralna Rada Związków Zawodowych	Central Trade Union Council
CSR	Československá Republika	Czechoslovak Republic
CSRS	Československá Socialistická Republika	Czechoslovak Socialist Republic
CZSS Społem	Centralny Związek Spółdzielni Spożywców Społem	Central Association of *Społem* Cooperatives for Distribution of Agricultural Products
DOKP	Dyrekcja Okręgowa Kolei Państwowych	Regional State Railroad Directorate
GG	Generalne Gubernatorstwo	General Government
GIGE	Główny Inspektorat Gospodarki Energetycznej	Head Office of the Energy Inspectorate
GIOS	Główny Inspektorat Ochrony Skarbowej	Head Office of the Treasury Protection Inspectorate
GKKFiT	Główny Komitet Kultury Fizycznej i Turystyki	Central Committee for Physical Culture and Tourism
GKT	Główny Komitet Turystyki	Central Tourism Committee
GRN	Gminna Rada Narodowa	Community National Council
GS	Gminna Spółdzielnia Samopomoc Chłopska	Community Farmers' Self-Help Cooperative
GUC	Główny Urząd Ceł	Central Customs Office
GUdWzLiSW	Główny Urząd do Walki z Lichwą i Spekulacją Wojenną przy Prezydium Rady Ministrów	Główny Urząd do Walki z Lichwą i Spekulacją Wojenną przy Prezydium Rady Ministrów
HIM	Herder-Institut Marburg	Herder-Institut Marburg
IPP	Instytut Problematyki Przestępczości	Institute for Criminal Problems

jgu	jednostka gospodarki uspołecznionej	Nationalized economy unit
KC PPR/PZPR	Komitet Centralny Polskiej Partii Robotniczej/Polskiej Zjednoczonej Partii Robotniczej	Central Committee of the Polish Workers' Party/Polish United Workers' Party
KERM	Komitet Ekonomiczny Rady Ministrów	Economic Committee of the Council of Ministers
KG MO	Komenda Główna Milicji Obywatelskiej	Police Headquarters
KP MO	Komenda Powiatowa Milicji Obywatelskiej	County Police Headquarters
KPD	*Kommunistische Partei Deutschlands*	German Communist Party
KRN	Krajowa Rada Narodowa	State National Council
KS	Komisja Specjalna do Walki z Nadużyciami i Szkodnictwem Gospodarczym	Special Commission for Combating Economic Fraud and Corruption
KW MO	Komenda Wojewódzka Milicji Obywatelskiej	Voivodship Police Headquarters
KW PPR/PZPR	Komitet Wojewódzki Polskiej Partii Robotniczej/Polskiej Zjednoczonej Partii Robotniczej	Voivodship Committee of the PWP/PUWP
KWar. PZPR	Komitet Warszawski Polskiej Zjednoczonej Partii Robotniczej	Warsaw Committee of the PUWP
KWS	Komisja do Walki ze Spekulacją i Nadużyciami w Handlu	Commission for Combating Economic Fraud and Speculation in Trade
MAP	Ministerstwo Administracji Publicznej	Ministry of Public Administration
MBP	Ministerstwo Bezpieczeństwa Publicznego	Ministry of Public Security
MHD	Miejski Handel Detaliczny	Municipal Retail Trade

MHW	Ministerstwo Handlu Wewnętrznego	Ministry of Internal Trade
MHWiU	Ministerstwo Handlu Wewnętrznego i Usług	Ministry of Internal Trade and Services
MO	Milicja Obywatelska	Citizens' Militia
MP	*Monitor Polski*	*Monitor Polski*
MRW	Ministry of the Internal Market (Ministerstwo Rynku Wewnętrznego, MRW)	Ministry of the Internal Market
MS	Ministerstwo Sprawiedliwości	Ministry of Justice
MSW	Ministerstwo Spraw Wewnętrznych	Ministry of Internal Affairs
MSZ, DK	Departament Konsularny	Consular Department of the Ministry of Foreign Affairs
MSZ	Ministerstwo Spraw Zagranicznych	Ministry of Foreign Affairs
MZO	Ministerstwo Ziem Odzyskanych	Ministry for the Recovered Territories
NBP	Narodowy Bank Polski	National Bank of Poland
NIK	Najwyższa Izba Kontroli	Supreme Audit Office
NKWD	*Narodnyj Komissariat Wnutriennich Dieł*	People's Commissariat for Internal Affairs
NRD	Niemiecka Republika Demokratyczna	German Democratic Republic
NRF	Niemiecka Republika Federalna	German Federal Republic
OBOP	Ośrodek Badania Opinii Publicznej	Center for Public Opinion Research
ODZP TVP	Ośrodek Dokumentacji i Zbiorów Programowych Telewizji Polskiej	Polish Television Documentation Center
OPZZ	Ogólnopolskie Porozumienie Związków Zawodowych	All-Poland Alliance of Trade Unions
ORMO	Ochotnicza Rezerwa Milicji Obywatelskiej	Militia (Police) Volunteer Reserve

OWIR	Otdel Viz i Registracii [inostrancev]	Visa and Registration Department
PGR	Państwowe Gospodarstwo Rolne	State Agricultural Enterprise
PHZ	Przedsiębiorstwo Handlu Zagranicznego	Foreign Trade Enterprise
PHZ	*Przegląd Historyczny*	*Przegląd Historyczny*
PIH	Państwowa Inspekcja Handlowa	National Trade Inspectorate
PISiPAR	Państwowa Inspekcja Skupu i Przetwórstwa Artykułów Rolnych	State Inspectorate of Purchasing and Processing of Agricultural Products
PiŻ	*Prawo i Życie*	*Prawo i Życie*
PKB	Produkt Krajowy Brutto	Gross National Product, GNP
PKC	Państwowa Komisja Cen	National Price Commission
PKO	Polska Kasa Opieki	Polish Bank
PKP	Polskie Koleje Państwowe	Polish State Railroad
PKS	Państwowa Komunikacja Samochodowa	State Motor Transport Enterprise
PM	Przemysł Mięsny	Meat Industry
PMS	Polski Monopol Spirytusowy, Polmos	Polish Spirit Monopoly
PMW	Polska Misja Wojskowa	Polish Military Mission
POM	Państwowy Ośrodek Maszynowy	National Machinery Center
POP	Podstawowa Organizacja Partyjna	Primary Party Organization
PPR	Polska Partia Robotnicza	Polish Workers' Party
PPS	Polska Partia Socjalistyczna	Polish Socialist Party
PRL	Polska Rzeczpospolita Ludowa	Polish People's Republic
PRM	Prezydium Rady Ministrów	Presidium of the Council of Ministers
PRON	Patriotyczny Ruch Odrodzenia Narodowego	Patriotic Movement of National Revival

PSL	Polskie Stronnictwo Ludowe	Polish Peasant Party
PSS	Powszechna Spółdzielnia Spożywców Społem	*Społem* Cooperative for the Distribution of Agricultural Products
PTTK	Polskie Towarzystwo Turystyczno-Krajoznawcze	Polish Tourist and Sightseeing Society
PUBP	Powiatowy Urząd Bezpieczeństwa Publicznego	County Office of Public Security
PZPR	Polska Zjednoczona Partia Robotnicza	Polish United Workers' Party
PZU	Powszechny Zakład Ubezpieczeń	National Insurance Company
RFN	Republika Federalna Niemiec	Federal Republic of Germany
RKS	Rolniczy Kombinat Spółdzielczy	Federation of Agricultural Coops
RM	Rada Ministrów	Council of Ministers
RP	Rzeczpospolita Polska	Polish Republic
RSP	Rolnicza Spółdzielnia Produkcyjna	Agricultural Produce Cooperative
RWE	Radio Wolna Europa	Radio Free Europe
SB	Służba Bezpieczeństwa	Security Service
SKR	Spółdzielnia Kółek Rolniczych	Farmers' Cooperative Association
SRR	Socjalistyczna Republika Radziecka	Socialist Soviet Republic
SS	Schutzstaffel der NSDAP	SS
TL	*Trybuna Ludu*	*Trybuna Ludu* daily newspaper
TPRR	Towarzystwo Przyjaźni Polsko-Radzieckiej	Polish Soviet Friendship Society
UB	Urząd Bezpieczeństwa	Security Office
UNRRA	United Nations Relief and Rehabilitation Administration	United Nations Relief and Rehabilitation Administration

URM	Urząd Rady Ministrów	Office of the Council of Ministers
USA	United States of America	United States of America
USRR	Ukraińska Socjalistyczna Republika Radziecka	Ukrainian Soviet Socialist Republic
WRN	Voivodship National Council	Voivodship National Council
WA	Wydział Administracyjny Komitetu Centralnego Polskiej Zjednoczonej Partii Robotniczej	Administration Department of the Central Committee of the Polish United Workers' Party
WC	*Wiadomości Celne*	*Wiadomości Celne* - Customs Service Periodical
WOP	Wojska Ochrony Pogranicza	Border Defense Force
WO	Wydział Organizacyjny Komitetu Centralnego Polskiej Zjednoczonej Partii Robotniczej	Organizational Department of the Central Committee of the Polish United Workers' Party
WPTB	Wartime Prices and Trade Board	Wartime Prices and Trade Board
WRL	Węgierska Republika Ludowa	Hungarian People's Republic
WRON	Wojskowa Rada Ocalenia Narodowego	Military Council of National Salvation
WSS	Warszawska Spółdzielnia Spożywców Społem	Warsaw *Społem* Cooperative for Distribution of Agricultural Products
WSW	Wojskowa Służba Wewnętrzna	Internal Military Service
WUBP	Wojewódzki Urząd Bezpieczeństwa Publicznego	Voivodship Office of Public Security
WUSW	Wojewódzki Urząd Spraw Wewnętrznych	Voivodship Office of Internal Affairs
ZM	Zakłady Mięsne	Meat Plants
ZMS	Związek Młodzieży Socjalistycznej	Union of Socialist Youth
ZMW	Związek Młodzieży Wiejskiej	Union of Rural Youth

ZSL	Zjednoczone Stronnictwo Ludowe	United Peasants' Party
ZSRR	Związek Socjalistycznych Republik Radzieckich	Union of Soviet Socialist Republics, USSR
ŻW	*Życie Warszawy*	*Życie Warszawy* daily newspaper
ZWZ	Związek Walki Zbrojnej	Union of Armed Struggle

Index of names

Warsaw Studies in Contemporary History

Edited by Dariusz Stola / Machteld Venken

Vol. 1 Maciej Górny: The Nation Should Come First. Marxism and Historiography in East Central Europe. 2013.

Vol. 2 Zofia Wóycicka: Arrested Mourning. Memory of the Nazi Camps in Poland, 1944-1950. 2013.

Vol. 3 Anna Witeska-Młynarczyk: Evoking Polish Memory. State, Self and the Communist Past in Transition. 2014.

Studies in Contemporary History

Vol. 4 Joanna Wawrzyniak: Veterans, Victims, and Memory. The Politics of the Second World War in Communist Poland. Translated by Simon Lewis. 2015.

Vol. 5 Jerzy Kochanowski: Through the Back Door. The Black Market in Poland 1944-1989. Translated by Anna Wróbel. 2017.

www.peterlang.com

www.ingramcontent.com/pod-product-compliance
Ingram Content Group UK Ltd.
Pitfield, Milton Keynes, MK11 3LW, UK
UKHW011004120926
8556IPUK00027B/13

9 783631 65585